T0243207

ALL OUT!

ALBERT ELLIS
with Debbie Joffe Ellis

ALL OUT!

An Autobiography

Prometheus Books

59 John Glenn Drive
Amherst, New York 14228–2119

Published 2010 by Prometheus Books

Inquiries should be addressed to
Prometheus Books
59 John Glenn Drive
Amherst, New York 14228–2119
VOICE: 716–691–0133
FAX: 716–691–0137
WWW.PROMETHEUSBOOKS.COM

14 13 12 11 10   5 4 3 2 1

Library of Congress Cataloging-in-Publication Data

Ellis, Albert, 1913–2007.
    All out! : an autobiography / Albert Ellis with Debbie Joffe-Ellis.
        p. cm.
    Includes bibliographical references and index.
    ISBN 978–1–59102–452–1 (pk. : alk. paper)
    1. Ellis, Albert, 1913–2007. 2. Clinical psychologists—United States—Biography.
3. Rational emotive behavior therapy. I. Joffe-Ellis, Debbie, 1956–

RC438.6.E76 A3 2009
362.196/89140092 B 22—dc22

                                                                    2009013235

Printed in the United States of America on acid-free paper

To

Debbie Joffe Ellis

The greatest love of my whole life, my whole life

Contents

PART 2

Acknowledgments

Many thanks to Tim Runion for, as usual, his beautiful word processing, great generosity, and excellent help over the years.

Introduction

On Writing an Impossible Memoir

In some ways this is a difficult memoir to write. Not the writing itself, for that slips off my head and typewriter as easily as it did eighty years ago, when I began my writing career at the age of twelve. No sweat. Writing comes easily to me—too easily, some of my critics say. It slides out at times without too much reflection and even less revision. I send it off, practically newborn, to the editor and printer. I have much to say, and I say it swiftly. Ten or twenty years later, maybe, I revise it. Not too much.

This autobiography is a little different. I started it and finished 250 pages of the first draft some nineteen years ago when I was seventy-three years old. Then I dropped it completely. Why? First, I have been too busy—really busy—writing other books (over 80) and many articles (over 800). Often, these were pieces that had been requested, but my memoirs were my own idea, and because I never mentioned them to a publisher, I had no one on my neck to finish them. No pressure.

Second, I had already determined to be ruthlessly honest, as I soon show, and I knew that some of the people I wrote about would be hurt, possibly devastated, by my revelations. Because I have taken my time—I am, as of this writing, ninety-two years old—some of these people have obligingly died. So although my "hurtful" revelations are still something of a problem, many of my subjects will not read them. Therefore, I can unremorsefully go ahead with some interesting stories.

I was seventy-three when I wrote the first draft and thought I had plenty of time to finish the two volumes of memoirs I had planned to publish. Now, I'd better step it up. At ninety-two, and with insulin-dependent diabetes, time creeps on apace. A dead Albert will write very little.

I have fairly well covered the topic of therapy in my books about REBT (Rational Emotive Behavior Therapy). Psychotherapists have a number of my books on the theory and practice of REBT, most of them pretty well up to date. Self-help readers use many of my books to cope with their problems of anxiety, depression, rage, procrastination, addiction, dating and mating, sex, eating disorders, you name it. Could they use more? Maybe. But enough is enough! Now it's time for me to get on with this autobiography.

Okay. So I'll finish it. I have a number of reasons for writing about myself—more, I believe, than do most people, including well-known ones. Let me see if I can list some of the main reasons without getting too presumptuous or boring. If I do, skip the next few pages.

1. I am reasonably famous, at least in the world of psychotherapy and self-help, and presumably a good many readers would like to see how I got that way.
2. Just *because* I am a well-known therapist, people would like to know whether I—as many therapists do not—reasonably follow my own teachings. Doctor, cure thyself. Well, do I?
3. I can show how my REBT principles really *worked* for me. Some brilliant therapeutic theories didn't work very well for Wilhelm Reich, Fritz Perls, Carl Jung, and a hell of a lot of other leading therapists I could name. How well do mine work?
4. In what specific ways did I have serious difficulties in applying my techniques to myself? What can be learned from my failures? Had my theories and practices better be revised?
5. Can some of REBT's best self-help principles be useful to my readers? Can my own case histories serve them as well as the scores of my clients whom I describe in my other books?
6. What can I learn myself about therapy and life by reflecting on my self-victories and self-defeats?
7. I can depict some aspects of human character and personality—of myself and others—as a writer and a psychologist. Better, perhaps, than a nonpsychologist writer.
8. Readers of memoirs of famous people are curious, especially about their sex lives. Won't they be eager to read the details of a psychologist and sexologist?

9. All my books, since 1957, have been written to sell REBT to both professionals and the public. I am, probably more than anything else, a salesman and a propagandist. These memoirs will give me a chance to do my selling in another—and I hope quite interesting—format.

10. If I'm lucky, this book will be a best seller.

11. Naturally, I'll include in this book some of the advantages of REBT over other forms of psychotherapy and help many readers to separate the wheat from the chaff. Even those who have been helped by other modes of psychological treatment may be able to gain what I call more "elegant" solutions to their disturbances and their lives.

12. Through my emphasis on solving the psychological problems of my life, which most autobiographies ignore or treat lightly, I give a unique picture of myself that is more multi-sided than memoirs that mainly stress adventure, business, sex, or relationships. Not that I'll omit those things, but rather I'll add to them.

13. This book will show how a psychotherapist's methods largely originated in his own experiences as much or more than they did in his professional training and his experiences with clients.

14. Yes, this autobiography will discuss a hell of a lot of REBT theory and practice. Yes, there is some sales promotion incorporated in its narratives. Yes, it is much more theoretical than the usual set of memoirs. But, believe it or not, that is I. I am a continual promoter. I am an incessant theorist. I am a steady proponent of REBT. In fact, in a sense, I am REBT. Not completely, of course, but in a hell of a lot of ways. Unapologetically. Yes. So let's see what this *I* consists of.

Another problem: How shall I arrange this retelling of my life? Shall I begin in chronological order, as most autobiographies are arranged and as I started to do in my first draft? A logical enough arrangement that shows how I slowly developed over the years and presumably got the way I am today. That would be okay, but I am not that interested in my early days, and readers might not be either. They might get bored witless before I finally got around to my adult and more fascinating life—especially my sex escapades.

Shall I start, then, with my love affairs and get off with a bang? Not such a bad idea, but perhaps it is a little too soon? Too sensational? Too misleading to those readers who may assume that I was only interested in sex and refused to work through more serious issues in life?

Hmm. How about focusing first on one of my emotional and behavioral problems, such as my low frustration tolerance (LFT), and exploring important aspects of that. Ah! That would be interesting to me, and I might also learn from it. My readers, too, might learn something useful about their own LFT and might benefit considerably. I could try that initial approach.

But . . . but . . . what about the other two considerations, which might get lost in the shuffle? Hmm.

Why not be quite unconventional and combine all three of these approaches? I could write a number of main sections, and in each one include three subsections: One, chronological development; two, problem-oriented issues; and three, sex and love memoirs. Oh, yes, another thought. A fourth subsection might be devoted to a critical review of the three previous subsections, to evaluate how honest I was and to strive for even more ruthless honesty and less defensiveness.

Quite an idea! These four subsections cover my main goals in writing this autobiography—to give my history, to focus on my main emotional problems, to recount my sex/love life and its vicissitudes, and to strive for ruthless honesty in all areas. I'll try it and see. Before I'm finished I well may change my mind and do something else, largely because of these important considerations. Let me see! H. G. Wells, who—as I mention a little later—inspired me to write my life *all out*, called his own memoirs *Experiment in Autobiography*. Why shouldn't I experiment, too?

So I shall try writing each section of this autobiography in four parts: A. *Chronology*: an account of my earliest to my later years. B. *Coping with Emotional Problems*: a description of how I handled my low frustration tolerance, anger, and self-downing, or self-condemnation. C. *My Sex and Love Life*: self-explanatory. D. *Critique*: an accounting for ruthless honesty in each previous section.

Of course, these four sections will overlap somewhat, as you shall see. The whole work is meant mainly to be a history and a study of my psychological being and well-being. I shall concentrate on this in part B of each chapter, *Coping with Emotional Problems*. But I shall also interpolate some of this relevant material in sections A, C, and D. You shall see!

{}

Can I really do the impossible in this autobiography and write every-thing *all out*? Obviously not—no one can. I can't do it, and neither could H. G. Wells, from whom I got this "impossible" idea many years ago. He said, back in the 1930s, that if anyone wrote his memoirs *all out*, none of us avid readers would be satisfied any longer with fiction.

I was very young—in my twenties—when I read this, but I could see that old Herbert George was probably right. Although famous for his novels and for science fiction—remember *The War of the Worlds* and *Tono-Bungay?*—he realized that fiction was subtle self-scripting and he contemplated making his writing more direct and honest. He partly—and he knew it was partly—succeeded.

So should I. If I live long enough and keep writing my ass off—as I fully intend to do—I should succeed. But only partly! I am now ninety-two and am an insulin-dependent diabetic. As I write about my doings with and feelings about others—especially the women with whom I have been intimate—I'd better be careful. Several of my ex-wives and women friends haven't had the decency to die yet. Some—damn it!—will probably outlast me.

Naturally, a doll like me "deserves" to go on forever, so that I can outlive all my inamoratas and thus avoid inconsiderately hurting them in this memoir. But really, I understand that, according to my noble the-ories of REBT, I—and you—cannot really "hurt" anyone except with a baseball bat. As I ebulliently tell my therapy clients: "Granted that John will feel depressed, even contemplate suicide, if you tell him that you no longer care for him—and especially that you are leaving him for Zack. Remember, however, a main principle of REBT: You can only hurt John with a baseball bat. If he feels very hurt when you honestly tell him you no longer care for him, he really *chooses* to sharpen up your words and meanings and to stick them into his own breast. That is *his* prerogative. So you can ethically tell him the truth—which is *your* prerogative—and then try to help him accept the truth in a less self-damaging way. He has a choice—and so do you."

That sounds laudable—and many of my clients buy it and over-come their guilt about "hurting" others. They then feel healthily sorry and regretful, but not self-damning, about taking the honesty-is-the-best-policy path. So, according to this credo, I could record that when Rhonda and I were in our twenties and she was living with and raising a young daughter with her lover, Roseanne, the whole time I was buddy-buddy with Roseanne and helping her with some of her most serious problems, I was secretly conspiring with Rhonda to have fabulous sex with her twice a week. We pretended to Roseanne that I was paying Rhonda for typing up some of my notes on sex, love, and marriage and that I was helping her, too, with some of her emotional problems. We almost split my bed in two with our constant, frenetic lovemaking. We continued to do so for more than a year, with Roseanne being none the wiser—and benefiting considerably from the free therapy I was giving her while I was still in graduate school.

I could easily disclose these gory details and risk my readers knowing, all out, what a psychopathic cad I have sometimes been. Frankly, I am somewhat beyond bothering myself about such "nasty" revelations. So *I* wouldn't suffer at all. I might even congratulate myself on my brutal self-candor.

But what about Rhonda, Roseanne, and their daughter? Are they still alive? If so, would they feel horrified and hurt? Would they resent my "complete integrity" in sharing this particular story? I know not. So, assuming they are all peacefully moldering away in their graves— for I am hardly a believer in reincarnation—can I ethically bang away at my typewriter keys and possibly hurt them or their surviving friends and family?

I think not. So I have changed some of the names in this story so that I might relate it in an unhurtful form. Similarly, I will change or omit other "salacious" details in this memoir. Not, I stress, to protect myself but rather to save the sensibilities—especially the disturbed sensibilities—of some of my other friends, associates, and partners. Some of the full details I shall leave for publication fifty years after my death.

{}

H. G. Wells made some snappy remarks about Marcel Proust's seven-volume novel, *Remembrance of Things Past*. I personally enjoyed this masterpiece because it seems to be a lightly fictionalized version of some outstanding scandals of late nineteenth- and early twentieth-century French society. Proust, to be sure, never revealed that his great love was not the charming Albertine but was actually his male chauffeur. Perhaps wisely, he was defensively secretive. But Wells found Proust's note-taking about French society too detailed—and hence almost as boring as reading a Sears, Roebuck catalog. Chacun á son goût!

Still, Wells had a point. This autobiography is about me and my ninety-two years of living. Naturally, I find it absorbing. But I'd better skip some of the Sears, Roebuck details. Outrageous, no doubt, but still potentially boring. Samuel Taylor Coleridge once said that art was emotion recollected in tranquility. And abbreviatedly!

A more important point (and one that I shall get back to later) is inevitable self-censorship. As far as I can, I shall present my bad and good, stupid and intelligent, weak and strong points. Why? Because, following H. G. Wells's recommendation, I want to go as all out as I can. I want to acknowledge my idiocies—and use REBT to feel sorry about but unashamed of them. I want to make the point that all humans are fabulously fallible—a central tenet of REBT—including, of course, me. We have no real choice about this, but we can unconditionally accept ourselves—our so-called essence or being—*with* our fallibility. That will help us momentously, probably encourage us to acquire Unconditional Self-Acceptance (USA), and possibly inspire other people to give it to themselves, too.

Maybe it won't. Maybe if I reveal practically all my blemishes and blotches, many readers will make themselves feel disgusted with me and the rest of humanity, thus encouraging their own hopelessness and despair. As a psychotherapist, I would say that some people will do this. Hopefully, most readers won't, and will instead use my confessions healthfully. We shall see!

Still, Freud was right. And, as Pogo self-disclosingly said, "We have met the enemy and he is us." In making my self-revelations, I shall consciously prevaricate—supposedly to protect others—and I shall also unconsciously dissimulate—to protect myself. Using REBT, I say, "To hell with it. If my readers and their listeners hate me, so they hate me. They won't fire me, jail me, or cut my balls off. I'll stubbornly refuse to agree with their calumniations, rue many of the things I have done and not done, but always accept me, my self, my being, no matter what!"

Brave words, but can I consistently live up to them? Probably not. I shall still protectively—and often unconsciously—forget, distort, exaggerate, and fictionalize. I'll watch it and try to disclose my undisclosures to myself and to my readers. Try!

Well, enough of this introduction. On to exposure. I shall mainly exposit my contradictory and paradoxical characteristics of high frustration tolerance (HFT) and low frustration tolerance (LFT). Using the former, I have made myself into a well-known and often acclaimed achiever. Using the latter, I have been my own worst saboteur in doing what I "really" want to do. On to some alluring and gruesome examples.

Part 1

Chapter 1A

Chronology
The Sidewalks of Pittsburgh and New York

The first sensible thing I can remember doing that helped me enjoy life and ward off potential misery happened when I started kindergarten at the age of four, in Pittsburgh. Did I really go to school that early in the city of my birth, when other cities like New York (as I discovered a little later) kept kids out of school until at least five, and sometimes six? To the best of my recollection, I did. Perhaps I was close to being five. Perhaps, since I was always big (at least tall) for my age, my mother simply lied about how old I was and pretended I was five. I really don't know. But I am pretty sure that I was still just a tot of four and not a very husky one at that. Who, me? Husky? Not even hardly ever. Simply, and no nonsense about it, never!

Anyway, one bright day my mother quietly told me that she was taking me to school, which, with no discussion, she promptly did. She walked me up a long hill to a large building about a block away from the small apartment house in which we lived, introduced me to the reasonably nice blond kindergarten teacher, and coolly left me in her tender clutches, saying that she would return at noon to take me home. The reasonably nice blond lady, in her turn, quickly introduced me to a motley group of youngsters, all of whom seemed to be (and probably were) a little older than I, irregularly sprawled around the large school room. They were acutely aloof, since they had already started their day's activities, and at first I was bewildered and didn't quite know what to do with myself. "A strange bunch!" I thought, seeing them so active, into themselves, and not at all inclined to stop their personal activities and welcome me.

The teacher, too. "Quite a character!" I said to myself. For, after greeting me for less than a minute, she also flew into her own thing—giving out crayons here, tidying up a child's chair-desk there, answering someone's questions, and bustling all over the room. I thought, "I'll ask her what to do," but I felt intimidated by her bustling and by everyone else's knowing what to do without being told. So I sat there for a while and watched the bustle, avidly wishing I were back home or back on the street outside my house where I knew the terrain, had a few cronies (including some grown-ups), and could quickly run into our ground-floor apartment if I got bored or frightened.

I was, let it be known, a pretty happy child *without* this god-damned new school routine. At home, I was the oldest of three, with a brother nineteen months younger and a sister just born. My mother was so impossibly busy taking care of those two that she let me run around and do practically anything I wanted. Did I feel neglected and unloved—jealous of the attention she had to give (and I mean *had* to give) to my two siblings? Like hell I did. I was always, possibly from the moment I scooted myself out of my mother's belly, an independent, my-kingdom-is-myself youngster. For the first few months of my entry into this world, my mother later told me, I was somewhat "difficult"—physically weak, colicky, and crying in pain much of the time. But once my colic, or whatever it was, passed, I started to enjoy being alive. I never seemed too needy of my mother, my father (a traveling salesman and promoter who was rarely around), nor anyone else. I was curious about everything—and I mean everything—and didn't give much of a hoot whether anything that happened was "good" or "bad." Whatever it was, I found it interesting—indeed, fascinating. "Nothing like learning!" I thought, so I learned and learned and learned.

Not from books or other reading material, for I don't remember anything like that, even when I started kindergarten. But I spoke to people of all ages. I listened to sounds—especially musical sounds. I began (again, according to my mother's account) to hum and sing tunes when I was less than two. I liked going shopping with my parents, especially in the big downtown stores. And whenever something new came my way, which seemed to happen continually, I thought about it, tried to understand it and figure it out, made some kind of sense of it, and widened my picture of the way the world really was and what I could expect of it. I thoroughly *enjoyed* figuring out things like that. I was, in my own way, quite a thinker. A philosopher and a theorizer? Well, yes—somewhat. In George Kelly's sense, that is, I was a little human scientist: one who observed how things were, made predictions as to how they would soon turn out, checked these predictions, revised them, and was amused and fascinated by the whole seeing-thinking-predicting process.

So, you see, I was getting along exceptionally well when—perhaps because she was so frightfully busy with my younger sister and brother or perhaps (more likely) because she wasn't ever a deeply nurturing parent—my mother packed me off to the outside world. I probably would have liked her to ask me if I wanted to go to kindergarten, thereby making the process somewhat more democratic. But my mother was not one to ask such questions! She was mean as well as being authoritarian in a highly Germanic way (her ethnic background was German-Jewish), she had enough conventionality, layered with her own inclination, not to let her kids interfere with her life too much, to solidly know that you didn't exactly consult your offspring about what they wanted to do. You mainly let them get along on their own, once they had the ability to fend for themselves, and you didn't give them too many superfluous rules. But when you thought it best for them to do something, such as start kindergarten at the age of four, you merely told them what they were to do and then you expected them to do exactly that. If they didn't, that wasn't the end of the world, and you didn't beat the shit out of them (at least, not too much). But you kept at them until they usually (not always!) did the "right" thing and fell into line.

So I didn't think of not staying in kindergarten once my mother put me there and the teacher introduced me and gave me my own chair to sit at. Or I thought of it only briefly. For I was at first so confused by the bustle of activity all around me, and the fact that in the midst of this bustle I was being completely ignored, that I did momentarily think of getting out of my seat, aiming myself at the door, walking down the long hallway to the entrance of the school, and wending my way downhill back to my own doorstep. Only for a moment, however. For I knew that *some* (though not exactly which) *unpleasant consequence* would occur if I bolted. I knew that neither my kindergarten teacher nor my mother (and father!) would take my bolting with wild enthusiasm, and that they would probably capture me and send me back to class, whether I liked it or not. And this kind of attention was not the kind I craved—unlike my younger brother, Paul, who, incredibly, seemed to *like* jumping up and down, shitting on the floor or pavement, yelling and screaming, and doing other "un-nice" things that got him huge amounts of attention and reprimands.

So I rethought bolting from kindergarten and did, as noted above, the first concrete, sensible thing I can remember doing to help myself enjoy life and to ward off potential misery. I sat watching the other children (and the flying-around-the-room teacher) and I said to myself, "Well, it really is a pain being cooped up in this class with nothing to do. And it is worse than having the full freedom of our apartment and doorstep. And it would be better if I were home and able to explore in my own fashion, talk to my friends, and run into my house to eat or play or do whatever I wanted to do. But, damn it, this isn't the worst thing that could happen to me. It's really not that bad. And, if I don't mess things up, it'll probably even get better. The teacher will soon give me something specific to do, and the other kids will stop their busyness and talk to me. So hold it! Don't do anything too rash. Wait a while to see how things turn out. You can always bolt later, if things get too rough. But why put your ass on the line when you don't have to yet? Wait a minute! Look around and see what's going on. Maybe you can learn something interesting. Watch it!"

Well, that was my first lesson—or the first one I can recall—in which I worked at acquiring higher frustration tolerance. I didn't like the situation I was in. I considered it unfair, since my mother had dragged me into it without giving me warning or asking my leave. I didn't know what was going to happen next, and I was a little afraid of the other kids, who knew each other well and who might easily gang up against me. I didn't quite trust the teacher, who seemed all right but was very busy doing her own thing and neglecting me. I could think of distinctly better, more interesting things to do. So I was clearly frustrated—not to mention scared.

At that time, moreover, I had not read much of Epictetus. In fact, I couldn't read at all. My mother's reading to me consisted of a stray fairy tale here and there. And, no, she wasn't very good at combing the fairy tale literature to see what little Albert might benefit by. More often she read me a cartoon or comic strip from that day's newspaper. So Marcus Aurelius, Seneca, Spinoza, and Schopenhauer were not exactly my daily diet. Emerson and Thoreau were unheard of. Bertrand Russell, later quite an influence, was alive and writing, but his books on practical philosophy—especially his *Conquest of Happiness*—were years into the future. I was born on September 27, 1913. So when I was four, in 1917, Russell was already famous for his *Principia Mathematica* but not for his writings on the good life. As for the other notable mentor of my adolescence and early adulthood, John Dewey, if anyone had mentioned his name in 1917, *I* would have surely confused him with the more famous Admiral George Dewey, who destroyed the Spanish Armada at Manila Bay on May 1, 1898.

No, I can honestly say: At the age of four I received little help from the brilliant philosophers who were later to contribute to my potential sanity. But, ah! I didn't seem to need it. With my own bent for philosophizing surging firmly to the fore, I met the enemy (i.e., my own catastrophizing thoughts of being cooped up in kindergarten) and knocked him and her for a loop. I *reasoned* myself out of the near-panic state in which I had put myself, *concluded* that my whole world was really *not* about to cave in, and *decided* to stay in class and see what was going to happen.

What happened turned out to be almost all to the good. My classmates started to talk to me and involved me in some of their activities. After a while, my teacher gave me my own crayons and paints and showed me how to apply them to drawing paper. Snack time arrived and was something of a friendly ball. Finally, my mother came at noon to lead a happy little Albert back to the "safety" of his home. Within a few days, I found that home was relatively boring compared to the kindergarten activities, looked forward to leaving for school each morning, and learned to walk up the long hill and back home again on my very own, without my mother to chaperone me. In fact, I liked it better that way, since I could dawdle almost as much as I wanted and explore the block and the people in it as I wended my way to and from class.

Oh, I almost forgot: that was another hazard I managed to overcome. For the first day—or was it two?—my mother brought me to school and back. But then, typically, she decided that she could leave me on my own, since the school was only a long block from our apartment and I could presumably walk to and from it by myself. My mother often decided things like this, not because she thought that leaving children on their own helped them to become more independent. Mainly it was because she wanted the freedom to do what she wanted to do and not be encumbered by her dependent offspring. So she started me off at the age of four on my road to self-sufficiency and simply told me that thereafter I would have to take myself to school and back.

Because that's the way she was and that's the way I was used to, I argued only lightly with her mandate, mildly protesting that the one street I had to cross to get to school seemed rather dangerous. As I recall, it was one of Pittsburgh's busiest and widest streets, on which ran a great many cars and wagons, including a double-tracked trolley car. Negotiating to cross that street by myself was something I knew I could do (for I had sometimes crossed it on my own, in the course of playing outside my house), but I wasn't enthusiastic about doing it twice a day. The cars and trolleys—not to mention the big horse-drawn wagons—were detestably noisy, and if you were unlucky enough to run in front of one, well, that was the end. Of you, of everything. No kidding! I easily figured that out and thought of refusing to go to school by myself and insisting that my mother bring me there and call for me when school let out.

I thought of it—and decided that it wasn't very practical. For one thing, my mother did have two very young children, in addition to myself, and my father seemed to be around, to my recollection, about two days out of seven, and then mainly on weekends when school was out. So the chances of being taken to and from kindergarten by either of them were hardly magnificent.

I could solve the problem by asking almost any stranger to help me cross the street. I knew this would work, having tried it several times before and being rarely refused. Women, especially, seemed delighted to help a fairly cute four-year-old boy across the street, and men were no slouches either.

But, alas, I was a slouch at asking. Somehow or other, totally unlike my highly extroverted mother and father, I seemed to have been born shy. Once I got to know someone, we got along swimmingly. I knew how to use my big mouth. I even had "good" models. My father was a fantastic salesman who sold and resold the Brooklyn Bridge many times, and my mother was a compulsive talker who got thrown out of school in the sixth grade because—according to her teacher—her mouth incessantly went like a duck's ass. With people I knew, I talked well. But *new* people? Oh, no! I normally—or shall I say abnormally?—kept my mouth closed and waited for *them* to make the first overtures.

That didn't work too well when I wanted someone to help me cross the wide street outside my house. I could stand on the corner facing the traffic, and *eventually* some kind soul would ask me if I wanted to be helped across. I would then smile and gratefully say, "Yes, thank you," and go along with my escort. But *eventually* took a little too long for my impatient young soul. Damn that. I'd rather negotiate the noisy traffic on my own (and remember, this was before traffic lights were invented).

After some rational cognition on my part, I soon began doing just that. For I knew that the traffic was not *always* thick and fast. I could see that at times there were long, one- or two-minute gaps between cars and carriages, and I knew (from experience) that it only took me five seconds to scoot safely across the street when one of these traffic lapses occurred. So I sanely, and quite ably, started saying to myself, "Hmph! It's really not that dangerous. Noisy, yes. Dangerous looking, yes. But if I just wait a minute or two, a gap in the traffic will occur and I can get across easily, safely. If I only wait. And waiting won't kill me. Traffic will, but waiting won't. So I'll be stuck for a while. So it's annoying to be stuck. So I don't like it. So what? I'd better wait and then run like the devil before the cars get me!"

Well, that sensible self-talk worked. I calmed myself down, went to and from school by myself every weekday, and negotiated the busily trafficked street with few qualms. At first I was afraid. Then I talked myself into being less afraid. Then I practiced acting against my fear and got myself used to this "fearful" situation. Then I lost my fear entirely. Then I actually began to enjoy the previously "frightening" situation. There I was, only four, and I figured out a model for overcoming "fearsome" situations about which I plagued myself.

Even at four, I was also strongly inclined to do the right things for the wrong reasons. For—remember—I could have assertively insisted that my mother bring me to school and back—something she would have balked at but still might have done. Or I could have kept asking adults to help me cross the dangerous street twice a day. But my shyness—a euphemistic word, of course, for scared-shitlessness—won out. I gave into my anxiety about making new acquaintances and therefore, perhaps foolishly, devised a way of self-sufficiently risking my own life. Once I indulged in my shyness for a while, I talked to myself pretty rationally and actually overcame my fear of the traffic. But for the next fifteen years or so I was left with the handicap of needless shyness in many social situations. In fact, you might say that I overcame the fear of onrushing cars and wagons rather than "intrude" on people. A Pyrrhic victory.

Be that as it was, I did accomplish something remarkable in my fourth year. I began to think about—philosophize about—the hassles and fears I encountered and how I could stop making myself unduly anxious, depressed, or self-pitying. I didn't always succeed. Either I did very well at licking my fearfulness, then fell right back on my silly face, or, as in the case of my slaying the frightful street traffic dragons, I conquered my fear for the wrong reasons.

People who are endogenously depressed tend to remember all the negative things in their lives and ignore the positive. Stubborn nondepressives, such as I, often do the opposite: egotistically remember only the positive events—how they bravely conquered or laughed off reality. Yes, I overcame my fear of crossing the heavily trafficked street outside my house in Pittsburgh, but what about the fears I didn't conquer? Hard to remember—but definitely existent. I wonder what they were. Probably something to do with shyness. But, as a result of (accidental or self-imposed) forgetfulness, I'll never know.

What about today? How would I react to a new, uncomfortable situation now that I am supposedly rational? Distinctly emotively, I am sure, for I still definitely wouldn't *like* it. But I would first look for the adventurous side and force myself to think about, and positively evaluate, what I could enjoyably *learn* from it. And the unpleasantness that still remained? I would, much more strongly than when I was four, accept that part. For, starting young, I have learned to accept what I cannot change. A little belatedly, considering that St. Francis started to do so in the thirteenth century, but quite determinedly!

Anyway, starting at about the age of four, I began to learn—or should I more accurately say, I began to *teach* myself—some major rules of stubbornly refusing to upset myself about virtually any unavoidable hassles or pains.

If you think that big things happened to me at the age of four, wait till you see what occurred at five. And how little Albert, little rational Albert, if you will, handled these things.

First of all, during my fourth year, my family and I moved to New York. Again, as I recall, I was not consulted by my parents about this move. Somehow, they assumed that they were to make the decision—which they unequivocally did. As I remember, I was told about the move only a few days before it actually occurred. Perhaps they knew about it months before. If so, they hardly bothered to tell me, my brother, or my (tiny baby) sister.

All I can remember is that a few days before the actual move a great deal of bustling and packing went on, and I, in my small way, cooperatively participated. Did I want to leave Pittsburgh for the wilds of New York? Hell, no. I was doing fine in this smoky city; I didn't even realize how smoky and smelly it was. To me, it was largely sunshine and light. When I walked to school and back every day—which I now did quite fearlessly and happily—the sky was blue, the air crisp and bright, and the river was clear and peaceful. I had friends in school; more amicable children and adults on my block; an attractive young godmother who always seemed fresh, beautiful, and sweetly attentive to my desires (and who, alas, was fated to die of cancer a few years later); and lots of interesting things to do—like running into our apartment to see how my mother was reprimanding my recalcitrant brother and how she was nursing my bland, passive sister. The Pittsburgh world was my oyster. What good would it do me to leave it for New York?

"No good," I thought, with some degree of disappointment. But only disappointment—not depression or anger. Having not yet invented the Rational Emotive Behavior Therapy (REBT) theory of healthy versus unhealthy negative feelings, I don't think I quite saw the difference between being disappointed and depressed. I can see, however, that early on I did somewhat follow my own later theory. I could have irrationally told myself, "Oh, fudge! Why must my goddamned parents tote me off to New York, away from my pleasures? How horribly unfair! They absolutely should not haul me away!" Instead of making myself angry and depressed, however, I used my high I.Q. to think differently—more rationally. I said to myself something like, "Oh, fudge! I wish they didn't jerk us away when I'm really beginning to enjoy Pittsburgh. But my father really has to go to New York for business opportunities there. And we are likely to see him more in New York than we now do, considering that he is on the road so much. So it will be a little disrupting, moving. So I'll miss my friends. So it will be annoying. Too bad. But not the end of the world!"

With these rational self-statements, I made myself feel only disappointed about the move, only healthfully sorrowful, instead of unhealthfully disturbed. "What is more," I added to myself, "look at the good things that may happen in New York. It's supposed to be much larger and more fascinating than Pittsburgh. It has the famous Statue of Liberty and the Woolworth Building. It has an exciting mover of people called the subway. And bigger and better stores. Maybe I'll really like it. Maybe I can learn more there!"

So within a day or two, I got over my disappointment and began to look forward to the adventure of New York. And adventure, at first, it was. Because my mother had three young children—and not for the life of her, pinchpenny that she was, was she going to pay extra train fare—we all traveled overnight to New York in a sleeping car. In fact, the four of us spent that night in one single bunk. A rather tight fit, as you might guess. Luckily, we had the bottom berth, or who knows what might have happened—with my brother jumping around half the night and my mother having to grab him, run after him (yes, down the aisle of the sleeper), and drag him back by the hair to our crowded cubicle. Fortunately, most of our travel was at night, so my sister slept most of the time and my brother (except for his hell-raising episode) got in a few winks here and there. My mother, I seem to recall, hardly slept at all, since she was so busy seeing that we were reasonably comfortable and, preferably, asleep.

Not that she was able to do much for me in this respect. For even though we boarded the sleeper late at night and were scheduled to arrive in New York early the next morning, I was my typical insomniac self. I never was a good sleeper and often spent what seemed a good part of the night getting to sleep and then getting back to sleep each time I awoke. On this particular night I was highly excited about boarding the train, watching the Pullman car conductor make up the berths, peeping through the curtain to see other passengers snuggle into their berths, and looking out the window to watch the city and country scenery roll rapidly by. All through the night I kept nodding off, then waking up, asking my mother how much longer the ride was going to take and what New York City would be like once we got there. So I stayed up most of the night, but in an exhilarated, enjoyable state, as opposed to the rather harried state of my mother.

When we finally reached New York in the dawn's early light, I was yawny and far from my usual rise-and-shine self. But I enjoyed the hustle of Pennsylvania Station, meeting my father there, finding the porter who helped us with our luggage, taking the taxi ride to our new domicile, and installing ourselves in our furnished apartment on 110th Street—at that time a ritzy neighborhood bordering Central Park.

Once settled, I often found life hectic and disruptive. My sister had some kind of childhood ailment. My brother was, as ever, a royal pain in the ass, continually running around, as my mother put it, "like a chicken with his head cut off," getting into ceaseless trouble. My mother, hardly the most organized person, had innumerable things to do. My father was around for a change, but he still ran off every day to some kind of "business meeting." I was largely left to my own devices, with no supervision, no friends, no kindergarten, and nothing much but the City of New York with which to occupy my waking (about eighteen- to twenty-hour) days.

Well, that wasn't so hot. Life wasn't meant to be that way. Hectic wasn't exactly horrible, but enough was enough! When were we going to get that homey apartment in the East Bronx that my father kept promising us would soon be ready? *When?*

I didn't know when. My parents kept telling me that we were about to move into our new apartment. Then that it still wasn't ready. Then that it would be in a few days. Then that it wouldn't be . . . and so on. So I at first decided to be anxious and miserable. That state was interesting—but a little too interesting to suit my hedonistic tastes. Then I decided to be less anxious and miserable. How? Well, I wasn't sure exactly how, but I thought I might work on that and see if I could find out how.

I did work on it and I did discover how to make myself less miserable. I don't remember, at this late date (over eighty-eight years later) exactly what I said to myself to make myself less anxious and disturbed about uncertainty. But I remember telling myself something like this: "I would like to move to our new home as soon as possible, because dallying around in this furnished apartment is just not for me. Maybe for some other child, who likes this sort of thing, but not for me. My parents are very vague about when we will move. They really don't seem to know when. What a nuisance! But it won't go on forever. *One* of these days our new apartment will be ready. Why does it have to be today? Why can't it be tomorrow? Or the day after? Or a week from now? It can. So I'll put up with not moving to a new apartment until things settle. Meanwhile, I'll go about my business as usual, enjoying myself as much as I can."

Which I did. I played by myself—for there didn't seem to be any other children in that neighborhood. I talked to the superintendent of our building, who was one of the few people around during the day. I took the elevator up and down to our tenth-floor apartment, so I could chat with the elevator man, who seemed pleasant enough. I helped my mother a little with my squalling sister and my bratty brother. And I played with the few toys I had; most of our things were still in our bolted trunks that sat stolidly in the foyer of our temporary apartment.

Not a good time in my life, all told. Not too fascinating once I got bored with our new surroundings. But not bad either, because I stubbornly refused to make it that bad. I, little Albert, was not (yet) a creator of a fine, vibrant existence. But I was, in my own quiet way, working determinedly to make myself into an *accepter* of (grim) reality. And I was doing, if not magnificently, at least okay.

Things got much better a few weeks later, when we finally moved into our new apartment at 1021 Bryant Avenue in the East Bronx. Was it actually 1021? Yes, I am certain, eighty-eight years later, even though we lived there only about two years before moving to a brand-new two-story house on Heath Avenue in the West Bronx. What was the number of the Heath Avenue house? I haven't the foggiest idea, though I think it was something like 2532. But the 1021 number on Bryant Avenue somehow sticks in my mind and always has. Maybe because I thought that seven was my lucky number, and twenty-one is three times seven? Who knows?

Anyway, I found Bryant Avenue, from 1917 to 1919, an almost ideal place. It sported many apartment houses pretty much like our own, most of them inhabited by middle-class Jewish families, each with two or more children. Directly across the street from our house was a large empty lot, where we children practically lived. A block away were local stores, most notably the popular neighborhood candy store, which specialized in all kinds of plain and fancy sodas. Not "two cents plain," which the radio comedians later brought to my attention, but "one cent plain"—yes, a single cent for a large glass of plain soda or seltzer, which our particular store dispensed. For two cents, if I remember right, you got one of five or six delicious flavors with the soda. This candy store, which was almost my second home for the next couple of years, also had the best damned delicious malteds I ever tasted. Thick, creamy, incredibly chocolaty. A thing of beauty and a joy forever—or at least for the five or ten minutes it took to bolt down the two huge glasses that came out of the steel mixing cup. Pittsburgh never had anything like this! And I was supremely happy that the Bronx was infinitely more civilized.

I found the availability of male companions on Bryant Avenue even better, including a couple dozen around my own age. I became particularly close with Steve, an eight-year-old who took a great shine to me, although I was a good three years his junior, and who showed me the ropes of the neighborhood. He introduced me to the ball games—especially to catch, hide-and-go-seek, follow the leader, and the other common games.

Steve also showed me how to spy on little girls who, not wanting to run home to use the bathroom and interrupt their play, shyly pissed against a fence. We boys watched them squat and desperately tried to see what their genitals looked like and how differently from us they urinated. Steve also took me to one of the largest streets in the Bronx, Southern Boulevard, which was three blocks away and inhabited by large stores such as Woolworth's Five-and-Ten. He told me some of the facts of life—such as the differences between boys and girls and why most fathers worked all day while most mothers kept getting pregnant and then took care of their young children. Steve was an enormous help, and when we moved to Heath Avenue, a couple of years later, he was the one I really missed and with whom I occasionally remained in contact.

Even more important, in some ways, was Don, a boy my own age who taught me how to read—or, rather, who encouraged me to teach myself to read. For, along with Don, I encountered the next great frustration of my life: our local public school would not allow us to enter until we were six. At the time I met Don we were both five. Technically, we were eligible for kindergarten, but our parents moved to Bryant Avenue too late in the year to have us registered. So we would have to wait till next September and then enter the first grade when we were six.

Neither of us liked this very much, especially me. I had enjoyed kindergarten and wanted to resume as soon as possible, and now the lousy school authorities—for no good reason that I could see—were going to cheat me out of it. What villains! Don agreed, and his parents thought he was ready for first grade. They had taught him how to read, and he, like me, seemed to be a bright boy who could have easily begun the first grade at five and done well. So we both felt cheated and spewed out many unkind words about the school system. In fact, we competed with each other to see who could defame the school authorities most. Being quite verbal, and having a garrulous mother who enraged herself over the school's not taking me off her hands, I think I won the defaming contest.

And yet, although intensely desirous of making my days less miserable, I did find some advantages to staying out of school. For one thing, I had Don, who was almost always available to play with me. For another thing, he was willing to read his illustrated books aloud to me and help me read them too. I soon learned that the picture of the boy was equivalent to B-O-Y, the drawing of the sheep was equivalent to S-H-E-E-P, and so on. After a few weeks, I began to read as well as Don did. Then I plagued my parents to get me some books of my own, which (to get me out of my mother's hair) they gladly did. Soon, like Don, I was reading at a third-grade level, even though he and I were refugees from kindergarten.

That was all to the good. But whenever I saw our other little friends leave for school every morning and then happily return around three, I cursed their sonofabitch school. What injustice! How could they possibly do that to a nice boy like me?

I soon decided that they could. Parents, other adults, and school officials obviously were often wrong and unfair. Not to mention arbitrary and stupid. But if that was the way they were, then that was the way they were. Inconsiderate. Idiotic. Unjust. But alas there was no way, not in the foreseeable future, of changing them. So I gave myself another lesson in the important philosophy of accepting things you can't change.

Having come to the observation that the world is often unfair, I also made some unchildlike conclusions from the observed data. Many children decide that the world and the people in it are indubitably unkind and unjust. But then they endlessly rant about this unfairness, upset themselves immensely, and often bring on their silly heads even more suffering. Don was such a child: he observed the harshness of the world but never really accepted it. The entire year we were out of school together, he whined about how shitty it was and how the school authorities—stupid jerks!—should be hanged from the rafters for hindering our academic progress.

I verbally agreed. But the more he raved on, the more I sensed that he was unduly upsetting himself. "Yes," I said to myself, "the school authorities certainly are unfair to Don and me. But will upsetting myself about this, as Don and his parents keep doing, make them let us go to school? Heck, no! Will it do any good at all? Not that I can see. Then why upset myself?"

At first, I couldn't give a very good answer to this question. It seemed only natural to feel upset when others were plaguing you. More than natural—it actually felt good. But in another way, it didn't feel good. It felt upsetting. It felt a little too arousing. And, since I could see how Don and his parents kept boring *me* with their endless complaints, I realized that complaining made one a real nuisance to others.

"Maybe," I thought, "there's a better way to feel. Maybe I can feel more like my mother feels when 'upsetting' things happen: first angry, but then fairly unserious and uncaring. She never seems to take anything too seriously. At least, not for very long. Maybe she's got something there! Unlike my father, who easily gets and stays enraged. And over very little. And he seems so unhappy when he's upset like that."

So I thought about how different people react to similar "upsetting" conditions. Hardly alike! Some were happy, some miserable, others fairly indifferent about the same event. There seemed to be a choice about your feelings. Yes, a *choice*.

And so, at the age of five, I made a choice. I decided not to make myself miserable about being forced to stay out of school. I didn't like it and occasionally remembered (with a moderate degree of discomfort) that I wasn't getting what I really wanted. But I decided to lump it rather than to whine. So I didn't like it. So why did I have to?

After choosing to enjoy myself in spite of life's restrictions, I threw myself into learning to read with Don and exploring the neighborhood with Steve—and I began to lead a good life. This, at first to my surprise but then to my normal expectation, invariably seemed to happen when I refused to indulge in misery-amassing. Whenever I was temporarily desperate about something and then decided not to be, I soon found enjoyable distractions that made me feel good. I not only was un-miserable but I actually became pretty happy.

Even at this tender age I began to combat incipient depression in two therapeutic ways: first, I determinedly refused to turn my frustration into a holocaust. Second, I looked for special things I enjoyed and wholeheartedly threw myself into them until one clicked and became what I later labeled (in *A Guide to Rational Living*) a "vital absorbing interest." At five, I managed to concoct two vital absorptions: learning to read and exploring the East Bronx with Steve. And both helped me overcome the potential disaster of being kept out of school for a year.

{}

Was I really as bright and rational at this very young age as I now retrospectively make out? Probably not. I am, of course, recalling only the "major" problems of those days and how I dealt with them. If they were major, as I deemed them to be, it is hardly surprising that they evoked deep protective thinking and that some of this thought was rational and effective. Obviously, I survived, so clearly I coped. To cope is to think and to think somewhat rationally. So I apparently did just that.

There were certainly things I don't remember about this period that were minor and less troublesome—which is precisely why they didn't make a memorable impression. But that doesn't mean I didn't worry about them at the time they occurred. On the contrary, I see myself as a *natural* worrier—and hence, I surmise, one who is often *driven* to think up anti-worrisome solutions to everyday dilemmas.

Because of my natural tendency to be anxious as well as the exigencies of my early life, I suspect that in some ways I was *more* worried than most of my peers. But my fears were repetitive and routine, and, being about less-than-life-and-death matters, they were intrinsically evanescent. If I worried, for example, about my mother returning home from shopping, she eventually did return. If I was tense about not getting what

I wanted for my birthday, that day came and that problem got resolved. So time and circumstances provided solutions to my angst.

But did they really? No. Because I worried just about as much the next time. I still *had* to know that my mother would return from her shopping. I still *demanded*, next birthday, a guarantee that I would get what I wanted. So although I rationally dealt with what I saw as the "big" troubles, I largely let external conditions take care of my "normal" problems. I was, consequently, less upsettable than I could have been. I remember, during my childhood, having hundreds of minor worries (so inconsequential that I can only vaguely recollect them) that I rarely dealt with but let circumstances resolve. Apparently, the greater the difficulty was, the more I persisted at solving or accepting it.

By the time I reached adulthood, the fallout from that practice was both good and bad. I began to solve my small worries in much the same way as I had begun in my early days to resolve my larger ones. Instead of waiting for time to clear them up, I actively schemed to improve them myself. This usually worked fine—and still does. I take care of potential problems so well that they often get settled before they develop. But I may be so preoccupied with planning them out of existence that my preparations themselves may be too time-consuming. So, if you are as naturally anxiety-prone as I am, you can't completely win. You only ameliorate, never cure. My habit of forestalling hassles, developed during my childhood, has often served me very well, but it is not without some disadvantages, such as underlying anxiety that rarely is profound but is continual. I spend so much time figuring out the "best" solutions to possible problems that I may well neglect dealing with deeper and more important issues.

A case in point: Years ago, Janet, with whom I lived for thirty-seven years, was sleeping in the patio room of our apartment, and I was sleeping in the adjoining living room because the bedroom was being renovated. She lit two candles to create a more pleasant atmosphere. Fine. But, as usual, she fell asleep while reading—with the candles brightly burning. I was a little alarmed, seeing them lit as I awoke to go to the bathroom. Actually, there was little danger, as the candles were tall, in solid candlesticks, and on a glass table. But they could have fallen and started a fire.

I didn't want to wake Janet, so I figured out what I would do if, by unusual chance, a fire did start. Thinking and planning about different things to do—though not actually worrying about the "horrors" of a fire—kept me awake. "Fuck it," I thought. "The worst that could happen is we could die, and that would be highly inconvenient but not awful." So I started to go back to sleep.

Then Janet awoke, argued that the lit candles were really very safe, but in deference to me, she put them out. All clear. I started to go back to sleep. But I didn't sleep. I kept thinking of various things I would do if, for any reason, a fire started in our apartment. Would I first call 911 from our apartment, more safely run downstairs to call 911, ring for the elevator if it was far from the fire, or what? Let me see what plan was best. Still not worried about the possible fire and its consequences, and far removed from feelings of panic, I was nevertheless so preoccupied with planning and scheming in case of a fire that I couldn't sleep. Finally, knowing I would be tired the next working day, I forced myself to focus on monotonous stimuli—listening to my regular breathing—and got myself to sleep. I would think about fire plans the next day. So there!

My main point is: I rarely catastrophize or "awfulize" possible dangers. But I sometimes "worry"—that is, plan to prevent them—so effectively that I waste the time I've saved from worrying about the dangers or worrying about preventing the dangers. So I am both "calm" *and* "worried" simultaneously. Is this a form of natural anxiety? I would say yes.

Chapter 1B

Coping with Emotional Problems: My Neglectful Father and My Low Frustration Tolerance

Was I always a dedicated problem solver? Yes, I think I was. Ironically enough, this may have stemmed from my low frustration tolerance—my LFT. As far as I can recall, my father was quite irritable and critical of other people's doings. He knew—definitely knew!—what was right and didn't hesitate to complain about what was wrong. No, I don't remember him yelling at me very much, but I also don't remember him being around very much to do so. Nothing ventured, nothing strained!

Am I like my absentee father in this respect? Yes, in more ways than one. I, too, usually know the right—meaning the more efficient—way to do practically everything, and am 98 and ¾ percent sure that others are often "wrong" or "ineffective." How do I know? Well, I bother—as those others *should* do—to figure out "better" ways to do practically everything, from masturbation to procrastination. Yes, I even procrastinate magnificently. I avoid doing onerous tasks briefly and unostentatiously. So I never get caught making a late presentation, losing interest on my savings, or being fined for back taxes. When I do things at the last minute, or even in a rush—which, of course, is moronic—I never wait till *beyond* the last minute. I still get it done on time. So there!

Somewhat like my father, I do not voice my criticisms very much. I'm far from being an ass-licker for love (though I'll later relate how I sometimes apple-polish for practical reasons), but I know that criticism seriously "hurts" people who allow it to. Almost always. So I think carpingly with my yap tightly buttoned. But me and my nutty father—boy, did we both often think and feel great censure for others. He usually proclaimed it from the roof of his mouth when his detractors were not around, but not so much from public rooftops. A pragmatist. I usually trumpet it only in my head but not at their heads. A super-pragmatist!

Nonetheless, I often *think* in the critical way my father did. *I hate* people's "cretinism" and *demand* their whiz-bang responses—but rarely overtly. So where he was often a long-range hothead, I note my internal rancor, acknowledge my own overreacting and overbearing-ness, and get back to my ideal of Unconditional Other-Acceptance (UOA), which is one of the main things we teach in Rational Emotive Behavior Therapy (REBT). I try to get back to this ideal pretty darned quickly. But then I may fall from grace again.

I sometimes tell my clients about my father's absence and neglect. He rarely spent more than a few minutes at a time with us, and when he did, he was hardly devoted. He seldom questioned us; he didn't helpfully tell us what to do or play with us. My Uncle Ben, however, did all of these things. On his trips to New York for a day or two, he always romped with the three of us, my brother, sister, and me in our living room or dining room—and *enjoyed* it. He even kept breaking away from conversing with his sister Hettie, my mother, to excitedly play little games with us on the floor. For an hour—yes, a whole hour!

Not my busy father. He awoke at 8:30 a.m.—just before I was about to walk to school—kissed me good morning while he was still prone in bed, and, well, that was about it. He was always smiling and pleasant. But interested? Hmph! His morning greeting took a few seconds. I thought it was fine to kiss my father good morning, but if he was away on a sales trip, for instance, I got by very well. No sweat.

I think he went back to sleep for a while. Then he went to work till about eight or nine or sometimes ten. First, at the office. Then business meetings. Maybe poker or pinochle games. Maybe—as we later suspected—some screwing around. By the time he came home to sleep, we three children were already in bed. No, we didn't see him at all.

Saturdays? He slept late and then went to the office till 5 p.m. We saw him briefly at six, but then he and my mother went out to dinner and a show or a movie, and we were left with our maid.

Sunday? He got up quite late—eleven or twelve—had breakfast, and by one o'clock was playing pinochle or poker for the rest of the day and half the night with several of his male friends. Once in a great while—maybe twice a year—he went on an outing with us, to visit family friends. There again, he played cards with the men while my mother talked to the women, and we three children played as best we could with each other or with other children. We had no radio or TV in those days, so maybe we listened to phonograph records. My family—I don't know at whose insistence—had a good collection of classical music, operatic arias, and operetta performances. So that, I thought, was fine.

In fact, my mother told me that at the age of two I sang a great deal in my stroller, lustily voicing many of the popular songs of the day and even making up some of my own. She was a fine singer herself and almost became a professional, so I somewhat take after her musically. I always seemed to have an innate talent for composing music and could—and still can—do so endlessly. Unfortunately, my low frustration tolerance stopped me from learning how to play or write down my compositions. But that's another story.

Back to my neglectful father. Was my father nasty and mean? No. Did he criticize or belittle me? No. He was always—well, almost always—nice to me and my brother and sister. Did he favor any of us? Perhaps my sister a little, but not much. Nice and pleasant. Affable. Generous. But only attentive for a few minutes. Then back to his own preoccupations: business, card playing, socializing, maybe reading the paper. And how was he with my mother? I would say pretty much the same. They rarely quarreled or fought. But were they intimate and loving? Not that I remember!

Was my father cold? Shallow? Unfeeling? Clearly no—if he really was as irritable and angry as I think he was. Moreover, he was publicly intimate with his second wife, Rose. He fondled her affectionately—never in a sexual way—and said incredibly sweet things about her.

My guess is that my father was always busily occupied—and preoccupied. Business, cards, conversation, politics—all of the above, and more, were interesting to him. I never saw him bored. Always alert, always absorbed in some kind of problem solving. Like me! Maybe earlier with my mother and with Rose, he had been wildly in love, like I was, with girl after girl, woman after woman. Maybe. But like many people who are incessantly highly involved with some project, game, or idea, he rarely seemed to be anxious or depressed. Just intensely concerned. Perhaps, in working with him in two (failing) businesses when I was twenty-three and twenty-four, I noted this asset and developed my idea of acquiring a vital, absorbing, long-term interest to achieve true happiness. Or perhaps—more likely—I got this idea from watching myself. Or both.

In one way, I surmise, I was one up on my father. I easily and spontaneously got myself positively absorbed in certain people and things. As I shall describe later on, I fell madly in love with a blue-eyed blond bombshell when I was five and a half and with scads of other blondes, brunettes, and redheads for the next eighty-something years. But I also had at least one other ongoing obsession with things and projects—again, from five and a half onward. Let me see if I can remember some of the main interests and the years I heartily immersed myself in them.

- Reading (5 1/2 years onward)
- Stamp collecting (7 to 9)
- Spelling (7 to 8)
- Arithmetic and algebra (7 to 12)
- Mechanical drawing (12 to 13)
- Writing (12 onward)
- Light opera and semiclassical music (13 onward)
- Philosophy (15 onward)
- Economic and political revolution (18 to 22)
- Songwriting (17 onward)
- Comic verse (17 onward)
- Psychology (17 onward)
- Sex and love revolution (22 onward)
- Sex, love, and marriage theory and practice (25 onward)
- Practicing psychotherapy (28 onward)
- Creating and practicing Rational Emotive Behavior Therapy (40 onward)
- Founding and building the Albert Ellis Institute for Rational Emotive Behavior Therapy (46 onward)

Quite a list. But typical. Seeing how involved I am with many aspects of therapy—doing it, teaching it, supervising it, writing about it—people sometimes ask, "Suppose, for some reason, you couldn't do what you're doing anymore—say, had a stroke, became deaf, couldn't sit up most of the day and talk with people. What would you do? How would you still make yourself happy?"

Answer: "I would probably find at least one aspect of what I do now—such as writing about therapy—and thoroughly involve myself with that. If, somehow, that was impossible, I would pick something else—composing music, for instance, or writing about people who conquered personal adversity—and throw myself, as thoroughly as I could, into that. Never fear: I am a natural doer, a Jack-of-at-least-one-conscientious-trade-at-a-time. Rest assured: I'd find something!" I would.

Again: training or conditioning? My father and mother were both unremitting doers, though my mother slowed down a bit in her nineties. Heredity? Same answer. Environment and genetics? Ah—very likely.

But what about my near-compulsive drive, which my close relatives seemed to lack, to master a field of endeavor thoroughly, almost perfectly? Where does that come from? We shall soon see.

Chapter 1C

My Sex and Love Life
My First Great Love (Besides Myself)

Before I reached the age of six, two near-holocausts occurred that gave me ample practice at mastering and reordering my initial semi-hysterical reactions. First of all, I fell madly in love with a charming and (to my highly prejudiced view) utterly beautiful blue-eyed blonde named Ruthie. In those days, following the lead of the famous movie star Mary Pickford, women and girls often had long curly hair, and Ruthie was the rule rather than the exception. My mother—as Sigmund Freud would have knowingly pointed out—was also a blue-eyed blonde and in her own way exceptionally good-looking, with perfect Germanic American (and almost completely non-Jewish) features. But, frankly, she (unless I am deeply repressing this) never really thrilled me sexually. Perhaps familiarity breeds contempt. Perhaps she was too thin and flat-chested. Perhaps it was her lack of devotion to fancy dress, jewels, and underwear.

Whatever it was, I lusted, from the age of five onward, for just about every attractive female except my mom. Heaven knows how many movie stars I madly loved. And how many performers . . . and teachers . . . and cousins . . . and nurses . . . and classmates I dreamed of kissing, cuddling, and (as they called it in those days) necking with. Dozens! Or was it scores? Actual intercourse was not on my mind, for, frankly, I didn't quite yet understand that concept. But practically everything else up to that was on my mind.

My love mates were almost always older women, such as nurses I hardly knew personally. Until I met Ruthie. This little blue-eyed doll lived in the next apartment house, and her parents were close friends of my parents. Like me, she was just five—in fact, I think we were both born in September. Ruthie and I often got together for a chat about school, about movies, about games, and about everything else dear to a five-year-old's repartee.

My friend Don and I would usually play together on the street, right outside my apartment door, but my cozier chats with Ruthie took place in the room I shared with my brother. (Throughout our childhood, my brother and I almost always shared a bedroom.) When Ruthie's parents and mine went to the theater or to dinner, which they frequently did on Saturday night, Ruthie and I were left to play with each other in this room, while my three-year-old brother was temporarily put to sleep in my sister's room.

Not that Ruthie and I were unchaperoned. My family was, at that time, quite well-to-do and in addition to employing a chauffeur for our electric-driven Cadillac, we also had a full-time maid. After Ruthie's parents and mine left the house, the maid would put my sister and brother to sleep, sit in the kitchen, and immerse herself in a Swedish newspaper, looking in on us every once in a while to see that we were not burning down the house. And since Ruthie and I were polite and unrambunctious, the maid rarely checked on us at all.

Her mistake, that wintry Saturday night! For not only were Ruthie and I practicing being loving, but, knowing our parents would not be home until late that night, we decided to practice being sexy as well. Not that we really knew what to do. The love scenes we had seen in the movies were not, in those days, terribly explicit. *Something* always seemed to happen to get our beautiful and frail Nell pregnant or into some other kind of sexual trouble. But once the movie showed our hero laying his hands on Nell and her finally succumbing to his vile clutches, the screen would suddenly go blank. Nine months later there would be a wedding, a childbirth, or some other interesting conclusion. But exactly *which* act led to *what* conclusion was never made clear.

So Ruthie and I, given this meager information, could only do our damnedest on our own. We knew, naturally, that boys and girls were different. We knew that they did something to each other with their lower parts. But we didn't precisely know what. Being bright and inquisitive, we were determined to find out. My bedroom had a long radiator covered with a cabinet with holes in the front to let the steam out and a wooden top, which served as a kind of seat or workbench. Ruthie and I used it as a kind of medical examination table. We both took off our clothes (knowing this was not the right thing to do but being determined to do it anyway) and we sat and hugged and kissed on this (nicely warmed) radiator cabinet. That seemed pretty cozy, and I think we snuggled for twenty minutes or so, exploring each other's bodies with our hands and tongues.

Ruthie's body, incidentally, I found perfectly gorgeous. She was, as I previously noted, a beautiful little girl and had a plumpish, well-constructed body. Just the kind a young boy likes to kiss, lick, fondle, grasp, and caress. I had always imagined that when she got her frilly clothes off, she looked and felt like that. And I was right! In some ways, in fact, her body, her hands, and her mouth and cheeks were even better than I had (incessantly) dreamed about. So now that they were fully revealed in all their glory, and now that she seemed just as intent on kissing and caressing my body (and penis!) as I was on fondling her top and bottom, I was wildly ecstatic. If I remember right, I fully confessed that I had loved her ever since I first met her (several months before) and that I dreamt of her day and night. And she said something like, "Oh, yes. I know. I could see by the way you looked at me. And I really like you, too. I like being with you this way."

Not exactly a proposal of marriage. But certainly, for the nonce, sufficient. My unrequited love was now, I thought, fully requited. Life had no more frustrating bounds or limitations. Heaven could surely never be any better than this! Now, if only this could continue forever!

But it couldn't. Our parents would come back reasonably soon and (we knew darned well) put a stop to all this. Besides, our kissing and embracing wasn't getting to the bottom, the very bottom of things. Ruthie could see everything, since my little penis was clearly revealed and could be nicely explored with her hands and mouth with no more mysteries about it. Not so her genitals. They, as I had sort of suspected, were much different from mine, and a heck of a lot more attractive. Nothing hanging down between her legs, only a beautifully curved nether region—and a slit, which seemed to be closed. I assumed that she somehow urinated out of that slit, but I wasn't quite sure. And I assumed that something else, something deeply profound, was going on deep within that slit. But I had no idea what it was. I put my finger down there and could get it a wee bit into that opening, but not too far. And it still didn't reveal what was really going on down there. What could it be? What was behind that mysterious slit?

Well, there was only one way to find out, and that was to really look. So I got Ruthie to lie on her back on the radiator cover and tried to discover what was inside, truly inside, her. I was not very successful.

Some pinkish tissue, as far as I could see. And a small hole that one of my fingers could slip into. But the hole seemed to continue and then go nowhere.

Being a budding scientist even in those days, I decided to explore further and with proper instruments. I reasoned that if Ruthie had a long and deep hole, starting at her external slit, it had to go *somewhere*. But how deep was it? And where *did* it go? I would use whatever technology I had at hand and try to answer these fascinating scientific questions.

I snuck into the kitchen, saw that our maid was dozing at the kitchen table, and surreptitiously found (1) a funnel and (2) a bottle of milk. I joyfully lugged my stolen booty back to the bedroom where Ruthie was still stretched out, lusciously naked, on the radiator seat. I stuck the end of the funnel gently into her vulval slit and prepared to pour the milk into it. Where would the milk go? Would it go down a bit and then stop? Would it keep endlessly spilling into her body and come out of her mouth? What would happen? What would this show me about the female genitalia and the female body? Boy, this was going to be revealing! Both Ruthie and I would thoroughly enjoy (for she was just as ignorant of her inner workings as I was) what we would soon find. On with the experiment, to the hopefully sweet end!

Alas, it was not to be. Just as I was beginning to pour the milk into her vaginal cavity and had gotten perhaps a few drops down the funnel, all four of our parents burst noisily into the room, reacting with absolute horror over what we were doing. I don't recall them actually screaming and yelling, and certainly they didn't hit us. But the gist of their message was: "Look, you little shits! What do you think we left you alone like this for—to become sex perverts? It's bad enough that you might think up a trick like this when you become mature adults like us. But to be that sexually creative at the age of five? My God, what the hell is this crazy world coming to! As for that goddamned maid, sleeping her ass off in the kitchen while the two of you were actively engaged in this horrible act of er, of er, of er, uh, sodomy, well, we'll certainly see about her. And right away, with not a minute lost! How could she *do* a thing like that—go to sleep and let you do what you did? How could she? Yes, how *could* she?"

"Apparently," I said to myself, "she could. And did." In fact, if they would only stop screaming for a moment and look at the facts of the situation, they would realize that the maid, Thelma, often acted that way, leaving me and some friend to do whatever we liked. That's why

I knew the coast was so clear when I started to play around sexually with Ruthie. Unfortunately, I forgot that while *she* was asleep, *they*, Ruth's parents and mine, were not, and would eventually return. Things just got so delicious between us that I lost track of time, as lovers—especially true lovers like us—always do. Too bad I had not set some kind of alarm.

Anyway, while I was ruminating along these lines—Lord knows what Ruthie was thinking, but I suspect something similar, since she seemed rather pensive—I was also calming myself down from the first shock of being caught. I noticed that while my mother and Ruthie's mother were batting away on all verbal cylinders, our fathers were largely silent and seemed almost quietly amused by the whole thing. My own father was smiling broadly as he helped me into some clothes and seemed almost proud of his wicked son Albert and the "awful" things he had just done. And Ruthie's father, though a little sterner (as he roughly got her into *her* clothes) and hardly enthusiastic about what she had done, also seemed to be smiling a little benignly about my iniquitous part of the proceedings. I didn't quite catch it at the time, but I can see retrospectively that both these men were honest and sincere MCPs (male chauvinist pigs) who somewhat enjoyed little whippersnapper Albert's taking advantage of the female sex and found something charming about his "vile" act.

Ruthie's mother, a typical FCS (female chauvinist sow), took a much grimmer view of the situation, and in stentorian tones vocalized that her daughter's reputation was ruined and since Ruth had been technically violated (and possibly devirginized!), she could only proceed to a life of sin and wind up as a streetwalker. "Of that I'm sure, I'm sure!" this outraged mother kept reiterating, while the other three parents sympathetically shook their heads in agreement. But to my practiced eye (I don't know about Ruthie's), I could guess that their agreement with this hysterical woman was mainly pro forma, and that the other three parents, including my mother, really didn't give that much of a shit.

Maybe I was wrong about this. Maybe our parents, all four of them, were thoroughly outraged by my "taking advantage of" poor Ruthie and devirginizing her with a funnel. But that wasn't the way I (wishfully thinkingly?) saw it. I saw, all right, that Ruthie's mother was incensed and that she, there but for the grace of God, might well have clipped off my testicles. But I saw—or thought I saw—that the other three parents were going to spume and froth at the mouth for a while, but do nothing else. Neither my father nor mother so much as raised a hand toward me, and Ruthie's father spluttered even less and (being considerably smaller than my five-foot-eleven-inch dad) seemed wholly uninclined to take the law in his hands and whale the living daylights out of me (or Ruthie).

So I felt a little shame and guilt—mainly at my own stupidity for not finishing my examination of Ruthie before our parents burst in on our "perversity." But except for a few minutes after we were first discovered, I wasn't exceptionally fearful. I somehow *knew* that I wasn't going to (publicly or privately) get my behind walloped. To allay my remaining anxiety, I firmly said to myself, "Okay! So you did a really stupid thing this time! Or, you foolishly let yourself be caught doing it. Maybe you shouldn't have sweet-talked Ruthie into what you did. Maybe it is wrong to stick funnels up little girls' slits-between-their-legs. Maybe you'd better watch that kind of thing next time. But it's done. And upsetting yourself about it won't make it undone. So let them scream, your parents and Ruthie's. Let them think you feel totally ashamed of yourself and that you'll never, positively never, do a 'horrible' thing like that again. Promise them anything, in fact, if just to shut them up. Promise them you'll never do a single thing wrong in the future. That'll quiet them and give you a chance to go to bed. So promise them whatever they want. What have you got to lose?"

I promptly followed my own advice, told them that I was terribly sorry for what I had done (which I really wasn't), and managed to quiet them down. On her part, Ruthie said practically nothing, she merely hung her head in (pseudo?) shame and acted as if she was not that guilty since I had led her, mainly against her will, astray. "Horseshit," I exclaimed to myself, when I saw her acting in that butter-wouldn't-melt-in-her-mouth way. But I realized that, with a mother like hers, what the devil else could she really do? So I forgave her for her behavior, figuring she had to do it to save her skin, and figuring (wrongly, alas!) that we would get together again and eagerly return to our fascinating sexual explorations.

I merely sat things out, pretending deep contrition. This was a wise move, as it turned out. After Ruthie's parents dragged her unceremoniously home, my mother and father reprimanded me more mildly than before, and I still thought (though I may have been projecting) that they secretly admired my guts. When I went to the bathroom before finally going to bed, and surreptitiously listened at the door to their room, I heard partly covered-up laughter, seemingly about my chutzpah in uniquely devirginizing a young woman at the tender age of five.

On a couple more deliberate trips to the bathroom that night I also heard what sounded like more sex noises than I usually heard on previous occasions of eavesdropping. So even if they were upset about their son's "perversity," they were taking some advantage of it too. Or so I (self-referentially) guessed.

As if to confirm these thoughts, the next day they seemed to be in exceptionally good moods, talked pleasantly to me about all kinds of things (and not at *all* about last night's incident), and said nothing about my escapade to my three-year-old brother, even when he asked them, at one point, "What was all that rumpus going on last night? Did we have a fire or something?" "Oh, no," they said, "that was really nothing. Ruthie's parents got a little upset about something, but it wasn't really important." He shut up, and so did they—forever, as far as I could see. Sex wasn't mentioned again. Ruthie wasn't mentioned again. Ruthie's parents weren't mentioned—or, for that matter, as far as I could tell, ever seen—again. Which was all right with me. Except—ah, woe! That was the end of me and Ruthie. From that day on I never spoke with her. Occasionally, for the next month or so, I saw her fleetingly on the street, usually held tightly by one or both of her parents. She studiously avoided even looking at me, keeping her eyes glued to the pavement while her parents dragged her along and made sure she said nothing—absolutely nothing—to me. What was worse, after a couple of months she and her parents disappeared entirely. They had moved, I was told by my mother, to the West Bronx, literally miles away, and, as far as I could tell, they never even went anywhere near our neighborhood again.

Gone! The fair—and I do mean fair, since she was incredibly blond and bright blue-eyed—Ruthie was completely gone. At first, I could hardly believe it, since I kept harboring the illusion that one of these days all would be forgiven and Ruthie and I would take up our idyllic romance again. I often dreamed it so. I frequently felt it, practically tasted it happening, our renewed (ah, so ecstatically renewed!) encountering. My, what a great dream! But, sadness of sadness, only that.

This immense loss gave me something utterly and uniquely tragic in my young life to cope with, for my great lust for Ruthie was hardly just that. No, indeed. It was real—and I mean 110 percent real, total, complete, and stupendous—love. I hardly even thought, in my constant day and night dreams, about her smooth, plump, naked body. Those images and reconstructed sensations were ineluctably delicious, as you may well imagine. But what I most—constantly—dreamed about was holding Ruthie's bewitching little hand (much smaller and smoother than my own fairly large one), as we sat together and intimately talked, just talked. *That* was what I wanted most (oh, so utterly most!): to sit next to Ruthie again, hold her hand, and talk, talk, talk. To tell her how much I adored her, how I hoped to marry her one day, and how charmingly we could rear our seven blond, bright blue-eyed children. I wasn't quite sure how those children would materialize, though I vaguely thought it had *something* to do with sex. But I knew that if we kept seeing each other, and if we eventually married, we would have our own little Ruthie and our own little Albert—not to mention a few other beautiful kids as well.

That was hard, really hard, not seeing Ruthie again, not telling her how much I loved her. And as the days without her went by, it grew even harder, for my fantasies of getting together again were obviously pipe dreams. And the evil act that we had done together—that I, for the most part, had initiated—seemed much more wrong because it had led to this gruesome finale. Parting may have been such sweet sorrow for Romeo and Juliet, but it tasted decidedly bitter to me. Ruthie, who objectively was probably something of a charmer, became, in my saddened mind, absolutely ideal. Fantastically beautiful, gracious, soft-spoken, feminine, brilliant, luscious—you name any outstanding characteristic of the perfect young woman of five, and I unequivocally granted it to her. Without qualification. Without cavil. How could she unceremoniously leave me like this, never to lighten Bryant Avenue again?

Well, I eventually decided, she could. Requited love was assuredly the best thing in the world, but unrequited love wasn't entirely bad either. For one thing, I could keep reliving our super-stupendous romance in my head. For another, I could fantasize life with Ruthie in the future—assuming, as I dogmatically did, that we would meet again. And I could show myself that unrequited amour has its distinct advantages: you can't possibly be rejected when your beloved is no longer around to criticize or spurn you. You can, in your fantasies, do anything you want to do with her—with no holds barred and no practical restrictions. You can dream the impossible dream and make it seem wholly plausible.

What I didn't realize then was that the way I reacted to losing Ruthie may have encouraged my future pattern of unrequited loves. Actually, the relationship with Ruthie was clearly requited because we did get together regularly, we did let each other know that we cared, and we finally did have some good old-fashioned (or was it new-fashioned?) sex. So my feelings for Ruthie at that time were hardly unreturned.

But they were completely aborted by our forced separation. And I could tell myself that even though her parents cruelly parted us, she somehow could have managed to see me (though how, I couldn't say) or could have sent me a note. So maybe she really did stop caring, in which case our love went from being requited to unrequited. She may have continued loving me, but since she made no effort to let me know, our love affair was over. Whereupon, typical of my resolve to stubbornly refuse to make myself miserable about anything, I adjusted myself to love's demise and within a few weeks managed to live pretty well without it.

Later in life, as I repeatedly fell in love and (out of crassly self-indulged shyness) got absolutely nowhere with my inamoratas, I managed to eviscerate misery and even to partially enjoy my unrequited feelings. Could this have been because I first trained myself to do this with Ruthie? Or, speculating more deeply, could I have unconsciously decided that unrequited love, with its risk of abrupt withdrawal, was just too dangerous? And could I *therefore* have cleverly managed, by using my "shyness," to avoid such temporary requitement again, and to "content" myself less riskily, loving females from afar?

I am afraid that I—and the world—will never know which, if either, of these brilliant psychoanalytically inspired guesses is true. I willingly subscribed for a number of years and then, equally willing, abandoned practically all "deep" speculations about why people act in a certain way, despite or because of their past experiences. At first, these psychodynamic guesses seem exceptionally brilliant and plausible. But they rarely can be falsified, since they are totally speculative and, by some weird stretch of reality, could possibly be true. They are fascinating *attempts* at explanation, but are they truly accurate? Rarely. Which is exactly why I abandoned psychoanalysis after I had practiced it for several years and arrived at many brilliant "explanations," with few real benefits to my analysands.

Back to Ruthie and me. I was devastated by losing her and facing the prospect (which eventually turned into a reality) of never seeing her again. I felt what, in REBT, we would call healthy sorrow, sadness, and even some amount of grief. But first, because I hoped against hope that she would return and Pollyannishly convinced myself that she would, my sorrow was muted, mixed with sweet expectations. I felt true loss of something remarkable, something unique. But not—no, not ever—

ALBERT ELLIS • 53

entirely. For although I lost Ruthie, my feelings for her never truly disappeared. I lost her; but not me.

That's the beauty of unrequited love. Your beloved may fly the coop, but your feelings for her or him zoom off slightly, sometimes escalate, for a long time remain the same. Which proves the old (but rarely believed) saw: *Being loved* is a nice but passive, almost blah, state. *Loving*, on the contrary, is an exceptionally involved, often impassioned feeling. Being loved and a Metrocard will get you into the subway. Being *in* love may get you some of the rarest ecstasies. Don't confuse the two!

❴❵

I can say with a fair amount of certainty that my love for Ruthie lasted long after the ostensible demise of her feelings for me. For months I thought of her almost constantly. For years I thought of her fairly often. For almost a decade I occasionally brought her back—and I mean intently, longingly brought her back—to mind. Not that thinking about her stopped me from falling madly in love with other little girls. But it kept me on my mental toes and furnished the prototype for some of my later affaires de coeur. Nor were all my later loves, or even the majority, blue-eyed, zaftig blondes. While my most profound love, my wife Debbie, is blue-eyed and blond, brunettes, in fact, predominated, and one was a raving redhead. But Ruthie, in some manner, shape, or form, was always there: somewhere in the front or back of my mind, dismally dead to me in real life but alive and well in the recesses of my heart. Oh, so alive! And oh, so well!

As time went by, Ruthie became less alive and more of a fantasy. I eventually gave up hope that we would meet again and that her parents would relent and let us walk off into the blue together. Then I thought it would only happen by sheer, miraculous accident. But I increasingly saw that although those puritanical bastards might forever divide me from Ruthie's corporeal existence, they were powerless to affect my fantasy version of her being, nor could they keep me from making that version into any marvel I desired.

That, I realized many years later, is why masturbation is so wonderful—indeed, one of the most useful, and in its own way most creative, human inventions. If I see a ravishing woman who completely snatches her body and mind from my coveting grasp, there is nothing—absolutely nothing—she can do to stop me from mentally "using" her and doing anything imaginable with "her." Even more marvelously, what I do in my fantasies with this "partner" I can easily enjoy more than if she actually deigned to give me her "all."

Actually bedding my imaginary partner invariably entails real hazards and limitations. Most likely, she has wrinkles and rings of fat that, of course, she doesn't have in my fantasies. Or, even if her body is as perfect as I envision, she will most likely be less sexy and more frustrating than I imagine her to be when I "use" her autoerotically.

I saw a dramatic example of this with a male client who recently saw me for sex therapy (after getting nothing from psychoanalysis for three years). He could come to orgasm only with prostitutes, not with any woman he actually had feelings for. His former analyst, as you may guess, tried to convince him that he viewed "nice" women as "motherly" images, and that his Oedipus complex (his resultant guilt about having sex with his "mother") blocked him from truly enjoying sex with women who weren't prostitutes. A "fine" explanation, which he bought for a few years. But he remained impotent with women he loved and exceptionally virile with low-priced hookers.

It took me only a few sessions to help this man to see that this special kind of impotence (from which he had suffered for twenty-two years) stemmed mainly from his masturbatory practices rather than from his Oedipal "horror" of copulating with his mother. Since the age of fifteen, he had trained himself to think of women doing what he considered "highly sexy" things to him—such as pressing his penis between their massive breasts or begging him to screw them anally— and through these fantasies, he had no trouble reaching orgasm. When he was with prostitutes—even those who had small breasts and who refused anal intercourse—he used the same kind of fantasy images he had previously employed successfully, thereby arousing himself to reach climax quite quickly. But when he was with a woman he truly cared for, he thought it wrong to think these masturbatory thoughts. I showed him that he *could* use the same kind of "dirty" fantasies with women he loved and suffer no impunity from doing so. Soon, he began to have great sex with women he loved.

What has this got to do with my love for Ruthie—or with my later unrequited love for other women? A great deal. Because I "used" my image of her to my own advantage. For years after our separation I fantasized the most delicious encounters with her, and I so greatly enjoyed them that it probably would have been enormously anticlimactic had we actually met and talked—or screwed. In my erotic fantasies, she was (of course!) always madly in love with me, always incredibly responsive, ever ready—nay, eager!—to do anything I wanted. Fantasy-Ruthie became creative, too, suggesting that we stick lollipops up each other's nether regions, kiss while passing ice cream from mouth to mouth, eat candy on a stick together until we ecstatically smeared our faces and naked bodies, and innumerable other inconceivably lovely things that little boy-little girl lovers ecstatically dream of. She became so imaginative that she even (in my vagaries) surpassed me.

Do you see what I mean? Left to the limitations of reality, Ruthie and I could do literally nothing together. And even if we had managed to meet and commune, how many of my incredible fantasies about our union could we have actualized? Paltry few. But in my fervid imagination we left nothing undone, nothing raptly, all-gloriously unenjoyed. And at no cost or risk—just at the bidding of an easily pushed imaginative button!

I think that was the prime lesson about refusing to be miserable and determining to be happy that I learned from this crucial period in my young life: that what we believe and what we imagine, rather than what actually happens to us, controls our emotional destiny. Not that I was the first to realize this. When I began reading philosophy in my fifteenth year, I discovered that a number of fairly sound philosophers had figured this out long before I was born. The Greek stoic philosophers, especially, had seen with remarkable clarity that we largely feel the way we think, and they had said as much in Athens in the fourth century BCE, when Zeno of Citium founded the Stoic school. Several centuries later, their descendants—especially Epictetus, who flourished in the first century CE, and Marcus Aurelius, the Roman emperor (121–180 CE)—stated that it is not the things that happen to us but our view of what happens that upsets us.

So I merely reinvented the Stoics' philosophical wheel some two thousand years after they first set it rolling. And, I almost beat a noted Frenchman, Émile Coué, to the punch. Following the lead of Hippolyte Bernheim, a psychiatrist who wrote a book on hypnosis in 1871, Coué realized that what we call hypnosis is largely autosuggestion, or self-suggestion. He consequently coined the famous phrase "Every day, in every way, I'm getting better and better." He wrote books and traveled around the world, convincing thousands of troubled people that they could conquer all their ills, mental and physical, by suggesting to themselves hopeful, optimistic phrases.

Coué—as most people don't realize today, since he had a flurry of fame in the early 1920s and then cascaded into near oblivion—not only advocated strong verbal autosuggestion but hotly endorsed the use of imagination. He laid the groundwork for the belief—later well publicized by Napoleon Hill, Norman Vincent Peale, Maxwell Maltz, and other devotees of positive thinking—that if you intensely imagine yourself succeeding at tennis, love, business, or anything else, your images may be miraculously actualized and you will achieve almost anything you want.

At the age of five, I was thoroughly ignorant of Émile Coué and his espousal of positive thinking. Nonetheless, I realized that imagination was a powerful happiness-creating tool. I have to admit, I didn't succeed as well as Coué and his (somewhat fanatical) followers cavalierly promised I would. By intensely imagining, and also devoutly telling myself, that Ruthie would return to my life and that we would ultimately mate and have five or six or seven delicious children, I in no way actualized these dreams and made them come true. But I did superbly enjoy reveling in the images themselves and adding them to my otherwise fairly humdrum existence.

So I found (or rediscovered) several important tricks of the misery-decimating and happiness-producing trade: First, convince yourself that bad things (such as the abysmally tragic loss of Ruthie) are not all bad, not horribly bad, and in some ways not that bad at all. Second, distract yourself into pleasurable pursuits (such as imagining good things that might happen with Ruthie) so that you divert yourself even more from your sorrowful and depressing thoughts. Show yourself that, in spite of troubles, joy actually can exist in this benighted and blighted world and that you can allow yourself to feast, via fantasy, on some of the fine pleasures that reality (for the nonce and perhaps forever) flips from your hot-handed grasp.

For a five-and-a-half-year-old, I think I did pretty well in dealing with my abysmal horror over losing Ruthie. From the standpoint of my current REBT thinking, I could, of course, have done much better, for I never saw or faced my behavioral commands: "Because Ruthie is so desirable, I *absolutely must* not be deprived of her, and if I am, the world is a rotten, joyless place!" But by optimistic daydreaming and focusing on pleasurable distractions, I immensely cut down my woe. Inelegant REBT, but not bad for a youngster.

It could be asked, of course, whether my early sex escapade with Ruthie significantly affected me later and helped make me into one of the most prominent sexologists of the twentieth century. Most probably, and to some extent, it did.

But one never knows. The fact that I was so curious—about sex and everything else—at the age of five may well have stemmed from an early developed, and possibly innate, investigatory tendency that first led me to explore Ruthie's genitals and later encouraged me to focus my curiosity into several fields, including political revolution, light opera, love, sex, marriage, and psychotherapy. Once I found the field of sex interesting and enjoyable—as I did with Ruthie—and once I had my own strong sex urges to favorably prejudice me, as I had from childhood onward—my picking sexology as a special field to study is easily understandable. But which came first—the chicken of sexual curiosity or the egg of early childhood experience—is an enigma that perhaps only Freudians can unravel. With dogmatic but highly suspicious "explanations"!

The same issue arises regarding my adolescent and adult sexuality—which, as far as I can tell, were both far above normal. During early puberty I think I had an almost continual erection. During later adolescence I thought about sex obsessively. Even in my nineties, I rarely encounter any females from sixteen to sixty without thinking about them sexually. Because I had repressed wishes to copulate with my mother? Because I never succeeded in screwing Ruthie? Because I was a very reluctant virgin until the age of twenty-four? I doubt it. Mainly, I suspect, because of hormonal tendencies that I probably inherited, as well as sexual socializing that I learned from my surroundings. My father and his brother Mike were both adulterers and roués in their early days. Although my brother Paul and I were both raised conventionally, Paul, too, was something of a ladies' man from adolescence until he married in his late twenties. So I'm mainly betting on biology as well as social learning.

The other notable factor in my sex writings and practices was my natural skepticism and ideological rebelliousness. I always tended to *think about* the rules I was taught at home, at school, at temple, and by my peers. Those that I thought silly or harmful I tended to ignore, unless some authority was around to enforce them. So I largely ignored many customs and conventions, such as saying prayers every night, only crossing the street at corners, listening to adults and taking them very seriously, and avoiding using obscene language.

So with sex. I knew that masturbation was "wrong." But once I accidentally learned to do it at the age of fifteen, I found it so good that I did it guiltlessly, and often, thereafter. I only worried, for health reasons, that I might be doing it too often. But fortunately a little reading got me over that idea.

During my teens and early twenties, I would have gladly engaged in virtually any kind of sex with any consenting female. But I was too damned shy to go after consent. When I did start, in my twenty-fifth year, to have fairly regular sex with women, I did not hesitate to perform several kinds of unconventional heterosexual acts—including "living in sin" for a year with my ex-wife Karyl after our marriage had been legally annulled. I just *assumed*, since conventional morality was not my thing, that any kind of sex was good as long as it did not harm the people involved. This is exactly the same view I later took in my (published and unpublished) sex writings.

In other words, I would say that my liberal sex views, which I began to express in public talks and unpublished writings in the 1940s, were influenced by my general skeptical and liberal moral philosophies (which I selectively chose from my very wide readings) and from my hormone-inspired sexual prejudices. I have long thought that, given the same kind of conservative upbringing, highly sexed people wind up by being more liberal in their sex views and actions than do lower-sexed individuals. This hypothesis springs from self-observation.

Chapter 1D
Critique of Chapter 1

"*I was always, possibly from the moment I scooted myself out of my mother's belly, an independent, my-kingdom-is-myself youngster.*"

Was I really? Looking back, I seemed to be. But I definitely don't remember my first two years, when I was an only child. My mother, who was later neglectful, may have been most caring and close to me *then*. Maybe, as most infants are, I was quite dependent on her. Maybe the birth of my brother, nineteen months after I was born, and of my sister, four years after my birth, forced me to become more independent. Or maybe my physical problems, for the first few years, *made* me an unusual coper. Who can say? I think my tendency to be independent, plus my early you'd-damn-well-better-cope environment, "made" me so. Anyway, I was more self-sufficient than my brother and sister were later. At least, I *think* I was.

"*I was, in my own way, quite a thinker. A philosopher and a theorizer? Well, yes—somewhat.*"

I *now* see it that way. I remember that *later*, from my fifth year onward, I philosophized and theorized. I *now* do. Are my memories, then, prejudiced? We have considerable psychological research that tells us that in experimental situations people remember inaccurately, falsely, with much fictionalizing. Even under hypnosis, they vividly "remember" many events that, when checked with eyewitnesses, never occurred. Hmm! Did I, at the age of four, really philosophize and theorize as well as I remember I did? Maybe. Maybe.

Being cooped up in kindergarten "*isn't the worst thing that could happen to me. It's really not that bad.*" Nice rational philosophizing for a four-year-old, but did I really do it? No, I don't recall being too upset. But maybe I forgot—repressed?—how terror-stricken I really was. If I did take my confinement in kindergarten as calmly as I remember I did, could I have been too shocked to react emotionally? Too numb? Too fearful of *showing* much emotion? All of the above?

"*Well, that was my first lesson—or the first one I can recall—in which I worked at acquiring higher frustration tolerance.*"

In the first part of my autobiography, I will mainly be discussing my struggles with low frustration tolerance and my fight to acquire higher frustration tolerance. But—remember!—I am the founder of Rational Emotive Behavior Therapy (REBT), which strongly teaches people how to cope with low frustration tolerance (LFT). So I am particularly biased about my own tendencies, innate and acquired, to have and to fight LFT. I will do my best to explain my own LFT and my fighting, from four years onward, to deal with it. But, naturally, I am biased by my latter-day theory and practice of REBT. Always keep this in mind!

"*There I was, only four, and I figured out a model for overcoming 'fearsome' situations about which I plagued myself. . . . I began to think about—philosophize about—the hassles and fears I encountered and how I could stop making myself unduly anxious, depressed, or self-pitying.*"

Pretty good for four years of age! But, again, was I *really* that philosophical? Yes, I think—remember—that I was. But at *four*? Maybe it was more like six or seven. Maybe even that is exaggerated by my much later prejudices in favor of reasoning.

"*So I'll put up with not moving to a new apartment until things settle. Meanwhile, I'll go about my business as usual, enjoying myself as much as I can.*"

Excellent philosophy, but it sounds too pat. Maybe I really was much more impatient than that. Maybe I just got distracted by other things. Knowing how I am today, I could have been worried about what the move to a new place would be like and what practical problems I would need to solve.

"*I decided not to make myself miserable about being forced to stay out of school. . . . I decided to lump it rather than to whine.*"

"Decided" is a key word here. It sounds like I knew I had a choice and *decided* to make the sensible one. Maybe I did—I remember feeling not all that upset that I couldn't start school yet. But I could have whined and screamed and then forgotten about it. Or somehow otherwise adjusted to this grim fact. But consciously deciding—that seems a little too much. That's probably the way I would now like to see it: developing a *decision* not to overreact. Possibly I did, but it seems questionable.

"Maybe it is wrong to stick funnels up little girls' slits-between-their-legs. Maybe you'd better watch that kind of thing next time. But it's done. And upsetting yourself about it won't make it undone."

I'd like to believe I was able to think so rationally, but I'm not sure I did. A more likely hypothesis is that, first, I really didn't see anything very bad in what I did to Ruthie. Exploring really wasn't that wrong! Second, because of my love for Ruthie, I didn't see *anything* we did as bad. So I may have philosophically thought what's done is done and upsetting myself about it won't make it undone. But I also probably didn't think what we had done was very wrong.

"For a five-and-a-half-year-old, I think I did pretty well in dealing with my abysmal horror over losing Ruthie."

Yes, I suppose I did. But my distraction into fantasy about enjoying Ruthie was done unconsciously and somewhat magically. For a fairly long time I thought that we somehow would get together again. So *"by optimistic daydreaming and focusing on pleasurable distractions, I immensely cut down my woe."* But not as an intelligent, thought-out technique. Not exactly rationally. I did it, perhaps, almost desperately and defensively.

Chapter 2A

Chronology
My First Hospitalization

I was pleased (and still am, over eighty-seven years later), with my handling of the contretemps with Ruthie and her skullduggerist parents. But there was worse still to come, ere my fifth year had ended. That year, grim tragedy struck my tonsils. I suffered an acute attack of tonsillitis, with some kind of serious streptococcus infection. Really, I don't know what it was or precisely when it first hit me, since I have only my impressions. But according to my mother's recounting (which she later repeated many times, although that still doesn't make it reliable or accurate), I had this tonsil infection, suffered a very bad sore throat, and was finally rushed to the hospital, where I was saved from almost certain death by the outstanding skills of a Dr. Copeland, who presumably later became a politician and ended up as a state senator or something like that. His prodigious skill as a surgeon snatched me from the very jaws of death. But apparently the ravages of the streptococci continued, and I ended up with nephritis (kidney trouble).

Now, I have some strange memories connected with my hospitalization and tonsillectomy at this time, but I am not sure how accurate some of them are. I particularly remember that, when I was five and a half my brother, who was playing with me in the lot across the street from our home on Bryant Avenue, coolly lifted a red brick and even more coolly let it fall out of his hands on to my left pinky, squashing it to a near pulp and causing it to gush out what seemed to be a huge quantity of blood.

To say the least, I was startled by this sudden and wholly unexpected event. To be in sound body one minute, and a few seconds later to feel a sharp pain in one's finger, see it split open, and watch the blood endlessly pour out of it, is hardly a thing of beauty and a joy forever. I remember not being angry at my brother for dropping the brick, for I could see that he had merely meant to drop it on the ground, not on my hand. I remember his look of shock and guilt, when he saw what he had done. I remember my friend Steve, who fortunately happened to be right there at the time, quickly bandaging my finger with a handkerchief, yelling for help, and getting me promptly across the street to my mother, who was home tending to my baby sister. I remember being rushed to our family physician, two blocks away, who told me that everything was going to be all right. I remember going around with my finger bandaged for the next few days, and then finally being allowed to see it naked again: with a cleft in the end of it that gradually got a little better but that is still there to this day. I remember being grateful for not losing the end of my finger, as might have happened. And I again remember being nice to my contrite brother and reassuring my parents that he had not really meant to harm me. I remember that, although they scolded him for his carelessness, they finally decided not to punish him—for which decision I was relieved and glad.

It was only a few days after this brick dropping incident that I ended up in the old Presbyterian Hospital at 68th Street and Park Avenue (where the main building of Hunter College now stands). And somehow I connected the finger-splitting incident with my being in the hospital, although the two, as far as I know, were not connected.

What probably happened was that I developed a severe sore throat shortly after my finger was busted. I was seen by the same family doctor who sewed up my pinkie. This time, after briefly looking at my severely inflamed throat, he ordered me to the hospital, and since the finger—which was still painful and whose injured appearance was quite visible—was more on my mind than my throat—which was really not that painful and which was invisible—I must have connected my hurt finger with going to the hospital rather than realizing that I was there for my throat.

This faulty assumption—I see in retrospect—may have actually been due to deliberate lying on everyone's part. Hospitals in those days were pretty grim places to young children, and having one's tonsils out seemed even grimmer. I vaguely recall that my parents deliberately told me I was going to the hospital to have my finger taken care of, so that I would not realize that I was near death (they later told me I was) and that I was about to have my diseased tonsils removed.

If they did lie to me in this way and for these reasons, they succeeded admirably, for on the day of the operation I had no idea what was going to happen to me. I know that my crib was wheeled down the corridor, put on an elevator, and wheeled to a special room in the hospital (they did not tell me it was an operating room). I know that I was lifted from the crib and placed on a surgical table, with several nice, genial, comforting nurses and doctors hovering around me, telling me that everything was going to be fine, just fine, and acting as if what I was about to go through was some kind of simple exam.

As part of this presumed medical examination, I remember a white-robed nurse, whom I think had some kind of surgical mask on, but may well not have had her face covered at all—as I could have later added that detail from seeing scenes of operations in movies. She handed me a metal cone, which looked like half of a ball with peculiar indentations. "Look," she smilingly said, "this is an orange, and I want you to smell this orange. See, it smells good, doesn't it? Doesn't it smell good?"

It didn't look like an orange to me, though it did have a smell, a not too unpleasant medical smell and not at all orange-like. I tried to raise myself from the table to tell the nice nurse, "No, I don't think this is an orange. It certainly doesn't smell like one," when—poof!—that was the sudden end of that scene. When I awoke, a few hours later, I was back in my crib in the children's ward and tightly wrapped up in blankets. My throat hurt like hell, I was very thirsty, and a smiling nurse was telling me how fantastically successful my operation—that is, my tonsillectomy—had been.

Dr. Copeland, according to the nurse, had been an outstanding whiz and had removed every bit of my inflamed and diseased tonsils. There had been very little loss of blood; my life had surely been saved; and now, even though my throat would hurt for a while and I was not allowed to drink anything, I would soon be all right, exceptionally all right, and would be up and around in no time, and would even be able to leave the hospital in a week or two. Wasn't that great? Wasn't I happy to know how well everything had gone? Wasn't it good to be totally out of danger and to have my tonsillitis cured?

Frankly, I couldn't quite agree with all that. I now realized that I had been totally duped. My stay in the hospital apparently had nothing at all to do with my split finger but with my diseased tonsils. The so-called orange that I was asked to smell had been an ether cone and, after a few whiffs, had put me into a deep, anesthetized sleep. And instead of merely giving me a medical examination, those "nice" doctors had abruptly ripped out my only set of tonsils, strapped me to the damned crib, and adamantly refused to let me have the gallons of water that I desperately wanted and that I knew would ease my throbbing throat.

What lies! What perfidy! How cruelly they had taken advantage of my innocence and had perpetrated, without the slightest request from me or consent on my part, this dire deed! What gall! What rottenness!

I must admit that, at least for a few hours after I awoke from my operation, and especially those hours that I was in pain, I wasn't very rational. I knew that they—my parents and the doctors and nurses—had bald-facedly lied to me, and I hated them bitterly. I think I even dreamed of dire revenge, such as never talking to my parents again or (poetic justice!) never telling them the truth again. As for those doctors and nurses, I didn't know how to arrange it, but I thought it would be nice if I could only maim their hands and feet, or do something else equally pleasant, so that they, too, would have to have major operations before they were restored to a normal life.

Yes, I was hardly entirely reasonable about what had happened, but, much to the credit of my burgeoning rationality, I will say that my anger and potential vindictiveness was short-lived; it lasted perhaps only a couple of hours or so. For one thing, the nurse gave me some kind of painkiller, and my throat began to feel much better. Then they let me have a small amount of ice cream, and that made my throat almost feel good. Then my mother and father came to visit and told me what a lucky boy I was, to have the great and noble Dr. Copeland save me from the very jaws of death. Then for the next few days the nurses and doctors continued to come by, seemed genuinely interested in my well-being and comfort, and kept reiterating how fine everything had gone and what a marvelous future I had to look forward to, now that my sadly diseased tonsils were subtracted from my no-longer-poor throat.

I finally let them convince me that it was all to the good and that the badness of the operation (especially their lying to me about it) was garnered in the services of an unusually fine cause—me and my life. Now that I had come back from the dead, I was in no mood to be permanently moribund. Now that I realized how diseased my tonsils actually had been, and (as they then told me) how useless tonsils were anyway, I was relieved to be rid of them. As for the future, it seemed, at this age of five and a half, to loom far ahead. By the time my life would really end, I convinced myself, I would probably achieve just about everything I really wanted—such as being accepted at school, learning how to read better than ever, enjoying ecstatic union with beautiful girls like Ruthie, exploring distant neighborhoods with Steve, and sundry other glories.

So, once again in my young life, I decided to let bygones be bygones and to focus on enjoying life rather than whining about its iniquities. I took the operation, and its immediate sequelae, with stoic equanimity. I considered it to be bad luck—because I had to have it at all—but also good luck—because it turned out well, and I was soon out of the hospital and back on Bryant Avenue, healthier than ever.

Unfortunately, my optimism was short-lived. I think I spent a few weeks out of the hospital when I had to return again . . . and again and again and again. For even though my tonsils were out and the immediate source of my streptococcal infection was removed, considerable damage had apparently been done to my system, and I was soon diagnosed as having acute nephritis. As a result of this new major ailment I was right back in the children's ward of the good old Presbyterian Hospital.

Acute nephritis, or at least the form of it that I had, is luckily not a painful ailment, and the only suffering I remember for the next several years consisted of a series of dreadful headaches. These would erupt frequently—every few days, if I remember right—and at times would hurt like the devil. Whether they really followed from the nephritis, I don't think was ever quite determined. But they first seemed to break out when I was in the hospital and they gave me a pretty bad time.

How did I handle these headaches? Well, at first I didn't. I thought they were awful, simply awful, and when they became quite acute—as they fairly frequently did—I more than once thought of killing myself. "If life were to continue to be this painful all the time," I said to myself, "who needs it? Not I."

I don't remember being taught anything about suicide. I vaguely remember being taught some ethical principles at Sunday school, especially, of course, the Ten Commandments. But suicide and its ethics? Not a word, as far as I can recall. Not that this seems strange—since even in these more liberal days of the twenty-first century, when we teach children things about death that we didn't mention in the 1910s, we hardly start them at age five or six on the morality of suicide. Not quite!

So I think I was merely pragmatic about the whole thing when I was first assailed by my headaches at the age of five and a half. I knew I really enjoyed life. But I also knew that acute pain, as from headaches, was a horrible, terrible thing, and that it was impossible for me to enjoy myself when such pain was at its height. What is more, I was wise enough, after suffering several headaches, to realize that my current one would hardly be the last. I saw that it was merely one of a series, and that even when it disappeared—in anywhere from an hour to a day or two—it would darned well return. And, horrors! It would be just as bad, if not worse, as the previous one.

A truly grim prospect! But, I reasoned, I could choose to not be alive any longer and therefore I would cease suffering. If I were dead—which I somehow knew to be a state of non-feelingness—I would presumably not be in any pain at all. Hardly a happy state, to be sure, and one that would be highly monotonous! But not *painful*. Not *excruciating*. Not *hellish*.

So I thought about that and half-decided that I might really end it all one of these fine—or not so fine—days if those sonofabitch headaches continued unabated. I didn't really have any specific suicidal plans. I suppose I thought that—à la the movies—death usually came from shooting. And I had no gun. Or else it happened by jumping off a cliff. I didn't know if the East Bronx sported a single suitable cliff. Rather discouraging, I'd say, if one really wanted to do oneself in and avoid those terrible headaches. Especially when one was lying in a crib in the children's ward at Presbyterian Hospital, constantly watched (yes, day and night) by nice, vigilant nurses.

So while I didn't think too seriously about killing myself, I certainly contemplated death as a peaceful, painless state. But I had other, less drastic solutions to try first. I spoke about my headaches to the nurses and doctors and sometimes got aspirin. I discovered that if I could go to sleep with a headache, I would often wake up the next day without it. I saw that by pressing my aching temples, I could relieve the headache, sometimes make it disappear. I tried cold compresses, laxatives, distracting myself by pleasant reveries, anything I could think of.

Because I (deludedly) believed in evil and good (godly) external forces, I prayed to the good ones and then, when doing so seemed to garner results (my headaches eventually went away), I felt (deludedly) sure that I had reached and persuaded those godly forces. But even though my superstitious belief in evil and good forces was chimerical, it ironically did tend to help me. For when I prayed to God to overcome my headaches, I implicitly included several solid, ungodly ideas that were beneficial: (1) I stopped telling myself that the pain would *never* go away, and instead told myself that (with God's help) it definitely would. (2) I distracted myself from the pain by thinking of God, goodness, forgiveness, what a good boy I would be in the future, and so on. (3) I stopped telling myself that I was completely powerless to overcome the pain and convinced myself, instead, that (through the Lord's mercy) I *did* have the ability to overcome it. (4) Whereas I previously thought of myself as a weak, inadequate individual who could not conquer pain and would have to passively continue to suffer (forever!), I now convinced myself that I was strong enough to conquer the forces of evil. I was strong enough, in other words, to *persuade* God to help me.

By these kinds of thoughts, which obviously had nothing to do with God, the Devil, or the forces of good and evil in the universe but which clearly had to do with my *belief* in such spirits and forces, I was able to distract myself from the pain of my headaches and to replace my sense of weakness and abjectness with one of strength and power. *What* I believed, to give myself this sense of strength, hardly mattered. Suppose I believed that I had a magic lamp and that by rubbing it I could summon a beneficent genie who would give me anything I wanted, including the removal of my headaches. As long as my belief worked—fine!

Almost any "religious" belief will work at times. Suppose I believed that I once helped Satan out of a fix and that now, when I asked, he was ready to help me out of my headaches. These types of beliefs, however bizarre or unrealistic, would have helped me to deal with the pain of my headaches just as well as did my belief in and prayers to Jehovah. It is my belief that pulls off the therapeutic trick—not the truth or objective reality of what I believe in.

What is more, my belief in anything that helps me is more a belief in *myself* than in that "thing." Obviously, I invent or create this "thing"— this God, Devil, force-in-the-universe, or what you will—and I give it its "helpful" qualities. Even if such a God, a Devil, or force-in-the-universe does exist (which is possible, but highly unlikely), I could, first, refuse to believe in its existence and, second, accept its existence but *ingeniously award* it demonic rather than helpful qualities. Thus, assuming that Jehovah indubitably exists and that eventually we humans all see, hear, taste, feel, and smell His (or Her) existence and completely validate it, I, as a unique and individual human, can still *view* this Jehovah as (1) having full power to do away with my headaches and relieve me of their pain; as (2) having only the power to give me headaches but not the power to remove them; or as (3) having no power whatever to create or relieve my headaches and their pain. Even, then, if Jehovah undoubtedly exists, it is still *my belief* in Her (or His) power over my headaches that actually affects the headaches. And it is *my belief* in the power of prayer that makes it influential over my pain.

I did not, of course, do this sort of analysis of religion at the age of five but from the age of twelve onward, when I began to give serious thought to the existence of God and His or Her supposed powers over humans. My philosophizing finally showed me that God is a completely redundant hypothesis when considered from a therapeutic point of view. For even when it can be shown that belief in a supreme being is helpful to emotionally disturbed people who exacerbate their pain because of their negative thoughts about it—as was probably true of me and my headaches when I was five—it is their *belief* that is helpful and not the *fact* (or *nonfact*) of God's existence. People's *convictions* about supernatural entities may indeed help them, but that does not in any way prove that the deity they count on exists, nor that *it*, their God, has been helpful.

Should we, then, not encourage belief in God for its therapeutic value, even if we cannot prove the existence of any deity, and even if there is much reason to believe that no such supreme being exists? Not usually. Just as belief in God may help people in some ways, so may a belief in fairies, hobgoblins, demons, Nazism, or Ku Klux Klanism prove helpful. If I devoutly believe, for example, that I am a member of an Aryan master race and that the reincarnation of Hitler will soon lead me and my fellow pure Aryans to rule the world, I may well deflect myself from the pain of headaches or from feelings of inadequacy, thereby helping myself feel less pain and suffering. But at what a cost! Isn't my Nazism-inspired "cure" worse than my original disease?

Even in less extreme cases, my belief in some supernatural god or supernatural creed will tend to be hypocritical and even harmful. If I believe, for instance, that there is a god called Jehovah and that he is all-wise and all-forgiving and therefore will help me overcome all my physical and emotional problems, I definitely may do myself some good. But by holding this belief I fail to acknowledge that I am responsible for creating this deity; that I *indirectly* give myself the power to ameliorate my emotional and physical pain; and that I could much more logically, and without any highly dubious assumptions about the existence of Jehovah, *directly* give myself this power. Whenever I devoutly invent some deity to help me, I am the god-creator, hence I am really my own god! If I want maximum power to help myself, I'd be better off accepting myself and my own ability to be my own "savior," rather than inventing the (highly dubious) "middlemen" of gods, angels, fairies, and genies.

I had also better watch my own creationism. For although I have the power to think, feel, or act like God, *am I* really Jehovah? Hardly!

I am I, the creator of Jehovah, and the creator and uncreator of my headaches. But I am clearly not a special, unique God called Jehovah, nor do I have, as He supposedly has, unlimited power. My imaginative and creative powers are notable, but they are not phenomenal or omnipotent, no matter how strongly I (and my devout followers) think they are.

I see this now. But I have to admit that, at the tender age of five, I did pray to Jehovah and did probably reap some benefits thereby. The true curative power, however, lay in me and hardly in any supernatural deity. I knew that I was in severe pain and I even partly realized that I was contributing to that pain by focusing on it. So I looked around for a solution to my problem, as I characteristically did when I was in trouble. All told, I didn't do too badly. Many of the headaches decreased or went away. Days often went by without a headache. Distraction techniques allowed me to live with the pain, even when nothing worked to minimize it. By trying everything I could, I improved somewhat.

But not enough. The blasted pain kept recurring and at times was excruciating. Whereupon I reinvented the wheel again, using some Bible passages I'd read (in highly simplified form) in Sunday school. "This too shall pass!" became my regular motto. Not in those exact words—which I only remember actually coming across years later, when I was about eleven or twelve. "This too shall pass!"—a great line, I thought, when I first heard it. But I already partly believed the philosophic essence of this line at the age of five, when the headaches first became acute and persistent.

I could see, after a while, that these pains in my temples *did* pass. They weren't *always* there. And once they went away, for some reason or for no reason, I felt immensely relieved and went back to my regular enjoyments. So I concluded: "Pain is terrible! A really rotten part of life! But it *does, invariably, disappear. And it is replaced, always replaced*, by glorious lack of pain—and then by even more glorious forms of enjoyment. Why don't I simply *realize* this, then?—plainly *see* that the pain of my headaches is fleeting, sooner or later it's over? Why don't I just *admit* that it never lasts forever, always (fairly soon) goes? For isn't that *true?*"

I fully acknowledged that it was. I still hated the pain, but I *accepted* the reality of its temporary nature. Whenever it assailed me, I *knew*—I stoutly reminded *myself*—that it was unfairly back again (for what bad thing had *I* done to bring it on?), but that it would go. Yes, go! Yes, go!

So I forced myself, whenever a headache returned, to focus on its ephemerality rather than upon its horror. I concentrated on the time it would *not* exist, rather than its present duration. I convinced myself that it was only *temporary* and that it would not, could not last. This view of its transiency helped me tolerate it pretty damned well.

I must admit that, along with this fine philosophy of the temporality of pain, I also threw in a few less legitimate tricks—notably some related to religion. I don't know exactly why my parents sent me to Sunday school regularly, starting at the age of four and a half. If I remember right, because the public school system was most unfairly keeping me out of its sacred classes at that time, and because the nearby Sunday school (a conservative Jewish one, I believe) was inclined to welcome anyone at almost any age whose parents provided him with a weekly donation to place in the collection plate, and because it was *some* kind of school, I think my parents picked it as a poor second choice. However, as they kept me (and later, my brother and sister) in it for years to come, they may have had other reasons, too. Not that they were ever very religious. My father, if memory serves, thought so little of the Jewish (or any other) faith that he had a perfect zero attendance record at synagogue. Not even the High Holy Days (Rosh Hashanah and Yom Kippur) lured him into temple, and the only time, in fact, I ever recall seeing him in one was when I was bar mitzvahed at the age of thirteen and went through a ceremony that he had managed to skip in his own early days.

My mother, on the other hand, went regularly to temple—especially when we moved to the West Bronx and she became a member of its only Reformed Jewish Synagogue, Tremont Temple. But, as I sort of always knew, she went for social and cultural reasons, hadn't the foggiest idea what the Jewish religion was about, and frankly didn't give much of a shit. She just insisted that because we were born of Jewish parents, we inevitably were Jews, and that was all there was to it. So even though her own family was as nonconforming and a-religious as any "Jewish" family could be, she always identified with Judaism and felt that the Sisterhood of her temple (what with its constant bridge parties, mah-jongg games, dances, dinners, and other social affairs) was the real "religious" high point of her life.

So, in spite of regularly attending Sunday school at the age of four and a half, I wasn't exactly raised to be deeply religious. And, honestly, that didn't bother me at all, since I viewed Sunday school as a little learning and a lot of great socializing with the other boys and girls. So

I was hardly devoutly religious. Until those devil-damned headaches started. Whenever the pain began and it looked like I was not going to fall asleep or feel relief, I started to think that perhaps, maybe, yes, possibly there was a God, a powerful Jehovah, up there somewhere, looking down on me, watching to see how (morally or immorally) I was doing, and determined to give me my just reward if I were behaving nicely and lambaste my behind if I were not. In between my headaches, I can't say that I thought very much about the Almighty and His power to reward or punish me. I just assumed that, having been instrumental in bringing me into the world, He really didn't care that much whether I lived or died, and left my (kind or unkind) fate largely within my own (reasonably competent) hands.

Not so when I was in dire physical pain. I decided that maybe the Old Guy really did have some power, after all. Perhaps, for some punitive reason—for I was hardly an angel—He had actually brought on my terrible headaches. Or, if that was not the case and they had come on accidentally for purely ungodly reasons, perhaps He, in His infinite compassion, could go to bat for me and arrange to excommunicate them.

So, at first reluctantly and then with flaring enthusiasm, I resorted to prayer. "Oh, God, dear God," I prayed. "I know that You have infinite power and illimitable mercy. I know that You can relieve this god-awful—er, devil-awful—pain. I know that You know that I am really a good little boy, who would not really harm anyone or do any serious wrong. So please, please help me in this, my hour of need. Please take away this pain, or at least reduce it. Then You will see—oh, I truly promise that You will see!—that as soon as this pain goes away I will become a fine little boy, oh, a marvelously good little boy, who will do absolutely nothing wrong in the days to come, and will show You that Your faith in me is entirely justified, and that I completely deserve to be free—ah, free!—from this kind of pain. I can't offer You too much, dear God, but I do promise, fully promise, to be good hereafter and to show You that You won't regret taking away this pain!"

Hypocritical? Well, somewhat. Manipulative? Definitely. But, in my great moments of pain, totally sincere. I really meant every word of my prayers. I knew I would carry out my promises to the Lord. And I knew—really felt—that He would heed my supplication and help me get rid of my current headache. Oh, I was certain—desperately certain—that He would.

With this kind of self-fulfilling prophecy, I could not lose. For eventually, of course, my headache went away. And once it passed, I was fully back to normal again, feeling my old chipper self. So when I prayed to God to relieve my pain, and it finally disappeared, I was 100 percent sure that He had intervened. Like the fanatic nut who is positive that the Devil is after him, who frantically flees and stubs his toe, and who then is 110 percent sure that the Devil made him stub it, I was just as fanatically sure that, whenever I prayed and my headaches eventually went away, God had personally interceded for little Albert.

As a psychotherapist, I now see that my praying technique was something of a sham and not a truly religious solution to my headache problem. As soon as my pain receded and I was in healthy shape again, I forgot about the King of Kings and Lord of Lords and went back to my former evil behavior. For a day or two—at the very most—I was nicer and kinder to others and gratefully followed God's (presumed) rules and held strictly to (my personal version) of the Ten Commandments. But as the days went by and my headaches stayed away, I reverted to my normal secular activity, lied and stole as much as usual, took God's name in vain, didn't honor my father and mother, and ignored virtually all the basic Judeo-Christian tenets and rituals. Two days, at most, after the all-merciful God had graciously forgiven my past sins and made a covenant with me to relieve my headache provided I would sin no more, I thought about God and religion perhaps three minutes every twenty-four hours—if that much.

Nonetheless, my "religious" psychotherapy, for all its hypocrisy, was effective. It provided me with an inelegant, superfluous hypothesis that helped "explain" my existing problems, and because I wasn't yet wise enough to see how inelegant and superfluous this hypothesis was—nor was I able to substitute for it a more realistic and sound theory of self-help—this "religious" theorizing worked. As I now see, in my current-day wisdom, God is always a redundant hypothesis when we use Him (or Her) for therapeutic gains. Why? Because, as I noted above, it is not God but our belief in Her (or Him) that actually helps us.

Take, for example, my praying to the Lord to rid me of the pain of my headaches. It may have helped me considerably, but not because any god—Jehovah, Jesus, Allah, Jupiter, or what you will—had anything to do with it. When I was in severe pain, I irrationally believed that this pain must not exist—that it was awful, unbearable, and that it absolutely should not be inflicted on me. Not merely that the pain was bad, undesirable, and preferably should not exist, but that it was so bad that it incontestably had to disappear.

Because of my foolish, dogmatic beliefs about my pain and its all-encompassing horror, I naturally (as humans almost invariably seem to do) made it worse than it was: focused intently upon it, thought of nothing else, and raised it to almost incredible heights. What is more, being a (human—all-too-human) screwball about this pain and devoutly believing that it should never happen to me, me, me, I easily and asininely concluded (as, again, humans continually conclude), "It will never go away! It will last forever! It will kill me!"

In so concluding, I significantly escalated the original pain of my headaches and made it excruciating (rather than merely unpleasant). Instead of appraising my headaches as being damned inconvenient (but still bearable) I evaluated them as monstrously hideous—and I therefore intensely felt them as the horror that I imagined them to be. Then (as we crackpots inevitably do) I perceived my feeling of all-surpassing pain as evidence that the headaches really were insufferable, and I became totally convinced that they were.

This is a strange but easily verifiable human propensity: people think up or invent "terrors"—ghosts and demons. Then, because of their phantasmagoric (and unrealistic) fancies they feel "terrified." Next, they perceive their feelings of "terror" as indubitable reality, sloppily confusing the existence of the feeling with the "existence" of the "terror," which they imaginatively invented. After a while, they inextricably merge their real feelings with their imagined "terror" and insist that the latter is just as "true" as the former.

In my case, my headaches were certainly real enough and were probably painful reactions to some underlying physical pathology (such as my nephritis). But once they became sharply painful, I viewed them as "horrors" or as "terrors." As I saw them in this light, I made them into nightmarish feelings; then I horrified myself about these feelings; then I convinced myself that the nightmares would never end; then I experienced (and this time really experienced) more intense physical pain. But I thought, as we frequently do in cases like this, that my acute pain was externally caused (e.g., by evil forces in the universe or by a punitive God) and refused to acknowledge that a significant part of this pain was internally caused—that is, by my own mental processes and by my physiological reaction to these processes.

Falsely blaming the evil forces of the universe for my painful headaches, I dreamed up (with the help of my Sunday school indoctrination) a beneficial external force—a force to which I (and others) gave the name God. I therefore tried to influence this force, by dint of prayer, to help me overcome the evil forces of the world, and I presumably succeeded in getting this help.

Along with my "religious" attempts to alleviate my headaches, I also used various kinds of problem solving. I always liked problem solving. First, I wanted to resolve the difficulty—get rid of it. And I enjoyed it immensely when I did. Second, I reveled in the solving process. As a youngster, I frequently took apart old clocks or watches, just to see if I could get them together again. Even when they never got fixed (which was often!) I thoroughly enjoyed working on them.

Therefore, when I had this serious problem of painful headaches, I did my usual thing: thought about various kinds of possible solutions, experimented with one after another, and hated the headaches but liked the attempts to deal with them. Practically all the potential solutions I devised—pressing my temples tightly or trying to sleep the headaches off—were simple and naturalistic. But when those methods didn't work I resorted to the supernaturalistic one of praying to Jehovah. Because this did seem to work to some degree, I retained it. The main point is not *that* it worked or *why* it worked but that I invented it as a problem-solving technique. That was what I enjoyed: looking problems in the eye and doing my best to solve them. Being by nature (as most of us probably are) a profound hedonist, my main problems consisted of warding off misery and trying to be happy. Being by my personal nature a determined hedonist, I think I worked more and harder at this sort of thing than most other people I know.

It has always seemed incredible to me that people so passively bear pain and trouble. My brother practically courted it. My sister whined and yapped and passively endured it. My mother distracted herself so beautifully with interesting and exciting things—dancing, for example, as well as singing and talking—that she never seemed to be miserable for more than a few minutes at a time. My father, similar to me, I think, more seriously undertook to solve his problems of everyday living and seems to have succeeded fairly well.

I can say what I did—which was to think carefully about the hassles of my life and to figure out solutions to them. Headaches were a great hassle. So I strongly worked to solve them. Finally, I did. The prayers to God were coming along all right, and I had no complaints about that solution. Unfortunately, however, although they helped me when I had a bad headache, they didn't seem to do much good to ward off the return of another one, a week or two later. What was I going to do about that unnicety?

The answer was: Bear it—and keep trying to change it. As to bearing it, I made myself realize that the headaches were ephemeral and relatively infrequent. They occurred, at worst, once a week, and usually every two or three weeks. And they lasted, usually, for a few hours. By trying my various palliative tricks, I generally managed to suffer acutely only a half hour or so before I conquered the pain or got myself to sleep in spite of it. And by calming down about the headaches and doing my best to avoid anything (such as eating the wrong foods) that might bring them on, I often managed to decrease their frequency, and sometimes only suffered about once a month from them. Not good, this kind of frequency. But also, not too bad.

And I always held out some fine hope for the future. Maybe I (and my doctors) would find out the source, and they would go away. Maybe they would disappear by themselves, just as they had rather suddenly come on. Maybe some new and better kind of aspirin would be invented to overcome them. I hoped for the best rather than assuming the worst.

"But what if they increased?" I asked myself. "What if God stopped caring or if He actually wanted me to suffer and made my headaches worse?" Hmm, that would be rough. That might even end up being unbearable. Not likely, but it might!

I pulled out my trump card for this scenario: I would simply kill myself. Life was (normally) good, but it was hardly sacred. And, if it got bad enough, excruciatingly painful, it didn't have to continue. I had never, at this young age, heard of euthanasia. But I figured it out for myself, especially as I grew older. By my seventh or eighth year, I heartily—at least in theory—endorsed it. It was fine to rely on God. With His help, life could certainly be pleasant and well worth living. But if He and everything else failed, there was always me. I could choose to live or die, and if the former state of being became untenable, there was always the latter. So let me optimistically assume that my days would almost always be enjoyable enough to merit their continuance. But if not, not. I could choose to end it all.

This was not exactly what I learned in Sunday school, nor what I picked up from my friends and family—all of whom, as far as I could tell, were pretty terrified about the possibility of death. Not I. I figured out that, while not exactly desirable or anything to look forward to, my demise offered certain advantages. Cessation of suffering. Freedom from headaches. Peace. Eternal nothingness. Not great. But not so damned bad!

Having settled this matter of ultimate dissolution—whether voluntary or involuntary—I went back to enjoying, as much as I could, my hospitalizations and subsequent invalidism. I made friends with the other children in my large hospital ward. I liked most of the nurses and doctors. I read many books—especially *The Wizard of Oz*. I played with my toys. I thought a lot. I kept quite busy and only slightly missed my home environment as, from age five to seven, I kept going back and forth to the hospital.

Now, the goddamned Freudians—and even the much saner Adlerians—are going to insist that just because I was restricted so much by hospitalization and largely kept from sports and childhood activities, I therefore compensated and became an unusually thinking and problem-solving creature. Great hypothesizing. But it doesn't convince me.

Even before I spent much time in the hospital, I remember that when my mother put me down for a midafternoon nap every day, I was too awake and alert to actually sleep. So I lay comfortably (and with no frustration or impatience) in my bed and enjoyed thinking, imagining, and problem solving. My brother and sister slept, while I thought. When I was hospitalized, I continued the same pattern: when the other kids in the children's ward were taking their post-lunchtime nap, I was wide awake as a jaybird, happily looking down into the hospital yard, observing the activity there, and figuring out solutions to world problems and the vicissitudes of life. Why? Because hospitalized or not, I enjoyed doing so. Yes, maybe I compensated for enforced inactivity. But my counter-hypothesis is that I was born a philosopher and have never given up my birthright.

Chapter 2B

Coping with Emotional Problems
My Compulsive Rhyming

started writing song lyrics at age sixteen and comic verse at seventeen, so at sixteen, I decided that I was going to be a great lyricist and make ten million dollars in royalties and ASCAP payments. Well, what imitator of Irving Berlin, Irving Caesar, and Walter Donaldson in the 1920s didn't imagine that? I was hardly unique. But why did I model my song lyrics after Caesar, who was a fine songwriter, rather than after Berlin, who was supposedly the greatest?

Simple: Because Caesar's lyrics, especially in "Tea for Two," were more complicated, more rhyme-filled, and therefore, to me, more "perfect" than Berlin's fabulously popular, but still very simple, lyrics for a song like "Always," which is casual and unpretentious.

Practically any talented lyricist could write something like "Always" in ten minutes. A piece of cake! Now, take Caesar's much more formidable and inner-rhyme-accented "Tea for Two" from the musical *No, No Nanette*. To me, "Tea for Two" almost completely achieves the rhyming potential of a "great" lyric, while "Always" falls far short of this ideal. So in my own lyrics I felt that I had to be a "complete" instead of a "half-ass" rhymer and music accenter. Otherwise, I would be a flop!

Take, for example, one of my most admired rational humorous songs, "I Wish I Were Not Crazy," with lyrics I set to the tune of Dan Emmett's "Dixie."

Oh, I wish I were really put together—
Smooth and fine as patent leather!
Oh, how great to be rated innately sedate!

But I'm afraid that I was fated
To be rather aberrated—
Oh, how sad to be mad as my Mom and my Dad!
Oh, I wish I were not crazy! Hooray, hooray!
I wish my mind were less inclined
To be the kind that's hazy
I could agree to really be less crazy,
But I, alas, am just too goddamned lazy!

Notice how I go to extremes to include as many internal and end-of-line rhymes as I can into this lyric. Dan Emmett was a piker compared to me! But I emphasize: My urgent rhyming is a near-necessity. It accentuates and dramatizes the music of the song—it adds to the notes. The musical tones would be bereft, lonely, without my ancillary rhymes.

I think so strongly about this, in fact, that although practically all those who sing or listen to my songs like the lyric the way it is—and many are wildly enthusiastic about it—I still see it as weak and incomplete. I tolerate the last line of the verse "Oh, how sad to be mad as my Mom and my Dad," but I still think it lacking and at times consider changing it to "How unglad to be mad as my sad Mom and Dad." And even this line doesn't perfectly use all possible internal rhymes. How sad!

Although I have written hundreds of song lyrics, I still "needlessly" work hard to perfect their inner rhyming when most of them would be quite okay without it. I tell myself that this is only artistic rather than neurotic perfectionism. But is it?

Take another of my song lyrics, written in the 1930s, when I was in my twenties, to the melody of Johann Strauss Jr.'s famous waltz "Roses from the South."

When Love's in Season

(Chorus)
When love's in Season
It's high treason
Using reason, Darling!
With libertine volcanity,
Give in to its insanity!
A hearty bite full
Makes the night full
Of bright and delightful joy!—

Love as a toy
Never will cloy
If just allowed unreasoned employ!
Care not a jot!—
Throw in your lot!
When love's in season, reason is not!

(Verse)
"Love lives ever."—
Possibly so, I'll not say no.
"True loves never
Ever dissever or go!"
Still I'll continue
Trying a new conquest or two.
Love lives ever—
But lovers, alas, never do!

I did the same thing when I wrote my considerable comic verse in my twenties. It usually had to be beautifully rhymed. For example:

Short Short Short Story: November 1929

My dear,
My love,
My wings,
My mate.

My peer,
My dove;
My things migrate:

My flat,
My boat,
My gain,
My sod.

My hat?
My coat?
My cane?—
My God!

In gathering material for an anthology of comic verse, I became enamored of the triolet—a highly formalized and restrictive mode that has only eight lines, the third line repeating the first and the last two repeating the first two. I found triolets so challenging to compose that I spent much time writing a number of them. Here are some samples:

Triolet on Love

I love a lass,
I love a miss
You can't surpass.
I love a lass
Who's of the class
That will not kiss.
I love—alas!
I love amiss!

Triolet on Wealth

"You love me, dear."
She said: "I? No!"
"Ah, have no fear,
You love me, dear—
For I have here
A lot of dough.
You love me, dear."

After reaching that unusual pinnacle of trioletdom, I guess I thought I had little place to go. So I have not written any in years.

The perennial question: Why? Why did I go to all this (unnecessary) trouble? First, a few sensible reasons: I wanted a challenge, preferred to be unusual and outstanding, liked my "artistic" goals, desired to be successful and make money—as did Irving Berlin, Irving Caesar, and Ogden Nash. Okay. Sensible preferences.

But did I escalate these inclinations into dire needs? Evidence that I did: I persisted too strongly and too long, gave up on easier solutions, and sometimes ruined my lyrics and verses by overemphasizing their rhyme schemes. I lost their point by grubbing away at perfectionism. Poor taste—or obsessive-compulsive disorder? I doubt it was the latter: When I failed to get exactly the lyric or verse I wanted, I wasn't horrified or depressed—

only frustrated and disappointed. I denigrated my efforts, not myself, and kept trying till I had some "successes." Even when I gave up on one goal—writing superb triolets—I went on with my other strivings—less intricate poems and other important life goals. Some ambitions I abandoned, such as teaching myself to play and write music and even to invent a new system of musical notation. But my life went—quite absorbingly—on.

Was my behavior compensatory, as some Adlerians might surmise? In part, probably. Because I wasn't outstanding at sports, speaking, singing, or dating, did I therefore have to excel at writing and philosophy—at which I had some talent? Not exactly, because I was even better at math and composing but didn't absolutely insist on achieving in those areas.

Reasons for passionate striving are hard to pin down in many cases. My father and brother both might have been outstanding chess masters, but for practical reasons they chose to do well at business. I was outstanding at business, too, but I chose to focus on writing and psychology. Had even one of my paper-and-pencil stock market schemes worked—which I started to figure out when I was sixteen—I might have been a renowned investment banker. Who knows?

My main point is: I am a perfectionistically inclined involver. I make choices—usually one or two main choices at a time—and I push my ass. Passionately. Fervently. And, yes, with some degree of obsessive-compulsiveness. I think that is one of my basic, biologically propelled (and otherwise aided) natures. I hope it will be till I kick the final bucket.

Chapter 2C

My Sex and Love Life
My Second Great Love

Somewhere around my sixth year, I was again caught in a sex act, albeit one of a minor nature. Between my fifth and seventh year, I went to the Presbyterian Hospital eight times, once for double pneumonia and the other times for nephritis. Most hospital visits lasted about a week or two, although on one of these occasions, I actually spent ten months in the hospital.

During my stays, and especially for the longest one, at least two notable sex incidents occurred. First of all, when I was only about five and a half, I was bathed regularly by the nurses and for that ritual was taken to a large bathroom that had a deep sink flanked by two enameled metal platforms. For bathing purposes, the nurse would seat me on one of the platforms, with my two feet dangling over the edge and into the gap created by the sink. I would be thoroughly soaped (by her or by myself), rinsed off by a spray hose, and then dried with a large towel.

I don't really recall whether being soaped and sprayed by the nurse was a sexy experience to me, though I suspect that it was. I always preferred the prettiest nurses to give me my bath. I enjoyed the soaping of my body and the warm spraying that followed. I liked being dried with the large towel. And I certainly liked being praised by the nurse for sitting on the platform uncomplainingly, for cooperating as well as I did, and for helping to dress myself (putting on my simple hospital gown) after the bath was finished. Whether I actually sexually enjoyed the nurses' handling of my body or their patting it with a drying and soothing powder after I was completely dried, I don't quite remember. I think I did. But I wouldn't bet on it.

What did excite and thrill me was the fact that because I had to be naked when I was washed by the nurse—which I may have been ashamed of and minded at the start but soon got used to—the other children who were washed with me (and who sat opposite me, on the other side of the sink) were also as naked as jaybirds. And some of those children were—yes, you guessed it—young girls.

Now let's be fair about this. The nurses, being reasonably well brought up in the highly conventional, and antisexual, manner of that (1919) day were never so uncouth as to wash me, a five- or six-year-old boy, in the same sink as, and sitting directly opposite to, a girl of my own age or older. Heavens forbid! The two of us would presumably be shamed to death to let ourselves be seen nude by another child, and especially an other-sex child of around the same age. I, certainly, would not want my little (but fast growing!) penis to be seen by, say, a six-, ten-, or twelve-year-old female, and would probably have resisted mightily being bathed in front of one, and perhaps would have run out of the bathroom screaming. As for the young woman—well, you can imagine how enthusiastic she would have been to let her fleshly naked-ness be seen by a young ruffian of six, who was curious as hell to finish the job I had been so sadly interrupted in performing when I tried to explore Ruthie's nether regions. Hmph! Not to mention double hmph!

Knowing this, and still wanting to get maximum use of the busy bathroom, the nurses fiendishly devised a system that would benefit them and supposedly still keep down the prurient interest of their charges. Whenever they bathed two children simultaneously, they made sure that one of them was an older child—like myself, five years or upward—and the other was younger—say, no more than two years. In this way, the younger child was so immature as to presumably have no interest in anything sexual, and the older one, whatever his or her sexual precocity, would have very little sexual interest in a one- or two-year-old, of either sex.

That was the nurse's theory, but it wasn't exactly my practice. Although still supposedly in the autoerotic stage—according to the crazy notions of Sigmund Freud, who as far as I can tell commenced almost all of his sex life after forty and believed that from six to twelve boys had only latent sexuality—little Albert was distinctly interested in heterosexuality—indeed, any kind of heterosexuality—tiny "pervert" that he was. Maybe the nurses thought that female infants of one or two weren't sexually fascinating to me. But they were wrong! I looked forward to every bathing occasion, hoping (sometimes against hope) that I would be seated opposite one of these infant females, quite determined to learn thereby more of the facts of life.

Not that I saw very much. Even when the nurse placed a fairly well-developed female infant facing me and obligingly turned her so that her genital region was completely revealed to my eager gaze (held her, for instance, and swabbed vigorously at her vulva with a washrag), I forgot about her infancy and focused only on her femaleness. What a nice slit (I thought to myself) she had! And what joys (for me and other males) could lie within it! If only those goddamned nurses would really leave us alone for a few minutes, so that I could see for myself more than I had managed to see with Ruthie, and so I could validate the proposition that little girls really were made of sugar and spice!

Why my eyes didn't completely pop out of my head, I know not. Sometimes I thought they would. But, knowing that it was not exactly nice of me to stare at the feminine pudendum, and being rather concerned about displeasing the nurses who might catch me staring—especially the really pretty ones whom I also had eyes for, in spite of the stiffly starched and form-secreting uniforms that they wore—I pretended to look in practically every direction except the genitals of the little women who were facing me in the bath. But—oh, so cleverly!—I still managed to do quite a bit of unadulterated observing. And rarely got caught in the act.

Well, that was really sexy, that (bathing) period of my life. Unfortunately, we were only washed, we denizens of the children's ward, a couple times a week. And, most unfortunately, I was often bathed either solo, or when, damn it! a highly irrelevant male was seated opposite me in the bathroom. I already knew what the male genitalia were like, having explored my own to a nicety. I still, however, had no real idea about what was behind that delightful female slit. And I was, by hook or crook, determined to know.

I almost found out during a later hospital stay. At that time, I think I was about six and a half, and I was friendly with most of the other patients on the children's ward, especially since by this time I was something of an old-timer and many of the others were in for their first time, and for a short stay at that. As this was about a year after the cruelly enforced breakup of my relationship with Ruthie, I was quite ready to fall in love again, and I did so—this time with a six-year-old girl who was almost Ruthie's opposite: taller, thinner, dark-haired, and dark-eyed. She was also (as my not-so-religious but still acculturatedly Jewish mother told me more than once) a shiksa. Her family, I believe, was Polish Catholic, and her name was Gloria. She and I, almost from the first day we met, took to each other: I to her because she was damned beautiful and she to me (I was somewhat convinced) because I was bright and clever. Oh, yes: she was very nice too—had a sweeter-than-pie disposition and was friendly with virtually all the children on the ward, even those who were mean and nasty. I can't say that I loved her as much as I loved Ruthie (who was still somewhat on my mind, though by this time pretty much a lost, lost cause), but I was quite taken with her, dreamed of what we might someday (when we finally got out of the hospital) do together, and was reasonably sure that she would acquiesce to my not-so-innocent desires.

One of the reasons for my confidence was the sex games that we and the other patients on the ward played almost every night. A number of us slept in a special part of the children's ward that was somewhat separate from the main part of the ward (which was largely occupied, most of the time, with specially covered small cribs in which newborn infants or other very young children resided). In this section, all of us were from about five to eight years of age and were fairly friendly. We were also nauseatingly energetic and had little intention of actually going to sleep at around eight p.m. each evening, when curfew was sounded and the nurses went around and tucked us all in. After the nurses were finished and the lights in our section of the ward were extinguished, we were still wide awake and would have long conversations with each other, often at the top of our lungs—until one of the nurses, attracted by the noise, came in and shushed us. Whereupon, we would shut our big traps, pretend we were going to sleep, and then, no more than a minute after the nurse left, we would practically jump out of our covers and go back to our long, and this time somewhat subdued, conversations.

One of our main topics of conversation—as you may well have guessed—was sex. Not that any of us knew very much about it. We knew that boys and girls (and men and women) were different, at least genitally. We suspected that children were not brought into the world by angels or delivered from peapods. We felt, but were not quite sure, that parents did more than "love" and kiss each other when they went to bed, and that this had something to do with our being brought into the world. We knew—from the noises of the newborn babies around us in the main children's ward and from the visits of their parents and relatives—that many babies were born in hospitals like ours and that they somehow erupted from their mothers. But since we all came from highly conventional Protestant, Catholic, and Jewish families—with an occasional Muslim or Buddhist family thrown in for good melting pot measure—we really knew damned little about the essential facts of life, and we hungered—O, how we hungered!—for more of these elusive facts.

So we talked and we joked and we guessed and we imagined and we invented. Sex, sex, sex, sex. Love, love, love, love. Birth, birth, birth, birth. My, did we chat away about what we hardly knew at all. And not occasionally, mind you. Not merely at special times. No, every—and I mean every—damned night. As soon as the lights were out, our mouths were open and our ears were perked. And we repetitiously told each other, with an amazing air of authority, exactly what we all knew about sex and love and, by inference, exactly what we did not know.

Being a little schemer, and in my own way a shy and polite child but still something of an egotistical rebel (at least, when I had other children to show off to and to urge me on by lauding any derring-do that I might devise), I invented a brilliant addition to our nocturnal verbal sex game. I had my parents bring me a little flashlight, ostensibly because I was afraid of the dark (which I certainly wasn't; I adored the freedom from the nurses it gave me), and I always kept it under my pillow. I maneuvered the other children in the cribs around me to induce their parents to bring them flashlights, too—which almost all of them promptly did.

Thereafter, whenever the lights went out, our little flashlights went on, and we played a thrilling sex game, which (I am totally unashamed to say) was my invention. Each one of us in turn would stand up in our beds and quickly, for only a second or two, raise our nightgowns above our shoulders or heads, thus revealing our naked bodies. As soon as we did this, we would yell out, "Now!" or "Gownup!" or something like that, and immediately the darkness of the room would be penetrated by several flashlight beams turned directly on our (presumably sexy) nudeness. A second after this occurred, and we saw that the beams were hitting their mark (especially their genital mark!), we then would (modestly, modestly!) lower our gowns and cover our bodies. Then the flashlight wielders would laugh, obscenely comment on what they had seen, and urge another one of us to risk revealing himself or herself.

What fun! What incredible risk taking! What elated chatter after each of us had revealed our glorious nakedness. I think I only played this game fifteen or twenty times (before our nurses, who were soon on to it, passed a rule that flashlights were no longer allowed), but I found it, easily, the most exciting part of my stay in the Presbyterian Hospital. For hours before lights-out time, I looked forward to it. I was usually the one to give the signal to start it ("Hey, fellas, let's reach for our flashlights"). I always volunteered to be one of the gown raisers. For about fifteen minutes each night our game continued, before the nurses came in (realizing that we were not sleeping and were, instead, fully inclined to stay up indefinitely and keep flashlighting our way into sexual knowledge), sternly said, "No more of this! I said 'Lights out!' and I mean flashlights, too!," and insisted that we get to sleep. After that, I remained excitedly awake for another twenty minutes or more, thinking about what I (and my little flashlight) had seen and trying to digest this knowledge and make something meaningful of it.

Of course, I had seen goddamned little. Each of us, either out of feelings of shame or because we made the game of the now-you-see-my-body-and-now-you-don't nature, revealed our nakedness very briefly, and, with our little flashlights, we could see exceptionally little. Being quite young, virtually none of the seven or eight nude females that I saw had real breasts. And the only thing I saw of their genitals, and that for no more than a second or two, was a slit between their legs, with a tiny mound above it. Not very much, really and, especially after several almost identical "revelations," rather monotonous and unrevealing. The real additions to my sex knowledge that I acquired in the course of the few weeks I played this game were minuscule. The excitement engendered by the game was great, but its contributions to my scientific understanding of sex swiftly partook of the law of diminishing returns.

The contribution this game made to my mental health—and possibly that of literally thousands of clients of REBT in later years—was of a much higher order. For, although I did not realize it at that time, the sex-oriented flashlight game that I invented at the age of six was the precursor of one of the main REBT techniques I created half a century later. This was, if I recall correctly, in 1968, when I was leading weekend marathon therapy groups with George Bach, one of the main creators of marathon therapy.

George had his own inimitable way of leading a marathon group for forty-eight hours straight, with no special intermission for the group's (or the leader's) going to sleep. The theory was that if most of the members kept awake for the full forty-eight hours, or at least most of it (they were allowed to conk out on the floor while the group was still continuing, as long as they did not leave the room for any length of time and take a real nap elsewhere), they would become so tired that their resistance to opening up and to having real feelings about the other members of the group (including, especially, real negative feelings) would be overcome and they would spew out honest reactions. That theory, as I later discovered by experimenting with it, was largely full of crap, since most of the marathon members (except me!) actually did go to sleep for from three to ten hours during the forty-eight and therefore weren't at all over-irritable or as fully revealing as they were theoretically supposed to be. So (as I will recount later in this book) I changed the system around and devised a better, more efficient one.

Anyway, George had his way of doing marathons—which was innovative, brilliant, and typically George-oriented—and I and the REBT therapists, who were simultaneously leading other marathon groups at the Albert Ellis Institute in New York, had our way. This way mainly consisted of the very large proportion of typical REBT group therapy, which was problem-oriented and showed the marathon participants how they upset themselves through thinking irrationally about various things in their lives, and how they could dispute those irrational beliefs and substitute rational, self-helping beliefs instead. In addition, the marathons included several encounter-type exercises, such as those created at Esalen by Will Schutz and Fritz Perls, as well as several that I invented.

The trouble with the Perls-Schutz exercises, I soon discovered, was that they were not exactly rational and, in fact, some of them were highly irrational. Quite a few, for example, were based on the Freudian-Reichian theory of abreaction, which holds that if you suppress or repress your feelings (such as feelings of anger), they will plague you forever and lead to your ultimate ruin (e.g., sabotaging your mate or boss or creating your own ulcers or high blood pressure). But if you honestly acknowledge and express these feelings (e.g., by telling people off in your encounter group or by pounding pillows), your anger will disappear, and you will end up by practically loving those you used to hate.

This, as you might expect, occasionally happens. You hate your boss, refuse to tell him how you really feel, and go home and beat up your mate or end up at your doctor's office with an ulcer or high blood pressure. Then, in your marathon encounter group, you tell everyone how much you hate one of the other male members of the group (who, coincidentally, has some of your boss's main characteristics); you also express these feelings to this member himself; you perhaps pound a pillow representing this man's head; and—lo and behold!—you suddenly wind up liking this group member and even (miracle of miracles!) liking your boss as well.

Great stuff, when it happens like this in a therapy group. Much more often, however (as the psychotherapy books favoring abreaction forget to say), you wind up by hating the member in your group who resembles your boss more and more and are angry at him long after the marathon has ended. You then go back to your office and not only still loathe your boss but do so much more openly, until he has no trouble in seeing how you feel about him, and you unceremoniously get fired.

An unlikely tale? Not at all. Literally hundreds of quite good psychological experiments—as I indicate in my book *How to Control Your Anger Before It Controls You*—show that almost any kind of expression of hostility, direct or indirect, literal or symbolic, usually helps people to become considerably angrier and more punitive. So REBT, although it helps people to acknowledge and honestly reveal their underlying feelings (such as those of hostility, anxiety, or depression), by no means encourages them to act them out, either in rational encounter marathon groups or in real life. Not by a long shot.

In REBT, however, we do have many encounter-type or emotive-evocative exercises (for reasons that I won't take the space to go into here but that can be examined in several of my books on psychotherapy). And in searching around for one that would be most useful for my marathon groups, I invented my now famous shame-attacking exercise, which has subsequently been adopted by other (REBT and non-REBT) therapists and which has also been widely used by other self-actualizing groups, such as the Forum. I also steadily employ this shame-attacking exercise in my regular therapy groups at our institute in New York and with many of my REBT clients. When I assign the exercise in group therapy (which I do regularly), I instruct the group as follows:

> I am now going to give you one of the most valuable REBT exercises that we have been using for years, and that has been exceptionally helpful to our clients on innumerable occasions. This is called the shame-attacking exercise, and I devised it many years ago and have been using it steadily ever since because, as I saw at the time I created it, shame is often the essence of what we call human neurosis or disturbance. For whenever anyone—including, of course, you—feels ashamed, embarrassed, humiliated, anxious, or self-downing, you are

foolishly and needlessly upsetting yourself; and no feeling of shame—yes, I mean no feeling—is really healthy. If you feel sorry, regretful, or displeased with any of your acts—such as your behaving immorally to others or asininely goofing at some task (like doing your REBT homework) that you know would be highly preferable to you, that is one thing. That is sensible and healthy. But if, in addition, you feel thoroughly ashamed of or embarrassed about that immoral or asinine act, then you are perhaps rightly not only putting *it* down as self-defeating or socially obnoxious behavior, but you are also putting *you* down for committing that behavior. And your self-putdown, or shame, will frequently help you to behave badly in the present and future. So feelings of shame, humiliation, or self-denigration are wrong: that is, self-sabotaging. And this shame-attacking exercise is one of the best methods we have devised in REBT to help you surrender these feelings.

Now, the exercise goes as follows, and includes two important parts. First, you do, and you do in public, some act that you consider quite foolish, ridiculous, shameful, humiliating, or embarrassing: such as wearing a very loud piece of clothing that you bought several years ago but have been too ashamed to wear. Or such as refusing to tip a waiter or a cab driver who has given you poor service. Or such as telling a very sexy joke in a public gathering. Some act, in other words, that you would sometimes like to do in public but do not have the guts to do, for fear that others would think you crazy or stupid.

Now, I warn you: Don't do anything that would really get you into trouble—such as walking naked in the street and getting arrested or telling a supervisor or boss that he or she is a shit, and thereby getting yourself fired. And don't do anything that would be harmful to another person—such as slapping someone in the face or being so disruptive in public that people are really bothered or frightened. Do something that is harmless but still generally considered "shameful" or "foolish," and do it in public, so that at least one person and preferably a good many people will see you do it and will possibly disapprove of you. So think, now, of something that you are really ashamed to do but that you are so embarrassed about that you virtually never would do it. And do that thing—and do it several times, and not merely just once.

This is the first part of the shame-attacking exercise. But the second part is even more important. As you do this so-called "shameful" or "embarrassing" act, I want you to do your best not to feel ashamed or embarrassed. Feel anything you want—but not humiliation, mortification, or self-downing. Do you understand? Do this "shameful" act, and preferably many times, but do it so that you prove to yourself that you don't have to feel ashamed. Do you see what I mean?

During the description of this shame-attacking exercise, I write down the "humiliating" act that the members of my group or my individual clients agree to perform (either immediately by going out and doing it then and there, or as a homework assignment to be completed the following week). I then check up to see (1) whether they have done it; (2) how ashamed they felt while doing it; (3) how they managed to feel little or no shame while performing it; and (4) how they felt after it was all over and after they thought about repeating the exercise again. When I induce my clients to do this kind of shame-attacking exercise, and especially when they do the exercise more than one time, they frequently make great changes in their attitudes and behaviors, and sometimes are able for the rest of their lives to do "shameful" acts in a highly unashamed manner. They thereafter may consider their act "wrong" or "shameful" and feel sorry about doing it but not feel like a bad person. When they succeed at this, they just about always make significant inroads into their self-downing and other anxiety-creating attitudes and begin to live happier, less disturbed lives. They achieve one of the main goals of REBT: Unconditional Self-Acceptance (USA).

I have found in the course of the past fifty years that this is a fine exercise, one that I am happy to have created. In addition to being quite therapeutic, it has truly added zest and amusement to the lives of (by now) perhaps millions of people. Many of the shame-attacking exercises that REBT clients do are, to say the least, startling and sparkling. They go out in the New York subway system and, at the top of their voices, yell out the stations when the trains stop ("Forty-second street! Change for Times Square!")—and they stay on the trains. Or they go to department stores and at a busy hour yell out the time ("Ten-twenty and all's well!"). Or they enter a drugstore and say, preferably to a female clerk, and in a voice loud enough to be heard by everyone in the store, "I'd like a gross of small condoms. And, since I use so many of them, I think you should give me a special discount!" Or they stroll down a sunny street on a Sunday afternoon, walking, on a long red leash, a banana and stopping every once in a while to pet it and feed it.

Some fun! But the main purpose is still serious: to show people that no matter what they do, and how "embarrassing" it supposedly is, they really do not have to feel embarrassed or ashamed at all—and, in fact, they can often make themselves feel amused, pleased, or happy as they are publicly disapproved of and laughed at, simply by telling themselves highly rational statements. As noted above, I devised this shame-attacking exercise in 1968, when I was in my mid-fifties. But the roots of it, I now see in reviewing my early life, go back to my days in the Presbyterian Hospital, when I was no more than six. For my flashlight game was really a shame-attacking exercise. Through it, I taught myself and my companions on the children's ward that you could easily do "shameful" acts, such as revealing your nakedness to the view of a whole group, and in the process not only feel unashamed but even delighted and amused.

For that was what happened to virtually all of us who participated in this nighttime game. The first few times we raised our nightgowns and were spotlighted by the others—"Look at me!" we shouted, "I dare you to look!"—almost all of us clearly felt embarrassed and instantly pulled down our gowns to cover ourselves and eliminate this embarrassment. But after we repeated this process only a few times—poof!—our shame largely vanished, to be replaced by a sense of exhilaration and self-congratulation for the "risky" and "shameful" act we had done.

Some of us went even further. At first, when my gown was raised, and five or six of my friends' voices screamed at me, "Oh, look at him! Look what *he's* got" or (more sardonically) "Look at him! Look at what he's *not* got!" I quickly covered myself and felt excited but ashamed. After two or three times, I felt excited but not ashamed. And after about five times, I said to myself, "I'll show them! I'll show them what a daring person with a real prick like mine can actually do!" So, instead of pulling my nightgown right down and falling under the covers again, I deliberately held it high over my head, refused to sit down, and stubbornly held myself (and my sacred cock) aloft until they became startled and somewhat ashamed and put out their flashlights. Having achieved that daring "victory," I wasn't ashamed an iota. In fact, I was damned proud of what I had done and of my courage in doing it.

The others, less daring than I, failed to follow suit—except for Gloria and another girl who, not to be outdone by me, did exactly what I did, and stood up for an indefinite period of time, fully revealing their nudity (including, in the other girl's case, since she was about nine, a fairly well-developed bosom). Well, that was really something! Not only did I get what I really wanted—respect and acclaim from the other children for being the first to be so brave and devil-may-care about exposing myself, but I also got a quite prolonged look at Gloria and the other girl—two beauties, thought I, who knew a good thing when they saw it (that is, their own luscious bodies) and were willing to share them so fully with the rest of us. When this great thing transpired, I was fully in seventh heaven.

Then came the crash. First, the nurses, though never precisely figuring out what we were doing but guessing (from the noise we made with our lustful, raucous laughter) that we were up to some kind of devilry and that it probably included something of a sexual nature, banned our flashlights and insisted that we go to sleep at the set hour of eight (so that we would be bright-eyed and bushy-tailed when they abruptly woke us up the next morning at six a.m.). Second, I fell more and more in love with Gloria—in spite of my parents' dire warnings about my getting too closely attached to a shiksa. Third, I discovered that this particular stay in the hospital was shortly to come to an end, since I was apparently (for the nonce) cured, again, and could therefore return to my home in the Bronx.

The second of these events—my falling in love with Gloria—was hardly a jolt but rather a boon. My nature has almost always been to fall easily in love with some female—and on one single occasion in my life, almost with a male—and to benefit immensely thereby. Love, as they say, makes the world go 'round. Maybe not for everyone. Remember, if you will, the tragic *Letters of a Portuguese Nun,* not to mention what happened to Abelard after he had his balls cut off. But for little Albert, hell yes. At the time I met Gloria, I was still thinking about Ruthie, but not exactly with the fervor of a year before, when I could hardly get her out of my mind for a moment. So I was open to a New Romance—which Gloria nicely provided.

Why? I cannot say why. She was beautiful, all right, as even my mother begrudgingly admitted when she learned (to her horror) that I was somewhat enamored of this Polish vixen. She had charm and popularity—as shown by the fact that a couple of the other boys in our ward obviously looked on her with favor, and even the male doctors stopped by her bed, when on their rounds, for an uncommonly long time. And she was—or I distinctly thought she was—exceptionally bright. So my falling in love with her was not exactly a total mystery. And yet, she seems, in my mind's eye, rather vague, while Ruthie, who preceded her by perhaps a year and a half, still seems exceptionally vivid.

Could be the length of time I knew both of them. In Ruthie's case, I knew her (in the nonbiblical sense) for half a year or so, in the course of which we spoke together continually, often for a few hours at a time. And then, as I have already recounted, we had quite a "sexy" episode together. In regard to Gloria, I think I knew her only for three or four weeks, and our sexcapade was purely a matter of seeing, with no touching whatever. Although we sometimes were in adjoining beds, and therefore had some intimate talks together, we were often (at the whims of the nurses) moved several beds away from each other—until I complained and maneuvered to get us closer again. So we never, for any length of time, got that close, and it was not till my very last day in the hospital, when I already knew that I was going to leave later in the afternoon, that we were able to tell each other (ah, so briefly, so incredibly briefly!) exactly how much we really liked each other and that we were utterly determined to meet again once we were both back in our respective homes.

Fond hopes that never in even the slightest way materialized— except once, several years later, when we ran into each other for a few minutes as we were attending the outpatient clinic of the hospital, where we both went for a while for regular checkups. Gloria's parents, from what I could gather, were just about as enthusiastic about our getting intimate with each other as were mine—and for equally bigoted reasons. They were devout Catholics and could no more welcome a little Jew-boy like myself to their family than could my intolerant parents frolic with joy at the thought of taking a Polish Catholic girl into our reformed Jewish domicile. When you add this to the fact that Gloria and her parents lived somewhere far out in Queens, and my family lived in some of the farthest regions of the North Bronx (in a day, remember, when neither the Independent Subway nor the Triborough Bridge were even in the planning stage), you can see that my and Gloria's getting together for a friendly chat (let alone the vastly more physical contact that I continually thought about) was hardly a matter of high probability. Add to this the grim reality that neither her family nor mine were yet in the category of those relatively few New Yorkers who were favored enough to have telephones at home, and you will again see that our chances of even talking to each other, and thereby continuing our amative intimacy, were minimal.

Minimal, indeed; they were nil. I persistently bothered my mother about arranging for me to see Gloria on some kind of (at least) occasional basis, and, from what I later learned from her on the one brief occasion when we talked at the hospital clinic, Gloria supposedly did the same to persuade her mother. To no avail. The second great Love of My Life had, for all intents and purposes, fallen off the face of the earth.

That was, I need not tell you, abysmally grim. Two Great Loves in a row, and both down the drain because of parental opposition. How unfair! Here, through sheer luck I had met two incomparable girls, and here, through sheer charm and brilliance, I had managed to win them.

To no goddamned avail. Unkind fate had totally cut me down—twice. Twice in a row! What the devil was the use, anyway? How, at this rate, would I ever make it with a delectable young woman? How?

As the days went by, and it seemed clearer than ever with each new dawn that Gloria was never to be mine, I became more depressed. With Ruthie, I at least had the glorious memory of what we had done, sexually and amatively, together, and that helped get me through for quite a while. With Gloria, I had no such memories. Not only no memories, but no real dice. Bah!

At first I resorted to invention. Having not much of a past with Gloria, I ecstatically imagined the future. She was, as I have noted, beautiful—a soulful dark-eyed brunette, and her nude body, thinner and taller than Ruthie's, was intriguingly inviting. So I intensely imagined—oh, how I fervently imagined!—the intricate mergings of our hot, lustful bodies and the impassioned osculations of our hot, panting mouths. In imagination, too, we talked and talked and talked. We always had an enormous number of things to say to each other; and we said them ad infinitum. What, exactly, were they? At this date, I frankly don't remember. But they were certainly voluminous—and endless. Whenever I felt really depressed about the loss of Gloria, I distracted myself mightily with these imaginary conversations and fantasized physical contacts.

Here again—though I certainly didn't recognize it at that time—I was using another therapeutic technique that I was later to incorporate in Rational Emotive Behavior Therapy (REBT): that of cognitive distraction. Not that this is one of REBT's most powerful methods: cognitive distraction temporarily sidetracks you from almost anything you are worried or depressed about, but it doesn't truly get at the basic source of your anxiety and depression, and therefore, once you momentarily discontinue it, it doesn't prevent you from flitting back to it again and again and again, like yoga exercises or Edmund Jacobson's progressive relaxation techniques, both of which are frequently used by REBT therapists (including, occasionally, myself). You are afraid, terribly afraid, for example, that you are going to function poorly in the important meeting of your firm's executives, and you are even more afraid of being afraid—for you know damned well that if you are anxious about this meeting, you will almost certainly be viewed as neurotic and will function poorly in the course of it. So, you are a waterfall of interlocking anxieties and you are about to go out of your mind and apply for admission to some nearby loony bin.

Ideally, in helping you to use REBT, we therapists would teach you to see what you are irrationally telling yourself about this meeting (and about the anxiety you have in connection with it). We would help you to zero in on the absolutistic musts that you are bringing to it (such as "I *must* do well and I *must* impress everyone at this meeting!"). Then we would encourage you to challenge, to dispute these musts, using the logico-empirical and other disputing methods that REBT has particularly applied to the process and alleviation of human disturbance. So we would show you how to see and to uproot your fundamental "musturbatory" philosophy, and the horrible fear of failure that accompanies it, and thereby to remove (or at least minimize) your original anxiety and your anxiety about this anxiety.

That is how we would try to help you, using basic or elegant REBT. But—as many of its cavalier critics sometimes fail to recognize—while it emphasizes disputing of irrational beliefs, REBT also includes a good number of other cognitive methods of therapy: one of which is cognitive distraction. So if you showed little propensity for the elegant REBT method of disputing, or if for some other reasons (such as the nearness of an impending crisis) you could not readily take the time or make the effort to use the disputational method, we would help you distract yourself by other palliative but still effective means. For example, we might teach you Jacobson's muscle relaxation technique, show you how to take ten or fifteen minutes off from your worries to go into a highly relaxed state, in which you would be instructed how to distract yourself from your worries and, perhaps (later), to be more capable of dealing with them more effectively.

Techniques of cognitive distraction are almost innumerable, ranging from reading, window shopping, and watching TV to various forms of deep meditation. Knowing nothing about such techniques at the age of six, I tended to invent my own. Feeling distraught and depressed without any contact with Gloria, and without any reasonable possibility of having future contact with her, I threw myself into my usual activities on Bryant Avenue—playing ball, exploring the neighborhood with Steve, discussions with Don, and (at long last!) attending nearby Public School No. 28.

I also threw myself into distracting imagery: that is, wildly imagining all kinds of sexual and nonsexual meetings with Gloria. As is often the case, my fantasies were not nearly as exciting as my brief participations with her at the hospital had been. But they served! For months after I left the hospital—until, in fact, I managed to fall in love with a little red-headed girl in my first-grade class—I thought and thought and thought about Gloria. My thinking and imaginings about her were so profound, so occupying, that I simply had no more time for being depressed. Besides, I think I reasoned, the enjoyment of daydreaming was clearly better than the "enjoyment" of self-pity and depression. So I focused on the former and pretty well drowned out the latter in my phantasmagoric visions—which I found infinitely more gratifying.

{}

Time passed and, eventually, so did my interest in Gloria. Not that I ever really forgot her; I don't think I have ever completely forgotten any of the sizable number of females that I have been madly in love with for any decent period of time. Even though she was in my life only about six weeks, her memory lingered on and on. But not forever, or not forever in any acutely painful kind of way. Gloria, I decided, was a hell of an interesting girl. But life held a good many other fascinating facets, too, and I soon got absorbed in them.

As I read this chapter over, I see that I have managed to exclude at least one notable point: how I dealt with my various kinds of guilt. I didn't really feel that guilty as I surreptitiously looked at the genitalia of the infants who were being washed at the same time as me. Nor did I feel guilty when I invented my nudity-revealing flashlight game (which I knew damned well would have been a horrible no-no to the nurses in the ward and to my parents, if they had ever discovered its gory details). And I definitely felt no guilt when I allowed myself to seriously consider being intimately attached to and (who knows?) ultimately married to a shiksa. No, I wasn't guilty, and yet, in another way, I really was.

I knew "right" from "wrong," as every good American—and Sunday school-raised—boy supposedly should. And I felt duly uncomfortable for doing these "wrong" acts. But I started to develop, at this early stage, an attitude toward guilt that seemed to astonish my psychoanalyst, when I told him about it some twenty-nine years later. It was a simple system, indeed, and it almost always worked very well. Once I considered an act like spying on infant females and pretending that I was doing no such thing, I would decide whether the act was (a) really very bad or evil and whether, if it was that bad, it was (b) worth paying a possible penalty for. In the case of all the "immoral" activities mentioned in the last paragraph, my major decision was that they really weren't that bad. At least, not to my way of thinking.

Spying on nude females, I reasoned, really didn't hurt the one on whom I was spying—especially when she was under two years of age and hardly knew what was going on in the world. Inventing a nudity game for me and my companions in the children's ward was also not (to my mind) that bad, since it was quite enjoyable and hurt no one. Being in love with—and even eventually marrying—a shiksa, that again, despite my parents' strong views, didn't seem particularly heinous, since love (as I of course knew from the movies) conquers all, and restricting myself to marrying only in one's faith—and against the noble laws of love—seemed easily the greater (by far!) evil.

So the main reason I did not experience any guilt about the presumably vile deeds I committed in the Presbyterian Hospital during my seventh year was because I refused to define these deeds as very bad. This, however, did not mean that I was a budding young psychopath, headed for a totally immoral pathway to life. On the contrary, I was quite moral, in my own thoughtful way, and held (even at that young age) that any behavior that needlessly and truly harmed others (such as a physical assault without any provocation) was quite wicked. And whenever I considered performing such an evil act—which, not too often but on occasion I definitely did consider—I simply ruled it out as untenable. I knew that I would indubitably make myself feel very guilty if I committed such a bad act, so I simply refrained, as best I could, from committing it.

Of course, I was a little prejudiced in my consideration of "goodness" and "badness" based on my second criteria: namely, whether a "bad" act was really worth paying the penalty for. Suppose, for example, I knew perfectly well that my spying on the nakedness of infant females or my inventing the flashlight game would have clearly brought enormous penalties on my head—such as my being soundly whipped or my being deprived forever of seeing a girl (such as Gloria) with whom I was ravenously in love. Under those conditions, I would definitely define such acts as undoubtedly "bad," "wrong," or "evil," and simply would have refrained from performing them.

My solution to the superego problem, then, was rather clear-cut and ingenious (as my neo-Freudian analyst later was eager to point out). Either the acts I did (such as my sex-love escapades) were defined as being "good" and "proper"—or else I simply didn't do them. What, by the way, didn't I do? Well, I virtually never, for example, gave my mother a really hard time, particularly in the gratuitous manner that my brother continually did. If he wanted a cookie and knew for a certainty that it was not only forbidden but that my mother would surely fly into an intense, almost apoplectic rage when he (for the thousandth time) went against her dictums and ate it, he nevertheless gobbled down the banned food. If I wanted a cookie and, like my brother, predicted my mother's hysterical reaction to my taking it, I refrained from taking it— and much more patiently waited for the time when I knew that she wouldn't care that much if I ate it. Then I took the forbidden food.

So, although you can easily see that I was often something of a rebel, even as a rather small child, I was (unlike my unsainted brother) more of a rebel *with* than *without* a cause. I managed rarely to get into fights, to hurt others, or even to do anything about which my parents and other adults would get themselves unusually upset. By this double-headed tactic of defining only certain things as "wrong," and by fairly rigorously refraining from doing those (few) acts that I did define in this manner, I remained unusually guilt-free all during my early years. Anxious and ashamed I frequently was, but guilty of doing something I deemed immoral or harmful to others, hardly ever. This "sensible" tactic may well have restricted my life—especially in comparison with that of my brother, who was much more carefree and, in his own peculiar way, joyous. But it had its great advantages, too, and it certainly helped me to get along with others.

The question is not "Was my solution to the problem of guilt and of social disapproval the best I could have adopted in order to gain a maximally happy kind of existence?" Nor is it "Was my brother's solution to the same problem, even though it would have been labeled 'psychopathic' or antisocial, a better one for him?" Questions like these are always, in part, unanswerable, since the individual and social variables involved in responding to them are exceptionally complex and never entirely ascertainable. For one thing, the "right" answer might well be that, since my brother and I were rather different people, with goals and purposes that were often as diverse as they could possibly be, his "psychopathic" method of being guiltless was fine for him while my "ethical" way of being equally guiltless was fine for me. The "goodness" and "badness" of any act, let us remember, are meaningless terms unless related to one's general and specific goals and purposes in performing (or not performing) those acts. Any absolute standard of "proper" conduct that would be good for all people under all possible conditions seems impractical and utopian.

Assuming that my brother's method and my method of remaining guilt-free were both "good" for each of us individually, or that neither could realistically be proven to be significantly "worse" than the other, the question could still be asked: "Even if his 'psychopathic' way was fine for his particular interests, wouldn't it, in either the short or long run, prove to be deficient from a social standpoint, because it would lead to a chaotic society?" A good question—but, again, not completely answerable. How "good" both of our behaviors were for the social group in which we resided at the time that he was "psychopathic" and I was "socialized" would depend on a multiplicity of factors, some of which (at least immediately) would never be ascertainable. Thus, an investigator of the social results of his behavior and of mine would have to determine: (1) What were the present and future goals of our society? (2) What resources existed to help or sabotage the fulfillment of these goals? (3) What kind of "rational" or "sensible" rules would have to be laid down so that the goals would be optimally achieved? (4) How likely was the biological "nature" and social upbringing of the inhabitants of the community (such as my brother, myself, and millions of other people who lived in it) to abet or sabotage the carrying out of these "rational" rules? (5) What is the socio-economic, political, and religious future of this community likely to be? (6) Et cetera, et cetera.

The point I am trying to demonstrate here is that while a good case could be made for my (as opposed to my brother's) guilt-free attitudes and behavior when I was a child, no unqualified judgment of my (or his) "rationality" could probably ever be finally arrived at. But that is not the issue. Even if my own choice of guiltless thoughts, feelings, and actions were (then or now) correctly judged to be "wrong" or self- and society-defeating, the manner in which I made that choice seems to have been unusually "reasonable" or happiness-oriented.

For, as far as I can remember, even as a child I fairly consciously figured out and chose a plan of "sensible" action for myself.

It really doesn't matter, then, whether my techniques of avoiding guilt were, for myself and for the social group of which I was a part, good, bad, or indifferent. At least they were mine and they were, for the most part, quite consciously mine. My brother's plan of living, as noted above, may well have been the best one for him and may even have had as much social value as my plan. But, although he was an exceptionally bright boy and later became the American amateur chess champion (following somewhat in my father's tracks, since the Old Man had been, at the age of seventeen, the chess champion of the city of Philadelphia), his method of using his head to figure out whether he had better think x, feel y, or execute z seemed (at least to my way of looking at it) relatively nonexistent. He appeared just to think, feel, and act, without premeditation or postmeditation.

This was the way it appeared to me, my mother, and almost anyone who had intimate contact with my brother. Actually, as we might have guessed, he used his head quite a bit to ascertain whether his behavior was "good" (that is, self-helping) or "bad" (that is, self-sabotaging). But if he did so consciously, with good intentions aforethought, none of us who observed him could see that that was his plan. I, on the other hand, did consciously figure out the "rightness" and "wrongness" of my feelings and behaviors. That is the main point I am making here: not that I did so "rationally" or "sanely," but that I almost invariably knowingly tried to come up with "rational" or "sane" answers. Maybe my brother, in his own way, did too. But that was hardly evident from the manner in which he spoke and acted.

Many times I have half-jokingly (and 49 percent seriously!) told my public and professional audience that the main reason I gave up completely on psychoanalysis and started to create Rational Emotive Behavior Therapy is because "I have a gene for efficiency and just will not tolerate the woeful inefficiency of psychoanalytic theory and practice." Some joke! Actually, I do abhor, and always have abhorred, ineptitude, and my deepest philosophy of life—yes, in many ways my utterly deepest—consists of the assumption (and, I must admit, the partially unprovable or undisprovable assumption) that the more effectively one thinks and acts, the happier one (and one's social group) is likely to be.

Regardless of whether or not this assumption is sound (or even, in the last analysis, verifiable), it and I are virtually synonymous and are so, I strongly believe, for reasons that are largely biological. The early environmental influences that I experienced in regard to efficient thinking and human happiness were hardly in the direction that I personally followed. My father, as I have noted before, was hardly ever around when I was a youngster, and the amount of any kind of philosophy of life I picked up (or at least remember picking up) from him was minuscule. Not that he didn't have pronounced views on the way humans should and should not act—for he certainly did. But I discovered his opinions mainly in my teens, when my brother and I would visit him every few months and have fairly long conversations with him over the fabulously cooked dinner that his second wife, Rose, would prepare for us. I then realized—and was somewhat surprised to realize—that he knew exactly the way the world should—and I really mean should—run and that he had no hesitation in telling anyone how he felt about this.

But up to that time I knew only very vaguely what his views on life were and I cannot recall being greatly influenced by them.

As for my mother, I knew her philosophy of life, all right, and knew that for the most part she was hardheaded and practical in her approach to things—particularly to monetary things, since she was always an extreme money pincher. But I also knew that she could be light-headed and lighthearted. She threw herself into the enjoyment of the moment, without giving much consideration (except economically) to the future. Her moods were highly varied and oriented to ceaseless whims. Although a bit dogmatic at times as to the "right" and "wrong" ways for people to live, she was rarely philosophically instructional and spent an incredibly small amount of time telling me and my brother and sister what to do and an extraordinarily large amount of time enjoying herself with temple affairs, with bridge, with mah-jongg, with gossiping among neighbors, with singing popular songs, and with various other kinds of not-too-serious enjoyments.

The philosophy of living that she taught us almost entirely con-sisted of a few selected proverbs, practically all of them extremely pop-ular and trite, such as "A stitch in time saves nine," "Out of sight, out of mind," and "Give them an inch and they take a yard!" If anything, then, my mother did not, as far as I could see, do much thinking for herself; and she only encouraged me to do my own thinking by neglecting me so much, as far as active child-care and the instilling of life philosophies were concerned, that perhaps she forced me, in a way, to think and act for myself. Such neglect I almost always considered a great boon—because I liked mainly being on my own and having a minimum of parent-imposed rules to follow.

Anyway, at the age of six I don't recall having any real philosoph-ical director of my life, and I didn't feel that I needed one. I enjoyed thinking about things, figuring out what was "good" and what was "bad" for me to do (or not do), observing what the results of my ideation and activity were, and then pensively deciding to continue or to change the pathways that I had chosen for myself as the "right" ones. The Freudians and the strict behaviorists, as you can well imagine, would insist that I developed this thoughtful, and in its own way unusually rational, approach to living—and did so at quite a young age—because of my earlier experiences with my father, mother, siblings, and others. Perhaps so. I am fairly sure that these infantile and post-infantile experiences had something to do with my becoming a highly cognitive youngster (and, later, adolescent and adult).

This influence of early childhood experience on personality, however, is vulnerable to having more than a few massive holes poked into it by almost any skeptic. For one thing, why don't *all* children in the same family, who tend to have quite similar experiences with their parents, develop in almost precisely the same manner? Second, what about the receptivity or responsivity that infants *bring* to their early experiences? Third, why do some children for the first few years react in one way and then later act much differently (e.g., my brother, who after early adulthood became unusually conservative, tactful, and not the least psychopathic)? Fourth, if children in the same family react quite diversely to physical stimuli (for example, one is allergic to milk and the other thrives on it), why should they not react with similar diversity to mental and emotional stimuli? Fifth, several research psychologists and psychiatrists have now shown that what we call temperamental traits appear in children within a few days or weeks after birth and that they usually remain fairly constant for the rest of these children's lives. Sixth—but why go on? I have no intention of logically or scientifically defending the proposition that young children's behaviors may well be influenced by their parents and other early associates but that they also have a will and way of their own, and that much of what we call their "personality" is backed by their strong biological predisposition to be pretty much the way they are.

What I am saying, however, is that in my own case I definitely seemed—always, I would say, though I cannot remember back to my early infancy—to have had a strong propensity to use my head to control my life. I think that I am naturally inclined to rationality or self-promoted happiness. I cannot by any means prove this, and I may well be wrong about it. But that's the way it has always felt and seemed to me. Just as Sigmund Freud (according to my own theories, again) was a natural archaeologist and a brilliant fabricator of (and overgeneralizer about) theories of the "origins" of human personality and disturbance. And just as Carl Jung was a natural devotee of mythology (and of much religious and mystical claptrap that inherently seems to go with that kind of thing). So I do believe that I innately and inherently *enjoy* logico-empirical thinking (as well as the enthusiastic ripping up of *il*logical and anti-empirical thinking). Therefore, I hypothesize, my early involvement with rational scheming and planning for my own comfort nicely evolved, and therefore, my lifelong interest in rational emotive behavioral processes has continued.

Scientists, in other words, are prejudiced by their own bents and natures—myself, as a scientist, included. Does this mean that REBT, like Freudianism, Jungianism, and so on, is scientifically limited? In a sense, yes. All supposedly logico-empirical theories, as Thomas Kuhn has convincingly shown, have their own built-in biases, and none of them is "purely" objective (as they often dogmatically claim to be!). As the postmodern thinkers have also shown, science itself is human-oriented and only seen through somewhat subjective human eyes. REBT, too? Yes, REBT, too. So, shall we scrap all these "biased" theories and begin anew? No, but let us be eternally vigilant, always skeptical (as good scientists are) about all of them. Including REBT.

Of course, my observation with keeping myself from misery can be looked at in another way—as a worrisome obsession. Perhaps I was so afraid of pain that I forced myself, at all costs, to ward it off. I could have had low frustration tolerance and felt that I couldn't bear being out of control and that therefore I had to find ways of coping with my potential emotional problems. So I kept desperately trying till I found them.

Perhaps. But isn't this a little too Freudian? The psychoanalysts assume that you really hate your mother when you do anything she objects to. If you then protest that you really love her and show evidence of favoring her in many ways, they then "prove" that your acts of "love" really are reaction formations and show that unconsciously you truly do hate her.

Interesting. But still mainly bullshit. Once in a great while someone truly hates his mother and masks his "shameful" feelings of hate by loving her to death. But always? Or usually? Hardly. So I may have sometimes felt horrified about letting my anxiety and depression get out of control and utterly overwhelm me. And I may have therefore developed a sensible philosophy of life to nip these potential horrors in the bud. But how can we prove that this was true? Where is the evidence? Nowhere that I can see.

Moreover, even if I did this, why was I not wise to do so? Frustration, let me admit, is not my thing. I am naturally eager to get going at many tasks and hate like hell to be thwarted. So I often plan and scheme, sometimes well in advance, to avoid what I hate, for example, being late to planes or trains. Therefore, I almost invariably arrive on time. I loathe being with boring people for any period. So I manage to avoid them or leave early. Anything wrong with that?

Similarly, I avoid other things I hate, such as anxiety and depression. And if, out of low frustration tolerance, I desperately avoid them, is that so bad?

Yes, it is, if by doing so I am really avoiding risks—and the adventures and pleasures that often go with them. Which, I have to admit, I often did during my childhood. But indulging in being upset, it seems to me, is a gratuitous risk. Where's the adventure, where's the pleasure in that?

What about my desperately avoiding panic and depression? Well, what about it? If I was desperate, that was not a desire but a dire need to avoid. But my plotting and scheming to be happy, from my early years onward, was sensible concern, not frantic anxiety. I think.

Chapter 2D
Critique of Chapter 2

"*I took the operation, and its immediate sequelae, with stoic equanimity.*"

Well, yes—eventually. But, consciously or not, I may be forgetting the fear I felt for a few weeks before I realized that all was well and that I was no longer in danger. Some children and adults vividly remember the horror of traumatic events like throat operations, and some are loath to let this feeling go. I eventually adjusted to the "horror" and so mainly remember my adjustment. My sister Janet never seemed to forget any horror, once she created it. My brother Paul rarely seemed to create any horrors at all. My father and mother would get temporarily upset about "gruesome" happenings, then they would adjust to them, forget about them, and return to the pleasant present. Luckily, I modeled them. Naturally or by learning? Probably both. So, for a while I was probably more upset about my tonsillectomy than I now "wisely" remember.

"*I was strong enough . . . to* persuade *God to help me.*" Yes, but I also probably thought that He would help me out of pity, because I was too weak to help myself. I sort of remember that my problem-solving tendency did give me a feeling of strength, but it was mainly strength to find my own solutions. I doubt whether, at that age, I thought I could persuade God in any way, nor could I find the strength to defy Him. That idea, that I could actually defy God, came to me at the age of twelve, when I became an atheist. By then, however, I didn't believe at all in God's existence, so I could safely defy his nonexistent power.

"*That was what I enjoyed: looking problems in the eye and doing my best to solve them.*"

Yes, when they were relatively minor and the pain of not solving them was mild. So I enjoyed games, arithmetic, and trying to persuade my sometimes stubborn mother to do things my way. But more serious problems I frequently avoided—like trying to converse with attractive girls or learning a new sport I thought I wouldn't do well at. Even my headache problems were avoided at first. I was too shy to keep after the nurses and the doctors. Then, as an excuse for my not seeking help, I tried to ignore the headaches. Finally, I got around to figuring out what I could do about them. Then I enjoyed coming up with possible solutions. But that was rather late in the game.

"I figured out that, while not exactly desirable nor anything to look forward to, my demise offered certain advantages. Cessation of suffering. Freedom from headaches. Peace. Eternal nothingness. Not great. But not so damned bad!"

Of course, this was just me contemplating the possibility of death. If I had actually been faced with it, and had the easy means of killing myself, I doubt very much whether I would have done it. It's more likely that, rather than dreading the uncertainty of what might happen to me after death, I would dread the uncertainty of my life had I continued to live. It might be quite free of headaches and replete with other good things. If dead, I would have missed all those goodies. That would be a waste and a shame! So I think my thought about the peacefulness of death was something of a trick to keep myself calm and invent a possible final solution. But I doubt if I ever would have used that end to my problems.

"I think that [obsessive-compulsiveness] is one of my basic, biologically propelled (and otherwise aided) natures. I hope it will be till I kick the final bucket."

But is my endorsing it rational—or largely a rationalization? Yes, my obsessive-compulsiveness has advantages, as I point out. No, I don't take it to impossible, self-defeating extremes. But isn't it time-consuming and wasteful? Wouldn't I, for example, be a more poetic and more moving lyricist—such as was Oscar Hammerstein II—without it? Am I not too hooked on it and do I not let my moderate obsessive-compulsiveness in some areas allow me to be too sloppy in other areas?

By taking care of problems quickly, have I sometimes sabotaged my long-range high frustration tolerance? Take my doing psychological research as a case in point. When I was a fledgling psychologist in my early thirties and quite intent (semi-obsessed) for ego reasons on producing a number of published research papers, I stayed several nights a week at the Northern New Jersey Mental Health Clinic in Morris Plains using clinic materials and other research data I had gathered and turning out a dozen papers, published in highly respectable psychological and sociological journals, within little over a year. Singlehandedly I did all the boring data gathering and statistical analysis for these papers—without any assistance from state-of-the-art technology. Oh, yes, I even typed all these papers—and revisions—on my old-fashioned typewriter myself. Moreover, I wrote—and typed—eight more non-research papers within the same fourteen-month period.

Quite high frustration tolerance! Yes, but it was sparked by the fairly desperate need to forge ahead as a published psychologist and doing so through ego raising, or what I now call conditional self-acceptance. I saw myself as a good person because I was so productive.

Twenty years later, when I had created Rational Emotive Behavior Therapy (REBT), made it quite popular, and headed a training institute, my research activity notably slackened. Studies of the effectiveness of REBT were more important than ever, and I had associates and technology to help me. I did damned few studies. I had several "good" excuses: (1) Other good researchers were doing them. (2) I (foolishly) relied on our paid researchers at the institute to do them—which they carelessly didn't. (3) Our institute is a nonacademic, clinical foundation and has never been able to get research funds. (4) My other activities—including seeing clients, giving workshops and lectures, and writing books—brought in money without which the institute would not have survived.

Great excuses! The fact remains, however, that while I work obsessive-compulsively at near-perfect rhyme schemes for song lyrics, and enjoy the challenge of doing so, I don't enjoy some of the grunt work of psychological research. So I happily let other researchers do it and at our institute often delegate it to others. Yes, I have participated in two dozen research papers on REBT, but this number hardly compares to the published studies of Aaron Beck and Donald Meichenbaum's research on Cognitive Behavioral Therapy. They apparently have higher frustration tolerance for research details than I have! Thus again, I have obsessive-compulsive high frustration tolerance for some tasks, but low frustration tolerance for some more important projects. A rather foolish inconsistency.

"Having achieved that daring 'victory,' I wasn't ashamed an iota. In fact, I was damned proud of what I had done and of my courage in

doing it. . . . I (got) what I really wanted—respect and acclaim from the other children for being the first to be so brave and devil-may-care about exposing myself."

Now that I review this incident I clearly see one of the failings of my famous shame-attacking exercise. It is designed to help people stop rating their self, their beings, and evaluate only what they do. By using shame attacks, they are to recognize that their "shameful" acts are disapproved of socially and are therefore "bad" but that they themselves are never rotten or bad persons. This presumably helps them "get" the REBT central philosophy, which holds that their specific behaviors can be legitimately rated (by personal rules and by social standards), but that their total personality cannot be accurately measured because it consists of thousands of ever-changing behaviors.

Marvelous!—and very helpful in interrupting the harmful self-rating tendencies of practically all humans. But, as can be seen from my experience at the age of six, self-evaluation cannot be so easily stopped. In getting myself to feel unashamed of my revealed nudity, I got rid of ego rating on the one hand but snuck it in the back door, as it were, on the other hand. Thus, *"I was damned proud of what I had done and of my courage in doing it."* Hmm! Pride is ego, or self-rating, and, as the Bible says, it goes before a fall (self-deflation).

So while supposedly throwing self-evaluation out the front door I simultaneously let it in the back door. What do you know—that's what many of my clients and readers who perform my shame-attacking exercise are probably doing! They are risking social criticism and refusing to put themselves down because of it. But they are also doing something "special" and "challenging" and thereby putting themselves up for doing it. They are simultaneously minimizing ego rating and bolstering this behavior. Ironic!

All of this tends to support the REBT theory of self-rating. It is usually so innate and well learned and practiced that it is almost impossible to rid yourself of it completely. Even my shame-attacking exercise, which is specifically designed to reduce self-rating, may be unconsciously (and cleverly) used to bolster it. Oh, vanity, thy name is man and woman!

"My thinking and imaginings about [Gloria] were so profound, so occupying, that I simply had no more time for being depressed."

Would that that were so! To be more accurate, it was only when I was imaginatively distracted and when I convinced myself that somehow we would meet again that I was able to not feel depressed about the loss of Gloria. At other times—many other times—I thought our separation was awful and horrible and I did depress myself. But I resorted to distracting myself with better-than-life fantasies and I also resorted to unrealistic wishful thinking. And they, inelegantly, I now think, helped. But six-year-old Albert was hardly a perfect stoic.

"Gloria, I decided, was a hell of an interesting girl. But life held a good many other fascinating facets, too, and I soon got absorbed in them."

This is another kind of distraction that I am naturally good at. I am easily absorbed in a variety of things, ranging from games to science to philosophy. I really get vitally, though not exclusively, interested in them. So when one of my pursuits, such as my love for Gloria, gets cruelly interrupted, I mourn and sometimes feel depressed for a while—but not forever. My other keen interests take over, and soon I am only intermittently depressed. This flitting to other or new concerns has real benefits, but it also curtails the depth of feeling that prolonged despair might bring. Perhaps it makes me affectively superficial. Perhaps that's why I haven't written any great stories, novels, or plays. My easily transferred, vital, absorbing interest in a number of things prevents my obsessive-compulsive tendencies from becoming one-sidedly fixed and has antidepressive aspects when one of my absorptions is blocked. So it has its advantages. But what about its not-so-obvious disadvantages? REBT holds that practically all human traits and behaviors have their benefits and dis-benefits. I had better think of both sequelae of my using my gains of other interests to distract me from the sorrows of lost interests before I cavalierly recommend this kind of distraction to my depressed clients.

"I . . . did consciously figure out the 'rightness' and 'wrongness' of my feelings and behaviors. . . . I almost invariably knowingly tried to come up with 'rational' or 'sane' answers."

Well, yes, but let's not gild the lily. I consciously and knowingly tried to come up with "rational" or "sane" answers more, perhaps, than did most other young children. But some of my answers were unconsciously constructed, and many of them were palliative and superficial.

Consider, again, how I dealt with not making myself feel guilty. Knowing that I was "wrong" in intently observing the female children during bathtime at the hospital, was I at all guilty? I think not. Not that at that time I used the sophisticated REBT distinction of considering an act to be bad but not evaluating myself as a bad person. That distinction was years away. Instead, I think that, like many children, I was something of an unashamed psychopath. I knew darned well that I was immoral and was dead-set against the rules of propriety. But I was so eager to get more sex knowledge, and so enjoyed trying to get it, that I ignored the rules—and praised myself for being clever enough to flout them without being caught.

Perhaps like most children, I had the psychopathic quality of first, viewing many "wrong" acts as not really wrong. After all, I was hardly hurting anyone by my secret spying on female youngsters. Second, I saw getting away with it as a challenging and good deed, and that view overshadowed its badness. Quite psychopathic. I would have been ashamed if I had been caught peeping by the nurses and would have been reprimanded for doing so. But I never was. So I greatly enjoyed this voyeuristic game. Yes, psychopathically.

Years later, when I ignored sexual conventions by engaging in frotteurism, having immoral (though consensual) intercourse with women, and engaging in some illegal acts (such as anal intercourse), I rationalized more effectively, in that I consciously upheld my deeds as "good" ones because they "justly" and "revolutionarily" combated the "fascistic" rules of society. I performed these acts to serve as a pioneering model! Nice rationalization. With just a little bit of psychopathy thrown in.

"Such neglect [on my mother's part] I almost always considered a great boon—because I liked mainly being on my own and having a minimum of parent-imposed rules to follow."

Exaggerated recollection? Probably. I did like being on my own and having a minimum of parent-imposed rules to follow. But at times, especially when I was sick, I felt that I needed my mother and resented her or depressed myself about her for being too occupied with other things, including my often disruptive younger brother and sister. I also liked being on my own because I received praise for being "a good little boy who could take care of himself." So I egoistically used this ability and my preference for solitude to make myself feel superior to other children—especially to my siblings, who were deficient in it.

"I definitely seemed . . . to have had a strong propensity to use my head to control my life. I think that I am naturally inclined to rationality or self-promoted happiness."

Maybe! But my unusual adversities when I was a child—such as neglectful mother and father and considerable illness—may have practically forced me to be more rational than most children are. Moreover,

I am now, and probably always have been, prejudiced in favor of ratio-nality. I admire sane and sensible people, including myself, who are more sensible and less upsettable, so I can easily have a prejudiced and distorted view of how thoughtfully self-helping I was as a child—and still supposedly am.

Yes, my mother always agreed that I was by far the most emotion-ally stable of her three children. But maybe I deliberately fooled her in that respect. Besides, in many ways my brother and sister were pretty screwballish, so I easily outshone them in well-adjusted behavior. Also, they may have more honestly revealed their disturbed feelings and actions to our mother and to others, while I dishonestly kept quiet. If so, I was in a way more rational than were they. But really?

"I do believe that I innately and inherently enjoy logico-empirical thinking. . . . Therefore, I hypothesize, my early involvement with rational scheming and planning for my own comfort nicely evolved."

Again, maybe! Some professors of logic—several of whom I have treated—are nonetheless severely illogical and disturbed. Why did they not, as I presumably did, use empiricism and logic to ameliorate their disturbances? Perhaps I am innately less disturbable, as—in several important ways—my father, paternal grandmother, and mother seemed to be. Or perhaps, as I said above, I prejudicedly see myself as saner than I actually am.

"What about my desperately avoiding panic and depression? . . . If I was desperate, that was not a desire but a dire need to avoid."

Yes, according to REBT, that would be a must. "I absolutely *must* not be panicked or depressed!" Then I probably would create panic about being panicked, depression about being depressed. Did I do this? Did I temporarily squelch my panic by convincing myself that "I *must* not be panicked!" and therefore sweep it under the rug, only to have it rear its ugly head again as it broke through my strong repression? Prob-ably not. I have been overconcerned or anxious about many things—such as being late to appointments. But I have practically never felt panicked—except once for a few seconds, when I was trapped in a dark room and saw no ray of light leading to a way out. Even then, I kept my panic under control by saying to myself, "I'll soon find the way out! I'll soon find the way out!" And I did.

So if I have repressed underlying panic, I keep it well repressed! It never seems to break out. Of course, the psychoanalysts could say that I just limit my life so severely and refuse to take notable risks that I thereby control my unexperienced panic. Hogwash! I avoid climbing

Mt. Everest (too damned cold!), but I have risked more "dangerous" love affairs, business ventures, public performances, and dissenting opinions than the vast majority of people—at least, since the age of nineteen, when I gave up most of my anxiety by surrendering much of my dire need for approval and success.

So, although I was born and reared to be quite anxious, I am now virtually unpanickable. As a child I coped pretty well with my anxiety, but it was still often there. Now, thanks to REBT, it is minimal. However, I still can be somewhat overconcerned about getting to appointments on time.

Chapter 3A

Chronology
Other Childhood Ailments

Please don't think that all my troubles in the Presbyterian Hospital were related to sex and love, for they weren't. My nonsexual problems were of a much higher order and sometimes required all the resources I could command to lick them. Because I complained about headaches, my doctors decided that I had some kind of intestinal problem. Whether they were right about this, I can't say, though I suspect that they were not, because the "cure" they created for my intestinal/headache difficulties proved to be somewhat worse than the disease.

Every afternoon, at four o'clock, a grim-looking cart would be wheeled around to my bedside with an even grimmer-looking bit of apparatus strung up on it. This apparatus mainly consisted of a large syringe bag, to which was attached a long piece of rubber tubing, at the end of which was a rubber nozzle. The idea, as you may have already guessed, was to give me a high colonic irrigation, in other words, to fill my lower and upper intestines with soapy water, which was then left (painfully) in me for a few minutes, and finally allowed to seep out into a sizable bedpan that was brought for the occasion.

This was no fun! The first part, where the nurse put some Vaseline on the rubber nozzle and inserted it into my rectum, wasn't bad at all; indeed it had some good points to it. For although the act of insertion was itself mildly unpleasant (somehow, in spite of Freud, I seemed to have totally skipped the anal-erotic stage of my childhood and never—no, never—got it back), the fact that it was being done by a pretty nurse, and especially one with whom I might be extravagantly in love at that time, made it almost thrilling. Not the insertion itself, I would say, but the fact that, in the course of handling the colonic irrigation apparatus and seeing that it worked properly, the nurses often—indeed, usually—had to handle me; that is, my body, my arms, my legs, and my buttocks. That—the touching and the handling of my body, was really something. *That* was what I kept looking forward to, and not (no, not at any time) the anal insertion.

Which, if you think about it, knocks the Freudian theory of early childhood conditioning into a cocked hat. For if a child of six experiences an enema every day for several months at the hands of his mother (or a mother surrogate, such as his pretty nurse), one would think that he would become obsessed with this pleasant rectal sensation and would make himself anally ruttish for the rest of his unblessed life. Not, dear Sigmund, little Albert! Although I sexually enjoyed, in more ways than one, these daily enemas, I became not in the slightest way either anal-erotic or anal-sadistic. I grooved on the external (buttocks and thighs) contact but not the internal (rectum and anus) touching.

"Well," the devout Freudians will doubtless say, "so you were a little different from the rest of us anally seduced males. Whereas we, when given enemas by a favorite woman in our young days, got conditioned to anal penetration and wound up as homosexuals or something like that, you focused on the external rather than the internal pleasure you received and wound up as a heterosexual male who vastly enjoyed, for the rest of your life, having your body (rather than your rectum) kissed and caressed. Big deal! You can still see, if you are man enough to admit it, that your early experiences with seductive women, and your guilty defenses against anality, had a great deal to do with the kind of sexual stimulation that you later favored."

Maybe so, but still, after all these years, I remain highly skeptical. My interpretation is just about the opposite: that because I never was (for partly physiological reasons) anally receptive, the penetration of my rectum by a good many attractive nurses just never took, and I always found it slightly unpleasant. But because, at the same time, I always was (again, for largely physiological reasons) sensitive to being touched, I did find the other aspects of my contact with the nurses exceptionally pleasant—and I therefore (partly for innate physiological reasons, again) became "conditioned" to tactile sexuality.

The Freudians will argue that, let's face it, I resorted to reaction formation or some other defensive maneuver and *that* is why I never emphasized the anal and why I *did* stress the tactile aspects of sex. They will claim, for example, that I really adored the inserting of the enema nozzle into my wee rectum; that I felt extremely guilty about that kind of forbidden enjoyment; and that I therefore made myself hate it and ended up substituting touch-pleasure for penetration-pleasure. Or, other fervid psychoanalysts (especially the Reichians!) will come up with some other surefire "proof" of my inherent, and of course deeply, deeply repressed, anality. This kind of clever circumlocution proves nothing—and never will prove anything—scientifically. It may have something behind it, but the probability of its accuracy is still about .001. As for me, I'll stick to my own explanation, even though it, too, is impossible to establish with any degree of certainty. At least, it is not brilliantly abstruse.

Be that as it may, although I enjoyed the initial stages of colonic irrigation—that is, the nurses' handling of my body in the course of preparing me for the rectal insertion—I by no means savored, as previously mentioned, what followed: What felt like gallon after gallon of warm, almost hot, water was poured into my lower and upper intestines, left in me for several minutes, and then was permitted to rush out of my anus and into the waiting bedpan. This—especially when the hot water got to my upper colon—hurt! And even the final evacuation of the water was no joy, as it left me with a somewhat painful intestinal and rectal feeling, from which it took me ten or fifteen minutes to recover. The whole procedure, from preparing for the irrigation to my final recovery from it, took about thirty minutes. It interrupted the other pleasurable activities I was doing (such as reading or talking to my friends), and it was literally and figuratively a royal pain in the ass. Despite its pleasant aspects, its total effect on me was a distinct minus. As four p.m. started approaching each day (including, I must ruefully say, Saturdays, Sundays, and holidays), I began to apprehensively anticipate what was about to occur, and if for any reason (such as an acute shortage of nurses or forgetfulness on the part of the nursing staff) it did not occur, I was quite relieved and enjoyed my late afternoon and early evening hours considerably more than usual.

The rationale for giving me these daily colonic irrigations proved to be almost entirely specious. My dratted headaches did not go away or even decrease in frequency. If anything, possibly because of my anxiety about the painful irrigations, they actually increased somewhat. So that was discouraging. I made sure I kept calling my continuing symptoms to the attention of the doctors and nurses, hoping they would see the light and would discontinue the "cure" and let me gracefully live with (as I had already taught myself to do) the disease.

To no avail. Week after week, especially during my longest stay of ten months in the hospital, they irrigated and irrigated and irrigated me. Never, it seemed, would they stop, and, until they finally did desist, after some three or four months of this "torture," I was utterly convinced that they would go on like this forever—and I mean forever.

So what did I do? Well, I simply put up with it. Knowing that my protests would avail me naught, and convincing myself that therefore my daily load of discomfort was truly inevitable, I reminded myself that the dreaded procedure entailed only a limited amount of suffering—about thirty minutes—each day. I showed myself that it had some advantages (the nurses touching me and the doctors promising that it would eventually do me a lot of good). I did my best to distract myself with pleasant thoughts (about running off and marrying one of the nurses or some other enjoyable thing). I focused on some pleasure I would engage in (such as eating supper or reading) after the colonic irrigation was over. I pictured myself in the future, beautifully rewarded for going through this horrible procedure, as an extremely healthy, nonhospitalizable child who would ultimately conquer the world and show everyone how strong and stoic he was. I boasted to my friends on the ward that it was excruciatingly awful, what I had to go through from four to four-thirty almost every afternoon, but that if anyone could take it, I could, and this clearly proved that I was outrageously superior to them (what with their whining and screaming over relative trivialities).

So, you see, I coped in one way or another with my daily painful experiences. I used several cognitive methods (though I hardly categorized them this way at that time) of accepting reality and making it (somewhat) less disadvantageous than it actually was: (1) I did what is called reframing and focused on the advantages of the pain I was undergoing. (2) I used cognitive distraction or the employment of pleasant thoughts. (3) I reminded myself that my discomfort was only ephemeral and would fairly soon be replaced by more enjoyable activities. (4) I imagined a great and glorious future as the reward for my present trials and tribulations. (5) I resorted to ego gratification and boosted my self-esteem (in my own eyes and, presumably, in the eyes of others) for the stoic attitude I was taking toward my distress. (6) I devised the substitute-gratification of impressing my ward mates and (again presumably) inducing them to pity me and like me more for my afflictions.

Pretty good coping, I must say, for a six-year-old child who was unfairly beset with a miserable chronic ailment, with hospitalization, and with daily medical treatments whose value was dubious and whose nature was clearly harassing. I am not even sure that I realized, except vaguely, that I was coping so well. Glimmerings of this kind of thing got through to me, since I repeatedly saw that the other children on the ward, or certainly many of them, were continually wailing about what was happening (and not happening) to them, and how unfair it was that they—poor things!—should be cooped up in this goddamned hospital and be subject to all kinds of medical iniquities while the other children they knew—especially their close friends and relatives—were freely cavorting in the streets and at school, totally unafflicted with any grim ailments.

As I pulled through the burdens of colonic irrigation, I was also beset with another hardship, from which I managed to suffer for the next decade or so: acute insomnia. And I mean acute. I don't recall staying awake at home, except on nights when I had headaches or other pains and therefore couldn't sleep. In the hospital, however, things were much different. For one thing, I didn't get much exercise but literally lay in my crib or bed almost twenty-four hours a day. For another thing, I did have my illness to be concerned about. Although nephritis itself didn't usually cause me any painful symptoms (even when I was afflicted with severe edema, or swelling of my bodily tissues, I did not experience this disorder as particularly oppressive), it did entail continual doctoring, accompanied by the constant reminder that there was something radically wrong with me and that my basic health (not to mention, ultimately, my life) was in serious condition. In addition, I was missing my freedom in the outside world, including attendance of first grade, which I had recently started. So I had a little more than my fair share of woes and worries, and I cannot say that they particularly helped me to slumber restfully when we were put to bed at eight p.m.

My main problem, however, again seemed to be more physiological than environmental. I had always been a light, restless sleeper who required complete darkness and silence to get and to remain dormant. Our sizable hospital ward, though it was flanked by streets conspicuously marked "HOSPITAL. QUIET PLEASE!" provided neither of my two sleeping requisites. Dark it certainly was not, since the nurses had to scurry around in the middle of the night, particularly if a child wanted something or suddenly erupted with pain. So although the top lights were doused, a number of the side bulbs (blue, as I recall) remained on all night, and whenever I opened my eyes (which I fairly frequently did after midnight) there they were, staring me right in the face and distinctly interfering with my going back to sleep again.

As for noise, that was even worse. Even on a quiet night, I could hear the trucks, including the horse-drawn trucks, in the street. "Giddyap!" and "Whoah! Stop!" rang out from time to time, and the gas-driven lorries, with their raucous motors and their booming horns, were a heck of a lot louder. Though our hospital ward was on the second floor, I could also make out the often clarion voices of the strollers-by, including the drunks, who (as far as I could tell) roamed the streets all night and had no respect whatever for those "QUIET PLEASE!" signs tacked to the lampposts.

All told, not the greatest atmosphere in the world for a light sleeper. Finally, to top things off, the ward was equipped with a large grandfather clock, which ticked away in an incredibly deafening way (at least in the middle of the night) and which actually had the chutzpah to resoundingly chime each and every hour—once for one a.m., twice for two a.m., and so on—ad infinitum. During the day, the ward was usually so noisy with the various things that were going on that one hardly heard this grandfather clock at all. But after everyone (except me) was asleep and all was (relatively) quiet, it seemed loud enough to me to wake the dead—or the light-sleeping living who were born allergic to that kind of noise.

With this kind of thing going on every single night (for the street lorries, the nighttime yellers, the newborn babies, and the grandfather clock knew not the meaning of the words *Sunday* or *holiday*), you can imagine how little sleep I generally got. I can't swear that I practically never fell asleep until at least midnight and that I frequently woke up and stayed up for an hour or two at a time thereafter, but that's the way I remember it. And I have a hunch, based on my later bouts with insomnia when I returned to my Bronx home, that I remember it right. It seemed to me that I did little but fitful dozing until around three or four a.m., and that if I had any solid periods of sleep, they usually occurred between about 3:30 and 6:00 a.m. Many were the nights, too, when I don't recall sleeping at all but only lying there, counting the hours on that blasted grandfather clock and accepting the fact that I just wasn't going to get any slumber that night.

That was really a problem, my childhood insomnia, and one that largely continued even after I got out of the hospital for good and that I only partially solved over the next ten or twelve years. Not that it completely incapacitated me, for although I was constantly tired in the morning, when the nurses came around at 6:00 a.m. to induce me to rise and shine, my tiredness soon wore off. By the time I had washed, eaten breakfast, and been looked over by the doctors making their morning rounds, I was in fairly fine fettle: not exactly as sharp as I might like to be, but no longer feeling the effects of my hours of nocturnal sleeplessness and eager to participate in the regular ward activities and in anything else that happened to come along.

The problem was: How could I bear being up half the night, while all the other children were peacefully sleeping? At first, I can't say that I did very well with this problem. I thought that I eventually would go to sleep, just because everyone else did—that it would simply take me longer to nod off. So I waited and waited, at first patiently and then increasingly impatiently, to see if this predicted sleep would soon overcome me. It didn't. Eleven p.m. arrived, midnight, one a.m.—on and on. Lots of rest. Lots of thinking various pleasant kinds of thoughts. But hell!—no sleep. Or just a few catnaps. Or very light sleep that was constantly interrupted by intruding noises. Damn, damn, damn!

I didn't take very kindly to that. I really needed more sleep, I thought, and I just wasn't getting what I desperately needed. Would I get weaker and weaker? Would I finally fade away into nothingness? I wouldn't know, of course, until either (or both) of these things happened. But it certainly looked like I was well on my way to some sort of deteriorated state.

I finally arrived, or half-arrived, at the solution that I was to formally discover when, a decade later, I went to the Fordham branch of the New York Public Library and took out a book—yes, a whole book—on how to sleep. The book told me, in exceptionally clear and no-nonsense-about-it terms, that the main reason for lack of sleep, or acute insomnia, is worry, and that the main worry insomniacs have is their intense worry about not getting to sleep.

According to the book—and I could easily corroborate this by checking my own experience—the process is as follows. Poor sleepers like myself go to bed and expect to fall asleep, as most normal people do, in a fairly short time—say, a half hour at most. Then they notice that that period of time has passed, maybe long passed, and that they are still awake. They tell themselves, "Oh, there's nothing to worry about. I'll soon be asleep." They turn over their hot and bedraggled pillow and try again. They still don't sleep. Then they say to themselves, "Maybe there is something to worry about. Maybe I won't sleep; maybe I can't sleep. Maybe there's something really wrong with me, and whatever is wrong with me stops me from, and will keep stopping me from, sleeping."

Then they *really* worry. In so doing, they naturally make themselves more wide awake than ever. Then they see that they *still* aren't sleeping—and, of course, they worry, worry in geometric progression. "One a.m. Oh, my! I didn't think it was that late. One-thirty a.m. Hmm, I think I'll probably make it by two. Two a.m.—I obviously haven't made it by two. Two-fifteen. Maybe I'll make it by two-thirty. But maybe I won't! What if I don't? What a wreck I'll be tomorrow! Two-forty-five. Oh, God! I'll never get any sleep if I don't doze off soon. But will I doze off soon? I bet I won't! I'm sure I won't! Shit, shit, shit, shit, shit!"

So the book said, and I could see that it was dead right. I had always known, ever since my sixth year, that my insomnia was related to the fear of being tired and ineffective the next day. But I hadn't quite realized that it also stemmed from the fear that—right now—while I was trying to sleep, I would never doze off. The fear of sleeplessness (like the fear of fear) was keeping me awake. When I read this great book on how to sleep, I immediately did as it advised: I stopped worrying about going to sleep, and as a result (almost like magic) began dozing off much sooner.

At the age of six, however, I had not read this book, but I did figure out a variation on its main theme. I first assumed that I was different from the other children in the ward: that they were natural or easy sleepers and I was not. I then looked for the advantages or superiorities of being different from them, in this way, such as being able to have pleasant wakeful thoughts and planning constructive things to do (writing a book that would be as good as or even better than *The Wizard of Oz*, for example). I thereby convinced myself that staying awake half the night was all right and would not interfere with my health or incapacitate me the next day. As a result of these accepting and distracting thoughts, I showed myself that I didn't have to worry too much about not sleeping. Because I stopped worrying so much, I sometimes slept surprisingly well. Or, if I slept fitfully, I often managed to go back to sleep again quickly after I awoke.

My solution to the problem of sleeping—or staying awake—in the hospital was not as elegant as it would have been had I been aware of and used REBT, because I didn't find and dispute my irrational idea that "I must sleep long and soundly, for if I don't terrible things will happen to me!"

If I had directly used REBT as I have taught my clients to do for fifty years, I would have asked myself: "*Why* must I sleep pretty long and soundly?" and I would have come up with an answer like "There is no reason why I *must*, though it would be preferable if I did." And I would have queried myself by disputing my irrational beliefs, which REBT employs: "Where is the evidence that it is *terrible* if I don't sleep long and soundly?" And I would have answered myself: "There is no such evidence. Because I wish to sleep easily, there is evidence that I am not getting what I want and that is frustrating or unfortunate. But if it were *terrible* or *awful* that I do not get the sleep I desire, it would be totally (100 percent) unfortunate—which of course it isn't (because much worse things than loss of sleep could easily happen to me). In fact, a *terrible* or *awful* event is one that is so unfortunate or inconvenient that it *absolutely should not* exist. But that is nonsense, because however bad it is, it *does* exist. So it is *awful* only by my definition. In reality, no matter how unpleasant it is for me to stay awake, it is *only* unpleasant, *only* inconvenient. Though I will never like it, I can definitely bear it, and if I bear it I may even find some aspects of it pleasant."

This kind of head-on disputing of my own irrational beliefs might have helped me arrive at a better solution to my sleep problem than the milder kind of accepting and distraction methods that I used at the age of six. But mine worked pretty well—particularly during my ten-month hospital stay. On occasion, I even became so accepting of my "handicap" of sleeplessness that I looked forward to remaining awake long past midnight and mulling over my pleasant thoughts. Usually, I had at least one favorite nurse whom—you guessed it!—I wanted to sleep with and marry some day. So I would have, in my nocturnal daydreams, all kinds of conversations and activities with this favorite. Later, I might have the additional thrill of having this same woman wake me at six in the morning and help me with my bedside toilet, to cap those glorious hours when we, in fantasy, had done just about everything under the sun—or moon.

Even when that particular nurse hardly spoke to me in reality (or when her stay in my ward had ended and she was whisked from my waking life forever), nothing stopped me from holding on to her (and our beautiful relationship) in fantasy. Although I wasn't completely thrilled by this phantomized solution to my sleeplessness, I made the most of it. So my days, weeks, and months in the hospital went fairly pleasantly by, and I have few remembrances of keen suffering.

Here is an interesting sidelight, which has important therapeutic implications: Whenever I stayed in the hospital for a month or more, my rational approach to coping with my sleeplessness worked well. I accepted my handicap and, as noted above, I even learned to enjoy it. I recognized that I was distinctly different from most other children, but I fully accepted this difference and made the most of it. Unfortunately, however, when I was in the hospital for shorter stays, or when I was afflicted with nocturnal wakefulness at home, I sometimes fell back to worrying and forgot about my previous solution.

This seems to be an amazing and common characteristic of humans. They experience some handicap or affliction and they cope with it rather poorly. More often than not, they resort to immense amounts of needless worry and a few spoonfuls of stoical acceptance. After they have plagued themselves for a period of time, they often find some kind of a reasonably satisfactory resolution—usually accepting it and living with it until (for one reason or another) it tends to abate. But once they deal with it, and even congratulate themselves on how well they are coping, they later fall back again. Either they stop confronting the issue and using their solution to it ("I've dealt with it long enough! It should stop by now! It's too *hard* to have to *keep* coping with it like this!") Or they experience a return of the problem and refuse to accept its resurgence ("Oh, shit! It's back again. Just when I thought I had it licked. I shouldn't have to deal with it all over again!"). Or they forget, once it returns, how they handled it last time, and go right back to their original awfulizing about it ("My God! I thought I'd never suffer from this again! It really is awful, now that it's back. I can't stand another minute of having it!").

I am not sure which of these self-defeating tendencies I reaffirmed. I do know, however, that after licking my sleeplessness in the hospital it later recurred in my home life. I shall return to this theme and show how I finally conquered my insomniac tendencies. I merely want to note here my allegiance to the human condition—the quite nutty human condition—of being prone (oh, how prone!) to rationally conquer one of my disabilities but then to fall (oh, so hard!) on my blasted face again and revert to my previous irrationality.

This was the basis for my somewhat famous argument with Joseph Wolpe in the early 1960s. Wolpe, at that time the most famous behavior therapist in the world, asked to meet me in my New York office to discuss our differences. He had read several of my early papers on REBT and acknowledged that, although I was already well known as a cognitive therapist, I was also a leading behavior therapist. But, he objected, "Why do you keep avoiding the use of the word *cure* in your writings? I think that in behavior therapy we really cure our patients. And you keep using the term *significant improvement*. Why not *cure*?"

"Because," I replied, as I had not given this problem too much thought prior to my conversation with him, "even though people may possibly get cured of a physical ailment, I don't think that ever really occurs with mental or emotional disorders. I definitely believe in change, or else I wouldn't be a therapist. But to be at least somewhat disturbed seems to be the human condition, and no one, I feel, ever gets cured of being human!"

Wolpe completely disagreed. He held that if someone has a bad appendix and a surgeon removes it, that person is cured. Similarly, in psychotherapy, if someone has an emotional disorder (e.g., a phobia) and a therapist shows the client how to remove it, the client is cured. I maintained, "Oh, no! Even removing an appendix may not be a true cure, since the underlying or systemic reason for its being inflamed or diseased might still be there and might result in some other kinds of infections. But, assuming that we may legitimately say that an appendectomy *cures* appendicitis, we cannot say the same thing about a phobia *or a more general emotional disturbance*. For the *so-called cured* individual may easily—and, in fact, often does—later turn up with the same phobia again, or a new one, or with some other form of disturbance. So physical *cure* and emotional *cure* are not the same."

Wolpe and I never agreed, though we battled out this same issue a year later, when he again came to New York to resume our argument. I am not saying that he was wrong and I was right, though I think that both of us held our original positions until he died. But I am saying that my own experience with giving up one particular disturbance—such as my worrying about my insomnia and with later reverting to it—has helped convince me that no matter how people improve emotionally, they rarely, if ever, become truly *cured*. Even I, with my strong tendencies to work against and (temporarily) solve my emotional problems, have never surrendered them completely. And if I haven't, who, I may arrogantly ask, ever will?!!!

Back to my trips to the Presbyterian Hospital at the age of six. I conquered my upsetness about my headaches and my insomnia, and in the process I think I helped myself considerably. The proof was how I reacted when a highly unusual event occurred to plague me. Being still afflicted with recurring nephritis (kidney trouble), I continued to get swollen ankles, swollen legs, and edema in various other parts of my body. It never seemed to be too severe, was generally painless, and I might not have even noticed it if my parents and others (warned about the symptoms of nephritis) had not seen the evidence and quickly sought to get medical attention.

One time I did notice, however, for, quite unusually, my entire stomach was so swollen that it looked like I was going to be perhaps the first seven-year-old male in human history to go through a regular pregnancy. I always, in spite of my painful thinness, had something of a well-rounded belly—as did my mother, who never weighed more than around 110 pounds in her entire life but still was fatter around the midriff than she was elsewhere. This kind of body configuration, I believe, is mainly hereditary, since my sister and father had it to some extent, too.

Be that as it may, my nephritic swelling was really immense this time, and my physicians thought it rather dangerous and decided to operate on me to reduce the swelling. The operation—which, once again, they did not tell me about until the morning when it was to take place—was rather unusual (and may have since that time been abandoned as a medical procedure). It was done right at my bedside, which was temporarily screened off from the rest of the ward.

I was asked to sit on the edge of the bed, while three busy physicians and a couple of nurses hovered around me. They told me that my stomach was to be punctured and that, through the small hole, some water would be drained off to reduce the swelling. This, they assured me, would be quite painless and I would soon be back in good shape and as lively as ever, with the hole in my stomach completely patched up. So there was nothing, they said again and again, to worry about, whereas, if I made a rumpus and refused to cooperate, my swollen stomach would really do me in, and heaven knows how long I would have to stay in the hospital.

Well, that sounded fairly okay to me, though I was of course somewhat apprehensive. I knew that my stomach was swollen and that that meant I had a return of the nephritic condition. I knew that until this condition cleared up, I would have to remain in the hospital—maybe, this time, for another long stay. Since the doctors and nurses had assured me that if they tapped my stomach and got rid of the superfluous liquid that had accumulated there, I would probably be out of the hospital within a couple of weeks or so. I decided to trust them, let them go through with the tapping job, and not put up any squawk about it. This time, they also assured me, I would be conscious during the whole procedure and would suffer no pain, thirst, or other ill effects either during or after the operation. I got myself to believe this, too.

So I bravely (squelching my natural fear) said, "Okay, go ahead. Let's see what happens." Whereupon they lifted my nightgown up to my shoulders, swabbed my stomach with some kind of analgesic lotion (Novocain, I think, but I really never was quite sure), punctured the area with a large needle to the back of which was attached a rubber tube, and then (holy cow!) let a white milky fluid run from the needle, down through the tube, and into a waiting basin.

Was I surprised! And fascinated. I had heard of operations before, and had even undergone the major one, under ether, of having my tonsils out. But I had never heard of an operation where the patient was fully conscious, where he felt no pain during the procedure, and where he could calmly watch some of his insides flow into a waste basin. Quite a thing!

As I watched this operation take place, and saw the milky fluid flow from my body into the basin—and also saw how surprisingly much of it there seemed to be—you would think that I would have been fairly upset. I wasn't. Maybe it was because I was fascinated by the unusual procedure, for certainly nothing like that had happened in my life before, and I never knew another person to whom it had happened. Maybe I was mainly trying to show how brave I was, so that the attending doctors and nurses would like and respect me. Maybe I was merely calm at the time of the operation—as people often are when suddenly confronted by an accident or emergency—because the whole thing had not quite registered in my mind yet, and I was going to experience (as, after a traumatic event, a great many people do) a delayed reaction.

All these hypotheses are tenable and possibly have some measure of explanatory power or "truth." Other explanations of my calmness and serenity, however, also seem plausible: Unlike most humans—including most sensitive young boys—I had already created (and partially adopted from the wiser adults around me) a philosophy of challenge. I viewed many obnoxious or dangerous happenings as a serious problem, all right, but as a process instead of a final problem—that is, as a difficulty to be explored and *to be met* rather than one to be thrown by or become devastated about. As a result of this philosophy, I focused on *what to do* about the events of the operation and their sequelae rather than on violently protesting against them and thereby concentrating on their "horror."

Concomitantly, and perhaps importantly, I largely ignored rather than centered my attention upon my worst feelings about this unusual medical procedure. When putting screens around my bed and explaining to me that I was going to have something surgical done to me—"a minor and painless operation," I think they called it—I did react with some immediate fear, since I didn't know exactly what they meant by this innocuous phrase and what they were actually going to do to me. To some extent, I feared (and quickly imagined) the worst. But I deliberately *lived with* and largely *ignored* these feelings, brushed them aside with astounding rapidity, and forced myself to focus on other aspects of what was going on. This is probably a crucial point, since agoraphobics and other individuals who are afflicted with serious anxiety almost deliberately seem to focus *on* rather than *away from* their fears and thereby wind up with fear of fear, or panic about panic, thus escalating their original fears enormously.

As a technique of not concentrating on the "dangers," the "horror" of my panicky feelings as the operation was getting under way, I (deliberately?) focused on the events and procedures that were taking place: the readying of the apparatus; the swabbing of my stomach to make the insertion of the needle painless; the curious absence of pain when the incision was made; the almost immediate flowing of my bodily fluid into the waste basin; the milky color of the liquid coming out of my stomach; and the rapid rate at which it was flowing. I *made* my curiosity about the operation get the best of me and concentrated on satisfying it, this curiosity, instead of worrying about what was going to happen to me later.

These were some of the things I did to live with, and nicely bear up with, this strange event in my young life. This is not to say that I was fully *aware* of what I was doing or how I was doing it (or even the reasons why I was doing it). In fact, there is a kind of Catch-22 here: Had I been fully aware of what I was doing, I might not have been able to do it effectively, since my concentration would have been different from what it was, and the main virtue of my technique of coping with my operation seems to have been that I chose (consciously or unconsciously) to concentrate, or focus, on one set of stimuli (the procedures of the operation) rather than on another set (my immediate fearful reactions to these procedures).

Now, from a distance of many years, I see much more clearly what I was doing, and therapeutically doing, than I (or anyone else) saw it then. I see this not only because I am reviewing the past in a more dispassionate and objective manner—wasn't it Samuel Taylor Coleridge or William Wordsworth who defined poetry as "emotion recollected in tranquility"?—but also because I have seen this same phenomenon very clearly over the years in many of my clients. I originally defined emotional disturbance as largely (though not entirely) a thinking disorder, and that is why I originated REBT early in 1955 and started to get far better results with it, and in much shorter periods of time, than I had been previously getting with psychoanalysis, psychoanalytically oriented therapy, and the other types of therapy I started experimenting with as I became more and more disillusioned with analysis. But as I began to use REBT with a great many clients, I began to see that it was not merely their thoughts, attitudes, or philosophies with which they needlessly upset themselves (as Epictetus and several other philosophers had clearly seen centuries before I began to accept this idea), but it was also their ways of focusing or concentrating on one set of thoughts, feelings, or behaviors rather than on another set.

There are several ways of looking at the "causes" or "explanations" of human disturbance, and most of them overlap and include some degree of "truth." The psychoanalysts, for example, tell you that feelings of guilt are the result of your conflict between your ego and your superego; and Rational Emotive Behavior therapists tell you that these same feelings of guilt stem from your telling yourself, "I *must* not act wrongly (e.g., steal), and I am a louse if I do." What the psychoanalysts really mean, however (if they were clear!), is that your ego (that is, your self-enhancing views) tell you that you *have to* act well and thereby be a good *person* and that your superego (that is, your self-critical and self-downing views) tell you that you have not really acted rightly (e.g., have stolen) and that you are therefore a *rotten person*. Your ego is in conflict with your superego, because (although psychoanalysis does not adequately explain why) one set of your views (the moral set) clashes with another set of your views (the immoral set) and with your desires (your id) to get away with doing the "wrong" thing. When this happens, you strongly condemn *yourself* (and not merely your *behavior*) for doing "immoral" acts.

The psychoanalytic view and the REBT view of guilt aren't exactly the same, but they significantly overlap in some respects. Similarly, the transactional analysis (TA) and the Gestalt therapy views of guilt overlap with the analytic and the REBT views. So, practically all the major therapies, although they may not honestly acknowledge this, state or imply that people's philosophies get them into "emotional" difficulties, and these therapies are therefore, in the final analysis, cognitive and philosophical as well as affective. I saw this when I first originated REBT—and that is why, right from the start, I emphasized that it is a highly philosophical form of treatment, since it consciously and directly discovers and helps people uproot their absolutistic assumptions. But I also realized, a little later, that it is not only their philosophy but the obsessive-compulsive manner in which they focus upon it that makes and keeps people disturbed.

To use the same example of guilt, mildly neurotic individuals not only conclude, "I have done the wrong thing (e.g., stolen) and therefore I am a worthless individual," but they soon allow themselves to turn away from this belief to other incompatible or conflicting ideas, such as, "Well, maybe so, but I only stole once and am not too worthless," or "Yes, I'm rotten for doing that thing, but everyone steals sometime, so I guess I can forgive myself." These mildly neurotic individuals suffer guilt *when* they focus on the wrongness of their acts and on their worthlessness for doing wrong. But also, and in fact much of the time, they focus on all kinds of other things—such as work, sports, sex, or reading—and therefore do not too often or too intensely feel guilty.

More serious neurotics and people with severe personality disorders focus steadily and intensely on how wrong their acts are, how worthless they are for doing them, what awful consequences will ensue, and how they *deserve* to be severely punished. Emotional disturbance, then, is not only closely associated with our self-defeating cognitions but with how we concentrate on these cognitions, obsess about them, and rigidly cling to them. Serious and prolonged disturbance partly arises from over-focusing. But when we over-focus on how bad a person we are for acting "immorally" or "stupidly," we also do so strongly and emotionally, and we do so actively and behaviorally.

Ameliorating our disturbance also involves focusing. Even if, on occasion, we focus on the right or rational idea, such as, "Yes, I did that wrong act but it wasn't that bad and I don't have to be eternally damned for doing it," we can obsess over it, go over it indefinitely, and end up spending so much time and energy on it that we remain neurotic. But if we have an extremely irrational cognition—for example, "I absolutely must never under any conditions steal, and I should be roasted eternally in hell if I do so!"—we may not, at least overtly, be too disturbed if we constantly use distraction techniques, such as indulging in sports, sex, or work. By doing this, we are then disturbed "underlyingly" (or, as the Freudians would say, unconsciously), but we may not, for quite a while, actually suffer strongly or feel overtly anxious, depressed, or guilty.

This is what I now see, and I think I see very clearly, after practicing REBT for over fifty years. I hardly saw it at the age of six or seven. But I did, somehow, sense the importance of focusing and of cognitive distraction. I realized, if not too clearly, that the more I concentrated on the dangers of having my stomach surgically tapped, the more I would most likely suffer from fear. So I concentrated on how the operation was going and what I could learn from it, and I got through it remarkably well.

The nurses and doctors kept congratulating me on my stoical attitude (not exactly realizing the kind of focusing I was doing in my head), and they seemed to be truly amazed that I accepted the entire procedure so well. From time to time, they would whisper to each other that I was taking it surprisingly nicely. Apparently, they thought that because I was a young child, I would almost certainly be scared stiff about such an operation, and I think they had debated whether to put me under some kind of general anesthesia during the entire procedure. But they had taken the chance of proceeding while I was fully conscious, and it looked like they were congratulating themselves on making the right decision.

Anyway, I benefited from their beneficent surprise and patted myself on the back for earning it. This ego inflating was, in terms of strict REBT theory and practice, a mistake, since I convinced myself that I was a good person *because* I was taking the operation so well (and, by logical extension, that I would be a real turd if I took it badly). But it did help me get through the procedure. My distraction methods had worked unusually well, and the reinforcement I received for using them (that is, my lack of overt anxiety during the surgical procedure) encouraged me to keep using other cognitive diversions in the future, whenever I thought I might be anxious about something.

That, for the most part, was the end of my childhood hospital experiences. After my seventh year, I returned only once more, several years later, for a thorough check-up. At that time, knowing that I was not ill and that I was only scheduled to stay in the hospital for, at most, a week, I relaxed and enjoyed my stay. I was also happy to learn that I had just about outgrown my nephritis—or, as my doctors now began to think my diagnosis may have been, acute nephrosis—and that I would probably experience no ill results from it in the future. My albumen level was consistently within the normal range. I had no more bodily swelling. I was allowed to have an unrestricted diet (instead of the salt-free and other diets I had been on from time to time). And I was, the doctors kept telling my mother, to be treated as any other normal young child. So I was quite happy about that, and assumed (correctly) that my affliction with nephritis was a matter of history and that my physical health was as good as anyone else's.

Oh, yes, one more important thing: An additional affliction I had to cope with during my hospital stays—and particularly when I was hospitalized for ten months—was that of separation anxiety. Up to my fourth year, I never recall being away from my mother, except for a couple of days at a time when she went to the hospital herself to bear my brother and my sister. And in each of these cases, I believed that she would return in short order, and I managed to go about my daily business quite well without her. I think I stayed over with friends of the family—such as my beloved godmother—during such times, and I don't remember resenting this or recall crying about my "lost" mother. When she did return home, I was genuinely delighted to see her again (and not in any way jealous, as I recall, of my new brother or my new sister). All told, I took the separation quite well. As for my father's being away, as he frequently was, I easily adapted and didn't make any fuss about it. I got used to it, and in some ways, because of his lack of monitoring and imposing restrictions, I liked it.

When I went to the hospital, my mother at first visited me twice a week, during the regular visiting hours (which I think were between seven and eight in the evening) and on Sunday afternoon. Occasionally, my father accompanied her, which was both unusual and good, as he rarely spent much time with his children, and if he ever talked or played with us (except briefly at some of our meals), I certainly don't remember it. So when I was lying in the hospital, trying to get used to this new and greatly changed style of life, and both my mother and father came to cheer me up, brought me little gifts, and told me how they were proud of the fact that I was taking my stay so nicely, I thought that was great and looked forward to their visiting soon again.

These frequent visits soon stopped, however, especially during my longer stays in the hospital. My father practically never came during those times, and my mother, busy as she was with two younger children and a whole household to take care of, came irregularly. Her main visiting time was on Sunday afternoons (from three to five, I believe), but during daily nighttime visiting hours, when most of the other children had their parents or others to visit with them, no one showed up to see me. And during the summer, when my mother, brother, and sister went away for two or three months to Wildwood, New Jersey, my mother could not easily take the seven-hour train ride between Wildwood and New York, and so she came to see me only about once a month.

So there I was, deprived of the nightly visits the other children on my ward received from their parents and others, and sometimes deprived of even a once-a-week Sunday visit. You can imagine how, when I first started to undergo this deprivation, I felt about seeing most of the other children's parents (and friends) regularly arrive and tend to them, while I had practically no one to talk to. My hospital friends were busy talking to their visitors, only a few of whom ever bothered to talk to me, too.

That was really a sad time. I usually knew that my mother wasn't coming, but I was not entirely sure, since she always told me, when she left on Sunday, that she might possibly drop in on one of the weekday evenings. So I always hoped against hope that she actually would surprise me and show up. But this rarely occurred. So I lay in my bed, reading or occupying myself in some other way and trying to convince myself that it wasn't so bad that my peers had so many relatives and friends who kept coming to see them, while I had only my mother (since virtually all my relatives on both sides of the family were in Philadelphia), and even she didn't show up that much.

I did manage to convince myself that it wasn't that bad. Usually. I showed myself that I wouldn't have wanted most of the other children's visitors, anyway—as they were often noisy, stupid, and ignorant of children and their ways. I even convinced myself, and correctly, that my own mother wasn't the best visitor in the world, since she, too, could be noisy, impossibly chatty, and self-centered in her own inimitable way, and that when she didn't come to see me I really wasn't losing that much. I also told myself that, just because I had nephritis and had to keep going back to the hospital, that in itself did not make the world *owe me* delightful visitors, and that pitying myself for not having them was not a very sensible thing for me to do. I finally convinced myself that although being by myself for an hour or two each day was not the greatest joy in the world—for I was quite sociable during my hospital stays and did a good deal of conversing with the other children and the nurses and doctors—it wasn't completely terrible and awful. It was just too damned bad—but that's the way it was. Unfortunate.

Of all the things I did to ward off misery during my childhood and to cope with the difficulties that life unceremoniously kept thrusting on me, I think that my handling this parental separation, with its accompanying feeling of rejection and loneliness, was about the most rational method I employed. In some ways it was a real precursor of REBT. For where I largely used, as shown in my handling of my stomach-tapping operation, the techniques of cognitive distraction, in regard to my loneliness and lack of visitation, I mainly used the REBT technique of Disputing Irrational Beliefs.

This is the most elegant, I believe, of all REBT methods and, to show you how prejudiced I really am, probably the most elegant of all the many psychotherapeutic techniques that have ever been invented. Many other methods—even some of those used in psychoanalysis—to some degree help people with disturbances. But the deepest, most pervasive, longest-lasting, and most far-reaching of these techniques is D (Disputing) the IBs (Irrational Beliefs) that people use to create their poor Consequences (Cs), their dysfunctional feelings, and undesirable behaviors.

To show what Disputing consists of, let me use the scenario of my not being visited in the hospital. The ABC's of REBT in connection with this lack of visitation may be outlined as follows:

G (Goal)—My desire to have regular visits by my parents.

A (Activating Experience or Adversity): My parents visit me relatively rarely in the hospital, while most of the other children's parents (and friends) visit them twice a week.

RBs (Rational Beliefs): "I don't like this! I wish my parents would visit me more and that I would have other visitors too. What a pain in the ass!"

HCs (Healthy Consequences): Feelings of sorrow, disappointment, frustration, and annoyance. Action—if possible—to arrange for more visitation by my parents and others.

IBs (Irrational Beliefs): "This state of affairs must not exist! My parents absolutely *should* visit me more often—and even arrange to have other friends or relatives visit me too. Isn't it awful that they're not doing as they *should*? I can't bear it! My parents ought to be damned and punished for this crummy behavior and forced to visit me more often. Poor me!"

UCs (Unhealthy Consequences): Feelings of anger and depression. Action of possibly telling my parents what bastards they are and letting the world know how horrible it is.

Assuming that these ABC's of REBT are correct—and I can assure you that tens of thousands of therapy sessions and many psychotherapy experiments have shown that they probably are—many things can be done to help people keep their Rational Beliefs and surrender their Irrational Beliefs (IBs) (at point B) or to distract them from these IBs and thereby help themselves to feel and act much better. Probably the best or more elegant of these techniques, however, is to help them to actively and forcefully Dispute (at point D) these self-defeating ideas and thereby not only give them up temporarily but ultimately basically disbelieve them.

What I essentially did to deal with my unhealthy feelings of anger and depression when other people were happily enjoying visits from their friends and relatives was to use the logico-empirical method of science (which REBT specializes in teaching people how to use) and to actively Dispute (at D) my Irrational Beliefs (IBs) along these lines:

Disputing: "Why must this dismal state of affairs not exist? Why must I have as many friendly visitors as the other children on the ward generally have?"

Answer: "There is no reason why this dismal state of affairs *must not* exist. If it exists, then it has to exist—and that's the only way it can be: deplorably existent. Nor is there any reason why I must have as many friendly visitors as the other children on the ward generally have. It would be lovely if I did, but just because such a state of affairs would be great, that never means that it *must* exist. If my having more visitors *had to be*, it *would be*; and since it isn't that way, this clearly proves that it *doesn't* have to exist. Too bad!"

Disputing: "Where is it written that my parents *absolutely should* visit me more often—and even arrange to have other friends or relatives visit me, too?"

Answer: "It's only written in my crazy head! Obviously no law of the universe commands that they should do what I would like them to do; otherwise, they'd have to follow this law. Clearly, they're not following it. Ergo, the law is a myth!"

Disputing: "Prove that it's *awful* that my parents are not doing as they should."

Answer: "I can't prove that. It's certainly inconvenient—a real hassle! I'll definitely never like being by myself when the other children on the ward are enjoying themselves with their visitors, so I won't! Why do I *have to*? Why *must* I be free of hassles and inconveniences? There's no damned reason why I must be. Sure, it's bad, quite bad that I am deprived like this. But if it were awful it would be totally bad—which it never is, as it could always be worse. Moreover, if I really mean that it's awful, I am viewing it as so bad that it must not exist. Which, of course, it does. Even if it is 99 percent bad—which, clearly, it isn't, because I can fairly easily survive my loneliness for an hour or so every day—it would never be 100 percent bad. Nor would it be so bad that it absolutely must not exist. So it never is awful—only a real bother!"

Disputing: "Is it really true that I can't bear having considerably fewer visitors than the other children usually have?"

Answer: "Of course it isn't! If I really couldn't bear it, I would die of this kind of deprivation, which I haven't quite done yet! Or, even if I wouldn't die, I couldn't be happy at all if I were in a truly *unbearable* state. Well, *can* I have some degree of happiness, even when I am deprived of visitors? Naturally I can. I can read; I can think my own thoughts; I can at times talk to other children's visitors; I can do lots of things to enjoy myself, even if I can't do exactly the thing that the other children, with their visitors and their gifts from these visitors, are doing. So I'd better do some of these enjoyable things and stop whining about my not being able to *bear* this kind of deprivation."

Disputing: "Ought my parents really be damned and punished for this crummy behavior of often leaving me without visitors?"

Answer: "How ridiculous! First of all, their behavior is really not that crummy. My father is usually away on out-of-town business trips and couldn't possibly get in very often to see me, and my mother, what with two young children to take care of and all the other things she has to do, may be a bit neglectful of me, but her behavior is hardly *that* bad. After all, I'm not the *only* one she has to be concerned about; she does have *other* important things to do. If she had more time, she would most probably come more often. And when she does come, she is obviously happy to see me, brings me things I want, and treats me very well. So how is her behavior so crummy?

"Besides, let's suppose that she's neglectful and that she could see me more often and simply refuses to go to the trouble of doing so. Even if she is acting in that wrong manner, how does that make her a *rotten bitch* or a *crummy person*? It clearly doesn't, since she does many other things very well and very lovingly. So, at the very worst, she is a person who acts badly (at least in *my* view) in this particular way. And although I may perhaps conclude that her deeds—or some of them—are rotten, I cannot justifiably conclude that *she* is rotten and that she should be damned and punished. After all, she's only human, and all humans are distinctly fallible. She's not subhuman, nor is any person. And, like all humans, *she's* never truly damnable, no matter how bad some of her acts are. As for her being forced, in some manner, to treat me better, that's ridiculous. She has a right to whatever she does—including the wrong things she does. And to force her to do the correct thing—or the thing that I really want—would be to take away all her freedom. I certainly wouldn't want my freedom taken away like that, nor would I like being forced only to do the so-called right things. So why should anyone force her to be angelic?"

If I had used REBT to actively and thoroughly Dispute my Irrational Beliefs about my lack of hospital visits, I would have done so along the above lines and I would have most probably changed my IBs and ended up with an Effective New Philosophy (E) or rationally revised attitude, which would have gone something like this:

E (Effective New Philosophy): "It's definitely sad and deplorable when I have few visitors, while the other children in the ward have a good many who come to see them almost every day. But that's the way it is—too damned bad. Life often is unfair and full of difficulties. But I can surely bear, though I'll never like, those hassles. Even injustice has its good points, because it gives me the challenge of being as happy as I can be in an unfair world. If I could change this situation, I would; but since there seems to be no way of doing so, I might as well gracefully lump what I don't like and keep figuring out how to enjoy myself even when I am deprived of visitation."

If I arrived at this Effective New Philosophy and kept going over it until I fully believed it, I would then experience the emotional Effect (of feeling healthily sad, regretful, frustrated)—and since I would not dwell on these feelings (or the Rational Beliefs that produced them) I would only experience them from time to time, rather than continually. I would also, simultaneously, tend to bring on the behavioral Effect of acting on my Effective New Philosophy and would do things like find enjoyable pursuits during visitation hours, see if I could sometimes turn the other children's visitors into my own friends, visit with some of the children on the ward who had no company that day, and do other pleasant things.

Being only six and a half at that time, and not yet having fully developed the principles and practice of REBT, I didn't do my Disputing (D) as well as I would do it today. But I did perform it in a rudimentary manner and I did arrive at an Effective New Philosophy that approximated my later rational emotive behavioral views.

My goal, when I was a young child, was essentially the same as it has been during the following years: to use my head to govern my feelings, but to govern them in such a way that I did not totally squelch them or arrive at Pollyanna-ish feelings of simulated joy. I wanted to retain some bad feelings, so that they would motivate me to keep trying to change the obnoxious events in my life and to activate myself to savor the present and the future. So I invented—though I did not realize it at that time—the REBT distinction between healthy negative feelings (such as sadness, displeasure, and irritation) and unhealthy negative feelings (such as depression, panic, and self-pity).

When, a good many years later, I started doing REBT and saw that many of my clients eliminated their baneful feelings (such as despair) by replacing them with equally or more hurtful emotions (such as flatness or intense rage), I realized that they were throwing out the baby with the bathwater, and that they had more, and much better, emotional choices than they were taking. Without having practiced an incipient form of REBT on myself for many years before this, I might never have realized how self-defeating my clients were, and might have helped lead them up the same kinds of emotional garden paths that so many other psychotherapists have done and still do.

Chapter 3B

Coping with Emotional Problems
Back to My Neglectful Parents and
My Low Frustration Tolerance

Like my father, my mother was also neglectful. Nice. Pleasant. Talkative. But she didn't listen too well—except to her own chatter. Sociable? Indeed, very! Tons of acquaintances and—what I then thought—friends. Later I realized they were practically all acquaintances—both steady and ephemeral acquaintances. Her brothers and sisters, too? Yes—even they were acquaintances. She liked them and talked endlessly with them (and with everybody else), but practically nothing heavy or intimate. All superficial. All on the surface.

Even her helpfulness was superficial. She helped me with my headaches, my nephritis, and my other health problems. She taught me how to cook, sew, and do other useful things. Lightly. Off the top of her head. Without any depth or real intimacy. She talked endlessly—but not as a discusser. She was a doer, not a great thinker. My father was a fine thinker—but not with his wife and children. Many years later, when in his seventies, he had many thoughtful discussions with my brother, Paul. But, as far as I can tell, mainly on business, investments, wills, and other practical issues. They were both outstanding at that.

Because I was not thwarted much by my parents, teachers, friends, or anyone else, where did my low frustration tolerance (LFT) come from? Biologically, I guess, mainly from my father. No, I don't think I learned it very much from observing him and his irritability. First, as I have said, I spent very little time with him. Second, when I was a child he rarely showed irritability—he was pleasant and affable with me, my siblings, my mother, and his friends. Third, he was a great business negotiator and salesman—he could, according to my mother, sell anyone the Brooklyn Bridge. Including her.

It was only years later, when I worked with him in two businesses and visited with him and his second wife in their apartment, that I could clearly see how irritable, opinionated, and critical of others (though not to their face!) he actually was. He always knew the Right Way—and they always did things the Wrong Way. He was an arch Republican who hated all Democrats, Liberals, and Radicals. He was often absolutistic and dogmatic. He had intestinal problems all his life—presumably from taking stressful conditions much too seriously. He couldn't stomach discontent. Or dissent.

So my LFT problem probably mainly came from his genetic tendencies to overreact to stressors—which his two cantankerous brothers, Joe and Mike, also seemed to have done. Mike, like my father, was outwardly affable and genial. But he was also an impossible alcoholic and an irresponsible husband and father. Joe, like all my father's close family members, was bright and effective—but quite grim, hostile, and vindictive.

Well, heredity and environmental influences are invariably combined, so I could have gotten some of my LFT from watching my father's irritability. Who knows? My main point here is that, for all of my manifestations of *high* frustration tolerance (HFT)—which I shall discuss later—I admittedly have a good deal of LFT. Item: I skip the more boring and repetitive parts of the fiction and nonfiction I read, even though I would benefit from more careful perusal. Item: I hate a good deal of the adulation I receive at my public talks and workshops, as I usually find it boring and repetitious. So I escape quickly. Item: In spite of my innate—and I think great—talent for musical composition, I never took the time and trouble to learn to play or write music. I once almost taught myself to do this but copped out after a few months of unenjoyable hard work.

Et cetera, et cetera, et cetera!

I said at the beginning of this chapter that my problem-solving ability, ironically, may have stemmed from my LFT. How come? Let me give an example. When I was only eight or nine, it was pouring one Sunday afternoon, so I couldn't go out in the street to play with my friends. Nor could I run through the rain for several blocks to see them in their apartments. We had no phones at our homes at that time, so I couldn't have phone conversations with them. My mother, brother, and sister were all visiting with people in other parts of our apartment house, and my father was out of town. So I was alone.

What to do to overcome my boredom and make myself active? I was forced to try to solve this problem. So I did. I had an old broken watch my father had given me that he said was not worth fixing. So I decided to try to fix it. Being practical, I knew I would probably not be able to fix it. But at least I might learn something about how it worked. So that would be interesting.

I took some of the small tools from my erector set, opened the watch, and started dismantling it. I did a great job! I had a score of watch parts on the table, when I realized more than ever that I would never be able to fix the watch—or even put it back in its original unfixed state.

No go. But I was still quite happy. I liked working with mechanical things and even at that young age I was the fixer of our house. My father, mother, and brother were not very mechanically inclined, though my mother (like her own father, who was a tailor) was an expert at sewing. But I watched our janitor fix things like broken chairs and electric cords, so I often tried my hand at fixing things. I even knew how to run our Cadillac car from watching our chauffeur and other people drive. But I wisely didn't try to drive it myself! I was not only practical but careful.

Anyway, I enjoyed dissembling the watch even though I couldn't put it back together again. More importantly, I learned to be on my own. I didn't *need* others to play with or talk to. I liked to be with them and almost always was with someone. I had already taught myself, from the age of five and a half, to enjoy reading. I certainly could do that alone. But now I saw that I could also be *active* alone. First, I could figure out what to *do*—find something interesting. Then I could do it. Then I could learn by trial and error. Then I could solve several problems I chose to work on. I could actually fix and master many things. Great!

Not that I didn't ask friends, or janitors, or others for help. I sometimes did. But I quickly learned what they taught me, skipped over some of their errors, and wound up by doing many interesting things myself. That was it: *interesting* things. I hated being bored. I abhorred being inactive. My father and mother were both very energetic people—always on the go. For all my childhood sickliness, I was endowed with similar energy. Doing nothing was boring. Even resting was boring, so I actively *thought* when I was told to lie down and rest. I figured out things. I asked myself why people—including myself— behaved certain ways, such as playing or working. I came up with many fascinating answers—some of them very questionable. No matter: I *enjoyed* both my questions and my answers. So my life was never boring. I *made* it interesting.

Looking back, I now see several possibilities for why I was like this. One: I was born with strong tendencies to be energetic, alert, curious, and mentally exploring. Two: I was, consequently, easily bored when there was little to be done. Three: I naturally hated being bored and tried to find something active to do. I may well have hated boredom more than other children did, thought that I *had* to be interested and active, and therefore was intolerant of it—had some degree of low frustration tolerance (LFT). Instead of having the kind of LFT that drives many people to withdraw and procrastinate, I usually propelled myself into finding and creating something active to do. I drove myself to solve my problems of boredom and usually constructed some activity. Four: My activity served to dissolve my boredom and/or master the practical problems I had set myself to solve (like dissembling a watch or fixing an electrical plug). Five: I received reinforcement—pleasure—from removing my boredom, mastering some procedure, and learning how to cope with problems right then and there. Six: The pleasure I received motivated me to get this problem-solving, frustration-removing process going again whenever boredom started to rear its ugly head.

If all this is correct, we can say that my LFT for being bored led me to become an errant problem solver. Misery is the mother of invention! An interesting hypothesis. But almost the opposite could also be true: My natural high energies and high propensities for enjoying problem solving led me to have *high* frustration tolerance (HFT). Therefore, when faced with boredom—which I healthily disliked—I refused to sit on my ass, whine about it, and thereby increase and prolong it. Instead, I uncomfortably propelled myself into constructive action, realizing that it would be worse if I did *not* do so; made my life less boring and more productive; saw the rewards (reinforcements) of doing so; and therefore continued to push myself until I made myself into a more habitual problem solver.

Which of these hypotheses or explanations is correct? Or are they both partly accurate? Who—without gathering much more evidence—can say?

This brings me to an important—and fascinating—question about psychotherapy and the accuracy of its interpretations. I have just given two different—though perhaps overlapping—interpretations of my childhood (and later) problem-solving propensities. The first "explains" that I have (native and acquired) LFT and that because I loathe boredom so much I do nothing about it—as LFTers often do—and intensify and prolong it. But paradoxically, I use my LFT to enhance my problem-solving abilities and thereby constructively alleviate—and keep alleviating—my hated boredom.

This hypothesis holds that I have strong—and probably innate—destructive tendencies to indulge in LFT and also strong constructive propensities to fight against my LFT, and that I use my constructive problem-solving predispositions to win this fight—and in the process reduce my LFT and perhaps even make it into HFT. So this hypothesis acknowledges—presumably, realistically—that I have *both* destructive and constructive inclinations and can (therapeutically) use the latter to minimize the former.

My second hypothesis somewhat differently holds that I start with constructive tendencies to have *healthy* feelings of frustration when I am bored and that I also start with constructive tendencies to have high energies and a love for problem solving, both of which lead me to bear with and fight against boredom, so that I build up HFT in dealing with it. My high energies, love for problem solving, and HFT all *constructively* propel me to uncomfortably take on problem-solving actions that eventually make me less bored and help me intensify and persist at gaining still higher frustration tolerance. Moreover, my realizing that it is better for me to undertake some pain—uncomfortably pushing myself to think and act against my feelings of boredom—is itself highly constructive, because it consists of using my native ability to think, to think about my thinking, and to think about thinking about my thinking. These two latter kinds of metacognition are especially human and particularly constructivist.

Once again, these two "explanations" of my problem-solving activity overlap but are not exactly the same. The first one emphasizes both constructive *and destructive* human tendencies, and holds that with hard thought and effort the former can be used to minimize the latter. The second "explanation" emphasizes constructive human tendencies and implies that merely by acknowledging them and using them—and not necessarily by disputing and fighting against human destructive thoughts, feelings, and actions—effective therapy will take place.

It is difficult to decide which of these two "explanations" for my problem solving is "correct"—particularly because they both, so far, only consider three important variables: my energy level, my propensity for problem solving, and my high and/or low frustration tolerance. Actually, in considering whether my low and/or high frustration tolerance really helped me to become better at problem solving (or vice versa), many other variables might be considered, such as (1) my intellectual ability, (2) my ability to think about my thinking and to think about thinking about thinking about my thinking, (3) my familial, cultural, and other influences on my problem solving and on my level of frustration tolerance, (4) my main goals and values in life, which involve important innate and acquired tendencies, (5) my physical health and disabilities, and so on. If we consider these variables, too—which would be a complicated and prolonged process—it is unlikely that we would ever definitively decide what, if any, is the "real" source of my problem-solving tendencies. The answer, if any exists, seems to involve a multiplicity of "explanations" and "solutions."

I am contending here that all interpretations, all explanations of why I was as a child, and still am today, a dedicated problem solver are partial, questionable, and inexact. It is amazing how definite and presumptuous such interpretations are often made by therapists, friends, biographers, and other explainers. In the field of psychotherapy it takes an exceptionally knowledgeable, wise, and reasonably unbiased practitioner to pick which of several possible interpretations he or she will go with—and then to try to convince the client that this is accurate. Even a sound therapist frequently errs!

What to do then? Theoretically—and "scientifically"—test out a number of possible interpretations to see which one works best. Meanwhile, the client is suffering and has limited time, energy, and funds to devote to this trying-out process. Not a very practical solution. Better yet—perhaps!—studies could be made in which clients with similar problems (such as severe LFT) were given several different kinds of interpretations for the origins of their problems—to see which worked best to help them solve these problems. Lovely—but it would be exceptionally complicated, expensive, and time-consuming to carry out these studies and check their results. Impractical in the short run—and perhaps equally so ultimately.

Meanwhile, back at the therapy session, the therapist is practically forced to pick an interpretation that sounds good to her head and heart and risk explaining it to the client. If the client accepts it or if it proves helpful, good. But not as good as you might think. A different interpretation might have helped the client more or at least done less harm. And another client might be helped considerably more by this same interpretation—or by a quite different interpretation.

What a mess. Whether a given interpretation of my LFT is good for me, for others, or for anyone is almost impossible to prove by individual therapists, by case histories of many therapists, or by experimental studies of clients with serious LFT. Maybe eventually, but hardly now.

If I were to see a therapist myself, the best she could do if she wants to help me is probably to study psychology and psychotherapy intensively, be especially knowledgeable about LFT, practice therapy with many clients, experiment with several kinds of interpretations, get much specific knowledge about me and my LFT over a number of sessions, put all her knowledge and experience together, and then take the risk of making an interpretation specific to me. Finally, she could discuss this interpretation with me, see how I respond to it, keep checking to see how well it works, acknowledge its lacks and disadvantages, observe what final results she and I seem to get with this interpretation, and use her increased knowledge to decide when, where, and how often to use this particular interpretation with other LFT clients in the future.

Whew! Quite a long-winded experimental process. So Aubrey Yates was on the right track when he said, in 1975, that every therapy session should preferably be an experiment. First the therapist experiments with his present client, then he uses the results to guess what interpretation and other procedures would probably be best used with future clients. Of course, if this therapist is rigidly wedded to one system of therapy, his experimenting will be highly restricted.

Is therapy, then, more of an art than a science? Not exactly. Art and science are not entirely different—especially as both really experiment with prospective "good" choices, and then check and revise to see how they actually work out. And both artistic and scientific decisions are only sometimes based on factual information but also importantly involve guesswork, whims, fancies, tastes, and other highly variable processes. Even so-called facts are seen and interpreted—yes, widely interpreted!—in terms of human goals, desires, values, and whatnot. Especially, often, whatnot! So we'd better watch it.

How do I personally do in this respect? Not too badly, if I do say so. I keep up with the scientific literature on psychology and psychotherapy pretty well—especially seeing how vast it now is. I subscribe to about thirty professional journals and selectively read the articles. I also read about thirty-five relevant books a year, particularly those on Rational Emotive Behavior Therapy (REBT) and Cognitive Behavioral Therapy (CBT). I now have more than sixty years of experience as a therapist since I started my private practice (part-time) in 1943. I have probably seen as many clients as any psychologist in the world, and up to 2003, when I had my major and lifesaving surgery, saw about ninety individual and group therapy clients every week. Only a few weeks after that surgery, I resumed seeing clients and running groups. I help supervise about two hundred therapists every year, particularly fellows and interns who regularly see clients at the Albert Ellis Institute for Rational Emotive Behavior Therapy in New York. I have my boards or other special qualifications in clinical psychology, clinical hypnosis, psychotherapy, sex therapy, marriage and family therapy, treatment of psychological trauma, and treatment of alcohol and substance abuse. I have written around eight hundred articles and more than eighty books on psychology and psychotherapy.

Enough already! I am obviously well grounded in therapeutic theory and practice. But I still am—or try to be—exceptionally experimental. I am reasonably sure, but never dogmatic, about the explanations and interpretations I give my clients. I know that I say them tentatively (to myself), though often authoritatively (to my clients), and I hope they are accurate and helpful, but I am far from sure about this. So I do my best to select from my training and experience and in the process use considerable guesswork, intuition (which is probably mainly, again, guesswork), risk taking (for I may well be wrong!), and experimentation. And, with the same clients and future clients, I continually revise and revise.

I do the same thing, as you might expect, with the many different cognitive, emotive, and behavioral methods that I use with my clients. I am usually risk takingly definite. But toujours experimental!

Still, I am sometimes overly risk taking and definite. I can be too sure that the particular theory or practice I am using with a particular client will work. I am sometimes deliberately authoritative (because I think this will work with a given client) but sometimes carelessly and grandiosely so. At times I fail to check carefully on the results we are getting—and consequently fail to revise my plans. It is easy to keep assuming that my current formulations and recommendations will work. So I allow my low frustration tolerance to rise again. When I acknowledge my mistakes, I try to correct them. But I can lazily fail to see and acknowledge them.

So, when my mistakes—including my LFT-incited ones—are obvious, do I flagellate myself for making them? Practically never. True to my basic REBT philosophy, I castigate my *performance*, not my essential *self* or *personhood*. So, back to working against my mistake making and LFT I go.

Chapter 3C

My Sex and Love Life
My Propensity for La Grande Passion

Gloria was the only girl I can recall actually falling in love with during my incarceration in the Presbyterian Hospital, even though there were a few others who almost made the grade. My choices, alas, were rather limited. Although the children's ward held about fifty boys and girls at any time, most of them were hardly suitable as objects of my affection. Over 50 percent, if I recall correctly, were neonates or children under the age of two, and although, as I have already noted, I could enjoy looking at the naked bodies of girls that young, I wasn't sufficiently pedophilic to fall madly in love with any of them.

As for the other twenty-five or so children, half of them were males and, of the remaining dozen or so females, a good number ranged from eight to twelve years, whereas I was only six and a half or seven. Just as my urge toward pedophilia was low, equally minimal was my gerontophilia. So I really had few potential inamoratas to choose from and, being somewhat selective, I rarely found any to my liking. I was friendly enough with most of the girls on the ward, but I can't say that I was strongly hankering to cart any of them off to the altar.

But! I almost forgot. One reason for my being so selective about the females who were close to my own age was that they often had unfair competition, as far as I was concerned, from the student nurses. The regular nurses were nice enough, as women in this profession, I have found, generally tend to be, and I liked some of them immensely. Many of them, however, were "old maids" of forty and upward—and definitely looked it. Nothing there, I felt, to get my hands and lips on to!

The student nurses were fillies of an entirely different color—and a very sexy color at that. Ranging from about sixteen to twenty and often beautiful enough to have given Miss America a run for her title, these charming youngsters had everything an adolescent female should—and I really mean *should*—have. They were almost all bright, alert, lovely, energetic—and unbelievably warm. I suspect that most of them greatly liked being on the children's ward rather than with grumpy and hopelessly ailing adults—and they showed it. Being females, I also think that they liked young boys like me, especially when that boy clearly favored them, smiled sweetly whenever they approached his bed, and made no bones about wanting to greet them in a distinctly nonplatonic way. That's the way I saw it, but I admit that my view was highly prejudiced and my wishes may well have been father to my lustful thoughts.

Anyway, I did fall in love with some of the student nurses. Usually, since I was selective, one at a time and, naturally, the prettiest and nicest one on the ward. Sometimes I was able to favor both a daytime and a nighttime nurse, which was rather great, since I could eagerly look forward to being awakened (oh, luck, oh luck!) by my favorite nighttime nurse, and then I would eagerly look forward, once again, to the change in shifts that would bring back my favorite daytime nurse, who (oh, real, real luck!) might bring me most of my meals and might even bathe me.

Fortunately, however, I didn't take my passion for any of these nurses too seriously. I realized that they were far older than I, that they most likely had husbands or lovers of their own, and that my relationship with them wasn't really going anywhere, much as I would have liked it to. So I reveled in the pleasure of loving them, and even in the pleasure of letting them know (at least to some extent) that I really cared for them. And I also enjoyed the enchantment of thinking about them, dreaming of them, and fantasizing what enormous intimacies were going to occur—but, of course, never actually did.

Why have I fallen in love so many times in my life? Starting with my mad passion for Ruthie at the age of five, I have rarely been out of love for more than a few short periods. Why so many? Why so intensely? Why, at times, only for a few weeks and at other times for several years?

I am not talking about loving but about being passionately—yes, romantically—in love. La grande passion. Not familial love, conjugal love, or what H. G. Wells once called (to distinguish it from romantic love) loving kindness.

Psychoanalysts, naturally, would have a field day exploring my (for the most part) mental amours. Mental? Definitely—for after quite verbally and physically expressing my profound feelings for Ruthie (briefly, alas, but pretty damned well), and a little later to a lesser degree to Gloria, it took me almost two decades to talk to any of my several inamorata. Pathologically shy, I didn't even try to be friendly, let alone date any of them, including Isabel, whom I madly adored between my twelfth and sixteenth years and with whom I never even had a single conversation!

Back to the topic of romantic love. The Freudians might say that because my mother was nice, kind, and caring, but never too intense about anything (except saving money), I (over)reacted by becoming decidedly more passionate myself. Possibly, but I doubt it.

Actually, my mother was warmer and more affectionate with my brother and sister than with me, because they seemed to demand it more and I didn't seem to need it, even though I was always on better terms with and—activity-wise—closer to her than they were. Although I always craved heterosexual peer love, I wanted no more than the gentle, moderate caring that my mother gave when I was young. So I felt no lack there.

What about my being deprived of Ruthie and then Gloria? Did that "make" me desperately plunge into other affairs of the heart?

Maybe. Those heartbreaks could have made actual contact with girls seem too "dangerous," so that I cleverly resorted thereafter to falling in love with those with whom I had almost zero contact. Could be. But, again, I doubt it. For if I had somehow been directly thrown into more contact with Reneé, Dorothy, and other girls I adored, I am sure I would have been delighted to become intimate with them. But, according to the mores of that day, they were waiting for *me* to make the first overtures. Which I was too scared to do. Alas!

My two main reasons for steadily falling in love were (1) genetic and (2) literature and the movies. I just seemed to be born a would-be lover. My father, I have reason to believe, was a distinct ladies' man and probably fairly promiscuous in his amours. He even seemed to be able to love (and marry) my mother—who was just about as compatible with him as a dog is with a cat. My mother, hardly a varietist, loved my father quite intensely, even after she divorced him for having an infamous affair with her best female friend.

My brother fell tempestuously in love with a woman he met in college, never got to bed with her (partly because she lived in the "foreign" world of Staten Island), "sacredized" a pistachio nut she once gave him, and remained friendly with her for years after both of them had married other partners. I thought he was pretty nutty to invest so much time and energy for so little return with this particular woman. But who am I to talk?

As for my sister Janet, she seems to have been deeply in love with her husband Norman when she married him in her twenties, and when he divorced her, she kept falling in love with a series of men, none of whom unfortunately wanted her or were suitable for marriage. So, although she had a lousy love life, she was no slouch at getting involved with the next unlikely customer.

That seems to make it a perfect score for my immediate family. All five of us were easily smitten with unsuitable people who were either not available, who weren't too keen on us, or who turned out to be incompatible. But you can't say we didn't try. So my diagnosis is: innate (as well as early-acquired) tendency to vehemently love.

The acquired part, in my own case, seems to have been influenced by romantic reading—from *Morte d'Arthur* onward—and Hollywood movies of the 1919 to 1925 era. Oh, yes!—and popular songs of the day. I saw my first musical comedy, Edward Hirsch's *Queen High*, in 1925, when I was twelve; and my first light opera, Rudolf Friml's fabulous *Vagabond King*, the next year, when I was thirteen. From that time onward, my head was filled, day and night, with romantic love songs. Even before that, from my fifth year onward, my mother (who had a fine soprano voice) introduced me to "Down by the Old Millstream," "A Bicycle Built for Two," "Moonlight Bay," "After the Ball," and scores of other sentimental ballads, all of which I loved to sing with her and my brother and sister. But I felt, right from the start, that the tunes and lyrics from the musical shows were much better and infinitely more moving. For many years later they (and other romantic music compositions) became my main hobby, and I listened to them on the radio and whistled them to myself incessantly.

That did it. Given, very likely, a strong obsessive bent to begin with, and reared with the stories, films, and songs that were rampant with romance in the 1910s and 1920s, it is hardly surprising that my propensity for deep amour flowered nicely. My particular family romance, as Flugel once called it, may have had something to do with this, too. I still remain skeptical.

Chapter 3D

Critique of Chapter 3

"*Pretty good coping, I must say, for a six-year-old child who was unfairly beset with a miserable chronic ailment, with hospitalization, and with daily medical treatments whose value was dubious and whose nature was clearly unpleasant.*" Yes, pretty good. But, as usual, not too elegant. Mainly distractive and palliative. Rather ego-inflating, too. This, of course, has its distinct dangers. For if I was a "superior boy" for being somewhat stoic and warding off profound misery, I left myself open to be "inferior" again when I took things badly. That is probably one of the reasons I was so anxious as a child. I praised myself (my essence) for conquering pain but was prone to damning myself (my totality) in case I failed to do so next time. A dubious trade-off.

My superficial "solution" to the problems of physical and emotional pain also stopped me from finding the more elegant REBT solution—to unflappably *accept* (though hardly *like*) the high colonic hassles I underwent just because I was powerless to stop them and to laud my *act* of doing so rather than my *self* as the doer. That would have been a better "solution," but REBT was still years away.

Come to think of it, this flawed "solution" to self-imposed misery was probably indigenous to some of the ancient Greek and Roman Stoics, such as Epictetus and his follower Marcus Aurelius. First of all, Epictetus was something of a pagan fatalist who believed that many Adversities were doomed by the Fates and could not possibly be changed. So he sort of had to accept them—or completely suffer. No good choice.

Second, I suspect that he and many other Stoic philosophers egoistically copped out by viewing themselves as more courageous and superior persons when they imperturbably dealt with the grim facts of life. So they gained high frustration tolerance (HFT), a fine asset, by sacrificing themselves to potential self-downing, a great loss.

Similarly, religious Stoics (Marcus Aurelius was a Christian) may have gained high frustration tolerance by devoutly believing that God helps those who help themselves and therefore were consequently "superior persons" in their God's eyes, and also dependent, in the final analysis, on His or Her succoring. So even "self-dependent" Stoics may resort to questionable means of bolstering their "rational" imperturbability. To some extent, shall we say that the weak shall inherit the earth?

"So my days, weeks, and months in the hospital went fairly pleasantly by, and I have few remembrances of keen suffering." My acceptance of my insomnia was perhaps atypical for a six-year-old. But perhaps it resulted from my many long hours of sleeplessness combined with my bent for problem solving. My use of distraction and pleasant (though often highly unrealistic) fantasies is probably much more typical for young children. This is an easy solution to difficulties, requires little cognition, and comes almost automatically. Fortunately. Without this, what is even an intelligent child to do? Not much. So let me not downplay it or insidiously compare it to theoretically "better" answers.

"I accepted my (sleeping) handicap and . . . even learned to enjoy it." Possibly out of some desperation. After staying awake most nights, I became convinced that I inevitably *had to* suffer from sleeplessness. That conviction—which may well have been false—gave me no other choice *but* to accept it or else keenly suffer. Back to Epictetus and his fatalism. He *too easily* believed in inevitable fate and made his belief stoically work for him. I, too, without exactly believing in inexorable fate, may have done a similar thing to get myself to enjoy my handicap. One of my clearest memories is that, after a while, I did enjoy my insomnia. Bien. Forsooth, little Albert at times went beyond distraction and fantasy to become a fledgling constructivist.

"My distraction methods had worked unusually well, and the reinforcement I received for using them (that is, my lack of overt anxiety during the surgical procedure) encouraged me to keep using other cognitive diversions in the future, whenever I thought I might be anxious about anything."

Fortunately—and unfortunately. That goes for most of the human race. People have beneficially used distraction for many centuries—as in yoga and meditation—to ward off anxiety. Many methods work quickly and wonderfully well. But often *too* quickly and *too* wonderfully. For example, if you become panicked when taking an exam or when about to enter an elevator, you can meditate or use various relaxation methods to quickly dispel your anxiety. Often, you will lose your panic—temporarily. But then you will be tempted to use the same distraction method again—and again and again. Easy. But you will keep yourself from getting to your fundamental "musts" that largely create your panic, such as: "I *must* pass this exam—and I may not!" or "I *must* have a guarantee that nothing will happen in this elevator—and I don't have it" or "I *must* never be panicked—as I always may be."

Your inelegant relaxation "solution" to your anxiety may actually stop you from figuring out an elegant solution to it. But, again, it is quick and easy, and that is why so many people, as well as therapists who help people, resort to it. That is why my focusing on various aspects of my stomach-tapping operation, for example, instead of on the "horror" of the operation itself worked very well for me. But it also likely kept me from finding the more elegant and permanent answer to anxiety until I originated REBT some thirty-five years later.

"Without having practiced an incipient form of REBT on myself for many years before this, I might never have realized how self-defeating my clients were, and might have helped lead them up the same kinds of emotional garden paths that so many other psychotherapists have done and still do."

Well! That certainly sounds arrogant, self-righteous, and exaggerated. For several reasons:

1. I used some incipient REBT, all right, to combat my depression and anger about being relatively neglected by my parents when I was hospitalized for ten months. But *incipient*—and *vague*—is really the term to describe it. I hardly saw that my Irrational Beliefs largely made me upset, and I certainly didn't actively Dispute them.
2. Once again, I focused on distraction methods, such as forcefully concentrating on playing with my toys or on reading, to shut out the views and sounds of the other children having visitors while I was often deserted.
3. The rational thinking I used was largely derived from many maxims and proverbs of our culture. REBT has often been called a "common-sense" approach to solving emotional upsets,

and it partly is. It upholds several popular views, such as "Shit happens," "This, too, shall pass," and "Every cloud has a silver lining." My incipient use of REBT during my childhood derived much from these maxims. I was using sensible, realistic philosophies that are frequently voiced and acted upon in our culture (and some other cultures) by millions of people, not uniquely by little Albert.

4. I keep forgetting that many—perhaps almost all—non-REBT therapies overtly de-emphasize rationality but actually sneak much of it into their treatment methods, because their clients largely are irrational, unrealistic, and illogical—but also are quite capable of being reasoned into greater mental health.

So, my six-and-a-half-year-old coping with my separation from my parents and other visitors was partly incipient REBT. But REBT, and particularly its methods of Disputing Irrational Beliefs, is hardly entirely original but rather is based on common human processes—yes, common-sense ways—of dealing with potential and actual despair. I didn't use REBT to a nicety when I thought my way out of loneliness and depression in the Presbyterian Hospital when I was young. But I did vaguely practice some parts of it, and that practice probably did contribute to my later creating it in more comprehensive ways.

Why am I so eager to see the innate and biological elements in my own and others' personalities when I was once prejudiced in favor of environmental explanations? Well, first, why my previous learning biases? I think they, too, come from innate tendencies to think crookedly. Being a do-gooder I, like most of this ilk, felt that if people largely learned their poor behaviors, they could change them more readily than if they were born with strong tendencies to indulge in them. True—but that merely proves that it would be nice if their dysfunctional habits were mostly learned; it hardly proves that they were acquired rather than inborn. So my do-goodism (and innate tendency to often think illogically) prejudiced me to overemphasize social learning.

I was still a staunch environmentalist, when I had a rude awakening as a young psychologist. First of all, I read much evidence that convinced me that serious disturbance, such as schizophrenia and manic-depressive illness, had strong biological elements. I could also see that normal disturbance or neurosis had a lot in common with serious mental illness, and that made me do some deep thinking.

Second, I saw several clients who were reared in almost ideal homes—and they were often more disturbed than my clients who were raised in nasty and abusive families. For example, Georgia, a bright, attractive, and talented actress of nineteen, was as disturbed as she could be in spite of her great career and social successes—she was a protégé of one of America's best-known directors and was sought after by many attractive men. She had only good things to say about her parents, and when I saw them a few times, I realized that her love for them was justified, as they showed themselves to be thoroughly kind and considerate, despite her giving them (and others) almost continual trouble. They were most puzzled about her behavior, especially her incredible and constant self-immolation.

The mystery of Georgia's borderline personality disorder was at least partially solved when I learned from her parents that she was not their biological offspring but had been adopted at birth when a good friend of her mother became "illegitimately" pregnant and couldn't tell her very strict Catholic parents about her pregnancy. The mother was secreted away, and Georgia was supposedly born to her adopted parents—and just about no one, including Georgia herself, knew about the adoption.

Well, this information put a new light on things. Georgia's birth mother, and several of her close blood relatives, I was told, were strikingly like her, and some had been hospitalized for mental illness. No wonder Gloria was having so many problems, despite the careful and loving upbringing by her adopted parents. Spurred on by this information, I investigated my other cases where disturbed clients came from good families, and I found that emotional problems in this scenario were much more frequent among people who had been adopted than those who had not.

I followed other studies in the 1950s of adopted children and found that they were more frequently disturbed than non-adoptees, whether or not they knew about their adoption. So I convinced myself that parents who give up their child for adoption tend to be more disturbed than parents who keep their children, and that these parents give their offspring a genetic dysfunctional tendency. I am still convinced, though not rigidly so, that this is true.

For these and other reasons, I favorably hypothesize that some of my own temperamental traits are inborn. Among the other reasons was my observation of the fact that, although raised in the same semi-neglectful way by my mother—who even when she was married to my father was for the most part a single mother—my brother and sister were in many ways radically different from me, and also from each other. Moreover, our natural differences to some degree encouraged all three of us to be treated dissimilarly by our mother, more than the different treatment *caused* the temperamental uniqueness. So I believe.

Of course, environmental factors *are* important. For example, I was more sickly than my brother and sister and therefore spent more time away from my parents. I thus may have, because of my fragility, been treated more kindly than they were, had more adversities to cope with, and so on. So I *therefore* may have been importantly affected in a different way than my siblings. We'll never really know. But my main conclusion is that I was largely born differently—and again that that *led to* divergent upbringing. This is my prejudiced—though possibly accurate—view. Keep it in mind, as I shall try to keep it in mind, as I write about my "inborn" personality. I am a biased observer.

"*. . . for all my manifestations of high frustration tolerance (HFT) . . . I admittedly have a good deal of LFT.*" But it is much harder for me to focus on it and keep it in mind. HFT is in many respects the ideal in our culture—not that many children or adults have it. Practically all my clients have serious elements of LFT. That is why they are clients! But who among us will cast the first stone? As I am fond of telling my lecture and workshop audiences—especially when I cite my book *Overcoming Procrastination*, which has been a paperback best seller for almost thirty years—college students are relatively bright and productive compared to other people. Yet what percentage of them procrastinate on studying for tests and on writing term papers, know that it is foolish to procrastinate, and still frequently put off to the last minute what they could more sensibly do today? Probably 90 percent. What percentage of them also procrastinate in arranging the details of pleasurable pursuits, such as parties, outings, and vacations? A hell of a lot.

LFT, then, is often the human condition. Murphy's sixty-third law: "Whatever can be foolishly put off for tomorrow instead of wisely done today *will* be." Often. Definitely. Steadily. Leading to—you guessed it—still more procrastination and self-castigation. For how can I, a good-for-nothing laggard, be *able* to stop my idiotic delaying? Not very easily.

Now the fascinating thing here is that virtually no one in our society—parents, friends, teachers, bosses—favors dawdlers. Au contraire, they usually are reviled and penalized. Does that stop them—or move them? Rarely. So they get the downside of asinine ass-sitting—

poor marks, piled-up work, lost interest, lack of promotions, tax penalties, and so on—*plus* social disapproval and self-beatings. Whew. Does that stop their procrastinating? Rarely.

The REBT theory of LFT presumably explains all this. In the normal course of events, it says, humans will strongly motivate themselves to do important, life-preserving things like escaping from a fire, eating when starving, wearing warm clothes in winter, and seeking shelter from the rain and snow. Promptly. Energetically.

They will also make distinct efforts to do intrinsically pleasurable things, such as eat tasty food, have sex when aroused, win a mate whom they are strongly attracted to, and engage in exciting and interesting games and sports. Again, easily, eagerly, actively. These propensities for pushing yourself are in the long run life preserving, for even when you engage in games and sports, your pleasure in doing so gives you an incentive to live and live longer. And, of course, to have more progeny for the preservation of the human race.

Unfortunately, however, besides efforts to motivate and preserve yourself, you have—as a human—LFT and consequent effort blocking. You often have inertia that may interfere with getting yourself moving quickly, even in a flood or a fire. You don't like some of the prolonged and boring work of fixing the roof and may risk a torrential flood in your living room the next time it storms. The bad things that may well happen to you—such as fire, a storm, or heart trouble from eating tasty and fattening food—may be long delayed or may not happen at all. You may get away with not writing the onerous term paper or business report—or you may suffer only a slight penalty. Not going out of your way to do things for family members or others may again bring fewer—or much later—penalties. Not preparing for a fulfilling career may result in your being "satisfied" with a less-desirable career and ignorant about the joys of a better one.

Often, long-range gains—like good health, a fine profession, and enjoyment of a sport—necessitate onerous expenditures of time and effort, especially in the short run. They do not seem—though they well may be—worth it. The pain of striving for future gains seems much worse than the waiting time (perhaps forever) of not having these gains. The pain of, say, stopping smoking may be acute, and the rewards of stopping—good health, better discipline, approval from others for stopping—are longer-lasting but, truth to tell, milder. Short-range hedonism, therefore, seems to be better than long-range hedonism. Even when the risk is fatal lung cancer.

Are humans, therefore, usually short-range hedonists, indulgers in LFT? Not always—but very often. In some ways they make great sacrifices today for tomorrow's benefits—especially, ironically, if we call what they are doing a sport. Or a love affair. Or a career. Even then, the number of people who vow to pursue, say, a sport or a career and then give up before they follow through is immense. Frighteningly so.

Psychological generalities are interesting, but this is not one of my professional or self-help books. Back to specifics—my concrete elements of LFT and HFT. Maybe, more than most people, I have strong degrees of both. My productivity certainly shows much HFT. I get things done. I persist. I don't complain about the shit work accomplishment requires. But I may have, at times, achieved something for what I and REBT consider the "wrong" reasons—ego bolstering. I am also most productive at things I do easily—such as writing and speaking. In both areas, I am rarely at a loss for words—as were my talkative father and mother. No pushing against the grain. No forcing myself to go through unenjoyable practice sessions. Piece of cake.

Well, no—not entirely. If I agree to do an article or a book and for some reason hate to do it, perhaps get bored with it, I nonetheless go through with my agreement and finish it. Too bad—but I promised. So I buckle down and polish it off, perhaps a bit sloppily and fast. But definitely.

Much more often, I hate doing parts of a book (e.g., the bibliography) or parts of a public presentation (e.g., the clerical material for continuing education credits). But I damned well do them, with no delay, sometimes with amazing promptness. Why? Because they have to be done sooner or later, and doing them sooner, and having them out of the way for the rest of my life, is much better than later. So HFT in getting them done is better than LFT in farting around.

However, my HFT gives me more private and public approval than my LFT does. So I'd better not emphasize my self-discipline and ignore my lapses in self-control. This part of my autobiography particularly takes the both/and rather than the either/or approach to low and high frustration tolerance. I am trying, if possible, to see the "truth." No, not the absolute truth, as there probably is none. But the best approximation to it. So I shall keep reminding myself, especially in this critique section of each chapter, to look for the negative side when I prejudicedly mainly stress the positive.

I have some LFT, then, about my LFT. At times, I find it "too uncomfortable" to face. Well, I'd better look it in the eye and face it. Truth, I hope, will thereby win out.

"True to my basic REBT philosophy, I castigate my performance, *not my essential* self *or* personhood." Always? Well, no. I sometimes partly fall back to self-rating, though I am ever trying to make myself allergic to it. I feel at least a *little* guilty for screwing up—and perhaps a little guilty about feeling, against REBT tenets, guilty. Guilt, meaning blaming your performance *and* blaming yourself, is natural—it is both deeply innate and deeply ingrained by social teaching. Reducing guilt to blaming only your performance but not at all damning yourself seems virtually impossible. Of course, psychopaths seem (usually) to do it. But isn't that because, sensing that they would beat themselves up for real blunders or wrongs, they defensively convince themselves that they are virtually always "right"? Being unconsciously afraid to be wrong, they make sure that they never are. Clever!

Not me, Albert. I got myself to admit practically all my mistakes and immoralities, once I was well on the road to REBT-type rationality, just because I knew I would never fully beat myself, my personhood, for making them. Largely I would feel sorry and remorseful for my wrongdoings but never very guilty—that is, self-downing. Because, as noted above, I condemned the deed, not the doer.

But there is often a fine line between regret about acts and self-flagellation for doing them. I sometimes slipped over the line, especially if I did something very stupid and it had prolonged pernicious effects. Like my steadfastly refusing, for many years, to initiate encounters with potential female partners and my being unassertive with them when, every once in a while, I was introduced to them. That was really bad, and I consequently made myself ashamed and self-downing.

Even when, in my early twenties, I was getting rid of this shame, I paradoxically kept some of it by going to the other extreme. When I met a suitable woman—and I found practically every one of them suitable!—I would feel a little ashamed if I did not soon proposition her and, of course, was somewhat proud of myself when I soon did. So the self-rating was somehow there, though greatly reduced. What a time I had truly beating it to a pulp!

"Given, very likely, a strong obsessive bent to begin with, and reared with the stories, films, and songs that were rampant with romance in the 1910s and 1920s, it is hardly surprising that my propensity for deep amour flowered nicely."

Motivated by my own passionate response to girls and women, I later became a noted sexologist as well as, as has never been fully recognized, an authority on love. My first PhD thesis, which Columbia

University prudishly made me abandon as a dissertation (but which I later published in several journal articles) was on the love emotions of college-age women. Before I even entered graduate school in psychology, I started to do a massive study of sex behavior, not knowing at that time that Alfred Kinsey had already begun to do his famous studies in 1938. But mine was to be more comprehensive than Kinsey's (and, than Masters and Johnson's later researches). It was to particularly include comprehensive investigations of love and mating aspects of humans.

Accordingly—being no slouch—I read hundreds of books and articles on love, including stories, novels, plays, and poems. You name it, and I read it. Through this reading, through observations of my own amative experience, and through my firsthand interview and questionnaire study of several hundred young women, I probably became the foremost authority in the world on love emotions by the time I was thirty-four. When Kinsey, with whom I was friendly, heard about what I was doing, he had me send him some of my questionnaires and data so that he could possibly extend his own sex studies into the love area.

Anyway, my researches and self-observation convinced me that the human propensity to love was partly innate, as John Bowlby later showed, but that was as true of romantic, passionate love as it was of child and family attachment. I noted, among much other data, that even in anti-romantic cultures, like ancient China, where young people were betrothed in childhood and were forbidden to fall in love with other males and females, they often did so anyway and eloped in spite of the penalty of death if they were caught. I found many other indications of spontaneous obsessive-compulsive in-lovedness, in myself and other lovers whom I interviewed and read about.

For example, I fell madly in love with my first wife, Karyl, when I was twenty-four and had already been passionately involved—at least in my head—perhaps a dozen times before, from my fifth year onward. For months I was completely (and ecstatically) obsessed with Karyl and could think of little else. Because of my long prior history of ardent attachments, I think my great propensity for love largely stems from innate temperament. Scratch an Albert, or give him half a chance to encounter a suitable female, and—voilà—he's off to the races. I thought of Karyl almost incessantly, even though I knew my obsession was time- and energy-wasting, and often tried to stop it. This was a real obsessive-compulsive problem, like none I have ever had before or since. So, in explaining it, I favor biological sources and similarly think that obsessive-compulsive infatuation in general has hormonal and other physiological underpinnings—like non-amative OCD usually has.

As ever, however, I am biased by my own personal reactions. As I shall tell in detail later in this memoir, my relationship with Karyl was in many ways most unusual. First, she was at that time the only woman other than Ruthie in whom I confided my passionate feelings. The many others I said nary a word to. Second, Karyl was the first woman with whom I had sex and came to orgasm. Third, she returned my love for her—but very stormily and erratically. Fourth, at the time we met, I had done little dating for years and consequently practically all aspects of my relationship with her were exceptionally new and exciting.

As you can see, several environmental influences helped me become thoroughly obsessed with Karyl. I stick to my guns, however. For all these influences, I think that biology won out. I was stubbornly born, as well as raised, with the tendency to become violently attached, and my upbringing oriented me to become attached to young, attractive females. My sex drives, which were again largely biological, helped, too, of course. Maybe low-sexed males also fall madly in love. But, I'll wager, much less often.

Chapter 4A

Chronology
More Early Frustrations

Let it not be thought that my life as a child was only one long series of tribulations that, with the use of brilliant rational emotive behavioral thinking, I cleverly overcame. Actually, I had a good and happy life and rarely was a miserable child who felt sorely deprived. One main theme I'd like to discuss is my philosophical attitude toward life's hassles and how this attitude helped me to feel less than greatly disturbed when they occurred, and to remain reasonably happy. So I am doubtless giving a one-sided view of what I experienced, and I would not want to pretend that what I have been recounting so far was typical of my entire early existence.

With me, as perhaps with most people, the memories of tragedies and miseries rather than of good times and consequent joys tend to prevail. My clients sometimes ask me why this is so. "Why do I dwell so much on the bad things and so easily gloss over the good ones?"

"For one thing," I reply, "this is probably because as a human you are so inclined for biological or self-preservative reasons. If we didn't dramatically focus upon and remember the accidents, pains, grim losses, and near-deaths that transpire as we meander along toward our final demise, wouldn't this end occur more quickly? For us vividly to recall that one day we had a glorious mile-long swim in a ripple-free, tepid lake will bring up considerable pleasure again, and that is nice, but will it especially preserve our health and longevity? While for us to even more vividly remember that on one of the many occasions when we were enjoying this same kind of glorious swim a motorboat came within a few inches of slicing us in half—will that dramatic recollection not encourage us to watch our step while swimming in the future, and carefully avoid another almost fatal occurrence? Indeed, it probably will. So isn't it natural, and highly self-preservative, for us to keep thinking about the bad rather than the good events and fairly often, and quite prophylactically, to dwell on them?"

For this and various other reasons, holocausts and catastrophes rarely become run-of-the-mill, taken-for-granted happenings in our lives, while pleasures and gratifications often do. We may also guess—though I am not sure that any experimental psychologist has as yet turned up the data backing this hypothesis—that most of us, as children and adults, have many more mildly or greatly satisfying experiences than we have truly grim ones. If our memory banks were as retentive about the former as they are about the latter, they would be replete with so many bits of information that we would hardly have any remaining storage space for the significant events that we'd damn well better, for our continued good, remember.

I point this out by way of noting that, for all the dismal events I have so far explicated, I have always viewed my childhood as happy and beneficial, and still do. My remembrance—which of course may be suspiciously inaccurate—vaguely holds on to days and years of pleasant occasions.

In Pittsburgh, up to the age of four, I remembering enjoying almost everything I did. At Bryant Avenue in the Bronx, I luxuriated in my friendships with Don and Steve. I rejoiced in my talks (as long as they lasted) with Ruthie. I relished playing in the lot across the street from my home virtually every day of the year. I explored, usually with Steve, the East Bronx neighborhood for many blocks around my house. I thought that Sunday School was rather interesting, although I wasn't entirely taken in by all the miracles from the Bible that we kept reading about. When I finally began public school—a few weeks before my sixth birthday, I believe—I liked virtually all the activities (which I found quite similar to those that I had participated in at the age of four in Pittsburgh).

I loved my mother a good deal, though she was at times a pain in the rear end. I liked, or certainly accepted with equanimity, both my brother and my sister. I got along well with the adults who visited our home (especially the portly businessmen who played pinochle with my father on many Sundays). I thought our maid was pretty helpful and I was glad that she rarely bothered me. On occasion I truly fancied going out for a long drive in our chauffeur-driven electric-powered Cadillac, which was far classier than any of the other automobiles I had ever seen and which (because of its lack of gasoline) was remarkably un-smelly.

When I was seven, we moved to Heath Avenue in the North and West Bronx, and I found life to be equally or even more pleasant. We lived on the second floor of a two-story house and therefore did not have any noisy people above us (as we did on Bryant Avenue). Our apartment was brand new and equipped with the very latest conveniences—including our own water and gas heaters, which we could turn on whenever we liked, even if the weather was only the slightest bit cool. In back of our home was a very large lot, with all kinds of bushes, plants, flowers, and trees and with a fairly sizable cleared space, in which my male friends and I could play ball or other games. My school—Public School 7—was within a fairly short walking distance of our home and was nice enough, with well-behaved children (some of whom came from the fancy Riverdale section of the Bronx in which the school was located) and with fine, friendly teachers.

Friend-wise, my situation was even better on Heath Avenue than it had been on Bryant Avenue. Although I seemed to be the only boy of seven for blocks around, on my own street there were over a dozen older boys, ranging from about ten to fourteen, who took a great shine to me and made sure I was accepted into their sports and other games. They let me play baseball or stickball with them (though I was by no means good at either of these games). They explored the entire neighborhood with me, ranging far into Riverdale and away up into Woodlawn Park. And although our immediate neighborhood had no movie houses (it was freshly building up and did not have too many inhabitants within a mile radius), my friends frequently took me by trolley all the way up the very steep Kingsbridge Avenue hill to Fordham Road (the main business section of the North Bronx at that time) and to the several movie houses in that area.

It was at the movies that I saw virtually all the current films of Charles Chaplin, Mary Pickford, Douglas Fairbanks, the Gish sisters, and other stars of that day. At the famous Keith's Fordham theater, which later became one of the key points in the RKO chain, I was introduced to what was even more popular in those early days—vaudeville. Keith's was then the largest theater in the Bronx and at first specialized only in vaudeville. But as movies became more popular, it provided—for about ten cents admission—a current popular movie plus six or seven vaudeville acts. And in that heyday of live entertainment, the stage show would consist, quite regularly, of outstanding performers like George Jessel, Al Jolson, Fanny Brice, Harry Houdini, Thurston the Magician, and even some personal appearances by a number of the leading ladies and gentlemen of the movies. All this, and a large and live orchestra in the pit, too!

I was utterly enthralled with both the vaudeville acts and the movies and was immensely delighted that my male friends would go to the trouble of taking me along almost every Saturday to see one or more of these popular shows. Not to mention the fudge sundaes, ice cream cones, candy bars, cookies, and other junk foods that we consumed before, after, and during the performances. Bryant Avenue had been okay—including the few outdoor night movies my parents had taken me to during the summer months—but Heath Avenue, along with Fordham Road and the Grand Concourse, was a heck of a lot better!

Another significant and extremely happy event in my life occurred when I transferred to P.S. 7 in my seventh year. Urged on by some of the older boys and encouraged by one of my teachers, I got up the nerve to take myself to the public library that was close to my school, filled out the application forms (which almost stumped my mother but which I was able to wade through mainly on my own), and got my first library card. As a young child, I was able, as I recall, to take out no more than two books at a time—one fiction and one nonfiction. But I interpreted that to mean, two a day for six days each week (the library was closed on Sundays).

Well, that was really something! The librarians, though fairly friendly, soon got sick of me and my traipsing back there day after day to take out two new books. "Have you really *read* those two you took yesterday?" they kept asking me. "Oh, yes!" And, in truth, I had. There was soon almost no classic or popular book in the children's rooms of the library that I had not read, and after a few months I started reading some of them over again until I knew them almost by heart.

Was this because we didn't have books at home? Partly, yes. My father read, I think, the *New York Times* and the *Wall Street Journal*, but I never remember him reading a book of any sort. My mother read lighter newspapers—like the *Daily News* and the *Bronx Home News*—and she did have a few books, but I doubt whether she ever read them.

Eventually we did own some books, but they were mainly sets—the kind that door-to-door salesmen sell you when you are not too bright and have little or no sales resistance. We had, for example, the complete works of O. Henry, Robert Louis Stevenson, William Makepeace Thackeray, and several lesser-known authors. Later on, of course, we had the *Book* of *Knowledge*—all twenty volumes, designed especially for children to read. But when I was seven we had virtually no books in the house that I can recall, except a few that I brought home from school. So the New York Public Library was a godsend, and I took full advantage of it. Everything in sight. I read lots of plays, poems, biographies, and other nonfiction works along with fairy tales, children's stories, novels, sports stories, and other fiction. Having practically no books of my own, which I then might read over and over, I don't recall any real favorites. I just gobbled up everything in sight.

And I learned to read and write that way. I am sure that we were formally taught to read in school, because I vaguely remember some lessons on the alphabet. But as noted previously, I originally learned to read by going through my friend Don's books with him, and I continued this process by going through innumerable other books. I not only acquired a fantastic vocabulary for a child that way—and therefore, perhaps, was a favorite with other children and with adults—but I also had no trouble writing.

Whereas most of the other children in my class would laboriously mull over writing assignments, I would sit down and rattle them off fairly easily. I not only had a conversational gift of gab—which wasn't strange, considering that both my father (on a fairly high intellectual level) and my mother (on a considerably lower level) could talk almost anyone's ears off, and frequently did—but I also was a fluent writer. At an early age, possibly eight or nine, I had already started writing my own little stories, and if I had to write notes or letters to my friends, relatives, or teachers, I was at no loss to turn them out quickly and effortlessly. No trouble at all. My teachers appreciated this, but some of my school friends looked at my achievements with a jaundiced, jealous eye.

My other real pleasure in life was my relationship with my brother Paul. I don't remember that we were too close when I was very young, but by the time I was six and he was four and a half (we were still living at Bryant Avenue at this time), we became quite close. Perhaps my return from several short stays at the hospital had something to do with it or, more likely, his "growing up" and becoming more tolerable. Also, he was very bright and imaginative.

We slept together in a double bed and always spent a half hour or more talking to each other before we felt tired enough to go to sleep. We invented mutual fantasies, in the course of which we were the favorite friends of our favorite heroes and were the lovers or husbands of our special heroines. Babe Ruth, Jack Dempsey, and Charles Chaplin were our buddies, and Mary Pickford, Mabel Norman, and Lillian Gish were our girlfriends. What great times we all had together!

Paul and I rarely disagreed or fought—though he still battled with my mother, my sister, and practically everyone else. As his older brother, I advised and taught him but refrained from censoring him when he got into trouble. Being less daring than he, I *liked* his risk taking, got vicarious thrills from it, and copped out by letting (and even encouraging) him get into adventuresome trouble. His taking too many risks, moreover, gave me a legitimate excuse to shyly take too few.

Although I had other close male friends, Paul was always there and was, on the whole, my closest companion. I often took him for granted, but I really missed him during my longest stay in the hospital and was happy to resume our camaraderie when I returned home. Although younger, he was better at sports than I was; was much worse at fixing things or doing projects at home; he was a poor student (mainly because of conduct problems) but was very bright and often superior to me at complicated card games and chess. I accepted his superiorities, however, and was more proud of his having certain skills and abilities than I was jealous of him. He, meanwhile, used me to help get him out of his scrapes. So we got along very nicely—and both of us largely ignored (when he wasn't actively fighting with) my pain-in-the-ass sister, Janet.

Janet died in her sixties several years before Paul, and although I got along quite well with her—particularly after I managed to forgive her "sins" when I was fifteen—I found her, objectively speaking, negative and whiney, did not really like her, and (guiltlessly) felt very little sorrow about her death. With Paul it was another story. I was quite concerned, while writing the original draft of this autobiography, about his heart condition. At forty, he had had a serious heart attack and almost died, and I was somewhat shocked to see how weak and pained he was when I saw him in the hospital shortly after his attack. He made an excellent recovery, however, and dieted and exercised in a most disciplined manner for the next thirty years, thereby keeping himself in good health despite a mild case of Parkinson's disease when he was sixty-seven.

Unfortunately, his heart began failing again in his seventy-first year. At his last meeting of the board of directors of our institute, he was mentally acute, in his usual highly organized, intelligent, and humorous form, and provided us, on several important issues, with outstanding insight, fine financial advice, and diplomatic suggestions for handling some of our personnel problems.

Physically, however, he was in poor shape and probably should have skipped coming from Lakewood, New Jersey, by bus for our early morning meeting. He had severe angina pains and seemed to be taking it very well but clearly thought it was serious. I was really concerned about him and urged him to go to the hospital soon to see whether an operation was necessary or feasible. Eventually he went to the hospital for a heart bypass operation. I called him right away, and he seemed tired and only wanted to talk for a few minutes. There were, however, some complications, but they were straightened out and he was about to be transferred to a new hospital for surgery. His wife Esther was upset and I helped calm her.

On Wednesday, his son David called from Florida to say that Paul had died in the ambulance while being transferred to a different hospital. David said there was to be no funeral because Paul had donated his body to Rutgers University Medical School. I had almost expected his death, but I was still shocked. "Oh, shit!" I said to David. "That's really sad." And I deeply felt so.

Oddly enough, although Paul had been a great help to me and the Albert Ellis Institute in recent years, my main thoughts about him reflected our close camaraderie as young children. Paul and I were always fairly close and almost never had serious difficulties with each other. He was just about my best friend all my life, yet it is the early relationship I best remember and that immediately came to mind when I learned of his death. What good friends we were. And what a fine brother he was. How sad to lose him.

Sad for others, too. I remembered how helpful he was to Esther, David, and many others. Always ready with good advice. Always there with jokes and good humor. Almost always sane and (unlike our father) usually slow to anger. Remarkably wise and financially adept. The sanest and soundest member of the board of directors of the institute. The most honest and loyal keeper of my own personal accounts, such that I never even had to bother to look after them myself. A good friend to many. A fine speaker and teacher. A former National Amateur Chess Champion.

Truly a man to remember! Hardly perfect. Sometimes critical and sarcastic. Sometimes dogmatic. But not often. Early in life, a rebel and a hellion. Later, conservative, polite, conciliatory. Remarkably balanced. Easy to talk to. Unusually alive and interested. Faults, some; virtues, many.

I was quite sad. Tears welled into my eyes. I thought of how unfair it was that he didn't have a chance to be operated on—a procedure that may have prolonged his life for five or ten years. Yes, unfair! But—I rationally reminded myself—the world was unfair. Often. Very. It was!

So I was not angry or depressed. Only very sad. And my sadness kept impinging from time to time on my therapy sessions. I had four individual half-hour sessions and one group therapy session to lead the night I learned of Paul's death. So I threw myself into them and got by very well—till the sadness intermittently returned, for a few minutes at a time, to partially interrupt the sessions.

Not the group session. Hardly at all. I was so busy running one large group, trying to give everyone his or her turn, strongly intervening when the members got stuck in their irrationalities, that I almost entirely forgot about my brother for that hour and a half. Then I went back to my intermittent sadness. I felt much more sorrow as I thought about what I might do to help Esther.

I slept somewhat fitfully. I dreamed of Paul, of early days with Paul, once. And I dreamed of somewhat related things twice more. But I knew I would not become depressed. I knew I could keep accepting his death. How could I not—when it was a given fact? Why rant and rail against it? We all, alas, die. Is it entirely bad, our dying, seeing that we grow older and feebler? I would want to live vibrantly forever. But old and feeble? Hmm. And Paul had a good life for seventy-one years. And, fortunately, he died suddenly. It could have been much worse. He had a light case of Parkinson's, which could have deteriorated. And he did have painful angina. Who needs it? Maybe death was not too unkind. Let me hope that when it takes me, it does so precipitously.

Did I ever wish to die? Yes, a few times—especially in my later years, when I spent an utterly miserable night after a shoulder operation, running to the bathroom about thirty-five times because the intravenous fluid they gave me during and after my operation flooded my enlarged prostate and made me urinate every few minutes. Imagine! Up all night right after an operation and in continual urethral discomfort and pain. If I had thought that it would always be this way, would my life really be worth it? Maybe not. But, imagining that I would soon get help (which I did early the next morning) and be out of pain (as I later mainly was), I didn't literally contemplate killing myself. But I thought of it.

I am not at all afraid of death—of being dead. As I tell many of my clients (and have written in my book *How to Master Your Fear of Flying*), death is most probably exactly the same state you were in before you were born. Nothing. Zero. No sensation. No pain of any sort. Zilch. Too bad, when you think about it while you're still alive. But not bad at all once you are dead. Not at *all*.

So I was not sorry for Paul, now that he was irrevocably dead. I was sad that he hadn't lived longer, enjoyed more life. And I was sorry for Esther, for their son David, for the friends and associates (including our board of directors at the institute) who would surely miss him. Too bad for us. But not for him. Not anymore. "He" is at peace. Not we who miss him and shall keep remembering our loss. But the lost one is himself not lost. He simply isn't. He and his troubles no longer exist.

Postscript: I went to Florida to give a talk and a workshop the day after Paul's death and met several people who knew him and David. All of them were shocked and sad. I saw how high they held Paul in their esteem, which was good to see. But I definitely viewed him as gone, as having only a *past* history.

I even became a bit confused about this. When someone in Florida asked me, "Was your brother ill before he died?" I mistakenly thought they were talking about David and replied, "No, he is not ill." I had somehow edited out the past and remained in the present and only a minute later saw that the question was about my *dead* brother. I wasn't denying he was dead, but I seemed to be concerned only with the *living*. Perhaps that is healthy. Perhaps merely confused.

Was my lack of intense or prolonged upsetness over the death of my brother Paul related to my own enormous fearlessness about dying myself? Probably. Not that I don't give a damn about *bringing about* my own demise, for that I clearly do not wish to do. Since childhood and especially since my early hospitalizations, I have been quite disciplined about taking care of my health and for over fifty years I have been one of the best-controlled diabetics in the world.

For example, up until a year ago, I took fifteen units of NPH and ten units of Humalog insulin every morning; took twenty-one more insulin units at 5:00 p.m.; ate twelve—yes, twelve—small meals every day to carefully balance the insulin; tested my blood about seven times each day; cleaned my teeth after each meal (including water-picking); studiously avoided sugar and salt; exercised (not too little, not too much); and followed other health rules, which are a great pain in the ass and (alas!) time-consuming. Result: no serious sequelae of my diabetes since I was first affected with it in 1954 (at the age of forty). Today, after losing my large intestine and being afflicted with osteoarthritis in my right knee, I have nurses around the clock and, with Debbie's help, strictly follow my doctors' complicated orders. No nonsense!

So I clearly don't *want* to die, in fact, I would prefer to live (and continue writing and therapizing) just about forever. But at the age of ninety-two, I never worry about—indeed, I hardly ever think about—

dying. I am occupied by my work, attempting to correct institute matters, and attending to my healthcare with many doctor appointments. And I am almost surprised when so many of my nutty clients, most of them in good physical health, are so afraid of their own death.

How come I have never been very afraid of dying, even though I have had my fair share of serious sickness? When I was young, I never considered it too seriously. At the age of eight, I saw the laid-out body of one of my childhood acquaintances and heard his friends and relations taking his demise with some degree of awe: "How young he was! How sad that he had such a short life!" But at that age, I never saw my own death as imminent (though it sometimes was). And I decided to be as happy as I could while I was still around.

As I grew older, acquired diabetes, and was more prone than ever to death, I still had no fear of it—nor do I now, at age ninety-two and with a good many infirmities. As I said some years ago, in my book *How to Master Your Fear of Flying*, dying itself may (temporarily!) be painful, but death is not. It is zero—nothing. No pain, no pleasure—nothing! So what's to be afraid of?

I hate like hell the thought not that I will undoubtedly die but that it might possibly be soon. For I still (and always will!) have many more things to do before I kick the bucket. I don't *have* to do them. But I would certainly like to. So I greatly want to stick around to do at least some of them. But if I don't, I don't. So I worry not a whit about dying. It would just, I feel, be highly inconvenient while I am still alive!

I kept in close contact with Paul's wife Esther for the next few weeks, and she appeared to be holding up well. But she was angry—and most people would have said justifiably so—at the poor medical attention that Paul had received and that she was sure had "killed him."

Esther angrily insisted that Paul would still be alive if not for medical incompetence. But I, who also missed Paul and would have been overjoyed to have had him alive for several more years, felt very sad but not angry. I told myself, "Assuming that Esther is right, as she probably is, that incompetent physician who may have contributed to Paul's death has every right to be incompetent. That, alas, is his nature and right now he cannot be any other way. Sad. Bad. Most unfortunate. But that's still the way he is!"

Of all the friends and relatives who heard the sordid truth about Paul's death, I think I was the only one who was not very irate. I was rational and only keenly disappointed. I missed Paul very much. But I fully accepted the fallibility of his doctors.

Back to my childhood. By the time I was seven, my hospital days were virtually over and I was getting along pretty well. But then disaster suddenly struck again in one of the strangest possible forms. When I first began attending Public School 7 in Riverdale, I was put in the second grade because, even though I was almost eight, I had missed a full year's schooling during my hospital stays and had actually attended the first grade sporadically. The principal spoke with me and my mother for a while and decided that he would try me in the second grade, as I appeared to be a bright young lad and he was not one to cavil about my relative lack of formal schooling up to that point. I was happy enough about this and settled down for the first two weeks of the term to do as well as I could.

Well, to my surprise—and my teacher's—I immediately rose to the top of the class in arithmetic, social studies, and particularly literature. I discovered that the storybook they gave us—a collection of stories about King Arthur's Court—was supposed to last us for the entire term. Not believing that this could possibly be true, I finished it by the second day of the term, and when the teacher asked us a few questions about chapter one, I obliged with an outline of the entire book—to the consternation of the other pupils (some of whom had been unable to understand even the first chapter). Then, when the teacher gave us some simple addition to do, I also quickly polished that off and asked for more (while most of the other children were still struggling to get the answer to the first few problems).

"This is going to be quite easy!" I thought. Whereas I had previously been afraid that my lost time in school was going to be handicapping, I now saw that the reading I had been doing before school started (and that I had also done during my hospital stay) had put me well ahead of the rest of the class, and that they were going to have a devil of a time catching up to me, rather than vice versa. I also saw that my teacher, a young woman of helpful mien, was as nice as could be, and that I was really going to enjoy a year's sojourn in her class and be well prepared (since she let me forge ahead of the other students) for the next year's work, which—I could see by spying on some of the blackboards in a third-grade class—included some formidable-looking long division, in addition to the short division that we occasionally did in the second grade. So I leaned back comfortably in my seat and looked forward to every day's school activities.

After no more than two weeks in this second-grade class, catastrophe occurred. Without warning, I was called into the principal's office and told that since my teacher saw that I was doing so well and since the principal quite agreed with her, I was immediately—yes, that very day—going to be transferred to the third grade, where I would doubtless be able to do all the work just as easily as in the second grade and where I would thoroughly enjoy myself as soon as I got settled there. Wouldn't it be great, skipping a grade like this, and being placed back on my age level, where the other children would be a little older and just as bright as me?

"No!" I thought. "It wouldn't be great at all. I *like* the second grade and how I am doing there. I love my teacher and how attractive and nice she is. I *take to* the reading and the arithmetic and know I can do it well on the second-grade level. I *saw* the complicated long division on the third-grade blackboard and I'm sure I'm not ready for *that* yet. Great? Hell! It's a grim tragedy that they want to transfer me to the third grade without even asking my leave. How can they *do* a cruel thing like this to me? It's *awful*! I'll never be able to survive it and be happy again. What a horrible world this is, where, when you do your best, they still harshly penalize you for it!"

This is how I thought, but I naturally said nothing of the kind to the principal or to my second-grade teacher. I was always a nice little boy, a polite little boy, and I did almost anything they told me to do. Besides, I knew it was crazy, perfectly crazy, to argue against a sudden, well-deserved, distinctly unusual promotion from one grade to another, and one that I had been "rewarded" with after spending only two weeks in the second-grade class. All the other children, I knew, would have been charmed with such a promotion and would envy me for getting it. My parents would be delighted. My friends on the block would think it was marvelous. Then what the devil was I so sad and miserable about? If I spoke up and told the principal how I felt, he would think I was a real nut and might be mad at me. So I'd better smile, seem to go along for his (and my teacher's) ride, grit my teeth, and go through with the goddamned "promotion."

I smiled—wryly, I am sure—and traipsed out of the principal's office. Because it was close to lunch time, and I didn't want to go back to my classroom and face my teacher—whom I now practically *hated*—I started crying in the hallway, ran out the front door, and continued to cry all the way home. My mother, who rarely saw me cry and who was quite enthusiastic about my being promoted, couldn't understand what I was crying about. Although she was not practiced at soothing me (as I rarely complained about anything, while my brother and sister constantly did), she took me in her arms and kept repeating, over and over, "But that's grand! You'll now be a grade higher, and get through school faster. That shows how bright you are—and that your teacher and the principal fully recognize it. Of course you can do the third-grade work. The long division will be nothing for you—you're good at that kind of thing, which I never was. You'll like it, in the third grade, when you're only there a short while. And I'm sure the new teacher will be just as nice and sweet as the one you've now got and will help you and like you just as much. You should be proud of yourself! Only two weeks and they already see how well you do! Of course you can do beautifully in the third grade. How nice, how nice!"

That helped calm me down, and by the time I had finished lunch I had stopped crying and began thinking about the advantages of being promoted. My mother was right, I told myself as I walked back. I would now catch up with the other boys and girls my own age. I would get through school sooner and be able to go to work or to college sooner. I would be less bored in the third grade than I was already getting to be, at times, in the second. I would be able to do the long division and I might even enjoy doing it. I probably would have a very nice new teacher. Everything really wouldn't be as bad as I was imagining it to be. And my friends on the block, I was sure, would think it was great that I was so bright and that I had, within two weeks, caught up on the whole year's schoolwork that I had missed by being in the hospital. So things, after all, would not be as horrible as I at first thought they would be. In some ways, in fact, they would even be pretty good.

With my mother's help, I was already well on the way, within an hour of my "disastrously" learning about my "horrible" promotion, to Disputing (at point D in REBT) my Irrational Beliefs (IBs). I was lightly using the ABC's of REBT—which I had not yet invented! Not that I was doing this with the thoroughness with which I would do it today or with the elegance that I would use to help my REBT clients to employ. I was then, at the age of seven, using the form of Disputing that I have named the realistic instead of the anti-musturbatory approach.

As I noted in the previous chapter, when a young boy notices something very "wrong" or "bad" in his life—such as my being promoted long before I wanted to be—he experiences an Activating Event or Adversity (A) that he evaluates as obnoxious or harmful. This is because he *brings* to this Activating Event a Goal (or set of desires or wishes) and soon discovers that this is being thwarted. Thus, my Goal, or wish, was that I continue to remain in the second grade, do as well as I was doing, and be favored by my nice teacher.

Bringing this purpose, or Goal to point A (Adversity), I soon concluded that I was not really getting what I wanted and that this was annoying or "bad." In REBT we call this a Rational Belief (RB), because it was an evaluation that helped me see that A was obnoxious and that, if I still wanted what I wanted (that is, to stay in the second grade instead of being promoted to the third grade), I had better do something about it—such as speak up to my principal and teacher, induce my mother to intercede, or refuse to attend the new class. So although I felt the emotional Consequence (C) of sorrow, regret, and frustration, and although these were uncomfortable or "bad" feelings, I at first had a Healthy Consequence (HC), because it was unlikely to help get me more of what I wanted and less of what I didn't want.

I also, however, had a set of Irrational Beliefs (IBs) about the undesirable or "bad" Activating Events (A's). That was: "Because I don't like promotion, it *shouldn't* exist. I *can't bear* its happening! How *horrible*! The world is a totally unfair, rotten place for inflicting it on me!" These IBs (and not the "bad" A's) directly created my feelings of anxiety, depression, and self-pity—such as the depression I felt as I cried all the way home from school.

If this model of human disturbance is correct—and we have over a thousand psychological studies that tend to show that it is—there were various ways that I could have solved my dilemma of not getting what I wanted and remaining only healthily sorry and regretful but not unhealthily depressed and angry. I could, for example, change the Activating Events or Adversities (A's) so that they no longer existed. Or let them exist but focus on other things in my life (such as my other diversions or enjoyments). Or show myself that they were really not as "bad" or "obnoxious" as I originally viewed them. Or see them in a still unfavorable light but wisely accept the fact that unfavorable conditions are not horrible or awful (that is, totally bad) and that I could still lead a pretty good life in spite of the fact that they continue to exist.

Of these possible solutions to my problem of being promoted to the third grade when I didn't want to be promoted, I made no attempt to try for the first one: that of changing A and getting the principal and teacher to let me stay in the second grade until I was ready, of my own free accord, to be promoted. I knew (or strongly believed) that this would not work; and I also knew that even if it did, it held other disadvantages—such as everyone thinking I was a real nut for not wanting to be quickly promoted. So I never thought too seriously of objecting to my promotion and inducing the powers that be to change A.

Nor did I think much about trying the second possible solution to my problem: focusing on other things in my life and thinking so strongly about sports, movies, reading, friends, and so on, that I put my "horrible" promotion out of my mind and hardly thought about it at all. For one thing, this would have been impractical—I was supposed to show up in my new class that very afternoon, and how could I not be reminded of my "awful" fate when that fate was being forced on me right away? For another thing, I was so upset, at point C (emotional Consequence) about the "horror" that had just occurred to me that I literally became obsessed (as people so often do) with thinking about its "frightful" accompaniments, such as missing my new friends in the second grade, being without the help of my nice second-grade teacher, having to face the third-grade teacher (who, I had already heard, was a lot stricter than my present one), being forced to do long division instead of short division, and so on and so forth. These "grim" specters were so much on my mind that I certainly would have had trouble, even had I tried hard, in thinking of other, more pleasant things.

The third solution—that of downgrading the "horrors" of A—was the one that I (with the help of my mother) started to use. I couldn't convince myself that being in the third instead of the second grade was not at all bad or that it was good, because I had too many "real" reasons for thinking that it was against my own goals and interests and that therefore it clearly was obnoxious. But I could at least partly convince myself that it wasn't as bad as I first imagined it was, and that it had some good as well as bad points.

This is what I call the realistic, or empirical argument—a form of Disputing (D) of Irrational Beliefs (IBs) that often works very well, but it still can be highly inelegant and, usually, short-lasting and limited. If I am afraid of riding in elevators because of the "great danger" of their falling and my being killed in such a fall, I am (on one level of conviction) telling myself that it is highly probable that an elevator will fall and that I consequently will get killed or maimed if I am in it. This self-statement is, of course, unrealistic, since the actual chances of any elevator falling, and of my being maimed or killed when it does, are exceptionally small—say, about one out of a million—and consequently I have practically nothing to worry about.

I can therefore fairly easily contradict my false statement—"If I ride in an elevator, there is an excellent chance that I will be maimed or killed, and that would be awful!"—with the correct Disputation, "If I ride in an elevator, there is an infinitesimally small chance that I will be maimed or killed, and therefore I'd better (as millions of other people do every day) continue to use elevators and stop worrying about how 'dangerous' they are." I thereby contradict my original unrealistic, or anti-empirical statement with a realistic, empirically based observation or argument, and I presumably give it up and start fearlessly riding in elevators.

The trouble with this kind of Disputing is that it frequently (in fact, usually) doesn't get at the real root of my unrealistic fear of elevators, which probably is: "Under no conditions must I endanger my all-important, sacred life. And there is some possibility that, even though elevators are generally safe, the particular one I am about to ride in may not be, and may fall and kill me. Therefore I *must* not take the slightest chance that this very small possibility will come to pass, as it would be absolutely *horrible* if it did and if a sacred person like I were to die or get maimed!"

No matter how well and realistically I prove to myself that I will most *probably never* suffer seriously by riding in an elevator, as long as I hold the basic proposition that I must have an absolute guarantee that I will not, I will remain (consciously or unconsciously) anxious about riding in elevators; and even though I temporarily convince myself that it is safe to ride in one, I will tend to return, again and again, to my underlying fear of them.

The realistic, or empirically based argument, when it is used in Disputing, is a fairly good one, but it is inelegant unless it is used in conjunction with the anti-absolutistic or anti-musturbatory argument. In the case of the elevator, I had better ask myself, "Why *must* there be no condition under which my life is endangered? In what way is my existence sacred? How can I ever get a guarantee that I will always be safe in elevators? Prove that it would be utterly *horrible* if I did get maimed or killed in one." If I ask myself these questions and give honest answers to them, and then use the realistic, or empirically based argument to show myself that there is an exceptionally small likelihood that any elevator I take will fall and hurt me, the latter form of Disputing may well be effective. But by itself, without anti-musturbational Disputing, it often works only temporarily and lightly and doesn't solidly uproot my irrational anxiety.

In my school situation, just before my eighth birthday, I used the realistic form of Disputing to show myself that being promoted to the third grade before I desired such a promotion did not mean that I would only suffer; that it *would* have some real advantages; that I *could* adjust myself to its hassles and losses; and that I most probably *would* learn to tolerate, and even enjoy, the new grade and the new teacher. Although this wasn't, for the reasons I have just given, the most elegant argument I could have used to combat my anxiety and depression, it worked. I went back to school that afternoon, forced myself to thank my teacher for promoting me, went to my new teacher and was assigned a seat in her room, and settled down to gracefully lumping my "great" promotion.

As it happened, my realistic arguments proved to be correct. Within a week I found that I liked the work in the third-grade class (because it was more interesting and challenging); that my new teacher was not quite as nice as the old one but was a pretty fine woman in her own right; that my third-grade classmates were quite okay, didn't know much more than I did, and were friendly to me; and that almost everyone I knew, especially my male friends on my block, were delighted and very proud of me for being promoted so quickly and kept telling me what a bright boy I was and how well I would keep doing in life. So the okay condition of being in the third grade that I had predicted in my realistic form of Disputing turned out to be factual. It soon became a more pleasurable kind of condition than the second-grade situation that I had just left.

The way in which the realistic argument worked, however, may have been partially harmful as well as helpful. For although it brought me good (temporary) results, and I was satisfied to find that the depressed picture that I had first taken of being promoted didn't materialize, I think that I (like, alas, most youngsters and oldsters) falsely kept repeating realistic forms of Disputing for the rest of my childhood and therefore only rarely arrived at anti-absolutizing methods of combating my nutty ideas. This is what probably happens to most bright, and not too seriously disturbed, children and in an important sense is part of the "normal" (but not necessarily "healthy") human condition. Like myself, they dream up "horrors" about riding in elevators, failing at school, or being rejected by others, and they thereby make themselves very anxious (before these hassles occur) and depressed (after they actually arise).

Partially "knowing," however, that life's hassles are really *not* the "horrors" they imagine them to be (and knowing this largely because other children and adults seem to survive and even are happy with similar "horrors"), children realistically show themselves that they *can* risk going into elevators, studying subjects they may fail at, or trying to make friends with others who may reject them. They tell themselves, rather weakly but at least semi-convincingly, that it won't kill them to get stuck in the elevators, fail at school, or get rejected by other people. And they convince themselves, again somewhat flaccidly, that the elevators probably won't fail, that they may pass or do well at school, and that even if they sometimes get rejected by others, they will also find those who accept them.

Because these realistic arguments to some degree work, and because children who use them therefore lose a good deal of their anxiety and depression (and sometimes completely stop fearing elevators or failing at subjects), they wrongly think that these are very fine techniques of Disputing and they stick with them, and often with them alone, for the rest of their lives. Such reality-oriented Disputes often turn out to be valid (since how many times *does* an elevator fall and hurt you, once you force yourself to start riding in elevators?). Youngsters therefore sloppily conclude that these are virtually the only good arguments, and they therefore do not go on to develop more elegant forms of Disputing, such as anti-musturbatory techniques.

I saw this continually in the psychotherapists we trained at the Albert Ellis Institute in New York, Los Angeles, and other parts of the United States and Europe. A client contends, let us say, that she is devastated and perhaps is thinking of killing herself because her lover has just left her. "Why are you so desperate?" the therapist asks this client.

"Because this keeps happening to me. And now that it has happened again, I know that I'll never be able to make a permanent relationship with a man. Especially since I am now forty years old. There are no good men over forty in this damned city. And as soon as people see that I've lost out again, they'll all know I'm hopeless and that I just can't keep any man that I go with."

Hearing this, the REBT practitioner, especially one who is a neophyte, almost always jumps right in to realistically prove to this benighted woman: (1) Just because she has lost another lover hardly means she'll *never* be able to make a permanent relationship. (2) Her being older may *partly* but not wholly handicap her in looking for a partner. (3) There are certainly, in her city, at least a *few* good men over forty. (4) People may think she is a difficult person to get along with when they see she has lost this latest lover, but all of them surely won't see her as *absolutely hopeless*.

As I show my REBT trainees, these realistic (or empirical) arguments are okay; in fact, some of them are quite good. But they miss the crucial philosophical point that this woman is explicitly or implicitly holding: that she incontestably *must* win and retain a good lover and that if she doesn't do as she unequivocally *must*, she is a hopeless, rotten *person*. These therapists, who are quite bright and highly sophisticated, still very often stick mainly to the realistic instead of to the realistic *and* anti-absolutistic methods of Disputing their clients' Irrational Beliefs. When even REBT practitioners are so prone to do this kind of thing, you can easily see how natural is this low-level, inelegant form of Disputation, and how prone almost all humans are to employing it. So it was hardly phenomenal that I "successfully" used it in regard to being suddenly promoted to the third grade.

The next problem I came across in my young life was that of oral arithmetic. I always had a natural talent for arithmetic and had no particular fear of it—which I could hardly say was the case for many of my classmates, who, even when they were good at other subjects, were terrified of the arithmetic lessons and did poorly at most of them. Our third-grade teacher often gave us ten or twenty addition problems to do, and I almost always finished them long before anyone else in the class did. In fact, I usually finished them so rapidly that I had plenty of time to go back and check my results, while many of the other children barely had time to finish them without any checking. As for multiplication and subtraction, I was also quite adept, although not quite so fast as I was at addition.

What, then, was I afraid of? Nothing at all—if we were given a written test. As soon as I saw the teacher passing out paper for a test and then putting problems on the blackboard for us to tackle, I felt elated, for I knew that I would do well and most probably excel over everybody else.

My third-grade teacher, however, pulled a stunt that I allowed myself to get rattled about. In the addition and multiplication oral drill, she first asked us to yell out the answers to the problems in unison. Thus, she would say, "How much is seven times eight?" And we would scream out, some of us at the top of our lungs, "Fifty-six!" and she would smile and go on to the next problem. That kind of testing was fine with me, since I was usually the first one to yell out the correct answer, and then she and some of the other students would look at me admiringly, acknowledging that I was remarkably good at this kind of thing.

Then she tried a variation that most of the other children became somewhat panicked about, and that I, too, greeted with anxiety. She would ask, in the same manner as before, "How much is seven times eight?" but instead of having all of us answer, she would point to one of the students and say, "Harry!" or "Mary!" or "Albert!" and expect the one whom she called upon to immediately give her the right answer. If he or she did not, then she would say, "Class?" and the entire class would scream out, in unison, the answer she wanted.

Well, that was a little too much! Although I invariably knew the answer the teacher wanted, and rarely missed it in my head when she called on someone else to give it, I frequently became so anxious when she pointed directly at me and said, "Albert!" that I gave the answer hesitatingly or stutteringly, and sometimes even flubbed it completely. This was because—as REBT theory will tell you—I insisted to myself, when I knew I might be called upon, that I *had* to—yes, absolutely *had* to—provide her (and the rest of the onlooking class) with the correct answer, and that if I didn't, I would not only lose my well-recognized superiority at arithmetic but would actually be thought of as, and therefore surely become, a real dummy.

Hmm—quite a problem. If the teacher went through thirty kids in the class before asking me the answer to an arithmetic question, I had no trouble at all, once she said, "John!" or "Mabel!" in knowing the right answer and muttering it happily to myself. But if somewhere along the line she called on me, me, *me*, I could hardly hear myself think. I *knew* that I wasn't going to do too well—and that is exactly what happened. I screwed up the answer.

I was really perturbed about this. I knew that I had not lost my arithmetic ability and that I really *could* give the right answers to the teacher's questions—as long as I was not specifically called upon to give them. But I also knew that I could easily, when called upon, give the wrong answer or blurt out the right one hesitatingly, stupidly, with no confidence whatever (at that moment) that it was correct. So I started dreading, utterly dreading, the simple arithmetic exercise and began to see arithmetic as a horribly bad instead of a marvelously good thing.

I knew that this feeling of dread was wrong—because it caused me such pain—and I also knew, or thought I knew, that it was conquerable. What the devil could I do to get rid of it? I racked my mind for a solution.

I finally found a rather unique one, which I had first applied in another area. Just as I was good at arithmetic, I was also fairly good at spelling. There were a few words that I kept screwing up—such as *niece*, which I often spelled n-e-i-c-e—but I had a good memory and read a great deal more than the other children did, so I was always one of the best spellers in the class. The trouble with that was, whenever we had a spelling bee, I was one of the finalists. The teacher would line up ten girls on one side of the room and ten boys on the other side and read out words for us to spell aloud. After a short while, all the other boys would be knocked out of the contest (because as soon as you misspelled one word you had to leave the line and retake your seat in class) while two or three of the girls would remain to compete with me.

This wasn't exactly the greatest spot for me to be in, because if I missed a word at this point, the girls would win and the boys would go down to "disgraceful" defeat. Moreover, as the game approached its end, and I was the only boy vying with two or three girls, I would get two or three times as many words as each of my opponents. All the rest of the children were now back in their seats; the boys were cheering for me and the girls for their team, so I had everyone's eyes on me—and every word I missed meant that the girls would win once again, as they usually did, and that the members of the male sex would have to hang their little heads in shame.

A rough spot for me to be in! And one that would usually end in defeat, because it was rare that I was the last one standing, and frequently by the time I missed a word (which the teacher made harder and harder as the game proceeded), two or three girls were still left standing. This proved, of course, that once again boys were shown to be schmuckier than girls.

Although I liked being the last boy standing, and although I usually was in this one-up (on the other males) position, I didn't like losing and being seen as the Great White Hope who had ignominiously led—and I mean *led*—the boys to another inglorious defeat. So, just as I had begun to hate the arithmetic exercise, I also was starting to hate the spelling bee. What to do about that?

Fortunately, I soon hit upon a solution to this enormous problem. Because our class consisted of about twenty boys and twenty girls, and because the teacher wanted us all to participate in the spelling bee, I was not always picked as one of the ten male contestants, and about half the time I was only an onlooker. At first, this seemed to be a boon; being a member of the audience I wasn't in any jeopardy and could relax and enjoy the game. But then I came to see this as a handicap. If I were picked three or four times in a row, I was anxious the first time or two but lost most of my anxiety by the third or fourth time. Playing the game and getting used to its "dangers"—including the great "danger" of losing for the whole group of boys—seemed to become less fearsome the more I played. On the other hand, a day or two of not being chosen helped me build up my fears all over again, so I was therefore more anxious when I returned to the fray than I was when I left it.

I discovered, by serendipity, the human law that governs and encourages in vivo desensitization. Years later, in reading accounts of soldiers on the battlefield (especially during World War I when trench warfare was very prevalent), I learned that when first faced with this kind of open field fighting, almost all the soldiers were exceptionally frightened of being wounded or killed and that a good many suffered severe emotional breakdowns. But if a soldier, quite against his will, was forced to fight on the battlefield enough times, especially day after day, he frequently became inured to the death of others around him and to the possibility of his own death, and he therefore became considerably less fearful and often survived the front lines.

Though my situation was not exactly that dangerous, I found a corollary in the spelling bee. The more often I participated, the more desensitized to my fears of failing I became. I realized that even when I conspicuously failed—for example, when I muffed an easy word like *thought* by failing to include the *g* and was laughed at by the other members of the class (especially the girls) for failing—nothing terrible happened. I remembered it for the rest of the day, but everyone else soon forgot it, and even the few who later mentioned it to me did so with good-natured joking rather than with real scorn. And when I almost singlehandedly won the spelling bees for the boys but was defeated at the last minute by a girl who correctly spelled a difficult word while I, immediately after, incorrectly spelled another one, I found that I was still respected as one of the very best, and certainly the best male, spellers in the class. So losing didn't exactly put me in disgrace, even though it did not give me the victory that I always wanted.

Noting this phenomenon of in vivo desensitization, I decided to deliberately apply it to the arithmetic exercise. Instead of avoiding my teacher's eyes when she called on one of us to recite, I did just the opposite: I looked her directly in the eye, smiled confidently, and used whatever facial expressions I could to encourage her to call on me more rather than less, which she soon started to do. I think she saw that many of the children in the class—including me, at first—were frightened of failing at the oral arithmetic and, being a nice person, she didn't want to scare them. So she favored those who didn't seem to be frightened but who were eagerly waiting to be called upon. When I changed my mien and deliberately tried to show her that I was in the eager-beaver instead of the horribly scared category, she called on me more and more, just as I wanted her to do.

And, as I hoped, that did it. Being called upon almost every day to recite the answer to a problem, I *expected* to be on the griddle and therefore I stopped worrying about whether or not I would be. In fact, I sometimes did the opposite and worried that I would *not* be chosen to recite.

Then, just as soon as the teacher met my eye and was seduced by my (at first) false confidence into choosing me, I focused on my answer, my answer, my answer, instead of (as I had previously been doing) on myself, myself, myself, and what a louse I would be if I muffed the right answer. I forced myself, in other words, to be problem-centered rather than self-centered and by concentrating on "Let me see! Eight by nine is *what*? *What*?" I was distracted from thinking about myself—or, as we would say in REBT, from *rating* myself—and I therefore tended to do better than I had ever done before.

This may have been the first real time, when I was barely eight and in the third grade, that I got fairly solidly on to Rational Emotive Behavior Therapy. I think that virtually all attempts at solving the problem of disturbed feelings and dysfunctional behaviors are, to begin with, cognitive. The very act of problem solving itself is basically an intellectual activity, since it is almost impossible to solve a difficulty (except by accident) if you do not observe, see, or notice that you are having trouble and if you do not focus on it and think about possible solutions. Even after you tentatively think of a way to resolve it, and you try out that way, you then have to observe what the results are and check to see if these are what you really want. Finally, when you have tried the thought-out solution for a while, you do not get very far with what you have done unless you keep checking to see whether the alternatives you have chosen continue to work and will probably work in the future.

Practically all animals, then, have some kinds of (primitive or complex) nervous systems that enable them to react to what is going on in their environment and to act or change their actions so as to survive (and presumably be "happy") in this (to them) somewhat dangerous world. The human nervous system is unusually well-developed and culminates in a large brain, which includes a sizable cerebral cortex. Although the brain has two different hemispheres—one of them, the left, seems to be more "intellectual" or "cognitive" than the right—both hemispheres, as well as the interaction between them, produce many kinds of thoughts, and these thoughts, and the emotions and actions that accompany (and, to some degree, are an integral part of) them, help us to exist, grow, develop, and actualize ourselves. Human thought, therefore, is crucial to our existence but not absolutely necessary.

When we are confronted with feelings of anxiety and depression—as I was during my childhood and as virtually every other child also is—we "naturally" or "automatically" tend to try to think our way out of our emotional predicament and to change our undesired and self-destructive feelings. We primarily seem to do so by some kind of thinking or problem solving, and we often, at least partially, succeed. We are born constructivists. But thinking—as a great cognitive therapist, George Kelly, aptly pointed out in the 1950s—is not enough. Our thoughts and feelings incite concomitant actions. We play them out in practice and we thereby (very often) reinforce or strengthen them. If we think it is terrible to be rejected by others and we feel anxious or shy when we encounter them, we tend to withdraw from them, speak badly when in their presence, or otherwise act on our thoughts and feelings.

An enormous vicious circle then results. We think, "I *must* have Mary's approval and it is terrible if she dislikes me!" We concomitantly feel anxious whenever we see Mary or even imagine seeing her. We act by making ourselves stutter or go mute in Mary's presence and then perhaps avoid her completely. Then, because we act so badly, we think all the more that Mary must like us and that if she doesn't, then we feel all the more anxious about being in Mary's presence. Finally, we frequently give up and cease acting on our desire—we never approach Mary (or other people like her) any longer, and we practically become recluses.

The cognitive-emotive-behavioral method out of this dilemma, as REBT advocates, is to clearly and forcefully change our thinking, to convince ourselves that it is preferable but not necessary that Mary like us and thereby feel unanxious in her presence. But even if we don't consciously do this kind of rethinking—or, in REBT, Disputing (D) our Irrational Beliefs (IBs)—we can often implicitly do it by *acting against* our disturbed thoughts and feelings. Thus, we can make ourselves—yes, literally make ourselves—confront Mary and keep talking to her many, many times, no matter how anxious or otherwise uncomfortable we feel while doing this. And although this technique of in vivo desensitization is not guaranteed to help us overcome our horror of confronting Mary, if we persist at it and refuse to back away from her no matter *how* discomfited we feel by doing this kind of homework activity, we will most probably get better and better at what we are doing (conversing with Mary) and will tend to lose our horror of doing so.

Our in vivo activity will show us—empirically *show* us—that Mary will not (very often!) vomit and run away; that she will hardly take out a stiletto and plunge it into our heart; and that even if she does act in a nasty, blaming manner, our entire life hardly comes to an end. Moreover, we will find that we are still capable of being attracted to other women besides Mary—one of whom may be equally attracted to us. And we can see that even though we continue to be unmated, our lives are full of a number of other things besides sex and love, and we can therefore still be reasonably (and sometimes ecstatically) happy.

Rational or Cognitive Therapy, as Buddha, Confucius, Zeno of Citium, Epictetus, the biblical prophets, and many other philosophers and scholars have shown, is a highly effective method of personality change. Freud, Jung, and Adler, and especially the last of these three pioneering psychotherapists of modern days, also saw this—though Freud and Jung often downplayed cognition and ignored its crucial role in the more dramatic and emotional aspects of therapy (such as in the so-called transference phenomena). These pioneering therapists failed to emphasize too much, although they made brief favoring remarks about it, the behavioral or practical aspects of self-change.

Even cognitions—as we especially emphasize in REBT—had better be worked on and worked through if they are to be used effectively. As mentioned in chapter 1C, Émile Coué, early in the twentieth century, proposed the seemingly magical formula "Day by day in every way, I'm getting better and better!" But he realized that unless you repetitively and vigorously *drill* this thought into your brain, you get it and lose it, get it and lose it—and ultimately (ah, so often!) *really* lose it. And virtually all the religionists over the centuries have specifically told you what to think if you are to see the Light. They have also advocated everyday rituals (or activity homework) to follow, ranging from the simple lighting of candles and saying of prayers to the complicated routines of using phylacteries, following dietary regimens, or adhering to other religious procedures.

Modern behaviorists, starting with Ivan Pavlov and John B. Watson and going on to B. F. Skinner and Hans J. Eysenck, have strongly emphasized the action rather than the thinking parts of psychotherapy. Although they drag in cognitions somewhat surreptitiously—Skinner, for example, talks about verbal reinforcement and Joseph Wolpe about helping clients to change some of their misperceptions of "factual" reality—they still emphasize action-oriented techniques.

Rational Emotive Behavior Therapy was one of the very first forms of psychological treatment to wed the cognitive and the behavioral approaches, and it gives about as much emphasis to in vivo desensitization as it does to cognitive restructuring. It is not that today's Cognitive Behavioral Therapy would not exist if REBT had not been invented at the beginning of 1955, for it was already, at that time, in the therapeutic offing. But its present popularity, and most of the hundreds of controlled experiments that have now been done to support some of its main hypotheses, would have been delayed by a number of years had I not, in the mid-fifties, started to loudly and persistently beat the drum, against enormous opposition from the great majority of my colleagues, for the rational emotive behavioral approach.

The main point I am making here is that without having tried in vivo desensitization on myself, and without having used it successfully from my early childhood onward, I probably would not have come up with REBT as a favored therapeutic tool—or else I would have done so, perhaps, in the 1970s or 1980s instead of the mid-fifties.

Whatever our innate propensities to think, feel, and act in certain ways, we still learn by evocative experience. Fred Skinner, although often one-sided, continued to propound a basic psychological truth: practically all of us are natural hedonists. We continue to practice what we like (or what feels good) and drop from our repertoire what we dislike (or what feels bad). We are easily reinforceable (or rewardable) by one set of stimuli (e.g., bonbons or social approval) and we are easily penalizable by other stimuli (e.g., bitter-tasting food or social disapproval).

Skinner often de-emphasized the biological element (our innate reinforceability and penalizability) and stressed the environmental element (the external or environmental events that we find reinforcing or penalizing). But he clearly implied, and at times even stated, that reinforceability (or what I still prefer to call *hedonism*) is largely innate and genetic, and that therefore we all are practically compelled to do what we do by the "good" or "reinforcing" things that our environment presents to us and to stop doing the "bad" or "penalizing" things that it also presents.

This means, as almost all psychologists agree, that experience is crucial in what we learn and do not learn—and that therefore we often learn more, or more thoroughly, by actions than we do by mere words. This point is used in most schools of psychotherapy—but often without recognition. I am sure that I used it when I was an analyst, putting everyone on the sofa, making them free-associate, and spending lots of time on their goddamned dreams. Therapists, of whatever persuasion, are not stupid, and they almost all realize that, in the final analysis, actions speak louder than words and that if their clients are to change, and really change, they had better push themselves to act differently.

My own experience, during my childhood and thereafter, helped me employ activity homework assignments with my clients—and even, though hesitantly (and somewhat guiltily) employ them when I still called myself a psychoanalyst. I supposedly knew that insight into one's childhood and the connections between one's early life and one's present hang-ups produced "real" therapeutic change. That was my analytic credo, and I stuck faithfully by it. But I also *sensed* that this was not, especially in some cases, quite enough, and that some good old-fashioned ass-kicking was also required with some of my DCs (difficult customers). So I kicked.

Being by nature a skeptic, and seeing that the ass-kicking sometimes worked well and that psychoanalytic interpretations worked poorly, I asked myself why this was so and began to experiment more with activity and less with analytic interpretation. My skepticism was probably born, I now realize, partly out of my own use of in vivo desensitization from childhood onward. When, during my early days, I first used this kind of technique to help myself, I cannot truthfully say. But I certainly did use it in the third grade, when I was in my eighth year. And had I not—or, had I used it and it had failed to work—I would not have so readily incorporated it into REBT. So my starting, around my eighth year, to employ in vivo desensitization on myself helped me considerably at that time—and beneficially influenced me and the tens of thousands of clients who have since profited from REBT.

Let me not, however, gild the lily by pretending that I had only good therapeutic experiences during my early life and that virtually everything that happened to me at that time was used to construct a rational attitude toward life and later to be incorporated into REBT. Psychotherapy itself has its grave limitations—as I tried to make clear in a final and, I think, pioneering chapter in the first edition of *Reason and Emotion in Psychotherapy*. It certainly had its limitations when I used it on myself during my childhood. Either I sometimes didn't figure out any good techniques to help myself with my emotional problems or I devised a workable method but did not apply it very well. Or, far worse, I simply indulged in my needless suffering, accepted it as inevitable, and made no attempt whatever to undo it.

This was evidenced, for a long, long time, in my shyness about approaching girls with whom I was madly in love. In Ruthie's case, she was a neighbor whom I kept meeting on the street in front of my house and whose parents were quite friendly (till oh, that fateful day when we were caught naked). Therefore, I had no trouble meeting her, conversing with her, and becoming close to her. And in Gloria's case, I met her when she was actually a bedmate of mine—that is, had the bed right next to mine in the children's ward of the hospital—and therefore was easy to get to know.

I never really had any trouble talking to people once I encountered them. My mother and father, as I have noted, were super-encounterers. Left with a total group of strangers in almost any set of conditions, they would soon start talking and would almost always make friends with some—indeed, many—of them. Then they would have little trouble continuing the opening conversation and going on and on, ad infinitum. I, partly a chip off the old block, could mimic them nicely in the second part—the going on and on once I got to know someone—but not the first part, the encountering itself.

This held especially true for the girls in school whom I kept falling in love with. I recall that during my first year in school, and my very brief second-grade sojourn, I became quite enamored of at least one or two girls in each of my classes. I raced down the stairs to the lunchroom every day, to try to sit at the same table with one of the bright, charming young girls in my class. Whenever I failed, I was pretty miserable. But, as far as I remember, I never talked to the girl at all, even when we sat at the same lunch table. Although I showed off as well as I could in front of her, and talked loudly and brilliantly to the other people (mostly males) at the table so she could see what a great fellow I was, I completely avoided any kind of a personal conversation with her and waited (both patiently and impatiently) for that banner day somehow to arrive when we would spontaneously start talking to each other and would (or course!) confess our eternal, long-held love. Well, that day, as you can well imagine, never came.

What about my bloody shyness? Was it really that bad or was it specialized?

The latter, I guess. I got along with both children and adults once I had made some initial contact with them. I expressed my feelings quite well, especially to my male friends. I assertively suggested that my companions do certain things with me—even risky things like spying on girls urinating and taking long exploratory walks to distant neighborhoods. With both Ruthie and Gloria I was somewhat daring—once I got to know them. After some initial shyness, I raised my hand frequently to recite in class whenever I knew the right answer.

With new people, however, I was much more shy. With female classmates whom I dearly loved, I never opened my big mouth. When asked to formally recite or enact a role in a play before a class or—horrors!—a whole auditorium full of several classes, I froze. Why? Why those particular forms of shyness?

My reluctance to approach new people may possibly have been sparked by some feelings of shame I had about my mother being all too willing to converse with everyone—yes, everyone. Whatever stranger she encountered—in the park, in the subway, in the grocery store, you name it—she unhesitatingly spoke to. And often quite inappropriately, since she was unselective—really promiscuous—and not everyone welcomed her blunt overtures. Noting this, I was sometimes ashamed to have, and presumably to be negatively identified with, such a mother. So although I got along with her marvelously at home and truly was her favorite child, I sometimes avoided going out with her in public. But tactfully I didn't let her know this. Anyway, she hardly gave meeting new people a good name. Maybe that was one reason for my social shyness.

But fear of rejection and ego downing was certainly a factor, too. To get along socially with people *after* you meet them and they talk to you kindly is fairly easy. To risk *not* being accepted by them when you first encounter them is much harder. Still worse, it is harder to risk rejection and ridicule by a slew of people to whom you are making a formal presentation. Could Albert's ego risk that kind of potential public assault? Not during my childhood and early adolescence. Not before I really started working, especially from nineteen onward, on becoming more rational.

With the girls I adored, even monolithic rejection would have been—or irrationally seemed to me—horrendous. What a fool I would have seen myself if one of *them* told me to get lost. Too bad I never risked it and tested my hypothesis, but I stubbornly refused to do so. As I tell scores of my psychotherapy clients these days, the best way to preserve and enhance a phobia is to submit to it and absolutely refuse to do what you are scared witless of doing. Quite a phobia preserver was I in those dear dead—or should I say *dread*?—days of my youth. Alas and alack!

Not for many years did I overcome my shyness in encountering girls with whom I was decidedly in love—or even those to whom I was merely attracted. The next major candidate came into my life in the third grade, when I switched to P.S. 33 in the Bronx, after my family moved from Heath Avenue to West 190th Street. Why we moved, I am no longer sure—perhaps I never was. Perhaps we could no longer afford the brand-new apartment on Heath Avenue (nor, for that matter, the chauffeur-driven Cadillac car). Perhaps we—meaning, of course, my sister and brother—were too noisy for the landlord, who lived downstairs from us. Perhaps my brother was all set for the first grade in school, and my mother didn't want him to walk up the big hill that I had to walk up every day to get to P.S. 7.

Whatever the reason, we did move to West 190th Street, in between University and DeVoe avenues, to a not-so-new apartment house where we had, on the second floor, a six-room apartment: one bedroom for me and my brother, one for my sister, one for my mother and father, a kitchen, a living room, and a dining room. Not a bad place to live, but not a remarkably good one either, especially considering the brand-new, much larger apartment houses on University Avenue, which started to go up soon after we arrived, many of them with elevators. This, however, was a highly respectable middle-class neighborhood, about half-Jewish and half-Christian. The only complaint I remember having about moving was that I lost my old male friends from Heath Avenue. They now lived only about ten blocks away, but those ten blocks included a long, almost impossibly steep hill on Kingsbridge Road, which ran from Heath to Webb Avenue. No one in his or her right mind wanted to negotiate that hill—at least not on foot. In summer, the climb was hot as hell, and in winter it was grim with ice and snow. Therefore, the residents on the top of the hill (where we were now located) and those at the bottom (where I had lived on Heath Avenue) were almost perfect strangers to each other.

So I missed my old friends and was quite sorry about that. I even walked down the hill once in a while to see them. Going back up was another thing. Our friendship quickly dwindled, to be replaced by the new friends I made on 190th Street and in P.S. 33.

I loved my third-grade class in the new school, even though I entered it in the middle of the year. The young female teacher was charming (and, to my delight, specialized in English and in arithmetic), and the children were mainly bright Jewish children who knew almost as much as I did—but not quite! Why so many Jews? Because the Christians in our neighborhood were largely Catholic and didn't go to public school but to St. Nicholas of Tolentine, which was the largest Catholic parochial school in the Bronx. Later on, when Junior High School 79 opened up on Crescent Avenue, I left P.S. 33 at the end of the sixth grade.

To get back to P.S. 33: This was an old, typical Bronx public school on Jerome Avenue, near Fordham Road. To get there, I had to walk about six short blocks, but what busy and dangerous blocks they were! Aside from the Grand Concourse (which was also a few blocks away), they were the widest and most traveled streets in the Bronx, and if anyone wanted to get hit by a car, or by one of the steadily decreasing numbers of horses and wagons still on the streets, these were the streets to choose.

Nothing daunted, I maneuvered them without difficulty. I didn't *see* them as dangerous and I saw walking as enjoyable. I also liked the *challenge* of crossing the streets safely—with no traffic lights, remember, in those days and with traffic cops on the corners only at very busy daytime hours. So, while the other kids in my class often complained about the "dangerous" cars and were safely conducted to school by their parents or maids, I fearlessly braved the traffic alone—because I *viewed* it as more of an adventure than a hazard.

Here, again, I used REBT-oriented reframing to help me cope with life's hassles and dangers. But I did so quite unconsciously, and only many years later did I fully realize what coping techniques I was actually using. As many professionals and laypeople have spontaneously noted when first introduced to REBT, it is a "common-sense" approach to psychotherapy. So, in good part, was little Albert's approach to life in the early 1920s. I used my common sense to confront any problems or suffering that arose in my life. When my desires for success, for love, for justice, or for comfort and safety were thwarted, I tried to figure out how to satisfy them—or to live with the continuing frustrations.

Isn't that what practically all of us humans naturally tend to do— remove or cope with life's difficulties? Isn't this one of our main inborn constructivist traits, and one that enables us to survive and to be reasonably happy—or, at least, not too miserable? Surely it is. We actively make ourselves—yes, *make* ourselves—feel frustrated and unhappy when we encounter frustrations, and we also, very actively, thrust ourselves into coping with our deprivations. Biologically, as well as by social learning, we are self-upsetting and self-caring animals. Yes, *both*. Else we suffer immensely. Else we die.

As for my own uniqueness, I would say that I saw, early in my life, that I *could* usually cope and care. And, consciously and unconsciously, I was determined to do so, and worked at implementing my determination. I sensed that I was sufficiently intelligent and competent to handle the exigencies of my life. I had the energy to do so. Best of all,

I *enjoyed* using my ability and energy to change what I didn't like and *not* to suffer too much when I couldn't change it. I was probably a born *and* made coper. Great luck—and enjoyable effort!

Having, I think, natural low frustration tolerance (LFT), as previously mentioned, I nonetheless have acquired some HFT. As to the former, I am easily impatient (particularly when under the stress of having many things to do *quickly*); feel "disgusted" at many people's stupidities and inefficiencies; keep order at my talks and workshops in a firm, sometimes harsh, manner; firmly detest my clients' self-sabotaging habits (while accepting *them*—the clients—nonetheless); somewhat impolitely get rid of bothersome questioners after my public presentations; solidly train my clients not to call me, except very briefly, in between sessions; am quite rough on unsolicited salespeople; and so on.

At the same time—peculiarly enough?—I meet big hassles very well and rarely upset myself about them. For example, during a week's stay in the latter part of the 1980s at Dempsey Hospital in Connecticut for an infected elbow, I suffered severe frustration with little emotional pain. I really regretted missing seven full days of work—including a three-day training practicum in Dallas and four completely scheduled days at the institute. I had to cancel about seventy clients, five group sessions, one supervision session, one interview with a fellowship candidate, and one board of directors meeting. Not to *mention* missing out on hours of reading and answering correspondence and many other activities.

Although I immediately substituted other work (such as writing and some rational song composing), and that was fine, I still was exceptionally frustrated about the missed (and rapidly piling up!) activities. But I kept firmly—very firmly—telling myself: "Too damned bad! So some important things won't get done. Tough!" This worked for a bit; then, when it looked like my stay in the hospital would be prolonged, I strongly told myself: "Tough again! Now I am not sure *when* I'll get out of here. However long it takes, it takes! If I can't be at the twenty-second anniversary party of my Friday Night Workshop, that would really be bad. As would another week or two away from my clients and groups. But I'll survive—and they'll survive. Even if these older-age infirmities of mine keep taking their toll and interrupting my New York and out-of-town presentations, as long as I'm still alive I'll get *some* of them done and still appreciably help the institute keep going with the funds I bring in. At worst, I may one day have to retire completely from clients, workshops, and other things like that. How restricting that would be. Even then, I'll always find something interesting to do—such as writing or composing. And I might even get some lovely things done that I would not have otherwise gotten around to creating. *That* wouldn't be bad at all. Whatever happens, I'll cope. For sure!"

Ironic contrast: though probably *more* frustratable than most—as well as more impatient to eliminate hassles—in several ways I have unusually high frustration tolerance (HFT). Because, one, I powerfully dislike but *accept* inevitable limitations. Two, I vigorously keep reminding myself that they're *only* inconvenient, never horrible. Three, I imagine the worst that could occur and prophylactically accept that. Four, I quickly arrange to limit some of the limitations (e.g., have phone instead of face-to-face sessions with clients). Five, I substitute other things to do (such as writing more than I usually would). Six, I throw myself into whatever I can do and almost always become distracted by it and truly enjoy it.

So I handle my LFT by a philosophy of HFT. After using the philosophy of HFT for a while, my feelings of low frustration tolerance—or what I have also named discomfort anxiety and discomfort depression—go, and I am mainly left with peace and enjoyment. My low frustration tolerance—which my father had, too—is probably innate. So, too, is my tendency to work at overcoming it. Odd that I should have two opposing strong predispositions like these. But why shouldn't humans be basically, and sometimes dramatically, inconsistent? No reason.

Another illustration of my using high frustration tolerance to fight my low frustration tolerance relates to my tendency to be easily bored—and my tendency to fight this tendency. One thing that my stay in the Connecticut hospital dramatized for me is my severe allergy to boredom. Not that I was often bored while incarcerated, for I made sure that I was not. I wrote (especially parts of the original draft of this autobiography). I composed rational humorous songs. I read Flaubert's *Sentimental Education*. I looked a little at TV—I had no radio. I talked to guests and had phone conversations and phone therapy sessions.

Pretty busy!

At times, caught up in the steady stream of medical procedures, I could do none of these things. Only wait . . . and wait . . . and wait!

What a bore! Nothing in life will probably ever drive me mad, but boredom might come close. I really hate doing virtually nothing. I always, of course, think, observe, reflect, plan, plot, and scheme. But waiting uncomfortably for twenty minutes with your injured elbow soaking in saline solution or holding "perfectly still" for five minutes at a time while all the bones of your body are being computer-scanned is not exactly the time for clear thinking.

I really tried, however—yes, I tried. While spending an hour in a series of awkward positions for the computer to scan, I composed some lovely songs in my head, and that relieved the monotony. While waiting for my elbow to soak—again, in a very uncomfortable position—I had some phone sessions with my clients. That helped!

But distraction didn't always work—and when I was bored I was truly bored. I could *stand* it, but who needs it? I can easily see now, more clearly than I ever saw before, why I almost always keep so busy. Relaxation? Rest? Vacations? Who the devil wants them? Not me.

One of my greatest virtues, ironically, is that I bore easily—and loathe boredom. So I incessantly therapize, supervise, dictate letters, write books and articles, give talks and workshops, administrate, attend meetings, and do other things—almost any other things—to short-circuit boredom, lethargy, and apathy. I almost always succeed. Even in hospitals. But not as damned much as I would like to do!

Another more recent example of coping with pain and hassles was around June 2003. I had been suffering from diarrhea, high blood sugar counts, severe itching, and other uncomfortable symptoms. The last weekend of May, Debbie was particularly concerned about my diarrhea and paleness. She called for an ambulance and traveled with me as it sped up Park Avenue. We arrived at the hospital not a minute too soon. Within twenty minutes of arriving I was passing copious amounts of blood and black fecal matter. My colon was found to be severely infected and could have burst at any moment, which would have killed me. I had to have my large intestine removed and an ileostomy procedure done. After surgery I was on painkilling medication through a drip and was pretty much out of it, but Debbie was constantly by my side, didn't leave the hospital, and watched me and the hospital staff like a hawk. She noticed my breathing was becoming more and more erratic and she called for the doctors. I was rushed to intensive care. The problem, they found, was that I had been getting too much painkiller medication through the drip, and this had affected my respiration and heart. Again, I could have died.

Being a diabetic, I have to have my blood sugar levels constantly monitored. Debbie pushed for nurses to do so more often than they were doing it, and she was often met with hostility. The next morning, about 3:30 a.m., I was sent down to get a CAT scan, as my white blood cell count was extremely high, and Debbie had noticed that my color was unusually pale. She tried to rouse me to give me barium solution to drink before the scan as the radiologist asked her to do, but couldn't. She screamed for doctors, who found my unconscious state was due to my blood sugar level being 23—dangerously low. Any longer, and I would have been in a deeper coma or worse. I was immediately put on a glucose drip and revived.

Debbie tried frantically to improve things for me, and because of her great love and caring for me, she suffered far more than I did. Her tears often fell. Without her I probably would have died.

The next day Debbie told me that I awoke initially disoriented but regained clarity as the day went on and that I asked her to conduct an interview with me that could be sent to colleagues, clients, students, and friends to let them know how I was doing. Back to work despite being in hospital—no nonsense! I tried writing a little each day, but my writing was wobbly and I soon felt too tired to continue. There was still weakness, pain, and discomfort, and much recovering to do. When I returned home on June 25, I needed round-the-clock nurse care and was limited in what I could do. But I pushed myself to do all that I could. On June 27, I gave a three-hour workshop to visiting doctoral students—in my bedroom. With Debbie's help I attended to my correspondence and returned to my writing. On Friday, July 11, I gave a two-and-a-half-hour lecture to the institute's summer fellows—again in my bedroom, and that evening resumed giving my famous Friday Night Workshop, which I had been doing for forty-something years.

I returned to seeing clients and running groups. I had been scheduled to speak at the August 2003 American Psychological Association meeting in Toronto that year, but doctors were adamantly against my traveling. So I participated via telephone.

On the whole, I think I did very well, considering. I tolerated the pain; I tolerated the interruption to my work; I put up with some incompetent nurses who at times screwed up; and when I became aware of unhelpful and unkind actions of some people, I never hated them, only what they were doing. I was mostly exceptionally patient as I endured many painful tests and procedures.

I am still handicapped by my physical afflictions. I walk with a cane and my hearing will never be as it once was. But this doesn't stop me from continuing on, doing the best I can. Thanks to using REBT on myself—my creative pursuits, work, and pleasure with Debbie are still very much alive and kicking. Pretty good, I think.

Chapter 4B

Coping with Emotional Problems
Still More of My Low Frustration Tolerance and My Anxiety

As I read over the last section, several things seem dubious. Too pat. Conclusions too easily arrived at. First, let's take my LFT. I still think my strong tendency toward LFT was largely inborn. Consider how even the brightest among us steadily procrastinate about important things—like paying taxes!—and do innumerable sloppy jobs when we could take a little more time and effort and do much better. The whole unholy human race seems to have a good deal of LFT. Some of it, however, may well be learned. Infants obviously cannot do too much for themselves and have to wait for others to take care of them. They are also excused for forgetfulness, neglectfulness, and goofing off. So they can easily be trained, not merely born, to avoid and delay. At first, they acquire LFT kind of sensibly—for what else can they do? But why should they keep indulging in it later? No good reason!

In my own case, I often got away with a good deal of murder, just because my parents were not around to see that I didn't. I therefore could dress myself—sloppily. I could neglect my homework—easily. I could be careless about my dress—constantly. Who was watching to correct me and teach me "proper" conduct? Not my mother. Not my father. Not my nonexistent older siblings.

Being a problem solver, I could also figure out how to get away with even more murder than could other children. I took shortcuts to school, including a lot of jaywalking. I read for hours at a time, until my mother came home from her bridge or mah-jongg game and asked me to do some chores. I avoided doing gym work because my parents didn't really read my report card to see what I was lax about in school.

I played with kids who were younger than me and easier to get along with because my parents, again, had no idea about with whom I was playing or how I was avoiding certain difficult situations.

So I often plotted and schemed to do what I wanted to do, rather than what I'd better do, knowing that there was no one who was going to check up on me. My environment, obviously, favored my getting away with things. So I did.

Well, well—not exactly! There's always another side, I see. I still had to be the kind of individual who would go out of my way to take advantage of my environment. Not everybody would. My sister, for one, definitely would not—though she had the same opportunities to do so as I had. My brother Paul definitely would, and did—perhaps even more than I, and he got away with things even more than I did. I did so quietly, and he did so effusively. He frequently threw spitballs in class, refused to do his homework, broke family rules, and did almost everything else that he "shouldn't" do. A real rebel! And a noisy one, while I was a quiet one. So it obviously wasn't merely our you-can-get-away-with-it upbringing. We *dared* to get away with it—and he much more than I.

I think that I mainly had a kind of passive LFT, while Paul had an actively rebellious kind. When I didn't want to follow a rule—such as obeying the traffic rules on my way to school—I calmly managed to avoid it in such a manner that I rarely got into any trouble. Not Paul! He ostentatiously avoided the same rule and, sure enough, got into trouble. His teachers would call me to their room to speak to me, since they knew that I was his older brother and a "good" boy in school. "How can your brother be the way he is?" they would ask in a genuinely puzzled tone. "He's really very intelligent and he does fine work when he wants to do so. But he keeps throwing spitballs and disrupts the class. Why doesn't your mother get after him and stop him?"

Yes—why? Because, of course, she just let things be. She supervised us minimally and went about her own happy life—talking, talking, talking to her friends, playing bridge (badly, I am sure), and running affairs at the temple—that is, running the making of the snacks and the serving of them. Certainly not doing anything complicated.

So we were both somewhat encouraged by our culture—or at least by our parents—to get away with things. That significantly contributed to my LFT. But again I insist that my brother and I were born to cut corners and to figure out how to avoid doing what we didn't want to do.

I began teaching myself, at quite an early age, some of the main REBT principles of USA—Unconditional Self-Acceptance. When my LFT did me in, and when I only got penalized by others for indulging in it, did I really stubbornly refuse to damn myself and only negatively evaluate my "rotten" behavior? Yes, I often did. But not always. After I had done something "wrong" or "bad" and was criticized for doing it, I decided to watch it much more carefully in the future, but not to castigate myself right then. It was bad, I concluded, but I rarely decided that I was bad.

On the other hand, I was suspiciously overcautious about not getting into trouble in the first place. As I noted above, I was a "good" boy. This means, of course, that I knew darned well what was the right thing to do—and I consistently did it. But if I did the wrong thing, I accepted my mistake and refused to denigrate myself for it. Here we have an interesting difference between, say, anxiety and depression. When I first created REBT, I said that anxiety and depression were philosophically similar. In terms of achievement and approval, when you're anxious about doing something, you tell yourself in advance of doing it, "If I do it badly—as I *must* not—and if other people disapprove of me for this—as they absolutely *must* not—that's awful and I'm no good!" When you're depressed, you tell yourself pretty much the same thing, but after the fact rather than before it. Thus, when you've actually done something you consider wrong, and when you think that you are being disapproved of by significant others for doing it, you tell yourself, "That was wrong—as it must not be!—and I am being disapproved of—as of course I must not be!—and therefore I am no good and it is awful!"

Pretty similar, eh? Aaron Tim Beck, who fathered Cognitive Therapy almost ten years after I created REBT, insists that the irrational beliefs with which you create your anxiety and the irrational beliefs with which you create your depression are quite different and only partly overlap. True in detail, but not in essence. Thus, when you depress yourself about doing something wrong or bad—particularly to other people—you can easily think, "I absolutely should not have done that immoral act and because I did what I should not, I am not only pretty worthless, but also I don't deserve any goodness in life and will doubtless suffer the torments of hell forever!" With anxiety, you probably won't go quite that far, so the two feelings often include some different irrational beliefs.

Specifically—but not generally. In general, both anxiety and depression usually include the ideas that (1) you are wrong or mistaken; (2) others notice this and look down on you; (3) you are rotten to the core because of this; (4) you will most probably keep seriously failing and being severely disapproved of. So both Tim Beck and I are probably right. But I still say: If I can somehow induce you to only rate or evaluate the goodness and badness of what you think, feel, and do, and just about never rate the goodness and badness of your entire personhood, your essence, your self, your being, then you will rarely make yourself feel either anxious or depressed but just concerned about performing well and being approved of by important others.

Well, even before I originated REBT I worked on my anxiety and partly got myself to believe in USA. But not quite. I was so concerned about doing well and avoiding big pitfalls in my life that I often made myself overconcerned, and, according to REBT, overconcern is anxiety. Concern—and fear—are intrinsic to the human condition. Without them we would not survive. But overconcern gets rid of some of our trouble at too great an expense.

For example, I almost invariably am on time for appointments. I like that, get a good reputation with others, and function well at my therapy and my public presentations—and even my writing—because of it. But I'd better admit: I often go too far with my promptness. When I have to fly to another city to give a presentation, I am concerned about confirming the time, getting all my things in order, making sure I do not forget anything essential, checking on my means of transportation, and sometimes arranging several other "important" things. So I'm practically never late for a plane or a presentation. But I am so preoccupied with being early that I actually may waste time (especially by avoiding some important tasks) by being "on the ball."

Debbie, my wife, tends to be very efficient, as do I. She plans most things in advance and organizes well. Since 2002, she has accompanied me to every doctor/dental appointment, to every event I presented in New York, and to the major conference in California at which I gave presentations in December 2005. Whereas I would prefer to leave for a nearby appointment one hour ahead of time, she might prefer thirty or forty minutes. Instead of leaving for the airport three hours before a flight, Debbie may favor two and a half hours. If there are no traffic delays, her way gives us more prep time at home. If there are delays, my way will be more likely to get us where we're going on time. Is her way risky, or am I overconcerned about being on time?

So, much more than I often admit, I am overconcerned—worried—

about time and about carrying off various things well. But once I'm done, that's it. "Yes," I say to myself, "I really screwed that up this time. I foolishly did the wrong thing and perhaps acted badly to others. Stupid!" And I am even happy to have made this error, so that I can watch for it and avoid it in the future.

Ironically, when my clients lambaste themselves mercilessly for something "bad" that they have done, perhaps a number of years ago, I get right to work to show them that, yes, it was bad, but it is done, cannot be changed, and never makes them a "bad person." But I do this almost routinely, because I am really surprised to see, not how they keep remembering their foolish or immoral deeds, but how they keep senselessly berating themselves for having done them. I effectively talk them out of this nonsense, but I really am not too empathic. I don't quite see—or feel—how they can damn themselves when the vile deed is already done, done, done. How silly! Why should I do that to myself? I rarely do.

Again, however, I'd better watch it. My so-called USA is really only partial. I may at times feel anxious, though practically never depressed. And ego anxiety, I insist—even though Tim Beck doesn't—is lack of Unconditional Self-Acceptance.

I can ask once again: How come I practically never put myself down for my misdeeds, including those against others? Yes, I feel some remorse—some sorrow and regret for having acted badly. And, as noted above, I nicely use this regret to encourage myself to act better in the future. But why aren't my regret and my guilt about my actions stronger, leading to self-damnation? I can think of several reasons for this, all of which may have some validity:

1. I am something of a natural-born pragmatist. What's done *is* done. So I have pragmatically accepted that fact since my teens, and perhaps before. What good will it do me to flagellate myself for my wrong deeds? Will it help me improve them in the future? No! If I am a louse for doing them, how can a louse act, in the future, unlously? Not easily.

2. Because I have practiced for many years not demeaning my self, my personhood, for my wrongdoings, I also easily forgive others for theirs. I don't hold grudges, I rarely keep remembering how others have wronged me, and I am certainly not preoccupied with vindictiveness. I don't see why they should damn themselves, so I practically never damn them.

3. I am solidly against needless pain—my own and other people's. I don't want any of us to suffer gratuitously. Therefore, I steadily focus on how uncomfortable pain is and what can quickly and decisively be done to eliminate it. Consequently, I don't feel much of it myself—real self-denigrating guilt—and I think that I gloss over, and hardly emphasize, other people's pain. I am so absorbed in helping them get rid of or at least reduce it that I have great difficulty awfulizing about it. Because I really don't focus on others' pain very strongly, I thereby avoid condemning myself if they think I cause them to experience it. I am just not that sensitive to it as I presumably should be. So I hardly down myself about contributing to their pain.

4. Actually, this may be the other way around. Not everyone is as sensitive to others' pain and troubles as he or she "should" be. Psychopaths definitely are not, and people with their own deficient feelings—some of them actually brain-injured—are not. Although I am hardly a psychopath in the usual sense—because I largely spend my life helping rather than bilking people—I could have some of a psychopath's kind of insensitive quality. If I do "naturally" have it, maybe that is why I easily focus on reducing my own and others' pain rather than on dwelling on it. Interestingly, however, I think that since being with Debbie I am more other-directed than I used to be, and more sensitive.

5. Still another possibility: Because I suffered so much pain and deprivation when I was a child—considering my neglectful parents and my long history of nephritis and other physical handicaps—I may have been so horrified by pain and deprivation that I was practically forced to defensively develop an early philosophy that drove me to avoid it. If so, I could have escalated my overconcern and anxiety and thus stayed out of the kind of social and school trouble that my brother Paul kept getting himself into. I could have also defensively reasoned that behaving badly was quite unfortunate, but what's done is done, so why beat oneself up about it?

Well, there I go again! The more thought I give to why I behaved in specific ways during my early and later life—or what is my so-called personality and what accounted for it—the more hypotheses I come up with. And conflicting ones! The whys of anyone's human nature are indeed difficult to accurately access. Often, probably, impossible.

Aside from what I have just said, let's look at the "facts" of my low frustration tolerance (LFT). Do I have some reasonably good evidence with which to back up my mainly self-made diagnosis? I think I do. I seem to have been born impatient. I do practically everything fast—not only because of my rapid-fire reaction time but because I want to get *started* pronto. Do I think before I leap? Yes, but briefly and semi-impulsively. When asked to do something, I usually immediately say yes or no. Why? Because I like to get things settled, and although I am well aware that I may make a mistake with my yes or no, I accept that fully—and lightly. So I'll be wrong! So people will hate me! I'll learn from my mistakes and use them to do better in the future. Put myself down for making them? Never. Well, hardly ever. I did this somewhat more when I was a child, but even then I was really anxious about being rejected by others—especially the young girls whom I loved—and not too much about my own acknowledged errors. I even liked making mistakes—I enjoyed *learning* by them.

As I grew older—especially after the age of nineteen—I abolished much of my anxiety about social rejection. I still *cared* for significant people's approval, but not that much. So, if my requesters didn't like my saying no to them, I wasn't particularly bothered. It was too bad, but hardly *awful*! My relative indifference enabled me to be even more quickly decisive than I was as a child. Today, more than ever, I can afford to be impulsive. And I like it.

Other people, however, often block my impulsive reactions. They talk slowly. They come late to appointments. They haggle—like my mother endlessly did!—over making simple purchases. They argue over insignificant details. They fart around. They do things at tortoise speed. They block my way on the streets and at airports. They procrastinate on promised presentations. You name it and they do it. Or refuse to do it quickly.

What a royal pain in the ass. Would I like to murder these slow-pokes and delayers? Frankly, I sometimes would, however, that would certainly be a little too bloody and I've never resorted to violence. I just wish—and I would say strongly wish—that all the slowpokes I encounter would quietly drop dead. Did I give much thought to their bereaved friends and relatives if my offenders did fortunately drop dead? No.

To make matters worse, although I have campaigned against bigotry and racism almost all my life, my impatience and other forms of LFT have made me quite bigoted at times. No, not against blacks,

Asians, or foreigners in general. But against ardent nationalists—including American nationalists. Even before Hitler showed me (when I was in my late teens) how bad nationalism was, I spoke and wrote against all kinds of extreme patriots, nationalists, and jingoists, because those I personally knew had not exactly been raised to be bigotedly nationalistic—they had *chosen* to be so. So I was bigoted against these bigots and despised just about all of them.

Similarly, I always resonated favorably to the famous statement of James Thurber and W. C. Fields, "Anyone who hates dogs and children can't be all bad." Right on! I liked children, of course, when I was a child, got along well with just about all of them, and even did some enjoyable babysitting when I was ten or eleven. But I lost it in my teens. I found most young children too noisy, rambunctious, and uncontrollable. Tell them what to do and they generally didn't do it. So I quietly avoided them, and only on occasion enjoyed talking to and watching my friends' and relatives' youngsters.

I frequently quote the famous statement of Mme. de Staël in this respect. Though a well-known novelist who portrayed many romantic and familial settings, she neglected her three children, stayed in Paris quite a distance from them, and rarely spent any amount of time at home. When chided for being a "bad mother," she replied, "I never find it interesting to converse with any person below the age of twelve." On the beam! I admire her sentiments—and her guts, for so honestly expressing them. I like to *observe* children, for I am curious about all aspects of human behavior. But being with them for more than fifteen minutes and trying to *converse* with them—not my thing! My impatience, my LFT, rises to the fore.

Having my own children, then, is not for me. So, with the full consent of my wives and mates, I never produced any that I raised. I tell people who ask me about this that I would make a "rotten father" and that this would be unfair to my possible children. True. Like Mme. de Staël, I would be too busy with other things—my fifteen-hour workdays consisting of (yes, alas, I sleep about seven and a half hours every day) continual rounds with my clients, supervisees, administration duties, lectures, workshops, writing, reading, and so on, not to mention my constant out-of-town traveling—for from one to three days, almost forty weeks a year when I was free to travel without nurses prior to June 2003. All this, I say, would be unfair to my children. So it would be.

But parenthood would be unfair to me, too. I probably wouldn't be overly impatient with my own brats. But in my heart and guts I would most likely seethe. About? The noise, the procrastination, the whining, the chores to be done by me and my mate to keep the children in order. And the time it takes to tend to all of the above. My lands! My life!

Now that I've mentioned time, let me note how important this is in my own general life and how it greatly contributes to my LFT. I think I have always, since my fifth or sixth year, been aware of time. Too aware. I have rarely been late to anything. I get to bed regularly before midnight to make sure I get enough sleep to be wide awake and energetic the next day. I set my alarm (since the age of seven) and get out of bed within two or three seconds of its going off. I set aside limited amounts of time every day for bouts of pure pleasure—such as listening to music, reading for fun, and even having enjoyable sex and lovemaking. Yes, pleasure is good, but more productive, long-range hedonism—such as I find in writing, reading the professional literature, and working hard to help my clients and supervisees—is even better. So I make sure I get enough of this kind of satisfaction by plotting and scheming to allot my available time.

As I grew into my early adulthood, I even developed a time neurosis and worked to overcome this during the period I was being psychoanalyzed in my mid-thirties. As noted previously, I was too careful about always being on time and saving time. This was largely because, although I had talked myself out of directly needing others' approval, when I was in my early twenties I still was too much in need of achievement. Or was I?

I most probably was born and reared with a strong desire for mastery and achievement. I didn't get this genetically from my mother's side, for she and her full brother Heinie and her sisters Sarah, Florence, and Teenie only seemed to moderately strive to do well in life. Her half-brothers Sol, Julius, and Ben, however, were brighter than her full siblings and were definitely more achieving. On my father's side, his siblings—Joe, Mike, and Rose—were quite bright and goal-oriented, as was my father himself. Did any of them absolutely need achievement to value themselves as persons? I suspect so, but I really don't know. Mike, the failure of the four, was an alcoholic and probably drove himself to drink for not being as accomplished as he presumably *should* have been. But I am guessing here, too.

Anyway, I can't remember a time when I was not achievement-oriented, especially academically. With the help of a friend, I taught myself to read at the age of five, before I started first grade. I then broke all records for reading, and when a curious public librarian asked me why I took out two books every day—the maximum one was allowed to borrow—and soon had trouble finding interesting books of fiction and nonfiction that I had not already read—I replied, "I just naturally like to read." She thought that was great and went out of her way to keep me supplied with new books.

Learning was my thing. I pushed myself to excel in all school subjects—notably literature, arithmetic, and spelling. I became a proud mentor to my friends, my classmates, and my younger brother Paul. I had great desires to learn and teach, to teach and learn. When I graduated from junior high school at the age of fourteen, my yearbook designation was "Encyclopedia—knows everything." Both the Freudians and the Adlerians might well say that I thereby compensated for my physical and athletic shortcomings.

As a very young child, I was tall and well built enough—though, like both my mother and my father, always on the thin side. So I ran and played in athletic games as well as the other boys did. But when at the age of five I was stricken with serious strep throat, I developed acute nephritis for the next few years, was hospitalized seven times, and was semi-invalided and kept away from physical sports between my fifth and seventh years. After I eventually recovered completely from the nephritis, I participated moderately well in baseball, handball, sleigh riding, and other sports. But I continued to be thin and frail and only excelled at walking and dancing. My brother Paul, nineteen months younger than I, was unusually good at most sports and consistently beat me at all the athletic games, such as handball and tennis, that we played together.

So maybe, maybe, maybe after the age of five, I gave up on trying to outstandingly achieve in physical pursuits and took to intellectual ones instead. Until, at the age of thirteen, I really found sex! My own guess, however, from over ninety years of self-observation, is that I was born distinctly more of a sexualist than a sensualist. Physical activity, especially walking and Ping Pong, is fine—but not exactly ecstatic. I like taking a warm shower or lying under a thick comforter on a cold night—but only for a short period of time. Not so with reading, writing, engaging in philosophical discussions, talking my clients out of their irrational beliefs, and various other intellectual pursuits. I can— and do—get lost in them for hours. And I wish I had more time—lots more time!—to pursue them, which brings me back to my lifelong preoccupation with time. Much—perhaps most—of it seems to be sheer desire, not dire necessity. I *enjoy* being alive and awake. I don't dislike being asleep too much, as I have hundreds, thousands of interesting dreams. But if I really had my druthers, I would love being awake all the time and extending each day for at least twenty-four additional hours. Life is good—and sleeping it away is often relatively dull.

I also realized, I think by the age of fifteen, that human life is short, and I fully accepted the fact that none of its precious minutes, once they have passed, can be regained. They are gone. Kaput. If so, I convinced myself, time is the essence. Money is good. Love is fine. Achievement is important. But all of these, once lost, can later be found or earned. Not time. The less time I have, moreover, the less I can enjoy money, love, achievement, and other pleasures. I'll be dead and unenjoying for a long time! So I'd better use, and use to the full, the meager time I have to be alive and conscious.

That sounds pretty realistic and practical—doesn't it? I like living, aliveness is limited, so let me not waste the time, whatever it is, that I shall actually have. Let me preserve it (health-wise) and use it (pleasure-wise). With what pleasures? Well, that's really up to me—and I'd better make it up to me. Let others enjoy what they will. They can recommend their personal and social enjoyments. Okay—let them. I'll listen—but consider. Seriously consider whether their thing is really and truly my thing. If it isn't, it isn't. If they dislike me for choosing my enjoyments and not theirs, tough. As long as I do not childishly rebel or needlessly harm them, I'm for me. Not exactly completely. But mainly.

In terms of the time I have available, I'm rather peculiar and partially compulsive. As a teenager, for example, I disliked jazz and the big bands when my peers were storming the Paramount Theater in New York to laud them. Later, in the 1950s and 1960s, I abhorred rock and roll, when almost everyone was mad about Elvis Presley, the Beatles, and scads of other noisy rockers. From childhood onward I loved melodic popular songs, and at thirteen, I became devoted to romantic operettas and within a few years was probably one of the world's leading authorities on the works of Jacques Offenbach, Johann Strauss Jr., Victor Herbert, Franz Lehar, and above all, Rudolf Friml. I could recite the composers, the date of composition, the lyrics of the leading songs, the melodic ratings of these songs, and other important facts about hundreds of well-known—and not so well-known—musical comedies and light operas. I won several prizes on the basis of my knowledge and letters of thanks from musical historians, such as J. Walker McSpadden, whom I gently corrected when they made mistakes in writing about this kind of music.

Did any of my contemporaries care about my favorite music? Hardly a one. Did I care about their poor tastes and their neglect of "great" songs and arias? Hardly a bit. I calmly and thrillingly went along my unusual merry way, listened most enjoyably to every operetta presentation I could dial on the radio, sang and whistled hundreds of fine songs to myself (and occasionally to my vocally inclined mother), and continue these somewhat odd pursuits up to the present day.

This is just to show that time I choose to spend on enjoyments is rather uniquely chosen largely in conjunction with my own fairly innate tastes. As I write this, I now see that these tastes are somewhat contradictory, even paradoxical, but that hardly stops me from catering to them. I said above that I am largely intellectual, rather than physical. But my musical tastes are (1) very sensual, (2) quite physical, and (3) far from intellectual.

Thus, although I admire classical (as well as semiclassical) music, I am easily bored by much of the "intellectual" music of Bach and his close relatives, by Palestrina, Handel, Haydn, and other (to my ears) nonmelodic composers. On the other hand, I love the romantic melodists like Grieg, Tchaikovsky, Delibes, Bizet, Verdi, Puccini, Debussy, Ravel, and Delius. So, obviously, I am sensual, romantic, and physical—*and/also* intellectual, classical, and academic. Not to mention clinical, helpful, and people-oriented. Not to mention, even in my therapy, theoretical, scientific, and experimental. Not to mention intuitive, guessing, risk taking, and once again experimental.

Am I really all of the above? Yes, but not necessarily at the same time or under the same conditions. Moreover, all these contradictions and paradoxes are not as contradictory as they may first appear. Science, for example, is rigorous, empirical, theoretical, and intellectual. But it is also intuitive, risk taking, directed by human goals, pragmatic, idealistic, and humane.

So why be surprised that I, as well as practically all people, have these important "contradictory" elements? Perhaps we really have to have them—and synergistically use them—to survive. Indeed, to happily survive.

Time out for reflection. Yes, I am contradictory and paradoxical, have both LFT and HFT, am too careless and too compulsive. Who isn't? Who can be consistently on the ball—or always sloppy? And nicely survive?

By way of illustration, look at my highly erratic—and steady—songwriting, which I mentioned in chapter 2B. When I was sixteen, I lived for a month at the Empire Hotel on West 63rd Street because my brother Paul had scarlet fever, our apartment was quarantined, and if I stayed at home I would not be able to attend school, take my final exams, and start preparing to go to college. So my father, for once, was very responsible, picked me up at school, took me to the Empire Hotel, paid a week's bill, gave me $50 in spending money (a huge sum!), and said I'd be on my own for perhaps several weeks until the quarantine was lifted.

That was startling, as I had never been away from home except for several hospital stays, and now I was literally alone, especially on weekends, day and night. Okay, I would make the best of it—and did. I did my school homework, read, and splurged like hell on musical films and shows—thirty shows, as I recall, in thirty days. That season was a heyday for both Hollywood and Broadway, and I adored seeing—and sometimes re-seeing—*The Vagabond King*, *Broadway Melody*, *The Desert Song*, *Rio Rita*, and other great musicals and stage shows at the Roxy, the Capitol, the Paramount, and other large movie houses. Stupendous! Ear-thrilling! And all within walking distance of the Empire Hotel.

One Saturday night, after seeing two musicals that afternoon and evening, I not only began to compose music in my head—an old habit of mine—but also to start writing lyrics for some of my tunes. That began, aside from other forms of writing, my most consistent hobby. First, I imitated the mushy songs of that day but with much more complicated rhyme schemes, then I moved on to more literary, anti–June-Moon lyrics. Finally, still in my teens, I took classic themes from Tchaikovsky, Grieg, Delibes, and other fine melodists and turned them into sensible, moving, highly singable songs. Here are some of them.

"Dead Liberty Will Rise Again"
(Tune: Tchaikovsky's Fifth Symphony)

As truth, beheaded by obscurant thrust,
Grows fiercely piercing eyes again:
So, fashioned subtly from skeletons' dust,
Dead liberty will rise again!
Not from mystical fancy or fating
Or luck that's rarely rife:
From psychophysical thirst unabating
Inciting to flesh-and-blood strife!

As passion, sacked by impuritan breath,
Knits reinflaming ties again:
So, resurrected from immature death,
Dead liberty will rise again!
Not from nature's logistical aiming
Or God's avenging knife:
From paveless graves of mere humans acclaiming
Their liberty dearer than life!

"My Heart Is In Repair Again"
(Tune: "Tales from the Vienna Woods" by Johann Strauss Jr.)

My heart is in repair again,
And I a love-splint wear again!
And languor fills the rest of me,
Since love has got the best of me!
I promised to take care again,
I swore that I'd beware again:
But love came calling kindly,
And before I knew it, well,
I just tried to woo it well;
I opined me that unblindly
I for once would do it well,
So I wouldn't rue it well—
And my heart's in repair once again!

"If I Loved Thee As I Love Me"
(Tune: "Narcissus" by Ethelbert Nevin)

If I loved thee
As much, dear, as I love me,
Our life would be
The sheerest of lunacy!
If you loved me
As you love thee,
The most insaniest,
Maddest, zaniest
Real crack-brainiest
Lovers we'd be!
If I loved thee,

As much, dear, as I love me,
Our life would be
A spree of the first degree!
So let's agree
That we love we,
And be emphatically,
Most ecstatically crazy!

"Love and I Are Quits"
(Tune: "In the Hall of the Mountain King" by Edvard Grieg)

Once I was a fool in love,
Just a wild mule in love;
Now I've gone to school in love—
And love and I are quits!
I've slipped the deadly stuff of love,
Known the real rough of love;
Now I've had enough of love—
The shoe no longer fits!
In loving one expects to see
Joy and sweet ecstasy;
Instead I was perplexed to see
Problems—and more!
I wanted just a touch of love,
Never too much of love,
But felt the steely clutch of love
Right to my core!
I asked for just a bit of love,
Not a wild fit of love,
But fell into the pit of love
And lost my very wits.
But now I'm through with pairing off—
Boy, am I swearing off!
At least, till our next squaring off,
Love and I are quits!

"Peace Be with Love"
(Tune: Frederick Chopin's Prelude)

Peace be with love
Now that peace is with men,
And the once-grounded dove
Is on high once again.
Peace be with love,
Where democracy's found,
And aggressors don't shove little people around.
War is behind us,
But let it remind us
That if we have a love of peace
Peace of love is bound to find us!
While liberty's light
Now shines down from above,
Darling, let us unite,
And let peace be with love!

I really loved my songs, thought they would be stupendous hits if published, and did some unusual things to get publishers to listen to them. For example, I would get a female friend to pretend she was a long-distance phone operator and call the president of a large publisher, giving him a spiel like, "This is Hoagy Carmichael. You remember me, don't you? I met you a while ago at an ASCAP dinner. Well, I'm now in Hollywood, working on a score for a new film, and I just met a young kid who's one of the best damned lyricists I ever saw. Incredibly good! An original. He has some songs like you've never heard. None of that June-Moon stuff. Really intelligent lyrics. Fabulous. His name is Albert Ellis and he lives in New York. You've got to hear him and his songs! When can you make it next week to listen to some of them?"

Believe it or not, this line worked several times, and no one questioned who was calling. I did make several audition dates with publishing bigwigs and brought along a friend to play and sing several of my songs. Result: total flop. All the publishers said that my lyrics were good—too good for mass audiences. Too literary, much too high-class. Wouldn't sell. No takers.

I got nowhere with publishing, but I continued my songwriting hobby, while I went about my otherwise busy life. Now here is how my HFT-LFT paradoxes helped me—and did me in.

HFT: I kept writing songs in the hope that one day they would be published.

LFT: I only occasionally tried for auditions, in person or by recordings, though I knew that songwriters who were published played in Tin Pan Alley constantly before they were accepted.

HFT: When my serious songs got nowhere, I went on to rational humorous songs, used them in my workshops and talks and with my individual and group therapy clients. Some of them have been raving successes, including these, from my recent book *The Myth of Self Esteem.*

"Perfect Rationality"
(Tune: "Funiculi, Funicula!" by Luigi Denza)

Some think the world must have a right direction,
And so do I!—and so do I!
Some think that, with the slightest imperfection,
They can't get by—and so do I!
For I, I have to prove I'm superhuman,
And better far than people are!
To show I have miraculous acumen—
And always rate among the Great!

Perfect, perfect rationality
Is, of course, the only thing for me!
How can I ever think of being
If I must live fallibly?
Rationality must be a perfect thing for me!

"Love Me, Love Me, Only Me!"
(Tune: "Yankee Doodle Dandy" by George M. Cohan)

Love me, love me, only me
Or I'll die without you!
Make your love a guarantee,
So I can never doubt you!
Love me, love me totally—really, really try, dear.
But if you demand love, too,
I'll hate you till I die, dear!

Love me, love me all the time,
Thoroughly and wholly!
Life turns into slushy slime
'Less you love me solely!
Love me with great tenderness,
With no ifs or buts, dear.
If you love me somewhat less,
I'll hate your goddamned guts, dear!

"You for Me and Me for Me"
(Tune: "Tea for Two" by Vincent Youmans)

Picture you upon my knee,
Just you for me, and me for me!
And then you'll see
How happy I will be, dear!
Though you beseech me
You never will reach me—
For I am autistic
As any real mystic!
And only relate to
Myself with a great to-do, dear!
If you dare to try to care
You'll see my caring soon will wear,
For I can't pair and make our sharing fair!
If you want a family,
We'll both agree you'll baby me—
Then you'll see how happy I will be!

"Glory, Glory Hallelujah!"
(Tune: "Battle Hymn of the Republic" by Julia Ward Howe)

Mine eyes have seen the glory of relationships that glow
And then falter by the wayside as love passions come—and go!
Oh, I've heard of great romances
Where there is no slightest lull—
But I am skeptical!
Glory, glory hallelujah!
People love ya till they screw ya!
If you'd lessen how they do ya

Then don't expect they won't!
Glory, glory hallelujah!
People cheer ya—then pooh-pooh ya!
If you'd soften how they screw ya!
Then don't expect they won't!

"I Wish I Were Not Crazy!"
(Tune: "Dixie" by Dan Emmett)

I wish I were really put together—
Smooth and fine as patent leather!
Oh, how great to be rated innately sedate!
But I'm afraid that I was fated
To be rather aberrated—
Oh, how sad to be as mad as my Mom and my Dad!

Oh, I wish I were not crazy! Hooray! Hooray!
I wish my mind were less inclined
To be the kind that's hazy!
I could, you see, agree to be less crazy—
But I, alas, am just too goddamned lazy!

"Makin' Whoopee!"
(Tune: "Makin' Whoopee!" by Gus Kahn)

If you should try
To bother me
I soon apply REBT,
Which gives me reason
In any season
For makin' whoopee!
So do your best
To make me mad
But I attest
"That's just too bad!"
With rational thinking
I keep from sinking
And acting loopy!
Try as you may to floor me,
You will never succeed.

Zap me with words quite stormy,
You'll see that I don't bleed!
So do your worst, dear,
From A to Z,
I still will burst out
Quite rationally!
Howe'er you treat me,
With REBT
I'm makin' whoopee!

LFT: I recorded a few of these rational humorous songs in 1977, and the Albert Ellis Institute has done well with a cassette and a songbook published at that time. But I have procrastinated on recording many of them for the last twenty-plus years.

HFT: I never specifically sit down to write new songs because I do so many other things. I wisely wait for my out-of-town trips to do so, thereby putting off immediate pleasure—for I enjoy writing the songs—for future greater gain. I write most of them in taxis on the way to and from the airport, when I am usually unable to read or do other productive work.

LFT: When I can write more songs or finish off old ones, I often don't feel like doing so, lazily procrastinate, and get fewer done than I might otherwise do.

HFT: I persist in writing highly complicated, cleverly rhyming lyrics when I could often get by with easier, simpler ones.

As you can see, I solidly labor away at my songwriting—and I don't. I procrastinate and goof—and I Push My Ass (PMA, in REBT) to stop such crap. My LFT and my HFT are both highly intermittent. I foolishly dawdle and I intelligently start all over again. Alfred Korzybski was right: I am obviously not a hopeless shirker nor am I a frantic worker. Something of both!

Chapter 4C

My Sex and Love Life
My Sex and Love Life Really Gets Going Full Blast

L et me get around to some aspects of my adult sex and love life. To give a more rounded picture of myself, I shall describe some of my dramatic sexuo-amative adventures, which have been an essential part of me since I was thirteen. Again, because some readers will be eager to hear how a renowned sexologist and psychologist conducted his own erotic life, this material may come soon enough to prevent them from being bored with much of my nonlibidinous material.

My "real" sex life began in November 1937, when I was twenty-four. I had already gotten over my phobia of meeting new women and was dating fairly selectively. Most of the women I knew were "nice Jewish girls" who were looking for a husband and who petted a bit but rarely had intercourse even with a steady boyfriend. They lived—if you want to use that word—with their parents and knew little about birth control. Even the women I met when I was active as a political revolutionist mostly came from conventional Jewish backgrounds and were not revolutionary in their love lives. They had to be madly in love with a man to allow him inside their sacred portals. They tended to be reasonably unattractive and loud and obnoxious. In fact, some of them were radicals probably because they were not too attractive to men and compensated by being politically super-assertive. At that time, I lived at home with my mother, brother, and sister, and I had very little money during those Depression years to spend on dating and no place to take a partner if she were sexually willing, as she invariably lived with her parents, too.

So I was becoming much less afraid of rejection by women but still getting nowhere sexually. Then I started palling around with Tom Trotter, who was a little older than I and was separated from his wife. My main attraction to Tom was that he used cleverness to be psychopathically promiscuous with women. The first night he met a woman—usually by picking her up because she was attractive—he would voice ardent love for her, say that he was about to take a fabulous trip to Persia, and invite her along. I was surprised at how many of them fell for this crap and quickly went to bed with him. Of course, he never mentioned his marriage.

Although I was very liberal sexually, I was moralistically opposed to lying to women to get them to give sexual favors. In fact, I always told women the truth about my feelings or lack of feelings for them—and consequently got little sex with women I liked but frankly did not love. I was so disgusted with Tom that I vowed to unmask him the next time he lied to a woman and tell her about his wife (with whom he was trying to reunite) and his nasty ways.

The next woman Tom used his "let-me-take-you-to-Persia" line on was Karyl, who later was to become my first wife. Here was my chance! When Karyl enthusiastically told me about her encounter with Tom and how she was all set to get engaged to him and to traipse off to Persia with him in a few weeks, I didn't hesitate to tell her the facts of life and of Tom. I met her on a cool November night, stayed up with her till one in the morning in the dim hallway of her apartment house (her parents were already asleep in their small apartment), and gave her all the gory details of Tom Trotter's (what an appropriate name!) perfidy. Karyl was hurt and livid. She was most grateful to me for my revelations, and vowed vengeance.

We worked out a plan where I visited her apartment when Tom was there and let him go on and on about their coming engagement and their three-month trip to Persia (where they would supposedly stay with some of his rich relatives). At that point, I coolly interrupted, "But what will your wife think about all this? Will she agree to these plans?" The cat leaped out of the bag. Tom's face instantly fell from ecstatic joy to grim horror. The jig was truly up—and he knew it. He quickly left Karyl's apartment. She and I laughed for the next twenty minutes. Her parents, who were in the other room, asked us what was so funny.

My peculiar love life with Karyl began that very night. Our conspiring against Tom put us marvelously close together. Our mutual glee, deliberately recalled and repeatedly reinforced, made us feel like lifelong buddies, although we'd known each other only a matter of hours.

Anything, everything was discussed, from politics to common friends. But mostly ourselves: our own dislikes and likes, characteristics, aims. We had no trouble being verbal. We were born for each other in that way. The talk went on. Somehow, mostly about sex. No matter where the conversation swerved, it inevitably came back to the central theme: What about this sex thing? And what part should we play in it?

I was doing my utmost to be frank without being vulgar, since Karyl shied at my down-to-earth language. In many ways, as a high school dropout of nineteen, she had much more experience than I, an incredibly well-educated college graduate of twenty-four. I had experience, but not sophistication. She had done things I had never dared to do: acted professionally for a short while; had lovers, including one who had practically supported her (though she still technically lived at home); played the great lady (and the little child) with her middle-class Jewish parents. But she was powerfully ethereal, somehow not for this crass, physical world. Maybe, in between her immersion in poetry and drama, she went to the john. But she made one wonder a little about that.

After a bit of this kind of evasion, I began to grow verbally desperate. After all, I was twenty-four and still a virgin. Not exactly virginal, for I had perhaps five or ten times as many heterosexually obtained orgasms as most of my friends, and many more than my girl-chasing brother. But not in bed, not even on a park bench. In the subway and other public places, and, as you might expect, with absolute strangers. Having an intimate, one-to-one talk with a girl was something that, up to this time, I had rarely done. I knew a fair number of females. I chatted with them amiably—in groups. But I didn't date them steadily, pet with them, fuck them. Because I wanted to "know" them sexually so much—too much—and was no longer afraid to approach them but was scared of refusal of sex.

This was it. Sheer luck, to some degree, had thrown us together. A mutual project against my ex-friend Tom had got us talking, talking, talking, talking. About her and my relations with him. Now we were still talking—this time about us. And I *had* to make it last, *had* to get somewhere with her. For she looked like a whore. Had tits like Mae West. And could talk almost as volubly and incessantly as I could. A beauty with a big mouth! Intelligent! Sensitive! Artistic! And, despite her holocaust at high school, extremely well read. Fallen, by great luck, into my conversational lap. Gad, if I screwed up this one, I deserved to go on being a virgin!

So, desperately afraid to be sent home empty-handed (and full-pricked) that chilly November night, I chattered on. And, partly to make sure I didn't cop out and let the intimacy—that is, the *sexual* part of the intimacy—wane, I recklessly plunged into shocking ideas. I said: "Maybe you won't believe it. But I really have no shame at all. Well, that's what I'm striving for, at least: to have none. Shame means that you give too much of a shit about what other people think of you. Well, why should you? What difference does it *really* make if I do something sexual and somebody doesn't like it? Will this somebody do anything to me other than think me nutty? So he—or she—will think I'm nutty. If I ignore this, I still may get what I want. Hell, if I wouldn't get arrested for it, I'd screw a woman in Macy's window. If she were willing, of course. You may think that crazy. But why do I care what our hundred viewers are thinking? I'd be concentrating on *her* and our fucking. Screw them!"

She didn't bat an eyelash. She didn't agree; neither did she argue. I now see, having known her for more than sixty years, that she probably wasn't listening too much to me. She was too obsessed with talking and listening to herself. Who, at nineteen, isn't? But Karyl especially was. She was an intense, passionate conversationalist. I loved her interminable flow. But I failed to see that I had *nothing* to do with it, except to serve as audience. True to her profession as an actress, she was always on. But because of my own self-centeredness, it only *seemed* like a conversation.

I wasn't merely impersonal about my super-sexuality and my lack of shame. With method to my madness, I fervidly avowed my interest in her. I must say that, for all my lack of previous practice, I was pretty damned good. Remember: this was my first heavy date. A few previous ones had been very light and chatty. No real interest on my part. I had gone to boy's high school, where we had no heterosexual contacts whatever, not even a prom. At the City College of New York, where I majored in business administration, we had about five boys for every girl in most of my classes, and, over-interested as I was in practically all these females, I hardly ever spoke, outside of class, to any of them. Even my post-college years, when I was something of a leader in the New York radical movement (where I was anti-Communist but highly revolutionary), were organized around my utter genius for remaining emotionally uninvolved, while my uglier and stupider male associates were screwing the ass off every female revolutionist in sight.

Still, I kept trying. I said: "You are incredibly attractive, almost in spite of your great intelligence, and I can almost get an orgasm just thinking about touching you." She went back to talking about herself. I said: "You just happen to have the kind of looks that I've always dreamed about. Billie Dove was my favorite movie star for years, with her classic features. You're not anything like her, but you're much sexier and real." She ignored me and went back to her near-monologue. I persisted. She parried. I returned to the fray.

She became downright discouraging. She kept averring that she was frigid sexually. "Oh, I know how I look. Lots of men have told me the same thing you have: that I appear to be so sensual and sexy. I'm afraid they're wrong. I am easily attracted. I become terribly infatuated with some men—often the wrong ones. I like them to like me. I like to be held by them, to try to please me. But I'm not really with it. I'm afraid I really am frigid. It might not look that way. But I think I am."

I didn't believe it for a moment. Doubtless, I didn't want to. But it was—or I convinced myself it was—more than that. No matter how discouragingly she talked about her disinterest in sex, her perpetual willingness to return to the subject seemed to belie her disavowals. She kept remarking what good "platonic" friends we were, and how she liked that and wanted it to stay that way. But I—pigheadedly? Wishful-thinkingly?—concluded otherwise. I deliberately reverted back to sex, back to sex. Despite the painfulness. She became tormentingly more attractive by the hour: so physically near, so demonstratively far, far away.

Another thing I couldn't believe. As she had consistently done from our first meeting a few days before, she kept baiting me on my non-sensuous appearance. "I just can't see you in bed with a woman," she said. "You look so cold, so intellectual. You're very bright. I like to talk with you. But I just don't *feel* you as a sexual being. I don't see you that way at all."

Maybe, consciously or unconsciously, she was baiting me. I don't think so, since later evidence showed otherwise. Anyway, I picked a rather peculiar track of reacting. I resolved to prove—with more talk, of course—that it was only my amazing self-control that made me appear unsexual and that, in reality, I could be very passionate. Looking back, this seems a thoroughly idiotic track for me to have taken. If I *looked* too cool to her and wanted her to think differently, why didn't I rip her clothes off and show her just how uncool I was? Reason: Wasn't I afraid that if I got moving I would *demonstrate* my inexperience and inadequacy? Quite probably.

Perversely—humans *are* incredible in their rationalizations—I kept complimenting myself on my self-control. She said I looked asexual. I knew that I wasn't. Well, I would calmly, unthreateningly *convince* her that I wasn't. That would show that I was very sexy but a nice guy, to boot. How could anyone resist *that* combination? It was only a matter of time till I would have her begging me for sex.

She couldn't really be frigid. She only thought she was. She was only terribly repressed, emotionally repressed. She surely wanted sex as much as I did. She only had to be, by the right method, released of her repressions. And I would find the key to that release. Then would the fur fly!

For a few moments, it almost did. She said, for the umpteenth time that evening, "I really don't see how you could possibly become passionate with a girl." Riled somewhat, I cut short a sentence, stretched my hands, fingers tensely pointed outward toward her, put histrionic feeling into my voice: "See! See those fingers. Well, I can feel sex in the very tips of them. And feel it from there to the center of my groin!" Pointing my fingers dramatically at her beautiful body, sprawled listlessly on the floor (while I sat forward in an armchair near her), I said: "I just have to touch your body—any part of it—and I can feel sex keenly. All over me! See!"

There was something in my voice and in my grim, half-tortured eyes that made her see exactly what I was driving at. Nothing further had to be said on either side. "Let's not talk about sex any more," she said hurriedly, embarrassedly.

"Yes," I acquiesced, as I slowly recovered my good humor. "Perhaps we'd better not." And, for a short while, we said almost nothing, as we mused individually over our thoughts and feelings.

But—fatedly, one might say—our conversation reverted to the old, half-bantering yet underlyingly serious discussion of sex. The hour was now well past one a.m. I was still seated sloppily in the comfortable armchair of her living room, she enticingly sprawled on the floor. I was thinking of calling it a night. Then I remarked that, if it was a matter of anyone's receiving caresses from her (she was fondling the family dog at this time), I would be delighted to be the one to receive them. Exactly the sort of statement I had made several times previously. And, as before, she began, "Oh, I just can't see you—" "I am passionate!" I doggedly said. "Verbally?" she questioned.

This time there seemed to be an extra note in her voice—a note of impassioned longing, a note of subconscious (or was it, could it be?) conscious desire. "Damn it!" I said to myself. "I've stood enough of this. It's now or never!"

Deliberately closing my glasses—which I had been swinging in my hands for a while—and clamping them in their case, I pulled myself to the front of the chair and calmly and clearly (to my own surprise) said: "Karyl, there seems to be something in your voice calling me down to that floor!"

Suddenly, with no wasted movements, I threw myself down beside her, and reached eagerly for her face and body. In passing, I got a fleeting look of what appeared to be great surprise on her face. But no anger—or not enough of it, at least—to deter me. I grabbed and kissed her, first blindly and summarily. Then, as no resistance materialized, with increasing passion and enjoyment.

At first, remembering my last experience with kissing about a year previously (from which I had received no pleasure from the girl's closely pressed and resisting lips), I shied away from kissing her face and concentrated on drawing the upper part of her body close to mine. But as soon as my lips touched her smooth-skinned cheek and neck, and I felt their warm, satin quality penetrate my senses, I was immensely thrilled and pleased. I hungrily tried to feel and to kiss any available part of her bare skin. I pressed my left cheek flush against her right one, rubbed it slightly up and down on hers, and was immensely joyed with the moment and with her.

Meanwhile, she hugged me close, as in a blindly compulsive embrace, sometimes giving the impression that she did not know what she was doing and that perhaps she wasn't too pleased with the whole business but was grimly going through with it anyway. But since she did not really resist, I pressed closer, hugged her back and her breasts, and began to seek out even greater joys in her body.

I tried to feel her bare breasts, to get at them and to kiss them. But her dress covered them almost completely, and when I tried to get under her waist, she pushed my hands away and nodded an almost painful no, whereupon I immediately desisted. Then I hugged her all the closer, kept changing my position so that I could get renewed bodily pleasure from every touch.

Almost guiltily—because I wanted to be thinking only of her—I began contemplating other things. I thought of her father and mother, who were supposedly sleeping in another room of their small apartment. I wondered with some amusement what might happen if they awoke and walked in on us. But—strangely, since I've always been something of a physical coward—I was not in the least afraid. So I pushed out of mind these outward possibilities and thought only of the two of us, and the wonder—the really perfect wonder—of our being together on the floor. The whole thing was so real, so joyfully true, that I couldn't quite accept it as a normal and natural occurrence.

Then I watched her tense, almost sleeping form for a while and wondered about her supposed frigidity. Was she really as responsive and encouraging as she at first seemed to be? Was she, out of kindness, afraid to resist my advances? Was she perhaps only testing herself, to see how frigid she really was?

Somehow, even these negative thoughts didn't worry me. Nothing did for the time being, as I tossed around on the upper part of her body, getting all the contact and physical pleasure I could, and firmly feeling that this was the greatest moment of my life and that this noble love (unlike the sexually unfulfilled ones I had been profoundly having since the age of six) would, could, absolutely should last forever.

For a while, I was afraid to let the lower part of our bodies have anything to do with each other, for I knew by experience that I was capable of reaching climax quickly and that if I did, I would then take relatively little joy in continuing to fondle her. But the pleasure and the temptation was too much. Soon, I was lying full-length on her, with our midsections sliding deliciously back and forth against each other. A great love for her filled my being. Everything was perfect, except that I was afraid of hurting her in some way and afraid that, if I did, she would tolerate it silently.

After what appeared to be a delectably prolonged period of plea-sure—but what was probably only five minutes—she motioned me away, and I quickly drew myself off, falling back on the floor, almost gasping for breath. Then, for what seemed to be interminable minutes, we said not a word, continuing the strange silence (especially for us) that started when I first pulled myself down beside her. Finally, after I attempted to break the silence with a few semi-humorous remarks, and noticed that she rather liked that way of breaking apart, I recovered my usual volubility and we began to talk.

"It was my fault," she said. "I asked for it."

"Well, I don't regret it. Not at all." Nor did I. I was exceedingly pleased with what had happened and felt unusually tender toward her.

But I didn't know how to tell her so—being afraid, as ever, that if I did, I would sound insincere. So I reverted to humor, and soon we were laughing and joking in an unusual way for two people who had just completed a period of tender nonverbal contact.

Ironically, I was somewhat ashamed of not being as passionate as I had alleged I would be. My tender feelings had got in the way—which I both regretted and didn't. I was rather surprised, and not a little suspicious, when she frankly acknowledged that she had been wrong. "You really are very sexual!" she said. My shame and surprise alternated with my joy at being complimented.

I had been genuinely surprised by her own ardor. Not so much at what she had shown during our embrace, but at what she had indicated she could, if she only would, let herself feel. Her demonstration of physicality was mild. Her demonstration of what she might, some day, demonstrate was utterly convincing. What a luminous day to look forward to—perhaps!

From the moment I recovered my breath, I longed to get into her arms again. I began to grow dejected as she indicated, especially by her light conversation, that she had had enough for the night; and that—shit, shit, shit!—there might indeed be no further nights of this sort. "I was really surprised at myself," she said. "I'm not really like this at all."

Back I went to my dismal musings. "Maybe she felt she had to go through with it, after egging me on like that. Maybe she was afraid to hurt me and only pretended to be involved. Maybe she liked it but was terribly guilty and won't let herself do it again." Maybe, maybe! One more negative than the other.

I had no intention of forcing any more physical attentions on her. But I did (Oh, hope springs eternal!) maneuver my body closer to hers. Just in case!

For about fifteen minutes, we lay side by side, about three feet apart, with our heads resting on the side of a low daybed, humorously and calmly discussing what had just happened and bringing in various side subjects into the bargain. I was skeptical, at first, of this sort of dialogue, feeling that I should be telling her straightly and sincerely how warmly I felt toward her. But she insisted that the humor took away our self-consciousness and encouraged me to keep it up. "I feel better joking like this," she said. "It relieves my pressure." So soon we were laughing gaily, as if nothing had happened and as if we were still only the best of platonic friends.

Then I decided to risk it. "This bed is uncomfortable as hell," I said. "Do you mind, Karyl, if I rest my head on you?"

"Certainly not," she replied. I immediately placed my head on her thighs and began to feel good all over again.

"Ah, that feels so nice!" I exclaimed, as I nuzzled my head, eyes down, into her soft, pliant flesh.

Then, as she started gently to fondle my hair and face, I experienced the greatest thrill of all—in some respects, the greatest thrill of my life up to that point. I had dreamed many times of having a woman do exactly that to me: fondle my hair and my face in a gentle, thoroughly loving manner. Now that this dream was being realized, it seemed that Karyl really cared for me and that I could feel no greater peace. I loved her, suddenly, with all my heart, wanted nothing more than to do something terribly kind in return. Then as she ardently kept stroking my face, there seemed to be no question that she loved me too, and I was ineffably happy and so desperately afraid that I was not returning her caresses acceptably enough and that she was getting nearly so much pleasure as I. I kept thinking that I never, never had been half so happy before—that all my long years of waiting for love were now being amply rewarded, that there could now be no question about the worth and enjoyment of my life.

Within a few moments, we were in another passionate embrace, and, after a while, deep in the throes of passion, I strove again to touch her bare breasts, to get at them underneath her dress. This time there was no resistance. In spite of the close fit of her brassiere, I felt most of her bare bosom and was shocked with exultation at its incredible softness and smoothness. My fingertips tingled at its touch. I strove to cup my hands around her full breasts. But as I touched her nipple, I realized that if I wished to go further, I would have to undress her completely, and that, I was panicked to contemplate, might ruin our lovely relationship of this moment. So I withdrew and went to feverishly exploring other parts of her body again.

One thing that surprised me greatly was my utter lack of desire to undress her below the waist and to have actual intercourse. That seemed so far away and so dangerous—she might well object to it strenuously—that I never even thought of attempting it. Besides, I knew that we had no contraceptives available and that there was always the danger of her parents interrupting us. So I continued to embrace her passionately, wanting to please her as much as myself, until she firmly waved me off.

Still ungratified, I nonetheless immediately obeyed. Her first remark, as we broke apart, was: "Whew! I didn't think I was capable of it!" We both smiled, half-humorously, half-embarrassedly.

For a while, we lay on the bed. Then we gradually embraced again, with slightly less intensity. Karyl cut short our entwining after a few minutes and removed herself to a chair several feet away from me. It now appeared that the night—the most glorious I had ever spent—was, in spite of our wishes, drawing to a close. The clock harshly showed 2:30 a.m. Suddenly the voice of her father boomed, "Karyl, aren't you in bed yet? Don't you think you'd better go?"

Obviously, our parting time had come. I slowly put on my overcoat, whispering to her as I prepared to leave, hoping that her father didn't realize that I was there. It wouldn't have been diplomatic to antagonize him, especially considering that, with his passive consent, there might be many more ecstatic nights like this to come.

We resumed our parting conversation in our old bantering tone, interrupted, however, by a short, ardent good-night embrace. Then I left.

It was raining sporadically outside: now hard, now soft. For once, I hardly minded. For once, I walked along almost on cushioned feet. I was ecstatically happy, thinking only of what had happened and of portents of joy to come. Thinking of those unbelievably delicious breasts, of that surpassingly satin skin. Thinking with almost foreign tenderness of the dear woman I had just left. All the way home, I thought of her; all through the hour in bed it took before I fell asleep; all through another hour I lay in bed after I awoke at the unearthly early hour of 8:30 a.m. Sunday morning and, with hardly a single let-up, all through the rest of the morning.

Then, after telephoning her at 11:00 a.m., I went to visit her at one in the afternoon and stayed talking with her (and a little with her parents) until 6:15. During our visit, not a word was said about what had happened the night before, for, under the depressing influence of her parents' presence, only the slightest hints to what had happened could be exchanged.

I haven't read the original detailed notes on which this chapter is based in several years. I still like reading them, for they bring back much of the flavor of my past feeling for Karyl—a feeling that has not existed for many decades. I didn't love like that anymore until my love with and for Debbie—a love the likes of which I have never experienced before. I was not sure that, before being with Debbie, as I approached my late eighties, I would love anyone romantically for more than a few days or at most a few weeks. And not then quite madly. For I knew up until then (ah, experience—which, as the proverb noteth, is a dear teacher) what would really happen to my feelings and to any relationship that may be constructed on romantic love's quicksands. I knew that my amorous interests would soon wither into sentiments of friendship or conjugal affection (which are fine and great and all that, but hardly L-O-V-E) or into emotional mildness). So even while my romantic feelings lasted, I hardly took them too seriously. My romantic, obsessive-compulsive loves soon died.

Besides, what work loving was! I devoted countless hours to thinking about Karyl, being with her, doing for her. Not that these hours were boring or a waste, for they certainly weren't! But who has time for that sort of thing? I'm a busy man—perhaps one of the busiest in the world. I have many responsibilities and commitments, things I really want to get done. Where would passionate love, of the sort I had for Karyl, fit into this super-busy, unusually filled life? It wouldn't.

As much as I adored Karyl, in the decades that followed, and now, I love *it*: my life work, my dedication to the cause of psychotherapy in general, of Rational Emotive Behavior Therapy in particular. How could an all-consuming romantic involvement fit into that dedication? It probably couldn't, unless my partner has the same dedication to that work. Fortunately, that is the case with Debbie. As a famous French proverb goes, "A new love drives out the old." Devotion to a vital absorbing interest dims the old romantic attachments, which have kept involving me, one after the other, until the present. But lightly, not too seriously. Absorbing interest in practicing and developing a therapeutic institute is not exactly the same thing, of course, as a series of romances. But in some ways, it is more satisfying. Incredibly, however, with Debbie I practically have it all—we are on the same wavelength, we are dedicated to the work and helping others, and we love each other deeply. Such compatibility is rare.

What about the rampant sexuality I so blatantly felt and exhibited with Karyl that momentous evening when first we fell—well, let's be honest, more like waddled—into each other's arms? Where are *those* snows of yesteryear?

Not exactly melted, I must say. Even up to the age of eighty-eight I still did reasonably well in that area, thank you. Not as well as many years ago, to be sure, when I (by accident rather than design) fucked three women in one day and reached orgasm six times. Nor even as well as several years later, when I had seven orgasms in about eighteen hours with one woman. In recent years, until my relationship with Debbie, I was lucky to get two climaxes a week. From the age of eighty-nine, my only love and sex partner has been Debbie, and, despite my age-related disabilities such as arthritis, she has been the best love and lover I have ever been with. We enjoy marvelous sex and great tenderness.

So, although I'm not a mere shadow of my former sexual self, I'm not exactly the "man" I used to be either in terms of having six orgasms in one day. But more startlingly: I hardly care that much. If Karyl had put me off completely—as she almost did that night and as she did with nauseating frequency on subsequent occasions, I could easily end up with a zinging case of blue balls. Even more likely, I would have with an obsessive interest in her tits, her ass, and her genitals thoughts that would preempt my waking (even dreaming) for the next fifty hours. Indeed, the less we copulated the more (intensely and prolongedly) preoccupied with her body would I be.

Over the past several years, prior to being with Debbie, I had voluntarily foregone many sexual conquests, most of them with women I found quite attractive, but I have only mildly regretted my sexual losses. Why? Because something more important than sex usually intervened. Something as mundane as a good night's sleep before I gave my next morning's workshop; an opportunity to write ten more pages on a book or article; a chance to fly back to New York that evening instead of staying over for the next day's flight.

How, in these instances, the mighty fell!—or never even got erect in the first place. I wouldn't have believed it, in my early days with Karyl. I, the person who had had an almost constant hard-on since the age of thirteen, actually refusing to fill a gaping, willing love-hole? Ridiculous! Impossible! Unhearable! Yet, less than a dozen years later, there I was, actually saying to a charming young woman over the phone: "No, dear. I'm really too tired. I'd love to come over. I thoroughly enjoyed being with you last time. But I have to get up tomorrow at six to go to New Jersey. Let's make it some other time."

Lies, mostly. I wasn't too tired. I didn't have to get up early the next morning. It could have worked out. A decade earlier, nothing would have stopped me from rushing over to her place and quickly ripping her clothes off. That's what this story of Karyl reminds me of: my incredible, undownable sexuality of my teens and twenties. Brimstone and fire would have been *easy* to risk for the temporary assuaging of *that* feverishness. But a few years later I was saying to myself (not to the woman) during this phone conversation: "Who needs it? Sure, it was all right last time. She really swung her ass like crazy! But she lives too far away. And her apartment is so cold. And I'll have a hell of a time getting a cab back when I leave at three in the morning. I'm not tired now, but I *will be* tomorrow! And I have clients from 9:30 a.m. until eleven at night. Who needs it? Not worth it. Let's see how I can put her off till the weekend."

But the image of Karyl pulls. I can still see us together, almost exactly as we were then, despite the intervening sixty-seven years and the contradictory facts of today. For I am hardly the compulsive lothario of my youth, and even if I were just as sexy as ever, in all probability fewer charming young women would want my aging, balding carcass today. Nor, in her latter years, was Karyl anything like the nineteen-year-old beauty she was in 1937. Never a sylph then—but zaftig, O, how zaftig! In the last ten years of her life, Karyl became many pounds heavier. Ugh! I never did like real fatness, though at times I have gone with women who were quite overweight, mainly because I could close my eyes during lovemaking and *feel* turned on by feeling flesh that is repulsive looking.

That's why I have always known that I could easily engage in homosexual acts, especially if I were on a desert island, with no women around. I don't like the looks of men. I hardly look at them when I am walking down the street or attending a social gathering. In this respect, I am a heterosexual pervert: a one-sided, narrow-minded fetishist who easily turns myself on by looking at a female's body—or even *parts* of her body—and who has no equivalent interest in the male form (though I know a good-looking male when I see one and can even objectively—and dispassionately—admire his looks). But if I *had* to make do with homosexual relations, I could easily do so. For the *feel* of a male's mouth on my hard prick, I am sure (though I have never actually tried this), is essentially similar to the feel of a female's. And I know that irrumation *feels* good. So I could easily engage in homosexuality—while imagining, probably, having sex with a woman.

Let me not sidetrack myself. A main point I wrote in my notes for an earlier version of this autobiography was:

In my old age, I could easily become sexually obsessed with and enamored of another Karyl—particularly if she were as young and beautiful as Karyl was when I first met her. But it would be different, much different, in one significant respect. I would have little hope for the glorious *future* of that relationship. For I now know—I really know!—what will happen to my obsessive-compulsive attachment after a few weeks or months. It will wane. It will become dull. It will become subservient to my *real*, perennially ongoing relationship: with my work, with my theory and practice of Rational Emotive Behavior Therapy, with me. I will continue to live, to find myself, to enjoy. *She* will become a mere *part* of that existence and, most probably, after a while, a relatively unimportant part of it. I *know* that, from the very start, these days. And, knowing that, my love for her will become ephemeral, not *that* important.

That is what I believed until being with Debbie, who *is* a profoundly important part of my life.

So I used to think that I would merely enjoy an inamorata. She is not me. She is only a part of, though perhaps still an important part of, me. That part will pass. Before Debbie, I thought, there will be, on the length of my cock and in the core of my head, other women. One of them, Janet, lasted some thirty-seven years. But not obsessive-compulsively. Not impassionately, romantically. No woman *is* me, as I once thought Karyl would be. *No one* is. I, only, am me. My work, in a sense, is me. And even *that* could conceivably change.

I am I. That is what I teach my clients. They are they. They, as long as their lives last, exist. They are themselves, and they can always—yes, always—accept themselves. But they never—no, they'd better not ever—rate themselves. They'd better not have self-worth, self-esteem, self-confidence. Only REBT advocates self-efficacy and self-acceptance.

And the same goes for me! I exist. I choose to continue to exist. I choose to look for, to seek maximum happiness and minimum pain or suffering. I *want* to live and enjoy. But I never *have* to. There are no necessities, no have-to's in my universe. Karyl, at the time I loved her, was a kind of necessity. I *made* her a necessity. I *needed* her. At least, I *thought* I did. Well, that was nutty. That was demanding. That was slavish. I felt that there could be no question about the worth and enjoyment of life, for Karyl was the worth and enjoyment of life.

Shit, she was! Here it is, over sixty-seven years later, and I still liked, still had some interest in Karyl until she unfortunately died about a year ago of complications from lung cancer. But let's face it: I really didn't grieve that much when she died. Nor was I lost, only sad and sorry when I broke up with Janet. But life went on. I knew damned well that it would very enjoyably continue. I *made* it enjoyably continue. And months after Janet went, the relationship with Debbie began full-force, though we'd been very close friends for some years prior.

That's really an immense difference, if you think about it. I still like sex. I still like love. But the *need* has gone. In a sense, it was never there. I wouldn't have died without sex or love, hence they were hardly *necessary* to my existence. But I *thought* they were. Now I *know* they aren't. And vive le difference! I like it this way. It's great, in a sense, to be driven by your love feelings. They run, motivate, your existence.

Give you something grand and great to live for. Structure your life. Make you *know* what you are aiming for. Without doubts!

Fine. But unnecessary. Or—in all honesty—is it? Aren't I still driven today, but by other things? Certainly not love. Certainly not sex. Nor (I think) ego. I could argue, however, that these "needs" have gone partly because they have been satiated. I have not only loved to a fare-thee-well but have been notably loved in return. Many women have gone batty over me, said (and probably meant) that they were ready to dedicate their lives to me. Nice. Pleasant. But also something of a pain in the ass. Who wants all that attention? Restricting, too. If you love me, you invariably want me to do something to keep earning that love. And a lot of the time, most of the time, I truly don't want to do that thing. I want to do my thing, not yours. So keep your love. I can do marvelously without it.

Sex, too, when you've had as much as I have had with as many different women over the last many years. Sure, it's exciting when your rocks are hard and you want to shoot them off into a screamingly waiting juicy woman. Imperious. Almost necessitous. But disadvantageous—as you eventually learn—too. What about after you've fucked—and she wants something more? What about when you're getting somewhat bored with your pubis whacking away at hers (which can, at times, get painful, too), and she still wants to bang-bang for another ten or fifteen minutes? What about when she wants to talk, talk your head off, far, far into the night? What about her breath smelling, her nails biting into your back, or her bouncing around in the bed, after sex is over, and reawakening you from a sound sleep every twenty minutes or so? Who needs it? Who wants sex very much under *those* conditions?

Just a few words here about my relationship with Debbie. Her immense love for me, and self-sacrifice in her care for me, continues to astonish me. As I look back, I see that, in all likelihood, most of the women in my life loved or wanted to be with me because of one or more of the following reasons: (1) I am unusual; (2) I am famous; (3) I was helping them with their problems and issues; (4) It was of benefit to them to be with me. I have never experienced or seen a love as unconditional and honest, without any expectations or needs from me, as is Debbie's love for me. She loves me more than she loves herself, which I think is quite nutty and I tell her that. But it is still something unique for me and quite lovely to receive. And clearly it gives her great joy to do so.

If anything happened to her, such as her dying, to deprive me of her in my life, I think I would still go on and continue to work and help others. Losing her would be, without doubt, the worst and saddest thing for me. But I would do my best to go on, even with the immense deprivation. I would never have believed that from the age of eighty-nine I would experience such a love, that I would have a true soul mate and love in my life. I hope forever. My neediness is gone—I do not have the demandingness that I had with Karyl. My appreciation and gratitude for the love and security that Debbie and I share is immense, immeasurable.

But back to my love and sex drives. As they indubitably diminished in my later years, haven't my nonloving involvements continued unabated, even increased? What about my seeing many individual clients and leading therapy groups? What about the interns and fellows I supervise? What of my writing, writing, writing—at least a dozen articles and a book or two every year? How about my continual brief trips to various parts of the United States or the world, to lecture, conduct workshops, lead marathons, and do other highly active (and often taxing) things? Are these kinds of drives any different from, less compulsive than, my earlier love and sex urgings?

In a way, yes. I still don't exactly see them as necessities. They clearly are enjoyments—they add appreciably to my life, make it much less boring than it otherwise would be. But I don't *have* to do them. In the mid-1970s, I took an enforced vacation from virtually all my regular pursuits, spending a month in the hospital after breaking my clavicle when I fell down a dimly lit flight of stairs in Oklahoma City and subsequently had a major prostatectomy. I missed my work, but I got by nicely, and I could have done so, presumably, forever.

In looking back, it seems that much if not all of my hardworking actions of the last seventy-plus years have been more or less motivated by sexual seeking. I began writing seriously when I was in college and completed a half-million-word novel. Shortly thereafter, I became political and helped found and run a left-wing anti-Communist group. I later published scads of scientific papers in reputable psychological and psychiatric journals, as well as some eighty books and monographs. I was a bigshot in several professional groups for a good many years. I rose from the psychological ranks in record time (a little more than two years) to become chief psychologist of the state of New Jersey. Clearly, I have been no slouch in these respects. I worked my ass off. I earned my just rewards. While doing so, I followed largely nonsexual pursuits and often neglected dating, relating, and fornicating.

My sexual goals, however, were not even subtle or unconscious as I thereby wended my way. I figured out, when I was about nineteen and spending about twenty hours a week typing away at my Great American Novel (which was so sexually oriented for its day that it never got published), that I would probably, eventually, get laid on an even bigger and better scale with this sort of activity than I would by trying to screw around with the nice Jewish women I knew in the Bronx. If I got somewhere in life, I thought, they would let me take down their panties. They would want me to do so. And I would hardly refuse!

It worked. The more writing I did (even unsuccessfully) and the more I became known in the psychological field, the more women loved me and fucked me. So there was method in my madness. It worked the other way too. I had almost forgotten this fact, but thinking about Karyl and my original sex problems with her helps me remember that it was this very thing that made me professionally what I am today. For the less able I was with her sexually, the more I ran to the library to find out what I lacked, and that is how I first became interested in sex as a subject of research and writing and what impelled me into the whole field of psychotherapy. Another story, that, but it is fascinating to think how my sex hassles with Karyl led me to become, ultimately, one of the world's outstanding authorities on sex and the treatment of love and marital disorders. Fancy my almost forgetting that!

Another very important thing I hadn't quite realized until I reread the contents of this last chapter. My main theory of Rational Emotive Behavior Therapy also stems from my early sex-love hang-ups and what I actively—most actively—did to overcome them. I practiced an incipient form of REBT with myself long before I tried it on anyone else. And, as was so often true in my own case, sex led the way.

My problem, a few years before I met Karyl, was twofold. Ever since I began falling in love with females at the age of five, I was too damned shy (meaning, as I now tell my clients, scared shitless) about my love feelings for them. Because of my shyness, I was afraid to get going on even a mild petting basis, so I confined most of my intersexual life to the New York subway system and became, from my fifteenth year onward, one of the city's most active frotteurs. Quite by accident, in returning home from high school one day on a crowded subway train, I was crushed against the body of a lovely female student from another school, and before the crowd finished crunching us together between the 161st Street and 167th Street stations of the Lexington Avenue express, I had a most delicious (and certainly unexpected) orgasm. Maybe the girl did, too (she certainly didn't seem to be trying to pull away from me), but I never asked.

Which was exactly the point: In the subway, I never had to ask. I would get jammed against the body of some "attractive" female—she could be anywhere from thirteen to sixty-three, as long as she was distinctly female—and she would either remain close to me or would not. She could invariably escape, to some degree, but she frequently chose not to do so. So we would pretend to look off into space, to close our eyes and half go to sleep, or to be interested in something else. But in actuality, we were grinding our sexual parts against each other and frequently (I, for sure; she perhaps) came to orgasm.

But no words! No express overtures. No friendliness. Pure anonymity. Even when I wanted it otherwise. The few times I tried to go further, I was invariably and solidly rebuffed. One beautiful young woman, for example, sat on a train with her thighs and hips pressed firmly against my eager thighs and hips until we reached the very last stop of the subway. Because most of the other passengers had left by that time, we had miles of empty seats to sprawl over. But she stuck close to me and did everything but sit in my lap. Yet, when I followed her out of the train (long past my stop) and asked her if she wanted me to accompany her, she seemed to shrink back in a kind of horror, shocked at my gall in making such a suggestion.

Another woman, at least fifteen years older than me but still very attractive, practically raped me as we were standing in the center of a not-too-crowded train, with a good many strap-hangers' backs turned to us. But when I followed her to her apartment house and spoke to her on the elevator, she smiled apologetically and said that no, I could not accompany her any further because she was married.

As far as I could see, my subway partners wanted the anonymity, the sex without risk, as much as I did—which didn't exactly excuse me. I was able to convince myself that nothing further would happen than our sex-on-the-subway encounter. It was great for me. I had my variety—sometimes several women a month. I had my adventure—who knew what would happen each time? I had my excitement—the whole thing was surreptitious and therefore additionally arousing. And there wasn't that much risk. Unless I tried to carry an encounter any further, I never really got refused. I got balked (even bilked, as some women at first seemed to cooperate and then suddenly, capriciously, turned away from me). But I could not get the worst turndown of all: verbal rejection. What safety!

My main gain, however, was really attitudinal and healthy. I could see, after trying this kind of subway sex for a short while, that many people disapproved of it. They knew damned well what was going on between me and my accepting partner, and they stared and stared at us in a highly censorious manner. Mainly women, especially older women, did this. But men, too, on occasion. And they certainly were cold and negative.

Whereupon—and here my Rational Emotive Behavioral Theory and practice really started and began working beautifully—I asked myself: "What are they going to do to me? So they despise me. So what? Most of them, I'll never even see again. And how long will they remember me? Even those I keep encountering again, what are their nasty thoughts going to do to me? As long as the woman who is making it with me doesn't complain—and I certainly know how to test her out and get the hell away from her if she seems disinterested or repulsed—what can these damned busybodies do? Let them think what they want. Only sticks and stones can break my bones—and their names will never, never hurt me!"

In fact, I sometimes enjoyed bugging them. There was one woman, perhaps twenty years older than I (I was then seventeen), whom I saw regularly on my way to college. We both deliberately took the same train, made sure we did not take a seat even if one were available, and maneuvered to stand close to each other, especially when the train was crowded. She was married; seemed completely disinclined to be verbally friendly; and, whether she was getting it at home or not, was always in a highly sexual mood. It was a rare week that we didn't get together for at least one mutual orgasm. I closed my eyes and pretended to be half asleep, and she seemed to be highly disinterested in me though our midsections were tightly glued together. We swayed against each other no matter the motions of the train or the stares of other people in the car.

Even after people got on to us, she impassively, at least facially, continued and so did I. Two other older women, whom we frequently encountered, did everything except push or pull us apart to show their distaste. Neither of us budged. After a time, I rebelliously *enjoyed* these other women's upsetness. "If they want to be that way," I humorously-sarcastically told myself, "let them! They probably haven't been screwed themselves in years! Nasty prudes! Well, that's their stupid business. She, my partner, ignores it beautifully. Why can't I?" And I did—except that, as I just said, I began getting an extra kick from the others' vicious voyeurism.

After a period of time, it really didn't matter. As long as I was in no danger of (a) my female partner objecting or (b) any of the onlookers acting on their objections, I simply didn't give a shit. Even my rebelliousness waned. I just didn't care. I focused only on what I and my partner wanted, and that was that. I thought it bad—too damned bad—that the busybodies were disapproving. But I fully realized that it was not awful, terrible, or catastrophic. Nothing like that was. Disapproval, usually, was just disapproval. Tough! Why bother my head about it? I didn't. And one of the main philosophic cores of Rational Emotive Behavioral Theory and Practice was thereby born.

So when I told Karyl, "I really have no shame at all," I was largely right. I would have screwed her in Macy's window if that were the only way to do it. I wouldn't prefer that; in fact, I probably would dislike it at first. But I'd determinedly focus on what I was doing and enjoy it as much as I possibly could. As for the curious and disapproving views of the onlookers, fuck 'em! That, at least, is how I felt about it then.

Now, as I teach my clients, "Fuck them!" is not a good solution to the problem. It takes the potential self-hatred one feels at being disliked ("Aren't I a shit for doing the thing they consider to be wrong!") and it transmutes it into hatred of them ("Aren't they shits for deprecating me in their bigoted heads!"). That's merely replacing one mistake for another. One is not a turd for acting "wrongly" and being disapproved of by others, but neither are they vermin for being disapproving. There are no human shits, worms, lice, rats, or vermin. There are only human humans.

So, the correct thing to tell oneself under these conditions is: "Fuck it!" Or, even more correctly, as I pointed out in an interview with Paul Krassner many years ago, "Unfuck it!" Fucking is a good thing, and we'd better not use it as a pejorative term. Anyway: "Unfuck it! It's most unfortunate that these people look down on me for doing a harmless, enjoyable act with a willing partner in the subway. But that's the way they behave. And, as long as they don't level real sanctions against me, it's not that important. Too bad! Unfuck it!" That statement is not hostile at all. It's really rational. Lenny Bruce, who used the term "Unfuck it" in his standup comedy routine at times, got it from me! Fine.

Chapter 4D
Critique of Chapter 4

"*So I was not angry or depressed. Only very sad [about my brother Paul's death]. And my sadness kept impinging from time to time on my therapy sessions.*"

I think that I really was only sad and not angry or depressed. In REBT, sadness, especially at the death of a loved one, is what is called a healthy negative feeling, even when it consists of profound grief. When you lose something very valuable—a relative, friend, fine job, or something else you truly love, you had better feel quite sad or keenly disappointed. Such feelings, along with other healthy negative feelings like regret, remorse, and frustration, motivate you to deal with such losses or replace them with other enjoyable people or things.

So my feeling very sad about Paul's death was healthy—as long as it didn't intensively last for, say, five or more years and did not severely incapacitate me. Then it would have been, in REBT terms, a feeling of depression—partly caused, in all probability, by my Irrational Beliefs that his death was so bad that it absolutely should not exist, and that because it did exist it was awful and I couldn't stand it.

If, when I was a child, I had said that I thought quite rationally and was only sad and grieving about Paul's death, but not at all angry and depressed, I would most likely have been defensively lying. But I was seventy-three when he actually died and had taught REBT and practiced it on myself for over thirty years. So I guess I can honestly say that my grief was not depressive or oppressive. I believed that his death was most unfortunate, but that sad situations like that should exist when they do. Alas. Fatal, but not, to me, terrible.

Did I not—to probe for the truth—really not love Paul enough to depress myself over his death? Am I so protectively ensconced in my own selfhood to bar my loving anyone too much? Do I use REBT and other philosophies to protect myself from all emotional hurt, and thereby prevent myself from getting too painfully (or risk-takingly) attached to literally anyone?

Quite possibly. I loved Paul, in what H. G. Wells would call a loving kindness (instead of a violently impassioned) way, more than just about any other person. But not more than me! And not very closely, in the sense that I had to be with him steadily or that I thought about him much of the time. I didn't miss him too much when, for years, he lived in Texas and we rarely got together. I was frankly too busy with many other things to acutely miss him.

To tell the truth, I am always busy. Incredibly busy. Preoccupied with doing things and pretty much immersed in them. It was the same with Janet as it was with Paul. At first, I was in love with her. But living with her under the same roof and sleeping with her in the same bed fixed that! I read Stendhal's *On Love* and Henry T. Finck's *Romantic Love and Personal Beauty* in my twenties, when I was becoming a leading authority on love. They both held that after you live with a partner for about three years at most, passionate romantic love is almost always replaced with a distinctly less ardent kind of loving. I agreed.

Janet and I weathered several storms in our long partnership. And, as in the case of my seventy-one-year-long relationship with Paul, we could easily be apart, in the same house or on a number of separate trips we took, and not greatly miss each other. Maybe, as we sometimes used to humorously remark, those numerous trips enabled us to get along. The other, and more realistic, reason is that we were both exceptionally busy. In particular, I was quite into myself. Not in the usual way, for I do not indulge particularly in sensory pleasures—except listening to music, until about 2003 when my hearing became too poor—the way many "selfish" people do.

No, but I am steadfastly, almost obsessively, into various kinds of work. I am constantly preoccupied—and partly, but not exactly, with people. Obviously, I see many people, every week, for individual and group therapy and for therapy demonstrations, which I gave at the institute and at many sites throughout the world till 2005. From late 2005 I've been giving my workshops in the building next door. But even in those situations, I am absorbed with people's *problems*, not exactly with *them*. So I relate to them and help many of them, but I don't relate intimately. As for the other things I do (and there are many of them), they aim to benefit people, but they are still projects, events, matters, operations—yes, things. Because I choose them and enjoy them, I can truthfully say that I am incessantly involved with me.

As I indicated earlier, my love with Debbie is quite different from any other I've felt. While I am healthily non-needy, I do miss her when she is out attending to matters for longer than usual. We are together for hours and hours on end without feeling put-upon. We enjoy it. She does not distract me from my work; she facilitates it. I trust her more than I trust anyone; I trust her completely with my life, to take care of my health issues, in our work, in our relationship, and to carry on my work when I am dead and gone.

As both a child and an adult, my feelings of depression have been mild and superficial. Not just because I practice REBT—which does help me feel keenly sad at events like my brother's death, but not really depressed. Am I, in fact, even that sad? I once was quite sad about failing to stop the National Council on Family Relations, of which I was an influential member, from electing a very reactionary, anti–birth control president. I dismally struck out in getting published a number of books on which I had worked very hard for hundreds of hours. I ran aground twice in trying to marry Gertrude, whom I passionately loved. When I wanted to become a professor of psychology, no college would have me, including my own Columbia University, because I was too controversial.

On these and similar occasions I have been duly sad but practically never depressed. Partly because I was using a version of REBT philosophy and not demanding that my losses not occur. But I was also saved by my vital absorption in my work—meaning, in me. I was so determined to get certain things done (and I really mean done) that I even sorrowed superficially. Sorrow, regret, and disappointment take time, take energy, and I had better things to do. Or I thought I had.

Come to think of it—and I really have been thinking about it during these last fifteen minutes of writing—I am predominantly a doer. Granted that I am normally thought of as quite a thinker. Correct. But I now see that I think largely to act, to perform. I think in order to do something quicker and better—like figure out better ways of studying for an exam. I think of ways to sleep better, improve my cooking, get back and forth to a new city more efficiently, help clients improve more quickly, write a superior article or book. Et cetera. I like efficiency. So I think out ways to get it.

More of this later. As for my choosing sadness rather than depression when something goes wrong with my life, I choose the former because it is more efficient, and I have included this choice into the essence of REBT. If you use REBT as I designed it to be used, you see that a healthy negative feeling like sadness works—is efficient—and that an unhealthy feeling like depression doesn't work—is inefficient. So you pays your money and you takes your choice. Fine—if you really want to suffer little misery.

Even before I founded REBT, I may have sensed and used this process to keep me undepressed. Depression just wasn't worth it—so off with its head! Sadness was sad, but also more worthwhile. So I used it. But I probably used it by mainly realizing that depression was too much to bear, especially for any period of time, so I employed methods of distraction to ward it off. Because I like being occupied, I used various forms of activity to distract myself from possible depression—and they worked, were reinforcing. Splendid.

I may have gone one step further. Because activity worked to turn off feelings of depression—and because even feelings of sadness were far from delightful—I may have also used the distractions of work to lessen my sadness. I became so intently—and enjoyably—occupied that although I was indeed somewhat—but not very—sad when Adversities occurred, my sadness was brief and mild, and my involvement in activities longer and stronger.

Now, once again, we have a choice of radically different interpretations to "explain" my behavior. On the one hand, I could be a "naturally" unflappable individual who gets himself vitally absorbed in projects mainly because he is unemotional and feels impelled to substitute action for feeling. The other interpretation is that I tend to feel all right and could easily be depressed but don't want to suffer from such strong negative feelings. Therefore, I consciously or unconsciously resort to concerted action to ward off my potential feelings of depression and even of real sadness.

Which of these interpretations is "true"? Or are both somewhat applicable? Who can say? My favorite hypothesis, on the basis of observing myself for many decades, is that I have "normal" negative—and positive—emotionality at various times, but that for practical and defensive reasons I am so hooked on activity that I definitely turn off unhealthy feelings of depression, and sometimes also turn down healthy feelings of sadness, in order to "best" get on with my own life.

This hypothesis, if correct, would still mean that I am often too absorbed in me and my doings to feel too strongly about the loss of other people and things. An interesting thought.

"But I knew I would not become depressed. I knew I could keep accepting [Paul's] death. How could I not—when it was a given fact?"

Yes, that's a truly rational—meaning realistic—philosophy. I always, to some extent, believed in it, but especially after many years of practicing REBT with myself and others, I believed it. Facts is facts, as I think Dickens once said. How can you not very well accept them?

Well, what of postmodernism and its phenomenological outlook, to which I largely—or at least partly—subscribe? According to Martin Heidegger, Jacques Derrida, and a host of modern thinkers, no absolutistic "facts" exist, because all "facts" are seen through human eyes and could fairly easily be seen differently. Well, yes. That seems to be so, though postmodernism can even question postmodern statements and find that they are not absolute.

Still, to be realistic, there is no certainty, but a high degree of probability, that specific things, such as bridges and death, exist and that we'd better acknowledge their existence. The bridge is there or it is not there—and it makes quite a difference to those wanting to cross it. Also, it is well built or rickety—and that makes a significant difference, too.

Similarly, a person is dead or alive. The two states are hardly the same, particularly if the person is you or someone you love. Maybe, of course, he is not totally dead and has a soul that will march off after his demise. Maybe, but I wouldn't count on it. Although there is no absolute certainty that a dead person is completely dead forever, you can bet, with a high degree of probability, that she is. Yes: dead, inanimate, a stiff.

I think that this is precisely where the law of probability saves us from radical postmodernism and its dangers of complete (to use a bad word!) relativism. According to radical postmodernism—à la Paul Feyerband—anything goes. So the bridge, however well built, is not to be trusted. And moral rules are always shaky.

In some sense, true. The bridge and the moral rules are not to be absolutely trusted. They could be wrong—a strong bridge could fall and a sound rule could lead to bad results. But we need not—as REBT keeps demonstrating—use certainty to decide whether we will risk using the bridge or using the rule. We only have to be probabilistically "sure" that they will serve us. If we had to be absolutely certain about crossing bridges or following moral rules, we could hardly do anything, hardly survive. We would soon be corpses—and probably be dead for a long time!

So the laws of probability save us—and literally preserve our lives. We build bridges that probably will not fall and we don't cross them when they probably are rickety. This is similar to the way we act in following Heisenberg's principle of uncertainty. This principle states that on a subatomic level our observation of particles significantly affects light and matter themselves. Therefore we cannot be absolutely certain that these particles in themselves act in specific ways. Good enough. If we are physicists we accept this law of uncertainty and carefully watch our experiments and their results.

On a nonatomic level, however, we need not be so careful. Our observation of how well structured the bridge is hardly affects the structure of the bridge. We still—on grounds of probability—pretty much rely on our observation (and certain other tests) to see whether crossing the bridge is too risky.

Probability, again, serves us in regard to death. I couldn't be absolutely sure that Paul was going to be nonexistent forever when he died or that I would never ever contact him again. But I was reasonably sure of these "facts" of human existence and nonexistence. So I accepted them and made peace with my loss. I would have done so even before I created REBT but perhaps did so more solidly after I created it.

Let me note an important aspect of the power of philosophy in controlling my and other people's behavior. Once anyone strongly believes that a certain attitude, whatever it is, will help him deal with emotional problems, it most probably will help. For several reasons. Take, for example, my belief in the principles of REBT when my brother Paul died and several ways it helped me feel sadness and grief but not feel depressed:

1. I believed that sadness was a healthy negative emotion but depression was unhealthy. Naturally, therefore, I tried to feel sad but undepressed.
2. I believed that if I demanded that Paul not die instead of strongly wishing that this be so, I would be depressed. So I surrendered my demands, kept my wishes, and got myself undepressed. Perhaps my lack of demandingness itself worked. If not, my belief in its working could have made it effective.
3. I believed that Paul's death was final and could in no way be reversed. Therefore, it was foolish not to accept it. What had to be just had to be.
4. I believed that the state of death was not painful, just entirely

nonfeeling, and that therefore Paul would be ignorant of his death and not suffer at all. So I felt sorry (for myself and his wife and son) that he died but not sorry about him. "Him" simply didn't exist.

5. I believed that, although it was probably very stupid and unfair for his physicians to have contributed to his premature death, stupidity and unfairness should exist—because they do and did—and I was therefore not angry at them, as was Paul's wife, Esther.

For many reasons, then, my beliefs in these REBT-oriented philosophies helped me to avoid feelings of depression. It does not matter so much whether these philosophies were correct (meaning that they would be useful for many people much of the time), but that I believed they were "true" was the vital issue—as Jerome Frank has said it is in practically all psychotherapy. Had I believed that Paul would quickly go to heaven and be sanctified—a conviction that most likely is not factual—I might even have been happy about his death, instead of healthily sad or unhealthily depressed.

Let me make another important point. As the creator and leader of the REBT movement, I—along with other gurus—have a powerful incentive not to allow myself to be panicked, depressed, or enraged about anything. REBT fairly clearly says that these disturbed feelings are needless and preventable. Therefore, I especially had better not feel them and thereby sabotage the theory and practice of REBT. Never! (My personal view of outstanding therapists like Freud, Jung, Reich, and many other seriously disturbed people is that either their therapies were largely hogwash or they themselves did not use them. Certainly, they were not very helpful to these leaders of therapeutic movements, or else these leaders were so innately disturbed that their methods didn't work for them. Take your choice!)

Anyway, as the King of the REBT May, I had better not be too crazy. So it is certainly possible that I defensively hide my dementedness—from others and from myself—or that I promptly push my ass to make myself less disturbed. Therefore, when a real Adversity occurs in my life, I strongly use REBT, or anything else I can use, to fight against my possible upsetness. So this determination to "prove" that REBT really is effective may underlay much of my emotional stability since I became its chief protagonist. Another interesting thought.

"I missed Paul very much. But I fully accepted the fallibility of his doctors."

I used REBT very well here. I am not angry at Hitler, who killed six million people, including some of my relatives; nor at Stalin, who killed, directly and indirectly, some fifty million people. They were fallible, screwed-up—very screwed-up—individuals who acted badly but were not bad. So, presumably, were the incompetent doctors who may have killed Paul. I hated what they did, but I didn't hate the doctors.

Again, however, I reminded myself that as the leader of nonviolent REBT, I had darned well better follow its philosophy and hate no one. No one. So founding and leading a philosophy that focuses on less disturbance and less disturbability really helps—if the philosophy is good and I actually use it.

"When even REBT practitioners are so prone to do this kind of thing [use only realistic arguments to combat clients' Irrational Beliefs], you can easily see how . . . prone almost all humans are to employing it. So it was hardly phenomenal that I 'successfully' used it about being suddenly promoted to the third grade."

Yes, when I first originated REBT, in January 1955, I got several realistic ways of Disputing IBs from Epictetus, Marcus Aurelius, and other philosophers. But they, too, almost universally ignored the musts and demands behind people's Irrational Beliefs. Karen Horney saw them—"the tyranny of the shoulds"—but failed to actively Dispute them. The beauty of REBT, and not of the several other forms of Cognitive Behavioral Therapy that have largely copied it (and sometimes added to it), is that it uniquely sees, points out to clients, and forcefully Disputes their musts in many cognitive, emotive, and behavioral ways. It thereby differs notably from therapies, like Tim Beck's and Don Meichenbaum's, which only mildly emphasize the place of musturbatory Beliefs* in human disturbance. So I lightly and vaguely used pre-REBT thinking in dealing with the "disaster" of my being suddenly promoted to third grade when I was seven. But I was far from yet inventing anti-musturbatory therapy!

"My low frustration tolerance—which my father had, too—is probably innate. So, too, is my tendency to work at overcoming it."

Here again we have my bias in favor of biological causation. If I am naturally afflicted with LFT, maybe that very fact created an environment in which I was practically forced to overcome it. Otherwise, I would have whined endlessly about my life's hassles and restrictions

---

*Musturbation: Rigidly demanding that things *must* be the way one believes they should be. Absolutistic thinking. Frequently results in anxiety, depression, and rage.

and thereby made them much worse. Thus, my early physical sickness may have practically forced me to develop considerable HFT to live a reasonably happy life to stop my whining and desist from producing greater pains.

A different hypothesis: My unusual tendency to whack my LFT in the behind and to minimize it may have made it seem that I had too much frustration and actually could have produced greater LFT.

A third hypothesis: Both processes could have taken place. My tendencies—perhaps innate—to have LFT and to make concerted efforts to overcome it could have reciprocally influenced and exacerbated each other. Which interpretation is more correct? Guess!

In this respect, I still prejudicedly think I took after my father, who was rarely around but who exerted a genetic influence. Come to think of it, so, to a considerable degree, did my brother and sister. My brother's LFT made him disobey practically every social rule he found onerous. My sister's LFT led to her whining and screaming interminably about all of life, even at its smallest hassles. My mother rarely complained about difficulties but marvelously avoided many responsibilities, like careful child care, watching her children's education, bothering to get more schooling herself, and other things that virtually all other wives and mothers easily did. So my whole immediate family had considerable LFT—though in different ways.

I am considerably different from all of them, perhaps, because I never was too suggestible or influenced by them. I thought about how they behaved, considered whether it would work for me, and if not, easily ignored it. Like my mother's compulsive gregariousness. I never considered mimicking her in talking endlessly to perfect strangers and making fairly good friends with many of them. How boring! So I was selective in making friends but got on very well with those I did select.

Let's not run this thing into the ground. Maybe I picked up some of my LFT from modeling after my LFT-inclined family. But not too much. Most of it, I still think, came from the human conditions and the family genes. I'm by no means certain about this, but I am strongly convinced.

My distinct tendency to beat down my LFT when it sabotagingly reared its ugly head was also uniquely innate—as I shall show later—when I signally overcame my procrastination in my second term in college.

"So I incessantly therapize, supervise, dictate letters, write books and articles, give talks and workshops, administrate, attend meetings, and do other things—almost any other things—to short-circuit

boredom, lethargy, and apathy. I almost always succeed. Even in hospitals. But not as damned much as I would I like."

Again the inelegant distraction method of warding off misery! Started in childhood and continued even into my seventies. Not that it doesn't work, for it mostly does. Practically everybody who is prone to anxiety, depression, and LFT can, as I have done innumerable times, ward off these disruptive feelings by becoming absorbed in what they find to be interesting pursuits. But are they really facing their basic emotional problems and the musts and demands that lead to them? Rarely. So I healthily scuttled my boredom and "disturbdom." They almost miraculously disappeared. Lovely. But, until I used deeper REBT solutions, and especially looked at and uprooted my errant demandingness, did I thoroughly solve anything? Probably not.

Moreover, the activities I chose to distract myself from potential pain and boredom were okay, but were they vitally absorbing, truly self-actualizing pursuits? Often, probably not. If I had really undermined my self-sabotaging musts and looked for greater self-actualization, I might have come up with more harmonious involvements. Many solutions to emotional problems are "satisfactory" but superficial. Because we have only one relatively brief life to live, we'd better watch it!

"So maybe, maybe, maybe after the age of five, I gave up on trying to outstandingly achieve in physical pursuits and took to intellectual ones instead."

Maybe, but I doubt it. I mainly gave up on heavy sports, like football, for which I was hardly built. I tried hard in touch football, baseball, and tennis. I even became quite good, because I persisted, at handball. So my intellectuality was—back to my prejudiced view again—largely innate. I thoroughly enjoyed mental gymnastics—math, chess, crossword puzzles, philosophy, problem solving, and so on. Maybe I focused more on them than I otherwise would have done because of some of my physical limitations. But my real, intense pleasure in these mental pursuits was my natural tendency. I prejudicedly insist.

Of course, when one is good at intellectual pursuits one frequently attributes this to nature and not nurture. Why not? If one is born and not raised smart, one presumably is a superior person. Yes? Well, maybe not—but that's the way most of us (smart) people see it. So I may think I am innately intelligent to "prove" how intrinsically "noble" I am.

Quite so. But don't forget that I think that my original shyness and my continuing LFT are also largely biologically based. These are hardly good or superior traits. So my prejudice in favor of innate temperamental tendencies is not exactly an ego-raising bias. Partly, perhaps, but not entirely.

Come to think of it, another relevant point: I have always, from childhood onward, known about my superior intelligence. I took my first intelligence test in the fourth grade, to see if I and some other students could qualify for a fifth-grade class of especially bright students. I not only did well in it but, with another girl, came out with the highest IQ score in the class. This kept happening with all the other intelligence tests I took in school. Of course, I was a very fast reader and the IQ tests I took were speed tests. So I answered more questions than most of the other kids and therefore got higher scores. So was I really as bright as the tests supposedly showed?

Anyway, from these and other indications, I thought I was quite bright and was proud of the fact. In REBT terms I not only (perhaps rightly) thought that my intelligence was superior but (mistakenly) thought I, little Albert, was a great person. So I had both (good) self-efficacy and (bad) self-esteem. Because I felt that I was a brighter, and therefore a better, individual, I had an incentive to conclude that I was just born that way—born to be bright. Therefore, the special intelligence may have started in my perception, whether it was right or wrong, of my high-ranking intelligence. That could explain some of my willingness to favor nature over nurture.

"Alfred Korzybski was right: I am obviously not a hopeless shirker nor am I a frantic worker. Something of both!"

I could also say here, who isn't? We *all* have some distinct elements of LFT and HFT. We have to have a good degree of HFT to survive all the pains, hassles, diseases, and other frustrations of life. Otherwise, we humans might decide to commit suicide in frightful numbers. But, perhaps to save our energies and preserve ourselves, we *all* seem to have a considerable degree of LFT. If we were continually ego aggrandizing and consistently productive, that might wear us out—and soon enough kill us.

I am stressing my own contradictory elements of LFT and HFT just because I am, as almost everyone will acknowledge, an outstanding achiever and producer in several fields, especially psychotherapy, writing, and public speaking. How come such a performer also notably, and often, sits on his rump and halts his own tracks? That question seems fascinating—at least to me—to pursue. So, I seek some answers to it. Am I too damned obsessed with it? Do I get unconscious ego-raising benefits in that my "honest" search for my LFT really highlights my HFT and my achievements? I doubt it, but it's certainly possible.

The main point is that I'd better not let myself off the hook too easily for indulging in my foolish LFT. I know pretty well the rewards of HFT, which I have experienced so many times when I persisted in doing uncomfortable activities—such as finishing difficult articles or song lyrics—until my onerous work became comfortable and then enjoying. I also know things I have missed out on, such as learning to play and write music, which have greatly handicapped me in achieving my goals and purposes. How come I still procrastinate?

Perhaps more to the point, I am probably one of the world's greatest authorities on procrastinating, have written a best-selling book, *Overcoming Procrastination*, and have helped numerous clients and readers to stop their foolish temporizing and be sensibly productive. The world, I daresay, has even greatly benefited by having available many works of art and science that, without my showing their creators how to get off their stubborn butts, would never have been produced.

Nonetheless, I sometimes idiotically fart around instead of getting going. Strange? Self-defeating? I would definitely say yes.

I used to be much worse and decided, at the age of seventeen, during my first year in college, to stop some of my worst procrastination. In high school, I boasted about never taking a textbook home, about doing my homework mostly in the ten minutes we had between classes, and about doing my term papers at the very last minute after frantically hurried research in the school library. Being bright, I easily got by and earned the seventh-best grade average out of 150 students in my graduating class. Intelligent, well-planned dilatoriness!

In my second term in college, I decided that this was stupid behavior. By the time I got around to doing my term papers, there were only two weeks to go, the library books I wanted were being borrowed by other (dilatory) students, and I had to frantically rush. I barely made it and got by just before the deadline, but I knew that my papers were not as good as they could have been had I started them earlier.

I decided to become a reformed crook. In my second college term I was given three term papers and about five months to do them. Well, I'd show my goddamned professors! I forthrightly went to the college library (which so early in the term was practically deserted), easily got all the resources I needed, unfrantically wrote my three papers, and handed them in within three weeks.

My professors were astounded. This had never happened to them before. Within three weeks! I was a fair-haired boy, and they preju-dicedly favored me in several ways, in addition to giving me A's on my papers. I could do no wrong. All my required papers for the term were out of the way, no longer hanging over my head. I was free!

I benefited so much from this anti-procrastination that I used it for the rest of my life. Whenever I contract to do a lecture or workshop presentation, write an article or book, or prepare another project, I quickly get to work, usually long in advance, and polish off my writing weeks or months before my promised deadline. With fine results. For although I rarely extensively revise my presentations and I edit them rapidly, editors, publishers, and chairmen of symposia frequently have corrections and additions to (sometimes stupidly) suggest, and I am able and ready for them.

So my deliberate and planned-aforethought nonprocrastination pays off. How much? Well, to the tune of about a thousand published articles and reviews, more than eighty books, and innumerable public presentations. Oh, yes: Thousands of letters, too, nearly all of which I type or dictate within a few days after I hear from people or decide to write them.

In many important respects, then, I am almost a compulsive anti-dawdler. Nicely so. But not always. Some important things I still put off. This autobiography, for example, which I started again after writing several hundred pages over sixteen years ago. My ever-postponed (for over some sixty years!) study of musical composition. My doing a score of research studies of REBT that I have contemplated doing for several decades. My taking more nonwork time with Debbie and several sadly neglected friends.

Of course, I have some "legitimate" excuses, such as my incessant busyness and the time it takes to do the many "important" things I actually do. Partly true. But I still self-defeatingly goof. Even on some health things. As I have pointed out, I am in many ways unusually dis-ciplined in taking care of my diabetes and other health problems. But though I exercise every day, it is not enough, and it is not often the aer-obic kind that would most probably aid my infirmities of old age, such as my wobbly legs and my other weak muscles. I could also walk much more than I do. I am lax in this and several other important respects.

Why? Because in the short run I dislike doing many things I could beneficially do. Like most of the human race, I am unhealthily avoidant in several ways. Despite my definite HFT I also have some abysmal LFT. How come? As usual, I credit some biological reasons. I naturally and easily—I think—stall. Maybe I learned to do so, for my mother was also something of an avoider and my father shirked many family-raising responsibilities. So I could have picked up, from observing them and how they got away with it, some of my feet-dragging. But I still favor my innate propensity for doing so as prime explanations. Maybe I'm wrong about this. But I still think that most of the human race, including me, stupidly puts things off till the last minute and beyond. Usually people do not defeat themselves so severely as to die because of procrastinating. But it brings on much needless pain and lack of plea-sure and self-fulfillment.

Why does humanity do so? Because it does. But we can more specifically say that people follow the law of inertia and often have dif-ficulty getting started on doing important things. Once they get started, following this same principle of inertia, people may easily continue. But then another law frequently kicks in: the law of boredom in doing the same thing over and over, so that whenever they do a good thing—build a road or mow hay—they may become bored, stop, take breaks and vacations, and then go back to procrastinating. Dire need—such as impending floods or starvation—often keeps them going. But not always.

So I am, perhaps, better than most people in some ways. My HFT, which I created because I eventually realized that my LFT often wouldn't work, may in some respects be better than most people's. But it is spotty and not too reliable.

Chapter 5A

Chronology
The Good Years from Eight to Fifteen, and Then . . .

MY LIFE AS A REVOLUTIONIST

I really don't remember too much about the years I spent from eight to twelve—largely, I think, because they were so good. We lived on West 190th Street in the Bronx, and I went to Public School 33 on Jerome Avenue and led a happy, carefree life. School was easy and enjoyable. As usual, I was perhaps the brightest child in a class of thirty or so middle-class kids. I excelled at math, spelling, and reading, and did my homework within an hour after I got home from school. I was friendly with all the boys in my class and very close to a dozen or so boys in my neighborhood. I was constantly in love with at least one of the intelligent and pretty girls in my class, but much too shy to talk to any of them personally. I was hardly a good athlete, but neither were most of the boys in my class, so I got by well enough at handball, stick-ball, and baseball and didn't feel physically inadequate.

At home, things were somewhat different, for the boys on the block who were my age were bigger and stronger than I, so I cleverly rejected them as much as they rejected me, and played with those a year or two younger, who accepted me because of my conversational ability and my superior knowledge. In those days of the 1920s, boys and girls tended to stick with their own sex, so my friendships with girls were minimal. In our apartment, I spent considerable time reading, and when we got our first radio, when I was about eleven, I listened to music for hours at a time, especially the popular ballads and semiclassical songs of the day. We had a piano, although nobody in my family could play it, and we all enjoyed singing popular songs when one of my mother's visiting friends would play for us. My mother was a fine singer, but I was no slouch myself and regularly sang to myself or others. I also incessantly composed songs in my head and sometimes fancied myself as the next Irving Berlin, Victor Herbert, or Rudolf Friml to light up the musical sky.

Life went along smoothly, especially when the Yankees, the pride of the Bronx, were winning pennant after pennant, and nearby radio stores were blasting World Series games into the street and painting each innings' scores on their windows. Most of my friends and I were rabid Yankees fans; Babe Ruth and Lou Gehrig were our fantastic heroes.

At the age of twelve I started junior high school at P.S. 79, which had just been built and was a few blocks farther from home than P.S. 33. I was the brightest kid in our Rapid Advance class and I found the teachers and subjects most interesting. Learning French wasn't so hot— I got bored with memorizing the vocabulary—but algebra and science were great. However, some of the other students in my class took a long time—too darned long!—to get the algebraic equations that I quickly mastered. So I sang songs to myself and drew cartoons in my seat at the back of the room and thought that the other kids were quite stupid for being so slow. And don't forget that I was in the brightest class!

Everything went well until my eleventh year, when things began to be a little troubled at home. My mother was neglectful, but happy and pleasant. She had many friends, put up with my father's busyness and absences, and supervised me and my brother and sister with amazing sloppiness. We had a few rules, like "You've got to be home by 8:00 p.m., even if the other kids are still out in the street playing." But she only rarely yelled at us or hit us. I was a "good boy," so I practically never got taken to task, and from the age of seven onward, I could see that my mother was nice but pretty crazy. So I humored her (as my brother and sister foolishly didn't) and therefore was her favorite. I tended to learn, at an early age, what I often have trouble getting across to my clients no matter how old they are: never take screwballs seriously. Nutty people act in nutty ways. Fascinating, but not awful.

In my eleventh year, life at home turned a bit sour. My father seldom came home and was presumably out of town. When he was home, he and my mother quarreled somewhat—which was unusual for them—and on one occasion had a real yelling brawl. My father almost hit my mother and left in a huff—with, apparently, some things packed. After that, we rarely saw him, and my mother had several interviews with a lawyer. Then I overheard my mother telling her visiting sister,

Fanny, that she and my father had gotten a divorce but for various reasons were informing everyone, including us children, that my father was on a long trip out of town.

Well, that was a shock. My mother apparently wasn't taking her divorce too badly. She was calm when she told my aunt about it, and every day she went about her motherly and social routines just as before—but obviously something was wrong if they were keeping their divorce a secret. Because I was eavesdropping when I heard my mother and Fanny talking about the divorce, I decided to keep it to myself, too, for the time being. I told no one, not even my brother with whom I was very close, and waited for my mother to reveal all—which she did a couple of months later.

The whole story was quite sordid and melodramatic. My mother had a "best friend," Rose, whom she saw regularly, went shopping with, and played cards with. Why they were friendly, I'll never know, as Rose was ten years younger than my mother, well educated, a musician, and from a wealthy southern Jewish family. What she saw in my mother, I can't say—and I suspect she was really after my father. If so, she got him. A friend of the family saw them together in a roomette on the famous Twentieth Century Ltd., going from Chicago to New York—a train on which my father often traveled, but presumably by himself.

That was that. My mother didn't want a divorce, but she felt that she had to get one. My father went out to Reno for six weeks and got one of the quick divorces that Nevada was famous for at that time. They could have got one in New York, based on a charge of adultery, but that would have been somewhat messy. The news of the divorce was shocking when I first heard about it—but not too shocking. My father, after all, was not the best parent in the world, and we children saw little of him. When he was around, he was a bit sterner than my permissive mother. So I didn't exactly shout out, "Good riddance!" but sort of "Good-bye, Charlie, let me know when you'll be in town again." For we poor semi-orphaned children were soon told: (1) My father was going to marry Rose. (2) They were to reside in an apartment in mid-Manhattan. (3) He was going to give my mother alimony and child support of $240 a month, which was plenty of money in those days for my penny-pinching mother to live on. (4) He was to visit us regularly. (5) Whenever he did visit us, he would be unusually charming, nice, and generous with money, so it was to be a pleasure to see him.

Well and good. Nothing really very bad. Actually, though he lived only a subway or car ride away, my father rarely did visit us—as I remember, only about once a year—but he did keep in touch by phone. My mother handled his absence very well, and went on with her busy social life, as we children were encouraged to do. Fortunately, all our close relatives were in Philadelphia, so they rarely came to see us and tell us what a rotten bastard my father was and how he was making our life thoroughly miserable. Not having to hear this grim version of events, we went on leading conventional happy lives. Practically nothing changed with my father gone, as he contributed so little to our lives when he was present.

What was notable was that none of us three Ellis children suffered very much, as children are supposed to suffer, when my father was married to my mother and was rarely around. If anything, we suffered still less when my father and mother were divorced. Paul and I certainly took his absence with great equanimity, and, as far as I know, so did my sister Janet. She seemed to be upset about everything else in the world, particularly when she didn't get her way. But I never heard her complain about her neglectful and unloving father. She seemed to think it awful that "the boys"—Paul and I—were around, but not that her father wasn't. Odd, how children will choose things to upset themselves about—and, often, not what child psychologists and family therapists think they should get upset about. Of course, as I noted above, our relatives were not around to get us more upset.

I was not exactly religious during my childhood, though I used God to fall back on in my hours of need—especially when I was plagued with violent headaches. My family certainly wasn't religious either. We were Jewish, despite the Christian-sounding name of Ellis, which my father said he got from a telephone book when he wanted to anglicize his name for business reasons. But we were Reformed Jews, rather than Conservative or Orthodox ones, and as a family we observed practically no Jewish holidays. True to her very mild form of Judaism, my mother had matzo for Passover but no dietary restrictions, and on Yom Kippur she fasted for half a day. That made her holy enough!

I went to Sunday school from five years on and enjoyed the socializing there but was skeptical of some of the biblical stories. Miracles didn't impress me, particularly when I heard that God opened the Red Sea for the safe passage of the fleeing Jews and then, quite conveniently, flooded it to destroy the Egyptian bastards. That seemed a bit too much.

I was one of the few people in our synagogue, Tremont Temple, to study Hebrew and I forget exactly why this was so. Although I was only a fair student of French, which I took at the same time as I took

Hebrew, I was for some strange reason unusually adept at this ancient language. I learned the vocabulary easily, though it was much stranger than the French vocabulary, and I was also able to speak Hebrew well, whereas I was only so-so at speaking French. Odd! My Hebrew teacher, Ms. Goodman, a beautiful woman in her early twenties, greatly encouraged me, saying that I would make a stupendous Hebrew teacher. Her tits, plus my fantasies of making love to them in fluent Hebrew, were powerful reinforcers. Before I knew it, I began to think seriously of becoming a Hebrew teacher. If my fellow students at the yeshiva and my own future students looked anything like my teacher, Hebrew would turn out to be a most rewarding profession!

I became temporarily religious for a few months, attended services every Saturday, and followed more Jewish laws and customs than I had followed in all my previous years. Suddenly, I got an ungodly revelation and was soon on the rocky road to hell, except that I no longer believed in any afterlife.

The main thing that moved me along the road from Judaism to atheism was a course in science in the sixth grade. Prior to this, I had had some seven years of biblical teaching every Sunday, when to my surprise I discovered that the world was most probably not created by Jehovah in seven days and that Adam and Eve, if they existed at all, started the human race millions of years ago. Their ancestors, moreover, were—yes!—lots of other animals, ranging from amoeba and protozoa to the great apes. As for the Garden of Eden, Cain and Abel, Noah and the Flood, along with a host of other biblical tales, they were just that—interesting tales. Most likely, in fact, an early form of science fiction.

The amazing thing is that as soon as I heard this astronomical and evolutionary exposé of the Bible, at the age of twelve, I thoroughly believed it. Not only did my science books and teachers seem thoroughly convincing, but the Bible appeared to be fantastically false. Tall tales!

What also helped me turn from a temporarily religious would-be Hebrew teacher—and who wouldn't be with the imagined promise of Ms. Goodman's nether regions wrapped around my beginning-to-be constantly erect cock?—to an unremitting atheist, was a great deal of other reading I was doing in my twelfth year. I had graduated from boys' books—the Rover Boys, Tom Swift, and Frank and Dick Merriwell—to more serious reading, both fiction and nonfiction. Hundreds of books—for I was an avid reader—by authors like Jack London, O. Henry, H. G. Wells, Upton Sinclair, Robert Louis Stevenson, Charles Dickens, Jules Verne, Percy Shelley, and scores of others. Most of them, as far as I could see, were liberal and unbelievers. In fact, in the decade before my twelfth year in 1925, dissent and heresy seemed to be the literary thing, and I sopped much of it up in my reading and found a whale of a lot of anti-religious fellow travelers. That helped a lot.

So I became a bold, almost brash atheist. No, not merely an agnostic, as a few of my friends became when they broke away from religion. I agreed with them that agnosticism was safe—you merely did not know whether God really existed and said, "To hell with it. Who cares? If He exists, let Him. I'll wait and see."

The agnostics made this argument: We couldn't exactly prove that God did or did not exist—for if He or anything supernatural did exist, we had no real evidence of it (many alleged, but no real, miracles). But we couldn't be certain, either, that God and the supernatural did not exist, because one day evidence might possibly present itself. So, either way, we couldn't be certain and therefore had better be agnostics.

Not for me! That seemed a coward's way out. I took a much firmer stand and talked my way into being a probabilistic atheist—but still a definite, card-carrying atheist. I reasoned this way: We obviously can't prove that there are no angels, fairies, fairy godmothers, or gnomes. But nobody in his or her right mind insists that they exist, and practically everyone believes that they don't. I, for one, credit this belief— that angels and fairies do not exist, even though we cannot absolutely prove that they do not. Why do I and billions of other people believe "No, there are no fairies"? On probabilistic grounds—because the probability is exceptionally high, though not absolutely certain—that none exist. So I'll hold to that degree of probability and say, "No, they don't exist."

By exactly the same token I believe that the probability of a God, and especially a personal God like Jehovah, is exceptionally slight. Therefore, until I obtain some decent factual evidence that He or She does exist—and so far I have not obtained an iota of that evidence—I shall fairly safely assume His or Her nonexistence. When He or She decides to produce such evidence and present it to me, I shall willingly accept it. Not till then!

I am happy to say that I largely developed this concept of being a probabilistic atheist in my twelfth year and have added to it somewhat since that time. A few years later I wrote an essay on what I called "pragmatic atheism," in which I held that although one could not absolutely prove that there is or isn't a supernatural deity, there were more practical advantages than disadvantages for not believing in one.

For, I said, an atheist is free and untrammelled to think for himself, to follow flexible instead of dogmatic inquiry, to subscribe to sensible instead of restricted rules of living, to be humanistic instead of theistic, and to figure out the best goals and purposes to lead a happy personal and social way of life. I still subscribe to this kind of atheism because, I think, it is likely to lead to a better human life than is any kind of superhuman-inspired belief.

My atheistic philosophy profoundly affected my life and goals from my twelfth year onward. I not only stopped swearing allegiance to a conventional God and religion but blossomed into a number of other unconventional practices. My teen years were filled with various kinds of intellectual heresy and revolt. Before they were finished, I became a fairly rabid anti-nationalist, anti-monogamist, and anti-capitalist.

No, this was not the result of my environment. My father was a staunch conservative, a capitalist Republican. My mother was apolitical and her relatives and friends were pretty much like her. My friends mostly came from middle-class conservative families—Jewish business-people and professionals who were most interested in professional status and making money. During my teens, I went to the High School of Commerce—yes, very commercial. Then, during my late teens, I went to the Baruch School of Business and Civic Administration of CCNY—a far from liberal or radical college. Until I became an active revolutionary at the age of eighteen, I don't recall being in close contact with a single adult or peer who had very liberal, let alone radical, ideas.

Where, then, did my revolutionary ideas come from? Largely, from my reading and from my thinking heavily about what I read. My hobby, at the age of sixteen, became philosophy. I was introduced to it by an intellectual friend a couple of months before I started college. But then I saw practically nothing of him, so I plowed ahead on my own, covering just about every noted ancient and modern philosopher—to whom I added all the best-known psychologists and sociologists. The Russell Sage Foundation Library, on 22nd Street and Lexington Avenue, was only a block away from my college and it allowed me to take out six glorious books at a time, which I very frequently did, while neglecting my accounting books, though accounting was presumably my major.

Well, that did it—reading and thinking about reading. My fellow students at college, except for Bernie Blau, who became the only friend I kept in touch with after I graduated, were philistines. Business, sports, dates, and parties were their main obsessions. Mine were reading, writing, and philosophical thinking. Not even a near match. I was preparing for my next career—political revolutionist.

I was developing, basically on my own, into an ardent dissenter who was determined to be a rabid revolutionist—but probably only with the pen and not the sword. I thoroughly enjoyed, in my little essays, contending with the world's greatest philosophers, as well as with a number of psychologists, sociologists, politicians, religionists, and other writers. Not that I didn't agree with a few of them—such as Bertrand Russell, George Santayana, and John Dewey—who were hardheaded and unmystical. But I took issue even with some of the best philosophers, including Kant, Schopenhauer, and Nietzsche, when I thought they went astray.

My point was to get to the unvarnished truth. I was, in those youthful days, something of a logical positivist. I believed in arriving at the truth by empiricism. So whenever I came across an idea, like Schopenhauer's view that will and idea were independent entities, I marshaled what I thought was good evidence to refute it, arguing against the theories with what I thought were irrefutable facts. I enjoyed these argumentative essays of mine intensely, and I suspect that I got ego satisfaction out of them. For here I was, teenage Albert, with little more than a commercial high school and college education, plus membership in several good libraries, jousting heatedly—at least on paper—with some of the best minds in the world. In my estimation, moreover, I was making some excellent dissident points and clearly "winning" this game. What intellectual fun!

So I loved my dissenting opinions and probably kept developing them to prove how damned clever I was—which was okay, of course, but a little on the passive-aggressive side. I wasn't really doing very much for my unconventional causes. Merely, in my personal journal, playing a good writing game.

My life in this respect radically changed when I met Manny Elston and Albert Ney in 1932. Although I never would have guessed it possible, they turned me into an active revolutionist. And I really mean active.

Manny was a handsome, cultured professor of music, who operated a small private conservatory on Webb Avenue, a few blocks from where I lived. But his real forte was public speaking. In a spellbinding manner, he could spout mellifluous, brilliant sentences and paragraphs that began with an elegant theme, worked up to a crescendo, and ended most coherently, with every punctuation mark beautifully in place and a most convincing summary and finale. Like my father, he could sell you the Brooklyn Bridge—but in a much more rhetorical and literary style than Harry Ellis.

Al Ney, a decorator, was, in his own way, more profound than Manny, not that much of a public speaker but a solid thinker, planner, and doer. Together, they had run the notorious Young Communist League (YCL) of America but had been thrown out for ideological differences. They were now quite opposed to the American Communist Party (CP) and its real leader, Joseph Stalin. So they were about to start a revolutionary party of their own, called Young America, which was to emphasize American revolutionary principle (vive Thomas Jefferson!) but be definitely socialist and collectivist. No, it was not Trotskyist, nor was it to follow the social democratic philosophy of the Russian Mensheviks. It was to really be revolutionary—stop at nothing, including perhaps some violence, to put its will across to the American public.

Well, this was just my meat! This appealed to my would-be activism in several respects. First, it was radical, not namby-pamby liberal or social democratic. Second, it was opposed to the Communist Party of America, which I considered Stalin's handmaiden and the apologist for his dictatorial terrorism and suppression of free speech. Third, it would fight against fascism, which had already taken over Italy, and against Nazism, which was about to take over Germany. Fourth, it might help save the United States from the Great Depression, which capitalism and the Republican Party had brought on and which was now entering its devastating third year.

You can see why I latched on to Manny and Al's brainchild, Young America, which I fondly hoped—super-optimist that I was—might help save the country and the world. I got several of my Bronx friends to go along with me, as they, too, were young people being preyed upon by the Great Depression, and soon the first branch of Young America was in full swing. We had over fifty active members, weekly meetings, a publication, and social affairs; and we became a vital part of the conglomerate of radical student, youth, and adult organizations that were then proliferating on the American, and especially the New York, scene.

This was a great time in my life, for it helped me overcome much of my lifelong problem of public speaking avoidance and social shyness. Because I was so enthusiastically in favor of Young America, Manny and Al—who were our close advisers and who led a group of adults who backed us—made me the leader of our chapter and I hesitatingly accepted. I was especially afraid of giving public talks for the organization but decided that if forced to do so, I would. If I died, to hell with it!

I then made one of the best and bravest moves of my life. I decided to become a real leader, whatever my speaking handicaps. So I gave myself the in vivo desensitization homework assignment of forcing myself, at least once a week, to give a public speech for Young America, telling my audiences who we were, what we were doing, and how they could add to their lives by joining and supporting us.

Did I suffer in giving my first few speeches? I truly did. I was so anxious, so afraid of making mistakes and being laughed at, that I really did make a number of errors and truly was laughed at. I didn't give up. Through thick and thin, I continued to open my big mouth. I stumbled on.

Then, as I half-expected from reading philosophy and psychology, I became more familiar with my speaking material and things got better. I acted like the children in John B. Watson's famous experiment who were afraid of animals placed several feet away from them. As the children were distracted, the animals were moved closer, and the children grew familiar with them and were soon petting them. I didn't exactly pet the laughing people in my audience, but I did get familiar with them and unafraid of them. Soon I was practically ignoring them and just focusing on my speeches. That really worked! The more I concentrated on my speeches, the less I was able to think of the "terrible" audience. That did it. I just kept sailing along.

To my great surprise, I found that in spite of my fears, I was a remarkably fluent speaker. Just like my father and mother! Just about as good as Manny Elston! I was able to put every single clause of a complicated sentence in place and usually end up with a banging conclusion. How? Completely unknown to myself, I was a great speaker. My anxiety had told me I would be hesitant and stumbling. Well, it was wrong. As my fears receded, I was remarkably fluent. Indeed, I was amazed at my own speaking ability. I soon enjoyed what I had been phobic about from early childhood on—public speaking. Now, as I frequently tell my workshop audience, you can't keep me away from the goddamned public speaking platform!

Let me emphasize: The main way you get yourself over almost any phobia—like avoidance of speaking in public—is first to convince yourself that it is only inconvenient and not terrible and awful to do what you are afraid of doing. Second, you deliberately make yourself uncomfortable—yes, uncomfortable—actually doing what is so "fearsome." Your "horror" exists in your head but not in your real life. Uninvent it, and keep going. If you define discomfort as a "horror," ironically, you get a self-fulfilling prophecy.

To conquer your phobia, steadily and persistently act against it. Do what you are afraid of doing. If you die in the process, good riddance. You then won't have any fears. But you won't die. You'll live to tell the tale—and probably enjoy it. Your phobia (holding back) will become an ongoing release (going forward). That, at least, is what happened to me when I made myself speak in public, even though it was highly uncomfortable to do so. I parachuted myself into a "dangerous" ozone that soon transformed into a joyous gliding. Within several weeks of speaking for Young America, I became something of an orator. From deep inhibition to gloriously free floating!

This experience made a profound impression on me and prepared my way, years later, to become a psychotherapist. For I learned several valuable lessons from it:

1. Don't be afraid of something that is not physically dangerous and that you haven't tried yet. Driving at 100 miles an hour, yes. Skiing and scuba diving, maybe. But not public speaking, interviewing for a job, or asking someone for a date. If you die, you die!

2. The worst that can happen to you when you try most of the things you are phobic about is failure and rejection. Failure is usually good—you can learn by it. Rejection is unpleasant—but you discover who will really accept you. Keep trying.

3. However uncomfortable you feel about doing some physically safe thing—such as speaking in public or riding in elevators— you are creating—yes, inventing—your "terror" in your own head. It is not "enormously uncomfortable" or "terrifying." You are making it so. You usually cannot change whatever "it" may be—the "fearsome" audience to which you are speaking or the "dangerous" elevator. But you definitely can change your view of it. You, not it, control your reactions to it.

4. As I note above, familiarity not only breeds contempt but, quite often, pleasure. Do, do, do many things you stew, stew, stew about trying, and, what do you know, you will frequently become adept at and truly enjoy them. As the classic proverb goes, nothing ventured, nothing gained. Try this with your phobias and inhibitions.

So my forcing myself, in spite of my discomfort and terror, to speak very often for Young America significantly changed my life. I was ready to be an active revolutionist. Young America was the vehicle and I, now brash and bold about speaking, as well as about writing, was to be one of its leading drivers.

And, for the next several years, I enthusiastically was. As you will see in other sections of this autobiography, when I take to something, I really take to it. As you might expect, I read hundreds of books and articles on revolutionary theory and activity. Including, even, those on how to make bombs, organize street fight cadres, fight with all kinds of weapons, and ultimately make civil war on the bourgeoisie.

Was I truly rabid about all this? I certainly seemed to be. Though a pacifist at heart, I figured out that if collectivism was to completely win out against capitalism—which I thought it definitely should—it had better not be by the social democratic way of voting it into power. That might eventually occur—as it had temporarily occurred in Russia, when the Mensheviks were in power for a while. But it would take much too long, and in the meantime, more Americans would die of poverty, starvation, disease, and suicide (all of which, I was convinced, capitalism pandemically brought about) than would be killed and maimed in an effective, and possibly bloody, revolution.

Was I really convinced of this? Yes. I had previously figured out, while I was studying economics and business administration in college, that no system was more inefficient and brutal than capitalism. For as several liberal writers had revealed, American technology was already so powerful in the early 1930s that it could wonderfully overproduce in both agriculture and industry—if all property were collectively instead of privately held and no one was able to exploit other people for private enterprise "gains." Actually, as I wrote in an essay in my journal, our technology was so efficient, especially with the assembly line method of producing consumer goods, that if it were owned by the masses and not by independent entrepreneurs and stockholders, and if work was properly allocated and divided, every American could work for about two hours a day for three to five days a week and could thereby support himself or herself.

Yes, six to ten hours a week! All the rest of one's time could be devoted to leisure—art, music, literature, science, sports, and whatnot. What a great life practically everyone could have!

My thing, as you can see, was efficiency. In the 1930s, most people lived only about sixty-eight years and then were irretrievably nonexistent; they had better make the most of their pitifully short existence, spend a minimum amount of time working at tasks they did not like, and devote practically all the rest of the time when they were not sleeping to doing vocational or avocational work that they really enjoyed. That was obviously the way to go, and society should clearly arrange things so that we could promptly and safely take that path.

A well-run collectivist state, I firmly thought, would do the trick. Not a sloppy, laissez-faire kind of socialist state, such as already existed in a few parts of the world. Not a tyrannical kind of communism that existed in the Soviet Union and that was leading to mass suppression and woeful inefficiency. No. This efficient collectivist state would be run—and at first quite honestly run—by a benevolent oligarchy or dictatorship. Later, as Lenin had said, the dictatorship would presumably wither away and the government would be quite democratic. But it would be, somehow, an efficient democracy and not an inefficient one like the "democracies" that capitalism spawned. It would be suitably run so that all of its citizens really could work the ten or less hours a week that our technology could make possible.

I was really hooked on this utopian idea for a couple of years and was even preparing to write a book about it. I certainly spoke about it enthusiastically to my fellow Young Americans, and some of them bought it. So did some members of the other leftist groups who quit their own organizations to join Young America. We were, peculiarly enough, a real revolutionary group with a distinctly American flavor.

My own views, along with those of Manny Elston and Al Ney, were truly revolutionary, as we strongly—and I am afraid devoutly—believed that revolution was desirable at all costs. Why? Because (1) capitalism was impossibly bad, (2) it could be only slightly reformed and not abolished by democratic voting, (3) the American voter might be so lax about voting it out of power that, in the meantime, millions of people would remain impoverished, diseased, anxious, depressed, alcoholic, and even suicidal. That, of course, would be a greater evil than the evil of, say, a few thousand lives, at most, that possibly would be lost in a violent, and even somewhat bloody, revolution. Moreover, if we, the revolutionists, were really sensible and efficient in our scheming and actions, hopefully our revolution would lead to only a small loss of life. The main victims would be die-hard reactionaries who had already wreaked so much capitalist harm that perhaps they really deserved to die anyway!

So efficiency was my grim rule, and in its name, I was prepared to risk my own young life—for effecting a revolution is admittedly a risky business—as well as take the lives, if necessary, of some evil counter-revolutionists. My views, I now see, were really a form of utopianism: that, come what may, virtue will triumph. Yes, it may be costly to some people, but truth, with a capital T, will prevail and the greater evil will for all time be abolished.

This is quite a naive way of thinking—as I now see and today's terrorists do not. But do-gooders often go wrong and of course fail to see how wrong they may be. I certainly did blind myself, so I'd better admit it. As the years went by, and Stalin and the Soviet Union so definitely botched up their revolution, I greatly modified my views. First, I realized that the temporary "dictatorship of the proletariat" could easily become a dictatorship over the proletariat—as Stalin obviously made it. Second, I realized that in no way did it have to wither away. In fact, it might go on forever. Third, I saw that a bloody revolution and its aftermath could easily be much more bloody than my fellow revolutionists and I planned it to be. (Stalin, I eventually learned, directly and indirectly killed some 50 million people, while Hitler, who was democratically voted in as führer of Germany, "only" directly killed 6 million anti-nationalists, mainly Jews and Gypsies.) Fourth, I saw, from the Soviet experiment, that although collectivism was theoretically "good" and capitalism was "bad," both factory workers and farm workers failed to recognize socialism's noble virtues and sabotaged it right and left. The result, I realized, was that capitalism, with all its failings, was in many ways more efficient than collectivism.

Realistically facing these facts, I gave up most of my allegiance to socialism and became critical of capitalism but hardly against it. After about four years of being both a theoretical revolutionist and (as I shall soon discuss) a paid active political revolutionist, I gave up the revolutionary obsession in my life and became (as I shall also tell) a somewhat less obsessive sex revolutionist. Quite a jump—but I fairly easily made it.

Meanwhile, for a little more than a year (from my twenty-first to my twenty-second years) I became one of the few paid revolutionists in the United States. The Soviet Union, of course, had paid revolutionists, and so did several communist satellite countries. In the United States very few paid revolutionists existed because the small revolutionary parties, such as the Communist Party, had many passionate volunteers and were not in need of paid devotees. Moreover, they usually had no money to pay them.

Such was the case with Young America, with one notable exception. Young America was controlled by New America, a group of highly intellectual adults, recruited largely by Manny Elston and Al Ney, who also took a revolutionary position and would have liked the United States to democratically vote in collectivism but sadly expected it not to do so. Like me, they thought revolution might be less bloody, in the long run, than evolutionary democracy. So most of them were hardly Social Democrats and, for one reason or another, hated Stalin, the Soviet Union, and the American Communist Party.

One of the leading members of New America was Richard Storrs Childs, grandson of the founder of Bethlehem Steel Company and heir to quite a fortune. Dick put up a great deal of money to support New America and was a very bright intellectual who tried to keep the organization on true revolutionary paths. I did some projects with him, and he liked me very much and thought I would help him keep both Young America and New America on the right active revolutionary track. So he offered to pay me a small salary out of his own pocket every week if I would quit the pants-matching business that my brother Paul had started and work as an undercover agent for him and New America. Only he and the few members of the board of directors would know I was being paid by him to do revolutionary activity, and the general membership of New America and Young America would think that, as usual, I was the volunteer leader of Young America.

Being at that time a passionate collectivist and revolutionist, but having to devote most of my time to my partnership with Paul in the pants-matching business, I was eager to accept Dick's offer and become a paid and full-time activist. Paul, who was a member of Young America himself but was much less devoted to political revolution than I was, agreed to take over our business and run it himself if Dick would also put up $250 to buy him a secondhand car. With this car, he could run the business by himself almost as efficiently as both of us could formerly do, because the business largely consisted of traveling to many pants and clothing stores, by subway, bus, and trolley car.

In those days, the 1930s, practically all men in New York wore suits, with the pants matching the jackets. Paul and I saw the opportunity to take a worn-out pair of pants, match them up with a similar material that we bought from large wholesale fabric firms on Hester Street in Manhattan, show a swatch of the new material to the prospective customer, and then make up a new set of pants that was similar to his still serviceable jacket. We would thus save the customer from the expense of buying a whole new suit.

So we had two regular routes—one covered by me and one by Paul—and we made up, all told, hundreds of matching or near-matching pants for stores on these routes. We only made two or three dollars on every pair of pants we sold to the stores, but we did well for a few years and kept our family, which my father was no longer supplying with money, provided for.

As time went on, some members of New America began to defect. Some of them became attached to Franklin D. Roosevelt and his New Deal. Some joined Norman Thomas and the Socialist Party. Some, I heard but was not able to verify, sold out to the Communist Party and actually tried to maneuver its taking over New America and Young America lock, stock, and barrel.

Included in the traitors who favored selling out to the CP was, rumor said, Dick Childs! I never did get things completely straight because the members of the different factions told me different stories. Each faction was, of course, completely right, and all other factions were, obviously, totally wrong. What a mess! New America was split into several pieces, staggered on for a few months more, and then quietly went out of existence. The field of political revolution now consisted of two main groups—the Communist Party and the Trotskyites, who hated each other intently. For a while the Trotskyites even infiltrated the Socialist Party, much to the disgust of many of its members. But the remaining Socialists held the fort against the Trotskyites, who again went off on their own.

I still was something of a revolutionary, but now I had no real home. With New America and Young America gone, I seemed to be the only real revolutionist in the United States who was a true-blue American. The CP was still slavishly attached to Stalin, and the Trotskyites beat the drum for an international revolution and were not attached to any country. I still thought that we revolutionaries could follow American ideals and be sensible, efficient, and practical. But I seemed to be alone.

I was influenced, at this time, by reading Harold Lasswell's *Psychopathology and Politics*. Practically all of us revolutionaries read Marx, Engels, Lenin, Stalin, and Trotsky, and from our reading we sensibly figured out that capitalism was wrong and brutal and was not going to be replaced by democratic collectivism for many years. So we became ardent, active revolutionists. Lasswell's thesis was quite different. Oh, no, said he, active revolutionists had severe emotional problems. Because of their childhood experiences—Lasswell was mainly Freudian, he said—they had feelings of inadequacy and childish rebelliousness and therefore they couldn't stand normal society and were pathologically compelled to fight against it, and even destroy it, to compensate for their own feelings of inadequacy.

I immediately sensed that Harold Lasswell was at least partly right, for just about all the revolutionists I personally knew—including Manny Elston, Al Ney, and Dick Childs—did indeed have some serious emotional problems. I wasn't a psychologist at this time, but I had read much of Freud, Jung, Adler, and other psychological writers, and I could see that Lasswell was largely on the mark. What is more, when I talked to my fellow revolutionaries about Lasswell and his theories, they all completely denied his contentions and stoutly held that their only reason for being revolutionaries was because their sane and sensible reasoning about the grim facts of capitalism and their rational reading of Marx, Engels, and other famous revolutionists, made them radicals.

"Bullshit!" I thought. "Their rigid defensiveness tends to prove Lasswell is right. They really are screwballs and they won't admit it!"

I particularly debated this issue when I experimentally joined the Young People's Socialist League (Yipsels) for a while, when it was being infiltrated by the Trotskyites. I wasn't a Socialist or a Trotskyite, but as a student of revolution I wanted to see how the Socialist Party actually worked. So I joined them to see their actual maneuvering—and saw more than ever how correct Lasswell was.

One leading member of the Yipsels, Beatrice, was a very attractive, bright woman of my own age with whom I madly fell in love for a while—until I saw how crazy she was. She was living with—and constantly fighting with—a male Yipsel who was even crazier than she. But as long as he worked hard for the party, she refused (as I suggested she do) to leave him.

I explained Lasswell's theory to her and admitted that in my own case he was largely right—because I could see that my revolutionary devotion was oriented toward making me King of the May and was at least partly based on my trying to make up for some of my own inadequacy feelings. At bottom, I wanted to be another Lenin—not, of course, a screwball like Stalin and Trotsky—and therefore, along with my other sensible reasons, I beat the revolutionary drumsticks. I thought that if I opened my heart to Beatrice in this manner, she would see the light and fully admit some of her own neurotic reasons for passionately devoting herself to the Yipsels.

Not a bit! Like the other radicals I spoke with, she insisted that her only reason for being a passionate revolutionist—for she really was something of a Trotskyite rather than a mild follower of Norman Thomas—was good political reasoning. So she stuck to her "logical" grounds for being a revolutionist.

I could see that Beatrice was defensive and was lying both to me and to herself. So were the other revolutionists with whom I discussed Lasswell's theory. They were, I now realized, much more emotionally than intellectually motivated to be radicals. They had serious personality problems that they were not facing, so they faced aggressive political activity, usually to show how "superior" they were to the non-revolutionists. By putting the conservatives and liberals down, they went up on the ego seesaw and thus felt less inadequate. They usually had genuine philosophical differences with the political establishment, but their main reasons for their rabid activism stemmed from their own personal problems.

I cleverly realized that I, too, was in this "psychopathological" group that Lasswell described. I had genuine radical political and economic views. But I also had the obsessive-compulsive need to cram them down the throats of "true believers" in capitalism. I was actually a rabid, ego-driven heretic—when I thought I was merely a sensible do-gooder.

My thinking about myself and my fellow revolutionists, and how frenetic we really were, soon got me out of the revolutionary movement. I saw the virtue of democracy, with all its faults and, presented with the facts of the debacle of the Soviet Union experiment, I even recognized that capitalism was in many ways the lesser evil than collectivism. Yes, it had its distinct limitations, to be sure, especially the exploitation of poor people and the deification of consumerism—what Thorstein Veblen called "conspicuous consumption." But by 1937, when I was twenty-four years old, I saw what it took for the Soviet Union (and to some extent Communist China) to admit a half century later—that capitalism had its distinct virtues, and that capitalist democracy was better than any kind of dictatorship.

Ironically enough, I became a somewhat different kind of revolutionist—one who strove for free speech and specifically for sexual revolution. I had always had libertarian leanings in these directions. My writings in my journals, as well as the novels I began to write from my nineteenth year onward, were rabid in their advocacy of anti-nationalism, freedom of speech, and the liberation of conventional social standards. Even when I was a political revolutionist, I paradoxically beat the drum for arrant individualism and freedom of expression. I reconciled my contradictory views by deluding myself, as Lenin did, that the "dictatorship of the proletariat" was going to be quite temporary, would soon "wither away," and would be replaced by untrammeled democracy. Lenin and I were idealists—and, as history showed, we were wrong.

So, although giving up political revolution, and withdrawing from all organizational activity, by the time I was twenty-four, I shortly thereafter began to call myself a "sex revolutionist." I still had the powerful urge to rebel against society—partly out of intellectual perspicacity that made me clearly see its inanities and cruelties, but also, as Harold Lasswell had accurately pointed out, because of my own emotional problems. I wasn't very anxious or depressed. But I wasn't succeeding at selling my writing, at getting an enjoyable and well-paid profession, or at copulating with the hundreds of women I avidly lusted after. I had no intense emotional relationship with a fabulous woman—or even an unfabulous one. All told, I thought I was something of a failure with a capital F.

I didn't depress myself about failing, for I was determined to succeed and I somehow thought that eventually I would. But my underlying rebelliousness was perhaps enhanced by my actual lack of achievement. The less I got what I dreamed of getting, the more I became convinced that rebelling against social convention would somehow lead to my getting it.

This, again, is precisely what Lasswell said about revolutionists. For various reasons, they don't achieve what they personally want, so instead of noting their own limitations, they find society at fault and desperately strive to overthrow it. By revolting, they directly or indirectly cover their own pathologies and "fulfill" themselves. Did I, therefore, cover up my deep-seated feelings of insecurity and depression by consciously and overconfidently seeing my radical ideas as prevailing and seeing myself as a triumphant leader of the greatest revolution in history? Then, when I gave up my notions of effecting a great political revolution, did I quickly turn to the notion of being the triumphant leader of a sex-love revolution?

Of course, this is one possible interpretation of my quitting politics and devoting the next epoch of my life to the cause of sexual freedom. We could also give quite a different interpretation of my devotion to this kind of libertarianism. We could say that I reacted poorly to the frustrations and limitations of my childhood—including being plagued by illness, spending much time in the hospital, being deprived of my first great love, Ruthie, and being kept out of school when I very much wanted to be there. Therefore, we could interpret that I developed strong rebelliousness against restriction, wrote essays against "horrible" conventionality from age sixteen onward, became a political revolutionist at eighteen, went on to be a paid revolutionist at twenty-one, and when I (with the help of Joseph Stalin and Harold Lasswell!) turned away from that kind of violent social change at twenty-five, quickly found another radical cause—namely, sex revolution. Finally, in 1955, in my middle age, I continued (successfully) with sex radicalism and also started a new revolutionary movement in psychotherapy by founding the first major Cognitive Behavioral Therapy, REBT. According to this psychodynamic (and Adlerian) interpretation, my early over-restriction led me to be allergic to all restrictions, so I have therefore been a consistent revolutionist all my life. Sounds like a good explanation, doesn't it?

Yes, but I don't quite buy it. My favorite explanation of my strong bent for revolutionary activity goes more along the following lines.

1. I was born and reared to be different and more contemplative than most children—a rugged individualist who largely thought things out for himself instead of following the usual conventional paths.

2. Fortunately, my lack of conventionality was not beaten out of me, because my parents were both neglectful and gave me, along with their neglect, much more freedom than the average child is given. Happily, too, my fairly conventional relatives (of whom I had many) all lived in Philadelphia, and so I saw them quite infrequently during my childhood and adolescence. They had minimal influence on me and my brother and sister.

3. I enthusiastically thrived on my childhood freedom and became my own person rather than a social conformist. While most of my childhood friends needed others' approval, I liked it and found it but didn't desperately seek it out.

4. When unduly restricted by childhood illness and its consequent restrictions, I put up with it fairly well, gained freedom in fantasy and in reading much literature, and plotted and schemed to make my life freer when I could do so. While restricted, I kept looking forward to future freedom, and in my teens I actually found some of it.

5. As I went my relatively merry way, my major self-restriction was my shyness in approaching girls with whom I was madly in love

and also immensely attracted to sexually. I was so enamored of them, and in my teens so sexually aroused by them, that I related to them only in fantasy—with which I obsessively pre-occupied myself. But my fantasy was always optimistic and activity oriented. Someday my loves and I would walk off in the blue together and be incredibly compatible in every respect.

6. I felt somewhat restricted by the routines of my school and family life during my later childhood and adolescence. School was somewhat boring because of my brightness. My mother, brother, and sister were continually fighting with each other over what I considered to be minor hassles. In my fifteenth year the Great Depression hit and left us economically strained. But I always thought that my future would be distinctly better. I read a great deal and figured that, as a budding writer, I was headed for fame and fortune, however gloomy the present looked.

7. The more limited my life actually became, the freer I made it, first in fantasy, second by my libertarian writing, and, third, by my actual political revolutionary activity. So I kept my free expression continually alive. When I curtailed my political activism, after several years, I looked for another kind of activism, and actually found it in the area of sex.

8. I was actually conscious of this change. When I became a sex revolutionist in 1938, at the age of twenty-five, I started reading hundreds of articles and books on sex, love, and marriage, and prepared myself to write a really radical multivolume work, *The Case for Promiscuity*. I half apologetically said to my former political friends and associates, as well as to my other friends who were less involved in the revolutionary movement:

> I have quit politics for the present, because I am no longer an ardent collectivist and political revolutionist. I see the pitfalls not only of Soviet Communism, which has become fascistic and anti-democratic. But I also realize that all forms of collectivism are in real danger of leading to fascism and of abolishing freedom. Socialistic democracy may be in some ways ideal, but its weaknesses have led to Hitler's Nazism and Mussolini's Fascism. Capitalistic liberalism seems far preferable, though it has its distinct deficiencies and had better be revised in many ways.
>
> Because many people are still trying to change the political world and may possibly still get somewhere, I have

chosen to work mainly in the sex-love area, which has few activists. Sexual freedom is today rarely fought for and even more rarely realized. Almost everywhere, in free and fascistic countries, we are tied down by social restrictions, nationalistic and religious bigotries, and other irrational proscriptions which needlessly bar sex-love liberties and lead to great evils. Because the great majority of would-be changers of the social scene are political and economic revolutionists, and are largely ignoring sexual liberty, I will be one of the few sex revolutionists, like Havelock Ellis and Bertrand Russell, and see what can be done for humanity in this extremely important area. Political freedom is fine and I greatly favor it, particularly in these days of tyranny, war, nationalism, dictatorship, and fascism. But the crucially important area of social-sex relations is being neglected by freedom lovers and is leading to immense harm. Let me concentrate, by writing, speaking, and other forms of activism, on that major area. Few among us dare to courageously speak out about free love, premarital sex, easy divorce, widespread dissemination of birth control, liberation of sex laws, and other aspects of sexual freedom. I, for one, shall take the risk of being unusually honest and crusading in this area. Let the chips fall where they may!

So from a political revolutionary (during my seventeenth to twenty-third years) I became a sex-love revolutionist at the age of twenty-five.

Actually, I had very little status and very great chutzpah for the role I adopted. I had only a Bachelor of Business Administration degree from the City College of New York. No, not a single graduate course. Since finishing college in 1934, I was unemployed for over a year, was in the pants-matching business with my brother, was a paid political revolutionist for a year, and assisted my father in two unsuccessful businesses. Then, at twenty-four, I married and quickly divorced Karyl but lived with her for a year after our divorce and earned a measly fifteen dollars a week as a jack-of-all-trades in a wholesale gift and novelty firm. With these questionable qualifications, I was determined to change the world—yes, in spite of my being a near-starving nonentity. It hardly occurred to me that I wouldn't succeed.

I really pushed my ass to make it—and finally succeeded to a considerable degree. I read, as I have stated, hundreds of articles and books on sex, love, and marriage. I founded the Love and Marriage Problem (LAMP) Institute for research and therapy. I fought my way, against odds, into the clinical psychology program at Columbia University and got my PhD there. I finished my book, *The Case for Promiscuity*—a thousand single-spaced pages that I typed myself—and several other books on sex and love, none of which were published. I began publishing many articles on sex and love in psychological journals and popular magazines. I gave many talks and workshops on sex and psychotherapy. I became chief psychologist of the New Jersey State Diagnostic Center, and then chief psychologist of the state of New Jersey. I published my first book, *The Folklore of Sex*, in 1951, followed by a long series of volumes and many more articles on sex and love topics. I had a part-time and later a full-time psychotherapy practice in New York and had more clients for sex and love therapy than any other psychologist.

Well, persistence won out. From practically nothing, I became a noted sexologist, the founder and first president of the Society for the Scientific Study of Sexuality, the author of several best-selling books on sex and love, and one of the most influential writers and speakers of the American (and European) sex revolution of the 1960s. Alfred Kinsey was, of course, most influential, but I, especially in the field of popular writing on sex, was widely followed, too. As a clinician and a writer, I probably helped to uproot more sex-love misery than any other professional. I did a good revolutionary job and was satisfied with most of what I had accomplished.

Chapter 5B

Coping with Emotional Problems
Overcoming My Social Phobias and Coping with My Early Sexual Frustrations and Irregularities

Did my LFT get into my sex life? Yes and no. First, yes.

I accidentally began masturbating at the age of fifteen, when I was somewhat stressed about studying for an important exam. I don't think I was that afraid of failing, but I had to memorize a great many dates and facts for my history exam—and that was a bore. Also, I was quite horny—which I had been from the age of twelve—and didn't exactly know what to do about it. So I went into the bathroom, locked the door, and massaged my penis for a few minutes until, to my surprise, I saw a white fluid spurt out of it and experienced my first full orgasm.

After that, I masturbated regularly—usually about once a day and sometimes twice. But I was concerned about the time it was taking. Massaging my penis was okay, but coming was infinitely better. So, using very sexy images of wild and eager girls, and various manipulative techniques, I taught myself to come quickly—in less than a minute.

No problem. But when I started having sex with women, either petting or intercourse, I found that I experienced premature ejaculation. Actually, not exactly, because I came quickly but just about never before entry or other contact. So really I just had fast ejaculation.

Anyway, like most males of my day—the 1930s—I thought it was "right" and "macho" to be able to take more time to achieve orgasm. But I made no real effort to do so and mainly relied on the fact that an hour after having sex with a woman I could be aroused again and could easily take five or more minutes instead of one or two to reach orgasm. So my LFT led me to keep having sex, and partially delayed orgasm, this easy way.

Yet, I persisted. I never avoided sex—no, never. I never put myself down for "failing" to come more slowly. I learned, mainly by reading, how to satisfy a woman with my fingers and tongue. I listened to my partners and tried to help them with their sex problems—appropriate, since I was working to become a sexologist.

So I did all right. My LFT over making myself come fast added to my natural high sexuality and kept me from achieving slower ejaculation. But my HFT (high frustration tolerance) helped me to have a reasonably good sex life despite my limitations. So things didn't work out too badly!

In regard to getting suitable women partners, my LFT was at first a great handicap. I simply copped out and refused to go to the trouble of approaching them and getting rejected. But at the age of nineteen, my HFT dramatically overcame my LFT. I figured out, by reading philosophers and psychologist John B. Watson, that if I wanted to get over such fears as public speaking and meeting women, I had to make myself consistently uncomfortable at those very acts. In the case of both speaking and women, I learned the lesson in only a few weeks— a lesson that not only lasted a lifetime with me but for thousands of my clients, as well as untold thousands of my readers, all of whom also learned this "grisly" lesson. I discovered that with practically all phobias, the secret of success is to make yourself uncomfortable—very uncomfortable—until you become comfortable, and then actually enjoying of whatever act you had previously feared.

How did I learn to deal with making myself uncomfortable enough to overcome my phobias about speaking in public and encountering strange females? It's hard to say, although this sensible idea is included in several sources that I bought into. The Zen Buddhists said and implied it in giving several painful exercises to their devotees. The ancient Stoics often advocated it. The Christian martyrs joyously put on their hair shirts. These inklings impressed me somewhat, but not wildly: because all of the thinkers and doers were a little on the masochistic side and often looked upon self-inflicted pain as a virtue in its own right—or as a sacrifice to some god or guru.

Not me! I was much more of an Epicurean than a Stoic. Pleasure was good. Pain, in itself, was bad. But I could also figure out, from my own phobic experiences, that every time I copped out from speaking in public or talking to a woman who seemed to respond to my flirtations that my painful anxiety increased. Yes, it temporarily vanished when I copped out. But the next time I thought about risking a speech or an encounter with a woman, I was more anxious than ever. More panicked! Why? Because, as I discovered after creating REBT, every time I copped out, I made it worse by telling myself, "It would be terrible if I got laughed at for speaking badly!" or "It would be awful if this attractive woman rejected me!"

I didn't see this when I was nineteen. But I did see that my phobic pain increased whenever I ran away from biting the bullet and doing what I horrified myself about doing.

I also began to see that there was no other way of overcoming my horror than painfully working through it. I was helped in this respect by being drafted as chairperson of the first public meeting of Young America, which was—as I mentioned earlier—a radical organization that Manny Elston and Albert Ney talked me into joining. Ex-leaders of the Young Communist League (YCL), but now solidly against the American Communist Party (CP), they got together to start Young America and recruited me and a few other radical youngsters to start the ball rolling.

Because I was a little older than my fellow Young Americans, I was "logically" chosen to chair our first general meeting at Manny's Conservatory for Music and, though scared shitless of doing so, I couldn't find a good reason to refuse. As the meeting day approached, my anxiety escalated. But I couldn't cop out and let down Manny and Al—not to mention my brother Paul and several of my best friends in the neighborhood, whom I had personally gotten to join, or gotten close to joining, Young America.

So, in spite of my anxiety, I chaired the meeting. All I really had to do was introduce the various speakers—our older advisers and our Young Americans themselves. That wasn't too bad! And I didn't exactly view it as giving a real speech.

So I uncomfortably opened the meeting and uncomfortably introduced each speaker.

Until—what do you know!—I became more and more comfortable. So much so, in fact, that I not only encouraged the people in our audience to join in the discussion after each talk, but I actually voluntarily started doing some discussing myself. Yes, myself. I soon enjoyed it and did all right. In fact, sometimes better than all right.

So my forcing myself, for even perhaps the wrong reasons, to uncomfortably risk a public presentation really paid off. Not that I was cured of my phobia yet. Being a chairman of a meeting was not exactly the same as giving a solo speech. By no means! And, being elected the leader of Young America meant that I should frequently speak for this budding organization. I really should.

What a conflict! In REBT terms, I had two important conflicting demands in the forms of "shoulds" and "musts": (1) I *must* have a guarantee that I will always speak well in public and be applauded by my audience. (2) No matter how phobic I was about speaking because of this must, as the leader of Young America, I absolutely *should* frequently make public speeches.

Quite a dilemma!

I somehow saw what most phobics stubbornly refuse to see: There was no easy, nor magical, way out of my dilemma. Making the speech was one choice—a most uncomfortable choice—or I could opt for an agonizingly uncomfortable copout. For if I did nothing I would only prolong my phobia, make it worse, be criticized by my comrade Young Americans, and feel thoroughly ashamed of myself.

Either way, a rough choice.

So I did what millions of addicts finally do—and what billions of other self-abusers don't do. I figured out the cost-benefit ratio and decided to pay the cost. I opted—for a change—for immediate pain to merit future pleasure.

Yes, I deliberately chose discomfort. I knew I had to suffer to get rid of my public speaking phobia. In spite of my painful panic, I made myself speak and speak in public—at least once a week, sometimes twice a week. Never, at first, even slightly comfortably. Always worrying that I would screw up. Always looking for my flubs and my voice waverings. Always finding them—whether or not they existed. Never feeling good or relaxed.

Well, hardly ever. No, never—at first. As the weeks went by, however, I thought many times of giving up and resigning my damned leadership—and to heck, as well, with the blasted revolution that Young America was dedicated to producing. I nonetheless persisted in bearing the pain, much like those inveterate smokers and drinkers who not only swear they will break their habit but actually succeed in breaking it. I used to wrongly think that most of them were aided by self-help groups like AA, by therapy, or some other real support. But no. The facts show that more people surrender their addictions on their own—without any notable help from others. How? Mainly by seeing, acknowledging, and emphasizing how hard it is not to stop and how much easier it is—in the long run—to suffer through the withdrawal process. Cost-benefit ratio!

I somehow saw this. I realized that nineteen years of suffering from public speaking anxiety was enough. And that unless I suffered, right now, *more*, I would prolong the agony of my anxiety forever. Even though I copped out and didn't speak? Yes. Although my panic immediately evaporated every time I avoided making a speech, how long did it stay away? Briefly—or not at all. I knew I was still anxious underneath and would be openly so as soon as the speaking issue came up again. No rest for the weary. Especially since I was the leader of this organization!

So I bit the blasted bullet—again and again. Once a week, at the very minimum, I made myself give a public speech on the virtues of Young America. Or anything else I could find to talk about. At college. At political rallies. Wherever!

As you might expect—and as I think I did partly expect from reading philosophy and psychology—it took me only a few weeks to overcome my enormous anxiety. I first became comfortable and then actually enthusiastically enjoying. To my surprise, I found that I had a hidden talent—really hidden!—for cogent, fluent, and phenomenally put-together speeches. I would start off a complicated sentence, interpolate some modifying phrases, and then (what do you know!) end up remarkably well, with every word, phrase, and meaning put beautifully in place. I certainly didn't get this way by practice—because, up to this time, my practice at public speaking was just about nil. But I seem to have been born with the ability to string words together very well, and even my nervousness about doing it didn't sabotage this ability.

To prove that I merely didn't see myself as a great speaker when I was merely okay, I had ample confirming testimony. Manny Elston, who never seemed to prepare his own talks in advance or to use notes, was nonetheless phenomenally good at batting out infinitely complicated sentences and making every single phrase logically lead to his final conclusions. He noted that I, too, had this remarkable ability. "I thought you were afraid to speak in public," he remarked. "But you are remarkably good at stringing phrases together and making a coherent whole. Where did you learn how to do that?" I learned by doing it!

About a dozen years later another noted public speaker, the gynecologist and writer Dr. Abraham Stone, voluntarily said to me after I had presented a paper on masturbation to a medical meeting, "Ellis, I don't recall any time when I've heard anyone talk as fluently as you do. You have an unusual talent with words."

Fine praise from two masters! My conclusions: (1) I had just about totally overcome my phobia about public speaking. (2) I had done so in a few weeks. (3) I conquered my anxiety without any therapy—exclusively with self-help reading and practice. (4) I found that deliberately making myself—and on several occasions keeping myself—uncomfortable was the real therapeutic trick. (5) I saw that practically any other hardy and hardworking soul who made the effort could do this. (6) I'd better induce my clients, when I started to do therapy at the age of thirty, to do something similar!

Simple—isn't it? Or is it?

What was there about me, when I worked my ass off to overcome my public speaking phobia, that made me do it, persist in doing it, and succeed at doing it? Would almost any other intellectual person, as I have sort of been concluding over the years, be able to do pretty much the same thing I did, even if he or she exactly followed my procedure?

It would depend on their level of effort, persistence, commitment, and determination. In my particular case I read a good deal of philosophy and psychology and thereby discovered some of the things that I could do. But I had the intelligence to understand what I read. I had the creativity to adapt my knowledge to my own ways and leanings. I had the very strong determination to change. I had sufficient high frustration tolerance to put my determination into action and to keep acting on it. I had the optimism to note that I would probably eventually succeed, even when for a while I was failing to make any great progress. I had the courage to resume after I fell on my face a few times. I had the innate ability to speak well, even without much practice, once I uncomfortably forced myself to start speaking and to continue to speak. I sensed, though perhaps not too clearly at the time, that I really had to go through much discomfort to finally get to comfort. I accepted that grim reality.

So in many ways—and others that I could probably dig up and mention—I was a "normal," intelligent, middle-class individual in a competitive American culture. But I was also uniquely myself, and any other equally intelligent individual in this same culture may have *almost* done what I did to overcome my phobia—but perhaps may never have quite made it. Many factors come into play.

Also, let us not ignore a particular situation I was in. I had been elected the leader of Young America. As a leading member, I was supposed to give public talks promoting its goals and aims. If I didn't, I would certainly be criticized. And at that time—and this was why I developed the phobia in the first place—I was still deathly afraid of being criticized.

I also, as noted above, was suffering a good deal of anxiety—even panic!—when I thought about public speaking and when I damned myself for copping out on doing it. So the situation I was in, as well as my own thoughts and feelings, brought me considerable real discomfort. Quite an incentive to see what bad shape I was in and to see that in all probability nothing but voluntarily incurred greater discomfort would get me over it.

Moral: There were a good many reasons, intrinsic to me and also part of the situation I was in, that pushed me to change. Made me change? Well, no, not exactly, because I stayed where I was, anxious and inactive, for quite a few years before that, and I could have continued to stay in that unpalatable kind of soup forever. So I didn't *have* to change, but I had several personal characteristics and situational conditions impelling me to do so.

This raises some crucial questions about therapy itself. I have seen more clients, in individual and group therapy, as well as in many public demonstrations, than almost any other therapist in the world. I always thought that the kind of therapy I was doing was working, and that it worked better than other kinds of methods—and I still definitely do, though, of course, I am not absolutely sure of this. But I am fairly—yes, fairly—sure that the theory and techniques that I use in my sessions definitely help people in most instances. Otherwise, why would I continue to use them? (No, not for the money. I could make more if I used other methods and if these worked better than the ones I generally employ. So it's hardly the money.)

The point is: I am pretty well convinced that my usual therapy methods work—and so are the great majority of other (varied!) therapists convinced about the effectiveness of *their* methods. And we can cite a number of studies, many of them by researchers who are not devoted to our system, that show the usefulness of our practices. REBT and CBT (Cognitive Behavioral Therapy), for example, are discussed in at least two thousand research studies showing that they "work" and often even work better than other kinds of therapy. Excellent! But can any of us really show that (1) our system is superior to different systems, and (2) that particular methods that we use with a client are better than other methods that we use?

I doubt it. Why? For many reasons—especially the one that I have proclaimed for about over twenty-five years: Studies of therapy effectiveness—not to mention reviews of case histories—almost always seem to test how much clients *feel* better rather than how they truly *get* better. To help clients feel better after even a few sessions of therapy is not too difficult; and research shows that they often, by their own account, do feel better, even though the methods used widely differ. Jerome Frank and other therapists have come up with the idea that if clients are uncritically accepted by their therapists and if they somehow believe that these therapists are competent and their practices helpful, they significantly improve. This is understandable.

To "get better," however, in the sense that REBT uses this term, clients additionally have to make a profound philosophical change, see that they usually needlessly upset themselves, discover how to stop doing this, work hard to use this discovery, and get themselves to a point where they not only overcome their presenting symptoms but also rarely upset themselves, in the present and future, about anything grim that occurs in their lives. A great goal! And, I say, often not achieved even by those who work at using REBT.

However, if clients are accurately tested on how they *get* better, and not merely *feel* better, and even if they pass these tests, what exactly they thought, felt, and did to achieve this fine result is never easily ascertainable. Humans are infinitely different and complex compared to other humans and also compared to themselves. One person, for example, stops drinking because he firmly believes that God will punish him if he doesn't, and another person stops because she strongly believes that God will reward her munificently if she stops. One client stops hating her mother after she savagely tells her mother off, and another stops hating his mother because he decides to stop damning her—as well as everyone else. One disturbed individual stops being phobic about elevators because he goes in a hundred of them in a few days, and another stops her elevator phobia by never going in an elevator but merely waking one morning to see that staying out of elevators is silly and incredibly harmful to her life.

Even if we assume that virtually all lasting change involves a distinct attitudinal change—which is probably a sound assumption—there are so many different ways in which an individual can make this kind of modification that it is almost impossible to prove that promoting one of them will work for a single person or for a good number more people than will another kind of philosophy. Thus, again, a client may stop damning herself for her failings because (1) a nice therapist tells her to do so, (2) she sees that self-damning just won't work, (3) she realizes that she is only a worthless individual by definition and that she can always change this definition, (4) she reads that Unconditional Self-Acceptance (USA) worked well for a murderer, (5) she thinks that God (or her fairy godmother) loves her unconditionally, (6) she thinks that she has suffered enough pain in life and now deserves to enjoy herself. Et cetera.

Face it: Humans are too complex, and the situations they are in are too complicated for us ever to be absolutely sure that a particular thought, feeling, or behavior reduced a person's emotional disturbance or that some combination of thoughts, feelings, and actions did the trick.

If we do enough research—which is very expensive to do these days—we can sometimes fairly accurately tell that one therapeutic method worked better for more of a particular group of people than did another method and, perhaps, that a combination of several methods worked better than a combination of several different methods. Fairly accurately. But the road to accurate and definitive research is paved with good—and bad—intentions. And humans are infinitely complex. So let's do more research, and still more research. Let's ask people—like myself—why they think they reduced their disturbances. Let's never give up asking these questions. But let's view all our research results tentatively—and keep on trying.

So my conclusions, stated above, about overcoming my own public speaking phobia may be reasonably accurate—for me. And perhaps they also apply to others who want to overcome irrational phobias. But not certainly. Let's give them some credence—and move on.

Which I did. Because of my conclusions, I forced myself to undertake my famous experiments in Bronx Botanical Gardens, which I deliberately designed to overcome my more important phobia of encountering new women and trying to date them. I had been a very sexy lad since the age of twelve and lusted strongly after 101 out of 100 young women. But I rigorously refrained from trying to date any of them, even those with whom I was madly in love. I ogled them, flirted at them with my eyes, and probably encouraged several of them to think favorably of me as a possible partner. But no moves!

A typical example was my doting for several years on Isabel, a very bright and attractive girl of twelve in my seventh-grade Rapid Advance class. She was a brunette, tall and athletic, exceptionally talented, and had unusually well-developed breasts. A beauty—as practically everyone else in our school agreed. I thought of her incessantly, had innumerable erections in the process, and kept looking at her significantly when either of us—especially she—did something notable in class.

Wonder of wonders, she definitely responded to my "advances." This was made crystal-clear at the end of the seventh grade when our class had to choose between starting the eighth grade in section 1 or section 2 of our Rapid Advance class. Section 1 required taking French and probably pursuing a nonacademic career, and section 2 required Latin and preparing for academic high school and, later, college. I, with most of the girls in my class, chose Section 1. I had already determined mainly to be a writer, rather than, say, a physician or a lawyer (which a nice Jewish boy should presumably be). But since I might well have to make a good living at some kind of work while writing great books that might or might not become best sellers, I was going to be an accountant, make a great deal of money for those 1926 days, retire by the age of thirty, and then be able to write any confounded book I wanted to write—whether or not it paid off very well.

On that momentous day, Isabel and I were in our art class, when we were asked to choose between section 1 and section 2. Immediately, we both anxiously—yes, I am sure, very anxiously—looked to see which section the other was going to choose. Horror of horrors!—Isabel raised her hand for the Latin class and I for the French, and we both looked shocked. I was certain, from that time on, that she cared—really cared—for me and that we might ultimately end up together.

Ultimately! For I did nothing, zero, not a damned thing to bring about our bonding. Up to then, I had never spoken to Isabel other than indirectly when we were both chatting with a group of other boys and girls. I didn't dare speak to her alone or go to her neighborhood after school and approach her. Yes, I had somehow ferreted out where she lived, in an Italian section (though she was Jewish) of the Bronx, about twelve blocks from my house. I think that at one time I even had her family's telephone number. To no avail! I did nothing. Nothing. I waited for a magical opportunity to meet with her, which, of course, never came. A couple of years later, we went off to different schools after we graduated from junior high, and I never, except for one almost magical moment twenty years later, saw Isabel again.

Poor old phobic me! My fear of public speaking was bad—but not that bad. I lived fairly comfortably, up to my nineteenth year, avoiding all kinds of public presentations. I was going to be a writer and then an accountant. So I didn't speak in public—fuck it! But my fear of approaching young women was a real disaster. I wanted to do this more, I am sure, than anything else in the world. I dreamed of doing it all the time. I enviously watched my brother Paul encounter girls from the age of ten onward—and make out pretty well with some of them. I knew that just about all my male friends dated, at least occasionally, and enjoyed doing so. From fifteen onward, I masturbated constantly, with hordes of women in mind. Women, and not girls? Damned right! Movie stars, of course—like Billie Dove and Loretta Young, but also most of my youngish teachers. And women on the streets, in the subways, in the movie audiences—you name it, and I lusted. Indiscriminately. Yes, I would say so—indiscriminately.

But I never spoke to any of these women. Except for one that my brother and I met at our seashore stay one summer in Wildwood, New Jersey—a gamine by the name of Annie—I never even made friends with any of them. Partly because I went to an all-male high school, the High School of Commerce. But so did Paul, and that never stopped him!

Well, I could go on and on about how I definitely did not do anything except prolong my phobia of approaching young women. But right after I overcame my fear of public speaking, I put that dreaded task next on my list, if it killed me!

I dreamed up innumerable punch lines and conversation openers. I invented charming and fascinating ways of meeting women. I acted on none of them. I even fell in love with another young woman, with whom I had gone to junior high school and who later lived in the apartment house next to ours on West 183rd Street. And I never spoke to her, either!—though she, like Isabel, seemed definitely interested in me.

Meanwhile, I added to my hobby of reading all the great philosophers that of reading practically all the noted psychologists as well. As mentioned earlier, I started going to the Baruch School of Business and Civic Administration of the City College of New York in its brand-new building on 23rd Street and Lexington Avenue in September 1930. Fortunately, the Russell Sage Foundation was only a block away and had a marvelous social science library. Better!—the librarians, when they got to know me from my constant visits, let me take out as many as six books at a time. So although I barely did my school homework, and practically never opened my accounting textbooks until two weeks before the end of the term, I read almost every notable psychology book in the Russell Sage Library.

Including those by John B. Watson. I was notably impressed by Watson and his coworkers, while I also devoured all the writings of Freud, Jung, Adler, and other psychoanalysts. But I could see that the analysts, except Adler, were anti-scientific. They still had most interesting material, and I got over many of my sexual hang-ups by reading their case histories—particularly those of Freud. I could see that these histories were partly fiction and that many interpretations of them were far-fetched. But I took what I could, and got some benefit from it.

What inspired me about Watson—and also his predecessor, Ivan Pavlov—was his method of in vivo desensitization. As mentioned earlier, Watson and his associates, such as Mary Cover Jones, would take a child of seven or eight and sit him at the end of a long table. Then they would put a feared animal, such as a rabbit or a mouse, at the other end of the table. At first, the kid was terrified. But they talked to and distracted the child, while they moved the feared animal closer and closer to him. Well, what do you know! Within twenty minutes or so, the child lost his fear and began to enjoyably pet the animal.

What a victory! Watson proved, to my satisfaction, that silly phobias—such as fear of a rabbit—could be extinguished by exposure, by in vivo desensitization. And in a short length of time I could presumably do the same with my own phobias. Therefore, I soon got to work on doing so.

The work I had to do on my fear of socializing with women was much harder than what I had done with public speaking. With women I had to risk direct rejection—being turned down to my face. Moreover, even if I succeeded in dating them—which was my first goal—I would then have to continue seeing them and could easily screw up, sexually and generally, in our relationships. That was really difficult to face!

Undaunted, I decided to try. As I tell my workshop and lecture audiences to this day: "If I die, I die!"

I planned to go to the Bronx Botanical Gardens, which was ten blocks from my home, every day during the month of August (as long as it didn't rain), reach Bronx River Parkway where there was a string of benches, and, instead of doing what I usually did—sit on a vacant bench that was about ten feet away from the one on which an attractive woman was sitting and then start flirting with her—I decided on a much more "dangerous" plan. If I saw a woman sitting alone, I told myself, "It doesn't matter what age, shape, or size she is. No excuses! I will sit on the same bench with her—not in her lap, of course, but next to her on the same bench. Then, having done this very risky act—for she might easily take offense about my sitting next to her and immediately waltz away—I will give myself one minute—yes, one lousy minute!—to open a conversation with her. Fuck it! If I die, I die!"

Well, I did carry out my remarkably astute—I would now say, brilliant—homework assignment of forcing myself to do what I was most afraid of doing. I went to the park every day that month—I told it not to rain, so it never did—and found, over that period, 130 women—again, all shapes and sizes—sitting on benches alone. I sat next to all of them—yes, all. Thirty of them got up and walked away immediately. Damn! But that was good, too: It left me with an even sample of one hundred—good for research purposes!

I then did what I had previously never done before: I opened my big mouth and said something. I made a comment about anything I could think of. The weather, the birds and the bees in the park, the woman's knitting or reading. Yes, anything. No nonsense! No excuses!!

All to no avail. Of the hundred women I spoke to, most said nothing back and only about twenty got into a real conversation with me. I did make one date, however. After a long and animated conversation with a woman, I walked her to the entrance of the park, kissed her on the mouth, and agreed to meet her later that night, on the same bench. But she never showed up! I stupidly had forgotten to get her phone number, so I never found out why she didn't. I suspected that she was at least ten years older than I—remember, I was only nineteen—and that she and her beastly mother or friends decided that it wasn't proper for her to date me. Maybe. I never knew, and I never saw her again, though I naturally kept looking for her in the park.

Actually, when I thought it over I concluded that my experiment went very well. One, I actually talked to a hundred women within one month. Two, I didn't die of it. Three, no one vomited and ran away. Four, no one took out a stiletto and cut my balls off. Five, no one called a cop. B. F. Skinner, who was then teaching psychology at Indiana University, would have thought I would be "extinguished" by one hundred rejections in a row. Actually, I was revived. I had a number of great conversations. I started learning how to talk to women about their jobs, interests, families, love lives, you name it. I began to get more adept at that kind of conversing. I saw that nothing really bad happened when the first twenty women clearly, but fairly nicely, rejected my invitation for a date. I got so used to being rejected that I easily sloughed it off. And I kept trying, in a less pressured way, to talk to other women. Out of the second hundred I approached, I actually made three dates. One I even saw for several times until she moved to another state.

Best of all, I got over my fear of talking to strange women in strange places, and for the rest of my life, I have been able to do so with relative ease. My failures and my few successes paid off handsomely—as had happened with my initial poor attempts at public speaking. Also, as the next few years went by I became one of the most successful daters in New York. Although I had no intention at that time of becoming a psychologist—I was still determined to be a writer—I soon learned what my male friends never seemed to get into their thick heads: The women we dated were rarely interested in our obsession with their tits and asses. In fact, they often resented that obsession, because that showed them that we were only interested in going to bed with them and didn't give a shit about their personalities or their goals. I saw this within a few dates, and thereafter developed a dating plan that got me into bed on the first or second night with many more women than my much more experienced male friends were able to "score" with.

My plan? I would date a woman—either through friends or through a pickup—and make sure that we did not just go to a movie or some other function where we remained in public. I preferably took her for dinner—say, at 7 p.m. or later. Finishing after nine, I would not take her to a bar or other public place for a drink, but I would somehow maneuver to get her alone to my apartment or to hers. From the moment of meeting her onward, I would mainly talk about her—her work, her family, her hobbies, her interests, her goals and aspirations. And, since I was interested in studying the philosophy of human happiness, I would concentrate on finding out about her personal problems. Did she have them? Almost always!

During all this time, I might hold my date's hand or interlock our arms on the street—but not much more physical contact than that. Then, three or four or more hours after we met, and after trying to help her with her worst problems and confessing to her some of mine, I would make a real pass: Kiss her, hug her, start a petting session, or whatever.

Well, it often worked. In spite of my limitations—for I usually had a low-paying job and only vague prospects about making money through writing—we would soon have most of our clothes off and, at the very least, have a heavy petting session. And sometimes, even, on this first night, full intercourse. Remember, this was before the advent of AIDS and some other serious sexually transmitted diseases, yet I was always prepared with a condom. But surprisingly, some of my partners had a diaphragm, and we soon were having "unsafe" intercourse. And none of my partners became pregnant.

More of this, again, some other time. My main success was not with women but with myself: I now had conquered my two main phobias and was well on my way to seeing how I, and presumably almost anyone else, could become remarkably less anxious and more enjoying of "dangerous" social pursuits. I really conquered me! I was extremely happy about that.

{}

It's about time I got around to the frustrations of my sex and love life and how I managed to cope with—or not cope with—my thwartings. As far as I can remember, I have always been sexually frustrated. Not that I went around thinking about sex all the time and loathing the fact that I couldn't get it exactly as I wanted. Not quite.

I think I can remember my very first acute sex drives, leading to a kind of orgasm, when, as I recall, I was only seven or eight. I was in the hospital for one of my several stays, and in the children's ward we had regular cribs, with bars on the side so that the nurses could put up the bars, lock them in place, and prevent us children from foolishly getting or falling out of bed.

One day, by sheer accident, I put my feet through the bars, so I could more easily talk with one of the children in a nearby bed, and found that when a metal bar pressed up against my genitals in a certain manner I received a pleasant, sharp sexual sensation—a kind of orgasm without any ejaculation. That was fine. I wasn't guilty or sorry about my genital manipulation but wary that I might be caught doing it by one of the nurses and therefore criticized. So I silently kept repeating it from time to time.

I didn't feel any great sexual frustration until I was twelve, when I began to get steady erections. This was pleasant enough physically, but I had not yet figured out how to masturbate and to bring myself to full orgasm, so I was quite frustrated. Moreover, I was ashamed that my erect penis would show through my pants and that everyone would know how horny I was—and would perhaps even figure out which girls I was lusting after. My male friends joked about having erections themselves and even mentioned "jerking off," which I did not fully understand (although I got little help from the many semi-sexy novels I read). But as far as I could see, my friends got erections only once in a while, and I got them all the time. So I knew I was different from them and was somewhat ashamed of the difference.

By the time I entered the High School of Commerce at the age of fourteen, things became worse. Although it was an all-boys' school, there were a few young female teachers who were to my eyes raving beauties, and I could hardly keep my mind on the goddamn math!

At that time, remember, I was very shy and had no female friends. My younger brother Paul and most of my high school chums had either regular girlfriends or female friends with whom they at least talked. I was too afraid to be rejected by attractive women and therefore never tried to get close to them. Being at a boys' school didn't help much either.

So by this time I knew perfectly well what I wanted to do sexually—kiss and hug practically every young woman, and innumerable older women, and wind up having full intercourse with them. Well, I never even got close to any of that stuff, so I was constantly frustrated. I thought of sex continually; masturbated once or twice a day; vowed to meet a girl and make some sort of advance but did absolutely nothing to get started. I had read about homosexual encounters, but my male friends just didn't seem to go in for that kind of thing, and I never even thought of suggesting it to them. I was hooked, mainly from reading and from seeing endless movies, on heterosexual sex. Even the few pornographic drawings and photos I saw were benignly heterosexual. So I remained hooked on being straight.

Even though I was exceptionally frustrated sexually, I took it well. I didn't make myself angry or depressed but vowed—vainly—that I would overcome my shyness and one of these days—or years!—get a regular girlfriend.

Meanwhile, I was becoming a semi-compulsive frotteur. As mentioned earlier, I deliberately sought out crowded elevated and subway cars, and made sure that my front was jammed against the back, or sometimes the front or side, of some woman. I also discovered that I could go into crowded movie theaters, deliberately stand in the back of the theater with the other standees, and press myself against the behinds of willing—or even not so willing!—females.

Did I ever get caught and balled out? Exceptionally rarely. Once, a woman actually yelled at me in the crowded subway train and called other people's attention to my molesting her sexually. But I pretended that she was entirely mistaken, and probably crazy, and quickly shot to an uncrowded part of the train.

Still, I felt more and more frustrated as the years went by. I kept masturbating and convinced myself that even twice a day wasn't "too much," nor did it make me "out of control." At last, when I was twenty-four, I met and began dating Karyl. We were at least able pet to orgasm, but no more. I couldn't even see her entirely naked, because we usually petted in her parents' apartment late at night, when they had already gone to bed. We were in their living room and could have been interrupted at any moment—which they wouldn't have taken to very kindly. They wanted Karyl to marry a rich man who could take them off welfare, and I, alas, was earning only fifteen dollars a week working in my father's automatic bridge game business.

Eventually we did get married—although it didn't last. However, we continued to see each other after our annulment. As for intercourse, that was out because Karyl had tried it with a few men and they couldn't enter her tightly closed vagina. A year after I met her and after I started living with her—ironically after we had our marriage annulled!—she was treated by a gynecologist, used a series of dilators, and was finally able to have intercourse—though never too smoothly even then.

So at first we engaged only in occasional petting—and never really in the nude. In fact, I later discovered that she never fully undressed because her ample breasts had large, brown areolas, which she was ashamed of. When I first stayed an entire night with her, she didn't want to take off her slip but was willing to let me see the lower part of her body and use it to my will. But I was so excited about getting even that far with her the first time I saw her semi-naked, that I had real premature ejaculation—came before even touching her. So that didn't exactly work out.

To add to my frustrations, a week later, when we got a room that we could be in by ourselves, she finally took all her clothes off; and I was so startled at the sight of her large breasts with the dark brown areolas that I again had an orgasm without contact. Frustrated again!

At one point during this period, Karyl found herself with no place to live. I was still living with my mother, brother, and sister in our apartment on Jerome Avenue in the Bronx, and I made a bold and assertive move. I took Karyl home with me at 10 p.m. and firmly told my mother that Karyl and I would be sleeping together on the daybed in our living room. Usually, I slept in the same bedroom with Paul, each of us having a comfortable single bed.

At first, my mother was horrified. "How can you do this," she asked, "in the same house with your innocent sister? She won't be able to live with it. You can't, you absolutely can't do this to her and to me!" But I could—and did.

I proceeded to make up the daybed, and Karyl and I, with very few clothes on, started to settle down there, even though the living room had no doors and was as open as it could be. I merely told my mother, quite authoritatively, "Look, you are entitled to your way of doing things, but Karyl and I are entitled to our way. We don't believe in conventional marriage or anything like that. Even though we are now annulled, we want to be together—and, as I told you, she is penniless and has no place to go. So we'll stay here a few nights, and then get a place of our own." My mother was speechless but finally went to bed, saying later that she didn't sleep all night. The next night she slept half the night, and the next, three-quarters of the night. By the fourth night, when I got home from work early and walked in on her bridge party, she was actually regaling her ladies with, "You should see what my terrible son, Albert, did. He actually brought that awful woman, Karyl, his ex-wife, home and slept with her the last few nights on the daybed here, right in the living room. You never saw anything like it! You wouldn't believe it!" In her own entertaining way, she was boasting to these women about how unusual I was and how I would do things that no other son would ever do—and get away with them!

As for my poor "innocent sister," my mother found her diaphragm a few weeks later and was shocked to discover that she and her fiancé Norman had been having regular sex for over a year. I teased her: "See! My poor innocent sister, Janet! Screwing around all over the place. And with Norman, her lover, whom she met in the temple! I told you people in this century don't follow the rules of your youth. Not that you followed them too much yourself. Don't forget that I am semi-illegitimate. Born six months after you were married to Dad. Well, there are no six-month children. Shame, shame, shame!" But I was laughing heartily and almost got her to laugh, too.

Finally, just to show you how sexually frustrated I was, my brother spent one day out of town so Karyl and I could have some privacy and sleep together in the bedroom I usually shared with Paul. We both slept naked together, and even after we had petted to orgasm and were going to sleep, I was so aroused by her naked, luscious body, that my cock went right up again. Though she slept peacefully through the night, I literally didn't sleep a wink. I remained almost ecstatically erect all night, delighted to keep touching her hot body and thinking that this was perhaps the most glorious night of my life. My long-standing sexual frustration made me enjoy sex more than ever, and I thought that I would never, never in a billion years get tired of it. Well, I was a little wrong, about that. But not very!

At this time, I had already started on my massive venture to learn all about sex, love, and marriage, and was doing my stint of reading ten books a day from the nearby libraries. Then, on Saturdays and Sundays, I went to the main reference library on 42nd Street—the Astor, Tilden, and Lennox Foundation of the New York Public Library—and, believe it or not, ran through as many as a hundred books each day. How did I do so? Well, I am a really fast reader and most of the material I read was repetitious. I took voluminous notes on all this stuff and had a deal with Karyl while we lived together. She was allergic to shopping, cooking, and housecleaning, as her parents raised her to be an actress—and to look for a millionaire. Although I did little housekeeping when I lived at home, I could easily take it on when I lived with Karyl. So I did practically all the cooking and housework when we lived in our two-room apartment on Bleecker Street, and Karyl typed up my notes from the marked-up books I had read that day, using the form of speedwriting that I had taught her. So for an hour or two a day she would type, while I would do the housework and more of my reading. That worked out beautifully.

I also gave up on some possible social and sexual pleasures. Once I get going, I can easily talk my head off, entertain myself and my friends, and stay up half the night doing so.

But I didn't. I saw my own friends only occasionally, and although Karyl was quite social and made lots of friends, and although some of them were bohemian types and therefore interesting to me (especially because I was a writer), I let her do most of her socializing alone and spent very little time at her friends' get-togethers. Even then, in my youth, I found cocktail parties and that kind of thing chit-chatty and boring. So, although I could easily get hooked into them, I rarely did. When Karyl was out socializing, I was normally in our apartment reading and/or writing.

Sexually, too, I could have done more than I did. We lived in Greenwich Village, where most of the people—certainly the ones we knew—were sexually liberal. Karyl and I always had an open relationship, mainly to give her leeway to fall in love with some dodo, although I, too, could have had women on the side. But that took time and money—neither of which I was willing to give. So I very occasionally went to bed with other women, but, for lack of time though not at all for lack of interest, I was mainly monogamous.

Was I jealous of Karyl and her sexual escapades? No, I worked through that very nicely. One night, for example, she told me that she would be going on a date with some charmer and might well end up in bed with him. I thought this was very unfair of her, but true to my principles of sexual freedom, I gave her full permission. That night, while they were out together, I took a long walk across the Manhattan Bridge—which I often enjoyed walking across—and then came home to read. At first I distracted myself with thoughts of Karyl and what she was most likely doing sexually. But I forcefully reasoned: "Look! No matter what she does with him tonight, this has nothing really to do with me. Besides, she is a pain in the ass in many ways, what with her disturbance and her childishness. So even if she waltzes off with him and I never see her again, the world will hardly end. On the contrary, I may be better off in several ways and certainly may find a better partner—including a better sex partner. So what's the horror? What do I really lose if I lose her tonight or forever? Not that much! And I really gain by being able to work on my own egoistic jealousy, stick to my nonmonogamous principles, and relish relationships with women on the kind of basis that I would truly like to have."

Well, I really convinced myself of all this. I spent a peaceful night reading (about sex and love, no less!). I calmly went to sleep about midnight and was awakened when Karyl came back at 1 a.m. Yes, she had actually gone to bed with this new guy and had enjoyed being "properly" devirginized. No, she wasn't serious about him, and she now loved me more than ever—partly because I let her do what she wanted to do that night. She was really interested, right then, in having sex with me, and so we most enjoyably screwed. She enjoyed it, but with my high sexuality it rarely lasted because her tight vagina grabbed my penis snugly and made fucking too enjoyable to last too long.

Finally, although our sex became better and Karyl became much more interested in me and wanted only me for a lover, living with her became very difficult. She was often exceptionally moody and depressed, talked about life not being worth living, contemplated suicide, and especially threatened to commit it if I dared to leave her. So after about a half year of living with her, I got sick of the situation. I really would have left on several occasions, but I thought, probably correctly, that her suicide threats were real, and thought that I would be guilty if I left her and she really killed herself. I stayed—and even at times berated myself for my "weakness."

Interestingly, Karyl was not the only woman in my life to have threatened to kill herself if I left her. There were a couple of other women who also made this threat when I told them I wanted to end the respective relationships with them. So I stayed with them longer for the same reason as I stayed with Karyl, when in retrospect it probably would have been better for me to have finished with them earlier.

Looking back, my motives were probably both self-interest—not wanting to feel guilt—*and* other-interest, as I did care about these women and believed they might carry out their threats of ending their lives.

However, I had a plan. I knew that Karyl would keep getting involved with other men, so while we lived together, I gave her plenty of opportunities to see others. As I suspected would happen, she soon met Tom, a young jeweler, who was mad about her, wanted to see her exclusively, and even wanted to marry her. I encouraged their getting together and even befriended Tom. I deliberately saw Karyl less and less for several weeks, and then was relieved to hear that they actually were getting married. Fine! I wished them luck and decided to go on my merry way—alone but highly interested in having affairs with other women. Which I did.

In addition to sexual frustration, I also experienced economical frustration. When I began living with Karyl in 1939, we paid twenty-eight dollars a month for our two-room apartment (with heat, no less!). We were able to afford this partly because Karyl was on welfare (due to a nervous breakdown), and because I managed our finances so well. First, I bought some of the cheapest food and materials and did not plague myself about being deprived of better sustenance. Second, I focused on my main goal: To be a writer of notable material on sex, love, and marriage. Third, I did not waste time envying other people who had more money and who lived higher on the hog. And, finally, fourth, I firmly sat on Karyl, who had some of her own money spending problems, and saw to it that she stuck within our budgetary limits.

Once again, then, I had reasonably high frustration tolerance. I hated debts and monetary hassles and so I made sure that they did not occur. And I hoarded time rather than money and put up with the distinct inconveniences of living in a semi-deprived manner. That was really my own choosing, so I did not whine about it. To be perfectly honest, my first sex irregularities probably began when I was twelve. At the age of five and a half, I was immoral by some strict standards—remember, I undressed my friend Ruthie and tried to pour milk—with a funnel, no less!—into her vaginal slit, and at the age of seven I invented the game of raise-the-nightdress-and-show-your-genitals among my crib-mates at the Presbyterian Hospital. Oh, yes: a little later I managed to get some books, such as Boccaccio's unexpurgated *Decameron* (with pictures, too!) and circulated them among my friends. Without, of course, letting our parents know what we were doing.

Sexually speaking, small potatoes. Socially inappropriate, but not terribly heinous. At twelve, however, my penis and I reached puberty head-on, and I began to lust, think, and fantasize without permission. Silently, for I certainly didn't overtly harass any of the girls and women I madly itched for. I was too scared to say anything to them even non-sexually, so my harassing them was strictly in my head.

To give myself a little credit, I was body-part selective. No matter how a young woman looked, I found some part of her anatomy to ide-alize and lust after. Face, ass, tits, hips, thighs, legs—something. Ah, gorgeous! Ah, curvaceous! Ah, big and busty! Ah, firm! Ah, petite! On and on and on. Did a given female have no outstanding part of her anatomy that I could obsessively cogitate about? Frankly, I can't remember a single one who had none.

Sometimes I even got paradoxically perverse. Just because Susan's ass was too big ("Ugh!") or Dottie's breasts were too small ("Shit, practically nonexistent!") I pictured myself inducing her to disclose that unsexy area, fondling it sensuously, and immediately getting an incurable erection. I creatively made the disappointing area of her body stupendously exciting.

As I signally failed to see at the time, all this was chauvinistically denigrating to the scores of young women I thought and fantasized about. Except for the one I "truly" loved, I ignored their personality and their personhood. Peculiarly enough, the object relations psycho-analysts—who in some ways are even more unscientific in their inter-pretations than are the dogmatic Freudians—mean that humans get attached to other people, whom they call "objects." But my sex objects, from twelve years onward, were often parts of people. I not only made the whole race of women "objects," and I saw only a few exceptions—my love objects—as minds and personalities. I could have easily had sex with a good many of their parts—had the women, of course, allowed it—without giving too much thought to the wholes to which they were attached.

Is that a little extreme? Yes, a little. I wasn't so much of a monster that I didn't want the full consent of the women whose body sections I lusted after. Indeed, I wanted that very much—wanted them to want my involvement with their tits, asses, and so on. I wanted them to enjoy my kissing, caressing, and fucking—indeed, to thrill to it. I wanted to satisfy my imaginary partners and I unrealistically fantasized that they would ooze with bliss as I fondled their steaming parts. For weren't they, too, focused on their particularly sexy appendages the same intent way I was? And just as obsessed with pleasuring these parts as I was?

Obviously, they weren't. I invented their having an obsession akin to mine. Very convenient of me! Therefore, I didn't see any iniquity in my objectifying these women and their "sexy" accessories. For years I was ignorant—marvelously so—of my misusing them. The feminist movement apprised me of this in the 1960s, but my own sex experiences made me see it two decades earlier.

Hell hath no fury like a sex fantasy lived out. I could do wonders in my head because my visions were never realized. The feminine torso—and special parts thereof—that I envisioned gave me endless pleasure, including countless orgasms. An amazingly shapely breast is a joy to behold and to cup in one's feverish paws. For a few minutes. But the owner of this twin paradise frequently requires hours—or days!—of stupid conversation, boring boat rides, socializing with her cretinous friends, expensive gifts and outings, and innumerable other odious "amusements." Indeed, her bosom itself, long after both of us have collapsed into orgasm, may demand limitless kissing, caressing, kneading, massaging, and other attentions. Long, long into the night!

Yes, people have delicious appendages, but appendages also have undelicious people attached to them. I saw while still in my early twenties that almost any woman was worth staying up all night for on the mere hope of her yanking off her clothes and offering her eager body to my hands, lips, and penis. For one night! After that the value of her sexual offerings became highly problematical, especially if she was stupid, drunk, or boring.

So I learned the iniquity of my fantasized lusting. It didn't work too well in practice unless a fairly intellectual person was attached to her delectable body parts. Not that I gave up my fantasizing. Not at all! That continued to work, because I could just imagine the luscious rewards of grasping a well-shaped thigh or ass and not focus at all on the insipid mind and personality that probably went with it. So I continued to objectify women's bodies—yes, and parts of their bodies— and have a fucking ball. That's the beauty of fantasy, and why it may have well, at least sexually, saved the human race. For sexual reality has great gains and hazards. Fantasy, however, is micro-tuned to unalloyed rapture. Only what you want to see shows. The unwanted is cached in oblivion. Physical warts and blemishes disappear, and unelectable mental and emotional taints are edited out. A neat disappearing trick! So you ceaselessly lust after your flame—until you actually bed him or her several times. Then your fantasy dies and adamant reality recurs—and recurs!

I'm not nutty enough to follow my fantasy, just wise enough to use it, despite my doubts. Fantasy does partially denigrate women by ennobling their bodies and ignobling their personhood. It doesn't see them for what they are—well-rounded, multifaceted personages—but for what they have—well-rounded tits and asses. It sees them, to use a bad pun, as holes instead of as wholes. It kind of sees them as passive recipients rather than vitally active doers. It is narrow and one-sided, not flexible and free.

Maybe that's inevitable. We say, "I love you" to a partner. Really? Do we truly love her as a whole—her essence, her so-called soul? Or, more honestly, do we love some of her main traits: her sensible problem solving, her cooperativeness, her sense of humor? And do we truly love, instead of the whole person, his character, his devotion, his achievement? Let's be honest now!

I could excuse my favoring—and mentally using—segments of women's torsos just as I could defend my honoring various of their personality traits. But am I not copping out? Am I still not, at bottom, something of a male chauvinist pig?

I would say I am. For I am defining a woman's worth largely in terms of her sex attributes, which are part but hardly all of her womanhood. Moreover, I am giving her breasts or buttocks my prejudiced ratings, for I may (today or forever) like them huge, medium, or minuscule. So I am hardly fair and open-minded.

Before I damn myself for my bigotry, however, let me acknowledge two important reasons why I am the way I am: heredity and environment. First, I was born a male and given certain hormonal, sensory, gustatory, and other sex-oriented endowments. I wasn't merely taught to lust after women; I also have strong biological tendencies to be sexual and to have women's bodies as one of my main sex objects. If I and billions of other males were not this way, the human race would probably have died out eons ago!

Second, when I was raised in the early 1900s, my society was clearly anti-feminist. It still is, though perhaps less so. During my childhood and adolescence a budding feminist literature existed—in the "high-class" writings of H. G. Wells, Havelock Ellis, Bertrand Russell, Virginia Woolf, Charlotte Perkins Gilman, Margaret Sanger, and other intellectuals. I read these writers in my late teens and was notably influenced by them—theoretically! But my guts were still with the masses:

with sex portrayals in the movies, popular songs, light novels, the radio, and other mass media. They stressed women's looks, bodies, passions—not their minds and personalities.

And so, not surprisingly, did my high-flying cock. You could almost say that I, a person, was interested in a woman as a person, but my Young Roger had something of a mind of its own—a male chauvinist mind—and doted on women's sexuality, not their personhood. It had been "conditioned" by the mass media to react this way, and I, Albert, did not a thing to recondition it. Indeed, I probably did my best to intensify my "conditioned" state. And succeeded!

So I was wrong. I "legitimately" was born and raised to sexually partialize women, but I "illegitimately" continued to indulge in this kind of discrimination against women. I did so till my late eighties. I favor the whole of a woman's body—its inclusion of "great" tits, and ass, and thigh, and face. But I can also thrill to a single one of its main segments. I esteem a potential partner's "whole" personality—her having outstanding intelligence, and charm, and vitality, and responsibility. But I can also avidly focus on none of the above while I single out one incredibly enticing "sexy" segment.

I could claim, in accordance with the theory of Rational Emotive Behavior Therapy, that I am healthy in this respect. If I were unhealthy—neurotic—I would say, "I must have a woman with an all-around perfect body. Absolutely nothing else will do!" Or: "I cannot be aroused by a partner who is not fabulously beautiful and stupendously personable." Obviously, I am not that rigid in achieving penile rigidity. So I am "healthily" flexible and alternative seeking.

No excuses! Until Debbie, I still cared un-ideally for women compartmentally. Pragmatically, this worked—for, at eighty-eight, my staff was alive and ticking. But I was "wrong" in the sense of being fractional and partial toward women. With some effort, I thought I might work on making my sexuality more holistic (instead of hole-istic!). I doubted whether, at eighty-eight, I would.

Then, at the age of eighty-nine, I did. My relationship with Debbie is holistic. I love her many good qualities: her unusual intelligence; her hardworking nature and outstanding work as a therapist, communicator, and in helping me in my workshops, lectures, and books; her caring for my health; her integrity and honesty; her great smile—and too many other things to go into detail about here. She is quite selfless, sometimes to her detriment, and by far the kindest person I have ever met. We enjoy the same sort of humor. We are on the same wavelength.

She is the best lover I have been with. I still thrill at her tall, elegant body with its lovely breasts and ass and beautiful long legs. Sexy. I love touching her, and her enjoyment of my doing so; and I love her way of touching me superbly, tenderly, and thrillingly well. And she doesn't need to talk for hours after lovemaking!

That at my age I still have regular orgasms is quite something. But even if, as time marches on, my testosterone levels march down, I think we will continue to rapturously enjoy touching and holding each other. We will enjoy, as we do now, the delicious sensual quality of our being together.

Do I still notice other women and their "sexy segments"? Yes, I do—(Can't a man have a little fun?)—but less and less so. And I would not risk my relationship with Debbie, who wants our relationship to be monogamous, by going to bed with another woman. Any temporary thrill would not be worth the risk of my losing Debbie or the sadness she would feel if I did play around.

Back to a recurring theme: The disadvantages of "good" changes. If I—and others—were to lead a "fuller," all-inclusive sex life, I might well become more purposive, committed, and "spiritual." I might thereby gain "deeper" sex-love relationships. But what of the possible disadvantageous "gains"?

By cultivating a more encompassing sexual garden I, for one, might reduce my intense arousals, might also reduce some of my nonsexual pursuits, might appreciably decimate the number and kind of my heterosexual involvements, might increase the hassles and boring aspects of my sexual engagements, and so on.

Hmm! A reward of postmodern thinking is that it helps reveal two sides—or multiple sides—of human choices. Because it sees nothing as absolutely good or bad—ethical-or-unethical-in-itself, as it were—it sees the potential "good" side of the "bad" and the "bad" side of the "good." Acknowledging both these sides, we humans then have more of a choice.

Postmodernism had better, moreover, admit that what is "good" for one person may be "bad" for another—and vice versa. If this view becomes popular—as it already has become in REBT circles and among sexual scientists, such as most members of the Society for the Scientific Study of Sexuality—our present views of sexual abnormality, perversion, and even crime may radically change. For who is to say that one's arousing oneself by concentrating, and even fetishistically concentrating, on sizable breasts or chests is "right" or "wrong"? Somewhat limiting, yes. But "mistaken"?

Again, I tend to quibble. I'd better acknowledge the past "errors" of my intensely focusing on certain "sexy" segments of women's bodies. To some extent, to do so *is* discriminatory and unfair—especially to those whose parts I prejudicially disfavor. It helps to dissever rather than to integrate male-female relationships. It limited my attraction to most older women. So it is "bad."

Therefore? I shall speak and write against male chauvinism, against overstressing women's body parts as the essence of their allure. I shall show men and women that while these social standards remain popular, they don't have to follow them, nor down themselves if they think their own bodies are "unattractive." I shall push educational teachings that emphasize the virtues of caring for people and not mainly for how they look. I shall favor sex attitudes and practices that are more varied and less restrictive than today's tend to be.

I shall do my best to fully acknowledge the limitations of my present and historical sexual leanings, and signally fail to excoriate myself for my one-sidedness.

{}

Did I commit any "really" immoral sex acts? To be honest, I certainly did. A few? No, many. In fact, hundreds. That many? Absolutely.

I am not talking about my many—indeed, many thousands—instances of lusting after girls' and women's bodies while giving little thought to relating to them as persons. As I noted before, frotteurism was a ubiquitous part of my life from my fifteenth year to my nineteenth year—during which time I bestrode the New York subways (and many of my female fellow passengers) with vim, vigor, and vitality. Lusting after women's fore and aft parts is only moderately reprehensible. Debatably, it can be viewed as minimally harassing as long as one keeps one's big mouth shut—which I invariably did.

Frotteurism is definitely another thing. As I previously indicated, I did it in a distinctly semi-harassing manner. I started pressing my body against a woman's flesh lightly and unintrusively, giving her ample opportunity to withdraw. I never boxed her in a corner, continued to press despite her revulsion, or groped her against her slightest disinclination. For one thing, I was scared that she would make an outcry. More to the point, I hate intersexual dishonesty, and I wanted my partners to know what we were doing and to voluntarily close the gap between us—which, to the best of my knowledge, practically all the "good" ones did.

That still doesn't let me off the hook as far as morality goes. No. Almost always, I started my pressing foray without any knowledge of how a new woman would respond, and I might bother her for a minute or two before she became conscious of what I was doing, especially at 8:00 a.m. when she was still half asleep! So before she frowned or moved away I was intruding. She might—who knows?—have felt very uncomfortable. Some of the more disturbed women might have obsessed about my—and other males'—frotteurism for the rest of their lives. Few, no doubt, but some.

As a result, I am now, when I think of it, guilty about my acts. I have remorse for what I did. If I could find those women I unethically annoyed and if they wanted some kind of restitution, I would try to give it. As usual, however, I am not guilty in the sense of defaming myself for my infamous deeds. No. I deplore the sin and accept the sinner.

As I think about this for the first time in years, I can see that I was more wrong than I had previously imagined. For my frotteurism was a palliative method that actually stopped me from devising and using more elegant means of dealing with my sex frustrations—and with my horror of "rightly" overcoming them. Like other young males who are not impossibly ugly I could have openly approached many women. I would perhaps have been turned down by hordes of them, but I might have turned on a few and had "real" sex with them. But I made myself scared witless of rejection and horrified about the time and trouble it would take to get what I truly wanted. So I indulged in my anxious self-downing (SD) and in my low frustration tolerance (LFT), and took the easy, instantly gratifying way out by "taking advantage" of my subway partners. Some advantage! Unknowingly, I *cultivated* my SD and LFT—preserved them forever.

Mainly, in fact, my LFT. As I describe in my woman-approaching sallies ("sally: *n.* a sudden rushing forth, as of troops to attack besieging forces") in the Bronx Botanical Gardens at the age of nineteen, I overcame much of my fear of sex-love rejection. So for years I could have "fearlessly" approached my subway partners, slipped them notes, or otherwise tried to get their *whole* bodies in bed. I didn't, because frotteurism was an easy, quick, and painless way to get hundreds of subway orgasms. No expenditure of time and money. No complications! No "infidelity" to the love affairs I was, from twenty-four onward, also having. No other great hassles.

Come to think of it, after all these years: At first SD but later LFT. I refused to pay the freight for more bedded sex—which I always,

always craved—and chose the "gravy train" (no pun intended!) of quick underground petting and orgasms. Pretty neat!—except that I *preserved* my LFT. So I forewent fuller for quicker—and kinkier—rapture. Too bad. If I had my earlier years to live over, I would push to correct this. And to work against my LFT.

Chapter 5C

My Sex and Love Life
My Love Life with Robin, Rhoda, and Shirley

I'd like to focus here on some of my main affairs—such as the highly dramatic one I had with Robin. Robin was one of the major loves of my life—along with Isabel, Karyl, Gertrude, Rhoda, Alma, Janet, and Debbie—but my mad love for her, as I shall soon tell, was short-lived. I am not psychic, but right from the start there was something about her that I didn't exactly trust. The sex, however, was great!

I worked with Robin, who was twenty-two, at the New Jersey State Diagnostic Center in Trenton, in the fall of 1949, while we waited for our building to be finished in Menlo Park. I was the first chief psychologist of this center, Robin was one of the nurses, and Ralph Brancale was to be the psychiatrist and director, so we became friendly. Lovely! I could see that Robin was something special. Bright and personable, and with a body that would start youngsters whistling, she talked mainly about sex and the fascinating affairs she had had from the age of ten onward. Knowing that I was already a published sexologist, and a liberal one at that, she soon told me about a number of her erotic adventures and about how she picked very sexy lovers but was never quite satisfied. This included Burt, her fiancé, who was okay in bed but not that thrilling—a typical New Jersey high school dropout who obviously was not up to Robin's intellectual level. Soon after we met, Robin, against her parents' wishes, married him.

Robin and I talked endlessly about sex and what she could do to either enjoy herself more with Burt or whether she should leave him. He was much more enamored of her than she was of him. But after two years, she was still contemplating leaving him and was feeling guilty about it. Meanwhile, she was obviously enamored of me and suggested that we meet at my place in New York every Saturday, spend the day together, and show each other some unusual sex tricks. Which we did! Robin was one of the sexiest women I have ever encountered. Not only at that time but for the next fifty years or so!

In fact, sex got so good between Robin and me—better, she swore, than she had ever had before—that she became thoroughly enamored of me, made Burt leave the apartment, and filed for a quick divorce. Now we had nothing to restrain us—and unrestrained we were. As she had predicted, her divorce went through a short time later and she insisted that we be engaged. Although I had some reservations—for I could already see that Robin had problems—I foolishly agreed. So for the first and only time in my life I got formally engaged. To satisfy Robin's prim parents, I even got her an engagement ring, though that was hardly my kind of thing. So we were sexier than ever and almost blissful—for a few weeks.

Then the roof fell in. I got somewhat suspicious of Robin's gadding about New Jersey when she wasn't with me, tracked her down through one of her woman friends, and was shocked to find (1) she was still living with Burt, (2) there had been no divorce, and (3) if I hadn't caught her in time, she would have been well on her way to becoming a bigamist. Well. That ended that—almost. Naturally, we got unengaged, and when she did ultimately divorce Burt, we began dating again, but on a less involved basis. Meanwhile, I was brought up on false charges by Sanford Bates, the commissioner of the huge Department of Institutions and Agencies of the State of New Jersey, largely because he and his devoutly Catholic administrative secretary hated my first published book, *The Folklore of Sex*, which came out in the summer of 1951. The book was quite liberal, while Bates and his secretary were staunch conservatives. Pretending that this had nothing to do with his decision, Bates claimed that I illegally had a private practice in New York while working for the state of New Jersey, and that I shouldn't be living in New York while officially working in New Jersey.

These were trumped-up charges. First of all, New Jersey had a law barring psychiatrists working for the state from having a private practice, but it was an old law and didn't include psychologists. Second, scores of state job holders in Trenton actually lived in or close to Philadelphia, which was in the "foreign" state of Pennsylvania, and commuted to New Jersey every workday. So if Bates fired me for living in New York, these Pennsylvania job holders would presumably have to be fired, too. They and the state of New Jersey would be in real trouble!

Knowing this, I could have easily gone before the New Jersey Civil Service Commission and fought Sanford Bates to a fare-thee-well. But I soon realized that Ralph Brancale was also unfriendly to me. As far as I could see, he was interested in having, or actually was having, an affair with Robin, and was very jealous of my relationship with her. Also, I had written a book, *The Psychology of Sex Offenders*, and generously made him a coauthor, although the book actually consisted of a study that I had done myself and on which I had only briefly consulted with him. But because he was director of the Diagnostic Center where I had done the study, he and Sanford Bates said that his name should go on the book as the main author. I refused to agree with this and cited the American Psychological Association code of ethics, which clearly upheld my position. Brancale and Bates were both angry about my refusal, and I could see that if I continued to work for the state of New Jersey they would steadily fight me.

Although I had previously decided to quit my job as chief psychologist of the State Department of Institutions and Agencies a year later, and instead do a full-time practice as a psychologist in New York, I now decided to make that change sooner. So late in 1951, I tactfully made a deal with Sanford Bates to resign my position and arrange an amicable break with the state of New Jersey. He agreed, and early in 1952 I left New Jersey, started to add to my part-time practice in New York, and was soon going strong in it from 10 a.m. to 12 midnight. Along with Rollo May, I was one of the few psychologists in New York City who was able to maintain a full-time psychotherapy practice.

Back to my relationship with Robin. I remained friendly with her, but we were not exclusive lovers. I had several casual affairs, and she, as far as I could see, had many. At first this did not bother me, as I began to see that Robin had serious emotional problems, and I by no means wanted to be too attached to her.

One thing I did clearly discover, however—Robin was far from an inveterate truth teller. Her lying about separating from Burt when she was actually still living with him was a shocker that made me question several of the other stories she had told me. She reported that she had published several articles and poems in the New Brunswick newspaper and that a number of her songs were published and used by prominent singers. I never saw reproductions of her articles or copies of these songs—she vaguely said that she had put them away in her parents' home and now couldn't find them. I strongly suspected that these were ego-raising lies. In fact, the more I knew Robin, the more I suspected that she was so insecure about some of her real accomplishments—which were okay but hardly outstanding—that she manufactured imaginary ones, including the story that she had committed several murders!

I stayed friendly with Robin, helped her get through scrapes with several more male and female lovers, and kept in touch with her for many years. Robin finally got a PhD in public health nursing, moved to San Francisco, and led a fairly respectable professional and social life. Pretty good for a double murderer! And damned good that I never married her.

What about my marriage to my second wife, Rhoda? All told, our relationship lasted two and a half years and included some real complications. These deserve a prolonged and detailed narrative, but I shall give a fairly brief summary here, which once again involves both my low and my high frustration tolerance.

Let me begin with the unique way in which I met Rhoda. I had had several affairs with women after I broke off with Robin in 1952, but none of them lasted too long. They were nice women and good enough sex partners, but after seeing them regularly for two or three months, I grew somewhat bored, knew they were not for me, also knew that most of them thought I was a capable, upcoming psychologist and writer and wanted to marry me, and I therefore thought it unfair to lead them to harbor unrealistic hopes of our ultimate mating. So I told them that we were just not born for each other and remained friends with some of them.

I kept looking for the "right" one, for I still thought I would meet her and settle down permanently. I particularly sought out professional women, including psychologists, who would be attractive and sexy, but also very bright. No luck.

The best of the lot was Jo Caro, a beautiful social worker whom I met at meetings of the American Association of Marriage and Family Therapists. Jo was not too happily married to a powerful but unsexy husband, Warren. I persisted in being friendly to her, however, with one eye on her head and the other on her lovely face and body.

My persistence paid off. In 1953, Jo divorced Warren and quickly jumped into my bed. What a partner! She was not only more attractive, brighter, and infinitely more honest than Robin, but in her own way, sexier. What way was that? Well, Robin, as I have noted, always—yes, always—wanted sex; and anything sexual, even plain, fast intercourse, gave her explosive orgasms. Jo was quite different. She was so interested in sex that she voluntarily took part in collecting regular data on her sex life for Alfred Kinsey's Institute for Sex Research at Indiana University.

Paradoxically enough, Jo was not a high hormonal sexpot like Robin. Au contraire, she liked intercourse and most other forms of sex, but she had some difficulty coming to orgasm. Therefore, logically enough, she experimentally tried everything and eagerly showed me a wide range of sex acts, some of which Robin and most of my other partners hardly even dreamed of.

We tried everything in and out of the sex books. Even a little drugs. Jo found that when she took a Nebutal capsule and deliberately stayed awake, she got a nice, pleasant high. At her bidding, I tried it too—but it just wasn't my thing. Sex and love were fine with me when I was cold-sober, and alcohol or drugs never enhanced things. Anyway, I thought my life with Jo was sexually and emotively the tops, and I even thought of possibly marrying her one future day.

That fantasy was rudely interrupted after we had been together steadily for three months. Jo began to see Mel, a psychologist, and eventually broke off our affair. I was sorely disappointed, but far from depressed. Jo was indeed outstanding, and I truly missed her. Many years later, I was one of her friendly circle to whom she sent a remarkable letter, which actually a few days later made the front page of the *New York Times*.

Jo had become afflicted with what was possibly fatal cancer, and in her letter she discussed how to painlessly kill herself and, with the cooperation of Mel and some of her other friends, actually did so. I was not surprised, as she had talked to me several times, when we were going together, about the advantages of death and the inalienable right of people to commit suicide, if that was what they really wanted to do. This was almost forty years before Dr. Jack Kevorkian dramatized the issue of the legitimacy of physician-assisted suicide in the 1990s. I am sure that if Jo were alive today, she would solidly support Kevorkian and his followers.

In spite of my steady dating, I did not replace Robin with a suitable partner. As I advised my clients and readers to do, I went to the "right" places where I might meet bright, cultured, attractive, and personable women. Not to bars and nightclubs, but to libraries, bookstores, museums, lectures, conventions, art galleries, and other places where intelligent people usually go. When I had the time! For I was very busy with my clients, workshops, research, writing, professional meetings, and other affairs—especially after January 1955, when I started to do Rational Emotive Behavior Therapy.

It was at this time that I was beginning to see how REBT worked so much better than the person-centered and psychoanalytic therapy, and even better than the eclectic therapy, and I quickly started to promulgate it to other therapists as well as to members of the public. As ever, I am a proselytizer and propagandist at heart. So just as I had previously beat the drum for great literature, for songs with sensible lyrics, for political revolution, for comic verse, and for my other vital interests, I now grabbed everyone I met and showed how REBT was presumably far superior to psychoanalytical, Rogerian, and other modes of therapy.

I did find time to attend a Christmas cocktail party held by the NYU department of psychology. First, I wanted to look for a possible sex-love partner among the women psychologists and graduate students, and second, I wanted to let all the assembled professionals know about my creation of REBT, how nicely it was working for me and my clients, and how they could read some of my material and use it themselves.

I was about to leave early when I spotted Warner Lowe, a friend of mine and an Adlerian, with whom I got into a long and interesting conversation. Warner's wife, Ruth, was an associate editor of the *American Journal of Psychotherapy* and had favorably reviewed and helped to publish in the journal my article "Psychotherapy Techniques for Use with Psychotics." So I talked with him about effective psychotherapy, and we agreed that most of the present popular methods—especially psychoanalysis and Rogerian therapy—were too passive and inefficient.

Before we parted, he asked, "By the way, Al, how is your love life going these days?"

"Not so good," I replied.

"Maybe I can help you find someone," said Warner. "What exact kind of woman would you want?"

I told Warren that I would like to meet someone who would be very involved in her own career and easily give me the leeway to keep avidly pursuing my own REBT work, and who wouldn't demand that I spend too much time socializing with her and her friends.

"I see exactly what you mean," said Warner. "I promise you, I'll keep my eyes open and if I find a woman like you describe, I'll mention you and your desires and do my best to get the two of you to meet and find each other out."

"Fine!" I said to Warner. "That will be great if you can help me find what I really want!"

Realistically, I thought there was little Warner could do to actually find a "perfect" mate, but I was wrong. A week later he called me and said, "Al, you won't believe it, but I think I've found exactly the woman for you. In fact, she's with me here at my office right now. I've been speaking to her for an hour and I find her to be very attractive; only twenty-four years old; dedicated to pursuing her career as a dancer; she already has a master's degree in dance from the University of Wisconsin; and, best of all, she's very bright and serious. Just the woman for you. And you, I am sure, are just the man for her. Let's get the two of you together right away. Here, let me have her talk to you right now. Her name is Rhoda. She's really a beauty!"

Warner handed the phone to Rhoda, and though both of us were a bit startled by his enthusiasm, we went along with it and made a date to meet at my office at 11:00 p.m. a few nights later—when I would be finished with my last client and Rhoda would be finished rehearsing for a dance production at the Henry Street Playhouse. The already famous Alwin Nikolais, then in his fifties, was directing one of his unusual modern ballets—no conventional terpsichore for Nick!—and his star, as ever, was the thirty-year-old Murray Lewis, his protégé and lover.

Great stuff, both of us meeting after work! We talked spiritedly and intelligently for an hour, sipping a little wine and getting along splendidly. As Warner had said, Rhoda was indeed an attractive brunette. Though a dancer, she was not painfully thin but had—somewhat against her own wishes—ample thighs and hips and more than ample breasts. She was both firm and zaftig—a marvelous combination. Most American males would have lusted after her full blast, in spite of her slight heaviness. Me included!

We both had to get up early the next morning, so we agreed to break off our introductory meeting at midnight and see each other again that Saturday evening, when we could spend more time together. Normally, I would have put her in a cab and let her go to her Upper East Side home—a low-rent apartment in an old brownstone house—by herself. But I was hot as hell and looked forward to some necking in the taxi. So I hailed one on Eighth Avenue, near my West Side Parc Vendome apartment, and we both jumped in.

Well, did we neck for the next fifteen minutes. Like fire! My left hand promptly went under her skirt, and my right hand opened her blouse, pushed up her bra, and passionately fondled her incredibly soft-firm breasts as she gasped with joy and pressed closer and closer to me. Then my hot mouth got to her nipples and almost sucked them off, pushing her to several explosive orgasms. I opened my fly, and she feverishly clutched my cock, quickly getting me to spurt a load of semen into her small, excited hands. "Boy!" I said to myself. "Am I glad I insisted on taking her home!"

All too soon our taxi landed at her door, and she invited me into her small apartment just as I, of course, hoped she would. "Wait a few minutes," Rhoda breathlessly said, "as I go to the bathroom and make some preparations. Meanwhile, you rest here on this bed. Take off your clothes, if you want, and rest a few minutes till I get back to you."

I certainly was in no mood to argue with her. Within half a minute after she closed the bathroom door, I was completely naked in her small bed. My cock was so straight and high that it raised the heavy bed quilt that I had partly thrown over me. Three minutes later a naked, rosy-bodied Rhoda hurtled herself out of the bathroom onto the bed, and for the next hour and a half we went at it hammer and tongs. Both our bodies sizzled, and our orgasms blasted ourselves and each other. We were both thoroughly exhausted—but kept fondling and talking to each other, and within ten minutes we were more than willing to try two-back horsey again.

I had three full orgasms within an hour and a half that night. But that didn't even come close to my record. A few years before, I slept with three women on a single day—Robin in the morning, my ex-wife Karyl, who visited me that afternoon, and a high-class prostitute, Maria, who fell madly in love with me—temporarily—after I had a friendly two-hour talk with her at a Christmas party.

Maria gave me a fervent invitation, which I could have easily for-gone this on this particular two-women-and-three-orgasms day. I was also afraid—in this pre-AIDS time—of catching gonorrhea or syphilis. But I considered her luscious big tits and pulsing mouth, and so quickly drove to her penthouse apartment, where she was waiting for me at the elevator—stark naked, with a glass of Scotch in her outstretched hand. I refused—as I drank very little even before I became diabetic—so she gulped down the drink herself, although she already seemed to be well liquored. As soon as we got in the door of her apartment, she ripped off my clothes, threw me on the heavily carpeted floor of the living room, frantically gobbled my willing cock for a minute and then, afraid that I would come too quickly, slapped a condom on me, thrust her pounding thighs over the rubber and bounced up and down on my rock-hard penis as if the world was about to come to an end and we were going to have our final orgasm before it could beat us to the punch. I took over ten minutes to come instead of my usual two or three. She was ecstatic about my lasting so long. With her kind of thrusting, most of her johns were finished in a minute, and she was pleased to get rid of them.

That was the last of me and Maria—her mad love for me was now apparently satisfied, and she presumably went back to being a less orgasmic and more money-making whore.

Obviously, before I met Rhoda I had quite a full sex life—including this experience of three women and five orgasms in a single day. And even that wasn't the tops! When I was around forty, I regularly had about one orgasm every day, mostly by masturbation and sometimes two or three if I was with a quite sexually interesting woman.

Like Sandy, who was only twenty-one, married to an idiotic husband she hated, and interested in writing a book on sex. Under the guise of conferring with me on this book, she would come to visit me at 11:00 p.m. We would rush to my foam-rubber mattress and experiment with all the techniques she was supposedly going to write about. Small, blue-eyed, and blond, and with a pliable body that could do almost anything, Sandy kept showing me a new trick or two—most of which, she said, she had picked up with boys on her block when she started having sex at the age of thirteen—and I would reciprocate.

Don't forget that by this time I had read hundreds of books on sex and love, had been the American editor of the *International Journal of Sexology*, and had published *The Folklore of Sex* and many sex-love articles. So I taught Sandy some things, as well as vice versa, and for several months, until her husband became suspicious, we made my foam-rubber mattress really earn its keep. Sandy was no great intellectual, but she had a charming, bubbling personality, and, as long as we spent only an hour or so together once or twice a week, I never got bored seeing her. Even though we did no actual writing on sex!

So, obviously, I was hardly a monk during the time before I met Rhoda. More of a roué. I still haven't got to my biggest sex feat, however. That happened a short time after Sandy's husband got suspicious and no longer permitted her to "work" with me. She came home one night, so obviously high from our "writing conference," that he decided that we were most probably practicing what we preached. So that was that.

My biggest sex feat occurred when I was invited to give the main address on sex and love at a well-known Catskills resort and, as part of my remuneration, to spend a free three-day weekend there. Such resorts are far from my cup of tea, as the people who go there, especially the women, are obsessed with finding mates—and I mean permanent mates. This particular resort had a singles weekend and was loaded with young Jewish women—mostly seventeen to twenty-five—looking for a well-to-do professional man for a husband. I would have been happy to screw the ass off almost any of these pretty young things; however, being heavily marriage-oriented, they would take off their clothes only after a man had dated them several times and proved that he was really serious.

By the first day, I could see that I was going to get nowhere with these conventional, boring virgins (definitely no good cock-sucking—more like cock-teasing!) and I expected the next day to be more of the same, with many charming women delightfully on view in their skimpy bathing suits. However, Miriam, the owner of the resort, had planned a special event for me. Her thirty-year-old niece, Shirley, a social worker in New York, was coming up that day just to meet me. She was, said my hostess, very intelligent, quite attractive, had read my book *The Folklore of Sex*, was most eager to meet me, and would be *quite available*, Miriam emphasized, for anything I wanted to do with her. Yes, *anything*.

That sounded fine—except that Shirley had a very plain though pleasant face and was, well, at least thirty pounds overweight. Not that I objected to heavy women—for thin, assless, and breastless women were not exactly my thing. Some males are tit-men and some are ass-men—I am both. Meeting Shirley was not completely discouraging. We had a pleasant breakfast with Miriam, but I was not exactly thinking of ripping off her clothes anytime soon. But we would see what we would see!

Miriam urged us to go for a walk in the surrounding beautiful woods. We walked about a mile, saw a plateau we could climb up to via a narrow pathway through the trees, and almost killed ourselves sliding up to it. We lay on the grass talking about psychotherapy, which she seemed to be quite sane about and was no more psychoanalytic than I was. Shirley was really bright and a free-flowing thinker. She had, I think deliberately, worn a low-cut, light blouse, and I could see two interesting full-sized breasts peeping out of it. I got off my back, moved closer to her, and found her fully receptive. Shirley was Rubenesque, I would say, and about five feet nine (I am five feet ten), good posture, plump breasts, thighs that were definitely well-rounded but athletically firm, and a sizable but still fairly trim ass. No great beauty, but not hard to look at. Although she looked fat when dressed, she had a firm, well-exercised body that looked—as well as felt—pretty good when she got her girdle off. I would have been somewhat ashamed to be seen with a "fat" woman, as I had not yet invented my famous shame-attacking exercises—which I included in REBT in the 1960s. I didn't want onlookers to think that I couldn't "win" a more comely partner. Stripped of her finery, however, Shirley looked fine. It was only ten in the morning, but she was hot to trot. While one of my hands undid her blouse—no bra!—and the other went under her flimsy panties, Shirley unzipped my fly and gulped my erect cock deep in her throat. Well, we were off!

What followed was to be a twenty-three-hour period that would rival any other sex experience.

We screwed twice, there on that grassy plateau, and I had two tumultuous orgasms, after which I suggested we go back to the resort and have some lunch. She reluctantly agreed. After lunch, we retired to my cabin, where we tried screwing in the shower. She was really too tall, but by leaning over and clasping her ankles, and by having me penetrate her vagina from the back, we finally succeeded. But I kept slipping out of her vagina and not getting very good penetration or friction, so she bent far over and pushed my penis up her anus. I like a tight female anus, especially when I have had one or two orgasms and am nicely stiff but find it hard to come. Although I think that a woman's vagina is more pleasantly suited to my cock than is just about any other part of her body, anal intercourse can sometimes be unusually stimulating. It was, this time, with Shirley.

The tally after our shower? Three for her and three for me—and in about two hours.

Later that afternoon, as we ostensibly prepared for my talk, Shirley gobbled my prick, scrotum, and balls to a fare-thee-well and gave me my fourth tremendous sexual avalanche of the day. And after the talk, there was to be no movie-going, comedy-watching, or any other entertainment. Shirley was sure that our own special kind of entertainment was the very best. She wanted to reward me for the "stupendous talk" I had given, so she told me that I was not to do anything to please her. "Don't lift a finger! Just gratefully accept what's absolutely coming to you."

"But what about you? Don't you want me to try to do something for you, too?"

"No! I've already had the greatest day of my life. Four orgasmic blasts, when, often, I barely have one. And even without the sex, I can't ever think of having a finer time. All that great talk! Getting to know the real you! Seeing how you became—or made yourself—what you are. Seeing how much greater you are going to be in the future. All that—and more. I can't thank you enough. Yes, I've told you how much I appreciate you. But now I'm going to show you."

I wouldn't have believed it, but she did. She used her wonderful mouth and lips to tease and warm all my sexual parts. Each time she did so, my staff of life would rise to the occasion and feel like it was about to erupt, but, having had four pulsing send-offs that day, it wasn't easily going to have a fifth. But Shirley was determined, and I had a semi-reluctant but still gracious fifth orgasm for the day.

At eight, Shirley permitted us to take another shower and a nap.

By midnight we—and my penis—were almost wide awake. Shirley had me lie on my side behind her and insert Oscar in her vagina, as her gorgeous ass whacked against my stomach. Shirley had such a violent orgasm, writhing up and down and in and out so powerfully that Oscar couldn't seem to stand being passive and had his tremendous sixth orgasm of the day.

I awoke at 9 a.m. to find my fully erect cock smothered by Shirley's lips and mouth, and her head jerking back and forth. She was going to give me a final orgasm if it killed her. It almost did. The way she was jerking her head up and down, I was afraid it would fall off. Miraculously, it didn't.

But no go. I was willing to come, but Oscar stubbornly resisted. Shirley was by now thoroughly out of orgasms but was still determined to give me a seventh and final one before we left the resort. Once again, she tried with all her heart and every part of her body. I was extremely aroused but still seemingly far from an orgasm.

Finally, almost in desperation to have me come, Shirley put Oscar deep in her mouth. As Oscar was beginning to pulse toward orgasm, she milked him for what seemed like a full five minutes, screaming through her half-closed lips, "We've made it! You and Oscar are magnificent! And I'm pretty damned good, too! Seven for you and just as many, I think, for me! I'll never forget this day. Now that we know what we really can do, we must repeat it frequently. At least every Sunday!"

When we got off the bus at the Manhattan terminal, we thought of going to one of our apartments, but we both had important appointments to keep that day, so we parted amicably with a good-bye kiss. Whether we really would have gone on to still more orgasms, we'll never know. But I doubt it! My Lucky Seven was quite enough.

Back to Rhoda, whom I married in 1956. She had a beautiful body—not perfect, but good, good! Artists like Leon Kroll and Raphael Soyer enthusiastically used her as a model—and I could well see why. Her face wouldn't exactly launch a thousand ships, but it was charming, at the same time slim and sufficiently rounded, and usually lit up with a personality-filled smile. She was naturally outgoing, talkative, pleasant, and interested in her partner. No deadhead—but no obnoxiously compulsive talker. She was interested in dance, of course, and in body movement, but she was also conversant about animals, art, people, politics, sex, and many other things. Never a bore, always alert.

Sexually, stupendous! When I described her to Alfred Kinsey and Wardell Pomeroy, they immediately wanted to take films of her phenomenal ability. We arranged to do this on our honeymoon trip to Madison, Wisconsin, where she had done her graduate work in movement therapy at the University of Wisconsin. Then we were to visit with Kinsey at his sex institute at Indiana University. Unfortunately, Kinsey died of a heart attack before this, so Rhoda and her multiple orgasms were never filmed. A real loss to the archives!

Could Rhoda really have thirty full orgasms in thirty minutes or less? Indeed she could—and regularly did. When we were married and lived together on West 56th Street, our daily routine would usually go like this. Rhoda would take a shower at midnight and get into bed with her face turned to the wall. I would shower and join her about ten minutes later. As soon as I got into bed she would wake up and, as I started to put my arm around her, she would have her first of many orgasms. Started to put my arm around her? Yes, indeed. I was often on my way to embracing her from behind, and—would you believe it!—before I even touched her she was jumping and writhing orgasmically. If I touched her with my arm merely bent over her side and my cock prodding her shapely ass, that would work, too. Off she immediately went on her orgasmic way.

Then, for the next half hour, stimulated mainly by my touching almost any part of her body, and only sometimes by direct clitoral stimulation with my fingers or by intercourse, Rhoda would have orgasm after orgasm. Each one was usually separate, explosive, and body-shaking. Then, less than a minute later, she would erupt again—and again and again.

After a half-hour of thirty or more orgasms, Rhoda was still capable of continuing but felt physically—more than sexually—exhausted, and usually said, "Fine!" and was fast asleep. Meanwhile, I always had at least one or two orgasms, usually during intercourse. On a good night, I would get fully aroused again after twenty minutes or so, and we would have our second copulation—which, even with her on top, would last no more than ten minutes if I made an effort to prolong it.

So I was okay sexually with Rhoda—but she was phenomenal. Our sex life along these mutually satisfying lines lasted about two full years. Then various things happened, mainly nonsexual things, that disrupted our "paradise."

According to my recollection, Rhoda injured her right foot and, instead of giving up dancing with Alwin Nikolais's unusual group for a few months, kept up her usual routines and perhaps interfered with her foot's healing. It never did completely heal, and she therefore stopped trying to be a full-fledged ballet and modern dancer.

This was sad, and I duly empathized with her. She took her loss remarkably well and continued, for many years thereafter, to remain in the movement and dance field, to teach, to direct physical activities at Philadelphia State Hospital, and to do many other vigorous things. But during our last half year together, our routines were distinctly changed.

Because of Rhoda's broken foot, she no longer had dance rehearsals until midnight; she now was available much earlier in the evening and wanted me to be with her and her friends. Not I! I stubbornly resisted, so she disappointedly saw them by herself. I still saw my clients and therapy groups till 11 p.m., and if I had some time off from them, I had plenty of articles and books to both read and write. Which I did.

To make things more interesting, some of Rhoda's friends were available males who loved to chit-chat and make passes at her for hours at a time. I had no objections to that, as I favored the principle of open relationships and willingly had them with Karyl, Gertrude, and other women. As tended to happen with them, as well, Rhoda fell in love with a couple of her lovers, and that put a strain on our relationship. We still had great sex, and Rhoda had her usual thirty orgasms each night, but for the first time she objected to getting on top of me during intercourse. Not because she objected to the acrobatics—remember, she was a great dancer. But one of her lovers—a dancer, too, I think—loved to take the top position himself and had a cock that was not as quick-tempered as mine, and so could screw in that position for half an hour or so.

Rhoda liked that—including the male pelvic thrust. She revealed to me that the very first time I had fucked her, she had the most sensational and exhilarating orgasm of her entire life, silently wished for more of the same, but went along with mounting me during intercourse mainly to prolong her and my satisfaction. So, after she voiced this preference, I then employed more acrobatics myself during our copulation—though we had no chandelier—and that was all right, but I lasted several minutes less than before, and less than her new lover did. So it really wasn't all that right.

Things got no better between Rhoda and me, though we seldom quarreled and remained good friends. One of our rare quarrels involved a friend, Ed Brecher, a good writer on sex, who was interested in Rhoda's young ass. He was then about sixty, I was around forty-five, and she was about twenty-six. He was quite a lecher and arranged with his wife, Miriam, foursomes at their home in Connecticut. Miriam was quite bright herself, somewhat younger than Ed, and presumably attractive. Ed and she had a good many of these "open house" arrangements.

I don't think that Rhoda was enamored of Ed, but she liked the idea of a day in the country and some new kind of sex. I was always ready for new adventures, so I said, "Fine! Let's try it!"

Actually, however, I finally copped out. Miriam was good to talk with, but was just not attractive to me physically. I went for a ride with Miriam but made no passes at her—which information she seemed to relay to Ed, who had been making passes at Rhoda—so the deal was off.

Rhoda didn't seem to care much, and we had our own usual good sex in their guest room that night. But instead of starting back to New York early that Sunday evening and beating the traffic as I suggested, she dallied over another dinner and we started out late. We did end up getting caught in traffic, and what would normally have been a two-hour drive took four and a half hours.

I had an article to finish up that night and was not in a glorious mood. When we finally parked the car, I quickly got out, started unloading our luggage, and began to bring our stuff into our apartment house. To my surprise, Rhoda had a fit. I had not gone around to the right-hand side of the car, opened the door for Rhoda, helped her to get out of the car, and escorted her into the house.

What a crime! She ordered me back into the car and for the next ten minutes told me what an impolite, autistic boor I was. Why? Because her father would never, never do a rude thing like I had just done. He was always nice, courteous, considerate, and loving. As all men should, of course, be. I continually neglected some of the main social graces with her. My mother had raised me to be a boor!

I was not exactly hurt by Rhoda's vituperation, largely because I immediately thought, and fairly calmly said, that she and her father were chauvinist pigs who put females in an inferior place. None of that for me! I realized, however, that Rhoda was not to be talked out of her male-catering-to-female values. I saw that she would keep resenting my nonfatherly "impolite" attitudes and actions. This wouldn't kill me—but who needed it?

I began to see that Rhoda and I were not so compatible, and I thought more and more about the advisability of a divorce. We arranged an amicable one with my paying all the divorce expenses and giving her alimony for two years—time to get resettled with someone else. I still got screwed financially, not by Rhoda but by one of my best friends, Robert Sherwin, who represented Rhoda in our divorce. Instead of just putting through the agreement we had settled between us, Bob insisted that I have my own lawyer, farted around for a number of needless hours "negotiating" with this other attorney, and ran up a pretty huge, and quite unnecessary, legal bill with both lawyers—which I had to pay. I didn't argue with my "friend" and quickly paid both bills.

Fortunately, while our divorce was going through, Rhoda took a trip to California, met a highly respectable urologist in his fifties, and arranged to live with him a few weeks after our divorce became final in November of 1958. He wanted to marry her before the end of the year to save on taxes, so they were soon legally mated—and I saved almost two years of alimony payments. Beautiful!

Rhoda quickly got in trouble with her second husband, Norman. He insisted on her becoming pregnant soon after they married, then objected to her losing weight—and losing, with the weight, her luscious breasts. Orange County, California, where he practiced and they lived, was a Republican stronghold and not exactly Rhoda's thing. Nor was being an upper-middle-class dowager.

I liked Norman, talked to him on the phone, and acted as a part-time unpaid therapist for the two of them. Their relationship may have succeeded in spite of their incompatibilities, but Norman, at the young age of sixty-three, had a sudden fatal heart attack.

Rhoda survived pretty well with a little financial security. She moved to Los Angeles, opened an unusual art gallery, couldn't make a go of it financially, moved back to the Philadelphia region, and became head of the recreation and physical training department at Philadelphia State Hospital for a good many years, until she finally retired and moved to Austin, Texas. At this writing, Rhoda and I are still friendly—and I would say, still incompatible. But what sexual memories I have of Rhoda!

Rhoda was the one woman in my life who easily put my own sexiness to shame. You name the women I went to bed with in my twenties, thirties, and early forties, and usually I was distinctly sexier than they were. In fact, I was often too sexy. For as soon as they took their clothes off, Oscar immediately rose to the skies, and even if they then took ten minutes to go to the bathroom and put their diaphragm in, he remained completely at attention, impatiently waiting for them to return. Then, when we caressed or got around to coitus, Oscar would often tend to spurt his load in anywhere from twenty seconds to five minutes—unless I did something to make him slow down. Fortunately, being a sexologist from my twenty-sixth year onward, I knew several things that worked. For example:

> I would use a rubber, and sometimes two rubbers, to deaden my penile sensations.
>
> At times I used an anesthetic solution, to slightly numb the skin of my penis.
>
> I would tell my partner to go slowly in caressing my cock, and not grasp or rub it too firmly.
>
> I would start intercourse slowly and avoid, at least at first, deep pelvic thrusts into my partner.
>
> I would encourage my partner to mount me instead of my mounting her, again to avoid my own pelvic thrusts, which quickly brought me to climax.
>
> I would contract my anal muscles during intercourse, which often helped to hold off orgasm.
>
> I would use breathing exercises during copulation, again to retard my coming.
>
> As soon as I felt too excited during coitus, I would deliberately think unsexy thoughts—about bookkeeping, politics, psychotherapy, the ugly roof of my building, or practically anything else.

Using these various methods, I usually lasted long enough to satisfy nearly all my partners who were really set on active copulation. Not all of them, by any means, were. A few didn't like coitus, and an occasional partner found it painful. Most of them enjoyed it but came to orgasm only with clitoral manipulation, and therefore wanted intercourse as a fairly brief prelude to five to thirty minutes of petting. Others could easily live without any penile-vaginal penetration whatever, had it only to satisfy their partner, and insisted on direct clitoral rubbing leading to orgasm either before or after they obligingly loaned their vaginas to their partner's penis.

As I have pointed out in this autobiography, I have no trouble falling in love with women, relating to them, and refusing to upset myself about their ways—as long as I am not with them too much socially. Unintimate socializing largely bores me, as it mainly seems to consist of chit-chat.

Chapter 5D
Critique of Chapter 5

"*W*hat was notable was that none of the three Ellis children suffered very much, as children are supposed to suffer, when my father was married to my mother and was never around. If anything we suffered still less when my father and mother were divorced.*"*

Of course, psychoanalysts would deny that this is possible. They would say that we really suffered very much unconsciously but that we repressed our suffering. I very much doubt this interpretation. I personally suffered very little when my father wasn't around during his marriage to my mother, and I remember being sort of shocked when I heard my mother and her sister talking about the divorce. But I quietly recovered and gave the matter only practical consideration—particularly in terms of the family income.

I was indeed affected by the divorce. For one thing, I saw that marriage wasn't sacred and that people could easily, after thirteen years or so, get divorced and still continue to get by. That probably influenced me in terms of arranging my first marriage to Karyl quite impulsively, when all the odds were against it, and also consciously making it an experiment. And I was influenced in my marriage to Rhoda in living with her for only several months before we married and not knowing her that well. But in both instances, thanks to my parents' experience, I realized that marriages were not written in stone and that just because I married, I didn't have to stay married.

Moreover, I didn't feel that my father had rejected me and my brother and sister in getting divorced from my mother. I felt that he had rejected her in favor of his second wife, Rose, but not his children. I also felt that he had never been too close to his three children, and so his permanently living away from us was hardly much of a rejection. I also saw that my mother was able to take his absences quite well, when he was married to her, and that she similarly took his divorcing her calmly. So that, again, helped me feel that one could be married, be attached, but not take separation too seriously. So I truly believe that I learned important things from my parents' divorce, and that I was not consciously or unconsciously traumatized by it.

I didn't in any way assume that my father's leaving had anything to do with my behavior or that of my brother and sister. This is not to deny that many or most children make themselves quite upset when their parents divorce. They do. But this depends on the temperament of the children, their closeness to their parent, and on their prior experience with the parent before the divorce. In my own case, my natural temperament was not to upset myself too much about anything; I was not by any means close to my father; and my experience with him was that he was largely absent prior to his divorcing my mother. So I was not a prime candidate for being upset over his absence.

For those and other reasons, I did not find it at all hard to permanently miss a hitherto frequently missing father. I suppose that in some ways I rather liked it, for now I was the real man of the house. My mother relied much more on me than on my less disciplined brother and sister, and was, moreover, easily persuaded to do what I wanted. So I was something of a quiet—not a brash or cruel—King of the May, with no competition whatever from my father. Not a bad deal!

"My point was to get to the unvarnished truth. I was, in those youthful days, something of a logical positivist. I believed in arriving at the truth by empiricism."

Yes, like most logical positivists, I didn't believe in anything supernatural or absolute. Yet I thought that there was something like empirical or factual truth. I am now something of a postmodernist, who believes that there are no absolute facts but that we largely see things through human eyes and in something of a social- and era-oriented framework. At the same time I am not against realism and science, as some of the radical postmodernists appear to be. I think there are some pretty hard facts and social realities out there, but we cannot be absolutely sure of what they are, and they change with new times and situations. So in my youthful days I had too much faith in facts, whereas today I do not. REBT was always anti-absolutistic and anti-musturbatory and it therefore liberalized me and made me somewhat looser than the strict logical positivists. Finally, I gave up rigid positivism in 1976 when I read Mike Mahoney's book *Scientist as Subject*, and was on my way to liberal but not radical postmodernism.

My early dealing with upsetness was also, probably, an issue. I loved my freedom from both my father and my mother from the start and by no means felt neglected by them when they were not around to supervise or help me. Whether this love of freedom led me to love not being supervised or vice versa, we'll probably never know. I think—as usual!—that I had a biological tendency to love freedom as most adolescents do. And I became a collectivist because I wrongly thought that it would lead to greater freedom—after all, we would all own the means of production and would be fair about sharing them—and because I thought that collectivism was much more efficient than capitalism, especially considering our high technology. But I was always something of a natural, freedom-loving youth (as perhaps most people are, especially when they are young). So I became a collectivist revolutionary in spite of this tendency; and when I gave up my political revolutionary activity and became especially critical of the communist-fascist kind of state, I reverted to my presumably natural individualism and became, rather logically, a sex and love revolutionary.

"Ironically enough, I became a somewhat different kind of revolutionist—one who strove for free speech and specifically for sexual revolution."

Yes, I was always somewhat ambivalent as a revolutionist. I was never a devout one, and I was always far from a rigid believer in Marx, Lenin, and others. I was opposed to Marx because I could see that he devoutly believed in surplus value in economics, and his thinking was absolutist. I saw that he and the communists were rigid thinkers, not open to change. I wrote a question-and-answer primer, simplifying the three volumes of *Das Kapital*, to show my readers that they didn't have to rigidly stick to some of Marx's main tenets and didn't have to endlessly discuss Marxism and keep going around in vicious circles that actually kept them from getting to revolutionary activity. Then when I saw that Stalin and his Communist Party were getting away from the true revolutionary causes and were never going to reach them, I broke away from political revolution and quite drastically went my own revolutionary way.

I was much more of a revolutionary idealist than a revolutionary collectivist. Like Lenin, I was deluded into thinking that the collectivist state would wither away into a socialist democracy. But collectivism had its own rigidity, so I went back to my original individualism and democracy, which my sexual revolutionism tended to embrace. It was much more individualistic than collectivistic. And it was certainly democratic.

"My main success was not with women but with myself: I now had conquered my two main phobias and was well on my way to seeing how I, and presumably anyone else, could make myself remarkably less anxious and more enjoying of "dangerous" social pursuits. I really conquered me! I was extremely happy about that."

I think this was a real turning point in my life. For in a sense I had been out of control of me—run by my phobias of public speaking and of approaching desirable females and not truly self-controlled. Now I saw that even my worst phobias could be under my control by my refusing to awfulize about the possibility of doing poorly and by my forcing myself, very uncomfortably, to do what I was afraid of doing. That was the secret: not being too scared of failure and what others might think of me for failing, and then acting against my fears until I became comfortable and later even enjoyed the fearful pursuits. If I could control myself in this way, what indeed was there to be afraid of? Dangerous heights, yes, or something like that. But not social situations!

Now nothing much was going to stop me in my social goals, and I was on the true way, or one of the true ways, to happiness. I was, as ever, interested in how humans could refuse to make themselves miserable about anything and thereby be able to make themselves happy. I didn't want to be a therapist and help people that way, but I did want to help them as a teacher and as a writer—to educate them so that they would be able to change themselves and not unduly upset themselves. Now, I thought, I had one great way of doing so—and I enlightened some of my friends about it.

My attitudes were also, of course, a precursor to my doing Rational Emotive Behavior Therapy. The methods I had used to overcome my personal phobias were clearly cognitive-behavioral rather than the insight-gathering approaches of psychoanalysis and other forms of therapy. Therefore, when I started to do psychotherapy at the age of thirty, I got on a cognitive-behavioral track. I mixed in a bit of psychoanalysis, and then later largely practiced psychoanalysis with some behavioral interventions. But I eventually abandoned nearly all analysis and created REBT.

"I hoarded time rather than money and put up with the distinct inconveniences of living in a semi-deprived manner. That was really my own choosing; so I did not whine about having chosen it."

My high frustration tolerance in regard to spending money has helped me considerably with my life. I am not exactly sure where I got the habit of saving rather than spending, since I did not get it directly from my parents. My mother always spent frugally and saved fabulously, and during my childhood she gave us children a measly ten cents a week for spending money. So we had to dole it out carefully and forego many things that other children had. But my father was a great spender, and, at his bidding, we lived quite well, in an upper-middle-class manner. As I have noted, at one time we had an electricity-driven Cadillac car and a chauffeur.

Whether I largely copied my mother or was naturally provident, I never greatly missed luxuries and things that other kids had. In fact, I was usually ahead of the game in terms of saving money, and when I began to sell newspapers during the summer in Wildwood, New Jersey, I saved a good deal of money for the winter months, whereas my brother Paul saved very little of the money he earned.

The point is that when it came to matters of work—such as my writing—I easily forewent pleasurable pursuits, hoarded time, and didn't regret it. During college, after the Great Depression had begun, I had twenty-five cents a day to spend on subway fare and fifteen cents for lunch. But I ate peanuts (five cents) for lunch and spent almost all my remaining money on postage stamps to send out my numerous essays, stories, and comic poems. With little monetary resources, I easily gave up expensive socializing (such as eating ice cream with my friends) and was very happy to have the time to do more writing.

I didn't regret the pleasures I missed and the time it would have taken to indulge in them. So I have high frustration tolerance in that regard. But I very much resented the interruptions with my writing and other work and was impatient with people and things that interfered with that time. To this day, I easily forego one kind of pleasure but am irritable about having to give up another kind, which many people would view as "hard work." You could, of course, say I do so for ego reasons. Giving up eating good food or socializing with my friends doesn't detract very much from my self-inflation. But giving up writing, and presumably the fame that might come from it, does put my ego on high. So I have had some high frustration tolerance for writing in order to perhaps gain fame and fortune, and also for my main purpose of helping people. But the work itself seems to drive me. I am uncomfortable with important writing projects hanging over my head. I like to get them done, and I am thoroughly absorbed while doing them. I have what psychologist Mihaly Csikszentmihalyi calls "flow" while I am writing. I enjoy socializing, watching sports at times, and doing other things, but I do not have too much flow with these activities. With reading, both fiction and nonfiction, I get thoroughly absorbed. However, this is partly because I am constantly figuring out how to improve the ideas, plots, and stories I read.

"I refused to pay the freight for bedded sex—which I always, always craved—and chose the 'gravy train' (no pun intended!) of quick underground petting and orgasms. Pretty neat!—except that I pre-served my LFT. So I went for quicker—and kinkier—rapture. Too bad. If I had my earlier life to live over, I would push to correct this. And to work against my LFT."

This, again, is an important point for therapy and for self-therapy. People, me included, find easier ways out and settle for quick fixes like casual sex, monetary gain, and drugs and alcohol. I would have found it onerous to talk to some of the strange women I had sex with in the subway, to date them, and to have "real" sex with them. It would have taken a good deal of time and money—and by money I mean extra time, for I usually did not work while going to school and writing. So I naturally had more time for both of these pursuits, especially writing. If I had worked, in order to get money to date, I would deprive myself of this time.

My subway adventures, moreover, took very little time, since they happened in the course of my regular subway riding. And they were inexpensive! Also, they led to very immediate and quick gratification, sometimes twice a day. So I took the easier sex choices. But in doing so I retained my phobia of talking to strange women and my horror of getting rejected by them, which is exactly what virtually all phobics do—cop out of the irrationally feared pursuits and thereby keep them potentially "horrible" forever.

This is a natural human tendency. Even when people pay good money and spend much time in therapy, they resist taking risks that would show them how to conquer their phobias and fears. They very clearly see how "dangerous" it is to speak in public—or to risk playing "bad" tennis. But they refuse to see how time-, energy-, and neurosis-consuming it is to fail to take those risks. So they continue to be phobic forever and never get over their self-created fears. Their LFT leads to much more pain than the "horrible" discomfort they are avoiding.

"Robin finally got a PhD in public health nursing, moved to San Francisco, and led a fairly respectable professional and social life.

Pretty good for a double murderer! And damned good that I never married her."

Yes, damned good. But the interesting thing is that I came within a hair of doing so and even bought an engagement ring for the occasion. Indeed, I almost committed bigamy, for if I hadn't accidentally found out that Robin was still legally married, we might have actually made it to the Justice of Peace (what peace!). I guess you could say I was pretty careless about this marrying thing. I had an experimental and secret marriage with Karyl when she was unemployed and I was earning fifteen dollars a week. It couldn't possibly have worked out; luckily her parents discovered our secret in time and then squelched our marriage.

Robin was another impossibility. She and I had great sex and some steady companionship, but our goals and values were too different. She became "respectable," ultimately, but much too sociable for my work-preoccupied pace.

Why was I so cavalier about mating with women with whom I was truly incompatible? First, because I definitely was in love with them. Second, because marriage was hardly a final step to me—only an experiment. Third, because I wanted to find out, experimentally, whether I could live with these women successfully, and the only way to find out was to find out. So I plunged or almost plunged. With Rhoda, I took it for granted that she would always, and I mean always, be devoted to her career as much as I was to mine, and that her sociability would not get in the way of my work. But I was wrong, and I probably should have lived with her for a few years instead of marrying her so quickly.

However, I have no regrets. I found out what I found out. I never greatly regret the breakup of an intense relationship. It is over, but I am not over. I always look forward to other relationships. And, of course, to getting back to my work. What was experienced, was experienced. I enjoyed it and I can use it for future relationships. Risk taking, even like marrying, is really not that risky if you look at it in terms of experiencing what, in all probability, you would not otherwise experience in-depth, and then you go on to other adventures. I have had great stability in my life with my clients, leadership of the Albert Ellis Institute (that is, until problems started there in a big way in 2004), supervision, workshops, and writing. I used to think: Let my affairs of the heart be much more risky!

"Sandy was no great intellectual, but she had a charming, bubbling personality, and, as long as we spent only an hour or so together once or twice a week, I never got bored seeing her."

All the women I was deeply attached to were quite bright and distinctly personable women. They tended to be great in bed, but that wasn't enough—I like speaking for an hour or so with a woman I've just met, but not unless she is highly intelligent and cultured. By the time I discover that someone is not really for me, and I have probably helped her somewhat with her problems (which interest me), I have little wish to continue. The sex may be excellent, but it isn't enough, and I am fairly soon exhausted with it.

Nevertheless, with some of the women I was with prior to being with Debbie, I enjoyed the brief sex and conversation, so long as I didn't spend too much time with a woman—and away from work. I continually had new and vital experiences. I also have many male friends—mostly professionals—and I do not spend any great amount of time with them either. I can see them for an hour or so, catch up with what they are working on, enjoy the time I spend with them—and then, again, back to work!

Women usually want to be "just friends" with me, but I almost always avoid that. As I told them when I was in my twenties, "Just being friends with you, or even with a man, is time-consuming. So I might as well be friends, and usually casual friends at that, with women I also have sex with. That is much better!" They rarely saw it that way, but I stuck to my guns. Even when I had sex friendships with them, I rarely saw them very often and seldom for hours at a time. Some women mainly want to have telephone friendships with me, but again I give them very little time—as I also do with my male friends. It is not that I would not enjoy talking to some of them, even fairly regularly. But I enjoy seeing clients, supervising, speaking, and writing even more. So I make my choices.

I am very lucky in that I never have enough time to do the things that I truly enjoy. Each day has only twenty-four hours, and I usually get about eight hours of sleep in order to perform effectively the next day. So by necessity in the past, I had to give up certain things and relationships for other things and relationships. Naturally, I missed out to some degree. But I didn't take my missing out too seriously. If I did, that would not give me the time to enjoy what I enjoy—which these days is being with Debbie and most aspects of my work!

I have already written some about my relationship with Debbie, and I shall later write more about it and her phenomenal devotion to me. We are amazingly compatible—practically made for each other. She is passionate about me, about teaching REBT, and about helping people. She is an outstanding practitioner in both education and therapy. We are a great team. Since late 2002, she has worked with me, co-leading workshops, lectures, and seminars. The remarkable amount of work I have done since being with her, especially after my 2003 surgery, would not have been possible without her help. She inspired me to write and present more about REBT and Buddhism, and other subjects, and did research for all my recent books and writings. Though my hearing is fading—a great impediment in my work—miraculously I can hear *her* clearly and well. Not to mention her saving my life at least three times.

She is indubitably my greatest love. We married in New York City at City Hall on Tuesday, November 15, 2004, the happiest day of my life. I want to be with her forever, as she does with me. Who could ask for anything more!

The relationship that began in 1964, when I was fifty-one years old, and only ended thirty-seven years later, was my relationship with Janet Wolfe. Yes, we lived together all those years. Quite a long relationship, compared to my many brief ones. How come?

Certainly, not mainly for the great sex—though that was good for a number of years. As I have noted throughout this volume, that in itself is far from enough. Janet is also very bright—and, when she got going, could even out-argue me. We really interested each other, and could make each other laugh. Janet, when she lived with me from 1965 till early 2002, was a mainstay of the Albert Ellis Institute—a real helpmate in that respect. In fact, because I chose to do many other things than direct it—such as see innumerable clients, supervise interns and fellows, train outside practitioners of REBT, give talks and workshops, and write books and articles on REBT—I gave over important administrative functions to her. She started as the office manager, was for many years the institute's associate executive director and then its executive director. She actually did more administrative work than I and was very capable in that respect. Also, she conducted a good many professional workshops with me, and gave lectures and workshops on REBT and about women's issues on her own.

I shall later write about my sex-love relationship with Janet, which has had some unique aspects. Best of all, as I shall describe later, it was the most open of my many relationships, giving me freedom to be with other women, but probably the reason it lasted for thirty-seven years was that it allowed me the freedom to be myself regarding my almost obsessive-compulsive devotion to my work. Karyl, with whom I also had an open sex-love relationship, was quite good in this respect; but Janet was even better.

Part 2

Chapter 6

1934 to 1937 and My Relationship with Karyl Corper

As I mentioned previously, it was around 1937 that I decided to be a political revolutionist with Young America, which was against capitalism and for an American collectivism. It was during this period that I developed from a shy nonpublic speaker to a confident and fluent lecturer. I was only nineteen and was the head of Young America.

I did very well—but the Great American Revolution did not. The Communist Party still ruled the revolutionary movement and attracted thousands of converts, many of them famous writers and playwrights. The Socialist Party, going back to Eugene Debs, was much milder and more democratic. For a while it followed Leon Trotsky rather than Joseph Stalin and was much more revolutionary, but did so inconsistently. I joined it for a while but became disillusioned with its "niceness."

By 1937, I fully realized that although Lenin thought that the "dictatorship of the proletariat"—which actually was *over* the proletariat—was *not* going to wither away and that Stalin was (like Hitler) a fascist, paranoid ruler. Back to democracy I started to go! My revolutionary activity waned, and I decided to become a sex-love revolutionist. Lenin and Stalin were puritanical. I was going to write a thousand-page *Case for Promiscuity* and prove that men and women were natural varietists and could succeed in having sex-love relationships as long as they disciplined themselves to have them with consenting adults. As a sex revolutionist, I respected René Guyon—but not his endorsers who held that "sex before eight or else it's too late!" Bertrand Russell's *Marriage and Morals* was more my cup of sex.

From the age of fifteen onward, my main hobby was philosophy, and I largely followed the ancient philosophers, such as Socrates, Epictetus, and Seneca, as well as the modern philosophers, such as Dewey, Santayana, Russell, and Wittgenstein.

I had better not forget economics. Although I received my Bachelor of Business Administration degree from the City College of New York, my desire to get a regular accounting job was thwarted by the Great Depression and by my determination to be a writer—a Nobel Prize winner—from the time I was twelve. So, from the age of sixteen to twenty-eight, I kept writing book-length manuscripts aimed to be best sellers. You name it and I wrote it—stories, novels, plays, poems, and several nonfiction books both to help my political and sex-love causes and to make me rich. Several of my manuscripts received editorial plaudits, but not a damned one got published. Only a number of comic verses and one measly article on my hobby of music.

When it came to women, I was extremely shy and fearful of rejection, so from fifteen to nineteen, I engaged in considerable frotteurism but no risk taking. The first woman I steadily dated was Karyl Corper when I was twenty-four and she was nineteen. By the time I truly overcame my fear of failure—when I was twenty-eight and was no longer timid with Karyl and other women—I started to have the kind of love life I alluded to in the first part of this book. I was raring to go—and did!

I was no longer shy about talking to strange females, although I rarely dated them or made specific passes at them. Why? (1) They were nice Jewish virgins who were looking for sex after marriage. (2) I was financially unable to marry them or even take them on expensive dates. (3) If I got them pregnant, I didn't have several hundred dollars to pay for an illegal abortion. (4) I was still getting regular orgasms—at no charge—from my steady frotteurism.

In the years between 1934 and 1937, however, I was active enough without any dating. I published comic verses in the *New York Post*, I revised my novel *A Prisoner of Manners*, and I read manuscripts for Dick Childs' Modern Age Books. I kept very busy and was not deliriously happy but made much of my life. I realized soon after I began seeing Karyl that I might have material for a "great" novel based on our relationship. So from December 1934 to November 1937, my twenty-first to twenty-fourth years, I started taking hundreds of pages of notes, mainly about my relationship with Karyl but also about other important events of my life.

Following are some of my diary entries and notes during this period, interspersed with comments made upon later reflection.

December 1934. Agreed with Paul, my brother, that we should start a pants-matching business. I didn't like the idea of going around and talking to people—in pants stores and clothing stores—into matching pants, but I decided that it would do me good and get me over some of my shyness about doing it. So I agreed and became an un-shy businessperson.

December 31, 1934. Urged by my father, I went to see Lester Marquell, the head of the Sunday department of the *New York Times*, and he said that I'd have to be a reporter first and get some experience before I could do anything for him. And he told my father that I looked too thin and unenergetic.

January 9, 1935. Went to the Paramount Theatre on the two passes that Leonard Lyons had given me for writing verse for him. He was a newspaper columnist for the *New York Post* and published several of my comic poems.

January 10, 1935. Went to speak to the Modern Discussion Troupe on the way out of the present economic dilemma. I said that the only way out was the abolition of the profit system and setting up a cooperative commonwealth. Saw that I was becoming something of a public speaker.

January 17, 1935. Heard Goodwin Watson give his first talk for New America. Good talk, but he wasn't as radical as I would have liked him to be. Later, in 1943, he became my thesis adviser when Percival Symonds was on leave from Columbia University.

Beginning to see that the *History of the Dark Ages*, which I was writing, wouldn't get published and I had better write something else. Thought of writing an operetta around the *Romeo and Juliet* theme. Continued to get comic verses accepted in Leonard Lyons's column in the *New York Post*.

February 1935. Was asked by Radio America to cut down my article on *Killing American Music* to letter size and then they would publish it. First real publication!

May 9, 1935. Went to Emil Conorson's house, and he thought my *History of the Dark Ages* was too diffuse, and I agreed with him.

May 16, 1935. I disagreed with Marx's surplus value theory. It wasted the time of radicals, who could not get around to any good revolutionary activity. So I decided to write *A Primer of Marxism* to show that it was unrealistic.

July 1, 1935. As I was lying awake in bed, I figured out that maximum happiness was intensity—live intensely in everything you do and you will be as happy as you can be. Take life laconically, following the line of least resistance, and you may enjoy yourself somewhat, but you will not truly be happy and certainly not maximally happy.

July 19, 1935. We were not receiving any money from my father for alimony, and my family was getting desperately poor. Maybe Paul's and my business will save it, but we are by no means sure.

August 1935. Played tennis with Manny and played intensively. At first was losing but then was getting better when we were put off the court. Confirmed my view that intensity does matter a lot in regards to success. Looked like I had found the secret of success!

August 12, 1935. Had a good social meeting and held the floor on philosophy, poetry, and everything else. But unfortunately it was not a good revolutionary meeting.

September 13, 1935. I finished my primer of capitalism. Eddie Cohen thought this the best of my works and that it had the best chance of being published.

January 10, 1936. Business pretty dead, but Paul bought a car and is going to take over the business with the car. I was learning piano by myself, studying German, reading a couple of dictionaries.

January 28, 1936. Discussed my manuscript *A Primer of Marxism* with Margaret Mitchelson of Oxford Publishing Company. Their report stated it was a great work and better than John Strachey's *Nature of Capitalist Crises*, and that the style was effective. Oxford hadn't published anything radical in forty years, and unfortunately the editor turned it down.

February 21, 1936. Emil Conorson was very enthusiastic about the revised *A Primer of Marxism* and recommended it to everybody, including Harry F. Ward. Introduced me to the famous novelist Henry Miller, who had just returned from a long sojourn in Europe. Oddly enough, I found him to be a typical businessman type.

April 2, 1936. Janet, my sister, has a boyfriend at last. Hooray!

Friday, April 17, 1936. Applied to Socialist Party membership and was interviewed by Torchey. I was mainly interested in seeing how it worked, but did not buy its mild philosophies.

July 16, 1936. Broke the world's record for reading public library books. I used a new library card in sixteen days, taking four books every day and reading them.

September 1936. Disgusted with the Socialist Party and was going to resign from it. The more I think about the coming American revolution, I think it is to be effected, if at all, by the present radical parties in America being abandoned and left to rot in their own mess. So apparently I was disillusioned with the effectiveness of American radical parties.

I got absorbed in musical ratings and in doing a thousand of them and trying to be an expert on some aspects of classical, semiclassical, and popular music. Did some work for Louis Birk, treasurer and acting editorial head of Dick Childs' publishing company, who gave me some manuscripts to read and report on. I got $5 a manuscript.

September 27, 1936. My twenty-third birthday. Not a success—that is definite—but by no means a failure either. I have an immense amount of knowledge gained during the past year and may soon be able to use most of it. Numerous prose and verse works already written. With revisions, some of them may be published. Not happy, but no real cause for unhappiness. If only I had a good-looking girl to sleep with every night I might be happy, but then I'd have to relinquish some of my leisure time to make money. Unfortunately, I shall have to get a job to make some money one of these days. Meanwhile, keep at my drab selling job.

October 10, 1936. Now at work on a short book, *The Art of Not Being Unhappy*, which I think has good selling possibilities.

March 26, 1937. Wrote what I thought was the best novel I ever wrote, about the convergence of two middle-class people to a revolutionary position. Emil Conorson said my novel was very sexy, and everyone was amazed that I had written it in a week.

April 13, 1937. Began work on a new, milder novel. I found that I could do 40 pages a day on a novel. With a couple of secretaries, I could probably do a couple of novels a week!

May 1, 1937. Wrote a list of my work accomplishments: Over 900 books read, 90 percent nonfiction; over 50,000 musical selections heard, 99 percent classical and semiclassical; four books written, also several articles and study courses; two businesses simultaneously operated and managed for most of the year; over 2,000 pages of type-written notes taken; much material gained for future books and articles; several thousand musical selections composed; over 100 poems and song lyrics written; some political activity done.

July 16, 1937. Started to do some work for Dick Childs as a paid revolutionist. Little pay!

October 18, 1937. I met a fascinating woman, Karyl Corper. Karyl was an actress and had recently been on the Works Progress Administration for a year and a half, because her parents were almost on welfare. Now she was trying for an acting career. At nineteen she was not extremely beautiful—she was about twenty-five pounds over-weight—but she was attractive enough and seemed to be great at acting. So her chances for a career were good.

I quickly took to her, because I liked her sexy, large-breasted looks, found her intelligent, and thought she was different from other women. So on October 18, I walked her to her nearby apartment house and we had a tremendous conversation in the hallway for hours.

From October 1937 onward, I kept seeing Karyl every other day or so and extensively writing about our relationship. We kissed and hugged lightly, but never for me enough!

October 20, 1937. Although it was difficult to do so, I forced myself to express my feelings for Karyl. I did tell her openly, badly, but still sincerely enough, I thought, that I did love her. I said all that I had to say up to the bitter end, while keeping doggedly to an unemotional, sometimes slightly humorous, manner of speaking. And while hoping against hope that at least a fraction of my tender feelings toward her were being aptly conveyed to her.

On her part, Karyl took an equally humorous attitude and told me that she had had several affairs before, while this seemed to be my first. So she was hardly madly in love, uniquely, with me. I was disappointed in her attitude and accepted the fact that it was a blow to my ego, if our loving—hers and mine—meant nothing more to her than the adventures and especially the sex adventures she had had with others, and if it meant that she did not especially care for me. If she had not loved me as much as she had seemed to do during our embraces, it would mean that she didn't have a really mutual affection for me. I had not thought of that much before, but now I realized that mutual passion was the most desirable thing. As I spoke to her, I couldn't say offhand what my reaction would be if I were certain that she was only in a casual relationship with me. But I thought more and more to myself that while I would not cease to love her under those circumstances, it certainly would be less than I did right now.

Comment. I'm usually protective. Maybe that's one of my main traits—to protect myself from being hurt. Now, sometimes I may go to extremes and protect myself by not being in love very much. Then I don't feel very hurt if I am rejected.

October 31, 1937. Though I didn't know yet what her feelings were for me, I saw that my relationship with Karyl was going to be somewhat special and that, however it turned out, I could use our romance for my long-projected Great American Novel. Therefore, I began to take long notes on my activities with her, which I titled *Notes for a Novel*, and I also took some long *Comments* on my *Notes*.

November 1, 1937. We had been talking quietly for several hours in the living room with her parents in their bedroom of their small apartment. Anything and everything we discussed, from politics to friends, but mostly about ourselves, our dislikes and likes, characteristics, and aims—but somehow, most of our questions were in regard to sex. No matter where the conversation stood, it inevitably came back to: What about sex? What about the part we should play in it, Karyl and I?

Comment. The reason we talked about sex so much is that I was fascinated with it and with her, and lusted after her continually. And she was very namby-pamby and talked a good deal, but we didn't get around to any sex because of her attitude. I would have liked to, but not she. And of course I was really trying to find how far she would go and how fast. I was particularly interested in how fast.

In chapter 4C, I discussed my first intimate night with Karyl. Later I would comment: "*That was certainly one of the most—and perhaps the most—eventful nights I had ever spent.*" I thought of it joyfully and looked forward to intimate bliss in the future. I was very optimistic, as I recall, that good things would continue to happen and that Karyl would continue to be receptive. I was convinced that, in her own peculiar way, she really loved me, and I loved the fact that she loved me.

Everything was great and glorious, even though I knew it would be very hard for us to get along economically if we ever lived together or even went steadily together. So I didn't love my realism, but I was still very, very happy about the whole affair.

Looking back on it, some sixty-seven years later, I realize that I exaggerated quite a bit. Karyl was by no means as beautiful as I thought she was. She also was a bad bet in many respects, especially because of her emotional disturbance, which I sort of knew about but wasn't exactly facing at that time. So although I was not completely unrealistic and was very madly in love, I just didn't see certain aspects of our future very realistically. But I am glad that I enjoyed it all. It was a great experience, even if it wasn't quite completely realistic. It added to my life then, and it doubtless added to my life over the years. I have very few regrets about it, even though in the final analysis, it by no means turned out, as I shall say, very well. But it boded far more good than harm and it showed me that I could be passionately enamored of someone and go up and down in my moods about her. So I was hardly an unfeeling clod and though even at that time maybe I had less feeling than some other people would have—though I doubt that—I certainly had a great deal of it. Biologically I was prone to feel, and I had been raised on novels and on movies to be able to feel. And I definitely did feel. But the handicaps and the problems that ensued also led to some depression on my part. But again, as I shall show, I got through that depression remarkably well.

November 4, 1937. I saw Karyl every other day, but we only continued our light petting—which I enjoyed immensely.

When I saw Karyl again, I convinced myself that I would confess my love completely for her and not be ashamed of it. I think I thought it was silly to some degree because when one is madly in love in an obsessive-compulsive manner, one *is* behaving in a silly way, but I was still going to confess it. I realized that it was only my sense of ego that kept me from wanting to love any woman wholeheartedly and be controlled by my love. It was just that I always thought that a self-reliant attitude was best and was the bravest and strongest philosophy. And I thought that falling madly in love with a woman—any woman— would deprive me of that attitude and make me a mere ordinary, weak mortal man. I'm afraid that my ego nonsense was pretty strong, because I didn't want to be a weak, mortal man.

But I asked myself, what of it? Why be ashamed of this tender, loving feeling, weak though it may seem to be? What was the good of being so self-reliant and self-sufficient if in being so one was deprived of this great, intense feeling of love?

Of course, I could rightly contend, I was not madly in love with her. To lose her would not make me commit suicide or pine away for the rest of my life. However, I could be hurt. But even when I acknowledge that I am in love, or deeply love with someone, I sometimes think that it may come to an end, and I thereby protect myself against depression.

November 7, 1937. She was tired and apathetic and not in a good mood, and I accepted that. I told her that men were usually desirous of sex, practically all the time, but women were not. And she seemed to appreciate my understanding her. But I still wondered, of course, since she was something of a mystery, whether sex with other men had anything to do with her moodiness with me at times.

Comment. Yes, I kept wondering about that, because at that time I didn't know that she was sensitive about her breasts or that her vaginal opening was extremely tight. And whenever she was in a normal mood (and she was a depressive, which I didn't fully recognize at the time), I thought that maybe she was moody because of me. So I kept attributing her moods to the wrong thing. I wasn't completely suspicious of her, and I wasn't exceptionally jealous, but I just kept realistically and skeptically wondering whether her moodiness had something particularly to do with me. From the distance of many years now, I see that it almost certainly didn't—that she was an exceptionally moody individual and was much different from night to night. And even later, when I lived with her and she wasn't, as far as I knew, having sex with other men, she exhibited the same kind of moodiness; sometimes she was much more sexually and affectionately receptive and other times more into her own depressed mood.

November 10, 1937. Saw Karyl and I tried to tell her my feelings, but I found tough treading again. My tender words just didn't come, and she seemed to be satisfied with my very apparent sincerity. She was, even though she tried to hide it in her humorous skepticism, really pleased, and I was very glad that she was pleased. "You don't have to keep telling me this," she said. "I'm not like those other women who keep asking, 'Do you love me? Do you still love me?' You know that." Yes, I knew it, but I insisted that "I want to tell you these things." I offered them quite gratuitously. And I did feel like gratuitously expressing them.

Comment. As I have said before, I am not really the expressive type. I like to talk and I especially like to teach, but I don't *have* to express my feelings. Many of my other women friends—not necessarily Karyl—disliked that. They liked to express how they felt, and they felt done in if you were not equally expressive. But in the case of Karyl, immediately after I started having some physical contact with her, I wanted, wanted, wanted to express my feelings to her, and I did.

In the early days of my relationship with Debbie, I was at times less expressive than she preferred. But with her constant expressions of her love for me, her asking of me that I do so more—without *demanding* that I do so—and because my love for her is so great, these days I do express my feelings for her more than I have ever done in my life to anyone.

> November 12, 1937. I brought up the subject of coitus, but approached it very reluctantly, and when we finally got to the bottom of it, she didn't want to have it. I didn't particularly care, since I was getting so much pleasure already, but I worried a bit about why she didn't want to go further.

Comment. As I discovered later, Karyl was afflicted with a very narrow vagina and very thick hymen and couldn't have intercourse with me or anyone until months later, when she had a gynecological procedure that enabled her to do so.

> November 16, 1937. I told Karyl that I was somewhat afraid of her love for me because she was so changeable. "Oh, not in that," she said. "That's different. You know how I feel toward others. That's changeable, but with you it's much deeper."

Comment. Now I didn't realize it at the time, but thinking about her consequent history and her absolute devotion to me over the years, I see that she really did love me more deeply than the others. She was infatuated with them, but she thoroughly and deeply loved me. Nonetheless, she was a moody individual and probably dysthymic, so even her great love for me had its ups and downs.

From my later vantage point, I can see now that she was deeply involved with me from about 1937 until she died in 2001. So despite her moods and fluctuations, she really had an unusually deep love with me, which was not infatuation but devotion in a sense, and I would say that a large part of that devotion was to my ideals. First, maybe, my revolutionary ideals but later Rational Emotive Behavior Therapy, which she used on herself, inconsistently. But it definitely helped her.

November 21, 1937. Karyl asked about masturbation and questioned me about Havelock Ellis's studies in sex, which I had recently read. She seemed to think that if women masturbated, they weren't virgins anymore. And she seemed to confuse sex with intercourse. As I later showed the world, millions of people—men and women—were under this misconception.

November 28, 1937. We discussed sex and women, and she insisted that women were not very sexual, and I thought that they really were so more than they admitted. On the way home, I thought that it would be great if she loved me passionately as a person, as she now partly seemed to be doing, but I wanted sex in the relationship, too.

Comment. It now occurs to me that Karyl really never was very sexual, but that she (1) got infatuated with men and (2) even loved them and was sexy enough to help them and get them pleased, and get them to love her, but that she never was very sexual in her own right.

December 1, 1937. I had a very bad headache, and Karyl comforted me, and I was very appreciative of that. But then she started caressing her dog more than me, and I was sort of jealous. She loved the dog more than me. I walked home not depressed but very dissatisfied. But I decided I would see my relationship with her out to the bitter end and watch my humor that I used in regard to it, somewhat defensively, and get to the bottom of things. Getting to the bottom of things is what I really wanted. That might mean the end of the relationship, one way or the other, but at least things wouldn't go on in this ambivalent manner.

I made very tender passes toward her and seemed to think that she wanted me to be rougher and more impetuous with her. But I was into my own thing and resisted that. She got cold at one point and turned herself and me off, and said that she didn't know why she got that way. Then she got a little warmer, but made no effort to get back to her former sexy and tender way. I turned off to her and felt no love, temporarily, for her, but I was more determined than ever to find out what her real feelings were and see it through.

After a long silence, she said, "Something tells me that you are very angry at me." But I heard myself saying, "Angry? Of course not. What is there to be angry about? I never get angry at things like that.

The only things I get angry at are when people deliberately act in a malicious manner toward others. And even then I try to realize that they are naturally malicious—they're not only born that way but their environment or other factors make them that way—and that moderates my anger a great deal." I paused a while and then said again, "Angry? No, not in the least. I could use a few other adjectives to describe my feelings at the time." I was thinking of hurt and disappointment. "But, no, I am not in the least angry. Why should I be?" But I think I really was.

Comment. In thinking this over, I see that I was training myself even then—maybe as a result of reading the works of Buddha, Seneca, Epictetus, and other philosophers—to not be angry and to forgive people for what they did, and to blame them only when they did something in a truly malicious manner. I believed at the time the sort of Freudian, environmental, and Watsonian view that people largely learned to be angry. But I still thought it was inherent in them at the time and that therefore they should not be blamed or damned for it. So I was doing pretty well with myself on anger, but of course I could have held it very much underneath the surface and not faced it myself or expressed it to others.

December 14, 1937. She was cold to me and I asked her, "How can I be more romantic with you, my dear? Sing to you? Write you poetry? How?" I somehow saw myself as unromantic, though in many ways I was romantic, and she was very satisfied at times with my romanticism. But I knew that I was blocked and didn't express any real romantic views or manifestations very readily.

Comment. Should I study the art of love? I thought at the time. Not a bad idea! At the very least I may get on much better with Karyl, and even if I don't, I may be able to put it to good advantage with some other women. Damn it, I think I'll actually do it. There are a lot of other things I have to learn, but it will be damned good for relationship conversation. At this time, I was very interested in sex and was already writing or gaining material for my great book on *The Case for Promiscuity*. But maybe as a result of my feelings for Karyl, I also got very interested in love. I found out later that Kinsey was doing a great sex study but was ignoring love, whereas I wanted to research both sex and love. So I became very interested and involved in reading about and thinking about and talking about romantic love.

I felt I must impress Karyl in some way—do something big in some organization or business or something. Then maybe she'd trust me more and have more faith in me. Well, I actually did big things, not in business but in REBT and in psychotherapy—although it wasn't to impress her. I did it because I really wanted to do it. I wanted to be successful, and I especially wanted to follow my causes, which I was devoted to. So I may have done it somewhat, at the beginning, for her, but not too much.

I thought at the time that if only I had her in business with me, I'd be so confident of myself. But now I see that I could be confident of *doing well* and yet not fully confident of *myself*—which is sort of self-rating and is a mistake—and could do business very well without her.

> December 20, 1937. Saw Karyl and had a sex talk. When I explained to her that men frequently masturbated and that women do, too, she seemed surprised about that. So I wondered whether she was lying or whether she really didn't have any inclination to masturbate. She then confessed to me that she loved sensual contact, even with another woman, and I could see that she wasn't in the least frigid. When she stopped me from lying on top of her for too long or rubbing against her, I thought she was sexually prejudiced against me.

Comment. I kept picturing various scenes with Karyl. For instance, I imagined saying to her, "If you have real maternal instincts, why not mother me? I think actually I have more of those kinds of instincts than you have. For I want to mother you, hold you close, caress you as I would a beloved pet, smooth your cares, generally take care of you."

My thoughts went on and on and on, and I am amazed now, looking back, that I did not get bored with them all. But I never did get bored at the time. Obsessive-compulsive love, presumably, is nonboring. Even other obsessive-compulsive rituals and compulsions and thoughts don't seem to be boring. They seem to intrigue the person. I wrote pages about my relationship with her and what it could be. And I was very, very fascinated and very, very interested. Now I'm pretty bored with a lot of it, and it seems especially repetitious. It's interesting. It shows things about me—how strongly I could feel when I was madly in love and what foolish things I could do. But really, it's boring, and I wouldn't spend too much time at it today. Maybe the reason I've never been a great novelist is because I refuse to obsess, as others do, about the scenery and people's feelings, their feelings, their feelings, and the details of what happened to them. It hasn't been my bent, but it definitely was my bent at this time, at the beginning of 1937 when I was so desperately in love with Karyl, and so anxious, anxious, anxious about whether she truly, truly loved me. As I read over my notes, I see that I did innumerable crazy things as a result of my mad love for Karyl and the inconsistent way in which she treated me.

> December 25, 1937. On Christmas Day, she let me embrace her. We got very sexy and sensual, and I was enthralled by her silken body. But I was more enthralled by her stroking my hair and neck and cheek and showing me that, presumably, she cared for me. And I actually got more pleasure from her being tender to me than from the sex, which was amazing to me. So I expressed my love for her, but had to do it somewhat humorously. And I didn't really reveal my true feelings.
>
> I recall that after our first intimate sexual experience, I stopped thinking of other women and was pretty much madly in love with her. But I still didn't think she was, by any means, in love with me, and I was putting myself down and thinking that I wasn't very attractive, and therefore she had no reason to be in love with me. But then she began to grow colder and colder, and I began to feel more miserable. I blamed myself for her coldness and said that I really didn't love her, but just enjoyed her body. But that sentence didn't seem very convincing to me.

Comment. I realized that I was cold in response to her coldness and that I thought—as I always thought—that love had to be mutual affection, mutual caring. I'm not the one for unrequited love at all. Being loved is just as important as loving. So I decided to tell her exactly how I felt, and then, if necessary, we would remain just platonic friends.

After writing Karyl a long letter in which I bared my soul, I had some feelings of shame about the letter. I by no means had Unconditional Self-Acceptance. So I would have been ashamed of the letter and my feelings, under certain conditions, but I also would have been ashamed, I think, of me, which is crucial. We teach people in REBT to be ashamed of anything they *do* that is wrong or immoral but not ashamed of *themselves* for doing it. At this time I would still have definitely been ashamed of me, though I was not a great self-damner and was working on the philosophy of Unconditional Self-Acceptance.

> December 28, 1937. Karyl's father had another heart attack and was taken away in an ambulance. I was glad that I had stayed there in her

hour of need. I don't think I was very concerned about the father, who still didn't like me because of my lack of money. When I finally left at 4:30 in the morning, I felt more secure because the family had sort of accepted me.

Later, I wrote to her, "I've known more unhappiness with you in four months than in my previous twenty years. You've ruined my disposition."

Comment. I really was miserable for an unusual period of time, and I was negatively obsessed about other things because of her. These feelings were very, very rare, and fortunately I don't recall any other time in my life that I was that depressed, especially for any period of time. I even let my worry interfere with my job interviews. "I'm not lively enough and I don't feel lively. Something holds me back." And of course that something was Karyl and my relationship with her. I knew that I'd better be lively at job interviews, but I was obsessed with her all the time. I resolved to keep sublimating my affection in poetry and pictures. I cried freely when composing some poems.

Did my thoughts and feelings in this respect get separated? Well, no, not exactly, because I told myself very logically and rationally that there was no good reason to be in love with Karyl, especially considering the reciprocation that I received (or lack thereof).

I was obsessed with her and kept thinking delicious sexual and other thoughts. I wondered whether I would ever be sexually unobsessed and amatively unobsessed, and I thought maybe I wouldn't. I saw, by the things she actually did, that at times she really cared for me, but obviously not in the manner that I cared for her. The question is whether I was really obsessed with Karyl with the possibility (and the nonpossibility) of her really caring for me. So I think at times I really was more obsessed with the question mark about her than with her. On the other hand, at times I got sexually obsessed with her as well as with my obsession about her and as well as with her doubts about me and the uncertainty it caused me.

December 30, 1937, I brought up the subject of marriage and that I would like to marry her. But she said she had no intention of getting married, that she didn't like the idea at all. Of course, I was pretty much against things like marriage—especially without the possibility of a pretty easy divorce—but I favored it with her. She then said that I was much too young for her, and that if she ever were to marry she would like a man of thirty-five or forty who would accept her and her childishness. Actually, that was a pretty good observation on her part, but I took it amiss.

> January 2, 1938. I decided that I might well end up with a mere friendship with Karyl, so I started looking at other women and desiring them. But I still couldn't banish thoughts of Karyl from my mind. She wanted to read the letter, and I finally left it with her and said, "Here it is, and just remember that it caused me great—well, I can't exactly say anguish—but great difficulty in putting my feelings of love on paper." My letter mainly consisted of my feelings of love for her and doubts about her feelings for me.
>
> Karyl treated my seven-page letter lightly, said that she was already aware of my feelings for her, but that she thought I had a temporary infatuation and not true, lasting love. I was aghast and thought that she was diminishing my infatuation and wrongly seeing it like the many infatuations she had had. How wrong! Horrors!

Comment. I was at first almost struck dead with Karyl's dismissal of my letter, resolved that my cause was hopeless, and for the fifth or sixth time planned to leave her. That mood lasted several days, but when she called me and wanted to get together again, it receded.

> January 4, 1938. Karyl had friends over, and it was impossible to get really close. When they left, she insisted on talking about her supposed lesbian tendencies, and for the twentieth time showed that sex indulgence with any male meant little to her. I tried to make light of her statements but wished that she had never started on that track at all.
>
> Karyl was neglectful of me for most of the evening, so I finally left without so much as touching her. I mused to myself on the way home that I was really getting a dirty deal. In fact, I told myself, I was getting tired of the whole affair. Here I was so much in love with her, whereas she was completely unresponsive.
>
> I definitely didn't like it and was getting goddamned tired of it. Why didn't she admit that she just wasn't suitable for me? Trying to be objective about it on the way home, I told myself that I'd be pretty surprised if we were together much longer. Therefore, I'd better keep looking around for another female partner. In the meantime, I would continue trying sex with her, but if I didn't make it, I didn't make it. So I wished I didn't have to reconquer her every night, as it were, and hoped against hope for more affectionate attention. I felt both more affectionate and less affectionate toward her and wondering what the deuce was going to happen next. A fine situation!

Comment. Remembering the letter and my feelings now, I think to some degree it was much ado about nothing. I certainly didn't have to know her feelings for me, and at any rate, I would eventually find them out. So at that time I was, let us say, anxious about knowing her feelings and I felt that I definitely had to know one way or the other. I don't feel that way about practically anything anymore. I've really used REBT on myself, so while it's highly desirable to know various outcomes, it's not necessary. Maybe my lack of anxiety would have happened to me anyway, just as I became older, but I doubt it. I think it's because I always look at the final analysis and say, "If it doesn't work, it doesn't work. I won't be *as* happy as I would otherwise be, but I can definitely be a happy human."

> January 13, 1938. I told Karyl that if I did marry her, it would only be under one condition—and that is if I slept with her first. I said it would be foolish to marry if we were not suited to each other sexually—if I couldn't satisfy her and she couldn't satisfy me. And the facts show that this is frequently the case between people who marry, even after they've known each other for a while.

> January 15, 1938. Karyl was warm, but I was still hesitant. How could I ask her for so serious a thing as intercourse, or her virginity? How could I induce her to get to the bottom of this matter? The more I thought about it, the less enthusiastic I felt about bringing up the question. In the end, I resolved to let matters take their own course for a while, and to at least await a very favorable opportunity before I dared to pose questions like this extremely important one.

Comment. At this point, I didn't realize that she was not able to have intercourse, but I made a federal case of taking it, for her and for me, and misread things. That's why it's very good to have knowledge of certain things, so you don't delude yourself and imagine things or give them super-importance.

> I asked her about all those passionate scenes, and then totally unexpectedly, she said with bitter words to me—the cruelest words I had ever heard in my life—"*Oh, no, I was only acting then when I was passionate.*" I was so shocked that I almost talked automatically for a few minutes, and then I said, "Frankly, I don't believe it. I can't believe it." "Well," she said, and her words went through me like the keenest blade, "For the first time, I'm really telling the truth!"

Hearing her tone—cold-blooded yet half-repentant—I believed her, believed her so much that I immediately thought that something in me seemed to die, and I became abnormally cold.

I wondered at my own lack of feeling and anger, and even felt like remarking about it to her, but I didn't do that. How did I really feel about her dreadful words? For the most part, cold and bitter. For a few moments, almost lifeless. Emotion seemed to be totally lacking for a while, and I calculated that only intelligence was left. I was out to get to the very end of all these incidences of my intimate relationship with her, to force her to get to the very bottom of her feelings toward me. But I realized that the hour was late and that she was tired and I had promised to leave soon, and resolved to let everything go for another time.

As I walked home and got into bed, my anger rose and rose. "The lousy bitch!" I kept telling myself. "To think how she led me on, how she cruelly played with my feelings, and all the time was merely acting herself. What a low and dirty trick to play on anyone! How selfish! What a rotten bitch she is!" The more I mused, the angrier I grew. Then I set about talking myself out of my anger. I would get myself very enraged and then talk myself out of it, listing fairly rational reasons as to why I should stay with her. I calmed down and was no longer really angry, just hurt.

Comment. At times, I would blame Karyl for her inconsistency, but then I would fully recognize that she had severe disturbances—though not as much as I saw later, when I was a therapist—and then I would blame myself for farting around and not doing something very definite about getting rid of her. Once, on the way home from her house, I began to pity myself immensely. I was definitely on the verge of tears and told myself that it would probably be best to relieve my feelings a bit by crying, I actually did cry a bit, which was unusual for me, because all my life I've had difficulty crying. Not that I wanted to but couldn't cry, but I just didn't particularly want to. I did cry at sentimental movies, but not at most real-life things. I cried when my brother Paul died. So it was very unusual that I was crying about Karyl.

Yes, I've cried very few times in my life. I very rarely cry when something bad happens to me, including the loss of somebody that I really cared for or the rejection by somebody I really wanted to care for me. I don't take it too personally and, consequently, even if I do, I don't put myself down. But I cry sometimes out of anger and sometimes out of self-pity and otherwise remain rather stoical—maybe because I adopted the stoic philosophy at the age of sixteen. I probably thought that such an outlook was not only sane but also that it made me a stronger person.

{}

It's very interesting, as I muse over my dismal up-and-down feelings about Karyl at the beginning of our relationship, that I seemed to have forgotten at that time my article, "The Art of Not Being Unhappy," which I wrote on October 4, 1936, when I was twenty-three, almost a year before I met Karyl.

Let me just review some of the major points I made in telling others how not to be unhappy, and see how I reacted to them. First of all, I discussed worrying—such as worrying about the loss of a job—and I said that the answer to worrying is an exceedingly simple one. The way to do away with totally unnecessary fears is to banish them or to forget them. Yes, that is right: banish or forget them. Simple—isn't it? I pointed out that you couldn't do much about the job that was lost, and that therefore there was no point in worrying about it. So you force yourself to focus on other, more pleasurable things.

"Be ruthless about this. *Dictate to your mind instead of allowing it to dictate to you.* Because otherwise, your fear of failure will help you fail. So you'd better stop worrying."

Well, that was very nice, but I wasn't specific about how to do it, and in the case of Karyl—where I kept worrying all the time, Does she love me? Does she really love me? Is she honest? Is she just fooling me? Is she trying not to hurt me? and so on—I definitely kept worrying, almost compulsively at times, and didn't follow my own advice. Now, maybe I had given no real way of following it, and I hadn't realized at the time that if you say, "I must not worry, I must not worry, I must put my worries behind me," then, paradoxically, you worry more. But, anyway, I certainly didn't follow my own view of worrying in regard to Karyl.

Then I dealt with shame, and I even mentioned shame about shame—what I call a secondary symptom in REBT. But I showed that most shame, such as shame of intercourse even with one's wife, is rather illegitimate. And I said, again, away with it. And I wrote in my essay: "All shame is unnecessary that does not directly or indirectly help us to avoid the present or future unhappiness." Thus, if going naked got us into trouble and was viewed badly by others, we could feel ashamed of *it*, but I didn't quite say, *not* ashamed of *ourselves*. So we could help ourselves stop going naked by our shame about doing so. And I said, "We should therefore try to realize, frankly, our own shortcomings and not try to mask them from ourselves. Then when others criticize or ridicule us, we will not feel so offended." And I advocated that we take a thick-skinnedness or tough-mindedness toward things we do that seem to be wrong. And I quoted, "Sticks and stones can break my bones, but names will never hurt me." And I said, "Wiser words were rarely ever spoken!" I went on to say, "Don't permit mere ego-deflation to cause you unhappiness." But I didn't say precisely *how* to accomplish this. In the case of my relationship with Karyl, I was ashamed of many things I did—such as not speaking up with her and being so goddamned namby-pamby about that. I was really disturbed about that behavior and felt ashamed about it, so I hardly followed my own philosophy, written a year or so before, about shame.

The next thing I considered in my essay was anger. I said that anger was legitimate in regard to its leading you to fight with people who may be offending you. Most people, however, don't do much about offending you and they don't fight you, so therefore anger doesn't help you fight them and is unnecessary.

Even if the offender is in the wrong, it'll do you little good to engage in verbal or physical battle or even to get angry. So I said, "Curb your anger as much as possible. Cut it short. Sidetrack it. Get yourself thinking in other channels. Smile. Laugh at yourself. You'd be surprised how good it makes you feel." I was telling people to push anger out of their mind and not look at what *they're* doing to make themselves angry. So that's not a great solution, but at least I warned them about remaining angry.

In the case of Karyl, of course, I got angry at myself, but I also got angry—very, very angry—at her, when she said she loved me and she didn't. Or when she wouldn't say whether she loved me or not. At times, I was just moderately angry and usually forgave her. But at other times, I was very angry and, as I point out in REBT, anger gets you obsessed with the person you're angry with. And I was obsessing myself with her and her behavior and how rotten it was and how it did me in. So I didn't follow my advice very well at that time.

I next showed people how to control themselves by not obsessing about their failures, but I hardly followed this advice with Karyl. I wisely told my readers not to concentrate just on winning a game but on the pleasure and experience they could get from playing the game itself. And I partly did that with Karyl—concentrated on the pleasure and the experience I got with her—but I also put myself down for not doing the right thing and doing stupid things with her, including my obnoxious ambivalence all the time about her.

Then I went on to discuss boredom. I recommended when one is bored one had better divert oneself; I called this a diversion technique. That is, find something interesting. "Look up, look down, look high, look low. Look everywhere until you find it. It could be music, painting, literature, anything." Interestingly enough, I recommended what Bob Harper and I recommended years later, in the first edition of *A Guide to Rational Living*. "Find a cause big enough and suitable enough for you to espouse. If you can find one creed that you can give your heart and soul to, and that you can fight tooth and nail for, then, good sir, you are blessed." I don't know whether I figured that out myself or got it from reading philosophy, but it was a pretty good idea. Of course, I recollected later that it was still distractive and diversionary. We didn't quite consider what one told oneself to make things boring, when they weren't necessarily boring in themselves. Such as, "I can't stand this repetition, and it's awful, and it's terrible, etc.," which one could have tackled. So getting a vital, absorbing interest was okay, but it didn't exactly solve the problem as thoroughly as one could otherwise do it.

Anyway, with Karyl in 1937 and the beginning of 1938, I did use diversionary tactics—thought of other things, causes, and especially political revolutionary causes I could get active in—and to some extent it worked. But it by no means worked well enough. I wasn't exactly bored with *her* at times—yes, I guess I was bored with *her*—but I was also bored with my own nonsense and my own repetitively going over and over how awful her ambivalence was, and could I get the truth from her, and all kinds of things like that. So I used distraction but didn't get to my musts, shoulds, and oughts—"It *shouldn't* be this way. I *shouldn't* be this way, and she *shouldn't* be this way"—which led to a large part of the boredom. So my advice wasn't bad, but I didn't exactly follow it.

I next considered dejection, or what today I would call depression, and especially wondering about the purpose of life, the world, and what the universe is, and having no answer to it, and therefore depressing ourselves for being purposeless. And here again, I recommended *looking the other way* and *ignoring purposelessness* as much as possible and forcibly directing our attention elsewhere. If something bad happened—our candidate lost the election—we could think of other things. Despair wouldn't do us any good, so why dwell on it? If we despaired of the intelligence of other humans, we could either do something about it or not, and if we couldn't, then why dwell on it? We could concentrate on other things.

Well, again, I got depressed at times over Karyl and sometimes ignored that and was able to concentrate on other things. But I definitely didn't see at the time that I was telling myself that I was no good, that it was hopeless, that I'd never get what I wanted. *Low frustration tolerance and self-downing.* So I didn't do much about that, other than use my distraction technique to not dwell on it too much, but I certainly dwelled on it somewhat.

I realized that we often used denial because we weren't doing well enough and we thought we should do better. So I spoke about that, discussing the "So-What technique": if you don't get what you want, that's too bad. So what? You could live with the deprivation and not whine about it. Again, I recommended all kinds of distraction, and I definitely recommended not whining. However, I didn't clearly understand people's low frustration tolerance, and that we are telling ourselves when we are deprived that it's horrible and awful and we can't stand to be deprived. We could change that to "It's a pain in the ass. Too damn bad!" So I recommended the "So-What technique" back then, but these days—and for many years—I tell clients *not* to use that. Because if they say "so what" they go from one extreme to the other and sabotage themselves. "It doesn't matter at all," when it *does* matter. So by all means, they can tell themselves that it does matter, but it doesn't matter TOO much and it's not awful and terrible when they can't get what they want. So I didn't give an ideal solution.

In the case of Karyl, I definitely was not getting what I wanted much of the time—probably the majority of the time. I got a little sex and a little love, but not enough of either. I *awfulized* about it, and then distracted myself from awfulizing, but I didn't really get to the core of "It's terrible, horrible, and awful, and I can't stand it." I didn't see that with her, and I don't think I saw that in my essay "The Art of Not Being Unhappy."

I recommended in the essay that just as we inhibit natural pleasures, such as overeating, should we not more easily be able to inhibit natural displeasures in order to stave off further displeasure? I realized that sorrow and regret were natural and normal, but that we could hold them back, and recommended that we do so. And it's very possible to do so. Even if we lost an irreplaceable mate, it is possible not to languish for days, weeks, or even years over him. If he died, it wouldn't do us any good to languish like that. And I said, "Sorrow is mainly a habit, and that if you did not see others participate in it and be expected to indulge in it yourself, you would hardly do it at all in many cases." But that, I guess, was quite an exaggeration. It's not only a habit. It's a natural, biological, and socially learned behavior, and practically nobody could never sorrow. To not get what you want is almost automatically to sorrow—but not to depress yourself.

I next considered loneliness. I recognized that we don't need others to talk to and be with, and that therefore we could reduce that need, but I didn't show people how to do so. The thing was to *do* something about your being alone: to join clubs, to meet new friends, to be as nice as you can be to the friends you already have, and to be alone relatively little.

If that didn't work, I said, you could occupy yourself with other things instead of with other people, especially interesting things. Interesting occupations can largely solve the problem of loneliness as well as fear, worry, rejection, and boredom. Today, however, I would only partially recommend this technique.

In the case of Karyl, I saw her continually, every day or two, and therefore wasn't lonely for her company but lonely in the sense that she didn't care for me in the way I cared for her. Therefore I was alone in my own heart, even though I was seeing her steadily. And of course I dreaded the fact that she might give it all up, and then I might truly be without any woman. So I worried about that. Again, I did my best to distract myself and even thought of throwing myself into more political activity, which I knew would be involving. But I didn't do that very successfully.

Next in the essay, I dealt briefly with envy and showed that feeling envy usually meant that we were rating ourselves lower than others, who we felt had better traits than we had. And we'd better curb our ego-mania, our swell-headedness, as I called it, and not put ourselves down. I said, "We should put off all envious ideas as soon as they occur, banish them and think of something else. Otherwise, they may do us much harm and little good." But, here again, I keep reverting to the tactic that so many people use, by themselves and with therapists, that of distraction. I call it cognitive distraction, and in REBT we teach people how to meditate, how to do yoga, and how to otherwise distract themselves, and especially to get a vital absorbing interest. But we also teach them to stop saying, "I *must* not be alone. It's *awful* to be alone. I'm no good for being alone." And that's the main method, because distraction only works temporarily.

With Karyl, again, I envied other men who were with her, those who were taller and especially those who had more money, and maybe were better sexually. I didn't realize how little sex she was really having with them. And I even envied her volatility, her emotionalism, and her being able to throw herself enthusiastically into things, but I didn't get at the source of real envy—my self-downing. So that didn't work too well.

I next dealt with disgust and showed my readers that they naturally would feel revolted or disgusted about certain things, but then they take it a step further and make that thing into a horror, thereby disgusting themselves even more. But I sort of thought that that was inevitable in some cases. Some things *were*, I thought, disgusting. So I recommended that one become familiar with disgusting objects. Try in vivo desensitization, as I used it on myself with my fear of public speaking and my fear of approaching young women when I was nineteen. If I disliked approaching disgusting things and dealing with them, I could force myself to do it. But in addition to that, since I don't think I had much faith in my readers doing disgusting things deliberately, I recommended not dwelling on the feelings of disgust, to shove them away as quickly as possible, and forcing oneself to think of something else, something nondisgusting. Good old distraction again, which was my main solution for practically everything.

In the case of Karyl, I was disgusted with a few of the things—physical or otherwise—that I did. But I guess I was really revolted about her indecisiveness and her not being able to be honest with me and maybe even with herself. But again, I used distraction and it didn't work too well. Instead of facing the fact that (a) she just was this way and mysteriously disturbed, and (b) that was too goddamned bad, I not only didn't have to dwell on it, but I could accept it. And in "The Art of Not Being Unhappy," I signally forgot most of the time the real solution of acceptance—*unconditional* acceptance of the things we find disgusting or of the people whose behavior we find disgusting, without damning them, or damning it, or damning the world.

I next dealt in my essay with confusion. But really I could have called it indecision. I pointed out that it was a normal state, and we could hardly help confusion and indecision at times. We could try to learn more about things and make better decisions, I recommended, but that, too, wouldn't often work. So I finally recommended from my standpoint of years later not to let our indecision and confusion affect us, as we may very well let it do. Why not let our indecision work its way out and finally come to a decision—and in the meantime not fret about it. Again, I saw the secondary disturbance very clearly, that it was not just our indecision and confusion, but our beating ourselves for being confused and indecisive. So if we refused to do *that*, that would be fine. But I wasn't too specific in how to tackle our secondary symptom and say, "Too bad. I'm indecisive, and it's bad to be, because I won't be able to make a perfect decision and solve my practical problems that I have. But it's not the end of the world, and I'm not a shit for being indecisive."

I next considered overstimulation. I realized while writing this essay that the people I was talking to—my presumable readers—could be born with a tendency to be easily overstimulated or could have acquired it from their social learning. In any event, they could try to control themselves, and if they couldn't control being overstimulated, they could consider seeing a psychiatrist or a psychoanalyst. Today, I definitely wouldn't say psychoanalyst; I'd say a good Rational Emotive Behavior therapist. They could control their overstimulation, I said, and they'd better make an effort to do so. Also, I realized that they could have a secondary symptom—they could worry about being overstimulated, and their worry would be a disturbance. But again I suggested distraction to stop worrying and think of something else.

Of course, I see today—and I've seen for years of being a therapist—that if you are overstimulated you could think of other things and distract yourself, but you'd better get at the source. Usually it would be that this thing that stimulates me is exciting, and it's too exciting, and I can't stand not being overstimulated or stimulated and therefore I *have* to be calm. But, of course, I *don't* have to be calm.

In the case of Karyl, I was definitely overstimulated much of the time—particularly, of course, sexually, but also I was overstimulated by her beauty, by her presence, by talking to her, by her negativism, you name it. If at any time in my life I took things too seriously, that was it. So I was continually overstimulated. I obsessed about her, almost had an obsessive-compulsive disorder. Being IN love by itself is partially obsessive-compulsive, as I now think. So I was overstimulated. I told myself to think of other things, and at times I did, but it didn't really work that well. So I did it for a while, but came right back to the overstimulation.

I next dealt with the horror of having difficulties, and showed that it was more than childish if we screamed and complained when we couldn't get what we wanted. I said, "We humans meet with some difficulty, start the ball over, gain no sympathy or comfort, and pity ourselves all the more. How puerile! How insane!" So I saw the stupidity of mulling over difficulty. Then I gave the answer. "So let's try to grow up. Let's accept difficulty and trouble as such, do what we can to overcome them, and then clamp our lips tightly and go on to think of something else. Let's be adults for once!" Yes, but I didn't by any means show that if we want to be adults, we again have to accept that the world and its problems will be difficult, and that's too bad, and we won't be able to solve many of them, and that's not *awful*. So thinking of something or someone else, which I recommended, was okay, but it wouldn't solve the problem.

Again, palliation, *cognitive distraction*, solves practically any problem temporarily, but it doesn't get rid of the underlying overgeneralization and our "musts"—our *must*urbating—that things *must* not be this difficult, and I *must* be able to find a great solution to them. Mainly it is the realization that things don't *have* to be easy, that they have to be difficult when they are difficult. And they don't have to be solved immediately, and I don't have to solve them, though I'll do my best. That will mean acceptance. But distraction will work temporarily. And, again, Karyl was as difficult a customer as I could have found at that time. When I discussed her and her doings with other people, they agreed she was a DC (a difficult customer) and that the situation— money, her living with her parents, my living with my parents—was very difficult. *So I distracted myself and enjoyed* myself as much as I could under those difficult conditions. *But I was very, very far from acceptance.*

Next, in "The Art of Not Being Unhappy," I tackled *compulsions*. What can we do if we have a compulsive thought or make a compulsive action, and know that it is compulsive and know that it is bad? Well, first we could use willpower and stop doing the compulsion. How? And I said, "Merely by stopping it." But I realized that, by trying to change our bad compulsions by force, we often actually encourage them, may reinforce them. I recommended taking them to extremes at times in order to stop them. So I advised my readers to see immediately how ridiculous their compulsions were and to make a definite attempt to get rid of them, fast and early.

Now, in all this, I really didn't see the biological elements of obsessive-compulsive disorder, and I was just talking about my compulsions, such as my compulsion to see Karyl: to think about her and to get things straight when I was madly in love. But today I realize, having had many clients with obsessive-compulsive disorder, that their serotonin or other biological elements are deficient, and they certainly in some respects are compelled to do what they know is pointless or bad and don't want to do. So *seeing* it is not enough, and stopping it will work only if one *persists* and cuts it down—usually slowly and gradually—and then one minimizes it but often never gets rid of it. Our tendency to be compulsive we never completely get rid of. So I didn't see that at that time. But I realized that one could partially stop one's compulsions if one worked very determinedly at it. Again, I recommended distraction, but not that strongly in this instance.

Of course, I didn't exactly get rid of my OCD for Karyl and sometimes probably made it worse by saying, "I must get rid of it! I must get rid of it! I must not allow myself to be compelled to do things with her, think of her all the time." That probably exacerbated it. But I didn't convince myself, as I have my clients now convince themselves, "It's only uncomfortable—very uncomfortable—to stop, but it's much more uncomfortable and harder not to stop, and therefore I'd better take the lesser evil and stop it, and cut it down, and live with it to the degree that I have to temporarily live with it, but not, of course, ever blame myself for being compulsive. That is fatal and leads to the secondary symptoms and will defeat you." So with Karyl, I would say that I wasn't very good at stopping my compulsions and my obsessions.

I concluded my essay with several rules. (1) We preferably should try to understand the cause of our trouble. (2) We preferably should try to eliminate the cause of our trouble. (3) We preferably should try to hold back the feeling of unhappiness to keep it from spreading. (4) We preferably should occupy ourselves so that we have no time to be unhappy.

These are not such bad rules, but they really don't get at the source of our convincing ourselves over and over that we shouldn't have this trouble, that we're stupid for having it, that it's horrible to be compulsive. REBT much more specifically faces compulsion, including obsessive-compulsive disorder (OCD), and deals with it. Even though REBT therapists have a difficult time with OCD clients, we probably help them much more than most other forms of therapy and even more than other forms of Cognitive Behavioral Therapy, which partly stem from REBT.

All those rules I listed above are ones I partially used with Karyl. But I didn't use them strongly or actively enough.

Now I must say, from a distance of over sixty-eight years, that my intention was to acknowledge that I had serious trouble with Karyl, with the world, and with me, and to do something about it. So I was always very active in looking for solutions. And the main solution I found—distraction—only worked to some degree. That's the trouble with it. It works temporarily, but then the problem comes back. So I didn't think things through in terms of shoulds, oughts, musts, and how to dispute them empirically, logically, heuristically, and pragmatically. I didn't even temporarily get rid of the musts. But I lived with them and sort of accepted myself with them, and refused to put myself down. So at the age of twenty-four, I was using a form of REBT.

This tends to show that having a solution, even a temporary solution, to an emotional-behavioral problem helps, but not enough. The essence of disturbance, which I came solidly to years later and which I just hinted at earlier—which, again, are the absolutistic musts, the shoulds, and the oughts—I just nicely glossed over and missed. I saw them in part but very vaguely, and didn't see how to dispute them cognitively, emotionally, and behaviorally.

I could say that I finally clearly saw the power of *must*urbation, partly by reading people like Alfred Korzybski and Paul Tillich, but also by continuing to persist in talking my clients out of their bullshit, even when I was an analyst; and for two years or so, from 1953 to 1955 while I was creating REBT, I was seeing clients and trying to talk them out of their Irrational Beliefs and giving them activity homework against it. Then I very clearly began to see the musts—see them the first year or so, 1955 to 1956, of my using REBT.

I definitely saw that my clients all had Irrational Beliefs and that they were perfectionistic, but I wasn't as clear on the musts. And finally, around 1956, when I was about to give my first paper on REBT at the American Psychological Association convention in Chicago, I started clearly seeing the three main musts: "I must do well, you must do well, and the world must give me what I want when I want it!"

I was definitely on the right track with Irrational Beliefs, and I saw later that they all included musts. But I didn't clearly get it—which shows that really getting something and *using it actively* is excellent. Seeing it vaguely is very good at times, but not enough. After Karyl told me that she had been lying to me and pretending to love me, and I was completely shocked and hostile for a while, my hostility kept returning. "She *must* not be that way!"

February 7, 1938. I got close to a suitable woman in the subway, and she and I were both passionate, the first time for me in a long time, since I was in love with Karyl. I was very surprised, and felt relief after I had an orgasm with this woman, but not much pleasure in the process. It seemed that it was purely physical and that I didn't enjoy it very much.

Comment. Of course, I would have enjoyed it before I met Karyl, since this was one of my main ways of getting sex. But compared to the great, great love I had for Karyl, the sex didn't seem very important. So sex can lead to greater love, but also greater love can lead to little enjoyment for other women.

> February 8, 1938. She criticized me for my sloppy clothes. But I resisted because I didn't dress up for her too much, since I expected to see her for years, and it was a waste of time. It seemed ridiculous sprucing up and taking half an hour to wash and dress. But on the other hand, I still need to impress her as much as possible since I'm not good-looking enough at my very best.

Comment. That need to impress Karyl seems almost amazing to me now, because up until I was about eighty-nine years of age, I didn't particularly spruce up. I washed up very briefly, usually in the morning, and when I went out I combed my hair a little, but used practically no lotion or soap or anything on it, and did a pretty scruffy job. So I was clean, but that's all. I never worried about dress, even when going to an important affair. I just maybe washed a little better. But I certainly didn't and don't need the approval of others, and don't try to get it by sprucing up. Since being with Debbie, however, I'm told I look very good: better than I've looked for many years. She cuts my hair and gets me very nice clothes. I tell her I don't need them, but she says she enjoys getting them for me and tells me over and over that I look handsome, that she loves my looks (with or without the nice clothes). So I let her!

> February 17, 1938. I saw Karyl and noticed she was wearing one of the few dresses that could easily open at the waist. So I got very sexy. I tried to tell her about the letter I had been writing, but she interrupted me. She got me to sit on another part of the floor for a while, not too close to her with my head on her lap, and I felt hurt.

> February 19, 1938. I was afraid she wouldn't call me again, and should have asked for another appointment. And I once thought that I was so stable. Good luck on that one! I wrote, again: "She was the only girl who ever loved me, a lovely intellectual girl, and I forced her to go. I'm an idiot." And I thought I was.

Comment. People are so damned neurotic. Maybe one can only hope till a suitable partner comes along. That is a statement I would endorse today. I keep quoting Alfred Korzybski that all humans are unsane, and I believe that they all translate their strong desires into musts. So the great majority of women and men are very neurotic, to say the least, when they're not severely personality disordered.

February 23, 1938. Karyl remarked in the course of a conversation that love should be free, without any ties, so that the lovers could part at any time. And I, who had previously believed just this, but now thought that philosophy meaningless in my own case, felt my heart sink. I felt that she didn't love me at all, and that was awful. So here again, we have this 100 percent change—that I used to be in favor of free love, and still theoretically was for other people, but not for me.

March 1, 1938. I kept working on my letter to Karyl and finally finished it. It took ninety-seven single-spaced pages. I list at length some of Karyl's worst traits and why I think they make us incompatible for marriage if she does not change them:

1. You have frightful health habits.
2. You insist upon being secretive with me.
3. You are a confoundedly difficult woman to handle.
4. You are hardly the most economical person.
5. You have little political knowledge.
6. You are a wastrel of time.
7. You have a pretty terrible bunch of friends.
8. You are frequently selfish and inconsiderate.
9. You have a definite propensity toward shallowness.
10. You are petty about numerous little things.
11. You don't exactly offer me things I desire for love.
12. You do not fit in well with the characteristics and qualities that I desire in my future wife.

I also point out how I annoy Karyl and what some of our incompatibilities are. Such as: "(1) I am too serious about most things, especially about myself and my relationship with you. (2) I am, according to you, too logical about practically everything. (3) I am at the present time a very bookish individual, and this again often causes you utter annoyance. (4) I am a smug and conceited person, and you naturally object to that kind of person. (5) I do not in the least fit in with your various minor and major phobias. These phobias that you have in rare abundance demand certain definite things from a man, especially, it is to be presumed, from your husband.

"Before I bring this letter to a close, I want to thank you sincerely for arousing my love emotions. I mean that, darling. When I met you I was practically incapable of falling in love with any woman. Now, to my own great surprise, I definitely am capable of loving a fine, intelligent young woman like you. So I will always be grateful to you no matter what our future may bring.

"Secondly, I want to thank you again for the most absorbing and exciting experience that I have ever gone through. Thirdly, darling, thank you for the great joy you have given me at intervals. Real happiness is rarely achieved in this dismal life, and some of the people never achieve it. Thank you, fourthly, for the many new things you have taught me during the hundreds of hours we have spent together, dear. I never knew women at all till I met you, and now I do to some degree. And I learned many things about myself, especially my many faults, which were well worth the time I spent with you. Again, I offer my grateful thanks.

"I close on a *note of optimism and hope that is quite unusual for me.* For your benefit and for my own, I have written this memorandum. I have already benefited by it more than getting certain things off my chest. Now that it has drawn to a close, I feel almost spiritually relieved. I only hope, darling, that it in some ways makes you feel better, too. We have been through many strange and beautiful things together, dearest, and I am sure that we could go through many more. We are still just at the beginning of our love and entering into a relationship. We are both so young, both so capable of living and learning. Yet, to have every opportunity of experiencing all the beauty, all the charm, all the indescribable happiness and mutually shared love, we should, we must attain all the joy and splendor that true love gives to life. We will! Finished, darling. P.S. I love you."

Comment. And that was the end of the letter. As I look over it now, I see that it was very, very honest. It was *obsessive-compulsive*, but I was anxiously afraid that she might not get all the details and so I overdid them probably, and some of the letter seems to be much, much too detailed. But my heart was in the right place, and I really honestly expressed myself. I told her about my letter, surprising her greatly. I promised to bring it to her when I finished it for our next meeting. I dreaded the thought that the letter might be destroyed by fire before I could give it to her. I had once read that it was Carlyle, I think, whose housekeeper burnt his whole history of the French Revolution, and he had to write the goddamned thing over. So I have an unusual fear that fire might somewhat destroy my great work and I've attended to it in a practical manner by sending fire copies until recent times to people who had room in their house to keep them in case anything happened to my original works before they were published.

March 11, 1938. Finished the letter and went to see her. Got close to her, even though she had a cold. I wasn't that concerned about a little thing like a cold. Said that I would keep writing, but not to make money at it, would do it on the side. And she was skeptical about my writing ability, especially my making money at it. Gave her the letter at her asking, and she began to read it, while I closed my eyes and rested. With many qualms. At the beginning she said, "He expects me to be so logical, just like a mature woman, despite the fact that I haven't had that experience yet. How silly!" I looked at her from time to time to see if she was still reading. She said, "I've read ten pages now, and I still don't know what you want. Do you want to be my lover? Do you want me to be your mistress? What do you want?" "Nothing like that," I said desperately. "I wrote it mainly for my own good." But I despaired now of it doing any good at all. She marveled at the section where I listed all her faults and said, "Oh, you know all those things about me."

Karyl finished my letter and said, "What can I say? I don't want to be in love with you. You're too logical. I want a wild impulsive lover. But I suppose I can't dictate to my heart, can I?" She was vague and I could get little out of her. She finally admitted that she had only read the letter hastily and under bad conditions. We discussed marriage again and she seemed unusually favorable for it, which was fine.

Comment. Now, many years later, I see that there are advantages and disadvantages to everything, including Rational Emotive Behavior Therapy. *That's the human condition—to be in a dilemma and have no total way out of it. There isn't any total solution.* So I saw it somewhat then.

March 21, 1938. Got in business with my father and The Four Aces, who manufacture an automatic bridge game, which looks like it might work out. We have $10,000 to invest and hope to be in production soon.

Seriously thought of marrying Karyl and her coming to live with my family. I was then living with my mother and my sister and brother, but that wouldn't work out too well. Went right back to "If only I was sure that she loved me." I never was, and I continually asked myself, "Does she, does she not? Does she, does she not?" obsessively. Read about an obsessive-compulsive love and said that I wouldn't love her obsessive-compulsively. But I damn well did!

March 30, 1938. I had started my new job—I think at Distinctive Creations—and was getting little money for it. But I didn't whine about the hard time I had. And she said, "You can stand it. You don't need anything exciting." I asked her what she thought of me, and she said, "No, you don't need anything at all."

April 1, 1938. Saw Karyl, and she said, "You can keep your letters and your clumsy advances," and that hurt me terribly. "I don't want any part of them." But I looked at her tense red face, becoming more fearful every moment, and wondered if she was deeply serious. "No, it's all off between us," she continued. "Men are all out after the same thing—dirty filthy brutes. So take your love to some other girl." Again, I was quite hurt and shocked. She went on: "All you want is sex. You keep making sex demands all the time. How can one write such an insensitive letter? Sex—that was all it was full of."

I got angry, because I said, "I write five out of ninety-seven pages about sex, and you stupidly accuse me." But she insisted that sex was in every line, and she may have had some sense about that. I thought that the letter had brought about a more loving atmosphere between us and I thought that was excellent. I resolved to make a real study of women—to read every good book on the subject, and if possible to have several platonic relationships with women. Began reading a book on women avidly since it seemed to explain so much about Karyl and her attitude toward me. Wondered if my case wasn't hopeless because she was so full of psychological feelings that seemed to hold her apart from me, which she might never overcome.

Mentally, I began to drift further and further away from her and to take it for granted that our relations were nearing an end. I introduced Karyl to my mother and saw that my mother had frightened her and made a bad impression with her loud-mouthedness. I thought again that Karyl was semi-neurotic and needed psychoanalysis, but I now see that she had a severe personality disorder and that psychoanalysis, again, would have helped bollix her up more.

Comment. I see now that Karyl may not have had obsessions or phobias, but she did exhibit very nutty ideas and behaviors. I thought that it might be better to live with a strange, interesting woman like Karyl than with a more sedate one who might fit in better with my character.

That was pretty nutty, because I might enjoy such a woman more but probably would not be able to live with her.

> April 3, 1938. Thought of preparing a letter to her now for submission in another six weeks. Then there would be plenty of time to outline it properly and get it together.

Comment. It looked like I compulsively liked to write letters, and I am a writer, and I was never done with writing her letters. Kept steadily reading every possible book on marriage, sex, and love, in order to understand her. And I think it was just about this time that I started to get really interested in writing *The Case for Promiscuity* and other works on sex and become a sexologist. Now, it's possible that my ignorance of her and of sex with her made me get this involved, but also it may have been a little before that. I'm not sure.

> She accused me of being an intellectual snob, and I said, "I am something of an intellectual snob—always have been, probably always will be. I don't apologize, for that's the way I am and I don't think you can change me." Karyl accused me of being a snob and conceited and smug, and I admitted that I did accept the fact that I did very well, especially with 1 out of 1,000 in intelligence tests, which I had taken with college and came up in the 999th percentile. And I was very good at writing. And I think I said that I'm one of the best comic poets in the country and one of the best musicians—because I realized then that I had a talent for composing. Not another Beethoven or anything like that, because I know my own limitations. That's what I like best about me—I do know a good many of my own limitations.

Comment. I'm afraid that in saying all this, I was really showing Karyl and myself that I had conditional acceptance—because I was good at various things such as writing, I was therefore a good person. So I had by no means come to the notion of Unconditional Self-Acceptance. I hadn't read Paul Tillich or the existentialists at that time, and certainly not Carl Rogers, who was in 1937, I think, still psychoanalytic. She accused me of being like other writers who feel that they have to write and can't do without it. And I said, "Neither can I. I'm just like them. I must write also and will continue doing so until the end of my days." That was something of a compulsion, to show how good I was as a writer, and then presumably also good as a human because I was good as a writer. So she was somewhat right about my being a compulsive writer.

April 5, 1938. Went to her house and no one answered the bell. Called later and found the parents just got in, and she had been out late the night before and apparently forgot about the appointment with me. So I walked home slowly, angry, saying, "That's what she really thinks of me—forgot the appointment. Certainly in love she is not! Even I wouldn't do that to her now, much less in a few days. Quite angry. That bitch! No, I shouldn't get angry like that, but still angry."

This was, again, atypical of me, as it wasn't my nature, usually, to get very angry. When I finally called and she answered, she was sleepy because she said she had been picketing for two nights. She was sorry she forgot the appointment with me. There was so much excitement going on. So I accepted her apology.

Comment. Suddenly I felt much better because I said, "To hell with it! I've decided not to take it so seriously after this. Later, I read about the miscegenation laws that prevented whites from marrying blacks. I told myself immediately that I would marry her even if I discovered that she had black blood and that it was illegal to marry her. Nothing like that would matter to me. I really, really loved her. Again, this shows how nutty I was at that time.

April 7, 1938. Went about the task of writing the new letter to her and got preoccupied with that. Started looking at pretty women again, and especially after every one I saw in the subway. Finally wrote my letter to her—seventy-six more pages—and gave it to her. It began, "Dear darling, this is a declaration of war. You completely ignored my last ultimatum to you—read it lightly, made little effort to understand it. In my country, that means war. I did everything but shoot myself in the last letter I gave you. It was an ultimatum because it said that this tomfoolery of yours has got to stop pretty damned quick. I want everything and all love from you, and I'm getting less than nothing at present—not even thanks for my letter.

"This will be my *last letter to you*. But let me explain at the start that I'm still in love with you. Not exactly as I was three weeks ago, but still. First of all, *I withdraw all offers of marriage to you*. I wouldn't think of marrying you at the present time, except possibly for spite. My reasons for not marrying you are, first, it has become very obvious to me of late that you don't love me wholeheartedly. I have tried my best to love you but have not succeeded in getting you to fully love me.

"Let us review the things I stated in my last letter that are demanded of true love. And let us see how likely you are to fulfill them: First, I want unlimited affection. This you have never in the least given me, nor does it seem that you ever will unless something unusual happens. Second, I want beauty, and you with your infernal reserve have given me only a fraction of that beauty it is in your power to give me—a damned small fraction. Third, I want your companionship. Again, with your numerous other important interests and your continual secretiveness, you have given me comparatively little companionship. Fourth, I want tenderness and you, who have so much to give, seem to deliberately evade the issue at practically all times. Fifth, I want relaxation in love. It is just as easy to relax with you in that respect as it is with a caged tiger. Sixth, I want children by you. This, oddly enough, seems to be one of the few things I have a fairly good chance at with you. Seventh, though I forgot somehow to mention this in my previous letter, I want intensity and passion in love. I want spirit, fire, ardor. What do I usually get from you? Lethargy, lifelessness, a turned-back, nerve-wracking passivity. Grrr.

"We know each other six months; I'm not sure of your love at all yet. I love you but with ups and downs depending on your reactions toward me; at present, I'm miserable five parts to one, and seem to have no power to make you happy. I can't help you—perhaps make you forget pain a little when I'm with you—but sometimes it makes things worse, apparently. We could go on like this forever, but it's getting us nowhere. We've had two breaks, so far, and we'll have more, so we might as well get married and see if we're made for each other."

April 8, 1938. She criticized at the opera a couple who were necking together and wouldn't listen to my telling her that it was not doing anybody else any harm. And I said to myself, "She'll never change—too much bad conditioning in her past." But now I see that it was more than just bad conditioning. She was an absolutist and believed that what she thought was absolutely right and people shouldn't do it.

She asked me why I was not applauding the opera when she kept applauding throughout. I said, "Well, the others will do it anyway. So I don't have to." I said that applauding was a little too artificial for me. She asked me if I didn't get the infectious spirit of the crowd applauding, and I said, "No. Practically never. I conserve my energies for other things."

On the way home from the opera she asked me about my emotional state, and I said it's hypo-emotionalism. And she thought I couldn't enjoy life like that, but I said, "I have my own enjoyments. I admit that I used to think the other way, that living—the emotional one—was bad because it always seemed to bring unhappiness to people. But I'm not so sure of that anymore, and I've just about given up telling people how to live. As for me, I find it better at times to show my emotions as much as I can."

Comment. This was something really new for me, now that I think back on it. I always have been very emotional, inwardly and outwardly, and usually about some cause or other. But on the other hand I've always fallen in love madly, and when I'm in love, then I'm hyper-emotional. And as I said to Karyl at this time, my emotionalism is a combination of control and hyper-emotionalism. And I said, "I'm not really so unemotional as I seem. I probably felt more emotional from the music we heard than anyone else in this place."

April 9, 1938. Talked to a very attractive woman I met the next day and almost fell in love with her, but warned myself that I didn't want to marry her or anyone and I'd better watch it. And I think I talked myself out of falling in love with her because of my relationship with Karyl, which had ended so badly.

Feeling very good these days, as if I had finally conquered love and could now take all its delights without all its pains. Thought that if I had been more good-looking, I would have had a real fling at this love business and get so much of its pleasures without feeling in the least hurt myself.

June 5, 1938. Thought of waiting at home for a call from Karyl, there being a bare possibility that I might get one. "No," I said, "to hell with it. Let her call!" So to some degree I was getting over her, but by no means completely. I had fantasies with other women in which I pictured conquering them sexually but not really loving them. So I was still distinctly hung up on Karyl.

She sort of urged me to try to have an affair with a woman I knew, but I resisted and said that it wasn't that good or interesting. She again talked about her desire to have a baby, and she might even have one without having intercourse. She said she might never marry, and I said maybe she should not marry because she seemed to be too focused on herself and not on any lover. Again, I got disgusted on the way home and thought that I would give her maybe three or four more times. Unfortunately I kept saying that and never went through with it.

Again, she accused me of being too mechanical in the lovemaking, and she said I was not a good lover. But she kept being very inconsistent about that. Tried again to get her to say whether or not she had orgasms without any intercourse, but she beat around the bush and wouldn't say yes or no. But then at times she hinted that she loved me and that I loved her, and I was a little surprised but accepted it as quite good. Went to kiss her, but she evaded me.

Comment. Kept going through hell on her account, or on my account. And then years later, when I read this over, seemed to think everything was so trivial and so silly, and how could I be so asinine as to have such doubts about her and insist that she love me. But at that time I was taking it much too seriously.

I was still very curious to see how it would work out, so I didn't quite give up on her. Pretty, pretty crazy! At the same time, my father's business was going bankrupt and I would soon be out of a job.

I realized that I was angry at her and then I saw that that was rather foolish. I didn't have the REBT theory of anger, that you create it and it's quite stupid. But I realized that it was wrong. So I thought that I didn't give her a chance. She moodily did stupid *things*, but they weren't her. They were just a part of her, so I'd better give her more understanding. Even before I created REBT I had a fairly good attitude toward anger, but I often didn't carry it out in practice.

I wrote down reasons why it would be beneficial to marry her. (1) To break down psychological barriers and have less reserve; (2) experience the experience of marriage; (3) maybe we'd have sex; (4) gain knowledge of her loving me or not loving me, once and for all; (5) make meetings with her easier; (6) be able to help her more; (7) save years, maybe, and see what was what. So I kept insisting to myself that there would be some good use to staying married. But I think a lot of it was rationalization.

She remarked that she wanted a baby very badly—that it was the only thing that would save her—and that she must have one within three years or so. Then Lover 4, with whom she had an appointment, knocked on the door and I left.

June 6, 1938. I saw Karyl and told her the truth about my writing notes on her, because I was going to write a novel from them later. And she was very, very angry and ordered me out of her life several times. She thought it was terrible that I had been writing those notes and wanted me to destroy them. And I insisted, oh, no, I would never destroy them. They were for posterity and were in an anonymous form so nobody could see who they were about. She ordered me out several times during the night, and I was quite sad and rather disturbed about her getting rid of me so quickly and easily and finally.

But then, very late in the night that same night, she allowed me to practically bare one of her breasts and kiss the nipple of it, and we got very, very involved sexually—at least I did—and she seemed to definitely go along with it. So I was ecstatic about that, and that made everything all right. I really felt, for a while, that she was going to end it all with me and couldn't conceive of how she could do a thing like that just because I had written those notes.

June 10, 1938. Got over to see her, and pretended that I was sicker than I was, hoping for some sympathy. She told me never to marry a Jewish girl—they were too demanding and wanted too much. Told her that I got sick after I got rejected by her and thought she was very cold to me. She said she wanted a baby again, and I told her she'd better be in better health before she had one. I told her that I used to think that beauty, intelligence, and character were important for marriage, and now I realized that the real thing was you had to be loved by the person you marry. I said I felt very sick because we'd been together a whole day and there was no affection between us, so it felt hopeless. "When I see you every day," I said, "I'm in good spirits, but then by the end of the evening it seems hopeless again, and that wrecks my spirit."

At one point, she said, "You're such a silly boy" and caressed my hair and was able to kiss me, and I was practically ecstatic about that. But I wasn't as happy as I could have been when she left, because I suspected that she was putting on some of her act and that she really did not love me.

Kept debating whether to keep seeing Karyl, but, after a disappointing evening with her, I went for a memorable walk in Bronx Botanical Gardens at midnight and faced the fact that I *needed* her, not merely wanted her, and that my *needs* created havoc. Went back to the philosophy of Epictetus and strongly decided that no matter how much I *wanted* her, I did not *need* what I wanted.

Solidly convinced myself of this, told Karyl of my giving up my needs and impressed her so much that she actually wanted to marry me. Although our marrying at that time was highly impractical, we agreed to do it *secretly* and to live together only when we got enough money to do so.

June 14, 1938. Karyl said that she didn't like being caressed during her period. She got too easily aroused but not satisfied. She told me that although she hadn't had intercourse with men, she had petted to orgasm with them and she was now willing to admit that. She indicated that she wasn't having that kind of sex anymore. I told her about my frotteurism with a number of women in the subway, and she said she had some, too, but was afraid she would be followed by the man who was rubbing up against her. She said that she hated to hear men use dirty words. She was rather prudish about that. I kept after her sexually, and she kept resisting. But I got to the point where I pressed against her and had an orgasm. Told her that I was, for the time being, stopping trying to leave her. I would stay with her and hope to get sex satisfaction. At that time, I wanted her and *needed* her. And that's why I was hooked on her. I noted that she was always a few minutes late and had a sense of responsibility but no sense of time, really. Now I think that she wasn't really responsible, either, and carelessly came late. I noticed her profile, her nose and her very bad teeth, and saw that she really wasn't that beautiful. But that didn't deter me from being madly in love with her.

June 19, 1938. When she said she might get a Saturday job, I felt exceedingly low and sagging on the way home. I didn't want to hurt her, but I did want to get away from this situation. I actually had some self-pity and thought I was neurotic. Thought of myself before I met her. How different! Preaching against jealousy, never in love, and all kinds of things like that. What a great change! At times, I was unable to concentrate on reading because of obsessive thoughts about her. I said to myself, "Eight months of constant thinking about her. I must love her." But on the other hand, I forgot our eight-month anniversary. I thought of telling her that I really loved her and wanted to live with her, but I must have a room of my own and not just a general big apartment where everybody could see everybody else and hear everybody else. I thought I got more pain than pleasure since I was with her. But at least I had those novel notes for a story.

June 20, 1938. Said I really had to see my songwriting partner, and she agreed to go with me. She talked in favor of trial marriage and living together for a while, not necessarily forever, and I agreed with her that it might be good to get the experience. And then I said, "Let's get married right away" and practically wanted to get married the next day. Because her parents would raise hell if we did get married, we agreed that we would keep it a secret. And she agreed that I would be under no obligation to support her. She said she would go out with other men but still be sexually faithful to me. And I said I would want her to tell me if she had affairs with other men, and she said she would, and she would even do it before she had the affair.

I said, "There is one thing that I have to ask you. Do you really love me?" And she said, "Yes, of course I do." She wouldn't marry me if she didn't love me. But she still refused to have any real sex with me. She laughingly said that I was getting the worst of the bargain, and I wondered even if I married her if there would be sex. I felt a little fearful about taking a step like marriage immediately, but then I realized that I had nothing to lose.

I almost got to her breast, but didn't quite get there. I kissed her breasts and neck and face and loved her immensely. I kissed her lips. I tried to be tender to show my love. I was very happy on the way home, but I wondered if things could really be that good. I remained somewhat skeptical, knew that our problems were by no means at an end. I thought that this was the only way, however—to marry her and make sure in short order whether she really loved me or not. Now it would just be a matter of a few short weeks, and I was certain after that I would know how she really felt about me.

June 21, 1938. Karyl was a little late meeting me, and she talked about seeing a new man. Despite my demurring, she said she would see him. I said, again, that I'd punish her by insisting on sex when she didn't stick to her own program, but so far it was mainly talk on my part.

Then I got the plan that she would read at least one book a week, otherwise I'd punish her sexually. It's interesting that I was not a therapist at the time but was using penalties to try to help her change. Later, although Skinner was against penalties and was for reinforcements, I included penalties in REBT. When people really wouldn't give up smoking, I told them to put the lit end in their mouth every time they smoked or to go to bed with a repulsive person. That, if they did so, often worked!

Comment. I had known her for months and she had never heard me sing. What intimacy! But that shows that I thought at that time that I had a very good voice. And my mother thought so, and some other people thought so. But in later years, I seemed to sing very well at times but then got off key. So I do it—as I tell my audiences for my rational humorous songs when I sing the song for them and lead them in song—I do it as a shame-attacking exercise, knowing that I won't sing very well.

June 27, 1938. Went to Hoboken to get the first papers to get married. Paid a man who accosted us for three dollars to serve as a false witness and say that he knew us for five years.

June 28, 1938. She called me in the middle of the night when I was sleeping soundly and said, "I just told my parents about the marriage.

Come over. They want to talk to you." Went to her house and was angry that she had told them when she wasn't supposed to. But I decided to be forgiving. Her brother was there, too, and they all wanted to know why we were getting married. I said I loved her. And they said, "Does she love you?" And I said, "Sometimes I think so and sometimes I don't. But if I get married to her, then we'll find out whether she really does." They just couldn't understand—especially since we were going to get married and not live together. That was amazing to them. I agreed that it was pretty crazy not to live together, but I said that if she demanded support, I wouldn't marry her because I was in no economic position to do that.

Her brother said, "She really doesn't love you at all and is just marrying you for her sake. You wouldn't want that, would you?" And I said no, not at all, if I really thought that. "Well, she is. I told you so several times before." I asked them if we could go in the other room and discuss it, and they said yes. I said to Karyl, "I'm still determined to go through with it. Their words haven't affected me in the least. They can't see our point of view and never will." "No, but it will hurt them. My father is a sick man." "They'll get over it." "No." "I may seem callow but I still think they will get over it. It's our lives, not theirs. They have had theirs, and we should have ours." She said, "You're not going to like the marriage." "I'll take my chances," I said. "There won't be any sex, you know." "I know there will be difficulties along that line." "Yes, I can't stand you at all that way." "You can't?" "No, I really can't." I didn't take her seriously, however, and thought her parents' attitude had just affected her. "Well, if you can't, it won't be a go, of course, but this is one of the things we'll see," I said. I asked her why she told them, and she said she got a job in Newark, at $23.80 a week in requisition. And I was glad about that, because I thought we would have money and maybe we could live together. "Then you still want to go ahead with it?" she asked. "Of course. Nothing they have said has influenced me." "All right, then. We'll get married tomorrow." Her look was very determined, and I had begun to feel good again.

She agreed reluctantly that we would go get married, but this time definitely not tell them. She seemed to give in, passively, because I wanted to do it. So we both went to see them and promised not to get married, at least for the present. They made us swear faithfully that we would not get married. We finally pacified her parents somewhat and went out for a walk. And she scolded me for being flippant with them, and I was angry at them because when I asked them if we wait for three months, will you then give us your permission? they said no.

June 29, 1938. I met her and we went through with the marriage ceremony in Hoboken with a judge and had to pay ten dollars, which she thought was very expensive, and the phrases about God and fidelity got on my nerves, but I put up with it. She then said that she couldn't keep the secret and she had to let it out, and she was going to tell them. And I said, "Okay, there will be murder, but if you want to do so, tell them about our marriage."

Comment. I felt quite good about having had the deed, the marriage, done. But otherwise I was pessimistic about the outcome, which seemed to be correct, finally. Her brother called, and I finally told him that we just got married, and he was shocked by that. Her parents said right away that we would have to get it annulled, because she couldn't stay on welfare and get her acting business settled, so she'd have to get thrown off it. They all jumped on her, including her brother, and she said I'd better not see them because they would pound me into the ground.

I agreed with her the night of our wedding that we'd better get an annulment right away. I didn't want an annulment, and I would have fought it through, but I was willing to get an annulment because she wanted it and objected to her parents' opposition.

She said that I was crazy to accept her on the terms of no sex, but I said, truthfully, that I didn't realize it was those terms, and I thought we would have sex now that we were married. She said, again, that she was affectionate with other men but not with me—and didn't feel like being that way with me because I was too aesthetic and intelligent and that didn't go with sex. And I was very hurt by the fact that she had no intention, even in marrying me, of having sex with me.

She insisted that there would be no sex, and I thought that there would be, but I didn't realize that at that time she knew that she couldn't have sex—she was too bollixed up vaginally—but she talked as if she just would not have it with me, and I was disturbed about that. She said that I was forty pounds underweight and that I wasn't a good lover, or at least I had a very bad history, and she couldn't have sex with me on that account. And, again, I was very hurt.

She said that she was crazy to marry me—couldn't find a good reason—and maybe she did it to help me. But she seemed very confused, and I could see that she was. She also said that because I had said I would marry her eventually, that she felt obligated to me and therefore she married me. I thought that she was much franker about not really being attracted to me and having affection for me but not love than she had ever been. So I was glad that I had smoked her out there.

I said that the marriage would stop me from going for another woman, but she said I really should go for one and that one would really like me, and she was sympathetic. She really didn't know why she married me, or at least couldn't see right away then why she did, and was very, very confused. We finished eating and went to her house, and I had to sit on the porch and saw her father through the window, and he glared at me—very hostile.

At times, she indicated that she really didn't want the annulment herself, but she agreed because they were so upset about it and therefore she had to do it. I was working with my father at that time, and I told him the next day that we had been married, and he thought that was a foolish thing to do. Told the woman I was friendly with in the office about it, and she said that Karyl really didn't love me if she didn't even want sex on the night of our wedding. And I thought that was pretty right—that was correct.

I thought that I would never find a woman again as good as her, and I even thought about committing suicide, but not very seriously. I felt very ambivalent—very optimistic and yet pessimistic—I wasn't really depressed or anything like that, but I was very confused about the issue and whether it was worth going on and trying to have any kind of relationship with her.

I wrote to myself, "You've driven knives into me, cut me into pieces. What do I care what happens now! You even did your best to undermine my self-confidence. Still I seem to love you—very strange." And I really felt that way—that it was strange, but I still did love her.

I was in no mood for masturbation, but I had a nocturnal emission, and I was rather bitter at the thought of having it on my wedding night. I cried that night somewhat and in the morning, but it was real sadness and not depression. So I wasn't really blaming myself, or putting myself down, and wasn't saying that the world was horrible.

I finally told my mother about the marriage and was rather flippant. And I told her that there probably would be an annulment, but I still hoped fervently underneath that there would not be an annulment and that we would go along and have a happy marriage. I was pretty crazy in that respect.

Karyl criticized me for not taking financial responsibility. We had very, very definitely agreed that it would be a secret marriage because I couldn't afford to keep her at all, and that I would have no financial responsibility. But she went back on that now, probably after talking to her parents, who were criticizing me severely about that.

I blamed myself for not satisfying her better sexually when we had a chance, and going by some of the mistaken books I read that said it wasn't a good thing to do. But I was probably very wrong about that. My not satisfying her sexually had very little to do with her not being attracted physically to me.

For once, I was quite unsexy and hardly thought of other women. I probably was so disgusted with Karyl and maybe with myself that it knocked off my sex desire. Found myself listening to music intermittently and not intensively as I usually did, and resolved that when I got over the *mishugaas* with her that I would go back to being really interested in it.

Sometimes I found myself crying and couldn't control myself. So, once again, I think I was exceptionally sad but not really depressed and self-downing. If so, that was pretty good, because she was putting me down, especially sexually. But I don't think I took it that seriously, though it was all correct. I read in the material I was reading on love, sex, and marriage that romantic love couldn't last, especially if you lived with somebody, which was Stendhal's view. And that made me feel okay.

July 1, 1938. I insisted on talking again, and told her that I really need—or think I need—understanding, sympathy, affection, and sex. And the sex might be last, and I would have one out of five chances of staying with her without it, but if I didn't have sex, I would have one in a thousand chances. I told her I might stay around a month or two more to see what happened, but if nothing happened, that was it. I told her that I thought we could be very happy together if the thread separating us was broken down. But I think that was very wishful thinking. I thought that sex was the main thing separating us and if that separation was broken down, everything would be fine. But I think, again, I was fooling myself.

I agreed that she wasn't charming, like a lot of women were, and that she was too self-centered for that. And I think that I was right. I told her that I warned everybody that we had a trial marriage and that we could see other people. She didn't like that because she thought people would whisper and talk behind her back. But I said that I didn't give a damn, and I really didn't. So even in those days, when I was madly in love with her, I still was a proponent of sexual freedom.

I told her that I was under a great strain and at least she could be nice to me and not nasty. It came to pass that it was after the eight-month anniversary of our first meeting, and I concluded that was certainly enough time for her to settle down and find out whether she really loved me, so I was very pessimistic about our relationship, but I wasn't that upset. In retrospect, I think that I really did like the experience I was having with her, and also the fact that I was, again, obsessively madly in love with her.

I said to her, "Darling, I'm afraid you'll shame me by showing how little you love me. You invariably do when I introduce you to my friends." Now I think that's probably important, because I would probably feel ashamed if I introduced her, especially if I was married to her, and then she showed negativism toward me. I would have taken that too seriously. So although at that time I was not very prone to be guilty, I was still definitely prone to be ashamed that I was doing poorly and that she would be showing that to her friends, and they would presumably look down on me.

I told people in Poe Park that I was married but didn't have any kind of a honeymoon and wasn't living with my wife. I was able to say that, but I was also somewhat ashamed because they would find out that I was married to a virgin. She objected to a little letter I sent her calling her "spouse." She said I should just call her by her name, and that her father read the letter too and didn't like it. Made a few passes, but she said I was too bony and that I hurt her. And then I left hurt by the fact she was so defensive and against me.

I foolishly said that I would have a great marriage if I could just have one hour of real love from her every week. But I had no great hopes and was going to give her six months to see how we would work out and then quit.

Her parents wanted her to live with me, or thought at least that I should take care of her. But she refused to live with me. I said she could come to my place, with my mother and sister, and live with me, but she refused to do so. So then they saw that it was her doing and not mine. Her parents were still only interested in money, and I saw how negative and rather vicious they were.

Karyl's parents kept bothering her to get money out of me, and she sort of agreed with them and tried to get it, but unfortunately I got very little money in the job I was working, and regretted that I couldn't give her more. I was so stupid that I probably would have given her more had I had it. But she and they were obsessed with money, money, money. She was partly mad at me for not having more money, but I showed her that for several years I did without money and ate peanuts in order to buy writing paper and that I just didn't have the money. It wasn't that I was a skinflint or anything, but I was determined to be a revolutionist and a writer, and all my effort went into that.

I kept resolving to get rid of her and then didn't, and now I don't know why, because she wasn't very friendly. I wrote that I must be childishly neurotic, and I really was very neurotic about my love for her, not to mention other things. At one point, I wrote, "I'll never be able to leave her, I'm afraid. That goddamned threat of super-happiness hangs over my head." But it was certainly an illusion on my part, to think that I could be super-happy with her.

July 2, 1938. Saw Karyl again, and she was almost in tears, saying that her parents practically threw her out of their house. Her parents had also scolded her for not getting a job and being too preoccupied with the acting, which was not making money. Her parents wanted her to keep the marriage a secret because I wasn't supporting her, and they were ashamed to explain that to others.

She talked about committing suicide if she got nowhere in acting by September 1, and it wasn't clear whether she meant that, but she was a depressive and easily could think about suicide. Once again, I thought I'd better leave her but resolved to stay around for a while to see what might happen. I was thinking that a miracle might happen. I was very dejected and had no incentive to work, since no matter what I would do I probably wouldn't win her love. I was, for one of the few times in my life, lazy, moping over the state of affairs. But then suddenly I got wild energy again and got back to doing my work.

I told myself I must see her every day, live with her, to make sure that she doesn't love me. That's pretty crazy. For the first time in my life, I thought about suicide seriously. "If I see you," I wrote, "utter misery. If I break off, deep regretting for the rest of my life. Worse misery. When by myself away from you, I use work as a dope." So I was really down, down, down in an unusual manner for me. I said, "If only there were some hope for the future, but the way I feel now is that if I don't leave you, I'll be perfectly miserable, and if I do, I'll be chastising myself for the rest of my days for just having missed something great by a mere thread." This shows that I was still a self-downer, because had I left Karyl and regretted it, then I would have beat myself up. That's unethical in REBT. I'd better blame what I did, but not blame myself. But I wasn't up to that point yet.

I told her that I suspected she mainly wanted me because I gave her money and bought her veal cutlets. And she was very guilty about that and said she wouldn't take any more money from me. But I said I was sure she would and that I would give it to her, but what I was really afraid of was that I wouldn't want to give her any more because I didn't love her anymore. I was afraid our love would come to an end, and that was a frightening thought. I said I lost a lot of respect for myself by being cowardly and staying with her for no good reason. And this shows that at that time I really was putting myself down—not my behavior—for being weak. I didn't want to be weak and that was bad. But I was not only saying that that was not so hot, but that

I was no goddamned good. So I clearly had conditional self-esteem at that time.

July 23, 1938. She said our marriage was now onerous to her because it interfered with her relations with other men. But that seemed rather humorous and sardonic to me.

She did say that she married me, again, to help me, but was too weak to really go through with the marriage. But her intentions were good. And that's possible. She resolved many things, but then she wouldn't go through with them. And the marriage may have been one.

I was taking my breakup with Karyl well, and I remember telling a friend who was going through a similar situation, "Why can't you do that? If you talk yourself into this love thing, why can't you just as well talk yourself out of it?" And there I seem to predate Rational Emotive Behavior Therapy, which says that you can talk yourself into things and out of love.

July 27, 1938. My song with George Segda, "Somewhere There's My Someone," was played on the air by the Kadoodlers.

July 28, 1938. I wrote, "I love you but don't respect you." And again, I didn't have UOA—Unconditional Other-Acceptance—with her. And I really did despise her at times for her weakness and her shilly-shallying.

At one point she said, "I can't stand your mere touch. It's different from that of any other man—shows how easily excited you are." She implied that that was very bad. So I could have easily concluded I'd get nowhere, but I think I stubbornly refused to conclude that. At one point, I said I think people should love each other completely, and that's all there was to it. Otherwise, what good are they to each other? But that was certainly a super-romantic attitude, which I didn't hold later.

I told her that she didn't need me, so we really didn't have true love, because for true love people needed each other. I didn't realize at that time that if you needed the person somewhat obsessive-compulsively, that wasn't exactly true love. I really was getting unattached to her. I got the idea that living together would be a good thing just to see if it worked—not that I cared for her that much, but I was very curious as to whether we could make it together.

I had been working for a publisher, Dick Childs and his publishing company, and now thought that publishing was mainly interested in money and I had lost some of my ideals in that respect. I told Dick that my big remaining interest was learning, learning, learning, from people, books, and things. My knowledge made me feel confident that I knew what I was talking about, where previously I didn't know and was sounding off without knowing too much. I even considered becoming a scientist and ending up there, because there I could pursue the many aspects of knowledge. I decided that I was going to spend the next few years on the serious study of sex, love, and marriage. I would try to be an artist, a writer, and so on, but I would only spend two or three hours a day as far as love was concerned, and therefore there wouldn't be a conflict.

Comment. So I was determined to have love and art and science, like I thought my father and stepmother had. For ten years, they had an ideal marriage. Of course, now I'm rather skeptical of that. I think my father got real value from his marriage and really did love Rose, but I think he verbally exaggerated his love for her in order to keep her happy. Also, he had failed in his first marriage and probably didn't want to fail in the second. So he seemed, on the surface, to have an ideal marriage, but I doubt whether he really did, because Rose was impossibly neurotic and as crazy as she could be in many ways.

July 29, 1938. Resolved for the ninetieth time to get rid of her, and said to myself that I'm a goddamned fool in regard to her.

I started listing her incompatibilities with me again. She was more poetic. I more sensual. She more gregarious. She more adventurous. Few common interests. She more superficial. She less energetic. She less educated and dogmatic. She less intelligent. I more bookish. I more staid. I much more logical. She indecisive. She unfrank. She neurotic. And I hoarded time. We certainly seemed to be very incompatible.

Comment. I can see now that I *acted* foolishly, but I wasn't really a total fool. I was predating REBT again by distinguishing my actions from my self.

August 1, 1938. Karyl surprisingly said, "I think Ron [one of Karyl's lovers] is in love with me, and I am with him, and therefore we'd better get the annulment October 18." I seemed to take this announcement fairly sensibly. We agreed to be friendly, and I seemed to take it rather well.

She said that she wanted to mother me at the beginning but was afraid of my love for her. I said I was foolish to love her the way I had, intensively and obsessive-compulsively, but now I thought I could get along quite well without that. And I said, again, to her that I would have bliss if we did get together, and that is why I married her. But it certainly hadn't turned out that way.

Comment. I said I was going to spend the next five years studying sex, love, and marriage and try to help people in that way, because I thought that marriage could be a good thing if you really worked at it and understood it. So it looks like this was the time that I decided to be a sex revolutionist and a marriage and love revolutionist. This was when I was still twenty-four. So maybe my being with Karyl and getting disillusioned with her had done me a lot of good. I was determined to forge ahead, naturally without her, and become a real expert—a sexologist and an amatologist (one of the few)—and stay in the field of marriage and family relations along that line and write and write and write on it. I also, I think, figured out at that time that if I wrote on love and not on politics and organization, that my books might really sell. So that would be a good thing.

I kept thinking of Karyl and wrote out 1,280 comments on her, including these: Number 45: Do her good points outweigh her bad ones? Number 732: What an insane thing love is—not worth it at all. Makes you make an utter ass out of yourself. Number 1123: Am I really affectionate, or is it only sex that I really want?

I kept telling myself, "I certainly picked the wrong girl to marry. Anyone else would have been better. No, that's not true either. I can't stand any other girl. If she only loved me, she'd be almost ideal." So I fooled myself about that.

> I made a long list of traits to change in myself: unromanticism, logic, assertiveness, weight, smugness, staidness. My list included pastimes I could take up for the future: athletics, museums, concerts, meeting people, and helping her with her writing. I asked myself, "Do I try so hard to make a success of the marriage because of my ego, and I don't want to admit that I'm a failure?" And I think there was a lot of crap like that there.

Comment. I had self-esteem if I won her, but self-dis-esteem if I didn't win her. I did not have Unconditional Self-Acceptance at that time, and only got it later through using REBT.

> I asked myself, "If she really hates me so much physically, why did she want to marry me? She must really love me. Yes, she must love me! See!" So I was pretty foolish in that respect. I said at one point, "I don't care if there's no sex between us, but at least I want affection. And you lean over backwards to avoid it." I said, "I sometimes love you when you're difficult, and when you're worse I love you more.

I'm not sure why." But I did. I certainly did sometimes love her more when she was a royal pain. I said at one point, "Damn it, darling. Why do I keep loving you? You've ruined my work completely. I haven't done anything in eight months. I keep two songwriting partners in despair and write a lyric every four weeks where I used to write one every four days. You're some terrible influence!"

Comment. I wrote to myself, "I'm no longer in the least sad about our impending parting over our bad state of affairs at present, though I do regret we can't love each other. I'm mainly angry now and resolved to end it on some basis. I can't love her as much as I used to. She's killed a great part of my love." That was a pretty good observation, but I think that I was angry because I was telling myself that she shouldn't have killed that part of our love. We had a great potential, and she killed it. And I was angry at her because I was demanding that she not be as crazy as she was.

I still had not seen the *musts* very clearly that led me to be so upset with Karyl. I would say that I finally saw them, partly by reading people like Korzybski and Paul Tillich, but also by continuing to persist in talking my clients out of their bullshit when I was an analyst. Even for the two years or so, from 1953 to 1955, while I was creating REBT, I was seeing people and trying to talk them out of their Irrational Beliefs.

August 3, 1938. Showed Karyl that I was reading *The Sexual Life of Savages* and was really interested in studying sex, love, and marriage. She put down my study of sex, but I insisted that it was really broad—which it was.

September 14, 1938. Karyl got after me for money, and I resisted but finally loaned her five dollars because I was intent on saving money for the annulment. I really was concerned about her money-taking propensities, and still resolved to resist her. I had little feeling for her, but my ego was so involved with trying to win her attention and sexuality.

Tried to avoid seeing her at times, largely because she would always want more money, and I knew that as soon as we got the annulment I could definitely see her less. I thought I might break off completely from her, but then I reminded myself I damn well better stay until October 18. I wanted the annulment now like I wanted just about nothing else—even more than I had wanted the marriage—but

I had to watch my step with her. I really wanted to be free of all responsibility from her, especially financial responsibility.

October 15, 1938. Saw the lawyer with her. Quoted from Havelock Ellis that love was a combination of lust and friendship. She didn't agree. Again, I kept after her sexually and was able to caress her and get an orgasm. I certainly persisted at the sex, even though I wasn't involved with her. She came over to my house again, and took the Bernreuter Personality Test, which showed her to be exceptionally neurotic, introverted, and submissive.

October 16, 1938. Karyl took more tests indicating that she had no self-confidence, was submissive, was unsociable. She agreed she would go through Bellevue Medical Center to see a psychiatrist that week. Her melancholia was present all the time. I resolved to live a life of controlled emotion and really, really live.

She talked again about having a baby once the annulment was out of the way. I was still attracted to her sexually but very definitely not involved too emotionally with her, and I realized that we could have sex without it affecting my love for her.

October 17, 1938. Finished the second draft of *Women: How to Handle Them*. Wrote two novels, one autobiographical. Little opportunity for song writing. Still working from 10 a.m. to 2 p.m. for Distinctive Creations.

Finished the second draft of the first volume of *The Case for Promiscuity*, got a good reception from Maxwell Perkins but a bad one from Quincy Howe. Much too long to be printed by a regular publisher. Will try a one-volume summary of it. I finally opened the Love and Marriage Problem Institute (LAMP). I may get into trouble with it and may have to go for a degree in psychology myself. I am starting work on *The Psychology of Love* and hope to finish it before they take me into the army.

October 19, 1938, to June 4, 1939. Kept working on my PhD degree.

June 30, 1939. Saw Abraham Waldbors, who gave me a recommendation for special entry to the New York Academy of Medicine Library.

July 26, 1939. My work at the medical library goes very well, and I keep reading their banned books. I often go up after work for a couple of hours in the afternoon. Working very hard on my book, *The Case for Promiscuity*. Read almost every restricted book in the medical library. They even allowed me to bring in my portable typewriter. Karyl is also helping me, working as my secretary.

September 12, 1939. Began working at Distinctive Creations from 8:30 to 5:30. Hated it, but had to take it the best I could because I needed to get the money for the annulment from Karyl.

October 11, 1939. Met a lawyer and practically promised him my annulment case for $125.00.

December 20, 1939. Saw all the cases go through very quickly for an annulment, and my case only took four and a half minutes. I was very good at testifying like a trouper. Everything turned out fine.

December 29, 1939. Went to the 42nd Street Library and got to work in earnest on my marriage book. Broke the record and read four books in two hours.

December 30, 1939. A friend called and said Karyl was about to commit suicide, so I went downtown to save her and found she wasn't as bad as he thought.

January 2, 1940. Started a new hobby—collecting song lyrics.

January 6, 1940. Gave Charlie, my boss, an ultimatum and got my hours reduced significantly because I didn't ask for more money. Now I'll come in at 10 a.m. and get off as early as work permits, which finally I got down to 2 p.m. or so.

March 7, 1940. Had a fight with Karyl and ready to break with her.

June 1944 to October 15, 1944. Was getting along with my PhD research, having interviewed over fifty women. After I interviewed them, we had very interesting discussions on love and sex. Most of them were very conventional women. I could have got into bed and had mistresses if I had more time, but I didn't.

Doing a good deal of volunteer counseling with people on sex, love, and marriage problems and getting very good experience. Karyl had a boy and is having her usual difficulties taking care of the baby.

{ }

I remained friendly with Karyl for the rest of her life. Even after splitting, we were sexually friendly at times. I helped her through difficult times and her depressions. We lived together for a year after our annulment, but her craziness (sometimes she was suicidal) was too much. I would say she had severe depression, with borderline personality and obsessive-compulsive traits. I helped her meet another boyfriend whom she later married. She kept unneedfully attaching herself to me in her later years, and our friendship was fine. She died of lung cancer and emphysema in 2001.

Though some of what I went through with Karyl was incredibly bad, I am grateful for what I learned about human disturbance and neediness. As I walked around the lake in the Bronx Botanical Gardens, I recognized that it was not my love for Karyl—but my *dire need* for her—that brought me much suffering. I realized what was later to become a main principle of REBT, and an important part of my growth and development. I realized I could love without *needing*. I realized the perniciousness of rigidly insisting that we must and should get what we want when we want it, and never suffer. I realized it is not awful, terrible, or horrible not to get what we want when we want it. Therefore the clarity about the harmfulness of shoulds, musts (*must*urbation), and demandingness helped me get over my own neediness, became a solid part of REBT, and has helped many others who learned and practiced REBT principles to suffer considerably less misery, depression, and anxiety in their lives.

Chapter 7

Was I an Irresponsible Parent?

My greatest moral lapse may have been having three "illegitimate" children by my ex-wife Karyl when she was still married to her husband Tony. For many years I did not acknowledge that I was their father; instead, I acted pleasantly but neglectfully toward them. Come to think of it, I almost duplicated, in this respect, the actions—or inactions—of my own highly neglectful father. Except that his three children were strictly legitimate.

The story of how I got into this "pickle" is complicated, and whether or not I truly was immoral for handling it the way I did is—I think—debatable. Let me tell the story, from my prejudiced perspective, of course, and then discuss the ethics of my behavior.

The year was 1945, and I was thirty-two years old, doing well at Teachers College, Columbia, on my PhD degree in clinical psychology. I was also immersed in my dissertation, "The Love Emotions of College-Level Women"—that is, before two nosy professors got wind of my "wicked" project and put the kibosh on it. Despite that, no real problems!

Karyl, my ex-wife, however, was not in good shape. She had married Tony in 1940, and her first child, Tommy, seemed to possibly be mentally deficient. He eventually grew up to be perfectly fine, but as a very young child, his mental capabilities were in question. Karyl, for perhaps good reasons, assumed that Tommy's "retardation" stemmed mainly from her husband's side of the family. She concocted a grand scheme that would enable her to have at least one "normal" child. She was, in her own way, still obsessed with me at the time, certain that I was exceptionally intelligent and well organized, that I came from a functional family, and that any children of mine would be unusually bright and capable.

Her scheme, therefore, was simple enough. She loved Tony, thought he made a fine father, and wanted to stay married to him. But she *had to have* a "normal" second child, and it *absolutely must* be fathered by me. No mere preferences here—utter necessity.

I was far from enthusiastic about Karyl's proposition that I father her second child, but I finally agreed, for several reasons. One: I was very friendly with Karyl, sincerely sorrowed about her upsetness over Tommy's "handicap," and wanted to help her recover.

Two: I firmly believed that both intelligence and character were inborn as well as acquired, and that I had good heredity in most respects. I had not developed diabetes at that time and both sides of my family seemed to be healthy and long-lived.

Three: The woman with whom I was in a relationship at the time—Gertrude—was never eager to have children and might possibly have fertility problems that would make motherhood impossible.

Four: Because I presumably did have good genes and so many millions of people with rotten ones were blithely overpopulating the earth, I "owed" it to the world to try to father two or three children to help reverse this dysgenic influence. If I were to let myself die childless that would be shirking my responsibility.

Five: Gertrude's indifference to raising children was matched, and even exceeded, by my own. I fully intended to be exceptionally busy with psychotherapy, writing, and a hundred other professional endeavors for the rest of my life, and therefore would make an unfairly neglectful father to any children I actually raised. Me take my sons to the ball game or my daughters to their dancing class? Horrors! Having other parents, especially their own mother, raise them was distinctly preferable!

Six: Karyl was an extremely attractive woman and a marvelous lover. Having intercourse with her several times until she became pregnant would be a real delight. Yes, sex with Gertrude was sublime and we were supposedly monogamous. But, as we both knew, I was a varietist, and she, too, had dated other men. She would hardly like Karyl's occasional communions in my bed and our goals of impregnation. Still, in some ways she would understand and doubtless forgive. Better yet, she would never—ah, never!—know. Not if Karyl and I fully, fully agreed on that.

As you can see, I had several "good" reasons for going along on Karyl's (no pun intended) ride. I talked things over with her for an hour and then "impulsively" agreed to try to have a child with her, providing that no one—absolutely no one—knew about my fatherhood. Karyl, whom I trusted, promised that she would keep the secret, and we had a great time in bed. We were on our way.

Karyl had her own method of arranging things—even up to inducing Tony to have anal intercourse to ensure that only my sperm entered her uterus for the next several months. Voilà!—it worked. Her second son, Philip, was soon in her womb and seemed to tumble out of it in admirable shape. I would say that he's had a good life, is a fine husband and father himself, does well as a psychiatrist, and takes after me in a number of mental, emotional, and physical ways, in spite of our sporadic and minimal contact over the years. When in his teens he did some paid secretarial work for me, and I now see him and his family when they are occasionally in New York. But I certainly didn't raise him, and our similarities and differences do, as we agree, mainly seem to be genetic.

What was my specific agreement with Karyl about my role as a father? Very concrete! I insisted—and she fully agreed—that my paternity was to be 100 percent secret, forever and a day, under all circumstances. Tony—obviously!—was not to know, would be hurt to the quick if he even suspected, would immediately divorce Karyl, and might resort to violence against me and her. So he was never—never—to know anything. This agreement was fully kept, and he had no suspicions while alive.

No one else—Karyl's children by me, her friends and relatives, Gertrude, my friends and relatives—was to know anything. No one! I kept to this agreement completely, but Karyl did so only for a number of years. For some reason—I think mainly to help Philip overcome some problems with Tony—Karyl told him about his biological paternity when he was in his twenties. He took it well, and he and I have had no problem with it since that time. We are both in the field of psychology and are fascinated by some of our similarities and differences.

Meanwhile, the plot thickened. Seeing that Philip was turning out remarkably well, Karyl wanted another child by me—and I, foolishly or not, consented. As I mentioned above, I thought that I had an "ethical" right to share my genes with the world in the form of two or three children. So Marty soon came into the world and was dutifully and lovingly accepted by his nominal father, Tony. Then Karyl had a fourth son by one of her lovers, and this child turned out to be seriously emotionally disturbed. So a few years later she insisted that she had to have a fifth child, and this time a girl—also with my great heredity. So in the 1950s she—or we—had Laurel.

Again, I could have easily lived without another child, but Karyl couldn't. My fabulous affair with Gertrude had ended by this time, so I was not even being nonmonogamous. Presto!—it worked. I was now a three-time father and saw no great drawbacks in that. It wasn't until a couple of years later that I developed diabetes, after my sister Janet had been similarly afflicted. So although my family's genes were not really in such marvelous shape after all, I had originally thought they were and incautiously fulfilled my responsibility to the population of the universe. Karyl kept her vagina wide open but her big mouth shut about Marty and Laurel's paternity until they were well into adulthood. Everyone took everything real well—and I was a reasonably happy absentee father.

Not that I took Karyl's revelations to our children with glowing warmth. I fully trusted her to keep our original pact, and had I known that she would violate it, I never would have agreed to father even one of her youngsters. I assumed at that time that once they were aware of my role in their lives, they would expect me to act in some kind of paternal manner. They would be deeply disappointed, perhaps feel hurt, and thereby be harmed. Not to mention their having conflicts with their other father, the real child-raiser, Tony. So I believed it to be most unethical to let them know the "truth" about their paternity.

At any rate, I truly believed that their real father *was* Tony, because fatherhood, like step-fatherhood, is mainly a social product. They *knew* him as their father and he *knew* them as his children. So, as the postmodernists would say, wasn't that the way it was? Assuredly.

I deliberately put my three children out of mind as much as I could—although, of course, I didn't deny that they existed. I rarely spoke to Karyl at length about them, took no part in their upbringing, and nicely assumed no responsibility for them. So now the question arises: Was I acting morally? Did I in some way do them harm? Did I cop out on responsibility that I preferably should have taken?

On the one hand, I say no. As long as they didn't know about my paternity—as Karyl and I had fully agreed—they expected and got nothing from me. So we were "even." When they did find out that I was their biological father, they may have had some serious expectations and disappointments—but since Karyl had been the one to break her promise by telling them the truth, I felt that outcome was her responsibility, not mine. I had kept my word and felt that I was in the clear. Karyl, one could argue, was unfair not only to lie to them and to Tony but also to finally tell the children the truth. She really couldn't win and in both ways was ethically at risk.

But wasn't I, too, unfair to Tony—who was a casual and by no means ever a close friend of mine? For years, as I have argued with my friends and clients, I was not unfair to him. Yes, I was definitely an adulterer—which, in our culture, is mostly considered to be wrong. Karyl, as an adulteress, was clearly wrong—and immoral—because she had a close, *trusting* relationship with Tony and she deviously harmed it by fertilely copulating with me behind his back. She had some "good" reasons for doing so—and even may have benefited Tony by her perfidy. He enjoyed having several children, and she would doubtless have stopped procreating after she had her first son. So Tony might have been severely deprived without her "help." Nonetheless, a good case can be made for her unfairness to him.

As an adulterer, however, I am fairly blameless for the same reason a business partner might be. You and I, let us say, are partners with a signed agreement that we have equal rights and responsibilities in our business and will devote ourselves exclusively to it. You trust me and I trust you. Behind your back, I make another partnership deal with Ms. Smith and spend half my time pushing her business and half my time devoted to yours and mine. I am therefore, by all reasonable standards, distinctly immoral because I am breaking our *trusting* relationship—not to mention our contract—and that isn't exactly kosher. So I'm something of a crook.

Let's, however, look at the case of Ms. Smith. She hardly knows you and obviously has no trusting relationship with you. In forming a relationship with me, then, even if she knows I already have one with you and is willing to accept that, she is not *intimately* bound to you. Therefore, is her forming an alliance—and we could say an adulterous alliance—with me truly unfair and unethical to you? In a thoroughly communist or socialist system, we can say that Ms. Smith is unethical—as she is not supposed to enter any private partnership—with me or anyone else. But in the capitalist or private enterprise system, we would have a hard time charging her with any kind of immorality.

So it was with me and Karyl. Not having a trusting relationship with Karyl's husband Tony, I was still an adulterer—and a liar. But was I, like Karyl, unfair and immoral to him? Arguably! I was, by omission, lying to my three children; however, I deliberately had no close or trusting relationship with them, so I therefore could be said to be fabricating a series of white instead of black lies. To tell them the whole truth might well have been considerably worse. Maybe I'll discuss it with them one of these days and see how they think and feel about it.

Anyway, I do not feel guilty about my hidden paternity. Maybe, if I were more in favor of "real" morality, I would. After all, I did lie. I abdicated—almost 100 percent—responsibility for rearing my offspring. I helped the three of them only very little over the years, when I could have helped them more. I don't make any effort to be close to them today, when they all know—and have told their own children—about their paternity. I am a rotten family man, just as I knew I would be when I decided long ago not to rear any "legitimate" children. And I am not guilty about all this! Doesn't this go to show how sociopathic I am?

Perhaps. Sociopathic individuals are usually defensive and self-protective. I clearly made a pact with Karyl—that I mistakenly thought she would keep—which, to my mind, defended me against possible blame while permitting me to do what I wanted to do. I protected myself from trouble, expense, and responsibility. I guiltlessly lied to other women about being childless. I managed to come out smelling like a rose when I did some exceptionally dubious things. In my own way, I selfishly plotted with Karyl to get what she rapaciously coveted. If I wasn't outrightly unprincipled, I was something of Karyl's partner in crime. Definitely!

Moral or immoral, I was a product—maybe a victim—of low frustration tolerance: LFT. I got what I wanted on some level—children—without assuming any responsibility. I had enjoyable adulterous sex, completely gratis. I managed to have some variety without having to tell my other partners about it. I enjoyed the present without thinking too much about a problem-filled future. I took advantage of Karyl's pursuing me sexually without having to spend too much time with her. I sometimes made easy sexual appointments with her so I wouldn't have to go to the trouble of getting more reluctant partners into bed.

Did I also fall into the ego trap of enhancing my estimation of myself by being proud of Karyl's pursuing me for my intelligence and efficacy? Or of thinking myself a better person because my children were doing fairly well in the world, even without my help? No, I think not. I was, and still am, happy about Karyl's preferences and my two sons' and daughter's achievements. But I do not rate myself, my being, one iota better because of these "proofs" of my ability. *It* is good, but that doesn't make *me* laudable.

Similarly, I acknowledge my possible immorality, and certainly my LFT, about my decision to procreate but not to rear my children. I did some highly questionable deeds in these respects. If I had the chance, I might not do them again. So I'm fallible, and at times I have (maybe!) behaved poorly. But I am still okay, even though some of my actions are not. I still give myself unstinting Unconditional Self-Acceptance.

As for my LFT—that's another issue. It wasn't enormous, but it still was mistaken—meaning self-defeating. I would have been stronger and wiser had I conquered it. I didn't.

I'll keep working on it.

Chapter 8

My Tremendous Affair
with Gertrude Birnbaum

As I did during my affair with Karyl Corper in 1937, I took copious "novel notes" on my affair with Gertrude Birnbaum. And, as in the chapter on my affair with Karyl, I will insert comments made both at the time as well as later, usually years after the incidents occurred.

September 1942. Gertrude, a teacher, was a cousin of Manny Birnbaum, and I was attracted to her mentally because she was very brilliant and a great conversationalist. But I didn't think her face was very attractive, though her body was fine. Also, she lived with her mother.

She was married, and her husband had been inducted into the army. She didn't seem to have too much feeling for him and said she might or might not get back with him when he returned from Europe. She had a very close friend, whom I think was divorced—Florence—and who was, to me, ugly, thin, and very much a pain in the ass. Florence was fairly bright and very literary, but she put on airs of being much more brilliant than she was.

Gertrude was only interested in a man who was romantically in love with her and would only go to bed with such a man. Both she and Florence were shocked when I told them about going to bed with a woman on the first night we'd met and having a great time, even though we weren't romantically interested in each other. Gertrude's mother, fortunately, was away for the summer, so that made me more interested in her. On our first real date, Gertrude told me that she and Florence had been very interested in me but were afraid of me because of my promiscuity. I made passes and wanted to get to bed with her right away, but she insisted, oh, no, she would never do that with another man, although she told me that she didn't have very good sex with her husband.

Florence was in a bad relationship with her husband and so tried to stop Gertrude from having a good sex relationship with anyone, including me, because it would take her away from Florence, who seemed to be hooked on Gertrude. Gertrude went on a vacation for two weeks and did end up having sex with another man, which didn't turn out to be very good. But that surprised me. So, now it looked like she might have sex with me, and though I was interested in her mainly for her mental attributes, her charm, and her brilliance, she was certainly attractive enough sexually. The next time I saw her, her mother was home and we had no place to go after dinner. So that was very disappointing. I could have taken her to my place, although I lived with my mother at the time, and it was a little too soon to introduce her to my mother and then have sex with her there—although we did do that later.

When I saw Gertrude again without her mother, she gave me a lesson in kissing. She was mad about kissing; I wasn't, but she showed me how to kiss very well. And I got so good at it that I was able to give her an orgasm through kissing alone—which sort of surprised both of us. I had hopes of getting to her fully sexually, and she was interesting enough mentally for me to keep seeing her. She was madly in love with me from the start and expressed it. I was holding back, because I wanted to be sure that she would have good sex with me. But, thanks to lots of telephone conversations and the fact that she was in great shape, I finally started to fall in love with her even though we had very little actual sex. She was going with several men and mainly teasing them sexually. But I wasn't jealous. I just wished that she would have more sex with them, so that she would loosen up and then have sex with me. She continued being very sincerely in love with me, and I became more and more in love with her. She was winning me over, mainly by her conversational skills and her brilliance. But I continued with my hopes of loosening her up sexually and having great sex with her.

After a few weeks, I knew that my involvement with Gertrude was the second-most emotional relationship in my life, after Karyl, and that she had much more on the ball mentally than Karyl had. So I thought, at the very least, we would be friends for life, because I was quite taken with her and the way she acted with other people, and the way she was brilliant with them. Although I still didn't think she was very attractive, we got closer and closer and I began to respect her more and thought that in many respects she could well be my so-called soul mate.

October 17, 1944. I wrote Gertrude a very passionate seven-page love letter. I said, among other things, "I love you, darling. Truly I love you. My love for you is keen, living, incessant, trenchant, intense. It is over and at once by me, around me, in me. It is lovely and frequent. Pleasing and exciting. Bracing and tender. It is a rare, great love in a life of loves." I said in the letter that I continually, continually thought about her despite my busy life and that I already forgave all her sins and rudenesses.

I closed my letter with "My sincere gratitude to you for having enabled me to feel firsthand and at a crucial point in my life, when I am deeply engaged in unraveling the facts of the theoretical foundations of human love, a warm, spiritual, personal experience of great love, which must surely make me and my life's work infinitely more worthwhile than without you I could ever have expected to be. Thank you, dear Gertrude. Thank you, my darling, indeed." It is clear from this letter that I was coalescing my deep interest in theoretical love, sex, marriage, and so on, with my great love for her. They went definitely together. She read my letter many times and said I would have to become famous so that people would read it and know how much I loved her. Quite egotistical!

Went for a drink with Gertrude, and she toasted to the first intercourse that we were going to have. I watched her teach for a while and saw how brilliant she was and how effective, and I was very proud of knowing her and being in love with her. Brought her to my place for the first time, and she loved the way I had all my bookcases lined up with great materials to read and to work with. Almost had sex at my place, but had great caressing and petting, and we were both completely in love.

I was concerned about sex with her, because of my poor sexual relations with Karyl, and I thought that if we didn't get to indulge in actual and complete intercourse that it would wreck the relationship. She liked my expressions of love for her but said that I was not up to my verbally expressing my feelings—which was correct.

We had arranged to get together for intercourse on Saturday, but she kept putting me off, and I was afraid it might never happen. She was restrained with me when friends were around, because they might communicate to her husband that we were in love. She wanted to have sex at my brother's place, which was available because he was away with his wife, and we would be completely alone.

October 28, 1944. She wanted me to be more romantic at my brother's before we actually went to bed. She dillydallied about getting into bed, but we finally made it. I was charmed by her body and her brilliant conversation. We had intercourse, but I came quickly and she did not reach orgasm at all. She scolded me for not arousing her more. I became aroused a second time and tried to get her aroused as well. We had intercourse a second time, and she was terrifically aroused—more than any woman that I had ever been with. She gasped and groaned and murmured endearing words over and over and writhed and jumped and quivered and the bed groaned and squealed under us. And I felt good and on top of the world with her.

We finally broke away from each other with my erection still very stiff and I in control of it. And she was very, very loving and warm, and said how great I had been sexually. She didn't seem to have a full orgasm, but her thighs and her stomach and her sex organs and her whole body were quivering all over. She was enormously happy, ecstatic, and free, and said that she loved me utterly, entirely, now that our relationship was really complete. At first, she didn't like being sexy rather than romantic, but finally she gave into it and loved it. And again I penetrated her, and she seemed to have a terrific orgasm. But then at 3:30 a.m. she got tired and wanted to go home. We were both exceptionally loving and excited, and I said that I completely loved her and that all my questions about her were gone. She hadn't yet reached a so-called vaginal orgasm, and she was a little concerned about that. However, she thought that she would reach it with me, and she was very happy, because she thought it quite important that she finally reach it—which she never had in her life. I was thrilled with the whole evening and thought that I was having with her, by far, the best relationship that I had ever had with a woman.

I wrote her a letter on October 28 about the night we had had in bed and how at first I was disappointed in my performance, but then she acted very well and I was able to recover. I also wrote her a letter on October 30, about our sex that night, and said that I appreciated greatly that she was concerned about me that I might not get full satisfaction. And that was the real thing that sent me into ecstasy—her concern about me and not just about herself.

October 29, 1944. Spoke to Gertrude on the phone, and she said she'd had to tell Florence everything, and that that was fine. When I saw her on November 5, she was not in a good mood—particularly because of her mother. But I was able to take her at her worst and still love her. Went to her place with her and was getting fairly warm sexually, but then her mother interrupted us.

November 10, 1944. I made a list of businesses Gertrude and I might do together: music publishing, book publishing, book selling, marital consulting, "How to win your man," dating service, an institute of sexual science, recording company, newspaper. I thought of starting a nonprofit group called The Intellectuals, which we would sponsor to help people meet each other and get married and have children.

There were scores of other plans I had for my future, which included organizing a great service organization, organizing a system of musical libraries, reorganizing the radio system of this country and this world, start a society for performance of neglected music, and organize a group for intelligent individuals called The Intelligentsia . . . and much more.

I didn't tell her that I thought her face was somewhat ugly, even though I thought her body was very beautiful; I thought she wouldn't be able to take that. She showed me how her husband was quite inadequate compared to her—nonsocial and not able to express himself, which she was.

November 15, 1944. I had a great nonsexual orgasm with Gertrude and wanted to satisfy her, but she had to leave early, so we never got around to it. She said that she wanted to be married to me at least for a short while, and I thought that was a pretty good idea, too. She felt that I gave her more than she gave me and she wasn't worthy of me. She said she also liked my affection and my consideration for her to not be out in the cold or the rain or anything like that. I had actually not wanted to see her that evening, preferring to get work done, but we had such a great time, I was grateful that she came over. She thought that she might add to the quality of my work, if not the quantity, and even if I didn't do more work, I was healthier and happier because of her, so that was a great trade-off. She didn't want to have intercourse, but I gave her an orgasm anyway. She thought that I was more important than she was sexually, because I thrilled much more to the sex than she did. Therefore, she was more interested in satisfying me than herself.

Comment. That was the way she wanted me: to be attracted to her and to want to please her but not much from her own intense sex desire.

November 16, 1944. Had the startling news that her husband might stay at his government job in Germany and get her to move there with him. And my heart sank at that, but I was willing to accept it if it did occur. Also, if she was with her husband in Europe for a while, she would find out whether she really did love me as she said she did. Thought about marrying her again, and felt that we were definitely meant for each other and should marry. If she was with her husband for a while and couldn't take it, then I would be very, very happy to marry her.

November 17, 1944. She had always worried about satisfying other men sexually, but I was vastly different—she wanted to satisfy me. She thought it was bad of me to make her so attached to me, because then she didn't know what she would do when her husband came home. And I said she could always get a divorce, and she seemed to accept that.

Listening to Debussy and Beethoven, we got passionate again. We both agreed that we were becoming definitely more loving toward each other and getting closer. I thought that she and Florence were both refined sexually—much too much so—and not really sensitive to art and music.

She thought that maybe we were wasting time—or I was wasting it—by seeing her so much, and that she should give me more leeway to do my work. She kept letting her girlfriends know that she was very involved with me and was no longer reluctant about that. She was going to take a day's vacation with me to relax, and we both agreed that we were tremendously in love with each other—more than we'd ever been.

In pushing me to drink, she commented that she was a driving woman and I had better watch that sort of thing—her pushiness. I said let her push; I wouldn't be afraid of that. I could hold my own ground.

We had a brilliant conversation about the production of the opera, and really had a great time doing so. She said that she shouldn't have gotten herself so involved with me and should have kept the relationship on a lighter plane, but I didn't like that point at all. I insisted that our heaviness led the relationship to be truly great and was to be cherished. She tried to discourage me about the thought of marrying her, but I would not be discouraged. I told her that when I decided on something, I normally went after it and got it. She said she did too, and I partly believed her and liked her for that fact. Then she went back to being very anxious about my varietist tendencies.

Comment. Gertrude's anxiety about my varietism seemed to be a part of her and was related to whomever she dated. Again, she *needed* security.

I saw that some of her problems were created by society—her mother or others—and I got a little bitter against society and resolved to change it again. I thought that being married to her for a while might be a good idea, because I didn't easily put up with people—including in-laws. She asked me how I would take it if she were a varietist, and

I said—honestly—pretty well, as long as her feelings for me were primary and for anybody else were secondary. She decided again that she wanted to marry me. On the way home, I saw that marriage had great disadvantages, and I might well be better off as her lover.

Comment. No matter how much I loved Gertrude, I always thought that marriage with her would seriously impede my freedom. Toujours freedom!

She decided that she was not going to Europe with Jack, because she really, really wanted me and thought that we were ideal for each other. Told her that I had decided that she was going to marry me, and she was thrilled by that. My statement made her see beyond doubt that I truly loved her. We loved the opera we saw and discussed various aspects of it and other opera productions that we might have some part in. At one point during the opera, she said, "I want so much to be yours, darling, and to sleep with you." And naturally I thought that was fine. We discussed her liabilities as a wife, but I said that I would accept her general neuroticism and her sexual neuroticism and not be happy with them but be happy with her.

The problem in marriage would be my varietism, but she might compensate by being varietistic herself in order to prevent herself from being hurt. She thought my varietism might stem from needing security and getting it from having a good many different women love me. But I thought that was not a good hypothesis. I said my varietism was mainly physiological, but that I could dispense with it and usually did. It was always there—I always looked at attractive women, even when I was with her—but I didn't need them.

She said that when Jack came home, she would be driven to call me and be in touch with me, and that might ruin things for her and the marriage and for me.

November 18, 1944. Wrote her an eleven-page letter. I wanted to relate in detail how I loved her and for what reasons. I said that I thought of her constantly during the day and of the glory of our relationship. "I think of the sweet, sweet loveliness of you—of the great undownable and yet so secreted kindliness of you, of the dear, dear tenderness of you. At night, I snuggle up to you, although you are not there. Even during the day, working, my arm is around you and I feel your warm body, and lustily feel the fleshness of you. And I laugh out loud thinking of how witty and radiant you are. I also dwell on how verbally loving you are and how great that is, and I want to put my love for you down on the printed page and get it down there for all time. I continually think of how to please you.

"I want to live with you and come home to you every night. I am exceptionally proud of you and your talent. When you think of going away, I get a real sinking feeling, and my stomach turns over. I want to declare my love for you to the world, though I am usually silent about those kinds of things. I want to go places—but I particularly want to go places with you. I really thrill to the sound of your laughing. Rather than just trying to save time and do work, I want to save it for you. I keep appointments open, hoping that you will be ready to see me. I am concerned when all is not right between us and I think, think about it. I take seriously your negative views of me. I see this letter has grown long and heavy, but I have not expressed myself long enough or well enough. You know that my heart is always here for you."

When people started gathering for her party, she blurted out: "I have something to tell you. I'm in love with Al." And I was very happy. Then I confessed to the others how much I loved her. For most of the night, she was involved with other people and apologetic to me for being so involved. She didn't want me to make passes after they left, because it would take an hour, she said, to calm down from the party. She said that if she had children—especially with me—she would be a devoted mother and would not devote much time to other people. We parted on a very high note.

November 22, 1944. Among other things, she blurted out, "I don't love you tonight; that's the way I am! That's the kind of night it's going to be." I thought that maybe she said that in order not to spend the night with me. I said I wouldn't sleep with her that night because of my sore throat—I didn't want to give it to her.

Got around to discussing why she didn't want to marry me. First of all, she said, I wouldn't give her the secure affection she needed. Second, I wouldn't be a good, financially responsible husband, because I would devote my time and money to my revolutionary work. Third, she said that she would have to live up to my level, and I was too good to live up to. She could easily do it with Jack, but not with me. I thought her points were pretty good. If Jack weren't around, then she would marry me, and she had even recently guiltily been thinking it would be nice if he would be killed.

December 30, 1944. Met her at the theater, and she remarked that her love for me was a tremendous and glorious thing. And we were very tender and affectionate for a while. She was concerned about the security of my love for her, but I said that I felt it was quite secure. Then she got enthusiastic about the *Partisan Review* and said we had to subscribe to it, just for us. And she also wanted to read a lot of the books in my own personal library. She said that since I had so much trouble with Karyl, she particularly wanted to only do me some good. And I said yes, that I desperately wanted to do her some good, too. She resisted me sexually because she said she just wasn't in the mood. And I didn't bother her too much.

January 1, 1945. I was looking for an apartment so that we could move in together, but I was having a very difficult time finding the right one at a good price. Had a serious discussion with her in the cold in the park. Told her that even if we were sexually incompatible in some ways, I was still definitely in love with her and wanted to be with her.

January 3, 1945. Met Gertrude and she was enthusiastic about a new way to teach refugee children English. We talked with her friend, and she caressed me and I caressed her quite sexually during the talk, but he probably didn't exactly see what we were doing. We were having a great evening, and on parting, I melted inwardly and told her that I loved her, adored her, and wanted to do so much for her.

January 4, 1945. Gertrude wanted to come to my place, and that was fine since I was not well physically. She was serious, and said she had been lying to me and now wanted to take on my own truthful attitude. She thought that Karyl was dumb and neurotic and that I was quite wrong to have been so attached to her. She criticized me for being so madly in love with Karyl, and I partly agreed with her and said that I was hard up at that time sexually. She now thought that Florence's love for her was really decadent and that I was right about Florence. Now she admitted she was lying to me and not taking my promiscuity too seriously, but really, she—and Florence—thought that I was very neurotic in that respect, and she had not let me see that. Some of her friends, too, had said that I was absolutely obsessed with women.

She thought that between the ages of seventeen and twenty-four I was not attractive to women and therefore I became compulsively varietist—that I had a need for new conquests and I might well continue to have this need after I married her. Then I would look silly in the eyes of her friends, and so would she for marrying me. If I was going to ogle girls in the subway after marrying her, then she wasn't going to marry me. She would still be my mistress, but she would not marry me. So she laboriously and uninhibitedly told me all those bad things about me. She had given me a great deal of affection, so now I wasn't too neurotic in the respect of needing it.

I rebutted her, first, that my being high-sexed was neurotic; second, that I had a great *need* for love; third, that I was sexually compulsive because I was unattractive to women. I said that at that time, I had no money and therefore couldn't do anything about going with women. Fourth, that after marrying her I would not run after other women compulsively. I was positive in my rebuttal, and that seemed to take her aback a little, and I also said that it looked like she was trying to avoid marrying me and was using these points as rationalizations. I thought that she was mainly concerned about what her friends would think of us.

January 14, 1945. Gertrude had a serious talk with me and said she had been depressed because she wasn't sure that I loved her now as I did a few weeks ago. She admitted that her feelings were very neurotic and much like those of her previous lover, when he was very neurotic. She told me not to act very nicely toward her right then, at the moment, to reassure her. I said that, yes, my love for her had changed somewhat, because of my preoccupation with my thesis and my general work, but in general it was as high as ever.

I said that actually, at this time, I felt that I was married to her. But in addition I was adjusting to Florence and to the fact that Jack was coming back. Also, I favored freedom in marital relationships and wanted to let her know that she had all the freedom she needed. There were other reasons, too, but I couldn't think of them. She seemed satisfied with these explanations. At one point she burst out, "I won't have it. I'm getting out of this relationship right away. You can't do that to me. You're too intelligent for me. I always run the relationship. I always dominate it, and I won't take it from you!" But then she relaxed and got more humorous about it.

She insisted I was trying to withdraw from the relationship for the last two weeks, and I said definitely not. We both put on the pajamas she had bought and had a grand time together.

January 19, 1945. She was tired from her busy week and wanted me to come over. Told her about my difficulties with a couple of people being upset about my thesis because of their prudishness. I was doing it on love, and so I might not be able to get a PhD from Columbia, or I might have to change my thesis. But I showed her how I was not putting myself—or them—down or getting upset because of these difficulties. Showed her how I had met problems all my life and had developed a philosophy to cope with them.

She said again that I had more self-confidence than she, and I pointed out that one reason was because I was devoted to my work. I had read that Sinclair Lewis only did one novel a year, and I thought that was very little. And I resolved that if I were a novelist, I would do more than that.

She referred to herself several times as Mrs. Ellis, and I liked that. But she insisted that she needed a man like Jack, that he gave her security because he would always love her no matter what she did. I realized that Gertrude did need that, and that I would not be the one to give her absolute devotion, the way Jack did.

January 24, 1945. Got her to my house and we fooled around sexually. We massaged each other, and then she suggested that we change to pajamas. She liked me to caress her wrist, because it was a thin part of her and she felt very fat otherwise.

She was ashamed that she went from 132 pounds to 142. But I insisted, rightly, that I liked her—loved her—at both weights.

February 14, 1945. I went over to Gertrude's in the evening, and we were soon ecstatically on the bed. She loved the Valentine's Day poem I wrote for her. But then she got guilty about having sex and love with me because of what she was doing or not doing with Jack, who still wasn't back from Europe.

She wanted to know more about me before she married me, and asked me whether I had had any breakdowns. I said no, that I used to get angry but now I used psychology mainly to overcome that. I still got myself angry with people's stupidities, but I rarely flew off the handle. She would have been unforgiving of me if I kept doing the wrong thing, but I said that I would be unforgiving for just a short while and then forgive her.

She said she had been very anxious at school, even though she was normally the best one in the class. She envied my not being tense and anxious, and I said, yes, it was very good, but sometimes it might really bother her. She said I was really good at not upsetting myself with my temper and was no longer as anxious as I used to be. That was great.

February 15, 1945. I told her about my thesis and how I might have to abandon my love topic, but if necessary I'd do it, because the PhD was going to be a union card for me. She was very interested, as usual. Had a long talk with her on the phone and parted amicably.

February 16, 1945. Wrote a letter to Florence, telling her what I disliked about her. I also thought she was in love with Gertrude, but let's fight fair for her. So I considered her my dangerous, most dangerous rival. And I thought she was a pernicious influence on Gertrude.

February 17, 1945. She had planned that both of us should do some work, but she continued the sex and talking, and we never got around to it. Parted at 1:30 very pleasantly, and I thought I had a great evening. But again I thought that I didn't *need* her and I could do without her, that I loved her consistently, if not excitedly.

March 10, 1945. She called and said she wanted to come over and I said, "Fine." I was still in bad voice but stupidly insisted on talking to her. She beautifully caressed my penis while begging me not to have an orgasm so she could caress it longer. Then she wanted intercourse, and I said I would only last a minute, but she still wanted it. So we had it, and I soon had an orgasm while trying to give her one. She lied about an orgasm so she wouldn't have to get me to exert myself more. I showed her that I had an orgasm while working on her, rather than her working on me, and she thought that was most beautiful. She was afraid that I was bored when trying to give her an orgasm, but I insisted that I wasn't. She wanted to passionately embrace, and that finally seemed to give her an orgasm. She said it would be too bad if we got too physically used to each other, and therefore became less arouseable. But I said that wouldn't happen. I thought I could easily have great sex with her for the rest of my life, but then I would miss out on experiencing sex with other women, which I still wanted to have.

March 17, 1945. It was a bright spring day, and I was definitely getting better and feeling quite good. She liked the article I had written against anti-Semitism in psychology and thought it was quite good. Then she started saying, after we listened to Beethoven, "A terrible pall has fallen over our relationship." She pointed to the circles under her eyes and showed that she was very serious. The excitement of our relationship had gone. I no longer loved her as excitedly as I had been. But I laughed, because at one point she accused me of being too aggressive, and at another point of not being excited at all and abandoning loving her rather than being in love with her. No, she accused me of *only* loving her, but not being in love with her. I said that she was unrealistic and expected too much of a relationship, and she agreed that she was an impossible woman. And I said that because I had been acting as a husband to her, some of the excitement seemed to be gone. But I didn't need the excitement like she needed it. But she still definitely loved me in spite of it all.

Then, while we were arguing, she got up suddenly and kissed me passionately, and I knew we would be able to work this through. I caressed her sexually, and this time she got very interested and said, "There! You have me again." She was very excited and, within a few minutes, she had her first orgasm and said that I was a wonderful lover. She was most nice to me and said, "I love you, darling," and everything was sweet and lovely once more. I told her how I bored myself with making love to her verbally, but wasn't bored by discussing things with her. And she thought that was good, since she had a need for telling how she loved me. We got back to caressing, and she even kissed me on the lips after taking some wine to stop her from catching my cold or cough. I went home quite satisfied.

March 23, 1945. She modestly covered her legs after we had sex, but I told her not to do so since I loved to look at her legs and thighs. She agreed with my distinction between in-lovedness and loving kindness, and said, yes, at times she had real loving kindness for me rather than in-lovedness. I was glad to hear that. She told me that Florence was definitely trying to knife me in the back and tell her how neurotic and disturbed I was. I pointed out that Florence had very definite lesbian tendencies, and Gertrude didn't quite get that.

March 24, 1945. Met her at Mozart's *Così Fan Tutti*. She got bored with Mozart and wished that she had heard more of Stravinsky. She was concerned about my illness and thought I had strep throat and that I had better go to a medical center.

Gave her one of her favorite orgasms, and she remarked that it was so good that I did because after she returned to life—because she was in something of a daze during the latter part of sex—she was so glad that I was there to be with her. With other fellows, she wished that they would be elsewhere after they had sex. And I said that the same thing happened after I had an orgasm with her—I was very, very happy that she was there in the flesh to talk to me. Then she suddenly blurted out, "I love you terribly, darling. I want you always with me." And when I was a little skeptical, she said, "I really mean it this time. That's the way I feel." And she talked about our living together again.

She didn't want me to see her hair, which was very messy, but I insisted and looked at it and said that it was fine and that I really loved her with it that way. And she was very pleased about it. I said that she could be with Jack for a year and then if she were unhappy I would make all plans for the divorce from Jack with her.

March 29, 1945. Showed her that I was quite emotional in going for artists like Sibelius and Tchaikovsky rather than Bach and Mozart, and that I lived revolutionarily on quite an emotional level of being, which she didn't. I talked about the essay I had written, "The Art of Not Being Unhappy," and I wondered whether I could teach it well to others, because maybe you had to naturally not be that way—not be miserable. She agreed that I had the philosopher's stone of not being miserable, but that I lacked her spontaneous joy and emotionality. But she said she had been teaching me how to have it, so I was much better at that.

She said that she could throw herself spontaneously into a high pitch of emotion, while I always retained some logic. But I showed her how some of her emotion could be sort of an illusion because it was not backed by any logic. She got an insight and suddenly saw that I saw things as a whole while she just took important bits by bits, moment by moment. And I tended to agree with her. I saw things in advance and planned them comprehensively, and she rarely did. Also, I didn't let myself down later, as she did. But I really threw myself into life as a whole and relished it greatly. I saw that her new insights were good, but I was glad that she and I pointed out that I could see things as a whole much better than she could. But on the other hand, I missed some of the high ecstatic moments that she was able to throw herself into.

Gertrude now said that her feeling of loving me was much greater than the in-lovedness that she had a couple of months ago, and I was delighted with this observation. Now she was enjoying her love for me more than ever, and I was glad about that. She said that she was much more neurotic than I, and therefore I enjoyed the upper hand in our relationship, as usually the less neurotic one would do. I had no compulsive need of her, and that's the way it preferably should be, and she was glad it was going to continue that way. But she said I was helping her to be less neurotic, and I said I was glad about that and would continue that. We both agreed that this was one of the best and deepest evenings we ever had.

April 1, 1945. Although I was not in the best of health, I agreed to come over to see her. She did some studying while I did some of my own. But then she came over to my chair and we got into some heavy sex. She got terrific satisfaction, but delayed mine and didn't get around to it until later.

She suddenly blurted out, "Wouldn't it be terrible if this lovely thing became too common with us and didn't last?" And I quieted her down and said that that was not going to happen. She seemed to be worrying about the future of sex with us, and I said let's enjoy the moment and keep it going and see what happens. I wasn't at all concerned about the future. I said that if I had not been so damned busy with other things, I would be the greatest lover she ever had, and she agreed. That was because I devoted a good deal of my creativity to science and to other things and not just to her.

Karyl came over, and I was affectionate to Gertrude in front of her but didn't want to hurt Karyl too much, so I restrained myself. Karyl talked about her bad family life, and Gertrude came over spontaneously and kissed her and seemed to be most sympathetic toward her. Gertrude tried to get information from Karyl about how it was to live with me. Karyl said she never saw me as a great lover but mainly as a scientist. Gertrude broke in to say that with her, I was a great lover, and I was pleased to hear that. Both women said very nice things about me, but as far as emotion was concerned, I was unemotional regarding Karyl but quite emotional regarding Gertrude.

A few days later, I saw Gertrude with Karyl again. I didn't think that Karyl looked very well, and I certainly wasn't attracted to her, and I was very happy that I wasn't married to her. Karyl complained about how lousy her marriage was, and she was stuck with the baby and wasn't happy. Gertrude tried to induce Karyl to put more energy into her marriage, but I thought that maybe Karyl should be seeking a newer and more satisfying mate than Tom, and then they agreed with me. Gertrude objected to Karyl talking that way in front of Tom, who seemed to be hurt. So Gertrude got after Karyl about that. I thought that was very nice of her and loved her. Gertrude saw that Tom could take it and obviously wanted to stay with Karyl, and she called off her dogs and didn't criticize him or Karyl.

Gertrude didn't like the fact that I had been so involved with Karyl, who seemed to be so neurotic and not have much on the ball. Gertrude and Karyl both agreed that I was, as Gertrude said, "the most terrific thing I think that ever hit New York and points west." Then Gertrude told them about some of her problems with Jack. Karyl said I had varietist needs and no one woman would ever satisfy me. But Gertrude thought that I loved her so much that I could just be with her right now. Gertrude said I was the only logical man for Karyl and Karyl should have held on to me, and Karyl agreed.

On the way to Gertrude's house, I told her that Karyl kept asking for reassurance from me, and that she—Gertrude—was somewhat like that, too. She admitted that she may have been reading into me some of her own promiscuous tendencies.

Later, she told me about the love letter that Florence had written her, and that Florence hoped she kept it with the love letters that men had written her.

April 7, 1945. Went to the show *The Tempest*, Margaret Webster's production. And Gertrude enjoyed it, and so did I. She thought I was a little depressed, and I resented her wanting me to be lively all the time. I didn't like the fact that she liked to be lively with other people and be in noisy places all the time. That wasn't exactly me. She kept saying how she loved parties and enjoyed them, and I wondered whether she was exaggerating again.

April 11, 1945. She and Florence had read an article I gave her, and she thought it was absolutely brilliant and that I should specialize in writing articles like that. Talked about changing my thesis topic to a non-love, non-sexual one, which she didn't like; she liked the original topic about the love emotions of college-level girls. But a couple of people at Teachers College objected strongly to it, so it looked like I would have to abandon it, and she didn't like that at all. But if I had to do it, I had to do it. Too goddamned bad! It was good to get the PhD one way or the other.

She thought I would get more fame by writing that thesis than the one on paper-and-pencil personality tests, which I was going to do instead. And I agreed with her, but I said that the thesis wasn't that important. Once I got it, I could do any goddamned thing I wanted, but that I mainly should get the thesis and go ahead with my career. Remembered what I had forgotten to tell her—that when I held her hand in the theater the other evening, I felt that it might continue my thrill of doing so for the next thirty or forty years, providing that she got the same thrill from holding my hand. She seemed to appreciate my feelings very much. She ended up our good conversation with, "I both love you and at the same time am in love with you." And I of course thrilled to that.

April 12, 1945. Called her about President Roosevelt's death, and she was upset about it. I said that it might be okay, because he was a compromiser and didn't stick to his guns about certain things. Even though I wasn't in good health, I thought that on that particular day I had better see her.

She said that she went up and down in her feelings toward me and wondered whether I did too. But, no, I said that mine were pretty constant and remained high practically all the time. Brought her my article—I think the one on hermaphroditism—and she liked it very much since I had done a great deal of work on it.

With other people, she said, she had a great need to be on high and usually was, but not always with me. And she thought that I might even look down on that, and I said it was okay that she was one way with one group and not with me. I said that her way was maybe even better, more sociable, than mine, because she did it with many people and I only with a few.

She said she missed my being compulsively in love with her, as she was with me. And again she accused me of loving her but not really being in love, as she was, and that might ruin our relationship. I still thought she had a neurotic need for excitement, and that it didn't do most relationships, including ours, much good.

That evening, she said I looked very good and my voice was quite well-modulated, and that made her more in love with me than ever. When I touched her I got so aroused that I could hardly think straight. I thought that she got dissatisfied with me and other men because she had to exert the maximum energy to please us and got tired of that. She couldn't get my feeling of love, and I described it as longing to do her good, the feeling of being at one with her, some attachment to her, and was based partly on her feeling of love for me.

April 14, 1945. Arranged to see Gertrude at nine on Saturday evening. She looked fairly ugly, but I was quite okay with her ugliness and still greatly loved her. On the train with her, she read Henry Miller and got very, very absorbed in it. At the group meeting we attended, she was very excited and was, as usual, the center of attention. She smelled a foul odor, and actually it was me farting, and I didn't want to tell her because she might take that amiss. She said she was more in love with me than ever, and that made her feel constricted. She said she had been trying to break me down like she broke down others, but now she was not doing that and was sorry she had tried. I was too strong in that respect, to be broken down.

Sitting on a park bench, she was difficult, but I told her and told myself—which was true—that that didn't turn me off very much. I explained to her, when she asked, how I used to be neurotic, but then I had made myself more stable. And she envied the fact that I was the happiest person she knew. On the phone, she said she had a real heavy feeling now for me. She was going to be with others but decided, finally, on April 15, Sunday, to be with me and came over and said, "I want to talk to you. I have found out something about myself that is very important. It seems that I must have two men, not one, then I can love you better and kiss you." And she came over and kissed me.

"When I am with another man, I can laugh and sing and be lighthearted, but not with you. But then I want to get rid of them." I said I had been trying to tell her that for a while. She got excited and came over and kissed me hard, while alternately saying that she loathed my nature and my stable way of doing things. For an hour and a half, we did some studying. Then she got sexy, and I was able to give her three orgasms. Then she gave me a terrific orgasm, and she posed naked. She wanted to do something tremendous for me but didn't know what it was. Did I know? And I didn't exactly. I said if she gave me children, that would be tremendous. She said that she would.

April 18, 1945. I spoke to Gertrude and decided that I might try to have some lighter relationships with her in addition to my great love. It wouldn't do me any harm, and it would do her some good.

April 19, 1945. Gertrude asked me to teach her how not to be desperately miserable, because her love for me was bringing her too much pain. I thought that, like other neurotics, she was running away from love and the pain of it. I showed her that she had one reason after another for not continuing the relationship with me. It was too bad that I hadn't gotten her to be less neurotic, but that was so. Still the idea of being totally in love with me frightened her. I showed her that love had pains, but I had no fright about it, and I had no intentions of leaving her. I was somewhat saddened by her neurotic feelings about love. I was sad about the fact that she could only love me neurotically and intermittently, not constantly. And I thought about my own tendency to love only neurotic girls, which I was now doing again.

April 22, 1945. I was having a business meeting, and she called to say that she just wanted to tell me that she had listened to a Debussy quartet and was overcome with joy and love for me. Told her about the business meeting, and said I'd like to take her in as a partner instead of my current partners. But she didn't have enough money and refused the offer, and I was disappointed.

April 24, 1945. I loved the fact that I could be very interested in something, then go right to her, then come right back to the thing I was interested in, and both were very fine for me. Not either/or, but both/and. Told her how much I loved her over the phone, and she said my speech should be recorded it was so good. We deliberately held silence for a minute or two to see if the silence could be beautiful because the other was on the phone. And we managed to do that. But I said it would be much better if I were actually with her.

April 27, 1945. On the phone, Gertrude said that two nights spent without me made her love me even more. Asked her again if she got bored with me recently, and she said no, if she tended to get bored, she did something to create excitement. And I saw that she was right about that—that was her tendency. I tried to see why she couldn't continue a long-term relationship, with me or Jack, that wasn't that exciting. Suddenly, she jumped on me and said I was trying to analyze and pull her apart. But I said I was just trying to help her prophylactically with some of her peculiarities and disturbances. But on second thought she may have been right about that—I pulled her too much apart. We had a good time analyzing and bantering with each other, as we often did, for the next two hours or so. She called off our Saturday date to see other people, and I said that was okay with me.

April 29, 1945. She accused me of dishonesty. She said I had been unaffectionate that day and therefore I didn't really love her. And I said we were in public and I didn't want to be seen to be too affectionate. I said I was sorry and could see how she could easily be hurt. She said she was very capable of steady love for me, but I was not capable of steadily loving her. Finally she agreed that I did love her very much.

Sexually she was still somewhat withdrawn, and I never quite aroused her. Went back to petting with each other, and the crisis seemed to be over. I persisted with my caressing and soon got her quite excited. She said she was thoroughly enthralled with my great sex technique—though it wasn't very different than any other time. She seemed to enjoy it immensely. She couldn't believe what was happening to her and had about seventeen orgasms, she said. Then we had great affection, too.

Got to her stomach and body again, and she got very aroused and unbelievably had another orgasm. And she expressed great joy, but she felt guilty that I was not getting as much pleasure as she was. She tried to give me other orgasms, but I only could have one that time. She said she only needed a night like this one out of four nights, and with more than that her nerve endings would become dull.

After her second orgasm, she got tremendously in favor of me and caressed me immensely. Then I gave her at least a third series of orgasms, and again they seemed to be very multiple and most ecstatic. Finally, it was too much and she had to run away from me. She could hardly believe her great sex receptivity of that evening and said it was far better than she ever had with any other male. She got so tired that at midnight I had to take her home. And that ended a great evening.

April 30, 1945. She was embarrassed because the previous night, for three hours, we were occupied with one thing: sex, and it had not been a well-rounded evening. It seemed to me that she was guilty about the one-sidedness of the sex. She kept viewing the evening only in a sexual vein, and I didn't like that. She still had some very puritanical notions that I wasn't pleased with.

May 3, 1945. Analyzed her critically somewhat again, but then she said that wrecked her warmth, and I stopped it. She said, "I want to be any way you want me to be, darling. What way is it?" And I said I just wanted her to be spontaneously herself. I said I was proud of my ability to not exaggerate an emotion, but on the other hand I sometimes wished that I could spontaneously have it as she did. But I convinced her that it was my love for her that made me suspicious of her, and hers for me that made her suspicious of me, and we both agreed on that. She was afraid the old wildness that I had for her was disappearing, but I said no. We brilliantly argued with each other and enjoyed the argument. I went back to being emotionally high, and she said that that was marvelous and that she would recommend that I have that technique when I spoke to other women on the phone.

May 5, 1945. Wrote her another poem, which ended, "This rarest numbness to myself and keen reactivity to you for me is a fearful thing indeed, but bodes but greatest good to us." And she liked that poem.

May 6, 1945. Called to tell me that once a week was not enough for her to see me. She had to see me at least twice a week—preferably for a long time on Saturday and Sunday. I thought that when she didn't see me for a day or two, she built up intensity for me.

Said she would come and see me at 5 p.m., but then said she'd see me at 8 instead of 5, and then she came a half hour late, so I fumed angrily at her. I was very hurt and tried to crawl into my shell and get rid of her. But on second thought, I decided to keep her as a second string, even if I got rid of her as a first string. Again she accused me of not loving her enough, especially since I said I didn't want to see her for a long time that day, and she practically broke off with me right then and there.

Discussed her beauty and my concept of it, and I said I sometimes saw her on an ugly duckling plane but still loved her. I loved the way she did herself up and looked well, but I also loved her without that. We embraced, and I showed her how sentimental and emotional I was. Talked about having children, and she said she really wanted them. Then got sexy again, and I insisted, despite her period, on arousing and satisfying her. Got her to tremendous sexual heights. Said, "This is good for you. Turn on your back. Let me manage it. I know what you want. I know how to give you great pleasure. I know what's best for you. I know how to do it. This is just a sample. We'll reach much greater heights than this. I have many tricks in the bag yet. It will always be like this, darling. I love you immensely. This gives me such great pleasure!"

May 7, 1945. Called her to say that the office was closing because of the great news. I think now that the news was probably the final ending of the war. Told myself to devote more time to writing about Gertrude and our love than to other things, and also I might make more money that way, and we could use the money. She said she was not putting any amount of pressure on.

May 12, 1945. To my delighted surprise, she called me at 9:45 p.m. to say that she would be over to see me in twenty minutes. I was a little suspicious that she was doing it mainly for me, but that proved again that she really loved me. I thought we would have a great night because of our lovingness.

She came, was quite affectionate, and said she would only stay an hour so I could get some sleep. She seemed exhausted sexually by the previous night, and didn't want me to be too sexy but wanted me to be very affectionate. I told her how much I loved her, and she seemed to agree, because she said I had been very expressive and my letters, particularly, had been very expressive. They couldn't have been better, she said. Said that I had aroused her tremendously the previous night because of the tone of my voice, which was excellent. I kept at her sexually and got her to a pitch despite her resistance, and she had an orgasm even though she wasn't cooperating that well.

She got so excited that she insisted on taking off her girdle, but she was somewhat standoffish and said she was really only a twice-a-weeker, and only got aroused with me because I was so good at arousing her. But I thought that she had a guilty conscience in terms of having so much sexuality, and that therefore she didn't fully enjoy it.

She also thought I would get satiated with satisfying her sexually, but I insisted that I absolutely wouldn't, because I had derived great pleasure from it. She seemed to have a guilty conscience in terms of having so much good sex, so frequently.

She said that we really should live together and get to know each other, and I agreed. She had previously been afraid that she wasn't good enough for me, but she now realized that she was one of the best in the world for me, and that if we parted I couldn't replace her. And I agreed with that. She stayed till one in the morning and had difficulty breaking away. And after she left, I was very tired but went to sleep thinking of her.

May 14, 1945. We both heard the VE proclamation, but it was sort of anticlimactic. She was saddled with Florence, who was very depressed and even talked about suicide. But she and I both agreed that we truly, truly loved each other and were very high about that.

Told her I would get around to working on my novel about Karyl, and she seemed to be fairly enthusiastic about my doing so. My eyes were bothering me, and I wasn't in the best of health, but I was planning to do a book on happiness, and she went along on that.

She said she wished she lived with me, so she could show me how she could take care of me. And of course I liked that. Told me to open my window, because I was catching a cold, and she thought that fresh air would help.

We talked about her husband maybe being released from the army, and I said that she'd better live with him a while to see whether they were really suited for each other, since she had never really found that out before he left for the army. She liked my telephone conversations with her, which were very loving, and I said I was doing very well at them mainly because of my feelings for her and not just because I was good at verbalizing.

Kept writing her poems, including one that said, "Can thinking be the curse of love?" And I debated it and then said, "Can thinking be the curse of love? Full thinking, no. That love which can't survive deep thought is better by you left. Ere you buy it." I wrote another poem, "Egoism for One": "Who loves in, of, and by himself loves but himself for sure. Thank you, my dear, for plunging that to my consciousness."

She seemed to object to our having too stable a relationship, but I wanted it even though I was madly in love, because I felt that we both had work to do—me in particular—and that with a stable relationship, I could get on with my love and on with my work. And she now saw that she hadn't given her husband, Jack, very much stability. He was always trying desperately to win her, so he couldn't do anything else in his life. We both agreed that we could just enjoy being in the same room together, that we really respected and loved each other, and that our relationship had everything in it—love, intellectual and artistic appreciation, sex, sensuality, respect, desire, and so on—and therefore we could be perfectly free to express ourselves and to be with each other and didn't have to be with other people.

She suggested a vacation for a day or two, and that she wanted to write. And I sometimes thought that she wanted to develop her writing more than she wanted to see me. I thought that we had much in common, and that she thought like me and I like her, and even if we didn't have great sex, it was very worthwhile being with her. If I should love anyone, there was no doubt that it would be her.

She liked the letter I had written her and said I really should write for a living, and she would scrub floors if necessary to see to that. I pointed out that the kind of writing I was doing just now was not very remunerative. She asked me how I did my writing, and I said I first had a thought, then I wrote it up.

May 19, 1945. I was in bad voice—had been for weeks. I think I had laryngitis, sore throat, and sinus trouble. And I wanted to be in good voice in order to talk to her. I could write about politics and other things when I was in bad voice, but I needed my good voice to express myself to her. Spoke to her very warmly over the phone, and she really liked that and so did I. We parted very affectionately.

I wrote a poem on relaxation, and I said, "For me, love is a function of perfect relaxation and tensionless of living correlative with caring."

May 24, 1945. Gertrude said that she wanted the best for me and I could even have other women if I wanted them. But I said that since I was so involved with her, I hadn't even wanted them—that I was attracted by looking at other women, but I really wasn't interested in them and was only interested in her. I said I hadn't been with any other women since her, and I really wasn't missing them. Talked about being married and whether we would get enough sleeping in. She finally left at one a.m. and said that things should be arranged so that she didn't have to leave me. And I agreed. I said I could hire an apartment for both of us for the summer, but she said no, only if she got at least two weeks off to go away for tennis. Told her my business deals with my partners weren't going well, and she said it would be better if I didn't have something like that and I was rash to go into it, but I said I was just taking a chance and experimenting.

May 26, 1945. Gertrude read some of my writings while I was with her and said they were beautifully written and I should devote myself mainly to writing since I had a great talent for it. She thought my writings about her were fine, but she objected to the ones about Florence. I thought that Florence was definitely not to be trusted and would probably tell Jack about our whole affair when he came home. She said that Florence was not really a lesbian, as I accused her of being. But I said she really was.

She got after me for not wearing a tie to work, and thought that some of my professors might see me without one, and that wouldn't be good. But I said I didn't give a damn. We argued about clothes, and she called me not only a sex revolutionist but a clothes revolutionist. I kept saying it was better to be comfortable, especially in hot weather, than to look good. She violently disagreed. She was afraid that people would view me as a crackpot because of the way I dressed.

Wrote a poem about tenderness and said that even if she were very ill, as long as she could look at me lovingly, that would be great with me. Wrote a poem about how great it was to have a vacation from her, temporarily, and that I could well use another one in thirty years or so.

May 28, 1945. She called at ten p.m. and said she was low and could use my help and she would be over in half an hour. And even though I was lacking sleep, I said, "Fine." She said that I was like Jesus, because I could look down on the world from the heights and be all-forgiving and all-wise, and she couldn't do that herself.

May 29, 1945. Gertrude seemed to get a so-called vaginal orgasm from my manipulating her clitoral region and was very happy about that. And I was very happy about pleasing her so much sexually. Emotionally, I seemed to get more pleasure than her, and therefore I wanted her to get maximum sex pleasure. She thought that her pubic hair was sexually disgusting, but I insisted that I loved to look at her blond hair and even to go down on her. I didn't like the wetness of her, but I was getting used to that too. I enjoyed working on her sexually more than her working on me, in a sense, because I knew that I was okay sexually and could easily get orgasms and other satisfactions and she couldn't do it that easily. She practiced caressing my penis, and after a while I got a terrific orgasm, and she was glad about that, too.

June 3, 1945. She was afraid that after marriage I might let down all bars, and she was disturbed about that. But I said, no, I definitely wouldn't. She asked me why I had once been so angry at my mother, and I said because she acted very stupidly, as did my business associates, and that I couldn't stand that. So at that time, apparently, in my life, I was easily angered by people like my mother and business associates, and thought that they shouldn't be the way they were.

I saw that we had a good deal of discussion to go before we could get married, but I wasn't perturbed about it and thought that we would manage to see it through and battle it out amicably. So I still wanted to marry her and have a great deal of pleasure, and I felt that

I would grow as an artist partly because of her influence. I also felt that we had resolved some things and were closer to having an amicable marriage.

She wanted to see a comedy show, rather than see me, on a given night, and I didn't like that. But I told her that at least I was the kind of person that could always find things to do if she wanted to do something else. I didn't need her to be around, and that would give her real freedom to be herself.

Wrote her a letter in which I said, among other things, "I love you, sweetheart, intensively, incisively, incredibly. I love you with full-bodied fancy, flesh, and with philosophy. I love you with a feathered sweetness, rampant might, piercing depth, and hale stability. I love you with indulgency and zealotry, tenderness and steadiness, hilarity and gravity, serenity and raw unevenness. I love you with a terrible, beautiful certitude, of knowing you are for me." And I really felt that way when I wrote it.

June 21, 1945. She had me come over to talk to her aunt and her aunt's son, who was a difficult boy, and I talked to them and saw that the mother was more difficult than the son, and I advised her to leave the boy alone. Gertrude thanked me for being so good during the evening, and said she missed me very much, especially this past week. I missed her, but at the same time I didn't want to see her too much, because it kept me from my work, which was very important. I saw that most of her friends were really trivial—not worthy of her and certainly not worthy of my spending too much time with them. I saw that she wasn't going to live up to her philosophy of giving me freedom to do what I wanted to do with my work, and I didn't like that. So I was disappointed with her.

June 24, 1945. She asked me if I had been difficult with Karyl, and we discussed some of the things, but I showed her that I only went so far with Karyl and didn't give in to her completely. She said she was so much in love with me that she was losing her sense of humor and wanted to go back to a lighter tone.

Went out on the rocks near her home, and I aroused her so much that she almost pulled me over a ledge. Then I got very aroused, too, and kept mumbling over and over, almost incoherently, "You're so beautiful, so beautiful, so beautiful." And I felt that all the way through me.

Then I got to caressing her vulval lips again and gave her a tremendous orgasm, so that we had to control her and me because we were out in the open. She said, "Promise me that you won't break off with me and stay away from me. I'm most serious about this and want to make sure that you never will leave me. You must listen to me. I never was like this before." And I promised her, and I noted that whenever we were close to parting, she made sure that we got together again.

Called Gertrude from my office to say that Karyl had called me and something was wrong. I was going to see her early that evening before I saw Gertrude. Karyl's child—I think it was her first one—was acting badly, and she was very upset. As far as I could see, the child was disturbed, but I calmed her down and was able to get her to take things much more calmly herself.

Gertrude jokingly said that we were two high-sexed people, and I agreed with her because sometimes I thought she was just as sexual as I was, and I was very sexual. In the midst of our highly sexed sexuality, she said that she loved me so much that it hurt. And then I went back to love more than sex with her. She said that because of her security with me, she was getting more love and sex satisfaction than she ever got before. She said as long as she was at peace with me, she was at peace with the world. And for once she seemed to mean it.

June 26, 1945. We discussed her husband Jack, and I said that he had spoiled her, was completely good to her, and I wouldn't be that good because I had too many other things to do in life. Discussed our getting an apartment and how she would fix it up. I said that that was okay as long as I could have some comfortable place to sit. It looked like my practical views might interfere with her aesthetic ones, but I thought there would not be too many conflicts.

I talked to her over the phone very affectionately, and we both thought we had a great evening. She asked, "Why do I find it so beautiful being with you—merely being in the same room?" And I said because she wanted to feel that way. No, she thought that I was the one who was making her feel that way.

I said she had an unhealthy approach to pleasure, especially sex pleasure, and she farted around too much. But no, then she insisted on undressing me, which she did, and I had an orgasm in the process. Then she wouldn't let me undress her, but I kept making passes at her and she got so warm sexually that she undressed herself. At first she didn't respond too well sexually, but then I got her aroused and got her to a terrific orgasm again. I said at times that I was so emotional that I couldn't really bring it out. But she said she had no trouble expressing her emotions, and she really didn't.

She thought we were having a low night, because we weren't having brilliant conversation. I said that was fine with me. And she said that having several minutes of great orgasms didn't make up for the lack of brilliant conversation. She didn't want to tell me a joke, because it was too low, she said, but she finally told it—about a man with a small penis and a woman with a large vagina and how she used lifesavers to "ring" him. I wondered about her thinking the joke was so low.

She was afraid that when Jack came home she would be very lonely and horrified about not being able to talk to me. I said that I could take it well if I knew that we would be apart for only six months or a year and then she would get back together with me. So that would be fine. She said when she was with others and heard my name, she had a thrill shock. And she was afraid that she would get a shock when Jack came back and she wasn't seeing me. Got her to go back to bed and aroused her greatly, and she finally made herself completely naked, which she usually didn't allow.

I was having a great time, sexually, and she liked the fact that I was sort of forcibly holding her down and making sure that she had enjoyment. The forceful element was what she liked, too. She rolled on to the floor and wouldn't get back on the bed for a while and said that she should be below me, humbly worshipping and adoring me, since she was actually below me and I was so great. This is what she never felt with anybody else.

July 4, 1945. Saw her on Sunday, the first time we had been together for a while. I made passes, but she said that I was too fast for her. Told her truthfully that I missed her a great deal that week, and she was very happy to hear that. She said that sometimes wanting sex and not getting it made it more desirable. But I said that I was not like that—wanting it and getting it was the main thing.

She said that she was not that good sexually, but she had great faith that I would be so, and that faith was justified. She'd better have faith in me, I said, because I was one to try everything and experiment to finally find out what was best for her.

With her, I said, and with the great work I had to do, I didn't have time to look for or go with other women. And I really felt that way. She was afraid she would be relegated to second place if I had other women, but I said she would be first. And I didn't want to become too involved with any other woman, because then it would take me away from other things, which were very important. She said that she wanted to work on a project with me, but I was very skeptical that it would actually come about.

She seemed to favor excitement rather than affectionality to go with sex. I said that I liked affectionality—especially the permanence of it—but it wasn't necessary because I had so many other things to do. She thought that my love for her did not depend on her, as I kept saying, but depended only on me. She said it was too bad we'd had sex so early, now she wasn't excited. But I said I could get excited again, so she caressed me and quickly had me erect again.

She said that things were so nice with Jack—with the outings, and the car, and music and everything—but agreed that with me it was even nicer, because of our great love. She said that living with a genius like me was worth it, even though it was very hard. Since we both went for greatness and magnificence, we might clash on that account, we agreed. She said, "I'll try to marry you if you want me to. Yes, I shall." And I said fine, but I still did not think that she had reached a final decision.

I agreed to take an apartment for a month, so we could be alone and sleep together a lot more. Had a hard time with her mother, who kept listening whenever the phone rang to see who it was she was talking to. Her mother had led a very hard life and seemed to resent Gertrude's leading a better one.

Read some of my stories to her, and in general she liked them very much, but she gave me some good criticism. Discussed with her some of the stories she had been writing. She had gloomy endings to her stories, but in my stories people got through their moods and glooms by the end.

I indicated that I could see her continually as long as I got in a couple of hours of work. She said that I didn't have the ability to really relish emotion for more than a minute, because then I got sexual. But I said that sex and emotional pleasure went together. I liked resting with her, but I wanted to get her going more. I got very powerfully sexual, and she got very, very aroused, as usual. She didn't need for me to use much energy, but I naturally did it in getting sexy. So I ignored her so-called protests and was very, very energetic with her and brought her to terrific orgasm again.

July–August 1945. Saw her several times and we got along quite well. However, she went away for two days and then came back with four dates in the offing.

I told her about my theory of technological revolution and how it might outdate political revolution. She admitted that for the past year my emotion for her had outdone her emotion for me. She said she couldn't marry me because that would interfere with my genius and her pain, which she sort of needed with her love, would interrupt our relationship and interrupt me. She said that many *Redbook* readers wanted the kind of excited, painful love that she wanted, rather than the nice, peaceful, affectionate love that I wanted.

Gertrude thought that she was much less sexual than I was, and that I could easily not love a woman who was not that physically satisfying. She resisted sex a little bit, then let me really go after her and satisfy her. And she had a terrific orgasm, and after she had sex she said she loved me immensely and asked me to please, please marry her. So it seemed to me that my hypothesis about her being greatly loving after sex, when sex was good, was a good hypothesis.

August 3, 1945. Got somewhat angry at her for not keeping in touch with me for a week, but I was busy writing a novel, so I wasn't too disturbed. We spoke the next day on the phone, and I prepared a list of things showing that we were not suited for each other because of recent happenings. She stayed away an extra week at a camp and didn't exactly apologize for that.

My general points to prove that she didn't love me were: (1) She was continually interested in trivia rather than me. (2) She was interested in non-intelligent things and especially didn't use her interest in regard to me when she wrote. (3) She was most insensitive to me in that she didn't see that things like not writing would be taken seriously by me. (4) She followed my negative predictions to the letter. (5) She treated me just as badly as she treated Florence. (6) She failed all the tests that I made up for her except for those few I announced in advance. (7) She was utterly dishonest in her relations with other men, never told them about me, never felt compelled to tell people about her love for me. Nonetheless, I decided not to leave her right away, because there was no one to take her place, and she did have great advantages. Eventually I would find someone better for me, but not right now.

I was particularly concerned about her emotional attachments—not so much about her occasionally being sexy and aroused by kissing another guy. I showed her that I had been interested in a few women, but then I thought only of her and didn't want to screw things up with her. She said, "Hello, darling," and we were in each other's arms and quickly got into bed. She said she had thought of me sexually all the time, and that interfered with her sex with other men. My condom broke as we were about to have intercourse, so I went back to satisfying her sexually with my hands. She kept saying how much she loved me and how I was the one for her, and that we would certainly marry eventually. I was very good in expressing my verbal love for her, and showed her that everything would come back, and we would be as great as usual sexually and otherwise.

I got serious and told her that I wasn't going to be satisfied with her with love and sex if she didn't do something worthwhile in life. So she'd better write or do something else and not merely teach. She said I was too finicky and that there was something wrong with me if I couldn't be satisfied with her unless she did something artistically outstanding, since she passed all her civil service exams and was teaching very well and doing everything else well. But I said that sort of stuff was way below her level, and I wanted her to reach fruition and accomplishment. Otherwise, I was bound to meet a woman who had more on the ball and was getting somewhere in life. I only respected people when they were making something of the traits they naturally were born with, I told her. But she said her creativity did not come out of writing and things like that but out of her emotional relationship with a man.

I wanted her to be as honest with me as I was with her and with other women. She said that her father had rejected her, so had her mother, and now I was rejecting her. She said she was exceptionally attached to me, thought of me during the weeks she was away, and would commit suicide if I really did reject her. But I was skeptical, and neither of us thought that she would really attempt suicide.

August 6, 1945. I started to go over the list of things I had against Florence with Gertrude, and she was flabbergasted, saying absolutely nothing at first. She objected to my interfering and not giving her freedom to do wrong. I said I was being strong for her own good. And she said even if I won over Florence, I would screw myself with her (Gertrude). But I stuck to my guns and said it was to be me or Florence. I said if Florence was really mentally ill, as Gertrude said she was, she'd better be institutionalized. Then she said she had already broken with Florence, but I didn't think so.

I heard about the atomic bomb—and it was going along the same day as our bomb—and I thought that it would greatly change history. Gertrude said she had dramatized her relationship with Florence and really was not that involved, but I was skeptical. I said I wanted to discuss the matter with her in more detail, and she said that she would see me soon. I said that I was giving her complete freedom except for Florence—that was the only way that I was restricting her. I said again that I loved her very much, and she said, "Really? Do you?" And I said yes. Then she admitted that I was at the high point of my love.

August 7, 1945. She told me what she had been keeping from me for a year—that Jack was not very interesting, that he had no real creative ability, and that he wouldn't get anywhere. He was definitely not up to her level. She said she felt that I never judged her when I was with her, and that was why she found it so comfortable to be with me. I was wondering, because in some ways I was more critical of her than anyone else she knew. Had actual intercourse for a change, because she was at the point of her period where it was almost impossible for her to get pregnant. So we enjoyed that.

August 8, 1945. She kept saying that we talked about her too much, but really she said, we should talk about me because I was very important and would get somewhere in life. As a matter of fact, when she was thirty-seven or so, she said I would be famous and she would be not so hot in looks and getting nowhere, that she was ordinary, and I was really extraordinary. I said that that didn't have to be so, since she had great talent if only she would use it.

Then we got sexual again, and I gave her another great orgasm. She said that she really wanted to have a child, for the first time in her life, and have it with me. Parted at 2 a.m., because she was considerate of my getting more sleep. I wanted to take her to the stadium the next day, but she said she would rather go to my place and work on some stories, which surprised me.

August 13, 1945. She wanted to discuss some serious things with me, especially now that she knew she could hurt me, and she never wanted to do anything like that. She wavered: Sometimes she was definitely going to marry me and other times she wasn't. But if she did marry me, she would still point out some of the rash things I do to antagonize people and block me—especially when I was doing some of that on my thesis.

I agreed with Gertrude that I might not marry her because of her ambivalence and the trouble of her getting divorced from Jack. She was also afraid that I might be very preoccupied with my work and not with her. I said that I would have great disadvantages in marrying her, but I loved her so much and it had so many advantages that I was definitely willing to do so.

She thought it would be better if she were my mistress, rather than my wife, because then I would do more work. But I said that I could arrange it after living with her a while to have her as a wife and also do the work I wanted to do. She said she was afraid of marrying me because I might leave her, but I thought that was a rationalization for the other things—the living together things—that would be a pain in the ass for her if she were married to me.

I said marriage could be a great experience for both of us, but she said she wanted roots, and in a sense, she did have roots with Jack. She also thought that she might be able to tell Jack the truth about the two of us and still stay married to him. She said there would be much pain in divorcing Jack, and I said she was cowardly because she could get over the pain if she divorced him. She also suggested that I might marry some nice woman and have her as a mistress. But she wouldn't like the idea of the woman knowing about her.

She said I was too clear-sighted in my love for her. And she really wanted somebody who was blindly in love.

I was somewhat depressed because she couldn't arrange to see me on that day (when the Japanese surrendered), and I thought it was a historic day and we should really be together. And I wanted a woman who was always available to me for special days. And she wasn't quite it. We agreed to forego sex for several days because she had some mid-section pain, but we were very, very affectionate. She finally agreed that I could stay over and sleep in her bed, because I pointed out that there was just about no chance of her mother coming in and inter-rupting us. But that was 3 a.m.

At first, Gertrude only wanted to satisfy me sexually, but then I really aroused her and we had a great time, and I satisfied her too. She couldn't sleep right next to me, but she did sleep, finally, and slept more than I did. When I got up to go to the john, she awoke and was horrified at my not being there and put her arms around me and clung to me when I returned.

Told her that I had written 700 pages of notes about her already, and she was not disturbed—as Karyl had been. The one thing that held me back from being eager to marry her is that I had work to do. But otherwise, if I were just a real hedonist, I would have definitely married her because it was such a delight to be with her.

August 17, 1945. Kept getting interrupted by phone calls, so we went back to bed and had a hilarious time with each other, and wished that it had been recorded. Agreed that we could write a Hollywood movie or at least a comedy for radio. Talked about having a baby and not making me pay any support for it. But we almost didn't care if she had the baby right then and there—at least she didn't.

Met Bob and Manny at the tennis court and had an intellectual conversation in which Gertrude far outweighed the other women with us. She was the life of the party. She said she had a lovely honeymoon with me that weekend. She said she was pained from loving me too much, again, when she called later that night, and felt that I might leave her and that would cause pain. Discussed her insecurity and her love for men's approval, and she agreed that she had no objective reason for insecurity with me. But I felt a little fed up with her for the moment, because we hadn't done anything for the past few days—just been with each other enjoyably—but hadn't accomplished much. So I was still hung up on doing things together and separately.

Felt that I loved her in practice, not theory, while she loved me in theory rather than in practice. And I still didn't like her not realizing her great capacity for intelligence and creativity, and that she probably never would realize it. I had fallen in love mainly because of her potential, and now she wasn't realizing it. I thought that she wanted to love me more, and felt that she should, but she never quite succeeded in doing it. Oddly enough, I thought if we were married, she'd shame me by her promiscuity. And even though I was in favor of promiscuity, I wouldn't do it against her.

August 22, 1945. She got very hurt and accused me of thinking that she was below me, which I hadn't thought at all. She ran out of bed, very hurt, and I was remorseful and tried to comfort her. But then she tried to prove her affectionality by saying: (1) She stuck up for me when her friends thought me gauche and pitiful; (2) Sexually she had been with me as with no others; (3) She had begun to take the prospect of our marriage seriously; and (4) She accepted me and didn't question my failings. Now she was very upset and despaired about our future and said that I was rejecting her as her mother had done for so long. I took the situation quietly and felt that I could talk her out of some of her upsetness. Then because of my calmness she accused me of not having real feelings for her. I said that I had been hurt by her, too, and there were actually tears in my eyes.

She said there would be lasting scars from this fight, and I said no, not unless we held everything in. She said she couldn't stand my being critical of her and accused me of wanting to destroy everything. Kept saying that I had no real emotion and no real affection. She said she was quite confused and not sure of anything now. She said I only knew how to be sexual and not affectionate. I finally did convince her that I loved her and as a result began to arouse her sexually. We had intercourse for only a short while, because I was very aroused, and she said it was the best intercourse she had ever had. Then she became very affectionate and warm and started calling me "pussycat," a new appellation. Then we were both affectionate and fell asleep at 3:30 a.m. I said that I was really trying to do good, but she seemed to need more and more cherishing, and I wasn't sure that anyone could give her that.

August 29, 1945. She came to my home after playing tennis in St. James Park. Got along beautifully and lovingly and had very good sex relations. Told her that after my analysis I wanted to study music, and she jumped on that because it would require money. I showed her that she sort of needed the marriage with me, but I didn't need it with her.

Then she started to walk out on me again. I insisted that if I married anyone, including her, my vital needs would have to be fulfilled. And she didn't like that. She blamed herself for her stupidity in always taking me back. I said I knew she was the best one for me at present, but I could still do without her and get along well.

August 30, 1945. She wanted to hear my songs, and I showed her some, and she was very impressed by them. She wanted to know what else I would do, and I listed forming an institute, writing a great novel, composing, setting up music libraries, working on love/sex happiness. She pointed out the dangers of my doing too much and thinking I would get it all done when there wasn't time.

September 9, 1945. Called each other twice, and I said during one conversation that a wave of love for her had gone over me while I was reading, and she loved that. Got in bed with her, but she again said I didn't really love her enough. We agreed that she'd better be less *in* love with me, and then she would be hurt less, because that was making her doubt me. And she agreed. She went over my reasons for her being in love with me: because I kept telling her how marvelous she was, I was a shining light in my own eyes, got her to appreciate herself because I was so stable, kept calling her regularly, and she could see my greatness. I said I'd fallen in love with her because I could see her intellect and greatness, and in spite of it all, how nice she was and how good she was at school. So I told her only her good points and omitted the bad ones, and she loved that.

I now saw that emphasizing your partner's nice points is probably necessary in good love relationships, and that my compulsive honesty wasn't so good.

Gertrude was afraid to buy a smoking jacket because it wouldn't agree with my tastes, and it was pretty awful that I didn't completely agree with her tastes.

I thought about us and I saw that we wouldn't be happy in marriage because I was a stronger person than she—and she wouldn't be able to take that.

Had intercourse again. She wanted to know why I didn't get control over my orgasm more, and I said I didn't have to because I could always come the second time with her and then it lasted much longer. But I said I would try more in the future. I was much sexier, really, in many ways than she, and therefore I didn't think I would last too long the first time.

We slept badly during the night, and I had a headache, but I was still solicitous of her. I felt more than ever that she could only love me because of the great good I did for her, and not because she really loved me in her own right. I still thought she got bored with me and thought she better have a succession of unboring lovers. But she said if I were married to her she wouldn't let herself be bored with me.

September 17, 1945. On the phone, Gertrude said she had been pushing her love for me downward the last few days, because getting out of love with me was the thing for her to do. And I said that I didn't need that kind of thing. I showed her that she liked new relationships because they were original and novel for a while, and therefore she could reach greater heights. But then being in love didn't last very long, so, as American women were inclined to do, they were very disillusioned. I thought I would be more in love with her if she stopped nagging me about it, and she partly agreed. I said that nine out of ten women would be very satisfied with my kind of love for them. And she agreed and said that therefore I'd better get a woman who was better for me. Agreed to take a week's vacation from each other to enhance our situation.

I thought about other women while away from her, but was grateful for the fact that I was in love with Gertrude and therefore I wasn't compulsive about them.

September 18, 1945. On the phone, told her that I might like to call her and tell her that I loved her even though it wasn't great in-lovedness. And she thought that was fine.

September 22, 1945. Talked on the phone, and she said that she had been following my suggestions and really getting down to doing her work. She told me about a big radio writer with whom she had been with the night before, and that he got so immersed that he wanted to marry her. Again, we both got to thinking that she most probably would marry me.

September 25, 1945. Wanted me to leave relatively early, because her mother might come back. But I got to her sexually and she had a tremendous orgasm again. We both thought the evening had been fine. A true experience again!

September 26, 1945. Gertrude was menstrual and not feeling good, and I volunteered to take her home from school. She was very tense and couldn't stay still, but I kissed her all over at home, soothed her, calmed her down, undressed her, got her to bed, and gave her a beautiful orgasm, which she loved. She didn't want me to leave, though it was getting late. Finally, at 11:30 p.m., she asked me to leave so I could get home early. It was nearly my birthday, and she got me several gifts. I realized that for all the goodness of the evening, I hadn't really been into it. Was afraid that if I married her, that our companionship would finally get boring to me. Again, I decided we logically should be lovers rather than married to each other.

September 27, 1945. Gertrude wanted to talk about philosophy—Berkeley, Hume, Spinoza, Schopenhauer, and so on. Went to a double-feature movie, and she was affectionate and sexy during the movie. We both thought that the evening had been good. Talked about marriage and whether love could last and thought that it could. But I thought that it would be better if both partners had some affairs from time to time. She thought that my affairs would lead to a real passionate relationship, and I said no, as long as I was working hard at my own thing and content with her, I didn't think it would.

She said she was changing over the year of seeing me and now was an "Al Jr." She was taking on some of my attitudes toward work and life. Everything went well, but I got a headache and therefore left at 12:30 a.m. to go home and get to sleep.

October 3, 1945. Gertrude was somewhat suspicious of me, and I was also suspicious of her. The reasons I gave for that were: (1) We were both a bit insecure, not daring to hope that we had won the other completely. (2) We were both very sensitive, really, and did not want to be hurt and were trying to withdraw before we were hurt. (3) We both had tremendous egos and couldn't see ourselves loving when the other did not, and feared that this was so. (4) We were both very capable of putting on an act—a sexual, amative act—with each other. (5) We were both very brilliant individuals and could see through the acting on each other's part. (6) Basically we both loved each other very much and were both sensitive because of our love for each other and afraid of being hurt because of this love. Therefore, we tried to withdraw immediately when we sensed that this love was not being returned. Gertrude agreed that my reasons were good ones. She said she had been very hurt recently, and I accused her of the tendency to break because of that. I said that she always satisfied my suspicions on a given time, but then they returned again. But she couldn't see why, since she had been giving up so many men in favor of me.

I insisted that our love was greater than ever—that mine for her certainly was—and only my in-lovedness vanished when she didn't seem to love me, but the loving her—the loving kindness—stayed forever. She said she really wanted to marry me when I asked her again, but said she wouldn't promise because of conditions. She might not, but she really wanted to, and seemed to mean this. I said I knew she had perfect taste, but that I also wanted to see her anomaly side. Super-refinement wasn't exactly for me, and there was some sexual puritanism on the other side of her. So I loved her artistic side, but I also liked her human lack of refinement.

On another night at my house, Gertrude said that she was grateful for the changes I had wrought in her, and she was afraid that her changes were not enough and that I would still not love her the way I said I did. So we temporarily resolved it and got into each other's arms. She saw that I was very emotional about her and liked that. My mother came in while we were talking, but she realized now that she could ignore that and saw how I had other women there before her, and they hadn't gotten upset about my mother. She satisfied me sexually and then got dressed to go. But she said my apartment was very restrictive to her, since she couldn't run around in it and undress and do what she wanted. Her dancing around naked and things like that enhanced her sexuality. I said I loved our honest discussion the first part of the evening, and I really had. And we parted very affectionately.

On another night, I was supposed to meet her for the movie *A Song to Remember*, and told her to come early because I had a bad foot, but she got tied up and came quite late. I was very angry at her for that and showed it. Got her to my house, and again she didn't seem to mind the fact that my mother was there. Told her that my whole life had been rebellious rather than going for love as children do. I decided I could live without the love of people, and that helped my rebellion.

As an adolescent, I refused to wear ties and refused to follow the freshmen rules, and in philosophy I was very rebellious. Then I fell naturally into radical activity. Gertrude's attitude, I thought, was one of ingratiation. She rebelled against her mother but not against others, and she had outgoing niceness and a definite compulsive need to be loved. Because of our different personality attitudes, we kept misunderstanding each other. She didn't quite agree with my analysis. She said I was insecure, but I thought that she was just projecting her own insecurity on me. Then she said, "Oh, how wonderfully well you verbalize! I bet there are no two lovers in the world who verbalize their love as well as we do." And I agreed with her.

She said I was greater than she because I did not love or need her compulsively and was given over to more worldly things. But I said that the only thing I had over her was that I had more creative drive and stamina. She said she was really animalistic in her sexuality, but I pointed out that she only let herself go animalistically when she loved her partner. She pointed out in detail how she got very aroused when I manipulated her genital region, but she said that if I stopped, then she didn't get frustrated at all, which seemed to be odd. And as manipulations continued, she went on to a climax, and her climax consisted of vibrations that lasted about thirty seconds or so. Even afterward, her vibrations could be aroused by her laughing, or by being touched on the stomach, or by other means. And the vibrations were most pleasurable to her.

Then I described my own orgasm: First there was a ticklish, pleasant, tingling feeling from the first touch or look, and then a period of not being able to hold, and it lasted quite a while then became more intense. Then on to a period of not being able to hold back, then a short orgasm lasting only a few seconds, then sexual relaxation, but pleasure of a sensual sort with her. She would have liked me to last longer, but I explained that the pleasure, all told, was most worthwhile and intense and made me feel amatively most tender to her and affectionate afterward. But if I didn't get an orgasm, then I would feel quite frustrated. She said that I hadn't had orgasms recently, and I said it didn't matter because I knew that she was going to get around to it. She did get around to it, especially orally, and I was very thrilled. But I really loved satisfying her as well as being satisfied, and I only hoped that she did the same. It got late, so we parted and arranged to meet the next day.

Throughout our six years together, during which time Gertrude divorced her husband, we continued to have great sex and few disagreements. By this time I was an accomplished and somewhat promiscuous lover, and we taught each other much about ecstatic sexuo-amative life. Things were going well; I got my PhD in clinical psychology in 1947, and the time to make decisions about marrying, or not, approached. As we looked for an apartment to live in, our crucial domestic differences became clear. I wanted an apartment with a room for myself in which I could be and work alone. Gertrude wanted an open apartment with *no* doors. She wanted to have people over for dinner or parties *at least* two times a week. She was a compulsive relater. At that point we mutually decided against marrying, though I still loved her. She looked for another husband—whom she met and married a few weeks later. I felt very sad and even shed tears, which was unusual for me. Though I kept my lack of neediness, which I developed during my time with Karyl, I thought I would never find a partner as compatible as Gertrude. And until I met Debbie, who is more compatible with me on practically every level than Gertrude or anyone else I've ever known, I never did.

Gertrude and I remained sex-love friends for over twenty years. During that time, she talked about divorcing her second husband and marrying me, but we kept our domestic incompatibility in mind and didn't marry. He died in an accident, and she remarried once more. Her life with her next husband was quite tragic—he was very controlling and later committed suicide. I remember with fondness my years of wild and romantic love with Gertrude.

Chapter 9

Important Influences

FAMILY INFLUENCES

My Mother

Like everyone else, for better or worse, I was positively and negatively influenced by my mother and father. First, my mother. When she bore me, she was a beautiful blue-eyed blonde with non-Jewish features, who had been having a ten-year affair with my brilliant, erratic, dashing father. She was thirty and he was twenty-nine, both lived in Philadelphia, and they married because she was several months pregnant with me.

Hettie Hanigbaum, as she was then called, was interested in singing, dancing, and acting, but *not* in motherhood. She had temporary jobs, mainly a salesperson job at Wanamaker's, but she soon quit work to be a wife and mother. We lived in Pittsburgh for my first four years. My mother soon gave birth to my brother Paul, nineteen months younger, and my sister Janet, four years younger than I.

My mother loved and somewhat frantically took care of her three young children and lived a middle-class life with them and my father. My father worked from nine till nine and gave her little help with the kids.

My mother loved me enough, but she also had to work hard to care for my younger brother and sister. So from the age of two onward, I was neglected and left largely on my own. I don't remember *feeling* neglected, and besides, I had a favorite godmother, who was blond, beautiful, and lively, and took good care of me. We sort of adopted each other.

My mother was very busy and seemed reasonably happy. At that time, four-year-olds were allowed to attend kindergarten in Pittsburgh. I was briefly terrified at being separated from my family and friends, but as I mentioned previously, I soon adjusted to school, found it fascinating, and even walked by myself one long block to and from school.

My mother spent little time with me but was loving and nice and, by the time I was five, socialized greatly and talked a blue streak with her female friends. I don't recall her conversing very much with my busy and not-too-helpful father. But everything was conventional and amicable.

My mother knew little about raising children, read practically nothing about it, and followed her friends' teaching—which was sparse. She was directive but not firm or critical, and I always got along with her better than did my brother and sister. Paul was a bright young rebel, and Janet, a whining depressive. I was quite friendly with Paul but had little to do with Janet.

In my adult years, I wrote many fond letters to my mother, such as these:

January 10, 1953

Dear Mother:

I am glad to hear that you are getting along so well. I am enclosing your check for next month, and I hope that you are doing all right financially. I do not want to see you going without anything that is necessary to your health and happiness.

On January 31 I am moving to a larger apartment, since I need one for my patients. I am moving to the Parc Vendome, 333 West 56th Street, New York, and will be there from February 1 on. It is a very classy development, including four apartment-hotel buildings, with elevator service and everything. I have two and a half rooms on the tenth floor—a large living room (13 by 22 feet), a full kitchen and dinette, a small dressing room, and a bath. Also a huge closet with two Murphy beds, if I want to use them, another large closet, and a foyer, which I can use for my patients. I am getting this very cheaply, for this sort of thing—$111 a month, since it is still under the old OPA regulations. I was very lucky to get it. For a place like this, in that part of the city, it usually costs at least $150 a month.

I think I shall be quite happy in the new place, and may be able to get some new patients from the building and the neighborhood, thus helping to pay for the rent.

Otherwise, everything is in good order, and I am quite busy, what with arranging for moving and many other things along that line. Let me know how you feel and how everything is going.

Love,
Albert

December 20, 1957

Dear Albert,

Your very nice letter came today, and I sure was glad to hear your book was in demand and I will be very glad to get the other one. Janet is reading it now. I received the card from Rhoda. I hope she enjoyed her visit in Wisconsin. Did you get the metal calendar for your desk I sent last week? Our mail is very poor and I don't send any parcels (as they are delayed for so long). I sure enjoyed the fruit cake that Paul and you were so kind to send me. I had a permanent and now look like me, that short haircut was awful. It hid my health, which I haven't got but felt lost without my curls and tonight I shall doll up and go to Xmas dance at the veteran's admit. and I enjoy it so much to give some old soul a little pleasure as I shall waltz like a teenager. Albert, thanks for the stamps, sure can use them and they are a treat and I see you do your share for charity. Those handicapped stamps are fine. I use them, so thanks for same. Enclosed is a buck. I want you and Rhoda to enjoy another cheesecake, as Paul and you have given me plenty. Not your sister, she only expects from me, and I give her linens (lace) she don't even care if I exist but sure go place. I have a ticket for December 26, *The Robe*. I didn't yet see it. I gave Norman a buck for his birthday on December 12, he didn't even thank me and has very little to say so that suits me. I am very happy and contented, as, Albert dear, I have everything I need. Paul is so good his letters are such a comfort to me. Our weather has been great (thank God), just a little rain, which was much needed. Now I do hope Rhoda and you will have a Merry Xmas and may the New Year bring you both happiness, health, and prosperity. With all my love to both of you. Keep well like your young old Ma. I know you are very busy, but I love and long to hear from you.

Lovingly,
Mother

February 2, 1972

Dear Mother,

I hope that you are very happy in your new residence. From what Janet [sister] tells me, it is a very nice place and I think you will enjoy it. I also hope that you are not worrying about anything in particular and that you are getting along well with Janet. It is just not worth your upsetting yourself about anything.

I have been very fine and free from all ailments and diseases in the past many months. Lots of people in New York City have the flu and colds, but I have not had anything like this. The weather has been rather warm here, with only a little snow, and it looks like we will have a mild winter. I know, however, that things are even better out your way and that you are enjoying a hell of a lot more sun than we get here, so I hope that the weather is fine and that you are enjoying yourself out there as much as possible.

I am still taking a good many trips throughout the country and recently got back from Florida where everything went well. I also still expect to be out in California in June and if I get to the Los Angeles area I shall certainly stop in to see you. Meanwhile, if there is anything that you need, don't hesitate to call on Paul or me for it.

Love,
Albert

I always liked my mother and got along very well with her, but I didn't love her too much and was easily bored with her compulsive talking and her many conventional friends. I was very responsible and wrote her every two or three weeks, whether I wanted to or not. She wrote me less often, but I couldn't make out some of her handwriting and found it very repetitive.

I wished her well, wrote her encouraging letters, sent her most of my books and some of my articles, sent her money, told her how well I was doing, and asked her about her life.

My Father

My father Henry was fabulously busy at work (9 a.m. to 9 p.m. weekdays) and with poker-playing friends on Saturday and Sunday, and so had very little time for his children. He kissed us hello at 7:30 a.m. and then rarely saw us for the rest of the day. When he did see us, he was very pleasant and nice but not really involved. He rarely taught us anything, supported the family generously, and kept to himself. He was the opposite of a control freak and he let my mother (and her friends) set the scene. He and my mother usually went to a show or a movie on a Saturday night, *saw* it, but didn't seem to talk much about it with each other. They most likely had sex briefly and regularly, although it was never mentioned. Years later, my mother told me that she enjoyed sex with my father—such as it was!

My Brother Paul

Paul's influences were exceptionally profound. From my fifth year, we were as close as could be and invented intimate, if imaginary, relationships with sports and movie stars. Later, we were close friends with Manny Birnbaum and other children. All our lives, we taught and learned from each other. In adulthood Paul (with our friend Eddie Cohen) was one of the trustees of the Albert Ellis Institute and helped it immensely. He also became a fine investor—and managed my stocks and bonds until his death.

Paul and I talked endlessly, and later in our adulthood I wrote to him regularly and received friendly letters from him. He was my true family, and we continued exchanging letters even when my mother wrote little. Our letters were often about my mother and sister and what they were doing, but many were about my funds, which Paul handled for me. As I have noted, he became an expert at investing and informed me of the gains in my investments, which he made for me. All told, from 1965 onward, he helped me accumulate a great amount in savings—which came in handy years later when I needed extra medical care and the problems started with the institute. This proved to be most beneficial for medical, nursing, and legal costs from 2004 on, until most of the savings got used up. At this time of writing, I feel very concerned about my financial situation.

A typical letter I wrote to Paul about his investing went as follows:

April 9, 1971

Dear Paul,

Many thanks for the check for $1,044.08, which arrived yesterday. You certainly seem to be doing as well as usual with our securities. I don't know how you usually manage to come out ahead, no matter how the market seems to be going, but you have an unusually fine record in that regard.

Janet and I will be glad to see you around June 15. If you want to stay here, just let us know and we will make arrangements for you.

Everything is going very busily and well and I am doing a great deal of traveling, as usual, around the country. I should also have at least two books and maybe three or four published this year. The institute is doing fine in most respects, and we have no complaints.

Is there anything special we could get David for his graduation? If so, please let me know.

Love,
Albert

Another letter to Paul went as follows:

March 22, 1973

Dear Paul:

Thank you for your recent letter and for the check for $4,000. I am glad that you sent all the material to Manny, since he will take care of it and it is not even necessary that I see it. I finally looked over my tax form and found out what is doing.

The check was a cashier's check, which was made out to you and not endorsed, so I had our office endorse it and put it through because it was desirable to have more money in my account. We tried to call you on this, but you were not available by phone. I assume that this is okay with you.

Everything is still exceptionally busy, and I am still getting more invitations to speak all over the country, so I am out of New York about two days a week these days, especially on weekends. I am glad to hear that you are enjoying your retirement and that all goes well with you and Esther.

Love,
Albert

My Sister Janet

Although I didn't personally like my sister Janet very much, later in life she lived near my mother in Los Angeles and took somewhat good care of her. I therefore wrote to Janet regularly, as a way of keeping in touch with my mother. One of my typical letters to Janet went as follows:

April 11, 1971

Dear Janet,

I am glad to hear that you are in good shape and that no one in the family has been harmed by the earthquake. I keep writing Mother, but, as you can imagine, I don't hear from her in return. I told her I'd see her when I get to LA early in October for the Behavior Therapy Conference at the Biltmore, for a workshop at Elysium Field, and for a talk to the Round Table. Then I go to San Jose for a workshop for the Humanist Assn. there. Incidentally, I get the Humanist of the Year Award for 1971 from the American Humanist Association in Chicago next week.

I am glad to have the old photos of me. I hardly recognize myself! But I'll keep them for the archives.

Good to hear that Joel is getting along so well. Sounds like his trip will be an interesting one. I'm going to Europe myself for the first time this summer, to speak at two conferences there.

About your new beau, the engineer: He probably can read *The Art and Science of Love*, and won't get upset by your suggesting it. *The Sensual Man* is an easy-to-read book, but it is not very deep. It mainly takes stuff from me and Masters and Johnson. It certainly won't hurt him to read it, but it's not half as good as *The Sensual Woman*.

Everything going most busily here, and, as usual, I do a good deal of out-of-town talking. I should have at least two books out this year: the one on *Murder and Assassination* is finally going through the press, and so is *A Casebook of Rational-Emotive Therapy* (which will probably have a more lively title by the time it gets through press). Other books are in the writing stage.

When arrangements for my LA trip are more definite, I shall let you know about them. But I may only be there for a few days and barely have time to do very much.

Love,
Albert

Paul's influence on me was huge; my sister's, very little. We largely ignored each other.

I was also mildly in touch with Janet's two children, and more in touch with my brother's son David and his wife Susan. I saw David, a lawyer, and Susan, a psychologist, when I had trips to Florida, where they lived. They both tried to help me years later, making efforts to try to protect me from some of my opponents at the Albert Ellis Institute.

All told, I had pleasant but not close ties to my relatives, as I think was suitable.

CULTURAL INFLUENCES

Childhood

When I was four, we moved to New York, and I started to have a good social life with the neighborhood kids on Bryant Avenue in the Bronx. I think I was much more influenced by my young neighbors than by my family members. But I was a "good kid" and didn't get in any trouble with my brightness and my teaching myself to read at the age of four. I also became more directive at helping other children.

When I was allowed to start school in the first grade at the age of six, I also became much more sociable with other children and, when I got a library card, became the best-read child for miles around. My socializing and reading interests at that time took precedence over my parental influences. Also, when I was five, my parents took me to the movies, which influenced me enormously, especially the stars of the day—Mary Pickford, Douglas Fairbanks, and others.

Oh, yes, sports. Like most boys, I soon became a sports fan, and made Babe Ruth, Jack Dempsey, and others my heroes. In our fantasies from five years onward, Paul and I lived a star-studded life with sports and movie people. We really "knew" them!

Ruthie

Yes, of course! As I have told elsewhere in this book, at five and a half, I fell madly in love with Ruthie (another blue-eyed blonde), was caught by our parents trying to pour milk through a funnel into her vagina, had her rudely removed from my presence, and never saw her again. A grim tragedy!—and for a while a real influence on my life.

{}

So I was little intimate with my mother, *very* little with my father, especially when I began to suffer from nephritis (kidney trouble) and went to the hospital nine times between the ages of five and a half and nine. I was often sadly neglected, compared to the contacts other kids had with their relatives and friends, but I dealt nicely with that neglect and became even more socialized with my other hospitalized friends.

How about sex? Did I have any latency period, as Freud might allege? By no means! When I was about six or seven, in the hospital, I put my legs between the bars of the crib, got semi-erections, and came to near-orgasms. Later, at seven or eight, I climbed gym ropes and again got near-orgasms. Damned good—and I almost became addicted!

INFLUENCE OF MY CLOSE COLLABORATORS AND COAUTHORS

Robert A. Harper

My first real collaborator and coauthor was probably my mother, since she helped me figure out many practical problems and how to solve them. But she was a lightweight thinker and planner, and hardly influenced my general philosophy of life or my creation of Rational Emotive Behavior Therapy. However, she rarely took things *too* seriously, nor was she upset over bad events for a prolonged period. Therefore, she was something of a good role model.

My collaborators from my twenty-fifth year onward were famous philosophers, especially Socrates and Plato and the Stoics—notably Epictetus and Seneca. Although I was hardly a pure Stoic, some of my main thinking went along with that of Epictetus: We are not upset by the unfortunate events that happen to us but by our *views* of these events. This philosophy was very influential in my life; Leon Pomeroy has called it the Epictetus-Ellis hypothesis (2005).

I met Bob Harper around 1950 at the American Association for Marital and Family Therapy and took to him immediately because he was anti-prudish, active-directive, sensible, and was opposed to the kindly but indirective teachings of Carl Rogers. We spoke together at AAMFC meetings and wrote a few articles together.

When I originated REBT in January 1955, Bob Harper was its first (and also its *only*) devotee. He endorsed my *How to Live with a Neurotic* (1957) and joined me in writing two key books on REBT: *A Guide to Rational Living* (1961) and *A Guide to Successful Marriage* (1961). Thereafter, we were always in the throes of the battle with prudes and conservatives!

Bob was active in professional meetings and affairs until he semi-retired in 1995. Until that time, he was president of several divisions of the American Psychological Association, joined me in dozens of presentations, and fought intensively with me against public and professional stick-in-the-muds. He was supported by his wife of thirty years, Mimi Harper. We had innumerable great get-togethers until his death at the age of eighty-nine in 2004. Never had I a better friend and rational collaborator!

Bob Harper was more handsome than I and more tactful, though he was as assertive as I. He was more loving to his four wives and more sociable than I. I was influenced somewhat (but not *too much*) by his sociability and would have been more of a terror without it.

In addition, Bob insisted on donating his share of the royalties on our joint books to the Albert Ellis Institute when I was still in charge of it. The institute continues to receive those royalties. In this way, he helped support the institute and REBT to the tune of well over a million dollars. I, of course, was very grateful. In addition, he wrote several books of his own. I am certain that if he knew of the recent institute treatment of me that he would no longer want his royalties going to them.

Oh, yes. Our humor with each other and against prudes with whom we disagreed was constant and (I naturally think) high-spirited. My wife and partner, Debbie Joffe Ellis, who heard some of our spirited exchanges and thought them hilarious, said that readers would greatly enjoy them in a section on humor in a future book. I've included some of our letters here:

December 19, 1957

Dear Al,

With the amazing speed, yet infinite care, for which I am famous, I dispatched the most recent crop of lies to M. Catharine Evans. Your progression to fellow in Division 17 reminds me that Division 13 to which I applied, courtesy of you and departed George, forgot all about its group of applications. So I must wait until next year to become a consulting fellow. Meantime, I'm struggling along being a counseling fellow and tremendously happy to welcome you into our highly select circle.

Having been able to think of no other absolutely certain way of getting you off to a real flying start in '58, I have decided to mail you my manuscript on *Psychotherapy for Marriage*, which should reach you about January 3. I have two chapters still to revise, which I'll do between ditch digging, wall papering, and related chores during our "vacation" in Nanticoke, December 22–January 1. You'll never know my true personality until you see me performing some muscular feat like diverting the creek that comes rushing down the mountain into the backyard into somebody else's backyard a mile down the road. Of course, I must admit that I don't recall your saying you *wanted* to know my true personality. But some day you and Rhoda will have to decide to hell with everything and take a trip to Nanticoke. But, anyhow, my book has boiled down to 10 chapters of 20 typewritten pages each, and, I trust it is necessary to say, every one of its 55,000 words is a god-damned gem. My, I envy you the pleasure of a virgin reading: I've had so many fucking readings of it I could puke.

Meantime, in this season of the Christ child, our thoughts naturally turn toward you, the messiah of rational psychotherapy, and your child bride. To both of you, my old bitch and I waft farts of Christmas joy.

Lovingly,
Bob

The Peter—not prick—of the Rational Psychotherapy Movement*

January 5, 1958

Dear Peter Peter Pussy Eater:

I have not written you over the holidays because I was so deeply depressed by not receiving this year's Duvall Christmas letter that I could hardly do any better than knocking out ten thousand words a day. But never fear: letting the punishment fit the crime, I have duly dispatched one of OUR progress reports to the Duvalls. If this does not get a (purely non-sexual) rise out of them, nothing will. After all, if we are to be relegated to the Harper class, we should also obtain a little of the rewards of iniquity. Knowing you should be sufficient reward for anyone in this connection; but, let us face it, it ain't.

Many thanks and all that kind of rot for the usual endorsement prevarications for the edification of Division 17. If there is any association, division, organization, or kiddy club in which we do not mutually infest by now, please let me know and I will do my best to outskunk you in it.

January 3rd has arrived, as you threatened, but still no sign of *Psychotherapy for Marriage.* Am I lucky enough to hope that it got lost in the mails, banned by the post office, or spontaneously combusted en route? Or am I luckless enough to learn that you merely neglected to send it as yet?

My calendar tells me that you and your long-suffering mate may be around these parts around the 24th. With peerless foresight, I neglected to tell my spouse (who answers to the name of Rhoda but we know what her true label is) that you might invade us in January, so she has got us about six and a half so-called social engagements on that weekend. However, some of

---

*Cock crowing or no goddamned cock crowing, I'll naturally deny the master whenever it is convenient to deny the master.

the people we are supposed to see then may drop dead or cut us likewise when they learn who some of our best friends are; or, such joys notwithstanding, we may still be able to find time to let you wine and dine us at the Waldorf. Let us know your schedule, so that we may plan a graceful escape.

Devotedly,
(Ration)Al

February 18, 1970

Dear Bob:

I don't know how you have managed to survive without hearing from me in so many months, but I imagine that you are a sturdy fellow and have got through most of the winter without my cheery epistles. Lots of nefarious things as you may well expect is going on here as usual, but we are still in business, no one has found out our true colors, and we are still very much a thorn in the side of various Establishments. Naturally we don't do quite as much harm as you do, unassisted, in Washington, but then it is not everyone who has a truly rare talent for this kind of thing.

Anyway, the main point of this letter is that I am about to sign a contract with Science and Behavior Books of Palo Alto, Calif., for publication of the *Casebook of Rational-Emotive Psychotherapy*. This will contain cases from several well-known RET people with annotated comments by me. What we need for each case is a type-script of a tape recording of an early session and of all or part of a later session of RET showing some kind of movement. I realize that you are still back in the 19th—or is it 18th—century as far as the technology of psychotherapy is concerned and that you do not ordinarily record any cases, however, if you can get me a tape recording of one of your early sessions plus one of a somewhat later session with the same patient I can certainly use this as a basis for a chapter by you in the casebook. Certainly it would be a good idea to have one of the founding fathers of RET—meaning you, buster!—contribute to this mighty tome.

Incidentally, we find it very useful at the Institute if many of our patients bring in their own cassette tape recorder and record all or many of the sessions that they have. Then they go home and listen to them and are able to get a great deal out of the sessions, often more than they get from the live session. You might think of using this technique with your own patients. If you do so you can borrow a couple of cassettes from them of an early and later session and fulfill the requirements for the casebook that way. Not that I want to twist your arm, but there are more ways than one of skinning a cat, even if that cat is a wily one from Washington!

How about it?

Love and kisses from Janet, me, Reason (our only remaining fish), who proved to be heartier than his sister, Emotion, and his brother, Suppressed.

Albert Ellis, PhD
Executive Director

August 19, 1976

Dear Al,

I personally am in favor of letting your strong unconscious resistance to fine southern hospitality win out and tell you to stay the unfuck away on Friday evening, September 3. Mimi, however, likes you in spite of your personality and rude ways and says that she'll have a box lunch here for you to munch and a cab pre-oriented for 8 o'clock to whisk you away to the humanistic prurients at the Hilton (it will take a cab only about 15 minutes to get you there from 4903 Potomac, N.W.).

Mimi and I are both presuming that you have overcome your male chauvinistic ways enough to let Janet remain for dinner. We'll get a sixth guest to take your place—which won't be a hard role for anyone to match in a positive sense even if we picked him randomly from Division 3. If such random selection doesn't work, we'll bring Rufus back in from the kennels.

In any case, we'll see you.

Love,
Bob

November 5, 1976

Dear Cousin Albert,

Your letter of October 14, 1976, in which you kindly accepted the great honor of participating in the famous Harper symposium on "Intimacy in Psychotherapy: Gallant Goal or Hollow Hoax?," neglected to list for you the particular topic of your particular contribution. Please correct this grievous error, so that I may fulfill the necessary requirements in submitting the proposed symposium to Aaron Canter.

George Bach has unreluctantly agreed to join the symposium with this title: "Creative Aggression—How I Fight for My Right to Be a Person-Intimate or Not-So Intimate in Getting the Job Done." Feel no need to have so nutty a title as dear old George.

Irma Lee Shepherd has not been heard from at this date, so I am turning to Erika Fromm.

Watch this space for further developments.

If you want some stimulating topic for conversation when playing hopscotch with Janet-wanet one day, please tell her she has never answered my query re a topic for my talk at the 1977 RET Conference and that I feel deeply rejected and that there is no use in going on and that nobody loves me and that Rufus has been mortally insulted along with me, Mimi, and my long dead mother.

Mimi and I are off for a week in Bermuda. Since Carter won rather than Jerry Boy, we have canceled our plans to sail on to Red China. After we knock a little religion out of Jimmy Boy (I'll give him free therapy), I think he'll make a good president.

Meantime,
Love,
Bob

November 9, 1976

Dear Bob,

I hate to have you kill yourself over Janet's neglecting your scrumptious offer to set the 1977 RET Conference aglow (somewhat à la manner of the Old Chicago Fire in Mrs. O'Leary's Barn) and arrange for the Second Coming (and First

Orgasm) of Christ (nee A. Ellis) the first weekend in June. But if you wait for Janet's reply, you may indeed live to a ripe old age and eventually die of natural causes ere you receive it. For, as far as I know, she has Ray DiGiuseppe, one of our Fellows here, working on the conference, and will do relatively little on it herself. Anyway, I shall send your death threat along to her and see if she decides to change her mind to drop you, Rufus, Mimi, and your long-dead mother a note.

As for the "Intimacy in Psychotherapy" symposium, I cannot hope to top Georgie Porgie in title-making, so how about something like "Intimacy, Schmintimacy: That Is the Question!" In case you and the APA committee on entitling talks raises questions about this lovely title (after all, I have nothing to lose but my solid reputation as a solid citizen of Psychology), you can consider another possible gem: "Does Intimacy, Like Virtue, Have Its Own Rewards?" Or, if you and the APA insist, you can put these two titles together and make one that is almost as long and as obnoxious as Georgie's.

That's all I can think of at the moment—for which you can thank the Lord!

Love,
Albert Ellis, Title-Maker Extraordinary and
Court Jester to King George the Abominable

August 7, 1983

Dear Al,

First of all, my present wife, whose name slips me, did not take kindly to being twice referred to as "Fran" in your last letter. When I explained briefly the nature of Alzheimer's disease to her, however, her rage subsided.

I shall try nobly to read the Ellis masterpiece in a quivering falsetto if necessary. Knowing, though, your tendency to frighten everyone to be on time, I suspect you will be there waiting for the rest of us. The rest of us, incidentally, may be you, me, Mimi, and Len Allen, for the APA program committee (no doubt, because they particularly hate you) have put Fred Skinner in an invited address at the same time as yours.

We'll have to do a catch as catch can social hour for the

three of us (four, if Fran shows up unexpectedly) in a post-speech planning. You may be pleased to note that I have cut my introduction of you down to 40 minutes, so you can read your speech at a slower clip.

Love,
Subgutagarter

August 18, 1983

Dear Bob,

Your hypothesis about my mistaking Mimi for Fran is a pretty good one. An alternate hypothesis is that I do not yet have Alzheimer's disease but other forms of senility.

Another hypothesis which I would beg both of you to consider is that I have always known that Mimi was much too good for you and therefore cannot accept the fact that you are actually married to her these days instead of to Fran. We won't say much about whether or not Fran is too good for you too.

Still another hypothesis is that I am still incestuously attached to my mother who was blue-eyed and blond and built much more like Mimi than like Fran and that therefore I cannot tolerate the fact that you are married to Mimi and wish you to go back to the great life you did not have with Fran.

I could think of other hypotheses but why bother? I look forward to seeing you and Mimi, not to mention Fran, briefly in Anaheim!

Love,
Al

June 17, 1987

Hi,

How about the four of us having an early dinner on Sunday, August 30, after the symposium? I could tell you were absolutely panting to have us take you, so I've once again demonstrated my great compassion. We can visit with our countless fans after the symposium, but let's not take them the fuck along for dinner. I don't mind the cost, but it changes the nature of the interaction. (Or are both you and Janet afraid of what people will think? Or possibly they might not *love* you?)

Love,
Bob

June 23, 1987

Dear Bob:

In response to your letter of June 17, I cannot quite understand why you are not giving me a full hour for my presentation and cutting the other panelists down to about 5 minutes apiece. Obviously, what they have to say will not compare to the glorious things I have to say, so it would only be fair if I monopolized all the time. However, since you take a slightly different view of this, I shall manage somehow to keep my presentation to 15 minutes.

Yes, Janet and I are panting for you and Mimi to take us to dinner again and Sunday August 30 immediately after our symposium would be as good a time as any. We will all somehow have to break ourselves from our millions of admirers after the symposium and that will be enormously difficult. But I have been working on my love slobbism for the last 40 years now and have it in reasonably good shape. What you and Mimi and Janet are able to do about *your* love slobbism still remains to be seen. But you'll probably all survive and be somewhat content with the mutual admiration society that the four of us will establish at dinner.

We are probably going to arrange a Saturday night party at the Institute for some distinguished APA members. If you strongly beg us to do so, we may somehow include you and Mimi in that gathering.

Love,
Albert Ellis, PhD
Executive Director

The Strange Case of Lyle Stuart

At various times, Lyle Stuart has been both one of my greatest helpers and one of my main lying detractors. I met him in 1956 and knew him to the present when Paul Krassner, who was working for his remarkably open-minded magazine the *Independent*, read some of my books he was remaindering, recommended them highly, and Lyle agreed. I soon began to write a monthly column for the *Independent*, which Lyle turned into one of my most popular books, *Sex without Guilt*.

Typically, although Lyle disliked some of my views on adultery and some of my down-to-earth language, he solidly backed me and began publishing many of my early works—particularly *The Art and Science of Love* (1960), which sold a million copies and gave me enough money to put a down payment of $200,000 as a donation to the Albert Ellis Institute.

Great, but Lyle also a little underhandedly got his employee Terry Garrity to take much material from my sex books and then published Terry's *The Sensuous Woman*, which sold many more millions of copies than my book and for which Terry sued Lyle for rewriting my material. Not so great!

For years Lyle was my publisher and best defender. I could never have built the Albert Ellis Institute without his help. I also donated money to him to help his near-bankruptcy when he supposedly slandered a gambling mogul and was sued. After he finally won this suit, established his publishing empire, and sold it for eight million dollars, Lyle was more solidly friendly than ever. My book *How to Stubbornly Refuse to Make Yourself Miserable about Anything—Yes, Anything!* was one of his publishing house's greatest assets. His new venture, Barricade Books, also published some of my recent books, such as my book on addiction with Emmett Velten.

Suddenly, things changed in 2004. Lyle's son, Rory, was part of the trouble between the members of the Albert Ellis Institute's board of trustees and me, and he and Lyle chose to believe the lies about me and my wife and partner, Debbie Joffe Ellis, that all but two of the board members were spreading. How this paragon of free speech could have gullibly believed these lies, I know not. But Lyle did and, in 2006 he became president of the AEI, replacing his son, Rory, who had replaced me after I had been unethically kicked off the board. (I was reinstated to the board by Judge Lehrer, who called the behavior of the institute in removing me disingenuous.) Regardless, Lyle told me that I would not be allowed to vote at board meetings, and that even if I did, I was in the minority on issues.

With his new power, Lyle first pretended to help me with my long-discussed Settlement Agreement with the institute, but then, for no good stated reason, became venomously opposed to me and Debbie and completely stopped the agreement. He joined other board members and officers of the institute in making up huge lies about me and Debbie and worsened my big fight with the institute. At times he was threatening: telling Debbie that she should influence me into signing the settlement he proposed (which I found unacceptable) or that the institute would counter-sue me and that I would have to go to deposition after deposition, and that it would wear me down, and I just would not be able to take it. Another time he told me that I should know that legally the institute was not obliged to let me continue to live on the sixth floor of the institute's building. Again, incredible!—as my supporters clearly saw. I took his words quite seriously. Debbie and I even talked about living in Australia if we were kicked out of the sixth floor, which had been my home for all these years.

At present, my case against the institute is stalled, and Debbie and I—against all American Civil Liberties rulings—are captives of the dictates of the institute, with no release date in sight. Practically everyone outside and some people connected to the institute clearly see this. But not Lyle!

How do I react to all this perfidy? I still factually see Lyle as the instigator of hateful—very hateful—actions, but I do not hate *him* as a person, and I am still grateful for all the constructive things he has done for me in the past. I don't understand his dramatic turnaround—though he has a history of other outbursts in the past—but I don't hate him, his wife, Carole, or his son, Rory, for their strange doings. REBT's philosophy regarding the removal of Debbie and me says that Lyle is not loathsome but that some of his acts are. But he is still a *forgiveable person*. I still remember my sending him a donation to ward off his bankruptcy for honestly publishing a book against a Phoenix mogul and I remember his writing me about a letter by the famous writer Dalton Trumbo to his son, in which, as Trumbo's son points out, his father says that my book *Sex without Guilt* is written "by a man who will take his place in history as the greatest humanitarian since Mahatma Gandhi—Albert Ellis, PhD." Yes, Lyle has treated me most contradictorily, but I still feel some great friendship for him.

Edward Sagarin (pseudonym Donald Webster Cory)

I had not heard of Edward Sagarin until he sent me a copy of his book *The Homosexual in America* in the 1950s. I immediately saw that although he was a stout defender of gay people's rights, he was also one of the few gay people I knew who fully accepted the fact that gays had their disturbances and that these disturbances often led them to be gay. Ed was also unusual in that he had a good supporting marriage, a son he cared for, and was an expert on perfume on which he had written a fine book.

I quickly became very friendly with Ed; we started a research study on homosexuality, and he sent me a number of gay clients. I didn't try to change them to be straight, but I did help them with their basic disturbances.

I wrote the foreword to Ed's book *The Homosexual in America* and collaborated with him in many ways. Eventually, he gave up the perfume business, got a degree in sociology, and was on the faculty of the City College of New York for a number of years.

Ed Sagarin was one of the sanest individuals I ever met, although he was sexually promiscuous and took too many risks. But he was unusually hardheaded, courageous, and close to my own psychological views.

He collaborated with me on my books, particularly *Nymphomania*, and defended me on many of my views. As I recall, he was the one who got me elected as an honorary member of the pioneering Mattachine Society, because of my liberal views on homosexuality. I addressed many of their meetings and became an important part of the early gay liberation movement.

All told, Ed Sagarin was one of the very best influences on me and supported me fully. I could well use help like his today!

Paul Meehl

Paul Meehl, one of the foremost scientists and psychologists of the twentieth century, practiced REBT together with some psychoanalysis in the 1950s and was a very good friend of mine (along with the famous philosopher Herbert Feigl) for many years. Paul particularly helped me to see that schizophrenia was importantly biological. He was another good example of coping with catastrophes, since he was sorely afflicted with physical problems for the last several years of his life, but he carried on his researching and other activities beautifully. Although treated very badly by one of his wives and not agreeing with his client, Saul Bellow, about her, he referred Bellow to me and I saw him for several months when he was in New York. Paul gave a talk on "Religion and the Maintenance of the Heart," which I thought included less bullshit than any other paper I can ever recall reading on similar subjects.

Paul was a prime contributor to scientific clinical psychology for many years and inspired me to see it as a science as well as an art. I did my best to follow his example.

Aaron T. Beck

The most unusual collaboration of my life has been with Aaron Tim Beck. I didn't *think* that I was collaborating with him on REBT and Cognitive Therapy. I thought that I had solely originated REBT in January 1955, especially in my book *How to Live with a Neurotic*, published in 1957.

I sent Tim Beck *How to Live with a Neurotic* when it was published, but I later discovered that he had written a paper on therapy and depression and that he was sort of claiming to originate Cognitive Therapy (CT) along with Cognitive Behavioral Therapy (CBT) at that time. That was news to me!

Actually, Tim Beck had *hinted* at the crucial role of thinking and depression in his first major paper on that subject, which was published in the *Archives of Psychiatry* in 1963. When I read it, I immediately endorsed it as a fine effort to establish CT. But it would have been miraculous if Tim Beck had not been aware of my *How to Live with a Neurotic* (1957) and *Reason and Emotion in Psychotherapy* (1962). In fact, he was working with Larry Treaker in 1960, and Larry was well aware of my early statements on REBT in 1956 and 1957.

I soon had a very cordial relationship with Tim Beck and was invited to present REBT to the department of psychiatry at the University of Pennsylvania. Some of our differences are mainly stylistic. As I showed Tim in a 1979 letter, we both directly teach people the ABC's of their disturbances, but then REBTers *actively and directively* dispute clients' Irrational Beliefs (IBs) while Beck's cognitive therapists do so more indirectly and slowly.

Also, Beck's daughter Judith, his main teacher and helper, came out in 1995 with her book on cognitive therapies, in which she accurately incorporated some of my emotional-evocative methods in her book—which I then approved of distinctly.

More recently, I, along with Tim Beck and Christine Padesky, have written about the similarities and differences between REBT and CBT. We partly agree that REBT stresses philosophy along with psychotherapy—particularly emphasizing Unconditional Self-Acceptance (USA), Unconditional Other-Acceptance (UOA), and Unconditional Life-Acceptance (ULA). Of course, Cognitive Therapy often does use these basic philosophies, too.

All told, both REBT and CBT can be done pretty much the same way, but I contend that if they include the specific, forceful teaching of USA, UOA, and ULA, therapists will achieve significantly better results. This has still to be shown with controlled experiment research.

In my disagreements with the Albert Ellis Institute, Tim Beck has been one of my major supporters, along with Judith Beck, Christine Padesky, Steven Hayes, and other leading CBTers. That's fine cooperation. William Glasser (choice therapy) has also been supportive of me.

A few of the typical friendly letters exchanged between Tim Beck and me follow:

October 18, 1965

Dear Dr. Ellis:

I just finished reading a review of your book *Reason and Emotion in Psychotherapy* in *Contemporary Psychology*. I was delighted to see that after such a long delay, the editors took cognizance of the importance of your work and gave it the kind of review that it deserves. On looking over your book again, I had some thoughts I would like to share with you. I think you have done a splendid job in delineating the moralizing and catastrophizing that patients do. For example, "I made a mistake and that's awful," or, "If I got hurt, that would be terrible."

I have found that you can carry the self-statements one step further in order to clarify *why* these things are horrible. The patient who pronounces bad judgment on himself for making a mistake, etc., says to himself "this is terrible because it shows how inadequate I am. I will go through life making one mistake after another, and will always be unhappy because of them." The mother who is upset over her child telling a lie thinks "this is terrible because it means he'll always be a liar. When he grows up, I will be disgraced by this. People will say, what an awful mother he has." The person who thinks that it is terrible to be rejected has thoughts such as, "This proves I'm unlovable. Nobody will ever like me. I will always be a social outcast, and will feel alone and deserted."

The point of this is that it seems to help the patient if he can recognize why a particular event is "horrible." The event or experience is classified as terrible because the patient makes a *prediction* of the dire consequences of this particular experience. This prediction then leads to his feeling helpless, trapped, hopeless, or frustrated.

I am currently completing a paper titled "The Cognitive Triad in Depression" and would like to have your comments when it is ready. I hope you will keep me posted on your latest work and ideas. With best personal regards, I am

Sincerely yours,
Aaron T. Beck, MD

October 29, 1965

Dear Dr. Beck:

Thank you for your comments on the moralizing and catastrophizing sentences I mention in *Reason and Emotion in Psychotherapy*. I entirely agree with you that what the patient is really telling himself is that the thing or the event in question is awful because it will lead him to have a very unhappy life in the future and that he is making a prediction. I don't recall exactly where I have written this up but somewhere I think I have stated that when the person thinks that he is no good or thinks that he is awful, he is usually saying several things, as follows: (a) I have never done anything well, (b) I am intrinsically the kind of a person who was born to do things badly, (c) I will always do badly in my performances, and (d) I deserve to be eternally punished for doing badly. Thus, he is making a prediction about the past in the sense that he is a kind of a mistake-making animal that he is because he was born this way and he is also making a dire prediction about the future—that he was always predestined to keep doing this kind of a bad performance.

The way perhaps, in which my formulation may differ slightly from yours is that I also include in it the idea that the individual may be punished by the powers that be for doing badly and that this idea of his perpetual self-punishment is also one of the reasons why he thinks that the situation he is in is horrible and hopeless.

I shall be most delighted to see your paper "The Cognitive Triad in Depression" and shall be glad to send you my comments on it. I shall also keep you informed of future works that we are doing here. I think that we sent you our latest bulletin of information, but just to make sure, I am enclosing one herewith. We are now actively engaged in giving courses and lectures in Rational-Emotive Psychotherapy here and one of these days if you are going to be conveniently in New York, we would certainly like to sponsor a lecture by you.

I am going to be in Phila. this coming weekend, talking on Sat. night at the Janus Society and Sun. morning at the Ethical Culture Society and Sun. afternoon under the auspices of the Penna. branch of the Institute for Rational Living and if I get a chance during my very busy schedule, which also includes a late Sat. night appearance on the Red Benson show, I shall try to speak with you.

Most cordial regards,
Albert Ellis, PhD
Executive Director

January 18, 1966

Dear Aaron:

Many thanks for sending me your paper "The Cognitive Triad in Depression." I think this is another one in your notable series of papers on the subject of depression and I certainly hope that you are thinking of gathering all this material and putting it together in a book since there is no good book on the subject that I know of that anywhere approaches the papers that you have been writing.

I think that the details you have gone into on the various kinds of thinking that lead to the different aspects of depression and also that differentiate it from anxiety states, paranoic states, and other forms of disorders are far and away superior to other materials that have been presented in the field and go beyond your original formulation. It is my feeling that as we get more closely to the actual sentences and beliefs that people have that distinguish their disturbances, we are really understanding what they feel as well as what they think, and that we are also lending clarity to ways of helping them improve, and I think that your attempts to go deeper and deeper into this area are most notable.

I can't see anything that I disagree with in the entire paper, otherwise I would be glad to present such differences to you. But you have covered almost everything I can think of in this particular aspect of your studies and there are no helpful suggestions that I can give you at the present time. If I think of any later I shall let you know about them.

Let me know exactly where this paper will be published when it is published and send me a reprint when it comes out since I want to quote it in detail in some of my own future writings.

Everything is going quite well with us. We have had our first semester of courses at the institute here and they have gone satisfactorily, especially our live demonstrations of Rational-Emotive Psychotherapy, which we give in our workshops every Friday night. If you are ever in this area, be sure to let me know, and I shall be glad to show you around the institute and show you some of the things we are doing. I've briefly been in Phila. in order to appear on a radio show and give another talk there a few weeks ago, but I literally had to race from the station to the meeting and then back to the train station since I was going to Montreal to next day, so I was not able to get in touch with you. If I am in Phila. for any longer stay, I shall be sure to call you.

Most cordial regards,
Albert Ellis, PhD
Executive Director

August 3, 1973

Dear Al:

I am currently involved in researching material for my new book on Cognitive Therapy, *Twisted Thinking: A Guide to the Emotional Disorders*. Consequently, I am writing to you at this time for a bibliography list on this topic and I would greatly appreciate a list of references. I am also in the process of checking publishers, and any suggestions you could offer in this area would be of tremendous help.

In the last few months I have often thought of your visit with us this last spring. Needless to say, the impact of your presentation was enormous, and I am looking forward to seeing you again this year.

I have enclosed a copy of the introduction and table of contents to my new book. Again, I would like to thank you for your help and interest.

Sincerely,
Tim
Aaron T. Beck, MD
Professor of Psychiatry

P.S. Could you send me a copy of the list of references you have been compiling on Cognition and Rational Therapies? Also, I would appreciate copies of your reprints of the last few years. Tim

---

August 7, 1973

Dear Tim:

Thank you for sending me a copy of the introduction and table of contents to your new book, *Twisted Thinking: A Guide to the Emotional Disorders.* I think that you are off to a great start, and it looks like the book will be a most valuable presentation and will go far beyond your classic work on depression. I would be glad to recommend a publisher for it, but am having some difficulties with publishers myself. They simply cannot be trusted to do much about the distribution of a good book, particularly a rational book. I am making sure in all my new contracts that I reserve the right to reprint paperback editions of my books through our institute here. Otherwise, publishers put out expensive editions and don't particularly push them. My experience with most of the publishers, mainly through having articles of mine published in regular anthologies, is that a firm like Holt, Rinehart and Winston seems to be a pretty good one for psychological and general distribution. However, it cannot be thoroughly trusted more than any of the other publishers can be. From my personal experience with Prentice-Hall, I certainly don't recommend them!

The long list of references that I have been compiling on cognitive and rational therapy approaches for the last couple of years is now fairly immense, but it is not in any typed form, but only on separate three-by-five slips. I hope to have a good deal of it typed up within the next few months for an article that I am doing on RET for the *Counseling Psychologist*. This will have a hundred or more references in it, in all probability. Meanwhile, I have mimeographed references to some of the main research studies on RET and related areas, and am enclosing this mimeographed list herewith. When I get anything more comprehensive in typed-up form, I shall certainly send it to you.

I am also having my office send you copies of my reprints of the past few years. Within the next few weeks I shall send you a copy of my new book on *Humanistic Psychotherapy: The Rational-Emotive Approach*. If there is anything else that you can use, don't hesitate to ask for it.

I, too, greatly enjoyed our contact last spring. I look forward to seeing you again in the not too distant future and certainly wish you the very best of luck with your new book on *Twisted Thinking*. Incidentally, I think that your title is an excellent one.

Cordial regards,
Al
Albert Ellis, PhD
Executive Director

May 22, 1978

Dear Al:

I appreciated your having written to Ruth Greenberg regarding my award from the Philadelphia Society of Clinical Psychologists. I was very flattered at receiving the award and I thought you might be interested in the "testimonial" presented by Erich Coche when I received the award. I am enclosing a copy for your interest.

I feel that we have not been in as close contact in recent years as I would like. A large part of this has been due to my being heavily overcommitted to various research and training programs. However, I do hope that we will have a chance to meet and chat before too long. Also, I would appreciate being placed back on your mailing list, so that I can keep abreast of your latest writings.

I have one other topic that I am sure would interest you. At the last meeting of the Association for the Advancement of Behavior Therapy, we organized a "special interest group" on Cognitive-Behavioral Therapy. Over a hundred people attended the organizational meeting. (We had not sent out any specific invitations but simply had made an announcement in the newsletter of the AABT.) The participants in the special interest group have expressed considerable interest in the similarities and dissimilarities in the approaches of the various people doing Cognitive-Behavioral Therapy. An informal program committee has suggested a topic at the next meeting of the group, which will be part of the program at the AABT. The suggested theme was Approaches to Cognitive-Behavioral Modification: Similarities and Differences. We thought that it would be good to have an exchange of ideas from people who are doing Rational Emotive Therapy, Cognitive Therapy, and cognitive behavioral modifications. We thought that it would be good to have a panel discussion led by Ellis, Beck, and Meichenbaum or their representatives. If this idea appeals to you, would you be willing to participate yourself or suggest some one of your people as a participant?

I am looking forward to our meeting again before too long.

With warm regards,
Sincerely,
Tim

May 30, 1978

Dear Tim:

I thought that the testimonial presented to you by Erich Coche was very appropriate and well deserved. I'm certainly happy that the Philadelphia Society of Clinical Psychologists saw fit to honor you in this manner.

Yes, I would be delighted to participate in a program on "Approaches to Cognitive-Behavioral Modification: Similarities and Differences" at the AABT convention in August. I'm scheduled to give a pre-convention institute on Thursday, November 16 and an address to the convention on Friday, November 17. If the meeting that you are proposing does not conflict with this, that would be fine.

I, too, am sorry that we have not been able to get together in recent years as much as we would have liked to do. I hope that we can have one of our old talks again in the not too distant future.

Cordial regards,
Albert Ellis, PhD

November 7, 1978

Dear Al:

I have returned from a trip to Israel and England and found that Cognitive Behavioral Therapy is growing strong among our overseas colleagues.

I am sorry about the long delay in responding to your letter of August 5, 1978, but I have been so far behind in my correspondence that I hope you will forgive me.

First, I want you to know how much I appreciated your having read the *Treatment Manual* and also your very kind comments about it. I have tried to rectify some of my references to RET in keeping with your letter.

Since the two paragraphs on p. 104 may be an incorrect view of RET, but one that is fairly widely held, I thought that it might be best to include as a footnote your response to these two paragraphs. I would, therefore, like your permission to cite your letter in the following footnote:

Footnote 1 (chapter 8, p. 104)

In a personal communication, Ellis states in reference to this section: "RET does NOT preclude getting what you call a 'solid data base' against which the patient's conclusions could be tested. Although RET therapists are not REQUIRED to do this as you seem to do it, they can easily CHOOSE to do so. In many instances, I would proceed almost exactly as your therapist did in the dialogue given in this section of the manual; in other instances, I might possibly proceed to discussing the patient's worth or her catastrophizing—and IN THE COURSE OF DOING SO derive the 'solid data base' information. In a few other cases, I might help her to fully accept herself or to stop catastrophizing without the data base information brought out in your instance—but with various other kinds of information brought out. RET does NOT have one special way of questioning and disputing."

We have decided that the best way to deal with your objection to the section on p. 187 would be simply to delete this so that we would not misrepresent your point of view.

I think it is reasonable that although we do share a great deal of common concepts and approaches, that we should differ in certain significant ways. In the past, I have been reluctant to dwell on these differences lest it produce some counterproductive divisiveness within our growing field. However, I do feel that right now there is enough solidarity so that we can stipulate the differences and perhaps come up with an empirical testing of some of them and, I hope, a new synthesis based on our shared clinical experience and empirical findings.

In this context, one of the problems that has troubled me in talking to and observing some of the RET therapists is that they are not very familiar with the research we have done on the psychology and psychopathology of depression and have not incorporated the specific methods that appear to be powerful instruments for effecting change (at least in controlled clinical trials). While this does not bother me personally, I certainly think it would help if we did have more sharing on this level. Perhaps we could talk about this more sometime in person.

Incidentally, I wanted you to know that I personally found the conference on "Reason in Cognitive Behavioral Modification" quite useful. I think our workshop went off quite well, and my various associates were quite pleased with the conference in general.

With best regards,
Sincerely,
Tim

January 2, 1979

Dear Tim:
    I've been very busy traveling around the country giving talks and workshops and therefore just got around to

answering your letter of November 7 during the present holiday season when I'm staying fairly close to New York. Yes, you can certainly place as a footnote in your book the personal communication from me that you quote in your letter of November 7.

I quite agree with you that although we both have the same basic cognitive and behavioral outlook, there are probably some stylistic and other differences in our methods that can be clearly stated and operationally defined and then put to empirical testing. The main difference that I can see offhand is that although you and your associates seem to jump in very rapidly with your depressed patients, to show them that they create their own disturbances and therefore have a good deal of control over uncreating them, and although you therefore show them as we do that A, the activating experiences do not directly create C, the emotional and behavioral consequences but that these are really directly created by B, their belief systems, you then go more cautiously and slowly about what we call D, or disputing. I personally go about disputing quite early in the game, even with some very depressed patients, and I am frequently very active about this. A good many other practitioners of RET, however, go about it much more slowly and in a rather Rogerian manner.

I quite agree that therapists who do RET and other forms of Cognitive Behavioral Therapy are often not aware of the research that you and your group have done on the psychology and psychopathology of depression and have not incorporated the specific methods that appear to be powerful instruments for effecting change in severely depressed individuals. I think it would be good if we talked sometime about how to spread the word on more of your findings in this regard.

I am glad that you found the conference on "Research and Cognitive Behavioral Modification" quite useful. We have only had good reports on the conference so far and therefore look forward to sponsoring it again in another couple of years or so.

If you are ever going to be in New York for a period of time, let me know and it would be good if we could get together again.

Cordial regards,
Albert Ellis, PhD

April 12, 1979

Dear Al:

I am enclosing a copy of an article including a review of the literature of studies designed to test the validity of the cognitive model of depression.

I would appreciate very much if you could give me your opinion as to the amount of support provided by these studies.

A number of writers have stated that there is little empirical support for this approach. Therefore, I would like very much to have your opinion.

Best regards,
Tim

May 16, 1979

Dear Tim:

Thank you for your letter of April 12 and for the article "Cognitive Approaches to Depression and Suicide." I have been exceptionally busy with out-of-town talks and workshops; hence this somewhat late reply.

You asked about my opinion as to the amount of support provided by the studies you cite in your article for the validity of the cognitive model of depression. My opinion is that these studies provide a good deal of empirical support for the cognitive model, though of course they do not provide incontrovertible evidence for it. But your hypotheses that depression is related (1) to a negative view of the self, (2) a negative view of experience, (3) a negative view of the future, (4) other negative consequences of a negative cognitive set, (5) the fact that a negative cognitive set can be rewarded, (6) that depression is correlated with a thinking disorder, (7) that depressogenic attitudes accompany depression, and (8) that Cognitive Therapy can help alleviate depression—all these hypotheses certainly seem to some extent borne out by the existing experimental and empirical evidence.

The points in your paper that I might quibble with in part include these:

1. "Situations that lower a person's self-esteem (such as failing an examination or being fired from a job) may precipitate a depression (p. 238). It is not the situations that lower a person's self-esteem, but his/her ATTITUDES TOWARD these situations.

2. "An individual may develop a depression when exposed to nonspecific stress of overwhelming proportion or a series of traumatic events (p. 239)." Again, it is not the events that are traumatic, but largely the individual's INTERPRETATONS ABOUT these events. You rightly, in the previous paragraph, speak about "the depression-prone person," and I think this is an accurate hypothesis. Such a person, I believe, is usually born with a strong tendency to depress himself or herself about "traumatic" events.

3. "It was anticipated that the death of a parent in childhood, because of the intensity and finality of the loss, might be expected to sensitize the child to regard future life deprivations and problems as irreversible and insoluble" (p. 252). This is one possibility; but the other is that the child is born with a distinct tendency to be oversensitive to frustrations and losses; uses this tendency to sensitize *itself* to the death of a parent (while other children do not); and also has a tendency to worry about future life deprivations and problems and see them as irreversible (even if it would *not* lose its parents). Studies like the Beck, Sethi, and Tuthill one usually forget, also, that there may well be distinct *reasons* why the parents of the depressed individuals died when they were young. For example, some of them may have committed suicide; others succumbed to alcohol; others were born with defective physiology, etc. These reasons may directly or indirectly provide the children with an *inherited* tendency toward emotional disturbance, in addition to the environmental fact that they suffered more deprivation than did children who did not lose their parents. Hence, the results of these studies are almost always contaminated by factors which are not always considered in the discussion of the study.

4. "It appeared that these data were consistent with the

concept that depressed patients may develop, as a result of traumatic life experiences, cognitive-affective patterns which, when activated, produce inappropriate or disproportionate reactions of deprivation and despair" (p. 252). For the reasons I gave in the previous paragraph, the phrase "as a result of traumatic life experiences" is probably too strong. They may develop these cognitive-affective patterns along with these experiences, but not directly "as a result" of them.

Other than the above comments, I still think that your article is a sound one and that it convincingly summarizes a good deal of relevant material supporting your hypotheses about depression. I would suspect that those who are not at all convinced by it have distinct prejudices of their own and are not too convinceable!

Cordial regards,
Al

June 29, 1990

Dear Al:

I was delighted to receive a copy of the book *Will the Real Albert Ellis Please Stand Up?* I very much enjoyed perusing it. It certainly is a great testimonial to your crucial contributions to the field as well as representing the affection that all of your former students and colleagues have for you.

I've been meaning for a long time to write a letter to you telling you how much I personally have appreciated your enormous contributions that have, in a major way, affected the course of my own professional career. You may recall that many long years ago when I was struggling with questions as to whether my own clinical observations and new theorizing had any validity, you contacted me and I was able to get some validation for my own new line of inquiry. Since that time, your own work has been a great influence on my thinking and my work. In the meantime I have gone into some related areas and I would hope to have a chance to discuss them with you (? at the Conference on Evolution of Psychotherapy in Anaheim). For example, we have carried out quite a few outcome studies using highly specific treatment manuals for depression, panic disorder, and drug abuse. Our theoretical formulations have extended to the concepts of cognitive vulnerability, cognitive specificity, and congruence between personality and stress in the precipitation of disorders. We also have prepared lists of the specific beliefs that seem to go with each of the disorders. Incidentally, your own postulations of the "irrational beliefs" did stimulate my thinking in terms of what I have labeled the "dysfunctional beliefs" that are idiosyncratic for each of the psychiatric disorders.

Now I have a request to make. On page 113 of the book, there is a splendid picture of you and me. I would love to have a copy of this that would be suitable for framing. I'd appreciate it very much if you could send that on to me.

Finally, I want to say how sorry I am that I've not been able to attend the various events honoring you. I've had considerable difficulty with a fragmented disc in my lumbar spine. This has made travel difficult for me and I've had to limit the number of trips that I can make. This is also the reason why I need to stay sitting when I give talks.

Thanks again for your inspiration and leadership.

Sincerely,
Tim

July 11, 1990

Dear Tim:

I am glad to know that you like the book, *Will the Real Albert Ellis Please Stand Up?* I want to thank you for your own significant contribution to it. We are now making a copy of the picture of you and me on page 113 and will send it to you soon. I agree with you that it is a splendid picture and am glad to have it in my own collection.

As you may have gathered by now, we had a fine thirty-fifth anniversary meeting of RET in Keystone, Colorado. I was delighted to get together again with many of the old RETers and to meet a good many new ones. It would have been great to have you there, but I can well understand your present limitations on travel. I myself have had something of a bad back for the past fifteen years and find that whenever I stand up even for an hour to give a talk I quickly develop pains in the small of my back. Like you, I therefore give practically all my talks and other presentations sitting down. If I sit up in my own reclining chair all day here seeing clients, I have no trouble. But as soon as I sit up in a regular straight chair for three or four hours in a row, I may tend to have difficulty. So I can well appreciate your having a fragmented disc in your lumbar spine and hope that it is possible that you will be able to do something about correcting this. In my own case, I find that light exercise is about the best I can do, but that it only helps my back somewhat and never quite cures it.

I well appreciate your recent studies using highly scientific treatment manuals for depression, panic disorder, drug abuse, and other specific neurotic disorders. I think that all your research in Cognitive Therapy has added appreciably to our understanding of many important problems in the field, and I was happy to see that the American Psychological Association finally gave you its Distinguished Award for Scientific Contributions to Psychology. You certainly well deserved it. Your contributions to Cognitive Therapy have been outstanding, and I, along with most of the other professionals in the field, have benefited immensely from them. No one has consistently done better research in the entire area of psychotherapy in recent years than you have done.

I hope to get back to you shortly with a copy of the photo. I shall indeed look forward to seeing you at the conference on the "Evolution of Psychotherapy" in Anaheim and will do my best to get together with you then to discuss some of your recent research.

Cordial regards,
Al

___

Arnold A. Lazarus

Arnold Lazarus has been one of my main supporters and collaborators since I first turned him on to REBT when he attended a workshop I gave in San Francisco in the late 1960s. Previously, and since that time, he is one of the most outstanding promulgators of behavior therapy— and, indeed, gave it (and Multimodal Therapy, which he developed) its name. But, peculiarly enough, recently, after writing a great chapter for one of my books on how therapists could achieve Unconditional Self-Acceptance (USA), he turned around and opposed their acquiring Unconditional Other-Acceptance (UOA).

Like Ray Corsini (mentioned later in this section), Arnie somewhat deifies *real* friendship and seems to have always resented my favoring and promoting him but not being, personally, *really* friendly to him. He may be right about this, since I never seem to have the time to be "really friendly" or personally very close to anyone except, in the past, to whomever my lover was, and now to my wife Debbie. I feel friendly toward my past lovers—such as I felt toward Karyl for more than sixty years after our intense love relationship ended—and I help them in various ways but do not regularly think and feel about them. I am *somewhat* close but not *very* friendly to them. Similarly, I have always favored most of Arnie's views and have defended him many times but have not been his *close friend*.

Today, I still like him more than I like other people and I still largely support him, but as I said before, I do not feel very *close* to him and still oppose some of his views. In turn, he often supports me but has not so far appeared to be a full supporter or backer in my disagreements with the Albert Ellis Institute.

Ted Crawford

Ted Crawford has been the most influential person who does not have professional affiliations—except in his collaborations with me. Ted got in touch with me after reading *How to Live with a Neurotic* (1957) and *A Guide to Rational Living* (1961) and (a little later) *Reason and Emotion in Psychotherapy* (1962). He was already well educated in psychology and psychotherapy, and my material quickly solidified his devotion to REBT. He always favorably contested its tenets and suggested changes and additions to them—many of which I have promptly adopted.

Ted is largely a relationship person—in his own life and in his philosophy. He had trouble with his main affairs and relationships, but he was rarely thrown by them and benefited immensely—and so did REBT—by his courageously dealing with his issues.

Ted particularly liked the anger-resisting philosophy of Marshall Rosenberg and made presentations on it. He incorporated this and other pro-relationship views in the articles and books he did with me—

particularly in our book *Making Intimate Connections*. Aside from his writings with me, he never became well known, but his thoughts and feelings on relationships helped a good many people.

I largely lost sight of Ted because of his physical issues. I learned a lot from him, for which I am grateful.

Ray Corsini

One of my closest psychologist friends, whom I met in the 1940s when both of us were fairly unknown, was Raymond Corsini. He later became the editor of the fabulous-selling *Currents in Contemporary Psychotherapy* and included a chapter on Rational Emotive Behavior Therapy.

Ray had a fascinating history as a psychologist, since he had first worked in prison psychology and then later became an Adlerian, but he also had therapy with Carl Rogers and adopted some of his main teachings. Still later, he formulated and promoted an unusual method of teaching schoolchildren some of the main elements of discipline and personality growth. I thought this method had some excellent points, but it never became as popular as Ray would have liked it to become. Some aspects of it were included by Bill Knaus and me when Rational Emotive Education (REE) was originated and we used it with children at the Living School from 1971 to 1975.

Although Ray, over the years, was one of my stalwart letter writers, he oddly enough did not think I was *friendly* enough with him, since we rarely saw each other. Like Arnold Lazarus, with whom I also exchanged many letters (and conducted many workshops), Ray was something of a *needer* of friendship and didn't think that I was personally "friendly" enough.

In turn, I thought he was one of my best friends and collaborators. Peculiarly enough, considering his unacademic achievements, he gathered a tremendous amount of knowledge that made him a great editor (of my work and others).

Among other things, I thought that Ray was *very* friendly in arranging for some women to go to bed with me (in Chicago and New York). But somehow he didn't *see* that as friendliness. Different concepts of "friend"!

Anyway, to this day Ray backs me in my disagreements with the Albert Ellis Institute, is very supportive of me and of Debbie, and for that and many other reasons, I still consider him one of my very "best friends."

Percival Symonds

A profound but somewhat peculiar influence in my life for many years was Percival Symonds, my main teacher and thesis adviser at Teachers College, Columbia University, during the 1940s and 1950s. Percival was a scholar of personality and published several influential and well-received books. But oddly enough, although he was a scientist, he was also a somewhat rigid Freudian. I saw this when I first studied with him in the 1950s, but I managed to cleverly ignore it and got in no overt differences with him about it. That was my wise decision! We were also collaborating members of the New York Society of Clinical Psychologists.

Percival supported the PhD thesis I was trying to do on the love emotions of college-level women until he went on a sabbatical to work for the US government in Washington for a couple of years. Then Goodwin Watson became my thesis adviser and helped me give up my topic for a less controversial one on personality tests when two bigoted professors strongly opposed my work on love. Percival supported me until his death in 1998 and didn't let our differences about psychoanalysis interfere with our friendship. Always a steady friend!

John Ciardi

When Twayne Publishers brought out my 1954 book, *The American Sexual Tragedy*, their executive editor was John Ciardi, an exceptionally fine editor, who was neither a therapist nor a political authority, but he made many corrections and additions to my book, which I thought were good and added considerably to it.

Thus, in December 1952, he noted, "I should like very much to see the anxiety-basis of jealousy more carefully examined." Also, "I especially see that the competition for mates in our society and the inferior position of unmarried women is an element that needs stronger pointing up."

In a February 18, 1953, letter, John wrote, "The fact worth mentioning is that *women are the human stars* when we see them with grown-up families." "We need to look at certain of the basic attitudes toward sex, love, and marriage formulated in the family." "What in our society makes it emotionally necessary for the man to be the provider and the girl the provided for?"

I agreed with and adapted many of these and other of John Ciardi's suggestions and thereby made him a prime collaborator of my sexual views. It was a pleasure working with John.

Richard Holbeck

A profound, though quiet, influence on me was Charles Richard Holbeck (currently known as Richard Huelsenbeck), one of the founders of the Karen Horney Institute. However, he was first an existentialist and a dadaist as well as a psychiatrist.

I found Holbeck in New York after he was recovering from an illness, and I selected him as an analyst in order to get accepted myself, later, as one. I was delighted to find that his personal library contained all kinds of books on existentialism.

My first session was notable because he asked me to free associate, and at the end of fifty minutes, he said, "My! You really *can* talk, can't you!" He indicated that I, unlike other clients, could *freely* associate. He largely listened to me for two years and made occasional existential and Horneyian remarks. He largely helped me understand *myself*. Then for two years he supervised my work with my clients. The Horney School did not at that time accredit psychologists, but he said that I was an (unorthodox) analyst, and I agreed.

Holbeck saw me through the end of my relationship with Gertrude and helped me sorrow over it without depressing myself. He thought she was quite erratic and that in some ways it was good I was rid of her. He also favored my PhD thesis topic on the love relations of college-level women and was glad that, under puritanical pressure to give it up, I changed it to a less controversial topic and got my PhD in 1947. I was friendly with him and his wife for several years after completing therapy but saw them only occasionally. Although I was something of a liberal existentialist before I saw him, I became more solidly so afterward.

LeMon Clark

LeMon Clark, MD, has been an outstanding liberal sexologist since the 1950s. He got the idea in 1953 of my doing a study of psychologists at the American Psychological Association Convention viewing color photos of nude and clothed women—all of whom were clients of LeMon's—and rating them for their sexual desirability. Our published study showed that the nude photos were considered more desirable even when they showed that the women had rather ugly scars. Among our psychologist subjects, nudity won out!

B. F. Skinner

The world-renowned psychologist B. F. Skinner was in many ways conservative. Skinner's *Walden Two* was revolutionary, as was his *Beyond Freedom and Dignity*. He was both a liberationist and a strong advocate of social discipline. Although Skinner was in some ways opposed to my brand of cognitive-behavior therapy, he was remarkably like me in that he ignored most criticism of his major views and courageously stood up against tremendous opposition. I therefore consider him something of a blood brother and am happy to use his reinforcement theory as a strong aspect of REBT.

Barbara Loden

Barbara Loden, one of the wives of the very famous Elia Kazan, was an unusual person who was first my client and later my friend. She was one of the loveliest people I ever met, physically and personally. She was often treated badly by her husband and others and at first seriously put herself down. With my help, she much more unconditionally accepted herself and used REBT to help her two children. She finally directed and wrote a film, *Wanda*, which the *New York Times* movie critic called "a small movie, fully aware of its limits, and within those limits lovely."

Barbara was not a professional, but she followed the progress of the Society for the Scientific Study of Sexuality and enthusiastically applauded it. Although she and her small film will not go down in history, she served as a fine example of what one can do when following the principles of REBT.

Artie Shaw

A famous jazz musician, Artie Shaw was a client of mine for several sessions and publicly said some nice things about me in an interview in *Penthouse* magazine in 1971. I appreciated his public support.

Saul Bellow

Saul Bellow, Pulitzer Prize–winning author (1975) and winner of the Nobel Prize in Literature (1976), was one of my most difficult clients when I tried to get him to be more rational about his ex-wife and some of his current associates; and I think I helped him get along with his future wife. But he strongly opposed some of my best rational arguments and said nothing good or bad about me—except that I farted too much during our sessions. He was right about that! He mentions me in his book *More Die of Heartbreak* (William Morrow & Company, New York, 1987), in which he writes: "Of course he had read classics like Forel and Havelock Ellis, Kinsey and the other sexual Ellis—Albert, the Thomas Paine of the sexual revolution—plus Masters and Johnson, and whatnot else."

Nelson Mallory

Nelson Mallory Jr. has been associated with the institute and has been a close friend of mine since the 1960s. He has run the Family Substance Service of Atlanta for many years, assisted me in many presentations, and written a book with me on sex and family relationships.

In his younger days, Nelson got into some legal trouble for his sex writings. But that did not stop me from taking one of his uncensored manuscripts, adding to it, and turning out a book I wrote with Nelson. This became one of my popular books.

Terry Garrity

Terry Garrity got together with Lyle Stuart and got temporary fame for her book *The Sensual Woman*, which she largely took from my sex books. She admitted this to me, was favorable to REBT, and went to bed with me once when Janet was not around. She was quite good in bed, and her book helped the popularity of using REBT with sex problems.

Roger Conway

Roger Conway, largely without my help, wrote a practical book, *On Sex and Love*, but got in trouble for it and for some of his practices. I thought his book had some excellent ideas; I rewrote it with more REBT in it, and it sold well as *Sex and the Liberated Man*. For many years, Roger was my supporter.

Arno Karlen

Arno Karlen, author of *Sexuality and Homosexuality: A New View*, got me to endorse it in 1971 by stating that it was "one of the most complete, objective scientific and many-sided works on homosexuality that I have ever read."

George Bach

I disagreed with George Bach, author of *The Intimate Enemy*, and thought he was irrational in his personal and professional life. His advice to people in relationships was likely to get them into *more* difficulties. But George was a risk taker and emotionalist and helped invent the forty-eight-hour intensive marathon. I took some of the best elements of his marathon and added some quite rational elements to it, including the Disputing of Irrational Beliefs. I gave marathons successfully for several years.

Gershon Legman

I was very friendly with the famous sexologist and writer Gershon Legman and endorsed his courageous book *Oragenitalism*. A most valiant promoter of banned sex material, Gershon helped influence me since the early 1970s.

Bernie Zilbergeld

Bernie Zilbergeld, world-famous author of *Male Sexuality* (and also of *The Shrinking of America*) was a very close friend of mine from the 1970s onward and visited me regularly. A fellow diabetic, we both did very well in dealing with our diabetes until Bernie finally died in 2002. He also was a remarkably good adoptive father to his girlfriend's child.

Al Goldstein

I personally helped Al Goldstein and *Screw* magazine and supported his free speech causes. He wrote me on July 19, 1973, "It has long been a joy to know you, be treated by you, and read your views in print."

Vincent Parr

Vincent Parr was an early devotee of REBT in the 1970s and was instrumental in inviting me, and in getting me kicked out of, the state of Arkansas by the notorious Governor Faubus. Fortunately, Faubus's reign came to an end, but Vince continued to sponsor me. He had been the director of the Albert Ellis Institute branch in Tampa, Florida, for twenty years and supports me in my fight with the AEI. In protest against the AEI, he was the first to secede his affiliated branch of the AEI in Tampa called Center for Rational Living. He is also, with Paul Kurtz (mentioned below), a leading humanist.

Paul Kurtz

When Paul Kurtz was a professor of philosophy at the University of Buffalo, he invited me to speak on REBT and has supported me ever since. He is a leading humanist and has sponsored several humanist manifestos. His papers and books on humanism are beautifully rational. He is the founder of the Center for Inquiry, publisher, and editor. He is one of my strongest supporters in my disagreements with the institute and a truly good friend.

Kishor M. Phadke

One of the most unusual influences on me and my work has been that of the psychologist Kishor M. Phadke, of Mumbai, India. An unassuming psychologist, he wrote me the first of a long series of letters on REBT on April 29, 1968, and continued writing me. He has also spread the word on REBT with several books in English and Marathi. He has always sought to understand the finer points of REBT and has always had his own followers and collaborators on REBT materials in Mumbai.

Kishor has collected all my letters to him on REBT and someday they may make a fascinating book. I would never have figured out some of the finer points of REBT without his detailed questioning, and I want to thank him for that. Although I only met him once on the visit to Mumbai he arranged for me, he has certainly been one of my finest friends and supporters since 1968. A long time!

Windy Dryden

A fairly early collaborator of mine was Windy Dryden of England. At first a counselor, he raised himself to become the first professor of counseling in the British Isles, partly by collaborating with me since the late 1970s on developing REBT. For many years, he was devoted to REBT and was a willing collaborator and promoter of its central philosophies. One of the best.

Then, to my great surprise, he took the side of the renegade people controlling the Albert Ellis Institute against me and my wife and partner, Debbie Joffe Ellis, and falsely accused her of running things on one occasion when my itching ears stopped me for twenty minutes in answering people's questions at a group therapy practicum. I *asked* Debbie to take over when my hearing got impaired, as I trust her excellent teaching ability, but Windy acted as if it was her *idea*. Anyway, Windy lied about Debbie's "taking over." I wrote him challenging his accusation but was not able to get him to retract it.

Assuming that Windy has sold out to the fake AEI, how do I feel about this? Very disappointed in what I see as his traitorism. But he still has many good traits and *partly* favors REBT. So I am sorry about his limitations, but I do my best to accept him with them. I shall still show people some of the "wrong" things he does without condemning *him* as a person. I was delighted with his being appointed the first full professor of counseling in Great Britain and predict that he will merit more honors and support.

Postscript: After I wrote this, Windy attended my Friday Night Workshop in the building next door, made faces at my counseling demonstration (this can be seen on a video that was filmed at that workshop), and said bad words about me in e-mails. Incredible how he could keep defiling me! But some people keep acting badly and like traitors when I have helped them enormously, people including Windy, Ray DiGiuseppe, Kristene Doyle, Michael Broder, Ann Vernon, Jim McMahon, and many more. Bad, but as REBT says, not horrible!

Michael J. Mahoney

I became a constructionist largely through the writings of Michael J. Mahoney and backed him when Northern Texas University summarily blocked his directing its department of psychology. Later on, he backed my serious disagreements with the fake Albert Ellis Institute. He is a brilliant psychologist and psychotherapist. You can learn much from reading him.

Michael Murphy

I was friendly with Michael Murphy, the head of Esalen Institute in Big Sur, California, did several popular workshops for him, and always admired his therapeutic open-mindedness.

Jack Gordon

Jack Gordon was not a professional but became fascinated with my writings in the 1960s and has been devoted to me and to REBT ever since. He had an important position in transportation in Great Britain but looked forward to returning to the United States and working with REBT. He retired, got professional training, collaborated with me on several papers, and also coauthored some good books with Windy Dryden. Along with Windy, he has probably been the prime promulgator of REBT in the British Isles. Up to the present time, he has thoroughly supported me in my disagreements with the fake Albert Ellis Institute. A real friend and helper!

James Bard

One of the early proponents of REBT was James Bard, PhD, who taught at Cleveland State University and had a practice with Harold Fisher in Cleveland. Jim and Hal led the Cleveland branch of the AEI and sponsored many presentations for me. Jim was always an original thinker, as was apparent in his book *I Don't Like Asparagus*, favoring Unconditional Self-Acceptance, which I thought was excellent.

Michael Bernard

Michael Bernard, PhD, achieved advanced fellowship in the AEI years ago and became devoted to REBT—especially to teaching it to children. He taught at the University of Melbourne, married an Australian woman, and had two children with her. When he was in Australia, he arranged two successful trips for me and managed them well.

Michael came back to the United States for several years and taught and practiced REBT in California. My talks with Michael here and in Australia were quite good, confirmed my REBT views, and were quite productive. I was on good terms with him until fairly recently when he decided to go back to Australia and teach there. He seems to have supported the people running the fake Albert Ellis Institute and has been ignoring me and not giving support to me. If he really is favoring the false AEI, I shall be very sorry about that, but, as usual, I will not upset myself. My work with him, including a book (recently revised) on REBT with children, is still satisfactory and has added to my and his influence.

Emmett Velten

I have been very friendly since 1969 with Emmett Velten, PhD, the author of a significant paper, "A Laboratory Task for Induction of Mood States"—the first to show how emotions are instigated by thoughts. Emmett has been one of my finest supporters over the years and as a member of the board of trustees of the Albert Ellis Institute, now keeps vigorously fighting for me, though earlier he believed the lies of the other board members opposed to me and Debbie. He is doing a biography of me, but it is taking quite a while!

Betty Dodson

Betty Dodson was the exceptionally sexually liberal author of *Liberating Masturbation* in the 1950s. It made her really famous, as did her liberal *Sex for One* in 1982. I helped her sell many copies of her books. She sent me a number of clients whom I helped with their sex problems. A thoroughly courageous woman who helped many people with her honest sex education groups.

Daniel Wiener

In the 1980s Daniel Wiener was a behavioral psychologist with some cognitive leanings who suggested that he do a biography of me. I was friendly with him and his wife, Phyllis, and visited them whenever I gave a workshop on REBT in Minneapolis.

I gave Dan much biographical material and had several long talks with him in New York. I thought it was a fairly good job but hardly ideal. It later got pretty good reviews.

When, in the 1990s, Emmett Velten started writing my biography, I was much more enthusiastic about his knowing me better than Dan

Wiener and being more accurate. Alas, he got sidetracked in doing other things and to this day hasn't finished the biography.

Jack Trimpey

Jack Trimpey was mainly an REBT practitioner and did remarkably good work with addictive and other clients in the 1980s. We were very friendly, and in a September 27, 1984, letter he wrote that REBT "has reinvented the mainstream of my professional armament to the benefit of thousands of my clients. It can be applied to virtually any human problem (that doesn't require surgery). I wish you many more years at the old stead. I salute you."

Very nice, indeed. But a couple of years later, Jack discovered Addiction Voice Recognition, a new technique for use with addicts that supposedly was miraculous and brief. He then kept insulting me, as well as most other addiction therapists, in a violent manner. Whether he is still at his vitriolic attacks, I know not. But I hope he uses REBT to calm himself down.

Jimmy Walter

For years, Jimmy was a great supporter of the institute and its mission, and he donated large sums of money to it, until the trouble started. For a while after that time, he helped me with some of my medical expenses after the institute stopped paying them but he could not continue doing so.

He visited New York for about a week in 2005 and spent hours daily standing on Park Avenue (Manhattan's millionaire residential area), near the institute, with a placard naming those he thought the worst of the perpetrators of the injustices—Broder, McMahon, and Doyle. He was filmed doing so by documentary makers, and this act may have had some media coverage.

It took guts and great conviction.

David Burns

David Burns, MD, a psychiatrist and professor famous for his book *Feeling Good*, has been very friendly to me since the 1980s and has promoted REBT when he was in Philadelphia and now on the West Coast. In turn, I have pushed *Feeling Good* and his forthcoming book, *When Panic Attacks*. He is supportive of me in the current situation with the institute.

Jon Carlson

Jon is an honored psychologist, professor, author, and editor. He conducted video interviews with me, and we have spoken on panels together. He was a most considerate host to me at the ACA Living Legends event in 2004 at which I was honored. He is a thoroughly kind and caring person, strongly supportive of me.

Jeffrey K. Zeig

Jeff Zeig is the founder and director of the Milton H. Erickson Foundation. A psychologist, author, editor, teacher and trainer of hypnosis, he regularly runs fine conferences, including the Evolution of Psychotherapy conference and the Brief Therapy conference at which I have given many presentations since 1985. He went out of his way to make it possible for me to attend the December 2005 Evolution of Psychotherapy conference in Anaheim, California, assisting Debbie and me with all of our needs—including bringing along two nurses to help with my medical issues. He did not succumb to the warning in a letter from the AEI that they would take legal action if he allowed me to speak and make any defamatory remarks in the state-of-the-art address I was scheduled to give. He acted with courage and integrity, defending my freedom to express. He supports me and my cause.

Martin Seligman

I was cited as a genius, along with Aaron Beck, in Martin Seligman's immensely popular *Learned Optimism*. He was president of the American Psychological Association in 1998. He supported me in disagreements with the fake Albert Ellis Institute. He also adapted some of my educational material for children.

William Glasser

William Glasser's choice theory came out in 1965—ten years after my introducing REBT—and includes some aspects of REBT. Despite our disagreeing with certain aspects of each other's theories, we have a very friendly and respectful relationship, and he supports me and my cause.

Frank Farley

Frank Farley is a former APA president, who from the 1990s organized panels and conversation hours in which I spoke at annual APA conventions. A professor at Temple University, he regularly brings his doctoral student classes from Philadelphia to hear me speak about REBT and my life, and then they attend my famous Friday Night Workshops.

Debbie Joffe Ellis

I have already written a little about my wife Debbie and our relationship, but I want to add more in this section on important influences in my life.

Debbie has had the most profound and positive influence in my life. With her I have experienced and received a depth of love, practically impossible to describe, that I would not have previously imagined possible.

She has inspired me in a number of areas of my work including REBT and Buddhism, love, kindness, and compassion. In addition to our great partnership in which we give presentations together, we have cowritten articles and the forthcoming monograph on REBT for the American Psychological Association. She is passionate about REBT, is an outstanding therapist and teacher, does a marvelous job in our writing projects, and is mindful about applying REBT principles in her life.

After my demise I trust her to have a prominent role in continuing my legacy of REBT.

Foreign REBT Affiliates

I have always seen REBT as American—and as non-American. Preferably, it should be promoted to clients, therapists, book readers, and others all over the world, especially if they hear about it and want more information. I have therefore widely communicated with North and South Americans, Africans, Europeans, Australians, Asians, and even Arctic residents about REBT and how to present it. In turn, their questions and comments have led to my revising and adding to REBT in principle and practice.

As I have noted before, my foreign correspondence has been extensive and interesting—particularly with K. M. Phadke, Jack Gordon, Jack Kokubu, Windy Dryden, Stephen Palmer, Lucien Auger, and many others. Some of them, like Phadke, have been *too* inquisitive and, for lack of more time, I have cut them back. But they have also led me to revise REBT and improve it, for which I am grateful.

Whenever possible, I have traveled many miles to give workshops in other countries. Thus, I spent five days in Kuwait in 1983, giving workshops on the management of stress. I also supervised the taped sessions of several of Tony Kidman's clients in Australia.

I particularly enjoyed two trips to give presentations in Japan, arranged by Yasutaka (Jack) Kokubu. He and his wife, Hisako, visited me in New York. In May 1989, he wrote, as the first translator of my books in Japan, "I love to procreate my understanding of REBT. I will be another Ellis in Japan." He was responsible for getting me many devoted followers there.

I also enjoyed several visits to Germany, particularly when Ursula and Horst Zimmerman were running our affiliate there. I wrote them on July 5, 1983: "It was great seeing both of you and observing how well you handled everything at the workshops in Mainz."

Stanley Krippner, PhD, psychology professor, writer, researcher, and a fellow humanist, invited me in the early 2000s to present with him in Mexico and at a European humanistic psychology conference.

The Summer Fellowship Program

In the 1980s, we added to our Fellowship Training Program the Summer Program, where we gave about twelve people a four-week scholarship and let them also participate in our Fellowship Practicum programs. We usually selected experienced therapists, often from abroad, to be in the program. It has gone very successfully since the 1980s, the participants seem to benefit considerably from it, and many of them have gone on to become fine advocates of REBT.

My Reaction to People Who Have Plagiarized My Work and Not Given Me Due Credit

Almost every month, people write to me and tell me that they are shocked to see how my work has been plagiarized without giving me due credit. The worst example is probably Wayne Dyer's *Your Erroneous Zones*, which sold millions of copies in the United States and many other countries and brought a huge fortune to Dyer. How did I, and how do I still, react to Dyer's using of my work? Here is part of my letter of September 1985, in which I wrote to him about it.

September 30, 1985

Dear Wayne:

Thank you for your letter of August 21 and for your latest book, *Gifts from Eykis*. I found it a remarkably good book and will comment on it in more detail below. I also want to thank you for referring several clients, over the last few years, to our institute. I saw a couple of them myself; and our other therapists, I think, saw some, too.

You say that over the years you have heard that I have directed disparaging remarks about you and your work. This is partly true, but I have always said that *Your Erroneous Zones* is a good book, that it has helped a great number of people, and that it outlines some of the main principles of RET quite well, and with great simplicity and clarity. I have personally spoken with about a hundred people who have benefited from it—several of whom came to RET through tracking down some of its sources—and only a few have spoken of it negatively (usually saying that it is too simplistic). So, although I naturally have some reservations about it, I like *Your Erroneous Zones* and think that it has considerably aided the cause of rationality here and abroad.

My disparaging remarks have been about your behavior, which seems to be quite unprofessional and unethical, in not mentioning rational-emotive therapy in any way in the book—when obviously you would never have written it without a good deal of contact with my writings on RET, especially with *A New Guide to Rational Living*. As far as my knowledge goes, you were partly turned on to RET by John Vriend, who in turn was a close friend of one of our early trainees at the institute (a student of Jon Geis); and in the late 60s or early 70s people kept telling me that you kept teaching aspects of RET when you were at St. John's. Then, around 1975 or 1976, you attended one of the workshops I gave on RET in groups at a Long Island hospital (was it Northshore?) and volunteered to be a member of my demonstration group. I could see, by the way you acted in the group, that you obviously knew RET quite well—and were using it very effectively. So I knew, when your book appeared in 1976 that it was based on RET right down the line; and since it has appeared, about 300 or more people have voluntarily told

[TEXT MISSING FROM LETTER] simplified form. When I finally read *Your Erroneous Zones* (about a year after it appeared) I could see that they were right and that it clearly was derived from RET—and not, as a defensive reviewer for *Contemporary Psychology* later tried to claim, from other writings.

So when people ask me, as they still often do, about *Your Erroneous Zones*, I tell them that the book is fine but that the author is still, to my mind, unethical in not mentioning its main source and not giving due credit to RET. This kind of significant oversight on your part, incidentally, is hardly atypical: since a large number of other authors have extensively used RET material and have given me and RET no credit whatever. To make matters worse, a number of highly reputable professional writers—notably Aaron Beck, Donald Meichenbaum, and Arnold Lazarus and Marvin Goldfried—at first gave due credit to RET for some of their formulations, but being rather ego-aggrandizing (as most humans are) and wanting to claim originality that they did not quite possess, they now often fail to cite the original RET sources of their ideas and pretend that they were completely original. Even Maxie Maultsby, who directly studied RET with me in 1968, now writes and talks as if his direct derivative of it, Rational Behavior Therapy (RBT), is entirely his own creation. This just seems to show more of the irrationality that you have Eykis say about humans in *Gifts from Eykis*.

Should I give a shit about this kind of gentle or outright plagiarism? For practical purposes, I'd better, since it deprives RET and our institute of very substantial backing. As a result of your failing to mention RET in your writings, for example, we have lost a great deal of mass support that otherwise, presumably, would have been ours—and would have been damned nice to have! Ironically—and sadly!—your writings and public presentations have not only "stolen" some large potential support for RET, but have even interfered with my own ability to spread it. Thus, when I now attempt to write a popular book on RET and present the ideas to mass publishers (including your own), they tend to look askance and say, "There's nothing new here. This has already been said—and widely sold—in other books. So why should we publish your new book?" This, to some extent, is of course only to be expected, but it still hurts—financially, I mean. Not me, personally, since for almost twenty years virtually all my income, from clients, writings, talks, workshops, etc., has gone directly to our nonprofit institute; and I literally get by, these days, on my social security and on income from money saved many years ago, when I was in private practice. But as a result of your, along with many other writers and public presenters, failing to give due credit to RET, the institute has lost, and still continues to lose, a very large amount of money that otherwise it would amass; and its work in spreading RET, both to professionals and to the public at large, is unfortunately restricted. This—as you might expect a true RETer to say—is hardly terrible and awful; and it doesn't mean that the ego-oriented individuals who fail to acknowledge RET's "legitimate" status are shits. But it is a royal pain in the ass, and I am naturally hardly deliriously happy about it.

The answer to your implied question about my hostility toward you was perhaps best given in a paper I wrote in 1978, "Why I Do Not Hate Wayne Dyer." One of my clients, who was connected with the *New York Times* and who was somewhat incensed about *Your Erroneous Zones* taking in so much money while the institute had its usual financial problems (since running a training program for RET practitioners loses rather than makes money), suggested that I write a piece for the op-ed page of the *Times* explaining why I was *not* very angry at you. He at first could not understand why I was not, and was intrigued by my answer, and thought that I should publish it. So I wrote the enclosed brief essay, "Why I Do Not Hate Wayne Dyer," and submitted it to the *Times*. For various reasons—including, probably, the fact that the *Times* has opposed my sexual writings for many years and has always taken a dim view of my objections to their censorship of ads for these writings—this great newspaper refused to publish my essay. So I have not done anything else with it, and it remains unpublished. But it does show, I think, how I used RET on myself to forestall my being really hostile to you, and, as far as I can see, it worked very well. I still very much dislike some of your *behavior* in not publically acknowledging RET's contribution to your work, but I really have no resentment against *you*. If anything, most of your major ideas—especially those in *Your Erroneous Zones* and *Gifts from Eykis*—overlap notably with many of my own; and if my ideas are really good and beneficial for humankind, then it really does not matter whether I or RET get credit for them. As long as they work, fine! And the more people who effectively promote them, as you have often done, the better! A hundred and more years from now, if RET continues to be useful (as I fondly think that it will), its main contemporary promulgators, including you, me, Aaron Beck, and others, will largely be forgotten by name. So be it. It is the philosophy of sensible living that counts—and hardly the names of the people who promote it. . . .

Enough for now: Since my passion for spreading RET drives me back to my work here at the institute. Once again, many thanks for sending *Gifts from Eykis*. It definitely surpasses all your previous writings that I am aware of. I wish you the very best of luck with it and hope that in its paperback edition it will turn on many more people to rationality. Even if it still sadly neglects RET!

Cordial regards,
Albert Ellis, PhD
Executive Director

Werner Erhard, the creator of EST, also lifted much of my early writings without giving me due credit. He came to visit me in April 1973 after he had become world-famous.

National and International Therapy Conferences

Because I have been a member or fellow of a number of national and international associations—such as the American Psychological Association, the American Association of Sex Education and Therapy, and the World Institute for Mental Health—I have presented papers and invited addresses in many cities all over the world. This involved much travel and constant meetings of important people in the professional field.

I have also been a speaker at the large Evolution of Psychotherapy conference every five years, ably run by Jeffrey K. Zeig and the Milton H. Erickson Foundation, as previously mentioned. These conferences have enabled me to interact with scores of well-known therapists and thousands of practitioners from many countries. At the 2005 conference, for example, I gave a state-of-the-art presentation of Rational Emotive Behavior Therapy and eight other presentations—all of which received standing ovations from thousands of attendees. While the bogus Albert Ellis Institute in New York was calling me "feeble," "over the hill," and "too old," I displayed constant vigor and hard-headed assertiveness for a real triumph.

My experiences with national and international therapy conferences have helped broaden my outlook and brought me widespread interaction with other professionals.

The Training Practice of REBT

I began to do one-day to five-day training practica in REBT in 1956, and the Albert Ellis Institute became registered as a New York State training facility in 1965. It has now sponsored scores of trainings all over the world and has presented about a thousand practica on three levels: (1) its primary practica for new students; (2) its advanced and associate practica; and (3) practica for those who have passed the other levels.

I can say that this training program has been a great success, since over 100,000 psychologists, social workers, and other therapists have graduated from it and most of them have continued to practice REBT since 1965. Fine! But one fly in the ointment has been that since 2005, after banning me from teaching in these and all institute programs, the bogus Albert Ellis Institute has run its own training practica and has "trained" participants in *partial* aspects of REBT but not in the full philosophical aspects of Unconditional Self-Acceptance (USA), Unconditional Other-Acceptance (UOA), and Unconditional Life-Acceptance (ULA). A tragic oversight!

Other People's Books and Articles

Writers constantly send me copies of their latest books and articles, hoping that I will endorse them and increase their sales or constructively criticize them. I frequently endorse them and make, I think, helpful comments. This aids the writers, but it also, of course, publicizes me.

I am sometimes accused of being too kind to others' writings, but actually I refuse to endorse most of them, and some of the comments I submit are negative. For example, I liked Julian Simon's *Unhappiness and Depression* but wrote him that he confused some useful and nonuseful ways of expressing himself. On the other hand, I had no reservations about Michael Mahoney's *Scientist as Subject* and wrote him,

"You have done a beautiful job of exposing some of the fallibilities of scientists, and I certainly hope that the book has a very wide and influential readership." It didn't have a wide and influential readership, but it did significantly influence me.

My endorsements of books were usually moderate. Here, however, is an immoderate one for a 1989 book by Hank Robb. "I thought your book was excellently done, and there was virtually nothing I could criticize about it. This is a rare statement for me to make about any book on REBT."

I also turned down Don Mullins, one of our own therapists, when he was enthusiastic about the book *Victory over Diabetes*, which seemed to be full of bunk to me.

INSTITUTE MATTERS

One of my most serious objections to the doings of the branch institutes of the Albert Ellis Institute was the case of Kurt Konnetan. In 1968, he directed the Philadelphia branch of the institute and did so nicely. But in the next year I heard that he was allowing untrained people to supervise some of the trainings of the branch and that he and his associates were teaching these trainees a number of non-REBT methods. I wrote Kurt about this, and after a while he stopped directing the Philadelphia branch of the Albert Ellis Institute and formed his own group of practitioners, which he was entitled to do.

Similarly, I now fight the bogus Albert Ellis Institute, which has taken over the training facilities of the real institute and has watered down some of the main principles and practices of the institute I established. The fight goes on!

Incidentally, a supporter recently asked me what I thought about changing the name of REBT to CEBT (*Cognitive* Emotive Behavior Therapy). My answer—NO. I want it to remain *Rational Emotive Behavior Therapy*.

Favoring Unpopular Causes

I favor a good many unpopular causes—such as gay marriage and the upholding of civil rights—and get vituperative letters for doing so. My views on homosexuality have aroused great ire from some of my readers. When I first noted that gay people were not wicked or abnormal but that a good many of them had emotional problems, I was severely castigated by many readers. But when, in *Sex and the Liberated Man* (1976), I changed my views and said that one did not *have* to be disturbed to be gay, scores of straight people wrote to tell me what a lowlife I was.

Similarly, when I defended Dr. Jack Kevorkian's espousal of assisted suicide, my mail became heavy with accusations of how anti-humanist I was. It seems to me I said that advocates of assisted suicide were usually quite humanistic, since they allowed would-be suiciders the *choice* of staying alive or not.

My stand against the bombing of birth control clinics—which I thought was quite anti-humanistic—again made me a target for many hostile letters.

Of course I wasn't surprised at these negative letters, because I thought, "That's what happens when you take risks—and that's what *should* happen, because many opponents *can't stand* your opposition. Too bad—let them eat their guts out!"

So, to this day, I often defend abortionists, those who assist in suicide, and many other courageous minorities. How can one fight for "good" causes that are unpopular? One had better take the *risk* of doing so. Sometimes, supporters of these unpopular causes win—as when the United States Supreme Court upheld the rights of women to get legal abortions. But even then, I continue to fight against the taking away of women's rights on abortion. I enjoy this kind of fighting.

I also favored and disfavored many viewpoints on psychology. For example, when Ray Corsini tried to stop the giving of diplomas in psychology of those who wanted to establish diplomas in psychoanalysis, I strongly backed him up. I agreed with Ray that some psychoanalysts covered wide and conflicting areas and that most of them were really eclectic. If a diploma is offered in psychoanalysis, then it should also be offered in REBT, Reichian therapy, and other therapies, and, of course, this is not the case. Ray's and my protests went unheeded.

Sometimes, I clearly favored or disfavored the goings-on regarding affiliates and their promotions. For example, although I trained Maxie Maultsby Jr. in REBT and favored his work in many ways, I also was skeptical of the ways in which he pushed ART, the Association of Rational Thinkers, which educates people in REBT. So, I wrote a letter in July 1976 to a critic of Maxie's addiction program wherein I said, "I may well disagree with some of his views on alcoholism, but we manage to live fairly well in peace."

When Samuel Roth was charged in 1957 with "obscenity" in publishing *Ulysses* and other books, and even went to jail for doing so, I heartily backed him—sometimes in vain.

I also supported and wrote in favor of a good many other censored works, including Maxine Sanini's *Housewife's Handbook on Selective Promiscuity* and my own *Case for Sexual Liberty*. I defended Brian Boylan's *Infidelity*, Shere Hite's liberal books on women's orgasm, Nena and George O'Neill's *Open Marriage*, and many other sexually liberal works. When we held a free-for-all sex affair—with no publicity!—at my home in the Albert Ellis Institute building in the 1970s, George was an active participant, but Nena sat in another room and was prudishly afraid to participate. Consistently enough, she later renounced their *Open Marriage* book.

In a triumph for the opposing side, Joseph Brill and I were at first banned from testifying in a New York Supreme Court case to prevent nudist magazines in public newsstands. Then when we appealed the case, the US Supreme Court in a landmark decision freely allowed public display of nudist magazines. A grand decision that I enthusiastically welcomed!

The Training of Individual REBT Practitioners

In addition to training many therapists in REBT in our practica and conferences, I and others at my institute also had more thoroughly trained, for a year or two, continuing education sessions with other practitioners. This works well but is often a losing battle financially, because we have to supervise therapists a few times each week, pay their supervisors, and have the institute charge only small fees for the supervisees' sessions with clients. We make up this loss in some other ways, but supervision of individual REBT practitioners is financially hazardous though worth its effectiveness. As mentioned below, since 2005 I have been stopped from giving any part of the trainings—with no written or spoken explanation given to me of specific complaints or reasons.

Rational Emotive Education

My goal from the start, with my clients and with those who attend our presentations, has been to spread REBT to the masses. Accordingly, we conduct many lectures, public workshops, and other public teachings. My Friday Night Workshops, given regularly since 1965, have demonstrated the most important cognitive, emotional, and behavioral aspects of REBT to about a million participants. In 2004, the former governor of Texas, Ann Richards, came to one of my Friday Night Workshops with her daughter. After the workshop, they came up to my apartment and visited with me and Debbie, and we had a great time. Ann Richards said she greatly enjoyed the Friday Night Workshop, laughed a great deal, and said it was the best and least expensive night out in New York City! We all seemed to share many views and got on very well. Worldwide REBT lectures, workshops, and audio-visual materials have introduced REBT to millions of more students.

In 2005, the institute stopped me from giving my Friday Night Workshops and any additional presentations in the institute building. To this day, they have not given reasons for the banning—in writing or otherwise. Debbie and I now rent a large room in the building next door and continue to give the Friday Night Workshops to standing-room-only crowds.

Bill Knaus and I promoted Rational Emotive Education (REE) in many ways since the 1970s and have trained other practitioners and educators to follow our lead. Debbie promoted REE very effectively in her native Australia during the time she worked there and will resume doing so here in the United States and overseas, as time allows. We're still going strong in 2006. Our goal is a little unreachable, but still real—to ultimately see that REBT is taught to every adult, child, and adolescent in the world. Some goal!—but we keep plugging away at it!

Humor

As a budding young philosopher at the age of fifteen, I took the Buddhists and the Stoics seriously, but not *too* seriously. I realized that we humans frequently awfulized about bad events and that we had better view them as *moderately* bad and invariably mixed in with good things. So I saw my early health problems as partly good (they gave me time for more reading) and very interesting; that is, I learned how to cope with difficulties. I rarely depressed myself about my neglectful parents, my physical disabilities, and my sports deficiencies. Bad, yes, but hardly *awful*. When they made me lose out on success, they hardly killed me.

As I developed REBT, I deliberately took a humorous view of things and taught it to my friends and collaborators. Here is a letter I wrote to the director of Jamaica Hospital in New York that shows how I used humor to prevent myself from feeling enraged about a very bad situation. It even includes a song!

August 20, 1974

Dear Dr. Marion:

I was greatly surprised the other day to receive from the Jamaica Hospital a bill for an emergency room fee of twenty dollars. This represents a charge for a service that I never really received and that I think your hospital is exceptionally delinquent about not giving me. And now this bill . . . !

If you will listen to the events that befell me on the Fourth of July of this year, I think that you, too, may well be shocked—and may even wonder why I have not yet attempted to sue your hospital for medical malpractice. At 9:10 that morning, while checking in for a 10:00 a.m. plane to Paris (where I was scheduled to give a talk and chair a panel at the First International Congress on Medical Sexology), I noticed that my insulin was missing from my luggage. Since it was a holiday, I soon discovered, too, that no drugstores at the airport would open until 11:00 a.m. and that almost all pharmacies in Queens were completely closed.

What to do—when I knew it would be dangerous for me to be without insulin (which, as a diabetic, I have taken regularly for the last twenty years) for even a single day? I decided to rush to Jamaica Hospital in a cab, get some insulin there, and rush back to the airport in time for my plane (which, at this heavily booked time of year, was the only one that would get me to Paris on time for my presentations).

After rushing like hell, I reached your hospital at 9:20 a.m., told everyone I met there that I needed insulin very quickly—and, in spite of my predicament, was put through an incredible amount of needless red tape. Now, insulin, as you doubtless know, is a nonprescription drug, as easily available as aspirin at every pharmacy in the United States. But *your* pharmacist, although I clearly explained to him my *immediate* need, insisted that I get a regular prescription from one of your emergency room physicians. Why? "Hospital regulations!"

Since I was given no choice, I ran to the emergency room (a good distance away) and went through more red tape to get a prescription for NPH U-100 insulin. Back to the pharmacy— again on the run! The time: 9:30 a.m.

Your pharmacy did not have U-100 insulin in stock but did have NPH U-80. Since I had been using this formula up to a few days previously and had just switched to the newly available NPH U-100, I explained this to the pharmacist and said I would take U-80—and be off to the airport. Oh, no! The pharmacist, who could have easily changed the prescription from U-100 to U-80, insisted that I return to the emergency room for a completely *new* prescription! Let me remind you, again: *all* insulin, in these United States, *is a nonprescription drug*. And I was about to miss a plane for Paris!

No sane argument prevailed. I had to rush back to the emergency room, wait idly for several minutes, interrupt a physician attending an injured child, get an entirely *new* prescription (when the physician, again, could have easily and quite legitimately changed U-100 to U-80), and go through various other kinds of rigamarole! Then I had to race back to the pharmacy with this new prescription. Nine-forty a.m.!

Everything was now in order—except that the pharmacist (a new man who seemed to have just gone on duty) insisted, in spite of my story about having to get out of there immediately to catch a plane, that I would have to wait my regular turn to have this prescription made up. (Insulin is *not* made up but is universally sold in its original box, with no patient's name or specific label on it!) How long would my turn take? "At least twenty minutes."

It was then, as noted above, nine-forty a.m. Kennedy Airport was about ten minutes (by my waiting taxi) away.

Naturally, I left Jamaica Hospital with no insulin. I made my plane with seven minutes to spare. Since I did not arrive in Paris until ten p.m. European time, I could not get any insulin that night, in spite of my racing all over Paris in taxis in a vain effort to get it. It was not until the next day that I was able to get any—after having been without it for about twenty-six hours.

I think it important that you know about this series of delinquencies on the part of your personnel and that you consider immediately changing your pharmacy rules to eliminate the use of the emergency room for non-clinic and non-hospitalized patients requiring nonprescription drugs—particularly on a Sunday or holiday when other drugstores are closed. Cases like mine admittedly happen seldom. But if I had had a severe headache and needed aspirin, I would also have been in trouble. For even had I had sufficient time to wait for it, I would have been required to pay for the aspirin (fair enough, of course) and also pay an emergency room fee of twenty dollars—such as the fee you have just billed me for. Being a professional in the field of mental health, I could easily afford this. But suppose I were a poor or lower-middle-class person. Twenty dollars and fifty cents for aspirin! Or twenty-two dollars for insulin! To pay for the red tape of Jamaica Hospital!

Let me not belabor this point. If you insist that I pay the emergency room fee of twenty dollars for the *dis*service I received on July Fourth, I shall certainly, though under protest, do so. The main point of this letter is: What are you going to do about your general rule requiring non-clinic and non-hospitalized patients to waste their and your personnel's time being processed through your emergency room before they can obtain nonprescription drugs? I await your answer with real interest.

Let me conclude on a less grim note. Instead of incensing myself about your hospital rules, as I easily could, I practice on myself the kind of rational-emotive therapy that I use with and teach to others. I thereby make myself highly displeased at the behavior exhibited toward me by your staff, but unangry at and nondamning of these people for their behavior. As I do this, my sense of humor comes back into play, and I am able to summarize the dismal incident I encountered at your hospital with this lyric (set to the tune of "Yankee Doodle Dandy"):

Insulin's a simple drug,
Filled without prescription.
You can get it by the jug
With no real conniption!

From every drugstore you have been
You can quickly take a
Quart or more of insulin—
Except red-taped Jamaica!

Again, I await your answer with real interest.

Sincerely yours,
Albert Ellis, PhD, Executive Director
Institute for Advanced Study in Rational Psychotherapy

In February 1958, when REBT was in its infancy, I wrote many humorous letters to my collaborator Bob Harper—which encouraged him to be lighthearted with me. Some of them are included earlier. We thought of eventually collecting our letters but never did so. Here is a typical letter that I wrote to Bob on February 28, 1958:

Dear Bob:

Yes, it looks like the P.O. has Petered (no pun intended) Out on those books. Rhoda (whom you may remember) was supposed to go see them sixteen weeks ago to get a tracer form, so that I could officially ask them where the fuck they are hiding the stuff. Eventually—say, 1968—she will probably pick it up. Meanwhile, leave us not worry about the lost books. One of these years, if they don't show up, you, I, or Emily Mudd will pick up an old copy of Ansbacher and Kelly, which we shall then gleefully share on a fuck and fuck alike communal marital basis. Or maybe you and Emily would prefer to share your communal copy without my horning in on such a glorious relationship. OK, sold: she's all yours. Never mind the change.

Rhoda and I are absolutely desolate over the grim prospect of missing your speech on "A Humanistic Value System for Marriage Counselors." Only our good common sense, our unwillingness to pay for Rhoda's fare, and our determination to drown our sorrows in bed prevent us from recanting on our oh-so difficult decision. But being grimly rational, recant we shall not.

Since my faith in the postal service has been multiply jolted of late (especially when the *Times* recently informed me that I shall soon be spending a nickel for the "privilege" of completing your education by mail), I am suspecting the worst and sending Frannie a duplicate bonus under separate cover. If this gets waylaid, too, my paranoia shall not have been avouched in vain.

Twice blessingly,
Al

Bob and I chaired a "Humor in Psychotherapy" presentation at the American Psychological Association convention in September 1976. Since I started to write song lyrics in 1928 when I was fifteen, by 1976 I had quite a few of them. So I picked what I thought was the best of the lot and recorded them on a cassette tape. I started to play this tape at the APA convention when—lo and behold—the recorder didn't work. Nothing daunted, I began to sing my humorous songs a cappella—in my "terrible" baritone. Luckily, the audience loved them and applauded loudly.

Since that time, I have often used my rational humorous songs with my clients and with professional audiences—and they are quite appreciated. A few of my songs are in my book *The Myth of Self-Esteem*, and I have included some of my favorites in chapter 4B of this book.

Devising Cartoons

Although I am poor at drawing, I have tried several times to devise and draw cartoons. I enjoy the cartoons featured in the *New Yorker* because they usually highlight delightful ironies. I particularly enjoyed the cartoon of two fierce bears who had tied up John Bradshaw and were saying, "He says he's John Bradshaw and is the head of white supremacy." The other says, "I think we should eat him." Just retribution!

For a time, I sent many of my cartoons to the *New Yorker*. No go! Their editor didn't have my sense of humor. The best of the lot showed two men kneeling down and holding a football for a kickoff. But instead of the football sailing in the wind, one of the men's heads was gaily flying through the air. The caption was "Oops—sorry!"

After a while, I stopped submitting my "great" cartoons. But thinking of devising them helped me see some of the great irony in life—which I enjoyed seeing and which helped me to be more realistic.

Music and Composers

My mother told me that I constantly sang the popular songs of the day when I was two years of age. I also remember, at the age of two and a half, being with my relatives in Philadelphia and being enrapt by a Victrola playing classical music and singing along with it, to the delight of my family.

I continued to sing and enjoy music all my life. My mother was a good singer, and I learned many popular songs from listening to her, one of my favorites being "A Bird in a Gilded Cage." I particularly enjoyed the musical comedy *Queen High*, on Broadway, which I saw with my mother when I was thirteen. *Queen High* turned me on to musical comedy and to the great composer of the 1920s, Rudolf Friml.

His *Firefly, Rose Marie, The Vagabond King,* and *The Three Muske-teers* were steadily sung at the vaudeville recitals at the Paradise Theater in the Bronx, only a stone's throw from where I lived.

I soon became an authority on the songs of Friml, Sigmund Romberg, Victor Herbert, and other composers of musicals. If one were sung or played, I could immediately recite the name of the song, the name of the operetta from which it came, the name of the composer, and the year of its composition. For example, "This song is 'The Indian Love Call' from *Rose Marie,* by Rudolf Friml, composed in 1923." I rarely missed, and I sang scores of these songs to myself—and sometimes to others—just about every day. Later on, I endlessly composed the words and music of my own songs.

This music, plus the symphonies and sonatas of the great composers—Beethoven, Chopin, Handel, and so on—highlighted my life and made me often think of how tragic it was that I never learned to play an instrument or write music. There is nothing I would have enjoyed doing more. I almost taught myself to do so a few times but unfortunately stopped. No, if I had not stopped, I might not have been another Beethoven, but I might have been a Rudolf Friml or Victor Herbert. I regret that I wasn't.

Anyway, music added immeasurably to my life, especially when I was poor and my writings were unpublished. I not only whistled hundreds of compositions but also harmonized to them and creatively jazzed them up—which again I taught myself how to do—and still often do. When I composed songs with other people, however, I always picked partners who could write down the music.

Radio and TV Shows

I started to do important radio and TV shows in the 1940s, before I started promulgating REBT. I was quite popular and had plenty to do, since I was active in the fields of sex liberalism, mental health, and other popular and unpopular causes. I appeared regularly on late-night radio, such as the famous *John Nebel Show,* and got in active conversations with audience members. Sometimes prominent psychiatrists and celebrities, such as comedians Anne Meara and Jerry Stiller, were part of the show and talked with me. I even did live therapy sessions by showing people how they upset themselves and how they could stop doing so. Many of them wrote me after the show, indicating how much they benefited from my brief conversation with them.

I was a guest on many New York and nonlocal TV shows, on various networks including ABC, NBC, CBS, and CNN news as well as early morning shows and a Chicago roundtable discussion. I appeared on late-night shows with famous hosts, and I participated on out-of-town shows in person or by phone. I never became a Jack Benny or a Dick Cavett, but I enjoyed the shows and being able to get my social messages to many grateful people.

I also enjoyed teasing some of the hosts. I appeared on the *Dick Cavett Show* in July 1965. Cavett proposed that I would talk only about mental health problems, but he fooled me and implied that REBT mainly said that gay people were healthier than straight ones. I made him look foolish about this, and he never invited me again. I later discovered he was probably gay. Oh, well. I remember being interviewed nicely by Barbara Walters.

On the *Merv Griffin Show*, I appeared with four comedians, and when I helped make one of them—a woman—look foolish for being against premarital sex, they cut my humorous attack from the tape of the show. Prejudice!

Several popular hosts, such Oprah Winfrey, gave me an appointment and, at the last minute, found out how liberal and anti-prudish I was and canceled my appearance. As usual, I stubbornly refused to upset myself.

In 1977, I appeared on the *Phil Donahue Show*. I debated with Margaret Mead, the liberal anthropologist, on a popular radio show. She stoutly said she would not allow her teenage daughter to use contraception. She didn't see that she thereby restricted her daughter's rights. On another show a prominent woman writer solidly opposed premarital sex—but came to the studio with her lover, which I pointed out!

I appeared on many more shows, but I can't remember the names of all of them. My radio and TV appearances were usually very lively and continue to be so. I don't go out of town anymore but do many shows over the phone. I received many letters and calls of appreciation following a fairly recent interview on National Public Radio.

Late in 2005, the Gold Anniversary edition of *Variety* magazine named me as one of the "Top 100 Icons of the Century."

Research Studies

When I formulated REBT, I intended to have it scientifically researched to determine whether its main tenets helped people get better results than people using other forms of cognitive-behavior therapy. Alas for my intentions!

Although hundreds of controlled studies of REBT have been done, the majority of them have been sloppy and therefore inconclusive. They indicate that, yes, REBT studies show effectiveness—often more than studies of other therapies—but still much better studies had better be done. Ah, but as yet only relatively few excellent studies have been done.

When I got after our research people to do more precise studies, they agreed with me, but they still didn't do them. Only recently were there some indications that such studies are being attended to. This, of course, is not merely the deficiency of REBT but of the whole field of psychotherapy. Thousands of controlled studies have been done but few conclusive ones. Take the studies of Aaron Beck and his affiliates, in which they seemingly showed that Cognitive Therapy (CT) works better than other therapeutic modes. They really only indicate that subjects *report* that changing their thinking leads them to make emotional and behavioral changes. Did conscious cognitive changes truly affect their unconscious thinking, feeling, and behaving? Perhaps—but who really knows? Definitive, sure-fire studies have yet to be done.

All I can say is that there is a good deal of evidence that REBT, as well as other cognitive behavior modes of therapy, often seems to work effectively. But hardly *always* with *all* subjects. Much progress, but no certainty! Considerably more research is required to substantiate my hypotheses. Back to the drawing board!

Supporters

Bill Knaus, Gayle Rosellini, and Will Ross have worked for my cause, and others in addition to those mentioned in earlier chapters have expressed support for me in my quest to be reinstated in the institute and in my fight for justice. Debbie Steinberg is lodging ethical complaints, and Jim Byrne and John Minor have written much in support of me. Some of the supporters I know, some I don't. Many of them are people I have helped considerably with their personal and professional lives. I greatly appreciate the efforts of all who want to help.

Will there be justice? Will I win back control of my institute? When I am no longer here, who will continue to be supportive of REBT and of my wife Debbie Joffe Ellis as she ably continues my work?

{}

Note: Dr. Ellis had intended to include in this chapter a section on each of the following people, but sadly he died before he could complete these sections. These are people he had contact with over the years, some of whom he jousted with privately and publicly. In all probability there were additional names he was going to include.

Albert Bandura, Rudolf Dreikurs, Hans Eysenck, Bob and Mary Goulding, Alfred Kinsey, Paul Krassner, Rollo May, Donald Meichenbaum, Fritz Perls, Irv and Miriam Polster, Wardell Pomeroy, Carl Rogers, Virginia Satir, Thomas Szasz, Joseph Wolpe

Chapter 10

My Relationships

Apart from my relationships with Karyl and Gertrude (mentioned in chapters 6 and 8, respectively), there were a number of women with whom I enjoyed sex and/or loving relationships. To be precise, from 1918 (age five), I enjoyed a total of fifty-three affairs, some serious, some casual.

Here are my recollections about just some of these relationships.

CINDY

I met Cindy, a very attractive blue-eyed blonde, at St. James Park in the Bronx, where we enjoyed several petting sessions—in the cold!—in the park because she didn't want to meet my mother, with whom I was living on University Avenue. Cindy was a teacher, quite bright and sexy, and our relationship was marvelous!—but nothing deep. After not seeing her for a while, she showed up, without notice, to visit me when I moved to 70 Park Avenue. Unfortunately, she had been hospitalized for bipolar manic-depression. I saw her a couple of times—and enjoyed great sex with her—but then she disappeared, possibly to be permanently hospitalized. A real loss to society—and to me.

DELPHI

Delphi was a bright, thin woman, married, and with two children. I saw her first as a client, and three years after we finished our sessions—with Delphi much less depressed—she wanted to have an affair, and we did. Unfortunately, I, like her husband, was too excited by her to slow down my orgasm, and so she became hostile. She broke off with me and told a few of her lovers that I was no good sexually. I was sorry, but felt: good riddance!

MRS. SHERMAN

Mrs. Sherman was my very attractive, well-built math teacher in high school when I was fifteen. She favored me because of my math ability, and I favored her because of her looks. I had many fantasized affairs with her, solving different math problems while we were screwing, but I never actually spoke with her privately. Marvelous fantasizing for a couple of years!

MONA

Mona was a beautiful, petite woman whom I had to keep putting off when I saw her professionally for manic-depression. After she stopped being a client and was distinctly improved, I still put off her advances for two and a half years. When we finally went to bed, I enjoyed her immensely and laughed with real glee. To my surprise, she said, "You're laughing at me. You think I'm no good in bed!" That was the end of our relationship.

SELMA

Selma was the Queen of the May in my college. A small but very attractive blonde with whom all the males were in love. She was friendly and seemed to like me, but at that time I was too shy to try to date her. So we got nowhere but remained mild friends.

JOSIE

Josie was fifteen and I was fifteen one summer in Wildwood, New Jersey. She was a tomboy and consequently quite honest. She was tall and slim, not a conventional beauty. We were very friendly because I was not shy with her, but I never made any passes—which I think she wanted me to do. We consequently were only friends, and both of us probably missed a great opportunity for some sex experimentation. She lived in Philly and I never even wrote her.

PAM

Pam was sixteen, John Gatto's daughter, and helped give us kids newspapers to sell. Something of a tomboy, but tall and very attractive. She was buddy-buddy with us boys, but never intimate and no dating. So I merely lusted after her for a couple of summers and never really talked with her. Another miss!

NETTIE

Nettie was drawn to me when we were twenty-four, soon after I broke with Karyl. She wasn't bright or informed, but I put up with her for several months because she was free with sex. Unfortunately, she wanted me to last longer than I did when she was my only sex partner, and I thought of more attractive women when I had sex with her. She became nagging, and I left.

RENA

I met Rena in 1947, when I was thirty-four. Our relationship lasted on and off for about a year. We never had intercourse during that period, because I was not assertive enough and she was prudish. She eventually moved to China and converted to Buddhism.

ELIZABETH

My relationship with Elizabeth lasted from 1948 to 1949. She was a nurse whom I met at Greystone Park. Although she had a fiancé, she was very sexy and easy with sex. She finally married her fiancé.

VANETTA

I met Vanetta in the early 1950s through Nelson Mallary, an Atlanta sexologist. At twenty-seven, she was tall, had a perfect slim but well-rounded body, and beautiful breasts

We first met at Nelson's whorehouse-decorated apartment, red lamps and all, and when I entered, she was already stretched out naked on his king-size bed.

What a sight. Lucidly white skin wrapped around a gorgeous torso, topped with jet black hair down to the small of her back. And bright blue eyes! I don't recall when I ever got my clothes off so fast. Excited as I was by Vanetta's looks and her receptivity, I came in, at most, twenty seconds.

I soon discovered, however, the somewhat shocking truth: she actually had semi-anesthetic nerve endings in her hauntingly beautiful skin. My caresses gave her only mild sensual and no sexual pleasure. Her vaginal lining, like most women's, was quite insensitive. Much worse, her vulva was also impervious to sexual and sensual stimulation. Only her clitoris seemed somewhat normal, but its nerve endings seemed to be hidden deeply under its skin, and only by strong direct stimulation on its small area could she ever come to orgasm. Even then, her orgasms were damned few.

I spent an unusual night with Vanetta and broke my record by having four orgasms in five hours. I enjoyed being with her, talking to her, and caressing her incredibly smooth, practically perfect body. But I was much less enthusiastic about spending hours of massaging her small, and largely nonfunctioning, clitoral region. It seemed to be so ungrateful!

So my sex life with Vanetta soon ended, though our friendship continued for several years later. When she was in her thirties, she got a fatal disease and died. A real loss for me and the world. Though I often thought of her sexually—particularly of her near-perfect body—it was my sensuality rather than my sexuality that was truly aroused—and my sense of esthetic appreciation.

JO

Jo, a social worker, and I enjoyed a relationship from 1953 to 1954. She was a beautiful blonde and at one point a Kinsey subject. We had great sex and great conversation, but she broke up with me to marry Mel Roman. Sadly, Jo committed suicide upon discovering that she had cancer years later.

CAROL

Dancer and mother of one child. Did work for me. Quite bright. Left to marry a boyfriend.

MAGDA

1963. Very bright psychologist. Mild petting. Became, hypocritically, a feeling therapist.

SANDY

1964. Married to a psychic screwball, one child. Small blonde, very sexy. Wrote part of *How to Live with a Neurotic Child*.

MARY

1969. Programmer. Very bright and crazy. Fine sex.

DRINA

1972. Psychologist, one son. Tall and thin. Sang my songs. Neurotic. Sex continued when she married and went to California, where I sometimes saw her.

RUTH

1977. Social worker. Married. Bright and ambitious. Very sexy.

BETTY

1978. Married, two children. Unusually sexy.

ANN

1979. Psychologist with boyfriend. Very enthusiastic. Good sex out of town.

VERA

2001. Housewife and mother. Occasionally came to New York and had sex—which was good.

JANET WOLFE

I met Janet at a party late in 1964 after John Wilcock introduced us. He had written an excellent review of my *Guide to Rational Living* for the *Village Voice*, and she had read the book and had been favorably impressed.

She was very good sexually, had lots of sex experiences, and had a fine body and reasonably attractive face. We dated every Saturday night, and since we were both poor, she would cook me dinner in her apartment, and I would pay if we ate out.

In June 1965, Janet got depressed and lonely, and I agreed that she could live with me. She was very nice and grateful, and for two months I fell in love with her. I soon fell out of love, but continued liking her for several reasons: (1) The sex was great. (2) She was quite loving. (3) She began to work well at managing the Albert Ellis Institute.

She had a long history of criticizing her female assistants and that culminated in 2000 with her fighting with our associate director, Catherine, and our assistant director, Kristene. Catherine was very lax and Kristine acted as if she was devoted to her. Janet almost got rid of Catherine—who totally cheated the institute, but Kristene—alas!—stayed.

After many years, Janet fought with the board over retiring as institute executive director and acted disturbingly with the members. I supported her, especially financially, because of her long years of service to the institute. She finally won and left the institute to practice REBT on her own and did well at it.

I generally got along with Janet—especially sexually—and we had an amicable relationship. But every three months or so, she would blame me for everything I did and refuse to talk to me for several days. I once got fed up with this treatment and planned on moving. Fortunately, her oldest friend, Jill, talked her out of her antagonism and we remained together until 2001.

My sex drive with Janet waned after twenty-five years of being together. As usual, I therefore thought of other women while having sex with her. No big deal!

Janet's sex interest in me waned after thirty-two years, and for the last five years of our relationship we had sex only sporadically. For the last four years, it practically stopped. But I enjoyed our professional partnership and didn't think of leaving her.

During our last two years together, in 2000 and 2001, things were amicably dull between us.

Janet decided, in 2002, to live by herself. I firmly supported her, and with my help, everything worked out peacefully and we remained friends—but not close ones.

I do want to say that Janet was a mainstay of the Albert Ellis Institute—a real helpmate. In fact, because I chose to do many other things than direct it—such as see innumerable clients, supervise interns and fellows, train outside practitioners of REBT, give talks and workshops, and write books and articles on REBT—I gave important administrative functions to her. She started as the office manager, was for many years the institute's associate executive director and then its executive director. She actually did more administrative work than I and was very capable in that respect.

Over the years, she left me free to do my thing over a long period of time. Without her backing, I would have still been a prodigious worker—but perhaps a less content one if I had had to do the administrative tasks that she did. For that I want to thank her sincerely.

DEBBIE JOFFE ELLIS

I first met Debbie Joffe in her native Australia during one of my teaching trips in the late 1980s. She was very taken with me and REBT. She was in her early thirties, younger than I, and an extremely attractive blue-eyed blonde. She is a licensed psychologist in Australia and a licensed mental health counselor in New York. She also has a doctorate in alternative medicine practice. In Australia she worked in her private practice, gave public workshops, and taught at a large college. She is an outstanding practitioner and teacher of REBT. She is the daughter of two Holocaust survivors from Poland who came to Australia, worked hard, and survived very well there. Unfortunately, her father, a remarkably stable man, died of heart problems in his fifties. Her mother, now in her late eighties, still lives in Australia. Her older brother also lives there.

Debbie started visiting the United States each year for a few months in 1998. We became very friendly; we would talk about many things, including her work with her clients in Australia, and she would help me in many ways with my work. We became more and more attracted to each other. We became intimate in 2002 when I was still living with Janet in an open relationship. Debbie and I became much more intimate when Janet decided to part from me and live alone.

I formed the best love relationship with Debbie that I ever had. Better than my relationships with Karyl or Gertrude. The best. In spite of some waning sex desire due to my ninety-two years, our love relationship is truly remarkable, unusually sexy, and profoundly loving. I still very much lust after her. Very much. I intend and expect to love her deeply until I die.

Debbie has 100 percent love for me, which more than matches my profound love for her. She is my full partner in all respects, helps with my writings and other work, and collaborates with me on my Friday Night Workshops and other presentations. She is incredibly competent, and many attendees of our various workshops and presentations have congratulated us on our close partnership.

Debbie has literally been a lifesaver. In May of 2003, my infected large intestine was about to burst—and would have killed me—and Debbie got me to the hospital just in time. During that hospital stay, she again saved my life twice—once by noticing that I was slipping into a diabetic coma and calling for immediate attention, and again by observing that I was going into respiratory failure. She never left my side during that and subsequent hospital visits. She stayed with me day and night.

Since my partial disability following that surgery, she continues to be lifesaving. She nurses me and supervises my nurses. In an earlier version of this autobiography, I wrote:

> She is my very competent assistant and partner, in my many presentations, research and writing. She arranges for my frequent medical visits and for conversations with numerous associates and friends. She is by far the best lover I have ever had, the most active and considerate. She is incredibly devoted to me. Because Debbie understands me far better than any other woman has, and communicates much better than all other women have with me, our sex life is greatly enhanced and could hardly be equaled. Debbie and I are naturally born for each other. As a result of all this caring—and more—I love her more thoroughly than any of the previous women in my life and one of these days we plan to marry. Who could ask for anything more? Certainly not I!

And marry we did—on November 15, 2004, at City Hall, New York. The happiest day of my life.

On special occasions—birthdays, anniversaries—I write my feelings and thoughts to Debbie. Sometimes I also write for her on *non*-occasions. My words bring her great pleasure. I include just a few letters, songs, and verses I wrote for Debbie here, along with one or two I wrote about her.

August 21, 2003

Dear Debbie,

Another birthday rolls around to make you, I hope, a little older and a lot wiser, and to merit my great love and appreciation for you. You have done many notable things for the institute during the past year—and far before that—but, in addition, I really honor the invaluable things you have done for me. Especially:

1. You have literally kept me alive in spite of my serious health problems. Without your constant love and caring, I would most probably have been gone months ago. Other people have indeed *voiced* their caring, but you

have remarkably implemented it. If anyone has constantly planned and schemed *more* for my welfare than for their own survival, it has certainly been you. I might never have believed this had I not seen it in the form of incredible honest devotion. No, you are not a saint, but indeed sainted!

2. You have often neglected your own health and happiness for mine. If anything, you have almost shamefully neglected yourself in favoring me. Many people would view this as quite nutty—for who will primarily look after you if you don't? As a recipient of your profound affection, I also think it somewhat nutty—but in its conscious self-sacrificing, splendid!

3. You have been, as I have told you, *too* perfectionistically overconcerned about me. Yes, *over*concerned and worried. So, again, you have often sabotaged your physical and emotional health for me. According to REBT, enough already! This had better stop.

4. You have risked the distinct disapproval and sabotaging of other people to protect and fight for me. Sometimes, to your own detriment, you have taken their barbs and other opposition much too seriously for your own good. Let them be nasty—and learn even more than you have been doing, to courageously and strongly ignore it. Make it keep rolling off!

I could go on and on about your rare ability to care for others and to enjoy doing so. Quite unique, but I think it adds greatly to your life. Cherish it—but try to reduce the suffering that sometimes goes with it. That would be quite a feat. Try for it as your years go caringly on!

Love,
Al

Happy New Year!
December 31, 2003

Happy New Year to you
And some ecstasy, too!

You completely deserve it
For just being—yes, you!

Happy New Year to me
And security, too!
I completely deserve it—
For just having—yes, you!
Albert

February 14, 2004
For Debbie

February's as cold as ice—
Not for us at any price!
But we'll warm it up but fine—
If you'll be my Valentine!

You're as sweet as peachy pie,
I'm a diabetic guy.
If I bite you, woe am I—
But what a lovely way to die!

August 21, 2004
Debbie's birthday

Roses are red,
Violets are blue
Another year's fled
And I still love you!

Violets are blue,
Roses are red,
My feelings for you
Are still thoroughbred!

Roses are red,
Lilies are white
My ardor for you
Is still dynamite!

Roses are red,
Leaves still are green.
My passion for you
Is still super-keen!

Roses are red,
Violets are blue,
With nuclear blasts,
I love, love, love you!

February 14, 2005

Roses are red, violets are blue—
What a grim year we have been through!
In spite of all this hullabaloo,
We have maintained a love that's true.
Affection and ardor keep sprouting anew,
Our passion and caring make real rendezvous,
When you love just me and I love just you!

May 15, 2005

Roses are red
Violets are blue
As years go by
I still love you!

Violets are blue
Roses are red
No Marilyn Monroe
Ever instead!

Roses are red
Violets are blue
Tickle my back
And I love you!

For Debbie
"Love, Love, Love"
Tune: "Barcarolle" from *The Tales of Hoffman*
Music by Jacques Offenbach
New lyrics by Albert Ellis

Love, love, love
Still is rife
When the world is rife with strife.
Love, love, love
Makes its call
When all kinds of troubles fall.
Peace will never decrease
And will take a long-term lease
If we never will cease to love,
Yes, only love, love, love.

For Debbie on her birthday
August 21, 2005

Roses are still red
Violets are still blue
And I, of course, am still true
And love, love, love only you!

Violets are still blue
Roses are still red
And my love for you
Is still greatly fed!

October 11, 2005

Roses are red
Violets are blue
I'm not out of my head
If I love, love you!
Violets are blue
Roses are red
I love, love you
And take you to bed!
Yes, take you to bed!

Roses are red
Violets are blue
Our love is real
And quite to come through.
Violets are blue
Roses are red
I'll think of you
When I'm half dead!
Yes, when I'm half dead!

(Note: Photographer Fred R. Conrad was taking photographs to go with the article about me and the situation with the institute in an article published in the *New York Times* on October 11, 2005. I was on my bed. Fred asked me to write something, as he wanted some natural-looking shots. The above poem is what I wrote for Debbie in a few minutes as the camera clicked.)

(From *The Red Mill*, by Victor Herbert)
Happy Anniversary!
October 15, 2005

Not that you are fair, dear.
Not that you are true.
Not your golden hair, dear,
Not your eyes of blue
When we seek the reason
Words are all too few
So I know I love you, dear,
Because you're you!

Things to Remember About Debbie

1. You are exceptionally considerate and kind-hearted, not just to me but to everyone except our real oppressors. You bring people joy and caring in many ways. You are quite compassionate even to me when I neglect and "hurt" you. You turn off for a while, but then come right back to compassionate caring—whether I "deserve" it or not. You present a royal degree of compassion because that is the way you are.

2. She is unusually loving toward me—puts me first. Yes, first and

foremost. 100% for me and less than 98% for herself. Pretty crazy!—but she consistently maintains it. Even Heloise wasn't better!

3. Handles telephone commitments unusually well. Yes, with people she hardly knows and also with people who are important to us. *Naturally* does this and doesn't even have to tell herself to do it.

4. Doesn't antagonize very difficult people. Doesn't like how they *act* but accepts them *with* their bad actions. Really has Unconditional Other-Acceptance (UOA). Despite difficult customers (DC's) being a pain in the ass.

5. Keeps track of time, not just for appointments with me but with her friends and relatives. She just is an exceptionally reliable person and considerately keeps others in mind.

6. Beats herself for not quickly finishing the impossible load of work inflicted on her, but actually does the most important parts of it. She feels most deficient if *any* of it was to be delayed.

7. Has to let some things go temporarily but keeps them on her mind and worries about them even though it is not her fault that they are delayed.

8. Doesn't just notice what hasn't been done but keeps figuring out what is missing and needlessly plagues herself about doing it.

9. Keeps asking herself what would be good to work at and gets independent ideas of what would be better to do to keep things under control.

10. Thinks about better things that I might do to improve conditions and suggests them to me in an uncritical manner.

"L'Amour Toujours L'Amour"
Music by Rudolf Friml
New Lyrics by Albert Ellis

Love, now at last I've found you!
Hold me and enfold me always
And let me put my arms around you!
L'amour toujours l'amour
Sing to me love's old sweet story—
Yearning, burning glory
L'amour toujours l'amour!

Tune: "Totem Tom Tom"
Music by Rudolf Friml
New lyrics by Albert Ellis

When we share and care for a person
We will risk and dare for that person
Damn it, pell mell!
We'll love like hell!
When you try to stop us from loving
We come by with more turtle doving
Damn it, pell mell!
We'll love like hell!

For love is great
An incandescent state
That fills your empty plate
Completely
It makes you feel okay
And keeps your cares at bay
And fills your life today neatly!
So give in to love's calling
Don't stop in-loveness
When you're falling
Try it pell mell!
Just love like hell!

"Cross Your Heart and Hope to Die"
Tune: "Cross Your Heart" from *Queen High*
Music by Edwin Hirsch
New lyrics by Albert Ellis

Cross your heart and hope to die
For I am yours as time goes by
Forever and forever, me oh my!
Cross your heart and hope to die
For I'm the apple of your eye
Forever and forever we shall try!
Morning we shall kiss hello
And evenings we shall sigh
Sundays we won't be apart—sweetheart
Days will come and days will go

Still I'll always love you so!—
Forever and forever, cross your heart!

For Debbie

February 14, 2006
Every day seems like Valentine's Day with you. Let's have lots more
of them!

The following was written for a chapter about me and Debbie, for
which she also wrote, for a relationship book by Daniel Eckstein, PhD.

My relationship with my wife and partner, Debbie Joffe, has been the
best one of several major relationships that I have had for a number
of reasons:

1. Debbie has intrinsic good character and kindheartedness to
   all living creatures, especially me.
2. She is unusually loving toward me and puts my health and
   interests *first* and *foremost*.
3. She keeps in mind and makes my appointments for health
   care, makes sure that I keep them, and accompanies me to
   my appointments.
4. She aids me in dealing with very difficult people in my life,
   including hostile people at the Albert Ellis Institute, and helps
   me refuse to make myself upset about them.
5. She warns me and corrects me when I go too far in my strong
   language to difficult people and when I excoriate them in
   press interviews.
6. She nicely and graciously puts up with the impossible
   demands that I put on her.
7. When important things do not work out right away, she
   keeps them in mind for the future.
8. She independently and ingeniously gets good ideas for both
   of us to work at and plans them out with me.
9. She encourages me to do sensible things to help myself but
   takes care not to plague and push me too hard about them.
10. Debbie also has an unusual, devoted, and helpful character,
    which very few people have. It makes her quite a strange,
    beautiful person. We both respect and *love* each other and
    expect to keep doing so forever.

March 16, 2006
To All Supporters of Me and REBT

I want to make sure that my wife and partner, Debbie Joffe, has a large part to play in stabilizing the REBT legacy. She has always been enthusiastic about doing so and can help immensely in making sure, while I am around and after my demise, in continuing to do so.

Albert Ellis

{}

Debbie and I have felt mistreated and isolated in the institute for these past few years. No end is in sight! We don't know if or when the original settlement agreement, given to me in December 2004, will ever be reinstated. Outside people who learn about our plight think it is pretty incredible, but Broder, Doyle, and McMahon, and the president of the institute, Lyle Stuart, persist with putting it off—seemingly indefinitely. Oddly, despite all their lies about us, our opponents have completely convinced themselves that they are doing no wrong and that we *justly* deserve our deserts. I stubbornly use REBT, refuse to upset myself, and feel only very displeased at *what* the "unholy fools" are *doing*. I am not angry *at them*. Debbie thinks I am doing a fine job of not upsetting myself and is trying to do so too.

Debbie has been frantically busy with my work, health, and legal issues for at least two long years, has had little sleep, and is knocked out. She still does a marvelous job of continuing with pushing her body to keep working, but she is burdened with too much. Because Rory was fed up with his involvement with the board and in my view was too gullible and made mistakes, he has been replaced by his father, Lyle, who became the president of the AEI. Lyle is very upset that I am not going along with what he wants me to do.

Debbie and I have real financial trouble. We may be penniless soon, and I need considerable medical drugs. There is still no resolving how to get more money to pay the nurses. The situation is getting desperate. Jimmy Walter can no longer help now with these payments, and we will go broke if we continue to pay for these nurses from our dwindling savings.

No Friday Night Workshops for months at the institute. Is it ever allowed to resume there? Will the board permit the civil rights infringement? We are determined to keep doing them and pay a lot of money each week for a place to do it next door. We now have a committee to support us, though for months we had no one supporting us.

Debbie is burdened with too much—organizing our work, our workshops, material for lawyers, my medical appointments, and much more. Sometimes I have to wait for her to finish a call or some other task before she attends to me. I am pretty patient but sometimes fall back to my old irritability—which I could have inherited from my father—and I might wave a dissenting fist at her or bawl her out very briefly. With all on her plate, she can feel super-sensitive, can make herself feel very hurt, and may be quiet for a while. I quickly apologize, but she still might feel hurt and quiet for a little while longer. I get over it and back to loving, but it might take her a little longer. But not very long. Even then, she is by far the most active and considerate lover I have ever had!

Debbie is my mate, partner, and soul mate. The only good thing in all that is happening in our lives is that we have each other.

Chapter 11

The Second-Worst Year of My Life— And How I Coped with It

I used to think that the year 2001, when I was eighty-seven, was the worst year of my life. However, now that the events from 2003 onward have occurred, I can say that 2001 was the second-worst year of my life.

At the beginning of that year, I was in good shape, considering my age, although I had innumerable minor ailments that slowed me down considerably.

I delight in performing projects rapidly, although rapidity has its limitations. Normally, I walk fast, talk fast, write very rapidly—I have even, for much of my life, copulated fast. But not in recent years. At about the age of eighty, I began to slow down—for a number of reasons. Let me see if I can remember some of them.

I began to develop wobbly legs, which slowed down my almost championship-speed of walking. Prior to developing this problem, I often beat the New York City buses. At the airports, I was one of the first off the plane—even when I was stuck in a middle seat. Once off the plane, I generally got to the taxis ahead of everyone else. I almost bowled people over, as I sped to my destinations. I was not frantic, just damned speedy. Waiting wasted my time, and I *hated* to waste any time. In my twenties, I decided that this was the only life I was going to have, so I'd better not waste much of it. There was much to do— especially my writing, from ages nineteen to twenty-eight, some twenty book-length manuscripts. So on with the show!

Not in my eighties, however, could I proceed quite so rapidly. I started developing osteoarthritis of the thumbs, which surprisingly slowed me down in many ways—dressing, bathing, shaving, cooking, writing, you name it. I still did everything *pretty* fast, but not at my usual exceptional speed.

Then, because of my minor health problems and the dangers of falling on my face, I had to spend what seemed like endless periods of time interrupting my busy schedule of writing, lecturing, giving workshops, seeing many individual and group clients, supervising therapists, traveling to give twenty-five or more national and international presentations a year, and so on. What interruptions? Here are just a "few."

- Constant wrestling with my hearing aids.
- Attending to my eczema and allergic itching.
- Cleaning my goddamned glasses.
- Sneezing for several five-minute periods a day because of my sinusitis and heat-cold allergies.
- Making myself two hot meals a day.
- Making myself about five peanut butter and jelly sandwiches every day.
- Taking two shots of insulin and ten bloody finger taps a day to control my insulin-dependent diabetes.
- Preparing my needles, finger tapping machines, and other diabetic supplies. Buying them.
- Eating about eight small meals a day to keep my blood sugar normal. Even in the middle of the night!
- Putting on headphones and hearing aids regularly, to hear my phone sessions and regular sessions with my clients.
- Going to the bathroom every one and a half hours.
- Walking up and down our building's stairs to get my mail and to talk with our employees and my professional associates.
- Changing the ribbons on my electric typewriter.
- Typing several letters a day. (This was faster than waiting for the institute's administrative staff.)
- Dictating several other letters to be (eventually!) typed by our secretarial staff.
- Dictating or typing about twelve articles and two or three books a year.
- Correcting and proofreading a number of letters and articles each week.
- Regularly visiting my various medical practitioners, including my

diabetologist, dentist, cardiologist, ophthalmologist, podiatrist, dermatologist, rheumatologist, and orthopedist.

- Doing two fifteen-minute exercise routines every day.
- Ordering and reordering various vitamins and medications for my blood pressure, thyroid, and dermatological conditions, among others.
- Actually taking my medication, usually twice a day, and especially spending some time applying my anti-itch lotions.
- Shaving at least twice a day my thick and relentless beard!
- Washing several times a day and taking a shower, including washing my hair, every single night.
- Packing for my many trips. Later, unpacking and replacing the used items.
- Arranging for my tickets for my trips—checking with my assistants for details of travel, schedules, program schedules, calls to organizers, meeting with the organizers, making hotel arrangements, mealtime routines and foods, etc.
- Outlining my lecture and workshop presentations. Steadily revising them.
- Shopping for my clothes and accessories, usually by mail order. Checking on orders and mailings. Writing out checks and credit card information.
- Keeping track of my bank balance and checks. Checking with our bookkeeper to pay my personal taxes.
- Putting away my worn clothes each day and setting out clothes for the next day.
- Arranging my night materials, food to keep available, arranging my bed covers, setting my noise machine and alarm.

I am sure there are many things I am forgetting to include in the above list. But doesn't almost everyone have such innumerable tasks to do? I think not, since I have my older-age ailments to take care of and I am busier than most people—even than most executives. Not that I'm complaining—for I *choose* to be busier and I *like* most of my doings. But what inescapable minutia they involve! And how the minutes and hours pass!

My goal, for many years, has been to get things done quickly without needless delay. I am therefore impatient with anyone's, including my own, needless slowness. But I am also naturally impatient—as was my impatient and angry father, Henry Oscar Ellis. He was rarely around, as I've earlier written, when I was a child, so I don't think I *learned* my impatience from him. I inherited, rather, my strong tendency for impatience from him and my mother. She was also somewhat impatient, but not, like my father, nastily so. She had three young children to care for, wasn't particularly inclined to be a mother (instead, to be a talker, singer, and actress), and therefore impatiently got through her caretaking swiftly and sloppily. No disastrous consequences, but she got by.

You could say, then, that I inherited—*and* learned—impatience from both sides of my family. Whether my impatience led to my fastness or my natural rapidity created my impatience is hard to say. Probably both/and rather than either/or. For I quickly talked, walked, ate, dressed—and *liked* doing so. In fact, I had trouble slowing myself down. When, on several occasions, I tried to eat more slowly, I barely succeeded and soon fell back to my steamroller gobbling.

FEBRUARY 2001

Suddenly, with no prior warning, Janet announced that she was leaving our thirty-six-year relationship, as I have described earlier in this autobiography.

Even before I learned about Stendhal's rule of love—that you are madly impassioned with a partner until you actually live under the same roof with her or him for a few years—I followed the basic precept. I never lived with Gertrude during our five years of high-spirited involvement. With Karyl, I loved her pretty intensely for a year, began living with her for a while—and that was that! With Janet, again a few weeks of living with her at the institute knocked off my passion. But my loving-kindness—as H. G. Wells called it—continued for her and for other women long after my extreme passion waned. So just place me living under the same roof with a woman for a while, and my amative intensity turns into loving-kindness, as Stendhal said. However, my relationship with Debbie is the exception that makes that rule.

In February, Janet told me that she was still going to live with me—as *friends*—for the present, and might later get an apartment of her own. Since she was then the executive director of the Albert Ellis Institute and I was the president, she was entitled to keep living in our apartment on the top floor of the institute's building. Convenient and comfortable enough for both of us.

Was it also *fine*? No. I *wanted* to keep my relationship with Janet going along well—as I thought it was going. I felt sorry, regretful, sad that it was ending. Considerably? Yes, *in part*. I could see and feel right away that the *additional* freedoms I would have from our breakup had some good points. I invariably *like* being by myself—arranging my doings, thinking my thoughts, never feeling (even on weekends by myself) desperately alone, as most of my clients often do.

I am, and have been since childhood, a *natural positive* "aloner." That is why I got along so well with Janet for thirty-six years. She left me to myself, for her own reasons, with few long periods of togetherness. She (fortunately!) had her own unusually busy professional and personal life. We saw each other every day, but briefly. We slept together every night—in a king-size bed!—and for many of our years had steady sex. For several *minutes*, not *hours*. No sweat. I even got bored easily with enjoyable sex. Too damned long and repetitious!

Janet, by agreement again, did things for me in addition to her institute work. She supervised getting our food, occasionally cooked for me while letting me regularly prepare my own hot and cold meals, watched over the laundry, took care of our maid, and managed other household tasks. In turn, in spite of her complaining that I really "never" listened to her, I usually immediately put aside my own multiple activities and, at her request, talked with her about institute matters, read and commented on most of her writings, discussed problems, talked to her visiting friends, and occasionally accompanied her to events. I helped Janet and she helped me. And at that time, I wanted it to continue that way—and I quickly saw that it could continue, on the basis of friendship, instead of mateship.

I really didn't have much to lose by our "changed" status. In addition, the change would free me to have other sex-love affairs. According to our original agreement—in June 1965, when we began to live together—Janet and I had an "open relationship." We both could, if we chose to do so, have sex affairs with other people, as long as we were discreet in doing so and didn't keep it a secret from each other.

I kept to this agreement and had about thirty-five short-term affairs with women, most of them on my out-of-town trips to give talks and workshops. Janet even arranged for me to have a couple of them. Splendid, since these affairs did not interfere with my (mainly working) life or lead to loss of sleep. I cut them short if they deprived me of sleep. Doing workshops was more important, though less exciting!

Janet also had several affairs—one for six months, very intense and very scary—and I never bothered myself about them. During her long affair, I was disappointed that she was so obsessed and partially neglected some of her institute work. But I had only slight pangs of jealousy and easily put up with them. If her lover was better in bed and lasted longer in intercourse—as she said he was—it wasn't *awful* and it didn't make me a *weak person*. Too bad! We not only stayed with our "open marriage" agreement, we *comfortably* did so. It worked—or *we* worked it.

Janet, however, had one brief attack of jealousy, when I spent a night with a woman, Dorothy, a couple of years after we started living together. I told Janet I was about to do so, and used a small bedroom elsewhere in the building to sleep with Dorothy while Janet slept alone in our huge sixth-floor bed. From Janet's reactions, I saw that the institute building (at least when Janet was home), was not the best place in which to be honestly unfaithful. So I only used the institute's premises to sleep with another woman when Janet was out of town. When I was out of town, no hassle.

When Janet ended our sex-love partnership in February 2001, I was already having an on-and-off affair with Sandy, a businesswoman who lived out of town with her husband and two children and who came three or four times a year to New York on business—and on monkey business. But I only let Sandy stay over on days when Janet was out of town. Otherwise, I had sex with her, rather briefly, on my office sofa. Somewhat restricting!

Those restrictions came to my mind in February 2001 and helped to ease some of my sorrow and disappointment about Janet's and my separation. Now I would be freer to stay with Sandy—and other possible partners. Not freer in time—that was always fully filled—but freer in terms of logistics. I was eighty-seven—but, as Don Marquis's cat Mehitabel used to say, "There's a dance in the old dame yet!" With Janet soon to be gone, my sex life might bloom! Hardly every night of the week, but more than ever!

As I keep telling my complaining clients, everything that happens seems to have advantages *and* disadvantages. So it was with Janet's leaving me in a "lurch." Some advantages: Increased freedom, more easily arranged sex with other women, more (time-limited) pleasures to come. I would see!

I was still, at times, sad about our parting—especially when Janet began to talk about buying her own apartment and seeing me a lot less. I would miss seeing her and having her around in case of emergencies.

I might go into insulin shock when my blood sugar got too low, which was quite dangerous. Once in the past I had a hypoglycemic reaction in the middle of the night, and Janet had to call a physician to get me out of it and avert my going into a coma. One could die of that!

I therefore felt safer with her than when I was alone. As I have said, however, I rarely worry about anything, even low blood sugar, and I had only ended up in the hospital two times with low blood sugar in almost fifty years of being diabetic. Janet could have learned to inject me with glucagon, but she didn't want to. However, on a few occasions when I had low blood sugar, she made sure I was taken care of. So living with Janet had its distinct advantages.

Did I blame myself for not acting in ways that might have kept her wanting to live with me? No, I accepted responsibility for failing to do so. I refused to risk a little discomfort and therefore risked much more discomfort: being without Janet. Idiotic! Discomfort intolerance! As REBT calls it, short-range hedonism.

I blamed my *behavior*, but not *myself*. I *acted* stupidly, but I wasn't a *bad person*. I was sorry and regretful but not depressedly awfulizing.

"Next time," I warned myself, "I shall watch it!" Which I am already doing.

I followed what REBT always advocates and what I almost always achieve: Unconditional Self-Acceptance (USA). I got this philosophy from the existentialists and particularly from Paul Tillich's *The Courage to Be*, which I read shortly after it was published in 1953. Tillich, a thriving lecher himself—which I saw when he tried to seduce one of my female clients when she was a student of his at Union Theological Seminary—forgave himself and others (as his friend, Rollo May, has written). He accepted *himself* in spite of his unchristian *behavior* and very clearly pushed unconditional acceptance in *The Courage to Be*.

"How right he is!" I thought as I read his book. "Good stuff! USA really solves the vast, ever-recurring human problem of self-deprecation. I'll use it!" I did—on myself and with my clients.

Though hardly a Christian, I was a "natural" for the Christian philosophy of accepting the sinner but *not* the sin. I did this myself since the age of five, when, during my exploration of the naked body of my first great love, Ruthie, we were caught by our parents. I acknowledged the "horror" of my act but managed to fail to denigrate myself. I forgave myself. Right—my *self*.

I used two basic philosophies to fully accept *myself* when I had *acted* stupidly. One, Tillich's Unconditional Self-Acceptance (USA) and

Alfred Korzybski's philosophy of acknowledging your specific behaviors and rating them as "good" or "bad" but not *over*generalizing and rating your *self*, your *being*, or your *totality* as "good" or "bad." This is what I had been teaching in REBT since 1955 and what I now effectively applied to myself.

Being the originator of REBT and, importantly, a follower of Korzybski, I could watch my feelings when put upon by unpleasant events and deliberately *make sure* I feel sorry and disappointed rather than depressed and self-downing when I screw up. I don't think I do this, however. I *naturally*, rather than consciously, do so. I don't depress myself and then make myself undepressed. I merely, with some feeling of sorrow, don't depress. I do this automatically, thanks to years of practicing—not to mention teaching—REBT.

MARCH 2001: SURVIVING AN ACCIDENT

Let me return to my "second-worst year," 2001, which began with the first "disaster" of Janet talking of moving out in February. I was doing very well, in spite of my health problems, and in March I was scheduled to give one of my regular three-hour workshops for the Learning Annex at 6:30 p.m. at the Holiday Inn on West 57th Street. Topic: "How to Avoid Procrastination." Over two hundred people signed up to start stopping their procrastinating. I was also scheduled to give a talk for SMART (Self-Management and Recovery Training) in Phoenix. Fine!

To make sure I got to my workshop early, I left my apartment at 5:45 to look for a taxi. Mistake! I should have ordered a limousine, but I was sure I could find a cab. Double mistake: I couldn't. Rush hour in Manhattan and no cabs available, I walked down Madison Avenue toward 57th Street. At the worst, I would get to 57th Street and take the crosstown bus to Ninth Avenue. Plenty of time yet.

The first five blocks were okay, but I began to tire, partly because of my fairly brisk pace. Sixtieth Street—already tired. Fifty-ninth and then 58th Streets, more tired—in fact, unusually tired. I continued plodding resolutely on to catch that 57th Street bus.

Suddenly, crossing 58th Street, I fell, landing on my face and head. I don't remember falling, but I did. I regained consciousness to find two cops leaning over me as I lay on the ground. I quickly became alert and told them that I was on my way to speak in a few minutes at the Holiday Inn, so please get me there fast.

No way! They explained that I was bleeding profusely, after apparently hitting the curb, and that I had to go to the emergency room. No nonsense: *had* to go. The ambulance had already been called and was on the way.

I was most reluctant to go. I felt fine and dandy and was all prepared for my workshop. Then I realized that I had a big towel wrapped around my head and face. Shit!—no escape from going to the hospital. No workshop that night—they were already calling the Learning Annex on their portable phones to tell them too damned bad—but that was that.

The ambulance from Lenox Hill Hospital—not my regular hospital—came and we drove off, sirens ringing, to the emergency room. It was a rough ride in traffic, and I thought, ironically, that we might well get in an accident, but we soon made it.

Because of the cops, the doctors at the hospital, and the identification papers I had with me, things were already in pretty good order. I was alert and in no pain—having already been given sedative shots—but I was bleeding profusely from my forehead, eyelids, and right cheek. A real mess!—as Janet cheerfully said when she came to see me. She even brought her camera, to take some gruesome—but also funny—photos.

Things proceeded apace. The doctors were at first undecided about keeping me in the hospital—mainly because of a shortage of beds. But in two hours they decided to do so. Meanwhile, I had all kinds of blood and heart tests. The doctors thought I may have had a minor stroke because I couldn't remember actually falling. I thought that I was merely tired by my long walk and by my wobbly legs, and that I therefore fell. But they carefully checked anyway.

Fortunately, Janet got a plastic surgeon to come to the emergency room to sew up my face. As it turned out, he did a very fine job.

Was I emotionally upset about this interruption of my life? Only to the degree that I teach people, using REBT, to feel *healthy* instead of *unhealthy* negative emotions when unfortunate events occur. I was distinctly sorry, regretful, concerned, disappointed, and frustrated by this sudden drastic impediment in my very busy schedule, but I was not obsessively or extremely sorry, since I have practiced REBT for many years and I am able to keep my sorrowful feelings at a moderate level. I was *distinctly* regretful about my situation, but I largely concentrated on more practical and enjoyable things and only *intermittently* felt real sorrow.

This, however, is my real point: I was *not* really anxious, depressed, or self-damning. Not at all! In spite of my culpability (in neglecting to call our limousine service), I didn't blame myself (or anyone) and just felt disappointed about causing and suffering from my condition.

I reacted similarly to Janet's ending our relationship: I briefly dwelt on its disadvantages, but I also (as I almost invariably do) considered its advantages. Being mated with Janet clearly had advantages, obviously, or I would not have continued it for thirty-six years. But the best partnerships, I always realize, have their restrictions and limitations. Freedom to do what I wanted was still, at eighty-seven, my *main* goal; I arranged with Janet an unusual degree of it *in* our relationship. Ending the relationship would make me even *more* free, though not remarkably more. Nice! And, as it turned out, it was a great thing for me that she left, as it freed me to be with Debbie.

Back to my injury. I brought on no depression or despair—not even real anxiety. I was *concerned* about my condition, how long it would take me to heal, when I would be back to my usual activities. But I did not *worry* about how long it would take, and I took the attitude that it would take just as long as it would take. Worry—as I tell scores of my clients—doesn't help to make things better. Au contraire! Drop it! So I did. I convinced myself, "Tough shit!" and the worry vanished.

Nor did I worry about my health and my physical condition. For the several days that I spent at Lenox Hill Hospital in their cardiac ward, they gave me test after test to monitor my suspected heart condition. Annoying, but good medical investigation, I realized. I optimistically assumed that my heart was all right—but, of course, I did not *know*. I was rationally *concerned* about it but not irrationally and obsessively *worried*. Mainly because I had strongly convinced myself that anxiety will not change things (except for the worse!) and I could do nothing for my "cardiac condition" until I found that I truly had one. I had more *practical* things to think about. So I thought about them. I answered my mail on a tape recorder that was brought to me. I read some professional journals. I planned for a few days ahead, when I expected to leave the hospital. I arranged, by videotape, to give a talk I was scheduled to give in Phoenix, on Tuesday, four days after I was hospitalized.

The one thing that I regretted most was that I was scheduled to spend three days in Phoenix, giving one of the training workshops in REBT that Emmett Velten, Michler Bishop, and I did regularly for therapists working for the Arizona Department of Child and Adolescent Offenders. This was important—and our Albert Ellis Institute in New

York received thousands of dollars remuneration for arranging and giving it.

There was no easy substitution. I was a favorite with members of this group, had spoken to them before, and we expected a big turnout—attracted by my name. Other staff members, though quite competent to replace me, wouldn't be acceptable; and we had no way of notifying the two-hundred-plus ticket holders, some of whom would come from a distance. Ugh!

However, arrangements were made for me to videotape the talk from my hospital room. I am a fast healer, and the plastic surgeon had done a remarkably fine job fixing the cuts on the left side of my face. I recorded a spirited talk before the TV camera, which filmed mainly the right side of my face. I focused, as I am able to do, exclusively on the content of the talk and not on my still-dismal situation (including some facial pain) and I more than got by. Everyone, including me, thought that my lecture was right on. I looked and talked well. Emmett, in his introduction, explained what had happened to me, and the audience, I was later told, was sympathetic yet enthusiastic. Ignoring my injuries plus focusing on the use of REBT with my audience won the day. We made lemonade out of our lemon and nicely lubricated everyone's throat and taste buds. I would say that using REBT on myself achieved this coup. My natural planning abilities came through—*after* I refused to upset myself.

MARCH 2001: DEALING WITH THE BOARD OF DIRECTORS

Catharine MacLaren, assistant executive director of the Albert Ellis Institute, began complaining bitterly about Janet, who was the executive director at that time. I calmly listened and told Catharine I thought that she and Janet were both acting like "fucking babies"—and acting against REBT principles. They were foolishly angering and hurting themselves—and, of course, blaming each other for their disturbed feelings. Catharine took my views lightly, obviously believing that she was 100 percent right and Janet was 100 percent wrong. Janet, when I told her what I told Catharine, also pooh-poohed my view and resented me for holding it. The only thing they both agreed on was that I was thoroughly wrong. Of course!

To calm things down somewhat, I told Catharine that hereafter she would take Janet's "orders" only through me. She would have no direct contact with Janet. I hoped that might improve things for a while, but Janet just stopped giving directions to Catharine, period, so I didn't have to relay them to her. Instead, Janet went on directing things by herself—and we somehow got by.

For a short while! Then yet another "disaster" struck. For some reasons I may never know, our board of trustees, *without even telling me*, gave Janet two months' notice as executive director of the institute. What they did and, particularly, the *way* in which they did it, was incredible and impossible to comprehend.

Janet was most likely on her way out, regardless of the board's decision. She was sick of taking care of the institute without any real support. However, I did spend considerable time planning to overcome the board's boxing me—and Janet—in. So I spent *some* time—but not *too* much—plotting and scheming.

First, I got rid of my anger. I was *very* angry at the board's actions with Janet. They summarily gave her two months—two lousy months!—to agree to their terms or quit. How unfair! She had devoted thirty-six *years* to the institute, and they summarily give her two months to make this decision. Of course, they wanted to get on with institute work and find another executive director to replace Janet. But they unfairly *forced* her to decide right away.

So I made myself *very* angry at their acts but did not damn *them*. I couldn't tell them how I felt—for I was, for a couple of months, incommunicado. But I made myself, during this trying time, mad at their *actions*. Not at the *whole* of them. I really followed REBT.

I was quite courageous about all this, too. The board was not opposed to me but to Janet, mainly because of her critical attitude toward some of the board members. By my telling them that they were wrong about her, I helped them get angry at me—naturally, to my great detriment. But I strongly held my ground, especially a little later, when the board finally resumed full meetings with me. I very firmly told them what I would do if they didn't change some of their ways, and I got them (rationally, I think) to consider my main points.

Among other things, I helped the board make a good contract with Janet for the future, thank her for her tremendous efforts over the years, and give her a good amount of money for the thirty-six years she had devoted to the institute. Janet was satisfied with this settlement, and things finally started going smoothly. We also shuffled the board, added some new members, and made it, I thought, distinctly much more functioning. I couldn't have been more wrong about that.

The main point I want to make is that I was very *determined* to see that justice was done in terms of Janet's dismissal. But despite the unfairness of the situation, I was not angry, hurt, anxious, or depressed. I was just very disappointed in the board's *behavior*. I succeeded in achieving my goals without harm to myself or anyone. Justice triumphed—and I triumphed. I felt great about that—but not at all like *a better person*. I was proud of my *actions*, but, as I warn my clients—not proud of *myself*. Many of my clients have a hell of a time seeing the difference between the two and figuring out these feelings for themselves.

Through August 1, I gave presentations, including at the American Psychological Association's annual conference in San Francisco, and for the Learning Annex in California. On September 4, I took a six-day trip to the Netherlands to celebrate the tenth anniversary of the opening of our training there. I gave several talks, workshops, and supervision sessions and a special presentation on Humor and Psychotherapy with Nando Pelusi. He is one of the regular trainers at our New York institute and is very funny, especially in his imitation of me. The Dutch people loved it, as do our American audiences.

SEPTEMBER 11, 2001

I was hardly back in New York, resuming my busy schedule of individual and group psychotherapy, when a staff member called me during my group session to announce that one of the buildings of the World Trade Center had been bombed by a hijacked plane and was on fire. A little after 10 a.m. I received another call, saying that the second World Trade Center building had been hit by another hijacked plane, and that both buildings were shattered and on fire. This was clearly, as President Bush soon announced, war on the United States by terrorist forces. War, with more than two thousand dead and thousands of injured. Terroristic war!

It was a full week for me, since I had twenty-three half-hour and seventeen full-hour sessions and four one-hour group sessions scheduled with my regular clients. I had no intention of leaving them in a lurch—especially *this* week. Several clients canceled or held phone sessions with me because they were so terrified by the events that they were afraid to take public transportation. Fortunately, I have had many phone sessions since I started to do therapy, so I am used to them. In fact, I hear very well over the phone because of the special headset I use. So I "see" several clients every week by phone all over the world.

I had several extra sessions with terrified people on September 11 and for several days thereafter. I volunteered to do free sessions and talks for a group of psychologists and social workers, but I mainly held in-person and phone sessions at the institute. I held my regular Friday Night Workshop, which I have been giving for thirty-six years and where I "cure" two volunteers every week with a regular REBT session, on September 14, but for the first time in our history I also gave a thirty-minute talk on terrorism. I held a discussion with my audience on what REBT could do to help people and possibly reduce their rage and panic and fear about terrorism. I also wrote an essay on the topic of September 11 to show how using REBT fights terrorism.

How did I personally react to the events of September 11? With great sadness and sorrow. I don't think I was close to any of the victims, though it is likely that a few of my clients who didn't show up for their sessions that day were killed in the explosions and fires at the World Trade Center, and possibly some of my friends and acquaintances were also killed or maimed.

The *general* havoc was simply appalling. I felt more mournful than I ever remember feeling before. Thousands of completely innocent people had been killed and many more were maimed and missing. I especially felt sorrow for the loved ones of the victims waiting at home—waiting, waiting for any word from their relatives and friends. How agonizing!

I also felt great sadness and compassion for the tens of thousands of people, in New York and all over the world, who were terrified by this experience. I especially felt compassion for one of my clients who witnessed the fall of one of the towers from his home in Brooklyn, a mile away, and could hardly speak to me in the phone session I had with him that day. He worked in a building next to the Twin Towers and was—fortunately!—late to work that day. He lost some friends, however, and was numbed by the shock of it all. I had to talk to him several times before I finally helped him calm down and resume his activities.

The last few weeks of September I gave workshops for David Lima in Syracuse and Albany, and one for a Canadian sponsor in Toronto on "Dealing with Resistant Clients." I gave three more workshops with David at the end of October. He is quite successful and is arranging more money-makers for himself and the institute. Dave is the most competent and reliable of all the people for whom I do workshops. He and his wife, Nancy, do everything that can be done—and more! He is a real gem and has been helped by his long-time practice of REBT on himself and his clients.

Debbie was visiting New York at this time. She extended her stay in order to do volunteer work with the September 11 recovery workers. It was good having her with me during this time. We worked together from about 10:30 in the morning until 9:30 at night; then Debbie did volunteer work at an around-the-clock drop-in facility from about 10:30 p.m. until 4 or 5 a.m.

NOVEMBER 2001: FINANCIAL PROBLEMS

On November 4, we received very bad financial news at our board. We always lose money each year on our regular operations—largely because of our expensive training program for the interns and fellows who visit for a year or two to work with our clients. But we almost always make up this deficit with income from our capital investment, which we have increased over the years.

This year, our investment portfolio lost three million in equities, owing to bad stock market conditions. Consequently, our income fell, and our net loss for the year was a staggering $783,000. This meant losing more money and suffering an equal loss the following year. At this rate, our income from securities would keep dropping and our yearly net loss would increase. Ultimately, if our finances continued dropping at this rate, we would have to go out of business—or else do much less training. Exceptionally bad!

How did I react to this grim blow? Grimly, but not depressedly. Sadly, but without terror. I did what I always do when the institute, to which I devote most of my life, is in jeopardy. I quickly imagine the worst outcome—and then show myself that I can still be happy.

Considering the possibility of the institute failing and ultimately going out of business, I first imagined thousands of our clients responding to our cause and contributing enough money to restore it to working order. Great—if it happened.

I then pictured even grimmer events—say, the institute in *no way* could continue. That would be *very bad*, and innumerable people, now and in the future, would be deprived of the benefits of the institute and its teachings. Truly rotten! But my close associates and I would survive—even, if necessary, on welfare. REBT would still go on—in writings and in therapeutic usage. Even without me! Much good would have *been* done during the institute's lifetime. Much more REBT would continue—after its funeral.

Suppose, however, REBT fell into oblivion and no one propagated or practiced it. Well, it would most likely live on in other cognitive-behavior therapies that it has influenced. Still, if *not*? If *none* of its influence remained? People would just have to get by without it. More miserably, most likely. But the human race would most probably stagger on.

And if the human race *didn't* stagger on? Well, so it wouldn't exist; maybe our planet would cease to exist; maybe all living things would die. Too bad. *Very* bad. But not *awful* or *unthinkable*. No me, no you, no any of us; zero. Conceivable, ultimately, anyway. And I, now very much among the living, could *accept* it. Dislike it, but still *accept* it— *if* it ever occurred.

Of course, as I thought these thoughts, the probability seemed very high that these disasters never would occur. Not for thousands, millions, or billions of years, if at all. Most unlikely. As I thought that, I was still *concerned* but not *panicked* about the state of the institute, of humans, of life, of everything else. Many setbacks for all of us. But complete annihilation? Unlikely.

Back to the drawing board: The making of the institute's fall and decline *very unlikely*. I would do my best—with the rest of the board— to save it and even expand its power and influence. What else was to be done? In spite of our lousy financial tidings, I forthrightly went back to work: steadily working at saving people in trouble through, largely, saving the institute.

Little did I know then what would transpire just a few years later, when my power to direct the institute was taken from me.

Chapter 12

A Better Year

The period from 2002 to 2003 was a very busy and productive year. The highlight of 2002 was Debbie moving to New York.

In addition to her fellowship work at the institute, she assisted me with practically everything. The burdens of making medical appointments, organization transportation, getting food, and so much more were no longer mine. Never was I so safe, and I felt very secure. I could devote more time to my writings and other work, which I enjoyed and which she also marvelously helped me with.

On December 12, 2002, I went to Orlando for a conference on brief therapy and gave seven presentations on REBT. It went over quite well, and I was the highlight of the conference because of my frank disagreement with several of the other therapists.

I, actually, had a good working year and was preparing to bring out several new books, including an *Anxiety Workbook* and my unfinished *Autobiography*. We also had some fine financial support for the institute. A pretty grim year—but we got by! And all the time Debbie and I were getting closer. Quickly. Profoundly.

However, on June 3, 2003, physical "disaster" struck. Prior to that date, I had been having severe diarrhea attacks on several of my out-of-town trips. My physician didn't think it was serious, but I began experiencing bloody diarrhea and wound up in Mt. Sinai Hospital for weeks.

Without Debbie, I might well have died. She got me to the hospital, stayed there day and night, supervised the nurses, was worn out herself, but got me through. I awoke after surgery with no large intestine, a plastic ileostomy bag, and from then on I would require a nurse attending to me around the clock. I took things very well—as I recounted in *Rational Emotive Behavior Therapy: It Works for Me— It Can Work for You*. No fear of dying, no horror, no awfulizing, and back to work quickly, mainly on several new books. For months, I was unable to see clients in my office, but I soon began "seeing" them by phone every Wednesday, starting in October. I also resumed with one of my therapy groups on Mondays, starting in November.

I gave a few workshops at the institute and for out-of-town venues that were not too far away. I resumed my regular Friday Night Workshops in September and gave a talk to the Nassau County Psychological Association in October. I participated in the annual August APA convention in Toronto by phone. I was supposed to meet the Dalai Lama at an event in Bloomington, Indiana, but doctors were against my traveling. I participated in various other conferences and presentations, including a Learning Annex Workshop on November 11. All my presentations went very well. I was in good voice and had plenty of energy. Debbie was a great help in assisting me to hear members of the audience. Everyone seemed to be pleased.

Meanwhile, we had trouble at the institute again. We had lost money because I'd been unable to see many clients or to travel to give workshops. The board of trustees arranged to pay for my nursing expenses and to keep me solvent. They seemed as nice as they could be, but that was not to last much longer.

Dom DiMattia was a different matter completely. He was made executive director in September 2001 and was very competent in some ways, but he tried to run everybody *too much* and to replace me. He fought with everyone and did immense damage. Finally, by July 2002, I determinedly saw that we would have to get rid of him. We gave him a very fair settlement, and that was that. We agreed to say nothing about him to the membership or the public.

By 2003, it was clear to me that I wanted to be with Debbie for the rest of my life. I loved her more than any of the previous women in my life. Who could ask for anything more? Certainly not I!

I celebrated my birthday with an all-day workshop, followed by an evening reception and dinner. I presented and was joined at times by others, including Arnie Lazarus, throughout the whole day. In the evening, messages from prominent well-wishers were read out. I include a few of them here:

William Jefferson Clinton
September 27, 2003

Dear Albert:

Hillary and I are pleased to wish you a very happy 90th birthday.

We hope you have a joyous celebration and a wonderful year.

Sincerely,
Bill Clinton

Hillary Rodham Clinton
United States Senate
September 27, 2003

Dear Dr. Ellis:

I am delighted to have this opportunity to wish you a Happy 90th Birthday!

I am profoundly impressed at the magnitude and breadth of your accomplishments. Your professional innovation is itself remarkable, but the spirit of your progress is even more so. The diligence, skill, and unflagging dedication you have shown to your profession is an inspiration to all generations.

On this special occasion, let me again express my warmest wishes for many years of continued success.

Sincerely yours,
Hillary Rodham Clinton

The White House
Washington, DC

Congratulations and best wishes for an enjoyable birthday celebration. May your day be filled with happy memories, bright hopes, and the love of family and friends.

Sincerely,
George Bush
Laura Bush

The City of New York
Office of the Mayor
September 20, 2003

Dear Dr. Ellis:

It is a pleasure to join with your family, friends, and colleagues at Albert Ellis Institute in wishing you a happy 90th birthday. As the father of cognitive behavioral therapy and Rational Emotive Behavior Therapy, you have achieved so much in your ninety years and, to the surprise of no one here, I am sure, you are still going strong. You are a mentor to therapists and psychologists around the world, a devoted doctor to the thousands of people you counsel and who read your books, and a source of inspiration to all those who know you.

I hope you have an enjoyable and joyous day, and on behalf of the residents of New York City, I wish you continued good health and great happiness.

Sincerely,

Michael R. Bloomberg
Mayor

State of New York
George E. Pataki
Governor
September 27, 2003

Dear Dr. Ellis:

On behalf of the citizens of the Empire State, it is a pleasure to offer sincere congratulations as you celebrate your 90th birthday.

This occasion provides friends and loved ones with the opportunity to convey their affection and admiration for you. In celebrating this special event, you can take pride in all you have achieved during your lifetime. Throughout the years, you have had many extraordinary experiences that contribute to a treasury of fond memories and serve as a testimony to the virtues of good living. In that regard, you serve as a great source of inspiration to many people who truly cherish you, and your gift for bringing joy and happiness to others is well-appreciated.

I applaud all you have realized in your ninety years, each of them marked by an appreciation for life that is displayed by your longevity. With my best wishes for a wonderful birthday and continued good health and happiness.

Very truly yours,
George E. Pataki

His Holiness the Fourteenth Dalai Lama Tenzin Gyatso also sent his thoughts and prayers and a white silk scarf called a *keta*, which was placed around my neck by a representative. His nephew also sent his wishes. Dr. Tony Kidman brought along his famous daughter, the actress Nicole Kidman. She told me I looked wonderful, and I told her that she looked okay, too. That resulted in much laughter from those who heard us, and the exchange was printed in the *New Yorker* magazine. Former students, now practitioners, from around the world were there—it was quite a crowded celebration, enjoyed by many. I thought it was quite fine, but I was glad to head upstairs with Debbie at the end of it.

Chapter 13

The Bogus Albert Ellis Institute

In this chapter, I would like to summarize the dismal state of affairs between me and my wife and partner, Debbie Joffe Ellis, and the bogus Albert Ellis Institute.

I was still president of the AEI in September 2004, and its affairs seemed to be in good order, when I suddenly found that its executive director for a year, Michael Broder, was lying to me and trying to take control of the institute, along with a main member of the board of trustees, James McMahon, and the passive and weak consent of the other members of the board of trustees. Two board members, Debbie Steinberg and Emmett Velten, who originally went along with the others changed when they finally realized what was really going on. I remember challenging Broder for making institute presentations too general (not REBT-specific enough), for promoting his own book at the institute, and for making the making of money more important than the promotion of REBT at the institute. Broder shouted back at me, "*I run this place, Al, not you!*"

Power corrupts, absolute power corrupts absolutely, as the saying goes.

I resisted this "palace revolution" and have been fighting with the AEI ever since. Joining Debbie and me in our recent war, a board-of-trustees-in-waiting was established, consisting of about two hundred prominent professionals and headed by me, Bill Knaus, and Debbie. This board-in-waiting promoted justice for Albert Ellis and tried to remove the traitors of the bogus board and take back the institute. Meanwhile, the group led by Broder, McMahon, the rest of the board—and later Lyle Stuart (who in 2006 became board president)—confined and restricted Debbie and me, took away our civil rights, tried to ruin the AEI financially, bowdlerized the AEI fellowship training program, and acted viciously against us, particularly by inventing and putting many lies and distortions about us on the AEI Web site. Debbie has been falsely maligned for trying to run me and take my life savings. Nothing could be further from the truth.

One morning in October 2004, when Broder and Doyle tried to convince me that Debbie was terrible and should be gotten rid of and replaced, Broder called my primary physician requesting that he prescribe tranquilizers for me because I was going to hear news that would upset me later that day.

Of course my doctor refused and with concern contacted Debbie and me to let us know that something strange was going on.

In many respects, we are fighting a losing battle, because:

1. The AEI has hundreds of thousands of dollars, which I largely built up for it since 1959, and it still receives the royalties of my books and innumerable services from me every year.
2. The bogus AEI has unjustly and unethically occupied our 45 East 65th Street building, jilted me from the presidency of the institute, stopped me from teaching there, and drastically cut down the remuneration for the considerable work that I do for it. In a lawsuit raised by me and my lawyer, a New York Supreme Court judge has ruled that the AEI is acting illegally, and another suit claims that it is illegally discriminating against my civil rights and using age discrimination against me.

This is just a brief summary. Many important professionals and friends of ours continue to protest how incredibly unjust the AEI is to Debbie and me. Incredible!

Meanwhile, I, Debbie, and our supporters have not given up and still hope to restore AEI to its rightful place as the first and foremost Rational Emotive Behavior Therapy training center, and to return to promoting its major philosophies of (a) Unconditional Self-Acceptance (USA), (b) Unconditional Other-Acceptance (UOA), and of (c) Unconditional Life-Acceptance (ULA). We strive for its past status and look forward to reviving it.

The current board of trustees of the AEI has illegally abrogated the long-standing basic contract between me and the institute, and we hope to fully reestablish it, so that it again provides me and Debbie with the following:

- Sufficient power to run the AEI as it was suitably run and greatly efficient since 1965.
- Sufficient income and support for the innumerable services we still do for the institute in spite of the unethical restrictions.
- Full use of the 45 East 65th Street building and rooms of the institute to promote REBT without the hindrance of some of the current staff of AEI.
- Full nursing care, which the institute promised me in 2003 for the rest of my life, to care for me after the loss of my large intestine while I was fulfilling much institute business.
- The restoring of the basic principles and practices of REBT to the training of professionals and of REBT educators.
- Publication and promotion of my and other people's REBT writings and audio-visual materials in the institute's regular catalog and presentations.
- The signing of a full settlement agreement between me and the institute that will ensure that provisions such as these are carried out.
- The full establishment of a substitute board of trustees waiting to take over the bogus board of trustees now running the institute, new REBT-oriented officers, teachers, and trainers to carry on former and revised REBT traditions.
- Election of a new competent and devoted board of trustees and removal of most of the present members of the board, who are toadies of Broder, McMahon, and Vernon, and who keep in power officers and trainers who weakly do their bidding.

Is Justice and Peace for Albert Ellis, Debbie Joffe Ellis, and the real Albert Ellis Institute too much to ask? We hope not!

Some people have said I took UOA too far with people who acted against me and the principles of REBT. I don't agree. Despite behaviors I consider atrocious, I have never stopped believing that they are fallible humans, acting very disturbedly and uncivilly, but despite that still have worth.

What I might have done differently, while maintaining UOA, was to have acted more vigorously earlier, before the troubles of 2004 began. Pity I didn't. There were instances prior to those years when the people who acted against my goals and interests—board members, institute directors, and certain staff members—showed themselves to be untrustworthy, not to be depended upon, irresponsible, or disturbed in ways that were not helpful to the institute. In retrospect, if those people were let go from the institute—and this goes back many decades in the case of some of them—then it is likely that the sad situation at the institute would not have happened. *Maybe.*

I mentioned earlier the state-of-the-art address I gave in December 2005 at the Evolution of Psychotherapy conference in Anaheim, California. Here it is, including the question-and-answer section that followed:

The State of Rational Emotive Behavior Therapy in the Twenty-First Century
Albert Ellis, Ph.D.
Evolution of Psychotherapy Conference
December, 2005
Anaheim, CA

I developed Rational Emotive Behavior Therapy (REBT) between 1953 and 1955, after I had largely abandoned liberal psychoanalysis in 1953 after practicing it for ten years. Even before that, I developed an approach to psychotherapy that Leon Pomeroy has called the Epictetus-Ellis Method. To be sure, it included cognitive, emotional, and action-oriented techniques, but it also was highly philosophic. It used many methods of ancient philosophies—such as Socrates, Epictetus, and Seneca; but it also favored the modern methods of Emerson, Dewey, Santayana, Russell, and Wittgenstein.

I first used philosophy on myself when I was fifteen years of age, and was anxious about my physical weaknesses, and I did so well in coping with them that I made a hobby of teaching them to relatives and friends.

I brought philosophy into psychotherapy when I went to graduate school in clinical psychology in 1942, and I more specifically incorporated it into REBT in 1955. I thus became a pioneering cognitive behavioral (CBT) therapist along with Aaron Beck, and with William Glasser and Steven Hayes. REBT particularly links psychotherapy to philosophy. What is the state of the art in Rational Emotive Behavior Therapy today and how do I use it on myself and with others?

The basic principles of REBT include the following:

1. People do not merely upset themselves because of unfortunate Adversities (A) that occur in their lives, but also with Beliefs,

feelings, and behaviors (B), which they *add* to these Adversities. Therefore, A plus B equals their disturbed (or non-disturbed) Consequences (C). They partly *construct* their disturbed (and non-disturbed) feelings by *reacting* (B) to undesirable A's.

2. People's *contributions* at B to C consist of thoughts, feelings, and behaviors, all of which *collectively* lead to their healthy and unhealthy Consequences.

   When A's are viewed as "bad," people have rational or sensible Belief-feeling-behaviors at B, such as "I don't like A's and wish they didn't exist. But they do exist and I can cope with them." They then feel what REBT calls healthy reactions, such as sorrow, disappointment, and frustration. These healthy reactions enable them to cope with Adversities (A's).

3. When people view Adversities as *terrible* and *awful*, and think they *can't stand them*, they have irrational Beliefs-feelings-behaviors and instead react at C with depressed, angry, and anxious reactions. They feel disturbed, and cope poorly with Adversities (A's).

4. When people view Adversities as *terrible* and *awful*, and think they *can't stand them*, they have irrational Beliefs-feelings-behaviors and instead react at C with depressed, angry, and anxious reactions. They feel disturbed, and cope poorly with Adversities (A's).

5. People have a *choice* of how they Believe-feel-act (at B); and when they make dysfunctional choices—which they often do—they can reconstruct them and choose to change them for more functional choices. They are born and raised to make several dysfunctional choices—because they are fallible humans—but they can almost always change their B's and come up with more functional choices.

6. People can learn (especially with psychotherapy) to see the difference between their functional and dysfunctional choices at B, can learn to correct their dysfunctional Beliefs-feelings-behaviors, and with practice can habitually come to prefer rational to irrational choices, and thereby make themselves less disturbed.

7. It is their biological and learned nature, however, for people to keep falling back to dysfunctional B's all their lives and not to be completely rational or functional. The human condition, as the Buddhists said 2,500 years ago, is to be unenlightened *and* enlightened, never thoroughly and perpetually enlightened.

8. According to REBT principles and practices, a person, you, can maintain considerable enlightenment when you consis-

tently—not *always*—acquire three important basic philosophies: (a) You have Unconditional Self-Acceptance (USA). You always—yes, always—accept *yourself* with your failings. You refuse to do what a notable philosopher, Alfred Korzybski, urged against your doing—that is, damn your *self*, your entire *being*, for your mistakes. You make many mistakes, of course—which humans do. But you always have other chances and never damn the entire you for any errors. (b) You have Unconditional Other-Acceptance (UOA). Just as you refuse to damn yourself for your stupidities, you stubbornly refuse to damn *other people* for theirs. You easily see how they screw up, but don't condemn *them* as *total screw-ups*. Korzybski, again. You feel compassion for wrong-doers. (c) You have Unconditional Life-Acceptance (ULA). You see what is wrong, unjust, and immoral in life, and work to improve it. But you don't conclude that life itself is hopeless and unchangeable. You accept *it*, when you temporarily can't improve it, as "bad" and "inconvenient" but not as "horrible" and "awful." You optimistically see that it *can* improve—and do your best to improve it. But not desperately, hopelessly.

Is this *all* you can do when you do yourself in, when others sabotage you, and life is pretty damned bad? No, not all, but a great deal to stop your silly whining and work at some winning. Work at USA, UOA, and ULA. You won't *always* succeed—but you'll learn!

So life still won't be easy—as Buddhists note. You won't get everything you want but you'll still have you—and many possible enjoyments—if you choose USA, UOA, and ULA. That's a hell of a lot!

Having decided, along with a number of rational philosophers, to strive for USA, UOA, and ULA, I applied these views to my own weaknesses—as I point out in my book *Rational Emotive Behavior Therapy: It Works for Me—It Can Work for You*. For many years I warded off depression, rage, and panic. Pretty good!

Then, as I never expected, I had a real test of my Beliefs-feelings-behaviors. In spite of many rebuffs and criticisms, I founded the not-for-profit Albert Ellis Institute in 1959 and, as its president, propelled REBT to unusual prominence. It became a pioneering leader in Cognitive Behavioral Therapy (CBT), it bought a substantial building in Manhattan, it trained hundreds of therapists in the United States and abroad, it had many affiliated institutes in North and South America and in several other countries, it gave widespread professional and public presentations, and it distributed scores of published materials on REBT. Quite successful and ever-growing. Meanwhile, I published over 75 books, about 800 articles, and many audio- and audio-visual cassettes on REBT and related aspects of psychotherapy. I can safely say that I and the Albert Ellis Institute significantly helped millions of therapists, clients, readers, listeners, and viewers from 1955 to 2003.

Then near disaster struck. Three main officers of the Institute began to be much more interested in absolutistic rulings and in profiting monetarily. They took absolutistic control of its presentations; they dropped its main philosophy of Unconditional Self-Acceptance, Other-Acceptance, and Life-Acceptance; and they radically changed its values and much of the main principles and practices that I had promoted for fifty years.

I fought vigorously against this controlling clique but soon lost almost every battle. I was unethically (and against the by-laws of the Institute) thrown out as President, banned from presenting professional and public lectures and workshops at the Institute, and forced to continue my famous Friday Night Workshops—which had been held at the Institute for 40 years—at an outside building. All this after I had donated millions of dollars to the Institute since 1959 and helped build up its power and its reputation. Unbelievable, but I, and even the Board of Trustees at the Institute, were made lackeys of the three ruthless people who still run it.

To make matters worse, a Separation Agreement was supposed to be signed by the Institute, partially reimbursing me for my keeping the Institute alive for 50 years, but the Institute's lawyer has abandoned this proposed agreement since September, 2005 and made it a dead duck. The controlling officers have made up about 30 lies about me and my wife, Debbie Joffe Ellis, and have published on the Institute's website more lies about their lies. Fantastic!

Debbie and I have naturally fought back with our own factual version of this holocaust and have mobilized hundreds of supporters—therapists and non-therapists—to petition the Board of Trustees and the gang who have restricted and vilified us. Over 500 and more supporters have petitioned the Institute's restrictors to change their ways.

Unfortunately, the Institute still has millions of dollars in its coffers—mainly built up by my donations over many years—and with my small net salary of $1,200 a month, added to a demand by the Institute that I pay for many health benefits that were paid by it for over 40 years, I have now spent most of my life savings over the last two years fighting the Institute. It looks like it will easily win out while I go bankrupt. Some of my supporters have donated sums of money to my defense, but so far this is a long way from enough. Money and power are in the hands of the three rulers of the Institute. Justice and fairness are not in their vocabulary.

To make matters worse—if possible—the three fascistic rulers who run the Institute have intimidated two members of the Board of Trustees into believing their lies about me and Debbie, nicely aided by the Institute's unethical lawyer, and have also intimidated the office personnel of the Institute by threatening the loss of their jobs if they are not cruel and restrictive to me and Debbie.

A late development is that the Executive Director of the Institute, who rigidly opposed me and Debbie, agreed to resign at the end of November. But—significantly enough!—he hasn't agreed to leave the Board of Trustees, and he has appointed as interim director a close friend of one of the Trustees, who has unethically and falsely accused me, since 2004, with lies about my behavior. So this new interim Executive Director is most likely not going to stop the slander and vilification of me and my wife, Debbie.

Can anything still be done to interrupt this dismal state of affairs? Yes, my hundreds of supporters who have protested my being unethically and illegally squelched by the Albert Ellis Institute can keep their protests going. Public opinion still has *some* power; so please let it go our way. Communicate with the three authoritative officers and with Dr. Raymond DiGiuseppe, Director of Education at the Institute, who joined them—Drs. Broder/Doyle/McMahon—in banning me (Dr. Ellis) from making presentations for the Institute. Give them a piece of your mind! Strongly! . . .

What else can be done?

1. More specifically my wife and partner, Debbie Joffe Ellis, and our supporters can preserve the original and modified theory of Rational Emotive Behavior Therapy, to see that its philosophy is practiced by its teaching professionals and students and that its integrity as a theory is backed by empirically oriented research. Is it REALLY more efficient and useful than Cognitive Therapy, Cognitive Behavioral Therapy and Acceptance and Commitment Therapy? Let's see!

2. Rational Emotive Behavior Therapy (REBT) is not to be fixed for all time, but nor is it to be watered down and made more general—as the current people who have presently taken over the Institute are now doing—to make it "more popular." If it is to be changed, let it be done on the basis, if any, of many hard-headed empirical studies.

3. The future of REBT shall be to continue its philosophy, to see whether this philosophy is really working, to add to and

modify it if it proves to be empirically lacking, and to spend more time and money in researching it and other cognitive-emotive-behavior therapies. Research and more research is the concrete answer to its particular therapeutic hypotheses. Those who follow it and teach it should preferably do their best to practice Unconditional Self-Acceptance, Unconditional Other-Acceptance, and Unconditional Life-Acceptance with their clients, themselves, and other practitioners.

Arbitrary authority had better go!

How about me and Debbie? We still keep fighting as long as we have any money to do so—and practicing the principles of REBT. We, first, will unconditionally accept ourselves even when many people, deluded by the Institute, continue to slander and vilify us. When we make errors—which we will—we will fully accept ourselves *with* these errors and do our best to change.

Second, we shall not damn the main three perpetrators of unfairness and injustice for their misdeeds. They act fascistically most of the time, but they are not "rotten fascists." They occasionally, no doubt, act nicely to their friends and relatives.

Third, we shall accept life with all its unfairness, and not desperately damn it. Life inevitably includes some arrant injustices which, for the present, we cannot improve. It is very bad—but not *awful* and *terrible*.

By continuing to promote Unconditional Self-Acceptance, Unconditional Other-Acceptance, and Unconditional Life-Acceptance, we shall, we hope, encourage others to use them, too. That won't improve the world and the people in it completely. But we think it will help.

QUESTION AND ANSWER SESSION

Question: Good Morning. I would very much like to be supportive of you. I trained under you many years ago. I'm a big fan of yours. Your presentation was wonderful but also quite general. I wonder if you would be willing to give us some specifics. When you talk about them speaking poorly of you or degrading you, I have no idea what you're talking about. I don't know if you're talking about malpractice, malfeasance. I have no idea what the accusations are. If you could give us some specifics, I'd greatly appreciate it. Thank you.

Answer: Well, first of all, they're saying that I'm 92 and feeble. That I'm unable to do what I did and control things. That I'm unable to do my presentations and my supervisions, etc., because of this. So they have age discrimination. Actually, I do all my presentations—especially the Friday Night Workshops, which I've been forced to do outside the Institute, next door. They won't let me—they're afraid. It used to make more money and popularity for the Institute than everything. And Debbie does it with me, and we have no complaints whatsoever. But they lied about my being feeble. Secondly, they made up lies about my attacking people—with my cane—and doing other things. (Audience laughter.) Pure lies, and then lies about lies. Read our website, and read their website, and I have listed about 30 of these lies. And next they told all the people who work for the Institute—the receptionists and the helpers, etc.—that I'm no good and that I and Debbie do bad things and talk against them, which we don't do. So they lie about us and make up much more lies. So, as I said, I have this one thing on our website that shows at least 30 different lies, and then it shows the facts in relation to the lies, and why they're unfactual and lying. So it would take too much time to go through them right now, but read our website and you'll find them.

Question: Dr. Ellis, I was at the Institute for training over the summer, for the primary and advanced practicums. And I noticed that, having read a lot of your things and been to other events where you were at, that the curriculum there was not solidly REBT, and I know REBT has been taken off the name, and the flyers, etc. And that what's going on there is more cognitive than REBT. Can you comment on that?

Answer: Yes, we have flyers put out by the Institute for their presentations for the next several months. One, they don't include me at all. Two, they have practica that I usually led, but I'm not in it. Three, they have toadies of the three unethical people who run the Institute who were not trained themselves in REBT but in general psychotherapy and sometimes in general cognitive behavioral therapy, and these people are presenting. So if you get the latest flyers of the Institute, you'll see that I'm missing and that Rational Emotive Behavioral Therapy is just mentioned slightly but really is not included in it. By all means, get the flyer.

Question: Dr. Ellis, I had a question regarding the thinking of something bad and inconvenient versus horrible and awful. But when it comes to something like the holocaust or any kind of ethnic cleansing, it's hard for me to not just think that that's horrible and awful and really be brought down by that. So can you comment on how you would use REBT to deal with a situation as bad as ethnic cleansing, or some seemingly horrible situation?

Answer: Well, REBT, I think, is the only cognitive behavioral therapy and the only one of all different 200 types of therapy which says that many things are bad—you don't get what you want or you do get what you don't want, so that's bad—and a few things are very bad—like the Institute's persecuting me and Debbie (audience laughter). So they're very bad. But nothing, nothing, nothing is awful, horrible, and terrible, because, one, even though a hurricane hits and 50,000 people are killed, there could be two hurricanes and kill 100,000. So things always could be worse. And no matter how bad things are—and they sometimes are exceptionally bad, like the holocaust in European countries—there could be two or three holocausts, and although between 5 million and 10 million people were killed, there could be more than that. So some things are bad. A few things are exceptionally bad and kill or harm or control the freedom of millions of people. But it's still not awful. And, what's more, no matter how bad it is, you can stand it. You can take it and not be happy about it—that would be abnormal—but in spite of it, you can lead a happy life. Debbie's family, for example, her mother and father went through the holocaust, but they got by and still later led a happy life. And many other people have. So it's never hopeless. It's never totally bad. It's just exceptionally bad. But you are an individual who can cope—and sometimes happily cope—with an exceptionally bad thing. So, again, nothing is horrible, awful, or terrible. And no matter how bad it is—unless they actually kill you—you can take it and still lead a pleasurable and happy existence. (Audience applause.)

Question: Dr. Ellis, one of the most profound things that has ever happened to me in my life—and the most profound thing in my graduate studies—was watching the video that you referred to earlier with Dr. Perls and Dr. Rogers. Is there any way to obtain that video today?

Answer: Perls fucked up as usual. (Audience laughter.) He was normally—not all the time—a very hostile, nasty, negative individual, and he was nasty to Gloria and she didn't like him at all. Rogers was very nice and accepting and fatherly. Rogers always gave Unconditional Other-Acceptance, so he accepted Gloria, and she liked him and corresponded with him later. And I gave her Unconditional Other-Acceptance, but I also showed that it wasn't terrible that she didn't have a man and she could probably find one. And I showed her how to do it briefly if she wanted to do it. So she corresponded with me and got married a few years later and said that it was partly a result of my session with her. So she led a better life, and about 10 years later she died. So she appreciated Carl Rogers and me, but not Fritz Perls.

Question: Dr. Ellis, you're such an inspiration—professionally and personally—and I want to thank you for sharing your personal struggles as you go through this time, and being really honest and open about that. I'm wondering if you—you're such a master at this—through this process, did you get depressed and then pull yourself out of it? Or does depression not even touch you any more, because you're such a master? Could you share a little bit about your process?

Answer: No, I never got depressed about the situation—or anything in recent years. When I was a child, and I wasn't loved madly by the little girls that I was in love with, then I stupidly depressed myself. But it only lasted a while, and then I turned it into sorrow and regret, but not depression. But even though these thugs are the worst thugs that I have ever seen in psychotherapy, they're not killing as many people as Hitler and Stalin and Mao, but they really are most thuggish most of the time—not only with me and Debbie, but with practically everyone. And they intimidate practically all the people at the Institute. But I don't hate them and I'm not depressed. I'm just very, very sorry that they exist. Too bad! (Audience laughter and applause.)

Question: First, I would like to ask where you found such a lovely lady as Debbie, and are there any more. And secondly, I would like to say that my fondest wish is that at 92 I will have your wit, your insight, and your therapeutic skill. If that's feeble, God help us all! (Audience applause.)

Answer: Thank you. I didn't find Debbie. She found me. (Audience laughter.) And she'd been devoted in teaching REBT and in being a therapist in Australia for over 10 years. And she decided that she'd like to keep visiting the United States and me, so finally we fell in love. And it was the happiest moment in my whole life. (Audience applause.)

Question: Dr. Ellis, I appreciate that your career is still a work in progress, but at this early point in your career, how could you characterize your legacy so far?

Answer: My legacy, I hope, is myself and the way I refuse to upset myself when bad things happen. (Audience applause.) And all the principles of REBT: You largely upset yourself. You can change it. You have choices. And you can choose, choose, choose, USA—Unconditional Self-Acceptance—UOA—Unconditional Other-Acceptance—and ULA—Unconditional Life-Acceptance. So go work your ass off and choose it. (Audience applause.)

Question: Dr. Ellis, I greatly appreciate your work. And when you asked for ideas and help, my young naive reaction was that I wondered if there would be a solution of starting just a new institute, with the support of the people that you have in the room that will support you. And just beat them by starting the real Albert Ellis Institute.

Answer: Well, our first choice is to get rid of the people who act bastardly most of the time. Throw them out. And that's why we appealed to the public—the professional public and the whole public. And leaders of professional training and self-help training. (Audience applause.)

Question: Dr. Ellis, I am a practicing psychotherapist and have appreciated your many contributions through the years. We've all been enriched by them. I've appreciated your optimism and what you described today. One area that has always puzzled me has been your ideas about religion and spirituality. I wonder if you can comment on your thoughts about religion and spirituality today and the role that it has in psychotherapy.

Answer: Well, people are entitled to be as religious as they want to be and as spiritual as they want to be. But I have shown in the *Journal of Individual Psychology* and in other places here, that if you're rationally spiritual, then you decide to be in favor of and to help other people and to make the world better. And if you're irrationally spiritual and religious, then you can be bigoted and knock down and kill other people. (Audience applause.) So spirituality and religion are very good as long as they have quite rational elements in them.

Question: Dr. Ellis, it really boggles my mind when I think about putting REBT in the same category as CBT and other cognitive therapies, because I think it has one powerful weapon that the others don't have, and that is the "too damned bad" factor. That has gotten me through many a tight spot, and people I worked with, so I thank you for that—for allowing me and others to be a child at times and to be able to stamp your feet and say "Too damned bad." Thank you.

Answer: Thank you!

Question: Dr. Ellis, 20 years ago I sat on your stage as a volunteer, and you helped me a great deal in less than five minutes. I am a licensed psychologist, and I have a chronic nightmare that there is *one more paper* I have to write. I wake up in a sweat every night. My question is: Can you address us clinicians who are ready to write, who have clinically treated clients, what do you suggest we write about to remove the nightmare?

Answer: There's *many* more papers! If you don't have to do them perfectly well and don't have to get universal acclaim for them, then as I do at the age of 92, I've written in the last few years five new books and two I'm working on at the present time. So there's many, many things you can do if you don't think you have to do them marvelously and perfectly well.

Daniel Eckstein, Moderator: Let me just say, Samuel Johnson once said, "A horsefly can bite a horse and make him wince, but a horsefly is always a horsefly and a horse is always a horse." We've had a magnificent steed—I didn't say stud, Albert—we've had a magnificent steed. And I think, Albert, this has been your finest hour. On behalf of so many of us, thanks for all the memories.

(Audience applause and standing ovation.)

The year 2006 is proving to be the most difficult so far. I spend hours reading and responding to e-mails and memos from Lyle Stuart and other institute people and lawyers. Time that deprives me of completing this book and others I am working on. Time that deprives me of more relaxing time with Debbie. I accept, while thoroughly disliking, this circumstance. For months I have been forced to do my famous Friday Night Workshops next door, and often return sneezing and coughing, as it is presently very cold.

In April I agreed that a group come to hear me talk one Sunday afternoon. Since there was not enough room in my office we used the lecture hall. Bob O'Connell—the director, who replaced Michael Broder—sent me a letter reprimanding me for my "unauthorized use" of the hall. I was accused of allowing people to wander freely through the institute—an utter lie, which I pointed out. Lyle Stuart then e-mailed me the following:

April 6, 2006
To: Albert Ellis
From: Lyle Stuart

This will respond to your note to Bob O'Connell and me concerning your unauthorized use of the Institute's premises last Sunday.

We do not accept your attempt to evade responsibility for your actions by parsing words. That you violated your responsibility to the Institute last Sunday is documented by our security tapes showing the numerous people whom you and Debbie invited to hear you in our auditorium and permitted to freely move around other parts of the building, all without the Institute's authority.

You must understand that you are an employee at Will and that acts such as you engaged in Sunday evening will no longer be tolerated.

Al, we have been overly patient with you, but you must understand that we will not continue to be if you insist on further abuses of your duty to the Institute.

If it is your desire to become a martyr by goading us into terminating your employment, please rest assured that we will oblige you.

Quite something, to be banned from freely presenting in, and using the lecture hall of, the institute bearing my name.

There are restrictions constantly. For the decades I've lived in this institute, it has supplied every floor, including the sixth floor on which I live, with a stock of toilet paper and tissues. On May 1, 2006, when we requested supplies, the lady who usually sends them up said that she was told that the president of the institute (Lyle Stuart) instructed that no more supplies be sent up for Dr. Ellis. When one of my nurses queried this, Kristene Doyle (associate director) called her and said that any requests for supplies for the sixth floor would be passed on to the president.

Incredible.

Back in 2005, Michael Broder instigated the rule that if I wanted any writing supplies I had to put in writing the time, date, supplies requested, and have Debbie give this to the receptionist at the front desk. Oh, yes—I had to *sign* the request. One day I sent a request down but forgot to write the time on it. The receptionist called Debbie and told her of this. Debbie apologized and asked that the receptionist fill in the time. The receptionist answered that she would only do it this once, and in future any requests not done properly would be immediately returned.

I am doing well at accepting this confining and restrictive behavior and attitudes from others. Debbie works harder at doing so, as she more directly receives the hostility and unfair treatment than I do.

I will continue to do my work, and to fight for justice, as long as I have the strength to do so.

Chapter 14

The Final Chapter
by Debbie Joffe Ellis

T he final chapter of the life of Albert Ellis is one that contains unimaginable pain, deep sadness and disappointment, victory, triumph, and profound love. His final chapter contained tests greater than any other in his life. It tested his capacity to practice his principles in the most dire of circumstances. And practice them he did. Heroically. Courageously. Unswervingly. Till the very end.

The victory was not one of achieving what he wanted in the outer circumstances of his life. For, sadly, regarding two important aspects—his health and his institute—he did not. The victory came from his remaining true to his philosophy, from remaining authentic and exemplary. Throughout the days of his physical decline he refused self-pity, he refused to damn people who acted against his goals and interests, and he continued to unconditionally accept others and the circumstances he could not change.

With determination Al made what appeared to be a *super*-human effort to recover, to regain strength, to return to an active life. He did not give up. It was his organs—his body—that finally broke down. Doctors were amazed at his willpower and persistence. He continued to contribute to others—giving interviews for books, newspapers, and magazines, dictating writings to me, speaking to students and groups from his hospital bed—even when his fatigue was enormous.

In his final weeks, when Al no longer had the strength to read or dictate, nor the energy to communicate much, our love—our touching, our tenderness, our being together—was the only good thing we experienced. Every day we expressed our thankfulness for having each other. Despite the bad things that were happening, Al continued to remember each day what was still good in his life.

One of Al's main goals in life had been to show people how to enjoy precious life as much as possible by teaching them how to reduce their suffering. He achieved that through his brilliant REBT theory, his tireless decades of teaching and writing, his work with individual clients and in groups, and—significantly—through the way he lived *and* the way he died.

Al returned from his outstanding presentations at the Evolution of Psychotherapy Conference, December 2005, tired but satisfied. He had demonstrated his vigor and commitment to continuing to "spread the gospel of St. Albert," and his presentations were received with enormous outpourings of appreciation and affection. Thousands of attendees also had signed petitions of support, although to our dismay, these petitions later mysteriously disappeared.

Back in wintry New York City, Al immediately attended to the numerous demands and activities awaiting him. The least pleasant of these activities—and greatly time-consuming—was responding to e-mails, memos, and letters from institute people or their lawyers. Rarely did they talk to Al directly; most communication was done via writing or through their lawyers and Al's lawyers. There were many days when Al would spend hours and hours responding to statements and accusations, and defending his position while expressing his truth. Doing this was very tiresome, and it prevented him from doing more of what he wanted to do. He wanted to finish this autobiography, and he would spend as much time as he could on it after the institute matters were done. Unfortunately, his eyes would get tired after the hours already spent on the prior work, so that limited him. In addition, he had started a new book about love, the two of us were cowriting books, there were articles to continue working on—and it was impossible to give each of these projects the time and energy he wished to give them. Like a trouper he kept going and going, forcing himself to do as much as he could every day. There just was not enough time to do all. Regular medical visits usually deprived us of half-days of work and were also often quite tiring. Al hardly ever complained—he simply accepted the circumstances—and kept going.

Each day we would respond to the e-mails and letters that kept coming to Al from colleagues, friends, clients, and those curious about the situation with the institute. He continued to help clients—giving both telephone sessions and face-to-face therapy sessions upstairs in his bedroom. He would wear his robe and sit in his recliner chair with the client sitting across from him. This saved the time and energy it would have taken for him to dress, go down to his office, and see the clients there. Having an ileostomy bag since his surgery in 2003, and painful arthritis, getting dressed and going down to his office did not take the few minutes it took prior to that surgery. So one way or another Al would find the most efficient ways possible for him to continue his work and conserve his energy.

He continued to give his famous Friday Night Workshops in a large room we rented weekly in the building next door. Getting there was quite an effort, but the workshop was a tradition he'd started over four decades ago and was very dear to him. He would give himself enough time to check his blood sugar levels, take insulin or have a snack—whichever was needed—groom, shave, dress, go downstairs in the elevator from the sixth floor, walk past the empty, silent first-floor lecture hall of the institute (in which he'd conducted Friday Night Workshops for forty-plus years until he was stopped from doing so in July 2005), out the front door, down the steps to the street, turning right and walking to the next building, up the steps and through the front entrance, into the elevator, and up to the second floor, through the room and into his seat. He was walking with a cane and leaning on me, and the whole process was exhausting for him. Nonetheless, when the workshop began, he was at it—vigorously disputing irrational ideas that volunteer participants shared, demonstrating REBT with his usual astuteness, wit, and wisdom, and answering questions from the audience. The room was packed—often standing room only. Regulars who'd been attending for decades, student groups, members of the public, and present and former clients loved these weekly gatherings and gained a great deal from them. At the end of the workshop, the tiresome return to the institute building was made.

In November and December 2005, and in the months of January, February, and March of 2006, the weather was often freezing; sometimes the temperature was *below* freezing with rain and/or snow, strong winds—very severe. Though Al would wear layers of clothing, gloves, scarf, and a bulky coat—he would usually be coughing and somewhat short of breath for a while after returning to the apartment. Even in April the weather was far from ideal. Despite the difficulties, it seemed that nothing short of hospitalization would stop Al from doing these workshops. It is fortunate that during this period John Fireman and Andrew Unger were recording many of Al's workshops and activities for their documentary about his life, so many people will be able to see Al in action during this challenging time.

On Friday, May 12, 2006, Al seemed more tired than usual, though progressively through the year from January onward, his strength had been lessening for reasons already mentioned. I suggested that we cancel the workshop scheduled for 7:30 p.m.—he adamantly refused. At 6:45 p.m., he was so weak that he could hardly get out of his chair without help. Though he preferred walking, he reluctantly agreed to be taken next door in a wheelchair instead. At 7 p.m. I had to call on a couple of men to help lift him into the wheelchair. I again said, "Al, let's cancel." "No," was his firm reply. He knew himself and his capacity well. For decades he had been monitoring his health, his sugar levels—often testing his blood over twelve times a day. He could tell from either giddiness, fatigue, or hyperenergetic states when his blood sugar level was extreme—one way or another. He was in touch with his body and in tune with its needs. If he thought he was up to doing the workshop, then he was. Had he recognized possible danger, he would have attended to that condition and probably canceled.

So we went next door, where the room was crowded as usual. Al was in good humor and did a great workshop. Those who knew him may have noticed that his voice sounded weaker at times, but other than that he was in good form. Following the workshop, however, he was *not* in good shape. He coughed more and was very pale. The nurse and I monitored him carefully throughout the night. He awoke every thirty or forty-five minutes, but that was not so unusual. At about 5:30 a.m., as he was sitting on the edge of the bed and I was helping get his slippers on, he fell back and shook. His eyes rolled back briefly. I immediately called 911, and within minutes an ambulance arrived.

That was our last time in the apartment until more than a year later, when we returned for the last seven and a half weeks of Al's life.

Al was found to have aspiration pneumonia. He was in great peril, and immediate action had to be taken. The solution was to provide Al with a feeding tube into his stomach. No more would he be able to take food or drink through his mouth. No more the sensation of taste or the oral relief of quenching thirst and relieving a dry mouth. Though diabetic, he had in the past allowed himself small portions of sweet foods he enjoyed. "No more strawberry shortcake," he would say jokingly. No more of anything. There he was, in this grave situation, still using humor.

The regular and safest procedure for inserting a feeding tube was nonsurgically through the mouth and down the alimentary canal. The doctors tried to do this a number of times, but it was not possible, as Al's inner organs were not in regular positions due to his previous surgery, and in addition to that, he had a hernia and there was some internal scar tissue. The only hope for him was for doctors to insert the tube surgically—and because of irregularities mentioned above—it ended up being inserted into his jejunum rather than his stomach.

Anesthesia is risky for anyone, but particularly for the elderly. Al took the prospect of the surgery with his characteristic calm; I was exceedingly concerned. The doctors tried to prepare me to face the possibility, and probability, of Al not living much longer—even if he did survive the surgery. Is he a "Do Not Resuscitate?" they asked. No—*Resuscitate*.

He came through the surgery. But what enormous physical suffering Al was to endure from that time on. I was with him day and night and witnessed what he went through. The hospital allowed me to put a fold-up bed in the room—at night I would unfold it and place it alongside his hospital bed. That way we could hold hands, I could stroke him, and get up in an instant if he needed anything.

But there was little rest for him to have. His skin was agonizingly itchy—no cause was found—and creams had only a temporary relieving effect. Stroking and massaging him helped, and I did that many hours throughout the day. (When I say "day," I mean the twenty-four-hour period. During the long stay in the hospital, day could easily merge into night as a blur, not a distinct change. Day, night—both seemed the same.) His body ached with arthritis. I pushed to get an airbed, which would relieve some of the pain and pressure. Digestive fluids would ooze out around his ileostomy site, and his skin would be red, raw, and burning. Similarly, acidic digestive juices would ooze out of the freshly made feeding tube site (about six inches to the right of the ileostomy site), causing the same skin degradation, leaving burning, weeping, raw tissue around it. His mouth was dry as sandpaper. "Water, water, water," he kept asking. He felt intensely thirsty. Many nights he did not sleep at all for this reason. All I could do was swab his tongue with a minimally dampened sponge. I'd first put it in ice water in the hope of providing greater refreshment and more relief. It hardly made a difference. It was too risky to allow Al to suck on ice (the liquid as the ice melted would go into his lungs, causing more pneumonia), and drinking—as already explained—was not allowed. Sometimes Al felt very hungry—he wanted food, any food. Not allowed. Can you imagine living for a year and three months without food or drink? Or for a year? For even three months? Three days? That was Al's experience—all nutrition being pumped into him via a tube into his jejunum for his final year and three months. And he didn't complain. He endured it.

Another reason that Al was unable to get any rest was that hospital staff came in every few hours to look, check, empty his ileostomy bag, test his blood sugar levels, and take blood . . . and more blood . . . and more blood.

Once Al's condition was stable, a couple of months after the surgery, I put a sign on the door saying, "Please do not enter between 2 and 5 a.m. unless necessary." I rolled up a towel to cover the large crack at the bottom of the door to keep out light, draft, and noise. Of course, I had the doctor's permission to put up this sign, and some carers respected the request whenever possible; others resented it and just did whatever they wanted to do.

This number-one-rated NYC hospital was also a teaching hospital, and as a result, interns would do rounds at all hours, including the early hours of the morning. When blood was needed for testing, and a phlebotomist wasn't immediately available, sometimes one of these inexperienced student doctors would attempt to take Al's blood. Some were fine at the task, but a few could not get the vein or artery and would keep trying and trying—putting fresh needles into his blood vessels again and again. Al would moan with pain. Once I just told them to stop. The young doctor was getting nowhere, and Al was not to be her experimental guinea pig if I had any say. Al would stoically bear the pain and not complain.

The challenge of Al's diabetes was another area that created disharmony with some hospital staff. He was what is called a "brittle" diabetic—meaning his blood sugars could unpredictably and erratically swing from high to low at any time. For this reason he tested his blood sugars more often than many other diabetics do. The hospital procedures limited their times of testing his blood to every four to five hours. This was sometimes not enough, in our view. We would use our own meter in between, and a number of times I had to alert medical staff to attend to him with extra insulin or immediate glucose when his sugars were extreme.

Some medical staff, especially the senior doctors, appreciated my involvement. Dr. Adelman, Dr. Seigler, Dr. Reid, and Dr. Lo Faso were incredibly kind and supportive. Others were irritable at best, hostile at worst, to me and to Al when we pointed things out to them and when we asked for urgent attention. Sadly, many of the so-called caregivers were far from caring. For this reason, when I had to leave Al's side for a short time to shower or to attend to other necessities, I would always arrange for someone to be with him. I would make sure he was never without someone by his side.

Back to the surgery. After some days spent in the intensive care unit, we moved to a room in another section of the hospital. At about 2:30 a.m. on the second night there, Al's breathing was abnormal and it was clear that something was wrong. Immediately I called for a nurse, who checked Al's vitals and then urgently pressed a call button on the wall. Doctors came charging in. I was told to leave the room, so I watched the activity from outside. Doctors were pounding his back, pressing on his front. "Breathe, Dr. Ellis, breathe," a doctor shouted a number of times. A machine was brought in that facilitated Al's breathing by ensuring that enough oxygen was entering his mouth and nose through the mask. These fine doctors had stabilized Al's condition. I was told later that we were close to losing him that night. After a few days Al no longer required the oxygen machine but had to breathe in sulphury fumes from a nebulizer every few hours. We were told it was necessary for his lungs, but it also unfortunately could lead to nausea and was most unpleasant.

Only days after this episode, Al asked me to get him his autobiography notes, pen and paper, and a copy of *Romeo and Juliet*. He wanted to write an opera, based on that Shakespearian work, and dedicate it to me. I got him those things, and every day Al did some reading and would attempt to write. I say "attempt" because initially he could scarcely grip the pen, and then when he did, his hand was shaky. But every day, sometimes for only a few minutes, he would try writing— first his signature, over and over, then on some days he'd write sentences. Eventually he could write pages. Unbelievable. Despite all the pain and deprivation, he pushed himself to be productive. Some days he was too weak or tired to read—but each day he'd attempt it. He would look at the *New York Times*. A few weeks into our time at the hospital, John and Andrew* brought in a gift of a massive volume of *New Yorker* cartoons. Al read a few each day. He pushed himself daily to do some mind-stimulating activity.

---

*John Fireman and Andrew Unger are currently working on a documentary about Albert Ellis.

Doing physical therapy was extremely painful and difficult, but again Al pushed himself to cooperate with the therapists to do the best he could. He wanted to get better. The goal was to get home. When asked by doctors what he wanted, he would usually give the same answer: "To get better, to finish my autobiography and other books, to keep helping people, and to be in charge of my institute again."

Through his extraordinary efforts, Al slowly and steadily improved. The doctors recommended that he go into a nursing/rehab home so that he could gain more strength before returning to a home environment. I looked at a number of places, some horrific in that they were dimly lit, with little or no welcoming atmosphere, and smelling of urine and worse. One place, which had the best reputation, I liked. It was bright and clean, it did not have unpleasant odors—*that* was the one I wanted for Al. But understandably there was a waiting list. I sought out the appropriate administrative staff, spoke with them, called them every few days, and luckily within the week a room became available. Another advantage of this place was that it was directly across the road from the hospital, so that if there was a need, Al could swiftly get to the emergency room. Good.

So in late July, we moved into the room on the fourth floor of the home. The kind director of nursing arranged for a recliner chair to be put in there. It would be good for Al to sit in it at times during the day, and I slept on it every night. Slept? Again, Al and I *at best* slept for about forty-five to sixty minutes at a time before he would wake—either thirsty, itchy, in pain—or all three. His late-night medications were administered after midnight, and morning ones started at around 5 a.m. Every single day. Al's body, and what it required to keep going, became nothing less than a torture chamber. The doctor and two main nurses on the floor were astounded by Al's lack of self-pity, the effort he made to recover, and his ever-magnificent smile at times, despite the pain and discomfort he was forced to endure. A few of the nurses were truly outstanding and caring. Some were far from it. Some of the aides whose jobs included helping to wash Al and changing the bedsheets could be rough and uncaring, and they clearly hated my being around. Too bad! I would stop them when they were too rough or rushed, and I would then request help from others and do whatever I could myself. But on weekends and public holidays, there were few regular staff members—you got who you got, no choice. I ended up having to hire a caring and competent person to assist at times, and whenever I could I did procedures myself.

The process of physical therapy proved to be difficult—but, as usual, Al went all out to make the best effort he could. The way for Al to regain muscle and strength was by appropriate exercise. The process of getting dressed and up to the therapy floor was painful, but Al willingly did it. His skin around the openings in his abdomen was burning, raw, and painful. His skin was itchy all over. His knee and other arthritic areas were exceedingly painful. Yet he would go up to therapy, and walk a few more steps each day. Soon he was walking almost the length of the long room with the aid of a walker. He would do leg and arm stretches and exercises. His pain and itching, however, were so intense that he would frequently exclaim, "Ow, ow" as he walked. Some of the therapists were understanding, but a few were critical. After a certain period of time, it was assessed that insufficient progress had been made within that time for them to continue the therapy. I could hardly believe it. Here was a man of ninety-three years, who'd recently come too close to dying. Was he expected to run around the block within the prescribed weeks? There was no doubt he *was* making progress. We were shown exercises Al could do in bed, and it was recommended he sit up and get out of his bed each day. The longer we were in the facility, the more disappointed we felt about the limitations of the physical therapy Al could receive in the home, and I started to inquire about physical therapists from outside the facility who could visit us. It was important to build up Al's muscles.

Al showed signs of improvement as the year progressed, though there was not a day without intense pain of many sorts. He continued to do as much as he could in terms of his REBT work. He gave interviews with writers, journalists, and professors, including those from the *New York Times*, a major London newspaper, a Scottish journal, *Psychology Today* magazine, and *New York* magazine. A psychiatrist from the hospital visited and asked Al questions about his REBT theory, and a psychology professor from a New York university interviewed him for her article about bullying.

It became too painful for Al to write, so he would dictate letters to me, including his final one expressing his views about the actions of the institute people and what he wanted. He would dictate to me information for this autobiography and for other writings.

Despite his enormous physical suffering, Al still showed interest and concern for others. His doctor thought that was astonishing and said that in his many years of working with the elderly he could hardly remember a patient in so much pain who wasn't mostly self-absorbed.

Al's reaching out to others in pain was highly unusual. For example, the brother of one of Al's best nurses had died suddenly in a car accident. The nurse had taken a few days off, and when he returned Al looked at him intently and said, "I'm very sorry about your brother. That's very, very sad. But remember that though you'll always be deprived of him, you can still have happiness in your life." Tears filled the nurse's eyes— very uncharacteristic for this man who was normally quite stoic and did not express emotions much at work. He thanked Al profusely.

Al frequently expressed concern about me and my lack of rest. I would tell him that I was fine and that there was nothing I would rather do than be with him every second of my life. Every day he would say, "Thank you." I told him there was no need. I thanked *him*. We continued to relish, appreciate, be grateful to the core of our beings that we were together. I would stroke and massage Al often, for prolonged periods, each day. We loved that. He particularly enjoyed having his head being stroked, with my fingernails gently moving from his forehead to the nape of his neck over and over. Once in a while he'd ask me to talk to him. "What about, Al?" "Anything," he answered. This wasn't to be a conversation, and I doubt that he was paying a lot of attention to what I was saying. It seemed that the sound of my voice was comforting to him. So I'd just talk for a while, until he'd say, "Enough."

Towards the end of 2006, a psychology professor who had in the past brought her classes to the institute to hear Al in his Friday Night Workshops contacted me to inquire about Al's condition. She wondered whether he was up to having students come to hear him speak at the nursing home. Al agreed to meet with them. The administrative people at the home allowed us to use a room for this purpose, and on two occasions the delighted students visited. It was a massive effort for Al to complete his early-afternoon bandage dressing changes, check his blood sugar levels, get medications, dress, get into the wheelchair, make sure the food pump was secure and working, and get to the room. Once there, though his voice was not as strong as it used to be and despite ongoing itchiness and discomfort, he was great. He would talk about REBT, we'd sing some of his rational humorous songs, he'd answer questions, he'd express compassion for difficulties students told him of, and he'd demonstrate his approach with volunteers. A typical Albert Ellis workshop! Incredible, given the state of his health. A story, with photo, appeared in the *New York Times* on December 10, 2006, about this.

Complications and setbacks, particularly from December onward, were happening with greater frequency. A number of times Al's feeding tube would slip out. This could be life-threatening as, if he was not getting enough steady food, his blood sugars would drop—leading to coma or worse. We'd be rushed to the emergency room for the tube to be re-inserted or replaced. Sometimes we'd be out of the ER within four to six hours; sometimes we'd be stuck there for much longer. It depended on how busy the ER was at that time or on the waiting time for transport back to the home.

One Saturday morning at about 5:30 a.m. I smelled a strong vanilla fragrance—the odor of the liquid nutrition that was being pumped into Al. Sure enough, his feeding tube was out, and the "food" was all over the bedsheets. Students were scheduled to visit Al at the home at two that afternoon, and Al did not want to cancel.

We were rushed to the ER. Al's blood sugar had plummeted to 32— very dangerously low. Glucose was immediately administered intravenously, and his sugar levels shot up into the 500s, but with time they dropped. A new feeding tube was inserted. By late morning we were ready to return to the home. We were waiting for transport, and Al said he felt okay. I asked him whether he wanted to cancel the students' visit. "Definitely not" was his reply. The kind ER social worker who had contacted transport was aware of Al's desire to get back quickly, as students were coming. She had studied his work in college and was quite in awe of him. Noon came by, one o'clock—no transport. Then at about 1:05 my cell phone rang. I ran into the corridor to take the call, which was from the home. I was told that students were waiting in the lobby, but since Al had been in the hospital all day thus far, the home's director didn't think he should exert himself, and so the students were asked to leave. The professor was also trying to call me at this time with the news, but I was engaged in talking with the director. I told the ER social worker, who was still trying to expedite transport, about the situation. She said, "You know, this is highly unusual, but since the ER is extremely quiet right now, if Dr. Ellis wants to still talk to the students, you can use the trauma room, which has a door we can close. But if an emergency comes in, everyone will have to immediately leave. If not, you can use it for fifteen to twenty minutes." "Al, do you want the students to come here?" I asked. He did. I called the professor who was on the street with her students outside the home, just across the road from us. "Get here as quickly as you can," I told her, explaining the situation.

So there we were. In the trauma room—a room where critically ill or injured people are taken to be revived, surrounded by tubes, machines, all sorts of medical equipment. And there was Albert Ellis—on the hospital stretcher, intravenous fluid dripping into his arm, nutrient fluid being pumped into his abdomen, surrounded by fifteen students, their teacher, and me. He talked magnificently about REBT, the importance of suffering less and enjoying life more. In the trauma room of the emergency room in New York's finest hospital. Incredible. One student asked him how he felt. "Great," Al answered. I responded, "Great? Al, how do you feel great, with all that's going on?" Without hesitation, he replied, "I use REBT." Another student, a nun, shared that she had worked as a counselor in Kenya and that Al's theories had helped her and her clients enormously. "A lot of people tell me that," replied Al. He continued to answer questions until, about fifteen minutes into the visit, the ambulette to transport us back to the home had arrived. How often does a brilliant pioneer inspire others from an ER bed after recovering from being moments away from coma and possibly worse? Not too often! But that was Albert Ellis. The one. The only.

From early 2007 things got worse. Al's white cell count was increasing. His liver function was declining. Pneumonia recurred. All extremely serious conditions. The worst part of returning to the hospital was having to wait long hours in the emergency room before a hospital bed became available and Al could be admitted. I can't remember his ever getting a bed within a twenty-four-hour period. Once we waited twenty-six hours, another time twenty-eight hours, the worst was waiting thirty-seven hours. The ER medical staff was under pressure to attend to many people, and it was clear to me during the times we were there that the ER was badly understaffed. I would have to constantly implore nurses to take Al's blood sugar to make sure it wasn't too high or too low. Sometimes a doctor would give directives, for example, "Give Dr. Ellis intravenous fluids," and this would happen only after hours of my continuing to remind nurses. The stretchers were incredibly uncomfortable for Al, whose arthritis caused him additional pain. I would find pillows and extra blankets and place them under him in an attempt to decrease his discomfort. The noise, the lights, going for CT scans or X-rays, returning to the ER frenzy—with no promise of a bed anytime soon. For many this would truly be crazy-making. Al accepted it, though at times bearing it was almost intolerable. Sometimes he would moan with pain. He was prevented from taking any medications that reduce pain, as they might adversely affect the other medications he was on. So more often than not he would have to endure the pain. Stroking his head sometimes helped. "It won't go on forever," he once said.

The thirty-seven-hour wait happened in March 2007. Al's doctor at the rehab/nursing home was very concerned about his high white cell count and creatine levels. We arrived at the ER on Monday night and did not get a bed until Wednesday afternoon. The experience of waiting was the worst we'd ever had. Shocking in some ways—including one neglectful nurse, one rough one, and a doctor who was rude and dismissive of concerns I had about Al. Thankfully the doctor who replaced him when a new shift began was attentive and respectful and seemed to move things along.

Despite the traumatic days we had just been through, Al remembered that a class of psychology students from Belgium was due to see him on Thursday. The professor had been bringing her students annually to New York, where they visited various clinics and therapy centers. Visiting Al at the institute was a highlight for them. In September we had agreed to the 2007 visit, hoping that Al would be home by then. He wasn't, so they were due to come to the nursing/rehab home. I suggested to Al that we cancel, and Al said, "No. Have them come here to the hospital." On Thursday morning Al looked so pale, and I again asked about canceling. "No," he answered. The students arrived early, and nurses insisted that Al see half the group at a time, as having too many in the room at a time was considered unsafe. The first half-class came in at 2 p.m. Al spoke for a few minutes and then invited questions. The first student to speak up said, "Dr. Ellis, thank you for seeing us. We are honored to be with you. But Debbie told us earlier what happened over the past few days. Why didn't you cancel?" Al's reply: "To continue to spread the gospel according to St. Albert!" Students laughed. Then Al said, "So I can teach you REBT, so you can learn to help yourselves. By doing that, you will be better able to help other people." Later he said, "So go work your asses off—do it! Do REBT!"

After about twenty minutes I asked Al if he was tired and wanted to stop. "No." After another thirty minutes I asked again. "No." The second half of the class had come in by now. Twenty minutes later I suggested, "Al, how about we just take one more question and finish for today?" "NO." "So how many more questions, Al?" "One hundred," he jokingly said. At about ten to five he said to the group, "One last question now." The class and teachers felt moved and deeply grateful for the precious time they'd had with him.

That evening a doctor told me that the blood work done that

morning revealed that Al had had a heart attack, albeit mild, some time prior to the blood sample being taken. I never ceased to feel astonished by Al's power of will. I can't even imagine how ill Al felt that morning, yet he refused to cancel the class; he continued to contribute and inspire all present.

We were able to return to the rehab/nursing home some weeks later. It would be for the final time. Though stable, Al was not getting noticeably stronger. The opposite. Occasionally, an interviewer or supportive person would visit. Al would still smile, thank them, answer questions— but for short periods only, as he would become too tired for a longer talk. His humor was still apparent at times. One interviewer asked Al why he thought New Yorkers had a reputation for being the most crazy of Americans. "Because they are!" Al replied. As always, he said it as he saw it, but with warmth, not criticism. He elaborated on contributing reasons and recommended REBT as an invaluable way to help.

Someone once asked Al what he thought of changing the name REBT (Rational Emotive Behavior Therapy) to CEBT (Cognitive Emotive Behavior Therapy). "No," said Al. "I want it to be *REBT*."

A colleague, who was doing a great deal of work in support of Al's goals, visited and gave Al updates about the situation with the institute. Al was deeply sad about what had been, and currently was, the status. When asked what he wanted, he would answer, "To run the institute, to have it be my institute again and have Debbie and the REBT people I choose work with me, to give workshops, to keep helping people, and to finish my autobiography and other books I've started." But by this time I sensed that he doubted that any of these goals would come to fruition. "I'm a realist," he used to say.

In May 2007 we were back in the hospital. Al's health was going from bad to worse. He once again had pneumonia. The doctors scheduled a procedure whereby, under light anesthetic, a tube with camera would be inserted into his lungs to allow the doctors detailed observation. Normally, I was told, this was a fairly simple procedure. I was allowed into the procedure room with Al, wearing a sterile robe, foot coverings, and a cap over my hair. I was told I could remain there until the first sedative was given, but then I would have to leave the room. Fine. The sedative was injected as I stood behind his head, stroking it. As I stroked I noticed that his chest was not rising and dropping—it appeared that he wasn't breathing. I shouted to the nurse who was just a few feet away, and she immediately put an oxygen mask over his mouth and began manually pumping it. The doctors rushed in, and I was rushed out, hearing, "We may have to intubate." And they did. The observation procedure of Al's lungs was never done. The sedative given to Al had affected his breathing. Al was hooked up to a ventilator and taken to intensive care. As usual, I was permitted to stay with him. I so greatly appreciate the senior doctors who allowed my constant presence. The ventilator, which was now doing the breathing, entered his mouth by a tube that created the sensation of his wanting to gag. No sound could be made by Al. His skin was unbearably itchy and he would scratch, but doctors were concerned that he would cause bleeding with too much scratching, so he was forced to wear uncomfortable protective mitts on his hands.

Couldn't talk, couldn't move, couldn't scratch, fully conscious. I would talk to him and stroke his head and tell him that this restriction was temporary, and not to try to talk, that soon he'd be free of it, and other reassuring words. Though I myself was not so assured. The doctors said that if he remained stable over the next few days, *days*, they would reduce the strength of the ventilator's activity. If Al's own breathing ability was strong enough, the ventilator would be removed, otherwise . . .

Al's breathing was adequate, and, again to the amazement of many, he was free of the ventilator and moved out of intensive care and into a regular hospital room. But the prognosis was *bad*. Al's doctor had a long talk with me. The time had come for me to decide about hospice or respite care. Al was not going to get any better. The doctor thought I was in denial, and I probably was. After all, I'd seen Al survive near death a number of times. We talked about his quality of life. I decided I wanted him in the home environment. With private nurses I would have more say and would be able to replace any staff who weren't suitable. In the nursing home I had no such choices. Al would get better care and be more comfortable in a home environment. So, at the beginning of June, we went back up to the sixth floor of the institute, to the place that once used to feel like home to him.

One afternoon I saw a tear fall from Al's eye. "Al, you look so sad," I said. "I am," he replied. "What about?" I asked. He said, "I am sad about the institute. I am sad about leaving you. I am sad about leaving you without me."

By July, any apparent improvements in his health were brief and short-lived. Ongoing and accelerating decline was undeniable. As the days went on, Al was too fatigued to speak. Nonetheless, he continued to express his love to me.

He cooperated uncomplainingly with doctors or nurses while they performed necessary, painful procedures. He would often nod thanks and convey gratitude even when so weak.

In the final three days of his life, he was conscious less of the time and semiconscious more of the time. He was excreting hardly any urine and mostly blood. The doctors told me the inevitable. His organs were breaking down.

After his wash on Monday night, he seemed fairly peaceful. At midnight his breathing became quite erratic, strange in its sound, but he did not appear to be at all distressed or suffering. I called the nurse in. She confirmed what I already knew. It was the beginning of the end. I told her I wanted to be alone with him, and she left the room, closing the door behind her. I held Al in my arms and stroked his head the way he liked it. I kissed him and kissed him, and communicated the words I wanted to say. I rocked him a little. He seemed very peaceful. Kissed him some more.

{}

At 12:30 a.m. on Tuesday, July 24, 2007, held in my arms, Albert Ellis exhaled his final breath. While being kissed.

{}

Al's funeral and burial took place on Friday, July 27, 2007. His body is buried under a large, stately, and beautiful maple tree in the Woodlawn Cemetery, Bronx, New York, minutes away from the homes and schools of his younger years and minutes also from the Bronx Botanical Gardens. Standing graveside, trains can be heard at times in the background—traveling on the very line Al rode so often before he moved to live in the heart of New York City.

A large memorial tribute, attended by many hundreds of people who came from New York, all over the United States, and overseas, was held at Columbia University on Friday evening of September 28, 2007. This was one day after what would have been Al's ninety-fourth birthday. The tribute went on for over five hours. A message from the mayor of New York, Michael R. Bloomberg, was read out. Speakers included one of Al's oldest friends, Manny Birnbaum; his nephew; distinguished colleagues; former students; one of his doctors; his lawyers; Janet Wolfe; a message on tape from his second wife, Rhoda Winter

Russell; and final words from me. Videotapes of Al were shown on a huge screen. A gifted musician sang and played some of Al's rational humorous songs on a grand piano. The memorial ended with a slideshow of Al from his childhood through his final months, with a tape of him singing some of his songs in his marvelous baritone voice playing in the background.

{}

"Time is precious. Once it's gone you can never replace it. So don't waste your time. Live the best life you can." Al would say this, and live it.

With his great capacity for joy, he experienced times of blissful happiness and deep satisfaction. He endured brutal times of difficulty and adversity with dignity and remarkable courage. He practiced his philosophy, as well as sharing it, until the end. And I'm glad to say, in his final years, he (we) experienced love more profound and remarkable than any he had ever known.

It is said that a hero is someone who has given their life to something greater than themselves. Albert Ellis was, and remains, a true and shining hero. A passionate hero. A daring hero. He wanted his life to be one that significantly and powerfully benefited others. Not for glorification, deification, or acclaim, but from the sincere desire to help reduce suffering and increase joy in the lives of as many as possible.

Albert Ellis changed the direction of psychology in the twentieth and twenty-first centuries. He contributed to changing attitudes and thinking about important life and relationship issues. His life was a model of, and proof that, his philosophy worked. He found true love. Indeed—a life well lived. Physically over, but in its greatness and influence, *never* out.

Epilogue
What Now?

The books and teachings of Albert Ellis will continue to benefit inestimable millions of people. People he trained, taught, helped, and inspired will continue to use and practice REBT and help many others. Research is being done by Shawn Blau, PhD, and others, and more will be done in the future. An Albert Ellis Tribute book series is being organized by Jon Carlson, PsyD, EdD; Elliot D. Cohen, PhD; and Bill Knaus, EdD. And I will continue, in every way I can, to share and spread the wisdom and philosophy of my beloved Al, as he wanted me to do.

D.J.E.

Appendix I
Final Letter

April 2007

This is a letter to Jeffrey Bernstein, Bob O'Connell, Kristene Doyle, Raymond DiGiuseppe, the Board of Directors and Officers of The Institute on the issue of their prohibiting me from using my name on my website.

I regret that this comes belatedly, but I've been in the hospital with pneumonia and other complications. Nonetheless, let me belatedly reply to their words and actions on the issue.

The real Albert Ellis Institute was formulated in the 1950s—actually the first Albert Ellis Institute was set up around 1957, coinciding with the release of my book *How to Live with a Neurotic*. The real Albert Ellis Institute Number 2 was set up at 45 East 65th Street in Manhattan around 1964. The real Albert Ellis Institute predates the fake Albert Ellis Institute by many years. Many references to the real Albert Ellis Institute appear in literature and elsewhere from 1957, so we have priority over the current people running the institute at 45 East 65th Street.

The current Institute uses my name, "Albert Ellis Institute," but I consider it fake. Since 2004, various REBT presentations have been watered down, the charter of the Institute was changed without my knowledge or permission, the Institute was not and is not run according to my preferences, and decisions were and are made and acted on without consulting me. It is well-known that in July 2005, I was forced by the Board of Trustees and senior staff to stop doing my Friday Night Workshop and any other work teaching or seeing clients for the institute.

The current Board of Directors of the Institute use my name without my permission and claim exclusive ownership of it for purposes relating to REBT and the institute. They were about to take legal action against my supporters if they did not remove my name from the title of my very own website—AlbertEllisFoundation.org. Sadly, my supporters have done so, for the cost of their defenses in fighting for me to keep the use of my name and the time involved would have been prohibitive.

The real Albert Ellis Institute has been working since the 1950s. Those at the fake Albert Ellis Institute thieved the name. I do not give them permission to use it with their fake Institute, and, yet, they refuse to let me use my name in the title of my own website.

This is gall. This is chutzpah. Suppose I take the name General Motors and use it without permission, or the name US Steel. This would not be legitimate without their permission. Therefore, the fake Albert Ellis Institute has no legitimacy. This is the worst chutzpah I have heard of in years.

There are many other things that have been said recently by some of the people of the fake Institute that are false, but I haven't the time to answer them right now. Dr. Bill Knaus and two other former directors of training have covered some of these points in their letter recently.

To Jeffrey Bernstein, Bob O'Connell, and the others, I say give me liberty to run the Institute my way, or what's the use of your running it in my name. The fake Institute people have behaved like pirates taking over a ship. Legal action may well be taken over this issue of who the Albert Ellis Institute gets credited to.

Appendix II
Letter from
Mayor Michael R. Bloomberg

September 28, 2007
Debbie Joffe Ellis

Dear Dr. Ellis,

I was saddened to learn of the passing of your husband, Dr. Albert Ellis.

Dr. Ellis was a true New Yorker—someone who wasn't afraid to make his voice heard and do his part to improve the community in whatever way he knew how. He will be remembered as someone who always spoke his mind with a wit and sense of humor that endeared him to students and followers. His work has helped countless people work through trauma and difficult times to become happier, more self-accepting individuals, and his contributions to the field of psychotherapy continue to resonate across the globe.

The effects of Dr. Ellis's work will forever be felt in the hearts and minds of those he treated and those who encounter his approach. My heart goes out to you and your loved ones during this difficult time.

Sincerely,

Michael R. Bloomberg
Mayor

Bibliography

I. THE WORK OF ALBERT ELLIS

1945

"The Case Study as a Research Method." *Review of Educational Research* 15: 352–59.

Review of *Sexual Anomalies*, by M. Hirschfeld. *Psychosomatic Medicine* 7: 382.

"The Sexual Psychology of Human Hermaphrodites." *Psychosomatic Medicine* 7: 108–25.

"A Study of Human Love Relationships." *Journal of Genetic Psychology* 15: 61–71.

"A Study of the Love Emotions of American College Girls." *International Journal of Sexology* 3: 15–21.

1946

Review of *A Psychologist Looks at Love and Psychology of Sex Relations*, by T. Reik. *Journal of Social Psychology* 24: 121–26.

Review of *Sex and the Social Order*, by G. H. Seward. *Journal of Social Psychology* 26: 133–36.

"The Validity of Personality Questionnaires." *Psychological Bulletin* 43: 385–440.

1947

"A Comparison of the Use of Direct and Indirect Phrasing in Personality Questionnaires." *Psychological Monographs* 61: iii–41.

Discussion of Heinlein's comment on *The Validity of Personality Question-naires. Psychological Bulletin* 44: 83–86.

[with J. Gerberich]. "Interests and Attitudes." *Review of Educational Research* 17: 64–77.

[with H. H. Abelson]. "Other Devices for Investigating Personality." *Review of Educational Research* 17: 101–109.

"Personality Questionnaires." *Review of Educational Research* 17: 56–63.

"Questionnaire versus Interview Method in the Study of Human Love Relationships." *American Sociological Review* 12: 541–43.

Review of *The Dynamics of Human Adjustment*, by P. M. Symonds. *Journal of Genetic Psychology* 71: 145–50.

[with M. R. Hertz and P. M. Symonds]. "Rorschach Methods and Other Projective Techniques." *Review of Educational Research* 17: 78–100.

"Telepathy and Psychoanalysis: A Critique of Recent Findings." *Psychiatric Quarterly* 21: 607–59.

1948

"The Application of Scientific Principles to Scientific Publications." *Scientific Monthly* 66: 427–30.

"The Attitudes of Psychologists toward Psychological Meetings." *American Psychologist* 3: 511–12.

"A Critique of the Theoretical Contributions of Nondirective Therapy." *Journal of Clinical Psychology* 4: 248–55.

Discussion of Mrs. Bernard's comments on research methods. *American Sociological Review* 13: 219.

"Questionnaire versus Interview Method in the Study of Human Love Relationships II, Uncategorized Responses." *American Sociological Review* 13: 62–65.

"The Relationship between Personality Inventory Scores and Other Psychological Test Results." *Journal of Social Psychology* 26: 287–89.

Review of *An Essay on Morals*, by P. Wylie. *Journal of Social Psychology* 27: 289–90.

Review of *Sexual Behavior in the Human Male*, by A. C. Kinsey, W. B. Pomeroy, and C. E. Martin. *Journal of General Psychology* 39: 299–326.

"A Study of Trends in Recent Psychoanalytic Publications." *American Image* 5, no. 4: 3–13.

[with H. Conrad]. "The Validity of Personality Inventories in Military Practice." *Psychological Bulletin* 45: 385–426.

"Valuation in Presenting Scientific Data." *Sociology and Social Research* 33, no. 2: 92–96.

"The Value of Marriage Prediction Tests." *American Sociological Review* 13: 710–18.

1949

[with R. M. Beechley]. "Assortative Mating in the Parents of Child Guidance Clinic Patients." *American Sociological Review* 14: 678–79.

[with E. W. Fuller]. "The Personal Problems of Senior Nursing Students." *American Journal of Psychiatry* 106: 212–15.

"Re-analysis of an Alleged Telepathic Dream." *Psychiatric Quarterly* 23: 116–26.

[with H. S. Conrad]. Reply to the Humms' *Notes on the Validity of Personality Inventories in Military Practice. Psychological Bulletin* 46: 307–308.

"Results of a Mental Hygiene Approach to Reading Disability Problems." *Journal of Consulting Psychology* 13: 56–61.

"Some Significant Correlates of Love and Family Attitudes and Behavior." *Journal of Social Psychology* 30: 3–16.

"Towards the Improvement of Psychoanalytic Research." *Psychoanalytic Review* 36: 126–43.

"What Kinds of Research Are American Psychologists Doing?" *American Psychologist* 4: 490–94.

1950

[with G. Groves, M. Brown, and H. Lamson]. "Articles of Interest to Marriage and Family Life Educators and Counselors." *Marriage and Family Living* 12: 106–10.

[with R. Beechley]. "A Comparison of Matched Groups of Mongoloid and Non-Mongoloid Feebleminded Children." *American Journal of Mental Deficiency* 54: 464–68.

[with R. Beechley]. "Comparisons of Negro and White Children Seen at a Child Guidance Clinic." *Psychiatric Quarterly* Supplement 24: 93–101.

Discussion of *Predicting Marriage Failure from Test Scores*, by L. M. Terman. *Marriage and Family Living* 12: 56–57.

"An Experiment in the Rating of Essay-Type Examination Questions by College Students." *Educational and Psychological Measurement* 10: 707–11.

"An Introduction to the Principles of Scientific Psychoanalysis." *Genetic Psychology Monographs* 41: 147–212.

"Love and Family Relationships of American College Girls." *American Journal of Sociology* 55: 550–58.

"Requisites for Research in Psychotherapy." *Journal of Clinical Psychology* 6: 152–56.

"The Sex, Love, and Marriage Questions of Senior Nursing Students." *Journal of Social Psychology* 31: 209–16.

1951

[with R. Doorbar]. "Classified Bibliography of Articles, Books, and Pamphlets on Sex, Love, Marriage, and Family Relations Published during 1950." *Marriage and Family Living* 13, no. 2: 71–86.

[with R. Beechley]. "A Comparison of Child Guidance Clinic Patients Coming from Large, Medium, and Small Families." *Journal of Genetic Psychology* 79: 131–44.

The Folklore of Sex. New York: Boni/Doubleday.

"The Influence of Heterosexual Culture on the Attitudes of Homosexuals." *International Journal of Sexology* 5: 77–79.

Introduction to *The Homosexual in America*, by D. W. Cory. New York: Greenberg.

"Legal Status of the Marriage Counselor: A Psychologist's View." *Marriage and Family Living* 13: 116–20.

"Prostitution Re-Assessed." *International Journal of Sexology* 5: 41–42.

"Report on Survey of Members of the Division of Clinical and Abnormal Psychology Who Are Presently Engaged in Paid Private Practice." *Newsletter of the Division of Clinical Psychology of the American Psychological Association* (August): 1–4.

Review of *Neurosis and Human Growth*, by K. Horney. *Psychological Bulletin* 48: 581–82.

"Sex—The Schizoid Best Seller." *Saturday Review of Literature* 34, no. 11: 42–44.

"A Study of 300 Sex Offenders." *International Journal of Sexology* 4: 127–35.

"A Young Woman Convicted of Manslaughter." *Case Reports in Clinical Psychology* 2, no. 1: 9–32.

1952

"Applications of Clinical Psychology to Sexual Disorders." In *Progress in Clinical Psychology*, edited by D. Browser and L. A. Abt. New York: Grune & Stratton.

[with R. Doorbar]. "Classified Bibliography of Articles, Books, and Pamphlets on Sex, Love, Marriage, and Family Relations Published during 1951." *Marriage and Family Living* 14: 153–77.

"A Critique of Systematic Theoretical Foundations in Clinical Psychology." *Journal of Clinical Psychology* 88: 11–15.

[with D. W. Cory (pseud.)]. "In Defense of Current Sex Studies." *Nation* 174: 250–52.

"On the Cure of Homosexuality." *International Journal of Sexology* 55: 135–38.

"Perversions and Neurosis." *International Journal of Sexology* 55: 135–38.

[with R. A. Harper, D. Dyer, S. Duvall, B. Timmons, R. Hill, and N. Kavi-
noky]. "Premarital Sex Relations: The Facts and the Counselor's Role in
Relation to the Facts." *Marriage and Family Living* 14: 229–36.

[with R. Brancale and R. Doorbar]. "Psychiatric and Psychological Investigations of Convicted Sex Offenders." *American Psychiatry* 109: 17–21.

"The Psychologist in Private Practice and the Good Profession." *American
Psychologist* 7: 129–30.

[with R. Doorbar]. "Recent Trends in Sex, Marriage, and Family Research."
Marriage and Family Living 14: 338–40.

"Self-Appraisal Methods." In *Progress in Clinical Psychology*, volume 2,
edited by D. Brower and L. A. Abt, 67–90. New York: Grune & Stratton.

[with R. Doorbar, H. Guze, and L. Clark]. "A Study of Sexual Preferences:
Preliminary Report." *International Journal of Sexology* 6: 87–88.

"What Is Normal Sex Behavior?" *Complex* 8: 41–51. Revised in *The Psychology of Sex Offenders*, edited by A. Ellis and R. Brancale, 120–32.
Springfield, IL: Thomas.

1953

"The Blacky Test Used with a Psychoanalytic Patient." *Journal of Clinical Psychology* 9: 167–72.

[with R. Doorbar]. "Classified Bibliography of Articles, Books, and Pamphlets
on Sex, Love, Marriage, and Family Relations Published during 1952."
Marriage and Family Living 15: 156–75.

Correspondence relating to *Marriage Counseling with Couples Indicating
Sexual Incompatibility*. *Marriage and Family Living* 15: 156–75.

Discussion of *Premarital Sexual Behavior*, by W. Stokes and D. Mace. *Marriage and Family Living* 15: 248–49.

"From the First to the Second Kinsey Report." *International Journal of Sexology* 12: 64–72.

"Marriage Counseling with Couples Indicating Sexual Incompatibility." *Marriage and Sexual Living* 15: 53–59.

Preface to *Sex, Society and the Individual*, edited by A. P. Pillay and A. Ellis.
Bombay, India: *International Journal of Sexology*.

"Pros and Cons of Legislation for Psychologists." *American Psychologist* 8:
551–53.

"Reactions of Psychotherapy Patients Who Resist Hypnosis." *Journal of Clinical and Experimental Hypnosis* 1: 12–15.

"Recent Research with Personality Inventories." *Journal of Consulting Psychology* 17: 45–49.

"Recent Studies on the Sex and Love Relations of Young Girls: Resume."
International Journal of Sexology 6: 161–63.

"Recommendations concerning Standards for the Unsupervised Practice of Clinical Psychology." *American Psychologist* 8: 494–95.

Review of *The Superego*, by E. Bergler. *Psychological Bulletin* 50: 192.

[with A. P. Pillay, eds.]. *Sex, Society and the Individual*. Bombay, India: *International Journal of Sexology*.

"Theoretical Schools of Psychology." In *Contributions toward Medical Psychology*, edited by A. Weider, 31–50. New York: Ronald.

1954

The American Sexual Tragedy. New York: Twayne.

[with R. Doorbar and R. Johnston]. "Characteristics of Convicted Sex Offenders." *Journal of Social Psychology* 40: 3–15.

"Classified Bibliography on Human Sex Relations." *International Journal of Sexology* 7: 228–39.

"Classified Bibliography on Marriage and Family Relations." *Marriage and Family Living* 16: 146–61, 254, 263.

[with R. Beechley]. "Emotional Disturbance in Children with Peculiar Given Names." *Journal of Genetic Psychology* 85: 337–39.

"Female Sexual Response and Marital Relations." *Social Problems* 1: 152–55.

"Interrogation of Sex Offenders." *Journal of Criminal Law, Criminology, and Police Science* 45, no. 1: 41–47.

[with H. Benjamin]. "An Objective Examination of Prostitution." *International Journal of Sexology* 8: 100–105.

"Private Clinical Practice." In *A Survey of Clinical Practice in Psychology*, edited by E. A. Rubinstein and M. Lorrs, 186–96. New York: International Universities.

"The Psychology and Physiology of Sex." In *Sex Life of the American Woman and the Kinsey Report*, edited by A. Ellis, 203–14. New York: Greenberg.

"Sex Freedom in Marriage." *Best Years* 1, no. 1: 3–7.

1955

"Are Homosexuals Necessarily Neurotic?" *One: The Homosexual Magazine* 3, no. 4: 8–12.

"Masturbation." *Journal of Social Therapy* 1, no. 3: 141–43.

"New Approaches to Psychotherapy Techniques." *Journal of Clinical Psychology Monograph* Supplement 11: 1–53.

[with R. G. Anderson, I. A. Berg, J. McV. Hunt, O. H. Mowrer, H. E. O'Shea, C. H. Rush Jr., R. B. Sellover, and W. H. Wulfeck]. "Professional Liability Insurance for Psychologists." *American Psychologist* 10: 243–44.

"Psychotherapy Techniques for Use with Psychotics." *American Journal of Psychotherapy* 9: 452–76.

[with J. Nydes and B. Riess]. "Qualifications of the Clinical Psychologist for the Practice of Psychotherapy." *Journal of Clinical Psychology* 11: 33–37.

Review of *Existence and Therapy*, by U. Sonneman. *Psychological Bulletin* 52: 275–76.

"Woman as Sex Aggressor." *Best Years* 1, no. 3: 25–29.

1956

"Adultery: Pros and Cons." *Independent* 61: 4.

"Another Look at Sexual Abnormality." *Independent* 55: 6.

"A Critical Evaluation of Marriage Counseling." *Marriage and Family Living* 18: 65–71.

"The Effectiveness of Psychotherapy with Individuals Who Have Severe Homosexual Problems." *Journal of Consulting Psychology* 20: 191–95.

"Evolving Standards for Practicing Psychologists." In *Psychology, Psychiatry, and the Public Interest*, edited by M. H. Krout, 186–200. Minneapolis: University of Minnesota Press.

"How American Women Are Driving American Males into Homosexuality." *Expose (Independent)* 52: 4.

"How Males Contribute to Female Frigidity." *Independent* 56: 4.

"New Light on Masturbation." *Expose (Independent)* 51: 4.

"On the Myths about Love." *Independent* 58: 6.

"On Premarital Sex Relations." *Independent* 59: 4; 60: 4.

"An Operational Reformulation of Some of the Basic Principles of Psychoanalysis." In *The Foundations of Science and the Concepts of Psychology and Psychoanalysis*, edited by H. Feigl and M. Scriven, 131–54. Minneapolis: University of Minnesota Press. Also in *Psychoanalytic Review* 43: 163–80.

[with R. Brancale and R. Doorbar]. *The Psychology of Sex Offenders*. Springfield, IL: Charles C. Thomas.

Review of *Sexual Hygiene and Pathology: A Manual for the Physician*, by J. F. Olivien. *Contemporary Psychology* 2: 86–87.

"The Roots of Psychology and Psychiatry." In *Psychology, Psychiatry and the Public Interest*, edited by H. Krout, 9–31. Minneapolis: University of Minnesota Press.

"Sexual Inadequacy in the Male." *Independent* 57: 4.

"When Are We Going to Quit Stalling about Sex Education?" *Independent* 54: 4.

"Why Americans Are So Fearful of Sex." *Independent* 53: 4.

1957

"Adultery Reconsidered." *Independent* 68: 4.

"The Advantages and Disadvantages of Self-Help Therapy Materials." *Professional Psychology: Research and Practice* 24: 335–39.

"Adventures with Sex Censorship." *Independent* 62: 4; 63: 4.

"Deviation, an Ever-Increasing Social Problem." In *Personality Problems and Psychological Frontiers*, edited by J. Fairchild, 138–51. New York: Sheridan House.

"How Do I Love Thee? Let Me Count the Ways." Review of *The Psychology of Sexual Emotion: The Basis of Selective Attraction*, by V. W. Grant. *Contemporary Psychology* 2: 188–89.

"How Homosexuals Can Combat Anti-Homosexualism." *One* 5, no. 2: 7–8.

How to Live with a Neurotic. New York: Crown; paperback edition, New York: Award.

"I Feel So Guilty." *True Story* 78, no. 6: 18–29.

Introduction to *The Jewel in the Lotus: A Historical Survey of the Sexual Culture of the East*, by A. Edwardes. New York: Julian.

"The Justification of Sex without Love." *Independent* 64: 4; 65: 4; 66: 4.

"On Sex Fascism." *Independent* 69: 4; 70: 4; 71: 4.

"Outcome of Employing Three Techniques of Psychotherapy." *Journal of Clinical Psychology* 13, no. 4: 344–50.

"Rational Psychotherapy and Individual Psychology." *Journal of Individual Psychology* 13, no. 1: 38–44.

"The Right to Sex Enjoyment." *Independent* 22: 4.

"Sex Problems of Couples Seen for Marriage Counseling." *Journal of Family Welfare* 3: 81–84.

"The Sexual Element in Non-sex Crimes." *Psychological Newsletter* 8: 122–25.

"Thoughts on Petting." *Independent* 68: 4.

1958

"Are Suburban Wives Af-fair Game?" *New York Mirror Magazine*, July 28: 4–5.

"Case Histories: Fact and Fiction." *Contemporary Psychology* 3: 318–19.

Comments on *Marriage Counseling Involving a Passive Husband and an Aggressive Wife*, by J. Crist. *Marriage and Family Living* 20: 126–27.

"Helping Troubled People." *Pastoral Psychology* 9, no. 82: 33–41.

"How You Can Get Along with a Neurotic." *New York Herald Tribune*, Today's Living section, August 3: pp. 4–5.

"Hypnotherapy with Borderline Schizophrenics." *Journal of General Psychology* 59: 245–53.

[with S. Kosofsky]. "Illegal Communication among Institutionalized Female Delinquents." *Journal of Social Psychology* 48: 155–60.

"A Marriage of Two Neurotics." In *Marriage Counseling: A Casebook*, edited by the American Association of Marriage Counselors, 104–97. New York: Association.

"Neurotic Interaction between Marital Partners." *Journal of Counseling Psychology* 5: 24–38.

"New Hope for Homosexuals." *Sexology* 25: 164–68.

"The Private Practice of Psychotherapy: A Clinical Psychologist's Report." *Journal of General Psychology* 58: 207–16.

"Rational Psychotherapy." *Journal of General Psychology* 58: 35–49. Reprinted, New York: Institute for Rational-Emotive Therapy.

Sex without Guilt. New York: Lyle Stuart; paperback edition, New York: Dell.

"Should Men Marry Older Women?" *This Week Magazine*, July: 8–9. Reprinted in *Marriage and Family in the Modern World*, edited by R. S. Cavan, 157–60. New York: Crowell.

"Ten Indiscreet Proposals." *Pageant* 14, no. 5: 6–15.

1959

"Case Presentation and Critical Comments on the Cases of Other Authors." In *Critical Incidents in Psychotherapy*, edited by S. W. Standal and R. J. Corsini, 88–91, 110–16, 154–58. Englewood Cliffs, NJ: Prentice-Hall.

Critique of *The Homosexual in Our Society*. *Mattachine Review* 5, no. 6: 24–27.

"Does Morality Require Religious Sanctions?" *Controversy Magazine* 1, no. 2: 16–19.

"Guilt, Shame, and Frigidity." *Quarterly Review of Surgery, Obstetrics, and Gynecology* 16: 259–61.

"Homosexuality and Creativity." *Journal of Clinical Psychology* 15: 376–79.

"A Homosexual Treated with Rational Psychotherapy." *Journal of Clinical Psychology* 15: 338–43.

"How Neurotic Are You?" *True Story* 79: 34–35.

"Over-aggressiveness in Wives." *King Features Syndicate*, July 26.

"Overcoming Sexual Incompatibility." *Realife Guide* 2, no. 4: 6–15.

"Premarital Relations—Pro." *Controversy* 1, no. 4: 24, 26–27.

"Psychological Aspects of Discouraging Contraception." *Realist* 1, no. 7: 11–13.

"Rationalism and Its Therapeutic Applications." In *The Place of Value in the Practice of Psychotherapy*, edited by A. Ellis, 55–64. New York: American Academy of Psychotherapists, *Annals of Psychotherapy*.

"Requisite Conditions for Basic Personality Change." *Journal of Consulting Psychology* 23: 538–40.

"The Seven Secrets of Sexual Satisfaction." *Pageant* 14, no. 12: 26–31.

[with Lehfeldt, ed.]. "Symposium on Aspects of Female Sexuality." *Quarterly Review of Surgery, Obstetrics, and Gynecology* 16: 215–58.

"What Is Psychotherapy?" In *Annals of Psychotherapy (Monograph 1)*. New York: American Academy of Psychotherapists.

"Why Married Men Visit Prostitutes." *Sexology* 25: 344–47.

1960

The Art and Science of Love. New York: Lyle Stuart & Bantam.

"A Brief for Sex Honesty." *Realife Guide* 3, no. 4: 31–38.

"A Case for Polygamy." *Nugget* 5, no. 1: 19, 24, 26.

Introduction to *Christ and the Homosexual*, by R. Wood. New York: Vantage.

Introduction to *The Housewife's Handbook for Promiscuity*, by R. Anthony. Tucson, AZ: Seymour. Reprinted, New York: *Documentary Books*.

Letter on the suspension of Dr. Leo F. Koch. *Balanced Living* 16: 175.

Letter to Norman Cousins on sex censorship. *Independent*, November: 3–5.

[with R. Felder and C. Rogers]. *Loretta*. Cassette recording. Salt Lake City, UT: American Academy of Psychotherapists Tape Library.

"Marriage Counseling with Demasculinizing Wives and Demasculinized Husbands." *Marriage and Family Living* 22: 13–21.

"Mowrer on 'Sin.'" *American Psychologist* 15: 713–14.

"The Psychology of Sex." *Realife Guide* 3, no. 3: 6–13.

"Research in Psychotherapy." *Newsletter of Psychologists in Private Practice* 1, no. 1: 2.

Sexual Intercourse: Psychological Foundations. New York: Institute for Rational-Emotive Therapy.

"There Is No Place for the Concept of Sin in Psychotherapy." *Journal of Counseling Psychology* 7: 183–92.

"What Should You Do about an Unfaithful Husband?" *Pageant* 15, no. 9: 6–11.

1961

"Art and Sex." In *The Encyclopedia of Sexual Behavior*, edited by A. Ellis and A. Abarbanel, 161–79. New York: Hawthorn.

"Coitus." In *The Encyclopedia of Sexual Behavior*, edited by A. Ellis and A. Abarbanel, 284–92. New York: Hawthorn.

[with R. A. Harper]. *Creative Marriage*. Secaucus, NJ: Lyle Stuart. Paperback editions: *The Marriage Bed*, New York: Tower; and *A Guide to Successful Marriage*, North Hollywood, CA: Wilshire.

Discussion on sex and censorship in literature and the arts. *Playboy*, July: 27–28, 74, 76, 88, 92, 95–99.

[with A. Abanel, eds.]. *The Encyclopedia of Sexual Behavior*. Vols. 1 and 2. New York: Hawthorn. Revised edition, New York: Aronson; paperback edition, New York: Ace.

"Fried and Freud." Review of *The Ego in Love and Sexuality*, by E. Fried. *Contemporary Psychology* 6: 38–39.

"Frigidity." In *The Encyclopedia of Sexual Behavior*, edited by A. Ellis and A. Ararbanel, 450–56. New York: Hawthorn.

[with R. A. Harper]. *A Guide to Rational Living*. Englewood Cliffs, NJ: Prentice-Hall. Paperback edition, North Hollywood, CA: Wilshire.

[with R. A. Harper]. *A Guide to Successful Marriage*. North Hollywood, CA: Wilshire.

"How Much Sex Freedom in Marriage?" *Sexology* 28: 292–96.

Introduction to *Sex Crimes and Sex Criminals*, by A. Bentham. New York: Wisdom.

"Myths about Sex." *Cosmopolitan*, February: 82–85.

"A New Sex Code for Modern Americans." *Pageant* 17, no. 6: 110–16.

"On Riess and Durkin on Ellis on Fried on Freud." *Contemporary Psychology* 6: 382.

"The Psychology of Sex Offenders." In *The Encyclopedia of Sexual Behavior*, edited by A. Ellis and A. Abarbanel, 949–55. New York: Hawthorn.

"A Rational Approach to Premarital Counseling." *Psychological Reports* 8: 333–38.

"Rational Therapy Applied." *Balanced Living* 17: 273–78.

[with T. Arnold, R. Ginzburg, M. Girodias, N. Mailer, O. Preminger, B. Rosset, and P. Krassner]. "Sex and Censorship in Literature and the Arts." *Playboy*, July: 27–28, 74–99.

"The Sex Offender and His Treatment." In *Legal and Criminal Psychology*, edited by H. Toch, 400–16. New York: Holt, Rinehart & Winston.

"The Treatment of a Psychopath with Rational Psychotherapy." *Journal of Psychology* 51: 141–50.

1962

The American Sexual Tragedy. Revised edition, New York: Lyle Stuart; paperback edition, New York: Grove.

"The Anatomy of a Private Practitioner." *Newsletter of the Division of Consulting Psychology of the American Psychological Association* 7: 26–28.

"Are Homosexuals Really Creative?" *Sexology* 29: 88–93.

"The Case against Religion: A Psychotherapist's View." *Independent* 126: 4–5.

"How to Live with a Sex Deviate." *Sexology* 28: 580–83.

Introduction to *Fanny Hill* [condensed]. *Eros* 1, no. 3: 82–83.

Introduction to *Single and Pregnant*, by Maddock, 5–7. Hollywood, CA: Genell.

"Is Nudism Anti-Sexual?" *Eden* 11: 6–9.

"The Lesbian." *Rogue*, September: 17–18, 28, 76.

"Morality and Therapy." *Columbia University Forum* 5, no. 2: 47–48.
"Myths about Sex Compatibility." *Sexology* 28: 652–55.
"Psychotherapy and Atomic Warfare." *Realist* 38: 1–4.
Reason and Emotion in Psychotherapy. New York: Lyle Stuart. Paperback edition, Secaucus, NJ: Citadel.
"The Seven Year Itch." *Dude* 6: 8–10, 71–72.
"Sex and Summer Violence." *This Month* 1, no. 6: 46–52.
"Teen-Age Sex Relations." *Realist* 31: 30–31.
"Twelve True versus False Ideas." *Balanced Living* 18: 140–41.
"What Is Normal Sex Behavior?" *Sexology* 28: 364–69.

1963

[with D. Susskind, A. L. Kingsolving, M. David, R. Ginsburg, H. Hefner, and M. Lerner]. "Banned Program: The Sexual Revolution in America." *Mademoiselle*, October: 112–13, 158–64.
"Constitutional Factors in Homosexuality: A Reexamination of the Evidence." In *Advances in Sex Research*, edited by H. G. Beigel, 161–86. New York: Harper & Row.
"Diane David on Sex." *Realist* 42: 1–12, 16.
"Dr. Albert Ellis on Fantasies during Intercourse." *Liaison* 1, no. 12: 1–6.
Foreword to *Advances in Sex Research*, edited by H. G. Beigel. New York: Harper & Row.
If This Be Sexual Heresy. . . . New York: Lyle Stuart. Paperback edition, New York: Tower.
"Instinct, Reason, and Sexual Liberty." *A Way Out* 19: 332–35.
The Intelligent Woman's Guide to Man-Hunting. New York: Lyle Stuart. Paperback edition, New York: Dell.
"Is the Vaginal Orgasm a Myth?" *Liaison* 1, no. 9: 2–4. Also in A. P. Pillay and A. Ellis, eds. *Sex, Society and the Individual*, 155–62. Bombay, India: *International Journal of Sexology*.
"The Myth of Nymphomania." *Gent* 7, no. 6: 31–33, 74–80.
"A New Sex Code for Modern Americans." *Mattachine Review* 9, no. 2: 4–10.
"Nudity and Love." *Independent* 135: 3, 6.
"Orgasm and Health." *A Way Out* 19: 240–42.
The Origins and Development of the Incest Taboo [bound together with E. Durkheim *Incest: The Nature and Origin of the Taboo*]. New York: Lyle Stuart.
"A Psychologist Looks at Adultery." *Rogue*, February: 15–16.
"The Psychology of Assassination." *Independent* 139: 1, 4, 5. Reprinted, New York: Institute for Rational-Emotive Therapy.
Rational-Emotive Psychotherapy. New York: Institute for Rational-Emotive Therapy.

"Rational-Emotive Psychotherapy: A Critique of Three Critiques." *Bulletin of the Essex County Society of Clinical Psychologists in Private Practice* (Spring): 7–11.

"Sex: Love or Hate?" *Independent* 131: 4–6.

Sex and the Single Man. New York: Lyle Stuart. Paperback edition, New York: Dell.

[with J. P. Pillay]. *Sex, Society and the Individual.* Bombay, India: *International Journal of Sexology.*

"Sick and Healthy Love." *Independent* 132: 1, 8–9; 133: 4–6.

[with C. Rogers, F. Perls, and E. Shostrom]. *Three Approaches to Psychotherapy: Gloria.* Film. Corona del Mar, CA: Psychological and Educational Films.

"To Thine Own Psychotherapeutic Self Be True." *Psychologists in Private Practice* 4, no. 1: 8.

"To Thine Own Therapeutic Lust Be True?" New York: Institute for Rational-Emotive Therapy.

"Toward a More Precise Definition of 'Emotional' and 'Intellectual' Insight." *Psychological Reports* 13: 125–26.

"The Truth about Nudity and Sexuality." *Bachelor* 4, no. 5: 18–20, 67–68.

Verbatim Transcript of a Recorded Interview with a Young Male Homosexual Treated with Rational-Emotive Psychotherapy. Orlando: Academy of Psychotherapists.

1964

"The Essence of Sexual Morality." *Issue* 2, no. 1: 20–24. Reprinted, New York: Institute for Rational-Emotive Therapy.

"A Guide to Rational Homosexuality." *Drum: Sex in Perspective* 4, no. 8: 8–12.

"How to Have an Affair and End It with Style." *Saga* 29, no. 1: 44–45, 89.

"How to Keep Boredom Out of the Bedroom." *Pageant* 20, no. 2: 14–18.

"In Defense of *The American Sexual Tragedy,* Dr. Ellis Answers the Charges of Dr. Levin." *Current Medical Digest* 31: 518–22.

[with R. Wolf]. "An Interview with Dr. Albert Ellis." *Campus Voice* 19: 6–11.

Introduction to *Casebook: Nymphomania,* by V. Morhaim. New York: Dell.

Introduction to *To Be Fully Alive,* by A. Maddaloni. New York: Horizon.

"Is Pornography Harmful to Children?" *Realist* 47: 2–3.

"Marriage Counseling." In *Handbook of Counseling Techniques,* edited by E. Harma, 147–53. New York: Pergamon.

"Must We Be Guilty about Premarital Sex?" *Modern Sex* 1, no. 1: 66–75.

"New Dynamics in Contemporary Petting." *Nugget* 9, no. 2: 16–20. Also in *The Search for Sexual Enjoyment.* New York: Macfadden Bartell.

[with E. Sagarin]. *Nymphomania: A Study of the Oversexed Woman.* New York: Gilbert.

Postscript to *Greek Love*, by Z. Eglinton (pseudo.), 429–38. New York: Layton.

"The Pressures of Masculinity and Femininity." *Independent* 143: 1, 4, 6–7.

[with J. C. Weaver and W. Thomas]. "Religion and Moral Philosophy in a Manifesto [Pan Humanist Manifesto of Ralf Borsodi]." *A Way Out* 20: 73–76.

"Should We Ban War Toys?" *Realist* 48, no. 1: 29–31.

[with C. Averit and L. Lipton]. "A Talk with Dr. Ellis." *Los Angeles Free Press*, September 10: 3.

"Thoughts on Theory versus Outcome in Psychotherapy." *Psychotherapy* 1: 83–87.

"What Creates Sex Hostility?" *Sexology* 30: 592–94.

"Wife Swapping." *Realist* 50: 19–20.

1965

"An Answer to Some Objections to Rational-Emotive Psychotherapy." *Psychotherapy: Theory, Research, and Practice* 2: 108–11.

The Case for Sexual Liberty. Tucson, AZ: Ray Anthony.

Introduction to *Dialogues of Luisa Sigea*, by N. Chorier. Hollywood, CA: Brandon House.

Introduction to *Guild Dictionary of Homosexual Terms*. Washington, DC: Guild.

Introduction to *The Love Pagoda*. North Hollywood, CA: Brandon House.

Introduction to *Oswald*, by K. Thornley. Chicago: New Classics.

Introduction to *The Story of O*, by P. Reage. North Hollywood, CA: Brandon House.

Introduction to *You Are Not Alone*, by M. M. Grossack. Boston: Christopher.

"Is the 'Myth of Negro Sex Superiority' a Myth?" *Fact?* September: 1–7.

[with R. Nathan]. "The Legitimate Pickup." *Mademoiselle*, May: 88, 94, 126.

"Morality and Rational Therapy." Letter to the editor. *Journal of Marriage and Family* 19: 417.

Rational-Emotive Psychotherapy. New York: Institute for Rational Living.

Review of *Sexual Fulfillment and Self-Affirmation*, by R. C. Robertiello. *Journal of Nervous and Mental Diseases.*

Review of *The Sexually Responsive Woman*, by P. E. Kronhausen. *Marriage and Family Living* 18: 101.

"Showing the Patient That He Is Not a Worthless Individual." *Voices* 1, no. 2: 74–77. Reprinted as *Showing Clients They Are Not Worthless Individuals*. New York: Institute for Rational-Emotive Therapy.

Suppressed: Seven Key Essays Publishers Dare Not Print. Chicago, IL: New Classics House.

Workshop in RET. New York: Institute for Rational-Emotive Therapy.

1966

"Continuing Personal Growth of the Psychotherapist." *Journal of Humanistic Psychology* 6: 156–69.

[with J. Wolfe and S. Mosley]. *How to Prevent Your Child from Becoming a Neurotic Adult*. New York: Crown. Paperback edition, *How to Raise an Emotionally Healthy, Happy Child*. North Hollywood, CA: Wilshire.

Introduction to *Secret Techniques of Erotic Delight*, by V. Howard. New York: L. Stuart.

"New Cures for Frigidity: New Kooky (but Workable) Cures for Frigidity." *Cosmopolitan* 160, no. 1: 30–35. Reprinted as *New Cures for Frigidity*. New York: Institute for Rational-Emotive Therapy.

[with R. Nathan]. "Our Soaring Suicide Rate." *North American Newspaper Alliance Syndicate: Long Island Press*, January 18–19: 37, 28.

Preface to *Sodom*, by J. Wilmot, Earl of Rochester. North Hollywood, CA: Brandon House.

"Psychosexual and Marital Problems." In *An Introduction to Clinical Psychology*. 3rd ed., edited by L. A. Pennington and I. A. Berg, 248–69. New York: Ronald Press.

"The Requisites of the Sexual Revolution and Their Relation to Nudism." *Sol* 7: 30–31.

Rules for Group Psychotherapy. New York: Institute for Rational-Emotive Therapy.

"Sex and Civilization." *Independent* 167: 1, 8; 168: 5–6, 8.

Sex without Guilt. Revised paperback editions: New York: Lancer; and North Hollywood, CA: Wilshire.

"Should Nonprofessionals Try to Do Psychotherapy?" *Newsletter Division of Clinical Psychology of the American Psychological Association* 19, no. 2: 10–11.

"Some Uses of the Printed, Written, and Recorded Word in Psychotherapy." In *The Use of Written Communication in Psychotherapy*, edited by L. Pearson, 23–36. Springfield, IL: Charles C. Thomas.

1967

[with R. O. Conway]. *The Art of Erotic Seduction*. New York: Lyle Stuart.

"Counseling Adolescents with Problems of Sex and Values." *Rational Living* 2, no. 1: 7–12.

[with D. Sandler and R. Liswood]. "Doctors Tell You the Best Time to Love." *Pageant*, August: 148–54.

"Goals of Psychotherapy." In *The Goals of Psychotherapy*, edited by A. R. Mahrer, 206–20. New York: Macmillan.

"Masturbation by Sexually Isolated Individuals." In *Sexual Self-Stimulation*, edited by R. E. L. Masters, 221–31. Los Angeles: Sherbourne.

"The New Sexual Freedoms." *Rogue* 12, no. 6: 12–13, 17, 83–85.

"Objectivism, the New Religion." *Rational Living* 2, no. 2: 1–6.

[with H. Hefner]. "Phone Dialogue: The American Sex Revolution." *Voices* 3: 88–97.

"Psychotherapy and Moral Laxity." *Psychiatric Opinion* 4, no. 5: 18–21.

Reply to D. H. Steding. *Rational Living* 2, no. 1: 30.

Review of *Human Sexual Response*, by W. Masters and V. Johnson. *New York State Psychologist* 19, no. 2: 38–39.

Review of *Lectures to Relatives of Former Patients*, by A. Low. *Rational Living* 2, no. 2: 29–30.

Review of *The Psychology of Science: A Reconnaissance*, by A. H. Maslow. *Salmagundi* 2, no. 1: 97–101.

Review of *A Sign for Cain: An Exploration of Human Violence*, by F. Wetham. *Annals of the American Academy of Political and Social Science* 370: 181–82.

Review of *Structure and Psychotherapy*, by E. L. Phillips and D. N. Wiener. *Psychiatry & Social Science Review* 1, no. 7: 4–6.

"Self-Acceptance and Successful Human Elations." *Newsletter of the Institute for Marriage and Friendships* (Winter): 8–9.

"Should Some People Be Labeled Mentally Ill?" *Journal of Consulting Psychology* 31: 435–36.

"State's Adopted 'Kinsey' Reports." *Los Angeles Free Press*, January 20: 16.

"Talking to Adolescents about Sex." *Rational Living* 2, no. 1: 7–12.

"Why One Out of Every Five Wives Is Having an Affair." *Pageant* 23, no. 3: 112–17.

1968

Biographical Information Form. New York: Institute for Rational-Emotive Therapy.

Discussion of *In Praise of Inadequacy*, by C. Jackson. *Voices* 4, no. 3: 88–89.

"Elbow Room." Letter to the Editor. *Playboy*, May: 4–5.

"Fifteen Ways to Get More Out of Sex." *Sexology* 35: 148–51.

"Havelock Ellis." In *International Encyclopedia of the Social Science*, volume 5, edited by D. Sills, 25–31. New York: Macmillan.

"Homosexuality: The Right to Be Wrong." *Journal of Sex Research* 4: 96–107.

"Is California More Sexually Liberal Than Other States?" In *The Hippie Papers*, 107–10. New York: New American.

"Is Psychoanalysis Harmful?" *Psychiatric Opinion* 5, no. 1 (January): 16–24. Reprinted, New York: Institute for Rational-Emotive Therapy.

"Let's Change Our Marriage System!" *Sexology* 34, no. 7: 436–39.

"Objectivism, the New Religion, Part II." *Rational Living* 3, no. 1: 12–19.

"A Rational Approach to Interpretation." In *Use of Interpretation in Treat-*

ment, edited by E. Hammer, 232–39. New York: Grune & Stratton. Reprinted, New York: Institute for Rational-Emotive Therapy.

Review of *Freedom—Not License!* by A. S. Neill. *Rational Living* 3, no. 1: 35–36.

"Sex and Revolution." *Modern Utopian* 2, no. 5: 3.

"Sex and the Young Adult." *Twenty-Five* 1, no. 1: 36–39, 50–52.

"A Sexologist Looks at Sexual Love." *Independent* 184: 5; 186: 1, 4, 6; 188: 7–8.

"Sexual Manifestations of Emotionally Disturbed Behavior." *Annals of the American Academy of Political and Social Science* 376: 96–105.

"Sexual Promiscuity in America." *Annals of the American Academy of Political and Social Science* 378: 58–67.

"What **Really** Causes Psychotherapeutic Change?" *Voices* 4, no. 2: 90–97. Reprinted, New York: Institute for Rational-Emotive Therapy.

1969

"Are You Secretly Afraid of Being Touched?" *Pageant* 10, no. 4: 132–37.

"Cognitive Approach to Behavior Therapy." *International Journal of Psychiatry* 8: 896–900.

Comments on C. H. Patterson's "Current View of Client-Centered or Relationship Therapy." *Counseling Psychologist* 1, no. 2: 37–42.

"Emotional Education in the Classroom: The Living School." *School Health Review*, November: 19–22.

"Emotional Problems of the Young Adult." In *The Young Adult*, edited by Forest Hospital Foundation, 83–102. Des Plaines, IL: Forest Hospital Foundation. Also in *Rational Living* 52, no. 2 (1971): 2–11.

The Essence of Rational Psychotherapy: A Comprehensive Approach to Treatment. New York: Institute for Rational-Emotive Therapy.

"Healthy and Disturbed Reasons for Having Extramarital Relations." In *Extramarital Relations*, edited by G. Neubeck, 153–61. Englewood Cliffs, NJ: Prentice-Hall.

"How to Increase Sexual Enjoyment in Marriage." In *Handbook of Marriage Counseling*, edited by B. N. Ard and C. Ard, 375–78. Palo Alto, CA: Science and Behavior.

How to Participate Effectively in a Marathon Weekend of Marital Encounter. Revised edition. New York: Institute for Rational-Emotive Therapy.

Introduction to *The Photographic Manual of Sexual Intercourse*, by I. R. O'Conner. New York: Pent-R.

"Mothers Are Too Good for Their Own Good." Syndicated article. *Boston Sunday Globe Magazine*, May 11: 26–30.

"Rational-Emotive Psychotherapy." *Journal of Contemporary Psychotherapy* 1: 82–90. Also in *Explorations* 17: 5–12.

"Rational-Emotive Theology?!" *Rational Living* 4, no. 1: 9–14.

"Rational-Emotive Therapy." *Explorations* 17: 5–16.

"Rationality in Sexual Morality." *Humanist* 29, no. 5: 17–21. Reprinted, New York: Institute for Rational-Emotive Therapy.

Review of *Adultery for Adults*, by J. Peterson and M. Mercer. *Psychology Today* 3, no. 2: 12–62.

Review of *Ego, Hunger, and Aggression: The Beginning of Gestalt Therapy*, by F. Perls. *Catholic World* 210, no. 1255: 36–38.

"Sex, Frustration and Aggression." *Rogue* 18: 27–30.

Sex, Sanity and Psychotherapy. Cassette recording. New York: Institute for Rational-Emotive Therapy.

Suggested Procedures for a Weekend of Rational Encounter. New York: Institute for Rational-Emotive Therapy.

"Teaching Emotional Education in the Classroom." *School Health Review*, November: 10–13.

"Toward the Understanding of Youthful Rebellion." In *A Search for the Meaning of the Generation Gap*, edited by R. Frank, 85–111. San Diego, CA: San Diego Country Department of Education.

[with D. Mace]. "The Use of Sex in Human Life: A Dialogue." *Journal of Sex Research* 5, no. 1 (February): 41–49.

"A Weekend of Rational Encounter." *Rational Living* 4, no. 2: 1–8. Reprinted in A. Ellis and W. Dryden, eds. *The Practice of REBT*, 180–91. New York: Springer.

"What Else Is New? Me!" *Voices* 5, no. 3: 33–35.

"Where Can We Go from Here?" *Psychology Today* 2, no. 8: 38.

1970

[with J. Baez, J. Campbell, and P. Goodman]. "The Authentic Man: A Symposium." *Humanist* 30, no. 1: 19–26.

"The Case against Religion." *Mensa Bulletin* 38: 5–6. Reprinted, New York: Institute for Rational-Emotive Therapy.

"The Cognitive Element in Experiential and Relationship Psychotherapy." *Existential Psychiatry* 7, no. 28: 35–52.

"Ellis on Kinsey: Part I." *Penthouse* 2, no. 4: 115–21.

"The Emerging Counselor." *Conseiller Canadien* 4, no. 2: 99–105.

"Frigidity." In *The Layman's Explanation of Sexual Inadequacy*, edited by P. Gillette, 192–209. New York: Award.

[with J. Henderson, D. Murray, and R. Seidenberg]. *Four Psychotherapies*. Cassette recording. Salt Lake City, UT: American Academy of Psychotherapists Tape Library.

"Group Marriage: A Possible Alternative?" In *The Family in Search of a Future*, edited by H. A. Otto, 85–97. New York: Meredith.

"Humanism, Values, Rationality, in Tribute to Alfred Adler on His 100th Birthday." *Journal of Individual Psychology* 26, no. 1: 11–12.

Introduction to *The Big Answer Book about Sex*, by P. Guilette. New York: Award.

Rational-Emotive Psychotherapy. Cassette recording. New York: Institute for Rational-Emotive Therapy.

Review of *The Psychology of Self-Esteem*, by N. Branden. *Rational Living* 4, no. 2: 31.

"Sex and the Family." In *Prophecy for the Year 2000*, edited by I. A. Falk, 176–78. New York: Messner.

"Sex and Violence in Society." *Independent* 157: 1, 4, 6.

"The Sexual Criminal." *Penthouse* 1: 83–86, 93.

"What You Should Know about the Sensuous Man." *Coronet* 8, no. 10: 18–24.

1971

"The Case for Sexual Latitude." In *Sexual Latitude: For and Against*, edited by H. Hart, 67–83. New York: Hart. Reprinted, New York: Institute for Rational-Emotive Therapy.

Critique of A. DiLoreto's *Comparative Psychotherapy*. In *Comparative Psychotherapy: An Experimental Analysis*, edited by A. DiLoreto, 213–21. Chicago: Aldine-Atherton.

[with D. Casriel]. "Debate: Albert Ellis vs. Daniel Casriel on Anger." *Rational Living* 6, no. 2: 2–21.

"Ego! Sex and the Great I Am." *Penthouse* 3, no. 1: 66–67.

"Ellis on Kinsey: Part 2: The Other Side of Kinsey." *Penthouse* 2, no. 5: 71–73.

"Emotional Disturbance and Its Treatment in a Nutshell." *Canadian Counselor* 5, no. 3: 168–71. Reprinted, New York: Institute for Rational-Emotive Therapy.

"An Experiment in Emotional Education." *Educational Technology* 11, no. 7: 61–63. Reprinted, New York: Institute for Rational-Emotive Therapy.

"Fifteen Ways to Get More Out of Sex." *Sexology* 38: 4–7.

[with B. N. Ard, H. J. Geis, J. M. Gullo, P. A. Hauck, and M. C. Maultsby]. *Growth through Reason.* Palo Alto, CA: Science & Behavior. Paperback edition, North Hollywood, CA: Wilshire.

Homework Report. New York: Institute for Rational-Emotive Therapy.

"Is There Any Cure for Nymphomania?" *Sexual Behavior* 1, no. 5: 13–14.

"Penthouse Casebook: Me, Myself, and I." *Penthouse* 3, no. 1: 66–67.

[with P. Lehman]. "Practical Applications of Rational Emotive Technique." *Rational Living* 6, no. 2: 36–38.

Rational-Emotive Therapy and Its Application to Emotional Education. New York: Institute for Rational-Emotive Therapy.

"Rational-Emotive Treatment of Impotence, Frigidity and Other Sexual Problems." *Professional Psychology* (Fall): 346–49.

"Reason and Emotion in the Individual Psychology of Adler." *Journal of Individual Psychology* 27, no. 1: 50–64.

Review of *Behavior Therapy and Beyond*, by A. A. Lazarus. *Behavior Therapy* 2: 300–302.

"The Role of Coital Positions in Sexual Relations." *Sexual Behavior* 1, no. 4: 12–13.

"Sexual Adventuring and Personality Growth." In *The New Sexuality*, edited by H. Otto, 94–108. Palo Alto, CA: Science and Behavior. Reprinted, New York: Institute for Rational-Emotive Therapy.

"Sexual Problems of the Young Adult." *Rational Living* 5, no. 2: 2–11.

"Sex without Guilt." In *Sexuality: A Search for Perspective*, edited by D. L. Grummon and A. M. Barclay, 226–55. New York: Van Nostrand Reinhold.

1972

The A-B-C's of Rational-Emotive Therapy. New York: Institute for Rational Living.

"The A-B-C's of Rational Sensitivity." In *Executive Leadership: A Rational Approach.* New York: Citadel. Paperback edition, New York: Institute for Rational-Emotive Therapy.

"Answer to Question on Aggression by M. R. Eldestein," *Rational Living* 7, no. 1: 12–13.

"Barriers to Sexual Spontaneity." *Forum* 1, no. 9: 12–16.

The Civilized Couples' Guide to Extramarital Adventure. New York: Widen. Paperback edition, New York: Pinnacle.

"The Contribution of Psychotherapy to School Psychology." *School Psychology Digest* (Spring): 6–9.

"Effectiveness of Telephone Interviews with Rational Emotive Therapy Trained Patients." *Daily Living* 1, no. 4: 13–15.

"Emotional Education in the Classroom: The Living School." *Journal of Clinical and Child Psychology* 1, no. 3: 19–22.

Executive Leadership: The Rational-Emotive Approach. New York: Institute for Rational-Emotive Therapy.

"Helping People Get Better Rather Than Merely Feel Better." *Rational Living* 7, no. 2: 2–9.

"How Does an Affair Affect a Marriage? It All Hinges on the Guilt Quotient." *Sexual Behavior* 2, no. 9: 48–49.

How to Master Your Fear of Flying. New York: Curtis.

"Humanistic Psychotherapy: A Revolutionary Approach." *Humanist* 32, no. 1: 24–28. Reprinted, New York: Institute for Rational-Emotive Therapy.

"Instant Therapy for Erotic Hangups." *Penthouse* 3, no. 6: 48–52.

"Intellectual Fascism." *Journal of Human Relations* 18, no. 1: 700–709.

"Is There Any Difference between 'Vaginal' and 'Clitoral' Orgasm?" *Sexual Behavior* 2, no. 3: 42.

[with J. Gullo]. *Murder and Assassination*. New York: Lyle Stuart.

"Philosophy and Rational-Emotive Therapy." *Counseling and Values* 16: 158–61.

"Psychotherapy and the Value of a Human Being." In *Value and Valuation: Axiological Studies in Honor of Robert S. Hartman*, edited by J. W. Davis, 117–39. Knoxville: University of Tennessee. Reprinted, New York: Institute for Rational-Emotive Therapy.

"Psychotherapy without Tears." In *Twelve Therapists*, edited by A. Burton, 103–26. San Francisco, CA: Jossey Bass.

"Rational-Emotive Psychotherapy: A Comprehensive Approach to Therapy." In *Innovations in Psychotherapy*, edited by G. D. Goldman and M. S. Milman, 147–63. Springfield, IL: Charles C. Thomas.

"Rebuttal of My Supposed Views on Gay Liberation." *Harper's* (December): 123.

Review of *Caring Relationship Inventory*, by E. Shostrom. In *Seventh Mental Measurements Yearbook*, edited by O. Buros, 560–61. Highland Park, NJ: Gryphon.

Review of *The Complete Immortalia*, by H. Hart. *Rational Living* 7, no. 2: 38.

Review of *Sexual Development Scale for Females*, by A. Senoussi. In *The Seventh Mental Measurements Yearbook*, edited by O. Buros, 958–59. Highland Park, NJ: Gryphon.

"A Revolutionary Approach." *Humanist* (January): 25–27.

"Sexperts—Do We Really Need Them?" *Forum* 1, no. 4: 6–9.

"Sexual Spontaneity." *Forum* 1, no. 9: 12–15.

Suggested Procedures for a Fourteen-Hour Marathon for Regular Group Therapy Clients. New York: Institute for Rational-Emotive Therapy.

"What Kinds of Reinforcement Can Cognitive-Behavior Therapists Receive from B. F. Skinner?" *Behavior Therapy* 3, no. 2: 263–74.

"Why Can't I Bring Myself to Kiss a Woman When I Want to Very Much?" *Sexual Behavior* (May): 7.

"Why I Am Opposed to Censorship of Pornography." *Osteopathic Physician* 39, no. 10: 40–41.

1973

Afterword to *Is Marriage Necessary?* by L. Casler, 181–84. New York: Human Sciences.

"Albert Ellis' Rationality Score." *Rational Living* 8, no. 2: 31.

"Are Cognitive Behavior Therapy and Rational Therapy Synonymous?" *Rational Living* 8, no. 2: 8–11.

"Autobiography." In *Counseling Children in Groups*, edited by M. M. Ohlsen, 79–80. New York: Holt, Rinehart, and Winston.

"Can There Be a Rational Concept of Healthy Personality?" *Counseling Psychologist* 4, no. 2: 45–48.

"Cognitive Therapy: Some Theoretical Origins and Therapeutic Implications." *International Mental Health Research Newsletter* 15, no. 2: 12–16.

Commentary on "The Bisexual." *Humanist* 33, no. 4: 18–19.

Comment on Judge Tyler's decision to cut the throat of *Deep Throat*. *Clinical Social Work Journal* 1, no. 3 (Winter).

"Definition of Rational-Emotive Therapy." In *Dictionary of Behavioral Science*, edited by B. B. Wolman, 716. New York: Van Nostrand Reinhold.

[with J. M. Whitley]. *A Demonstration with an Elementary School Child*. Film. Arlington, VA: American Association for Counseling and Development.

[with J. M. Whitley]. *A Demonstration with a Woman Fearful of Expressing Emotions*. Film. Arlington, VA: American Association for Counseling and Development.

[with J. M. Whitley]. *A Demonstration with a Young Divorced Woman*. Film. Arlington, VA: American Association for Counseling and Development.

"Emotional Education at the Living School." In *Counseling Children in Groups*, edited by M. M. Ohlsen, 79–94. Reprinted, New York: Institute for Rational-Emotive Therapy.

"How to Experiment in Bed." *Sexology* 39, no. 12: 6–10.

How to Stubbornly Refuse to Be Ashamed of Anything. Cassette recording. New York: Institute for Rational-Emotive Therapy.

Humanistic Psychotherapy: The Rational-Emotive Approach. New York: Julian. Paperback edition, New York: McGraw-Hill.

[with C. Shorkey]. *Human Sexuality Concepts*. Videotape. Austin: Audio-Visual Resource Center, University of Texas.

Introduction to *I Love the Person You Were Meant to Be*, by W. Emmett. New York: Warner.

"Is Transpersonal Psychology Humanistic?" *Newsletter Association for Humanistic Psychology* (May): 10–13.

"Mad People May Eat Improperly—but a Good Diet Won't Cure Them!" *Sexual Behavior* 3, no. 3: 8.

"My Philosophy of Psychotherapy." *Journal of Contemporary Psychotherapy* 6, no. 1: 13–18. Reprinted, New York: Institute for Rational-Emotive Therapy.

"The No Cop-Out Therapy." *Psychology Today* 7, no. 2: 56–62.

[with D. Riesman, D. Viscott, T. S. Szasz, L. B. Ames, and E. J. Lieberman]. "The Psychological Fallout [of Watergate]: How Other Professionals See It." *Today's Health* 51, no. 8: 19, 64–66.

"Rational-Emotive Therapy." In *Current Psychotherapies*, edited by R. J. Corsini, 167–206. Itasca, IL: Peacock.

"Rational-Emotive Therapy." In *Direct Psychotherapies*, volume 1, edited by R. M. Jurjevich, 295–327. Miami: University of Miami.

"Rational-Emotive Therapy: A Comprehensive Approach to Personality Change." 2 cassettes. New York: Institute for Rational-Emotive Therapy.

Review of *Between Man and Woman: The Dynamics of Intersexual Relationships*, by E. Shostrom and J. Kavanaugh. *Rational Living* 8, no. 1: 43.

Review of *Growth through Reason*, by D. Wargo. *Psychotherapy* 10: 362–63.

Review of *The Occult Conceit: A New Look at Astrology, Witchcraft, and Sorcery*, by O. S. Rachleff. *Rational Living* 8, no. 2: 36.

Review of *Overcoming Sexual Inadequacy*, by S. Neiger. *Journal of Sex Research* 9: 270–71.

Review of *Without Guilt and Justice: From Decidophobia to Autonomy*, by W. Kaufman. *Rational Living* 8, no. 2: 34.

"Sexual Mores a Quarter of a Century from Now." *Psychiatric Opinion* 10, no. 3: 17–21.

"So verlangere ich maine erektion" [So prolongued is my erection]. *Animus* 8: 8–9.

"Toward a New Humanist Manifesto." *Humanist* 33, no. 1: 17–18.

Twenty-five Ways to Stop Downing Yourself. Cassette recording. Philadelphia: American Academy of Psychotherapists Tape Library.

Twenty-five Ways to Stop Worrying. Cassette recording. New York: Institute for Rational-Emotive Therapy.

"Unhealthy Love: Its Causes and Treatment." In *Symposium on Love*, edited by M. E. Curtin, 175–97. New York: Behavioral Publications, 1973. Reprinted, New York: Institute for Rational-Emotive Therapy.

"What Does Transpersonal Psychology Have to Offer to the Art and Science of Psychotherapy?" *Rational Living* 8, no. 1: 20–28.

1974

"Albert's Answers." *Stoic* 1, no. 1: 2.

"Barnum Was Right! Or Why Supposedly Intelligent People Believe in Exorcism, Astrology, Tarot Card Reading, and Other Unmitigated Claptrap." *Rational Living* 9, no. 2: 2–6.

"Cognitive Aspects of Abreactive Therapy." *Voices* 10, no. 1: 48–56. Reprinted, New York: Institute for Rational-Emotive Therapy.

Cognitive-Behavior Therapy. Cassette recording. New York: Institute for Rational-Emotive Therapy.

[with G. Clanton]. "A Conversation with Albert Ellis." *Alternative Life-Styles* 2: 243–53.

[with H. Greenwald, V. Satir, and A. Seagul]. *Dealing with Sexual Material*. Cassette recording. Orlando, FL: American Academy of Psychotherapists.

Demonstration of Rational-Emotive Therapy. Cassette recording. Saratoga, CA: Cognetics.

A Demonstration with a Woman Fearful of Expressing Emotions. Videotape. New York: Institute for Rational-Emotive Therapy.

Disputing Irrational Beliefs. New York: Institute for Rational-Emotive Therapy.

[with S. Moore]. "Dr. Albert Ellis in His Own Words: 'Sex Is the Worst Reason to Marry—or Divorce.'" *People Weekly* 1, no. 4: 28–31.

"The Education and Training of a Rational-Emotive Therapist." *Voices* 10, no. 3: 35–38.

Epilogue to *Sex and the Intelligent Woman,* edited by M. F. Martino, 266–86. New York: Springer.

"Experience and Rationality: The Making of a Rational Emotive Therapist." *Psychotherapy: Theory, Research, and Practice* 11: 194–98.

Foreword to *Emotional Well-Being through Rational Behavior Training,* by D. Goodman and M. C. Maultsby Jr. Springfield, IL: Charles C. Thomas.

Foreword to *Help Yourself,* by J. M. Lembo. Niles, IL: Argus.

Foreword to *Youth: Toward Personal Growth,* by D. G. Tosi. Columbus, OH: Merrill.

[with R. A. Harper]. *Interview with Dr. Albert Ellis.* Cassette recording. Salt Lake City, UT: American Academy of Psychotherapists.

Introduction to *Homer the Homely Houndog,* by E. Garcia and N. Pellegrin. New York: Institute for Rational-Emotive Therapy.

Introductory remarks to symposium on human sexuality, A. Ellis, chair. *Proceedings of International Congress of Medical Sexology, Paris:* 1–3.

"Is Nudity Anti-Sexual?" *Ace Annual* 16: 44, 66.

[with P. A. Hauck]. *Overcoming Frustration and Anger.* Philadelphia, PA: Westminster.

"Questions and Answers on Patients' Problems: Is There an Appropriate Length of Time for Foreplay?" *Medical Tribune* 15, no. 35: 24–25.

"Rational-Emotive Theory: Albert Ellis." In *Operational Theories of Personality,* edited by A. Burton, 308–44. New York: Brunner/Mazel.

"Rational-Emotive Therapy: A Few Corrections." *Humanist* 34, no. 5: 35–36.

"Rational-Emotive Therapy Revisited." *Professional Psychology* 5: 111.

Rational Living in an Irrational World. Cassette recording. New York: Institute for Rational-Emotive Therapy.

"A Rational Voice." *American Academy of Psychotherapists Newsletter* 3: 1.

Review of *Abnormal Psychology: An Experimental Clinical Approach,* by G. C. Davison and J. M. Neale. *Rational Living* 9, no. 2: 41.

Review of *Decision Therapy,* by H. Greenwald. *Psychoanalytic Review* 61: 486–87.

Review of *Emotional Common Sense: How to Avoid Self-Destructiveness,* by S. Parker. *Contemporary Psychology* 19: 307–308.

Techniques for Disputing Irrational Beliefs (DIBS). New York: Institute for Rational Living.

[with M. C. Maultsby Jr.]. *Techniques for Using Rational-Emotive Imagery (REI)*. New York: Institute for Rational Living.

"The Treatment of Sex and Love Problems in Women." In *Women in Therapy*, edited by V. Franks and V. Burtle, 284–306. New York: Brunner/Mazel.

"What Rational-Emotive Therapy Is and Is Not." *Counselor Education and Supervision* 14: 140–44.

1975

"Albert's Answers." *Stoic* 2: 2.

Bibliography of articles and books by Albert Ellis. In *A Bibliography for Adlerian Psychology*, edited by H. Mosak and B. Mosak, 88–99. Washington: Hemisphere; and New York: Wiley.

Comments on Frank's *The Limits of Humanism. Humanist* 35, no. 5: 43–45.

"Controversial Issues." In *Controversial Issues in Human Relations Training Groups*, by K. T. Morris and K. M. Cinnamon, 3–4, 21–22, 30–31, 42–43, 52–53, 63–65, 73–74, 82–84, 93–94, 100–101, 107–10. Springfield, IL: Charles C. Thomas.

"Creative Joy and Happiness: The Humanistic Way." *Humanist* 35, no. 10: 11–13.

[with H. Greenwald, V. Satir, and A. Seagul]. *Dealing with Sexual Material*. Cassette recording. Salt Lake City, UT: American Academy of Psychotherapists Tape Library.

Demonstration with a Family. Videotape. New York: Institute for Rational-Emotive Therapy.

Demonstration with Woman with Sexual and Weight Problems. Videotape. New York: Institute for Rational-Emotive Therapy.

"Does Rational-Emotive Therapy Seem Deep Enough?" *Rational Living* 10, no. 2: 11–14. Reprinted, New York: Institute for Rational-Emotive Therapy.

"Do Sex Deviants Have a Redipus Complex?" Review of *Pornography and Sexual Deviance*, by M. J. Goldstein, S. Kant, and J. Hartman. *Contemporary Psychology* 20: 621–22.

Foreword to *Behavior, Law and Remedies*, by V. A. Church. Dubuque, IA: Kendall & Hunt.

Foreword to *Help Yourself to Happiness*, by M. C. Maultsby Jr. New York: Institute for Rational-Emotive Therapy.

Foreword to *Rational Emotive Therapy*, edited by K. T. Morris and H. M. Kanitz. Boston, MA: Houghton Mifflin.

"How Might I Best Turn One of My New Year's Resolutions into a Practiced Commitment?" *Stoic* 3: 2.

How to Be Happy Though Mated. Cassette recording. New York: Institute for Rational-Emotive Therapy.

"How to Get along with Neurotics without Going Crazy Yourself." *Glamour* 73, no. 9: 194–95, 210, 216.

How to Live with a Neurotic. Revised edition, New York: Crown; paperback edition, North Hollywood, CA: Wilshire.

How to Live with a Neurotic: At Home and at Work. North Hollywood, CA: Wilshire.

"An Informal History of Sex Therapy." *Counseling Psychologist* 5, no. 1: 9–13.

Life without Any Kind of Magic. Cassette recording. Orlando, FL: American Academy of Psychotherapists.

"Minimizing Irrational Proto-Thinking." *Journal of the International Academy of Preventive Medicine* 2, no. 4: 38–40.

"Myths and Other Sexual Nonsense You Can Forget Right Now." *Brides* 42, no. 2: 120–21, 124.

[with R. A. Harper]. *A New Guide to Rational Living.* Englewood Cliffs, NJ: Prentice-Hall. Paperback edition, North Hollywood, CA: Wilshire.

[with K. Morris]. "The Perls Perversion." *Personnel Guidance Journal* 54: 91–93.

"A Rational Approach to Leadership." In *Leadership Development: Theory and Practice,* edited by R. N. Cassel and R. L. Helchberger, 22–54. North Quincy, MA: Christopher.

"The Rational-Emotive Approach to Sex Therapy." *Counseling Psychologist* 5, no. 1: 14–22. Reprinted, New York: Institute for Rational-Emotive Therapy.

"Rational-Emotive Psychotherapy." In *Issues and Approaches in Psychological Therapies,* edited by D. Banister, 163–86. New York: Wiley.

Rational-Emotive Therapy: Four Interviews. Cassette recording. Salt Lake City, UT: American Academy of Psychotherapists Tape Library.

"Rational-Emotive Therapy Abolishes Most of the Human Ego." *Psychotherapy* 13: 343–48. Reprinted, New York: Institute for Rational-Emotive Therapy.

"Rational-Emotive Therapy and the School Counselor." *School Counselor* 22: 236–42.

RET and Assertiveness Training. New York: Institute for Rational-Emotive Therapy.

RET Group Therapy Demonstration. Videotape. New York: Institute for Rational-Emotive Therapy.

Review of *Depression: A Reincarnation. Contemporary Psychology* 20, no. 3: 221–22.

Review of *Homework in Counseling and Psychotherapy,* by J. L. Shelton and J. M. Ackerman. *Behavior Therapy* 6: 582–83.

Review of *Pornography and Sexual Deviance*, by M. J. Goldstein, S. Kant, and J. Hartman. *Contemporary Psychology* 20: 621–22.

"You and Your Fantasy on Film." *Gallery* 5, no. 6: 95–97.

1976

"After Masters and Johnson: Where Is Sex Research Going?" *Village Voice*, September: 32.

"Answering a Critique of Rational-Emotive Therapy." *Canadian Counselor* 10: 56–59.

"Basic Clinical Theory of Rational-Emotive Therapy." In *Cognitive Therapy and Emotional Disorders*, by A. T. Beck, 356. New York: International Universities.

"The Biological Basis of Human Irrationality." *Journal of Individual Psychology* 32: 145–68. Reprinted, New York: Institute for Rational-Emotive Therapy.

"Books on Marriage." *Voices* 2, no. 3: 83–85.

The Certification of Sex Therapists. Cassette recording. Baltimore, MD: Hallmark Films.

Conquering Low Frustration Tolerance. Cassette recording. New York: Institute for Rational-Emotive Therapy.

Dealing with Conflicts in Parent-Child Relationships. Videotape. Austin: Audio-Visual Resource Center, School of Social Work, University of Texas.

"Hazards in Practicing RET: An Answer." *Rational Living* 11, no. 1: 19–23.

"Healthy and Unhealthy Aggression." *Humanitas* 12, no. 2: 239–54. Reprinted, New York: Institute for Rational-Emotive Therapy.

"How I Made the Success Trip." In *The Success Trip*, edited by R. Firestone, 7–8, 102, 108–109, 149–51, 167, 248, 255, 279, 280. Chicago: Playboy.

"The Influence of Therapists' Image of Humans upon Their Therapeutic Approach." *Rational Living* 11, no. 2: 2–7.

"A Message from Albert Ellis, Ph.D." *Newsletter American Association for Sex Educators* 8, no. 3: 6.

"Nobody Need Feel Ashamed or Guilty about Anything." In *The Naked Therapist*, edited by S. Kopp, 59–72. San Diego, CA: Edits.

[with D. Block]. *The Pros and Cons of Extramarital Sexual Relationships*. Cassette recording. Logan, UT: American Association of Marriage and Family Counselors.

[with J. Barry and K. Heiser]. "Questions, Issues, and Comments regarding Continuing Education for Consulting Psychologists." *Newsletter for Division of Consulting Psychologists of the American Psychology Association* 28, no. 1: 27–52.

"Rational-Emotive Psychotherapy." In *Psychotherapy and Counseling*, 2nd ed., edited by W. S. Sasakian, 272–85. Chicago, IL: Rand McNally.

Review of *Clinical Behavior Therapy*, by M. R. Goldfried and G. C. Davison. *Rational Living* 11, no. 1: 38–39.

Review of *The Hoax of Freudism: A Study of Brainwashing the American Professionals and Laymen*, by R. M. Jurjevich. *Psychotherapy Bulletin* 9, no. 1: 19–20.

Review of *The New Psychotherapies*, by R. A. Harper. *Rational Living* 11, no. 1: 38.

Review of *Rational Behavior: An Explanation of Behavior That Is Especially Human*, by M. I. Friedman. *Rational Living* 11, no. 1: 39.

Review of *Treating Relationships*, by D. H. Lolson. *Rational Living* 11, no. 1: 38.

Sex and the Liberated Man. Secaucus, NJ: Lyle Stuart.

"Sex Differences." *New Dawn* 1, no. 3: 83–87.

"Techniques of Handling Anger in Marriage." *Journal of Marriage and Family Counseling* 2: 305–16.

1977

"Achieving Emotional Health." In *Human Health and Action*, edited by W. R. Johnson, 110–47. New York: Holt, Rinehart & Winston.

Anger—How to Live With and Without It. Secaucus, NJ: Citadel.

"Becoming More Becoming by Coming." Review of *Becoming Orgasmic: A Sexual Growth Program for Women*, by J. Heiman, L. LoPiccolo, and J. LoPiccolo. *Contemporary Psychology* 22: 763–64.

"Can We Change Thoughts by Reinforcement? A Reply to Howard Rachlin." *Behavior Therapy* 8: 666–72.

"Certification for Sex Therapists." In *Progress in Sexology*, edited by R. Genne and C. Wheeler, 251–58. New York: Plenum.

"Characteristics of Psychotic and Borderline Individuals." In *Handbook of Rational-Emotive Therapy*, edited by A. Ellis and R. Grieger, 177–86. New York: Springer.

Comments on *RET's Place and Influence in Contemporary Psychotherapy*, by R. A. Harper. In *Twenty Years of Rational-Emotive Therapy*, edited by J. L. Wolfe and E. Brand, 48–51. New York: Institute for Rational-Emotive Therapy.

Comments on *Values Revisited*, by C. Curran. *Voices* 13, no. 3: 26–28.

Conquering the Dire Need for Love. Cassette recording. New York: Institute for Rational-Emotive Therapy.

"Creative Marriage." *Love* 1, no. 7: 15–20.

Dealing with Sexuality and Intimacy. Cassette recording. New York: BMA Audio Cassettes.

"Does the Sex of the RET Counselor Affect the Efficacy of RET Procedures?" *Stoic* 5: 3.

Foreword to *This Will Drive You Sane*, by B. L. Little. Minneapolis, MN: Compcare.

"Fun as Psychotherapy." *Rational Living* 12, no. 1: 2–6. Also a cassette recording, New York: Institute for Rational-Emotive Therapy.

A Garland of Rational Songs. Cassette recording and songbook. New York: Institute for Rational-Emotive Therapy.

"Getting Shrunk: Then and Now." *Village Voice*, June: 31.

"Getting Shrunk: Then and Now, Reply to Editor." *Village Voice*, July: 6.

[with R. Grieger, eds.]. *Handbook of Rational Emotive Therapy*. Vol. 1. New York: Springer.

"How to Be Efficient Though Humanistic." *Dawnpoint* 1, no. 1: 38–47.

How to Live With—and Without—Anger. New York: Reader's Digest. Paperback edition, *Anger: How to Live With and Without It*. Secaucus, NJ: Citadel.

"In Memory of Paul Frisch." *American Academy Psychotherapist's News* (November): 5.

"Intimacy in Psychotherapy." *Rational Living* 12, no. 2: 13–19.

Introduction to *Total Sex*, by D. Abelow. New York: Ace.

[with W. Knaus]. *Overcoming Procrastination*. New York: Institute for Rational-Emotive Therapy. Paperback edition, New York: New American Library.

"Question: What Was the Absolute Worst Mistake You Ever Made in Your Entire Life?" *Extra*, June: 8.

"Rational Love Songs." *Emphasis* 14, no. 2: 19.

"Reinforcing and Punishing Thoughts." *Behavior Therapy* 8: 659–65.

"Religious Belief in the United States Today." *Humanist* 37, no. 2: 38–41.

Review of *Individual Education. Journal of Individual Psychology* 33, no. 2a: 391–96.

"Skill Training in Counseling and Psychotherapy." *Canadian Counsellor* 12, no. 1: 30–35.

"Why 'Scientific' Professionals Believe Mystical Nonsense." *Psychiatric Opinion* 14, no. 2: 27–30.

1978

Albert Ellis on Rational-Emotive Therapy: The Development of His Theories and Practice and the Application of His Procedures. Cassette recording. New York: Harper & Row Audio Colloquies.

"Atheism: A Cure for Neurosis." *American Atheist* 20, no. 3: 10–13.

[with E. Abrahms]. *Brief Psychotherapy and Crisis Intervention; Relationship Breakups; Disasters; Job Loss/Retirement; Betrayal; Terrorism; Fatal Illnesses*. 6 cassette recordings. New York: Institute for Rational-Emotive Therapy.

[with E. Abrahms]. *Brief Psychotherapy in Medical and Health Practice*. New York: Springer.

Cognitive Methods of Sex Therapy. Cassette recording. Washington, DC: American Association of Sex Educators, Counselors, and Therapists.

"Critical Reaction to Personal Mastery Group Counseling." *Journal for Specialists in Group Work* 3: 160–64.

Dealing with Conflicts in Parent-Child Relationships. Videotape. Austin: Audio-Visual Resource Center, University of Texas.

Dealing with Sexuality and Intimacy. Cassette recording. New York: BMA Audio Cassettes.

[with E. Abrahms]. *Dialogues on RET.* 2 cassette recordings. New York: Psychotherapy Tape Library.

"Feedback: A Genius for Lousing Up." *Wharton Magazine* 2, no. 3: 72.

Foreword to *Human Autoerotic Practices,* by DeMartino. New York: Human Sciences.

I'd Like to Stop, but . . . Dealing with Addictions. Cassette recording. New York: Institute for Rational-Emotive Therapy.

The Intelligent Woman's Guide to Dating and Mating. Secaucus, NJ: Lyle Stuart.

"Is Cognitive-Behavior Modification Sufficiently Cognitive?" *Contemporary Psychology* 23: 736–37.

"The Male as Sex Object." *Playgirl* 6, no. 1: 47–51.

"Personality Characteristics of Rational-Emotive Therapists and Other Kinds of Therapists." *Psychotherapy: Theory, Research and Practice* 15: 329–32.

"The Problem of Achieving Scientific Cognitive Behavior Therapy." *Counseling Psychologist* 7, no. 3: 21–23. Also in *The Behavior Therapist,* edited by C. E. Thoresen, 42–46. Monterey, CA: Brooks-Cole.

"A Rational Approach to Divorce Problems." In *Breaking Asunder: Before, During and After Divorce,* edited by S. M. Goetz, 42–46. Greenvale, NY: Post Center, Long Island University.

"A Rational-Emotive Approach to Family Therapy. Part I: Cognitive Therapy." *Rational Living* 13, no. 2: 15–19. Reprinted, New York: Institute for Rational-Emotive Therapy.

"Rational-Emotive Guidance." In *Helping Parents Help Their Children,* edited by L. E. Arnold, 91–101. New York: Brunner/Mazel.

"Rational-Emotive Therapy and Self-Help Therapy." *Rational Living* 13: 2–9.

Review of "Changing Sexual Values and the Family," by G. Sholevar. *Journal of Marriage and Family Counseling* 4, no. 1: 152.

Review of *Clinical Guide to Behavior Therapy,* by S. Walen, N. Hauserman, and P. Lavin. *Rational Living* 13, no. 1: 37.

Review of *Cognitive-Behavior Modification: An Integrative Approach,* by D. Meichenbaum. *Contemporary Psychology* 23: 736–37.

"Self-Help and Sex Therapy." *Sexual Medicine Today* 2, no. 11: 34.

"Sex Magazines as Vehicles for Sex Education." *Humanist* 38, no. 6: 47–48.

"Sexual Violence." *Penthouse* 1, no. 8: 83–86, 96.

"So-Called Alienation of Sex in America." *Psychiatric Opinion* 15, no. 2: 25–27.

"Solving Your Sex Problems the Rational-Emotive Way." *Interaction* 6, no. 2: 1–5; 6, no. 3: 1, 4, 5.

"Swinging and Affairs: Their Place in Marriage." In *Man and Woman in Transition*, edited by D. S. Milman and G. D. Goldman, 141–61. Dubuque, IA: Kendall/Hunt.

"Toward a Theory of Personality." In *Readings in Current Personality Theories*, edited by R. Corsini, 298–311. Itasca, IL: Peacock.

[with J. Marcano]. *Un psicologo puertrriqueno entrevista a Albert Ellis*. San Juan, PR: Taller de Comunicaciones.

[with Abrahams]. *Use of Rational-Emotive Therapy*. Cassette recording. Glendale, CA: Audio-Digest Foundation and American Psychiatric Association.

[with J. Wolfe]. "The Vaginal-Clitoral Orgasm Controversy Re-Examined." In *The New Sex Education*, edited by H. A. Otto, 313–24. Chicago: Association Press.

"What People Can Do for Themselves to Cope with Stress." In *Stress at Work*, edited by C. L. Cooper and R. Payne, 209–22. New York: Wiley.

1979

"Accepting Men the Way They Are." *Cosmopolitan*, December: 32.

"The Biological Basis of Human Irrationality: A Reply to McBurnett and La Pointe." *Individual Psychology* 35, no. 1: 111–16.

[with J. Marmor, H. Kaplan, J. Wolpe, and C. Socarides]. "Can Homosexuals Change in Fourteen Days? Differing Perspectives on Masters & Johnson." *Behavioral Medicine* 6, no. 6: 23–25.

"Dialogue and Quotations on Sex and Masturbation." In *Ah men!* edited by B. Avedon, 43–46, 62–65. New York: A & W.

"Differing Perspectives on Masters and Johnson." *Behavioral Medicine* 6: 23–25.

"Discomfort Anxiety: A New Cognitive-Behavioral Construct (Part I)." *Rational Living* 14, no. 2: 3–8.

Discomfort Anxiety: A New Construct in Cognitive Behavior Therapy. Cassette recording. New York: BMA Audio Cassettes and Association for Advancement of Behavior Therapy.

Foreword to *Change*, by F. Macnab. Melbourne, Australia: Hill of Content.

"The History of Cognition in Psychotherapy." In *Comprehensive Handbook of Cognitive Therapy*, edited by A. Ferman, K. M. Simon, I. E. Beutler, and H. Aronowitz, 5–19. New York: Plenum.

"Is Rational-Emotive Therapy Stoical, Humanistic or Spiritual?" *Journal of Humanistic Psychology* 19, no. 3: 89–92.

"The Issue of Force and Energy in Behavioral Change." *Journal of Contemporary Psychotherapy* 10, no. 2: 83–79.

"Negative Linking of RET to Positive Thinking." *Contemporary Psychology* 24: 1058–59.

"A Note on the Treatment of Agoraphobia with Cognitive Modification versus Prolonged Exposure." *Behavior Research and Therapy* 17: 162–64.

"On Joseph Wolpe's Espousal of Cognitive-Behavior Therapy." *American Psychologist* 34: 98–99.

"The Rational-Emotive Approach to Counseling." In *Theories of Counseling*, 3rd ed., edited by H. M. Burkes Jr. and B. Stefflre, 172–219. New York: McGraw-Hill.

"A Rational-Emotive Approach to Family Therapy. Part II: Emotive and Behavioral Therapy." *Rational Living* 14, no. 1: 23–27.

"Rational-Emotive Psychotherapy." In *Psychopathology Today*, 2nd ed., edited by W. S. Sahakian, 439–48. Itasca, IL. Peacock.

"Rational-Emotive Therapy: Research Data That Supports the Clinical and Personality Hypotheses of RET and Other Modes of Cognitive-Behavior Therapy." In *Theoretical and Empirical Foundations of Rational-Emotive Therapy*, edited by A. Ellis and J. M. Whitley, 101–73. Monterrey, CA: Brooks/Cole.

"Rejoinder: Elegant and Inelegant RET." In *Theoretical and Empirical Foundations of RET*, edited by A. Ellis and J. M. Whitley, 240–67. New York: Brunner.

Review of *The Briefer Psychotherapies*, by L. Small. *Contemporary Psychology* 24, no. 12.

Review of *Incest: A Psychological Study of Cause and Effects with Treatment Recommendations*, by K. C. Meiselman. *Society* 16, no. 6: 87–88.

"A Reviewer Sees Familiar Landmarks in E/R Therapy." *Patient Care* 13, no. 14: 100–101.

"Sex and the Liberated Man." In *Modern Man*, edited by G. D. Goldman and D. S. Milman, 69–104. Dubuque, IA: Kendall/ Hunt.

"The Sex Offender." In *Psychology of Crime and Criminal Justice*, edited by H. Toch, 405–26. New York: Holt, Rinehart & Winston.

"The Untired Rational-Emotive Therapist." *Voices* 15, no. 2: 34–35.

1980

Comment on "When the Therapist Wants to Terminate: From Pessimism to the Grotesque in Therapy," by M. Gottesfeld. *Voices* 16, no. 2: 16–17.

The Control of Stress in Everyday Living. Cassette recording. Hauppauge, NY: Alison Audio.

"Discomfort Anxiety: A New Cognitive-Behavioral Construct (Part II)." *Rational Living* 15, no. 1: 25–30.

Foreword to *The Principles and Practice of Rational-Emotive Therapy*, by R. A. Wessler and R. L. Wessler. San Francisco, CA: Jossey-Bass.

Foreword to *You Can Do It!* by L. Losoney. Englewood Cliffs, NJ: Prentice-Hall.

"An Overview of the Clinical Theory of Rational Emotive Therapy." In *Rational-Emotive Therapy: A Skills-Based Approach*, edited by R. Grieger and J. Boyd, 1–31. New York: Van Nostrand and Reinhold.

"Psychotherapy and Atheistic Values: A Response to A. E. Bergin's *Psychotherapy and Religious Values*." *Journal of Consulting and Clinical Psychology* 48: 635–39.

"Rational-Emotive Therapy and Cognitive Behavior Therapy: Similarities and Differences." *Cognitive Therapy and Research* 4: 325–40.

Review of *Gender and Disordered Behavior: Sex Differences in Psychopathology*, by E. S. Gomberg and V. Franks. *Journal of Marital and Family Therapy* 6: 94.

"Sex in the 80's." *Penthouse Variations*, December: 6–7.

"Sexual Abuse by Therapists." *NOW NY Woman*, October: 3.

"Some Cognitive Additions to Eysenck's *The Conditioning Model of Neurosis, Behavior and Brain Sciences*." 3: 459–82.

[with R. Wessler]. "Supervision in Rational-Emotive Therapy." In *Psychotherapy Supervision*, by A. Hess, 181–91. New York: Wiley.

"The Treatment of Erectile Dysfunction." In *Principles and Practice of Sex Therapy*, edited by S. R. Leiblum and L. A. Pervin, 240–58. New York: Guilford.

[with S. G. Weinrach]. "Unconventional Therapist: Albert Ellis." *Personnel and Guidance Journal* 59: 152–60.

"The Use of Rational Humorous Songs in Psychotherapy." *Voices* 16, no. 4: 19–26. Also in *Handbook of Humor in Psychotherapy: Advances in the Clinical Use of Humor*, edited by W. F. Fry and W. A. Salamed, 265–87. Sarasota, FL: Professional Resource Exchange.

"The Value of Efficiency in Psychotherapy." *Psychotherapy* 17: 414–19. Reprinted in *The Essential Albert Ellis*, edited by A. Ellis and W. Dryden, 237–47. New York: Springer, 1990.

1981

[with A. Lazarus, S. Gordon, C. Franks, P. Russianoff, R. Diekestra, H. Greenwald, and R. Harper]. *Albert Ellis "Roast."* 2 cassette recordings. New York: Institute for Rational-Emotive Therapy.

"Dr. Albert Ellis' List of 21 Irrational Beliefs That Lead to Sex Problems and Disturbances." In *The Book of Sex Lists*, edited by A. B. Gerber, 46–48. Secaucus, NJ: Lyle Stuart.

The Intelligent Person's Guide to Dating and Mating. Cassette recording. New York: Institute for Rational-Emotive Therapy.

"Is RET Ethically Untenable or Inconsistent? A Reply to Paul E. Meehl." *Rational Living* 16, no. 1: 10–11.

"The Place of Immanuel Kant in Cognitive Psychotherapy." *Rational Living* 16, no. 2: 13–16.

"The Rational-Emotive Approach to Thanatology." In *Behavior Therapy in Terminal Care*, edited by H. V. Sobel, 151–76. Cambridge, MA: Ballinger.

Review of *Disorders of Sexual Desire*, by H. S. Kaplan. *Archives of Sexual Behavior* 10: 395–97.

"The Seven Most Frequent Sex Problems." *The Book of Sex Lists*, edited by A. B. Gerber. Secaucus, NJ: Lyle Stuart.

"Teoria e prassi della RET" [The theory and practice of rational-emotive therapy]. In *Cognitivismo e Psicoterapia*, edited by A. F. Guidano and M. A. Reda, 219–37. Milan, Italy: Franco Angeli.

"Why Some Women Can't Find the Right Man." *Beauty Digest*, August: 10–13.

1982

"Albert Ellis' List of the Greatest Jewish Psychotherapists." In *The Book of Jewish Lists*, edited by R. Landeu, 191–93. New York: Stein & Day.

"Becoming Self-Directed: Notes from Albert Ellis' Workshop." In *Mental Health for Coaches and Athletes*, edited by T. Orlick, J. T. Partington, and J. H. Salmela, 37–42. Ottawa: Coaching Association of Canada.

Comment. In "How Much Is Too Much Sex?" *Forum* 12, no. 3: 52.

"Dream Watch." *Penthouse* 13, no. 5: 167–70; 13, no. 6: 159–62; 13, no. 7: 155–59; 13, no. 8: 151–54; 13, no. 9: 153–56; 13, no. 10: 155–58; 13, no. 11: 155–58; 13, no. 12: 149–52.

[with I. Becker]. *A Guide to Personal Happiness*. North Hollywood, CA: Wilshire.

"The Honesty of Laura Perls and the Basic Dishonesty of Gestalt Therapy." *Voices* 18, no. 2: 49–50.

"If You're Constantly Angry and Resentful. . . ." *Woman* 3, no. 3: 48–49.

"Intimacy in Rational-Emotive Therapy." In *Intimacy*, edited by M. Fisher and G. Striker. New York: Plenum.

"Must Most Psychotherapists Remain as Incompetent as They Now Are?" *Journal of Contemporary Psychotherapy* 13, no. 1: 17–28.

"Psychoneurosis and Anxiety Problems." In *Cognition and Emotional Disturbance*, edited by R. Grieger and I. Z. Grieger, 17–45. New York: Human Sciences.

Rational-Emotive Therapy: A Documentary Film Featuring Dr. Albert Ellis. Film. Champaign, IL: Research.

"A Re-appraisal of Rational-Emotive Therapy's Theoretical Foundations and Therapeutic Methods: A Reply to Eschenroeder." *Cognitive Therapy and Research* 6: 393–98.

Review of *The Sex Profession: What Sex Therapy Can Do*, by P. Schiller. *Journal of Sex Research* 18, no. 10: 84.

"Self-Direction in Sport and Life." *Rational Living* 17, no. 10: 26–33. Also in *Mental Health for Coaches and Athletes*, by T. Orlick, J. T. Partington, and J. H. Salmela. Ottowa: Coaching Association of Canada.

"The Treatment of Alcohol and Drug Abuse: A Rational Emotive Approach." *Rational Living* 17, no. 2: 15–24.

"When You Find You Can't Live without Him: What to Do When You Become Attached to an Ineligible Male." *Complete Woman* 2, no. 5: 59–61.

1983

"Albert Ellis' Opinion." *American Academy of Psychotherapists Newsletter* (June): 2.

"Al Responds to Allyn." *American Academy of Psychotherapists Newsletter* (September): 2.

The Case against Religiosity. New York: Institute for Rational-Emotive Therapy.

Comment on *Psychotherapy Focus: Old and New*, by Erika Wick. *Voices* 18, no. 4: 40–41.

[with R. Wessler]. *Conversations with Albert Ellis*. 2 videotapes. New York: Institute for Rational-Emotive Therapy.

"Dream Watch." *Penthouse* 14, no. 1: 145–48; 14, no. 2: 149–52; 14, no. 3: 159–62; 14, no. 4: 169–72; 14, no. 5: 171–74; 14, no. 6: 145–48.

"Failures in Rational-Emotive Therapy." In *Failures in Behavior Therapy*, edited by E. B. Foa and P. M. G. Emmelkamp, 159–71. New York: Wiley.

"The Future of Rational-Emotive Therapy (RET)." *I'Act Rationally, News and Views* (February): 2–4.

"How to Deal with Your Most Difficult Client—You." *Journal of Rational-Emotive Therapy* 1, no. 1: 2–8. Also in *Psychotherapy in Private Practice* 2, no. 1 (1984): 25–35.

"How to Take Advantage of Being Single at Your Age." *Woman* 4, no. 1: 32–33.

[with P. Krassner and R. A. Wilson]. "An Impolite Interview with Albert Ellis." *Realist* 16: 1, 9–14; 17: 7–12. Reprinted, New York: Institute for Rational-Emotive Therapy.

"The Origins of Rational-Emotive Therapy (RET)." *Voices: The Art and Science of Psychotherapy* 18, no. 4: 29–33.

[with M. E. Bernard]. "An Overview of Rational-Emotive Approaches to the Problems of Childhood." In *Rational-Emotive Approaches to the Problems of Childhood*, edited by A. Ellis and M. E. Bernard, 3–43. New York: Plenum.

"The Philosophic Implications and Dangers of Some Popular Behavior Therapy Techniques." In *Perspectives on Behavior Therapy in the*

Eighties, edited by M. Rosenbaum, C. M. Franks, and W. Jaffe, 138–51. New York: Springer.

"Rational-Emotive Therapy (RET) Approaches to Overcoming Resistance. 1: Common Forms of Resistance." *British Journal of Cognitive Psychotherapy* 1, no. 1: 28–38.

"Rational-Emotive Therapy (RET) Approaches to Overcoming Resistance. 2: How RET Disputes Clients' Irrational, Resistance-Creating Beliefs." *British Journal of Cognitive Psychotherapy* 1, no. 2: 1–16.

Review of *Psychotherapy Focus: Old and New*, by E. Wick. *Voices* 18, no. 4: 40–41.

[with R. Wessler]. "Supervision in Counseling: Rational Emotive Therapy." *Counseling Psychologist* 11, no. 1: 43–49.

"Two's Company, Three's a Crowd." In *Psychopathology: A Casebook*, by R. L. Spitzer, A. E. Skodol, M. Gibbon, and J. B. Williams, 99–104. New York: McGraw-Hill.

1984

"Autocontrol: El metodo de la Terapia Racional Emotiva" [Self-Control: The Rational-Emotive Therapy Method]. *Avances en Psicología Clinica Lationoamericana* 3: 35–43.

Comment on Gearhart's *The Counselor in a Nuclear War: A Rationale for Awareness and Action. Journal of Counseling and Development* 63: 75–76.

"Curing Hyperbole." *APA Monitor* 15, no. 7: 5.

"Current Psychotherapies." In *Encyclopedia of Psychology*, edited by R. J. Corsini, 339–41. New York: Wiley.

"The Essence of RET." *Journal of Rational-Emotive Therapy* 2, no. 1: 19–25. Also foreword to *Rational Emotive Therapy: Fundamentals & Innovations*, by W. Dryden. London: Croom Helm.

Foreword to *Rational Emotive Therapy with Children and Adolescents*, by M. E. Bernard and M. R. Joyce. New York: Wiley.

Foreword to *A Therapist's Manual for Cognitive Behavior Therapy in Groups*, edited by L. L. Sank and C. S. Shaffer. New York: Plenum.

How to Maintain and Enhance Your Rational-Emotive Therapy Gains. New York: Institute for Rational-Emotive Therapy.

Introduction to *The Work of Howard S. Young*, edited by W. Dryden. *British Journal of Cognitive Psychotherapy*, special issue 2, no. 2: 1–5.

"Maintenance and Generalization in Rational-Emotive Therapy (RET)." *Cognitive Behaviorist* 6, no. 1: 2–4.

"The Place of Meditation in Cognitive-Behavior Therapy and Rational-Emotive Therapy." In *Meditation: Classic and Contemporary Perspectives*, edited by D. H. Shapiro and R. N. Walsh, 671–73. New York: Aldine.

"Rational-Emotive Therapy." In *Current Psychotherapies*. Revised edition. Edited by R. J. Corsini. Itasca, IL: Peacock.

"Rational-Emotive Therapy (RET) and Pastoral Counseling: A Reply to Richard Wessler." *Personnel and Guidance Journal* 12: 266–67.

"Rational-Emotive Therapy (RET) Approaches to Overcoming Resistance. 3: Using Emotive and Behavioral Techniques of Overcoming Resistance." *British Journal of Cognitive Psychotherapy* 2, no. 1: 11–26.

Review of *Rational-Emotive Therapy: Fundamentals and Innovations*, by W. Dryden. *Journal of Rational-Emotive Therapy* 2, no. 10: 36.

"Treating the Abrasive Client with Rational-Emotive Therapy (RET)." *Psychotherapy Patient* 1, no. 1: 21–25.

"The Use of Hypnosis with RET." *International Journal of Eclectic Psychotherapy* 3, no. 3: 15–22.

1985

"Anxiety about Anxiety. The Use of Hypnosis with Rational-Emotive Therapy." In *Case Studies in Hypnotherapy*, edited by E. T. Dowd and J. M. Healey, 3–11. New York: Guilford. Reprinted in A. Ellis and W. Dryden, eds. *The Practice of Rational-Emotive Therapy*. New York: Springer; and *Progress in Clinical Psychology*, vol. 1, 467–80. New York: Grune and Stratton.

"Approaches to Overcoming Resistance 4: Handling Special Kinds of Clients." *British Journal of Cognitive Psychotherapy* 3, no. 1: 26–42.

[with M. E. Bernard, eds.]. *Clinical Applications of Rational-Emotive Therapy*. New York: Plenum.

"Cognition and Affect in Emotional Disturbance." *American Psychologist* 40: 471–72.

"Conceptual Thinking and the Criminal Personality." *Journal of Counseling and Development* 63: 589.

Conversation Hour with Albert Ellis. Cassette recording. Garden Grove, CA: Infomedix.

Critique of D. B. Wile's critique of Albert Ellis's method of cognitive restructuring in couples therapy. *British Journal of Cognitive Therapy* 3, no. 1: 81–83.

[with W. Dryden]. "Dilemmas in Giving Warmth or Love to Clients: An Interview with Albert Ellis." In *Therapists' Dilemmas*, edited by W. Dryden, 5–16. London: Harper & Row.

[with P. Dell, G. Steinfeld, and J. Grunebaum]. *Ethical Issues in Family Therapy: Accountability, Awareness, Advocacy*. Cassette recording. Highland, IN: Creative Audio.

[with M. Goulding]. *Evolution of Rational-Emotive Therapy and Cognitive Behavior Therapy*. Cassette recording. Garde.

"Expanding the ABCs of RET." In *Cognition and Psychotherapy*, edited by

M. Mahoney and A. Freeman, 313–23. New York: Plenum. Also in *Journal of Rational-Emotive Therapy* 2, no. 2 (1984): 20–24.

Foreword to *Managing Parental Anger: The Coping Parent Series*, by H. H. Barrish and I. J. Barrish. Shawnee Mission, KS: Overland.

"Free Will and Determinism: A Second Story." *Journal of Counseling and Development* 64: 286.

[with R. Goulding, S. Minuchin, and Z. Moreno]. *Group, Individual, or Family Therapy*. Cassette recording. Garden Grove, CA: Infomedia.

A Guide to Personal Happiness. Cassette recording. Washington, DC: Psychology Today Tapes.

"Horney Credited by Non-Freudians." *New York State Psychologist* 37, no. 1: 28–29.

"Intellectual Fascism." *Journal of Rational-Emotive Therapy* 3, no. 1: 3–12.

"Jealousy: Its Etiology and Treatment." In *Contemporary Marriage: Special Issue in Couples Therapy*, edited by D. G. Goldberg, 420–38. Homewood, IL: Dorsey.

"Love and Its Problems." In *Clinical Applications of Rational-Emotive Therapy*, by A. Ellis and M. E. Bernard, 32–53. New York: Forum.

[with D. Tascher and L. McGehee]. *Manual for RET/EAP Workshop*. New York: Institute for Rational-Emotive Therapy.

The Mind of Addiction. Cassette recording. Van Nuys, CA: On-site Tape Services and Institute for Integral Development.

Overcoming Resistance: RET with Difficult Clients. New York: Springer.

"A Rational-Emotive Approach to Acceptance and Its Relationship to EAPs." In *The Human Resources Management Handbook: Principles and Practice of Employees Assistance Programs*, edited by S. H. Klarreich, J. L. Franeck, and C. E. More, 325–33. New York: Praeger.

"Rational-Emotive Therapy." In *International Encyclopedia of Education*, edited by T. Husen and T. N. Postlethwaite, 4189–90. Oxford, England: Pergemon.

"Rational-Emotive Therapy (RET) Approaches to Overcoming Resistance. 4: Handling Special Kinds of Clients." *British Journal of Cognitive Psychotherapy* 3, no. 1: 26–42.

"The RET Theory of Irrational Beliefs and Inappropriate Feelings." *British Journal of Cognitive Psychotherapy* 3, no. 2: 84–86.

"Why Alcoholics Anonymous Is Probably Doing More Harm Than Good by Its Insistence on a Higher Power." Review of *Alcoholics Anonymous*, 3rd edition. *Employee Assistance Quarterly* 1, no. 1: 95–97.

1986

"Awards for Distinguished Professional Contributions: 1985." *American Psychologist* 41 (April): 380–97.

Comment on *Gloria. Psychotherapy* 23: 647–48.

Comments on the Evolution of Psychotherapy Conference. *International Journal of Eclectic Psychotherapy* 5: 239–41.

"Do Some Religious Beliefs Help Create Emotional Disturbance?" *Psychotherapy in Private Practice* 4: 101–106.

Effective Self-Assertion. Cassette recording. Washington, DC: Psychology Today Tapes.

"Fanaticism That May Lead to a Nuclear Holocaust: The Contributions of Scientific Counseling and Psychotherapy." *Journal of Counseling of Development* 65: 146–51.

[with R. Grieger, eds.]. *Handbook of Rational Emotive Therapy.* Vol. 2. New York: Springer.

"Rational-Emotive Therapy: A Case Presentation." In *Psychotherapist's Casebook: Theory and Technique in the Practice of Modern Therapies*, edited by I. L. Kutash and A. Wolf, 277–87. San Francisco, CA: Jossey-Bass.

"Rational-Emotive Therapy Applied to Relationship Therapy." *Journal of Rational-Emotive Therapy* 4: 4–21.

"Rational Way to Sell." *Personal Selling Power* 6, no. 5: 16–18.

Review of *Cognitive-Experiential Therapy*, by M. Wiener. *Journal of Reviews and Commentary in Mental Health* 1, no. 3: 29.

1987

"Cognitive Therapy and Rational-Emotive Therapy: A Dialogue." *Journal of Cognitive Psychotherapy: An International Quarterly* 1, no. 4: 205–55.

[with J. Young and G. Lockwood]. "Cognitive Therapy and Rational-Emotive Therapy: A Dialogue." *Journal of Cognitive Psychotherapy* 1, no. 4: 137–87.

"The Evolution of Rational-Emotive Therapy (RET) and Cognitive-Behavior Therapy (CBT)." In *The Evolution of Psychotherapy*, edited by J. K. Zeig, 107–32. New York: Brunner/Mazel.

"The Impossibility of Achieving Consistently Good Mental Health." *American Psychologist* 42: 364–75.

"Integrative Developments in Rational-Emotive Therapy." *Journal of Integrative and Eclectic Psychotherapy* 6: 470–79.

[with W. Dryden]. "Rational-Emotive Therapy: An Excellent Counseling Theory for NPs." *Nurse Practitioner* 12, no. 7: 16–37.

"Rational-Emotive Therapy: An Update." In *Current Issues in Rational-Emotive Therapy*, by W. Dryden, 1–45. London: Croom Helm.

"Reply to Parker on Fanaticism and Absolutism." *Journal of Counseling and Development* 66: 156–57.

"A Sadly Neglected Cognitive Element in Depression." *Cognitive Therapy and Research* 11: 121–46.

"Self-Control: The Rational-Emotive Therapy Method." *Southern Psychologist* 3, no. 1: 9–12.

"Speaking Out on AIDS." *Humanist* 47, no. 4: 23.

"Testament of a Humanist." *Free Inquiry* 7, no. 2: 21.

"Treating the Bored Client with Rational-Emotive Therapy." *Psychotherapy Patient* 3: 75–86.

1988

"Albert Ellis Responds." *Free Inquiry* 9, no. 1: 63.

"Are There 'Rationalist' and 'Constructivist' Camps of the Cognitive Therapies? A Response to Michael Mahoney." *Cognitive Behaviorist* 10: 13–17.

"Ask Dr. Ellis." *Journal of Rational-Emotive and Cognitive-Behavior Therapy* 6, no. 3 (Fall): 196–200.

"Can We Legitimately Evaluate Ourselves? A Reply to Robert C. Roberts." *Psychotherapy* 25, no. 2.

"How to Live with a Neurotic Man." *Journal of Rational-Emotive and Cognitive-Behavior Therapy* 6: 129–36.

How to Stubbornly Refuse to Make Yourself Miserable about Anything—Yes, Anything! Secaucus, NJ: Lyle Stuart.

"The Shortcomings of Spiritual Healing." *California Journal of Rational Recovery* 1, no. 2: 3–4.

The Treatment of Borderline and Psychotic Individuals. New York: Institute for Rational-Emotive Therapy.

Unconditionally Accepting Yourself/Others. Cassette recording. New York: Institute for Rational-Emotive Therapy.

1989

"Albert Ellis: 'At Least Three Errors.'" In *The Imperfect Therapist*, edited by J. A. Hattler and D. Blau, 114–16. San Francisco: Jossey-Bass.

"Comments on My Critics." In *Inside Rational-Emotive Therapy*, edited by M. E. Bernard and R. DiGuiseppe, 199–33. San Diego, CA: Academic.

Comments on S. Warnock's *Rational-Emotive Therapy and the Christian Client. Journal of Rational-Emotive and Cognitive-Behavior Therapy* 7: 275–77.

"Countering Perfectionism in Research on Clinical Practice I: Surveying Rationality Changes after a Single Intensive RET Intervention." *Journal of Rational-Emotive and Cognitive Therapy* 7, no. 4.

[with J. L. Sichel, R. C. Leaf, and R. Mass]. "Countering Perfectionism in Research on Clinical Practice: Surveying Rationality Changes after a Single Intensive RET Intervention." *Journal of Rational-Emotive and Cognitive-Behavioral Therapy* 7: 197–218.

"A Dictionary of Rational-Emotive Feelings and Behaviors." *Journal of Rational-Emotive and Cognitive-Behavior Therapy* 1: 3–28.

Foreword to *Beyond Revolutions: On Becoming a Cybernetic Epistemologist,* by DiSalvo. New York: Vantage.

"Four Decades of Experience with the Media." *Psychotherapy in Private Practice* 7: 47–54.

Overcoming the Influence of the Past. Cassette recording. New York: Institute for Rational-Emotive Therapy.

"Re-examining Freud." *Psychology Today,* September: 50.

"The Road to Happiness Lies in Accepting That We Are Responsible for Our Own Happiness." *Boardroom Reports* 18, no. 17: 13–14.

"The Silver Anniversary." *Voices* 25, nos. 1 and 2: 154–55.

"Thoughts on Supervising Counselors and Therapists." *Psychology* 26: 3–5. Also in *Association for Counselor Education Newsletter* (Summer 1986): 3–5.

"Using Rational-Emotive Therapy as Crisis Intervention: A Single Session with a Suicidal Client." *Individual Psychology* 45, nos. 1 and 2: 75–81.

[with R. Yeager]. *Why Some Therapies Don't Work: The Dangers of Transpersonal Psychology.* Amherst, NY: Prometheus Books.

1990

"Albert Ellis: My Life in Clinical Psychology." In *History of Clinical Psychology in Autobiography,* edited by C. E. Walker, 1: 1–37. Homewood, IL: Dorsey.

Albert Ellis Live at the Learning Annex. 2 cassettes. New York: Institute for Rational-Emotive Therapy.

Commentary on *The Status of Sex Research: An Assessment of the Sexual Revolution. Journal of Psychology & Human Sexuality* 3, no. 1: 5–18.

Comment on *A Competence Paradigm for Psychological Practice. American Psychologist* 45: 783–84.

"Communication Apprehension and Rational Emotive Therapy: An Interview with Dr. Albert Ellis." *Journal of Social Behavior and Personality* 5, no. 2: 203–10.

"The Courage to Grow Old." In *The Courage to Grow Old,* edited by P. L. Berman, 131–36. New York: Ballantine.

"Divine Intervention and the Treatment of Chemical Dependency." *Journal of Substance Abuse* 2: 459–68.

"Does Ellis's Rational-Emotive Therapy Constitute a Humanistic Therapy? Interview by Alec Duncan-Grant." *Changes* 8: 130–38.

"The Ellis-Tisdale Dialogue: Transpersonal Psychology." *Interest Group Newsletter* 9: 4–12.

[with W. Dryden]. *The Essential Albert Ellis.* New York: Springer.

"In Praise of Phone Therapy." *American Psychological Association Monitor* 20, no. 5: 3.

"Is Rational-Emotive Therapy a Humanistic Therapy? A Reply to Duncan-Grant." *Changes* 8, no. 2: 139–45.

"Is Rational-Emotive Therapy 'Rationalist' or 'Constructivist'?" In *The Essential Albert Ellis*, edited by A. Ellis and W. Dryden, 114–41. New York: Springer.

"Let's Not Ignore Individuality." *American Psychologist* 45: 781.

"Living with Diabetes." *Journal of Rational-Emotive and Cognitive-Behavior Therapy* 8, no. 1: 1–39.

"Rational and Irrational Beliefs in Counseling Psychology." *Journal of Rational-Emotive and Cognitive Behavioral Theories.*

"Rational-Emotive Therapy." In *The Group Psychotherapist's Handbook: Contemporary Theory and Technique*, edited by I. L. Kutash and A. Wolf, 298–315. New York: Columbia University Press.

"Rational-Emotive Therapy." In *What Is Psychotherapy? Contemporary Perspectives*, edited by J. K. Zieg and M. Munion, 146–51. San Francisco, CA: Jossey-Bass.

Reply to critics of *Divine Intervention and the Treatment of Chemical Dependency. Journal of Substance Abuse* 2: 489–94.

Reply to Len Sperry's *Recent Developments in Psychoanalysis. North American Society of Adlerian Psychology Newsletter* 23, no. 5: 4.

Reply to Walsh of Transpersonal Psychology. *Journal of Counseling and Development* 68: 344–45.

"Rumors about My Anti-homosexual Views: A Reply to Kristin Gay Esterberg." *Journal of Sex Research* 27, no. 4: 645–46.

"So, What Makes Me Tick?" In *So What Makes You Tick?* edited by D. Sharpe, 96–97. Berkeley, CA: Ten Speed.

"Special Features of Rational-Emotive Therapy." In *A Primer of Rational Emotive Therapy*, edited by W. Dryden and R. DiGuiseppe, 79–93. Champaign, IL: Research Press.

"Treating the Widowed Client with Rational-Emotive Therapy." *Psychotherapy Patient* 6, no. 3: 105–11.

1991

"The ABC's of RET." *Humanist* 51, 1: 19–49.

"Achieving Self-Actualization." *Journal of Social Behavior & Personality* 6, no. 5: 1–18. Reprinted: New York: Institute for Rational-Emotive Therapy.

"Are All Methods of Counseling and Psychotherapy Equally Effective?" *New York State Association for Counseling and Development Journal* 6, no. 2: 9–13.

[with L. Lega]. "The Case Study of Donald Green's Treatment by Rational-Emotive Therapy." In *Five Therapists and One Client*, edited by R. J. Corsini. Itasca, IL: Peacock.

Cognitive Aspects of Abreactive Therapy Reviewed. New York: Institute for Rational-Emotive Therapy.

"Counseling in the Classroom. Interview with Albert Ellis." *Journal of Rational-Emotive and Cognitive-Behavior Therapy* 9, no. 4.

[with W. Dryden]. *A Dialogue with Albert Ellis: Against Dogma*. Milton Keynes, England: Open University.

"How Can Psychological Treatment Aim to Be Briefer and Better? The Rational-Emotive Approach to Brief Therapy." In *The Handbook of Medical Psychotherapy*, edited by K. N. Anchor, 51–88. Toronto: Hografe & Huber. Also in J. K. Zeig and S. G. Guilligan, eds. *Brief Therapy: Myths, Methods and Metaphors*, 291–302. New York: Brunner/Mazel.

"How to Fix the Empty Self." *American Psychologist* 46, no. 5: 539–40.

How to Get Along with Difficult People. Cassette recording. New York: Institute for Rational-Emotive Therapy.

How to Refuse to Be Angry, Vindictive, and Unforgiving. Cassette recording. New York: Institute for Rational-Emotive Therapy.

Humanism and Psychotherapy: A Revolutionary Approach. Revised edition. New York: Institute for Rational-Emotive Therapy original publication.

"The Philosophic Basis of Rational-Emotive Therapy (RET)." *Psychotherapy in Private Practice* 8, no. 4: 97–106.

Psychotherapy and the Value of a Human Being. New York: Albert Ellis Institute.

"Rational-Emotive Family Therapy." In *Family Counseling and Therapy*, edited by A. M. Horne and J. L. Passmore, 403–34. Itasca, IL: Peacock.

[with L. Lega]. "Rational-Emotive Therapy: A Case Study." In *Five Therapists and One Client*, edited by R. Corsini. Itasca, IL: Peacock.

"Rationale und irrationale ideen inder Klinischen Psychologie." *Zertschrift fur Rational-emotive therapie & Kognitive verhaltens therapie* 2, no. 2: 5–23.

"Rationality, Self-Regard and the 'Healthiness' of Personality Disorders." *Journal of Rational-Emotive and Cognitive-Behavior Therapy* 9, no. 1.

"Reminiscences of My Psychology Days at City College." In *Reminiscences of City College Days*, edited by L. Nyman. New York: Psychology Department, City College of New York.

"The Revised ABC's of Rational Emotive Therapy." *Journal of Rational-Emotive and Cognitive-Behavior Therapy* 9, no. 3: 139–72. Also in J. Zeig, *The Evolution of Psychotherapy: The Second Conference*, 79–99. New York: Brown.

"The Revised Documents of Rational-Emotive Therapy." *Journal of Rational-Emotive and Cognitive-Behavior Therapy* 9, no. 3: 139–72.

"Suggestibility, Irrational Beliefs, and Emotional Disturbance." In *Human Suggestibility*, 309–25.

"Using RET Effectively: Reflections and Interview. In *Using RET Effectively*, edited by M. E. Bernard, 1–33. New York: Plenum.

[with P. Hunter]. *Why Am I Always Broke?* New York: Carol.

1992

"Are Gays and Lesbians Emotionally Disturbed?" *Humanist* 52, no. 5: 33–35.

[with M. Abrams and L. Dengelegi]. *The Art and Science of Rational Eating.* New York: Barricade.

"Brief Therapy: The Rational-Emotive Method." In *The First Session in Brief Therapy*, edited by S. H. Budman, M. F. Hoyt, and S. Fieman, 36–58. New York: Guilford.

"Cherchez le 'should'! Cherchez le 'must'! Un entrevue avec Albert Ellis, l'initiateur de la methode emotivorationnelle." *Confrontation* 14: 3–12.

"Does Psychotherapy Need a Soul? Response." *Psychotherapy and Its Discontents*, 212–20.

"Do I Really Hold That Religiousness Is Irrational and Equivalent to Emotional Disturbance?" *American Psychologist* 47: 428–29.

Foreword to *Overcoming the Rating Game*, by P. Hauck. Louisville, KY: Westminster/John Knox.

"Group Rational-Emotive and Cognitive-Behavioral Therapy." *International Journal of Group Psychotherapy* 42: 63–80.

"My Current Views on Rational-Emotive Therapy and Religiousness." *Journal of Rational-Emotive and Cognitive-Behavior Therapy* 10: 37–40.

"Rational-Emotive Approaches to Peace." *Journal of Cognitive Psychotherapy: An International Quarterly* 6: 79–104.

Response to G. Edwards's "Does Psychotherapy Need a Soul?" In *Psychotherapy and Its Discontents*, edited by W. Dryden and C. Feltham, 212–20. Buckingham, England: Open University.

Review of *Rational-Emotive Counselling in Action*, by W. Dryden. *British Journal of Guidance and Counselling* 20: 119.

"Therapists' Most Influential Kooks." *Voice* 28: 85.

"What Are Sexual 'Perversions'?" *Humanist* 52, no. 3: 35.

[with E. Velten]. *When AA Doesn't Work for You: Rational Steps for Quitting Alcohol.* New York: Barricade.

1993

"Changing Rational-Emotive Therapy (RET) to Rational Emotive Behavior Therapy (REBT)." *Behavior Therapist* 16: 257–58.

[with L. Lega]. "Como aplicar algunas reglas basicas del metodo cientifico al cambio de ideas irracionales sobre uno mismo, otras personas y la vida en general." *Psicología Conductual* 1: 101–10.

Coping with the Suicide of a Loved One. Videocassette. New York: Institute for Rational-Emotive Therapy.

[with L. Lega] "Diferencias transculturales en el uso de algunas tecnicas de terapia racional-emotiva: Ejercicios para atacar la verguenza." *Psicología Conductual* 1: 283–88.

"Fundamentals of Rational-Emotive Therapy for the 1990s." In *Innovations in Rational-Emotive Therapy*, edited by W. Dryden and L. K. Hill, 1–32. Newbury Park, CA: Sage.

"General Semantics and Rational-Emotive Behavior Therapy." *Bulletin of General Semantics* 58: 12–28. Also in *More E-Prime*, edited by P. D. Johnston, D. D. Bourland, J. Klein, 213–40. Concord, CA: International Society for General Semantics.

How to Be a Perfect Non-Perfectionist. Cassette recording. New York: Institute for Rational-Emotive Therapy.

Living Fully and in Balance: This Isn't a Dress Rehearsal—This Is It! Cassette recording. New York: Institute for Rational-Emotive Therapy.

"Rational Emotive Imagery: RET Version." In *The RET Resource Book for Practitioners*, edited by M. E. Bernard and J. L. Wolfe. New York: Institute for Rational-Emotive Therapy.

"RET and Hypnosis." In *Handbook of Clinical Hypnosis*, edited by J. W. Rhue, S. J. Lynn, and I. Kirsh, 173–86. Washington, DC: American Psychological Association.

RET Approach to Brief Therapy. 2 cassette recordings. Phoenix, AZ: Milton Erickson Foundation.

"The RET Approach to Marriage and Family Therapy." *Family Journal: Counseling and Therapy for Couples and Families* 1: 292–307.

"Vigorous RET Disputing." In *The RET Resource Book for Practitioners*, edited by M. E. Bernard and J. L. Wolfe, 117. New York: Institute for Rational-Emotive Therapy.

1994

[with H. Robb, eds.]. "Acceptance in Rational-Emotive Therapy." In *Acceptance and Change: Content and Context in Psychotherapy*, edited by S. C. Hays, N. S. Jacobson, V. M. Follette, and M. J. Dougher, 91–102. Reno, NV: Context.

[with R. DiGiuseppe]. *Dealing with Addictions.* Videotape. New York: Institute for Rational-Emotive Therapy.

Foreword to *More E-Prime*, edited by P. D. Johnston, D. D. Bourland Jr., and J. Klein. Concord, CA: International Society for General Semantics.

[with M. Abrahams]. *How to Cope with a Fatal Disease.* New York: Barricade.

[with A. Lange]. *How to Keep People from Pushing Your Buttons.* New York: Carol.

"Life in a Box." Review of *B. F. Skinner: A Life*, by D. W. Bjork. *Readings* 9, no. 4: 16–21.

"Radical Behavioral Treatment of Private Events: A Response to Michael Dougher." *Behavior Therapist* 17: 219–21.

Reason and Emotion in Psychotherapy: Revised and Updated. New York: Birch Lane and New York: Kensington.

"REBT Approaches to Obsessive-Compulsive Disorder (OCD)." *Journal of Rational-Emotive and Cognitive-Behavior Therapy* 12: 121–41.

1995

"Dogmatic Religion Doesn't Help, It Hurts." *Insight in the News,* March 6: 20–22.

1996

Better, Deeper and More Enduring Brief Therapy. New York: Brunner/Mazel.

1997

[with R. A. Harper]. *A Guide to Rational Living.* 3rd ed. North Hollywood, CA: Wilshire.

[with C. Tafrate]. *How to Control Your Anger Before It Controls You.* New York: Kensington.

[with W. Dryden]. *The Practice of Rational Emotive Behavior Therapy.* New York: Springer.

[with L. Lega and V. Caballo]. *Teoria y Practica de la Terapia Racional Emotivo-Conductual.* Madrid, Spain: Siglo XXI.

"The Uniquely Human Science of Treatment Development: Commentary on 'Science and Treatment Development: Lessons from the History of Behavior Therapy.'" *Behavior Therapy* 28: 559–61.

1998

[with S. Blau, eds.]. *The Albert Ellis Reader.* New York: Kensington.

[with E. Velten]. *Optimal Aging: Get Over Getting Older.* Chicago: Open Court.

[with V. Gordon, M. Neeman, and S. Palmer]. *Stress Counseling.* New York: Springer.

1999

How to Make Yourself Happy and Remarkably Less Disturbable. Atascadero, CA: Impact.

Rational Emotive Behavior Therapy Diminishes Much of the Human Ego. New York: Albert Ellis Institute.

2000

How to Control Your Anxiety Before It Controls You. New York: Citadel.
How to Maintain and Enhance Your Rational-Emotive Therapy Gains. Revised edition. New York: Institute for Rational-Emotive Therapy.
[with T. Crawford]. *Making Intimate Connections.* Atascadero, CA: Impact.
"Spiritual Goals and Spirited Values in Psychotherapy." *Journal of Individual Psychology* 36: 279–84.

2001

Feeling Better, Getting Better, Staying Better. Atascadero, CA: Impact.
How to Stop Destroying Your Relationships. New York: Citadel.
Overcoming Destructive Beliefs, Feelings, and Behaviors. Amherst, NY: Prometheus Books.
[with Windy Dryden]. "Rational Emotive Behavior Therapy" in *Handbook of Cognitive Behavioral Therapies.* 2nd ed., edited by Keith S. Dobson. New York: Guilford Press.
[with L. Lega]. "Rational-Emotive Behavior Therapy (REBT) in the New Millennium: A Cross-Cultural Approach." *Journal of Rational Emotive and Cognitive Behavioral Therapies* 19, no. 4: 203–24.

2002

[with Ira Reiss]. *At the Dawn of the Sexual Revolution.* California: Altamira Press.
Overcoming Resistance: A Rational Emotive Behavior Therapy Integrated Approach. New York: Springer.
[with M. G. Powers]. *The Secret of Overcoming Verbal Abuse.* North Hollywood, CA: Melvin Powers.
[with D. Joffe]. "A Study of Volunteer Clients Who Experience Live Sessions of REBT in Front of a Public Audience." *Journal of Rational Emotive and Cognitive Behavior Therapy* 20, no. 2: 151–58.
[with L. Lega and V. Caballo]. *Teoria y Practica de la Terapia Racional Emotivo-Conductual* (2nd ed.). Madrid, Spain: Siglo XXI.

2003

[with W. Dryden]. *Albert Ellis Live!* London: Sage.
Ask Albert Ellis. Atascadero, CA: Impact.
[with R. Harper]. *Dating, Mating, and Relating.* New York: Citadel.
Sex without Guilt in the Twenty-first Century. Fort Lee, NJ: Barricade.
"Similarities and Differences between Rational Emotive Behavior Therapy and Cognitive Therapy." *Journal of Cognitive Psychotherapy: An International Quarterly* 17, no. 3: 225–40.

2004

Foreword to *Beat Your Addiction*, by K. Peiser and M. Sandry.
"How My Theory and Practice of Psychotherapy Has Influenced and Changed Other Psychotherapies." *Journal of Rational-Emotive and Cognitive-Behavior Therapy* 22, no. 2: 79–83.
[with G. Halasz]. "In Conversation with Dr. Albert Ellis." *Australian Psychiatry* 12, no. 4: 325–33.
Rational Emotive Behavior Therapy: It Works for Me—It Can Work for You. Amherst, NY: Prometheus Books.
The Road to Tolerance. Amherst, NY: Prometheus Books.
"Why I (Really) Became a Therapist." *Journal of Rational-Emotive and Cognitive-Behavior Therapy* 22, no. 2: 73–77.
"Why Rational Emotive Behavior Therapy Is the Most Comprehensive and Effective Form of Behavior Therapy." *Journal of Rational-Emotive and Cognitive-Behavior Therapy* 22, no. 2: 85–92.

2005

Discussion of *Science and Philosophy: Comparison of Cognitive Therapy and Rational Emotive Behavior Therapy*, by C. A. Padesky and A. T. Beck. *Journal of Cognitive Psychotherapy: An International Quarterly.*
Foreword to *Online Therapy: A Therapist's Guide to Expanding Your Practice*, by Kathleene Derrig-Palumbo. New York: W. W. Norton and Co.
The Myth of Self-Esteem. Amherst, NY: Prometheus Books.

2006

How to Stubbornly Refuse to Make Yourself Miserable about Anything (Yes, Anything!). Revised and updated. New York: Citadel Press.
[with Michael E. Bernard, ed.] *Rational Emotive Behavioral Approaches to Childhood Disorders—Theory, Practice and Research.* New York: Springer.

2009

[interview] *Stage Fright*, by Mick Berry and Michael Edelstein. Tucson, AZ: See Sharp Press.

2010

Foreword to *REBT for People with Co-occurring Problems; Albert Ellis in the Wilds of Arizona*, by Emmett Velten and Patricia Penn. Sarasota, FL: Professional Resource Press.

"Rational Emotive Behavior Therapy," chapter in *Current Psychotherapies*, 9th ed., edited by Ray J. Corsini and Danny Wedding. Belmont, CA: Cengage Learning, Thomson Brooks/Cole.

2011

[with Debbie Joffe Ellis] *Rational Emotive Behavior Therapy* (monograph). Washington, DC: American Psychological Association.

II. ALBERT ELLIS IN THE MEDIA

Enormous numbers of articles about Albert Ellis and his work have appeared in the print media throughout his professional life. Near the end of his life, prominent and prestigious publications, including the *New York Times*, the *New Yorker* magazine, *Variety* (Gold Edition), and many others continued to write about his books and articles, comment on his opinions on psychotherapy and other topical issues, express astonishment regarding his amazing stamina and professional contributions, and chronicle the brutal and difficult circumstances with his institute during his final years. Included in the following section are the titles, dates, and sources of some of these articles:

Benedict Carey. "Judge Orders Psychologist Reinstated to Institute." *New York Times*, January 31, 2006.

Benedict Carey and Dan Hurley. "A Psychologist, 92, Is at Odds with the Institute He Founded: In the History of Psychology, Many Personality Clashes." *New York Times*, October 11, 2005.

Aura Davies. "Chill Out. Wellness for Body, Mind and Spirit: Shrinkraps: At 91, Famed Psychologist Albert Ellis Is Still Helping People Learn How to Suck It Up." *Time Out New York*, July 21–27, 2005.

Matt Dobkin. "Behaviorists Behaving Badly." *New York Magazine*, November 7, 2005.

"Following Up." *Time Out New York*. November 17–23, 2005.

Adam Green. "The Human Condition. Ageless, Guiltless." *New Yorker*, October 13, 2003.

Dan Hurley. "The Scientist at Large: Albert Ellis: From Therapy's Lenny Bruce: Get Over It! Stop Whining!" *New York Times*, May 3, 2004.

"Icons of the Century: Pop Pabulum: We're So Sorry, Doctor Albert." *Variety*, November 2005.

Michael T. Kaufman. "Albert Ellis, Provoker of Change in Psychotherapy, Is Dead at 93." *New York Times*, July 25, 2007.

Robert Langreth. "Patient, Fix Thyself." *Forbes*, April 9, 2007.

Nando Pelusi. "Final Analysis: Albert Ellis on Confidence." *Psychology Today*, April 2007.

Anthony Ramirez. "Despite Illness and Lawsuits, a Famed Psychotherapist Is Temporarily Back in Session." *New York Times*, December 10, 2006.

Index

Tampa branch of, 479
See also Friday Night Workshops
Albert Ellis Institute for Rational
Emotive Behavior Therapy—
2004 and afterward, 453–54,
480, 490, 522–23, 545–59
age discrimination against Albert
Ellis, 553–54
banning Ellis from making presentations at the institute, 552
stopping Friday Night Workshops, 558, 580
demand that Ellis pay own health
benefits, 551
Ellis's 2005 presentation on "The
State of Rational Emotive
Behavior Therapy in the
Twenty-First Century"
including Q&A, 548–58
Ellis's supporters, 457, 472, 473,
479, 480, 481, 482, 483, 484,
545, 551–52
final letter from Albert Ellis to
Albert Ellis Institute board
(2007), 579–80
negative changes in the institute, 554
final letter from Albert Ellis to
Albert Ellis Institute board
(2007) explaining, 579–80
summary of Albert Ellis's complaints against, 546
people seen as traitors to Ellis's
cause, 480, 482, 483, 522,
545–46, 552
Separation Agreement, 551
Settlement Agreement, 453–54
summary of Albert and Debbie
Ellis's requirements from, 547,
552–53
Albert Ellis Tribute book series, 577
Alma (lover), 305
American Association for Marital
and Family Therapy, 444

American Association of Sex Educa-
tion and Therapy, 490
American Civil Liberties Union,
453–54
American Communist Party, 261,
266, 268, 278
American Counseling Association
Living Legends event, 484
American Humanist Association,
441
American Journal of Psychotherapy,
310
American Psychological Association,
197, 362, 475, 484, 485, 490
awarding Tim Beck Distinguished
Service Award for Scientific
Contributions to Psychology,
471
code of ethics, 307
Ellis presentation at 2001 annual
conference, 536
American Sexual Tragedy, The
(Ellis), 474
anger
and abreaction, 90–91
and Albert Ellis
believing it is inherent in people,
346
feeling as a result of parental
neglect, 136, 154
feeling during hospitalizations,
66, 136, 154
feeling when board of AEI dis-
missed Janet, 535
learning from mother, 36
learning to handle, 16, 346–47,
352, 372, 535
of Albert Ellis's father, 36, 42,
140–41, 526
not feeling anger as a principle of
REBT, 31, 372
as obsession with the person angry
at, 354

as a subject of essay "The Art of Not Being Unhappy" (Ellis), 354

unhealthy consequence of, 135

Ann (lover), 510

annulment of Albert and Karyl Ellis's marriage, 292, 377, 378, 383, 385, 386, 387

anti-communist beliefs of Albert Ellis, 221, 234

participation in Young America, 261–64, 265

anxiety, 129, 154, 180, 186, 459

and Albert Ellis, 38, 39, 106, 533

dealing with as an adult, 115, 201–202, 204, 248, 277–78, 281, 282

dealing with in school, 27–30, 29, 178–79, 180–81, 183

dealing with separation anxiety, 133–39

during hospitalizations, 118, 132, 153

in relationship with Karyl, 348

being anxious won't change things, 533

Cognitive Therapy viewing depression and anxiety as different feelings, 200

ego-anxiety, 202

and Rational Emotive Behavior Therapy

applied to fear of public speaking, 262, 278, 280

use of shame-attacking exercise to counter anxiety, 14, 91, 93, 97–98, 154, 176, 351, 388

viewing depression and anxiety as similar, 200

ways to ward off, 153–54

See also fear; worrying

Anxiety Workbook (Ellis), 540

APA. See American Psychological Association

"Approaches to Cognitive-Behavioral Modification: Similarities and Differences" (AABT program), 463

Archives of Psychiatry (journal), 456

arithmetic and Albert Ellis, 181–82

Arizona Department of Child and Adolescent Offenders, 533

Art and Science of Love, The (Ellis), 453

arthritis, 229, 562, 564, 571

osteoarthritis, 171, 524

"Art of Not Being Unhappy, The" (Ellis), 339, 352–61, 409

aspiration pneumonia, 563, 564

Association for the Advancement of Behavior Therapy, 463

Association of Rational Thinkers, 493

atheist, Albert Ellis becoming an, 258–59

athletic activities. See sports activities, Albert Ellis not involved in

Auger, Lucien, 485

Autobiography (Ellis), 195, 251, 561, 566–67, 568, 573

continuing work on in 2002, 540

earlier versions of, 232, 513

process and thinking used, 13–19, 61, 159

autosuggestion, importance of, 56–57

"awfulizing" situations, 39, 124–25, 131, 203, 238, 355, 356, 495, 530, 541, 549, 553, 554–55. See also "catastrophizing" situations; "terriblizing" situations

Bach, George, 89–90, 449, 478

Bach, Johann Sebastian, 209

bad

bad things not always bad, 57, 61

with Rhoda, 317
with Sandy, 313, 329
Albert Ellis's dislike of, 142–45, 196, 438
efforts to overcome, 159, 195–96, 247–48, 355. *See also* distraction
as a subject of essay "The Art of Not Being Unhappy" (Ellis), 355
Bowlby, John, 161
Boylan, Brian, 494
Bradshaw, John, 500
Brancale, Ralph, 305, 307
Brecher, Ed, 319
Brecher, Miriam, 319
Brice, Fanny, 166
Brill, Joseph, 494
Broadway Melody (musical), 210
Broder, Michael, 480, 483, 522, 545, 552, 558, 559
Bronx, Albert Ellis's early years in, 30–37, 164, 442
Bryant Avenue, East Bronx, 33–34, 63, 66, 98, 164–65, 442
Heath Avenue, East Bronx, 34, 165–66, 191
West 190th Street, Bronx, 191–92, 253
Bronx Botanical Gardens experiments to lose fear of meeting women, 283–84, 287–89, 303
brother, Albert Ellis's. *See* Paul, Albert Ellis's brother
Bruce, Lenny, 238
Bryant Avenue, East Bronx, 33–34, 63, 66, 98, 164–65, 442
Buddha, 187, 346, 495
burial of Albert Ellis, 575–76
Burns, David, 483
Bush, George W., and Laura, 536
letter to Albert Ellis on Albert's 90th birthday, 542

business efforts of Albert Ellis
Albert and Paul Ellis's pants-matching business, 267–68, 274, 337, 338
project with his father and The Four Aces (automatic bridge game), 366
work at Distinctive Creations, 367, 386, 387
working for Dick Childs' publishing firm, 336, 339, 382
Byrne, Jim, 503

Caesar, Irving, 79, 81
Canter, Aaron, 449
capitalism, Albert Ellis's dislike of, 264, 265, 266
deciding a lesser evil than collectivism, 270
learning to prefer capitalistic liberalism, 273
Capitol theater, 210
Carlson, Jon, 484, 577
Carmichael, Hoagy, 213
Caro, Jo (lover). *See* Jo (lover)
Carol (Albert Ellis's relationship with), 509
cartoons, Albert Ellis's interest in drawing, 500, 566
Casebook of Rational-Emotive Therapy, A (Ellis), 442, 447
Case for Promiscuity, The (Ellis), 273, 275, 335, 346, 368, 386
Case for Sexual Liberty (Ellis), 494
"catastrophizing" situations, 27, 39, 238, 457–58, 464. *See also* "awfulizing" situations; "terriblizing" situations
Cavett, Dick, 502
CBS, 502
CBT. *See* Cognitive Behavioral Therapy
CCNY. *See* City College of New York

CEBT. *See* Cognitive Emotive Behavior Therapy
censorship, Ellis fighting, 494
Center for Inquiry, 479
challenge, philosophy of, 128
Chaplin, Charles, 165, 167
children
    Albert Ellis as father of three children with Karyl, 389–95
    Albert Ellis's feelings about, 205–206, 390
Childs, Richard Storrs "Dick," 267, 268, 269
    Albert Ellis working for
        as a manuscript reader, 336, 339, 382
        as a paid revolutionist, 340
choice
    choice as a major principle of REBT, 556
    choosing how to handle pain, 67–73, 76–77, 109, 119–20
        dealing with colonic irrigation treatments, 116–19, 152–53
        escalating the amount of pain felt, 75
        focusing on temporary nature of, 71–72, 77, 119
        using religious thoughts, 69–72, 75–76
        ways Ellis family members dealt with, 76
    choosing how to handle phobias, 279
    choosing how to handle sleeplessness, 122–26
    choosing how to handle surgery, 132
    choosing not to be unhappy, 56–57, 61–62
    choosing sadness rather than depression, 170, 239, 241, 242–43, 244–46, 378, 379, 538

choosing to live or die. *See* suicide
    See also coping
Chopin, Frederick, 213, 501
Ciardi, John, 474
Cindy (Albert Ellis's relationship with), 505
City College of New York, 221, 273, 286
    bachelor's degree in business administration, 260, 275, 336
    Ed Sagarin on faculty of, 455
    writing college papers quickly to overcome procrastination, 250–51
civil rights, 492
Clark, LeMon, 475
clavicle, broken, 234
Cleveland State University, 481
Clinton, Bill (letter to Albert Ellis on Albert's 90th birthday), 542
Clinton, Hillary Rodham (letter to Albert Ellis on Albert's 90th birthday), 542
CNN, 502
Coche, Erich, 462
cognitions, self-defeating, 131, 139, 154
"Cognitive Approaches to Depression and Suicide" (Beck), 467–69
Cognitive Behavioral Therapy, 110, 146–47, 187, 456, 557
    based on REBT, 188, 361
    differences between CBT and REBT, 246
    REBT as first major cognitive behavioral therapy, 272, 550
    similarities with REBT, 456–57
    studies showing that system works, 282–83
    See also Cognitive Therapy
cognitive distraction, 97–99, 112
    Albert Ellis's use of incipient REBT

Elizabeth (lover), 508

Ellis, Debbie (Joffe). *See* Debbie (wife)

Ellis, Havelock, 274, 299, 345, 386, 477

Ellis, Henry Oscar. *See* father, Albert Ellis's

Ellis, Hettie (Hanigbaum). *See* mother, Albert Ellis's

Ellis, Janet. *See* Janet, Albert Ellis's sister

Ellis, Paul. *See* Paul, Albert Ellis's brother

Elston, Manny, 260–61, 262, 265, 267, 269, 278, 280, 338

Emerson, Ralph Waldo, 26, 548

Emmett, Dan, 79–80, 216

emotional consequence, 176, 177

empiricism, Albert Ellis's use of, 260, 324

Engels, Friedrich, 268, 269

environmental factors in mental illness, 157

environmentalism and Albert Ellis, 155

envy as a subject of essay "The Art of Not Being Unhappy" (Ellis), 357–58

ephemerality of pain, 71–72, 77, 119

Epictetus, 26, 56, 130, 152, 153, 187, 246, 346

Epictetus-Ellis hypothesis, 444, 548

Epicureanism, 277

Erhard, Werner, 490

erotic fantasies, 55–56, 305

Esalen Institute, 90, 481

Esther (wife of Paul), 169, 171, 172

Ethical Cultural Society, 459

Evolution of Psychotherapy conferences

Albert Ellis as a regular speaker at, 484, 561

Ellis's 2005 presentation on "The State of Rational Emotive Behavior Therapy in the Twenty-First Century" including Q&A, 548–58

exercises in Rational Emotive Behavior Therapy

emotive-evocative type, 91

encounter-type, 91

shame-attacking exercise, 91–93

flashlight game as a precursor to, 89, 94

Experiment in Autobiography (Wells), 16

Eysenck, Hans J., 187, 504

"factual" reality, 187

Fairbanks, Douglas, 165, 443

Family Substance Service, 477

Farley, Frank, 485

fascism, Albert Ellis's dislike of, 261, 273, 335

fatalism, 153

father, Albert Ellis's, 24, 28, 103–104

anger and irritability of, 36, 42, 140–41, 526

divorcing Ellis's mother, 255–56, 323–24

and feelings of love, 150

impatience of, 527

influences on Albert Ellis, 439

interest in reading, 166

neglectfulness of, 40–44, 140, 154, 254

infrequent visits to Albert Ellis in the hospital, 133

remarriage to Rose, 255, 383

sisters and brothers, 141, 206

fathering children, Albert Ellis, 389–95

Faubus, Orval, 479

fear, 258–59

Albert Ellis learning to deal with fear at young age, 29, 37–38, 61

fear of rejection, 191, 236, 263, 336
    learning to handle, 135, 204,
        288, 357
    sex-love rejection, 218–19, 277,
        278, 283–89, 303
    Watson experiments on over-
        coming children's fears of ani-
        mals, 262, 287
    See also anxiety; phobias, over-
        coming
feeding tube, use of, 563, 564–65,
    570
Feeling Good (Burns), 483
Feigl, Herbert, 455–56
Feyerband, Paul, 243
Fields, W. C., 205
Fifth Symphony (Tchaikovsky), 210
finances, Albert Ellis's handling of
    dislike of debt and monetary has-
        sles, 296, 326–27
    having brother Paul handle invest-
        ments, 439–40
    for Karyl and himself, 296
Finck, Henry T., 240
Firefly (musical), 501
Fireman, John, 562, 566
Fisher, Harold, 481
flashlight game, 88–89
    Albert Ellis's use of, 94, 110–11
    as a precursor of shame-attacking
        exercise, 89, 94
Flaubert, Gustave, 195
Florence (Gertrude's friend), 396–97,
    399, 401, 404, 405, 406, 408,
    410, 411, 417, 418, 424, 425
Florence, Albert Ellis's aunt, 206
focus, 71, 75, 131, 132
    on distractions, 57, 62, 132, 154,
        176, 177, 353
    focusing on something makes it
        worse, 129, 131
    use of as a coping mechanism, 72,
        99, 119, 128–29, 130, 132, 154

Folklore of Sex, The (Ellis), 275,
    305, 313, 314
Forel, Auguste, 477
Frank, Jerome, 245, 283
freedom, Ellis's love of, 325
Freud, Sigmund, 19, 85, 105, 187,
    245, 269, 286, 287
Freudian theory, 106, 297
    of abreaction, 90–91
    of early childhood conditioning,
        117–18
Friday Night Workshops, 194, 197,
    480, 485, 512, 522–23, 537,
    541, 551, 554, 558, 562–63
    AEI board stopping Friday Night
        Workshops from being held at
        institute, 563, 580
    attempts to meet with students at
        the nursing home and hos-
        pital, 569, 570–71
    first workshop, 494–95
Friml, Rudolf, 151, 208, 254,
    500–501, 519–20
Fromm, Erika, 449
frotteurism, 113, 235–38, 291,
    302–303, 328, 336
funeral and burial of Albert Ellis,
    575–76
"Funiculi, Funicula!" (Denza), 214

Garrity, Terry, 453, 477
gay marriage, 492–93
Gehrig, Lou, 254
Geis, Jon, 487
Gertrude (a love of Albert Ellis),
    241, 305, 390, 475, 512
    Albert never living with, 527
    diary entries of Albert Ellis from
        1942–1945 about, 395–433
    obsessive-compulsive nature of the
        relationship, 402–403, 405,
        420
Gestalt therapy, 130

learning how to deal with, 67–73, 76–77, 109, 119–20

escalating the amount of pain felt, 75

focusing on temporary nature of, 71–72

using religious thoughts to deal with pain, 69–72, 75–76

ways Ellis family members dealt with, 76

health of Albert Ellis

accidents

accident in street in 2001, 531–34

breaking clavicle in a fall while in Oklahoma City, 234

acute nephritis, 67, 84, 120, 126–29

dealing with surgery for, 127–29

outgrowing, 132–33

arthritis, 229, 562, 564, 571

osteoarthritis, 171, 524

colonic irrigation as treatment for headaches, 116–19, 152–53

declining health in later years, 561–63

diabetes, 14, 17, 525, 565–66

and 2003 emergency hospitalization, 196–97

hypoglycemic reaction, 530

insulin, 14, 17, 171, 525, 562, 565

poor treatment of Albert Ellis at Jamaica Hospital, 495–98

problems caused by feeding tube, 570

treatment for, 171

eczema and severe itching, 196, 480, 525, 568

edema, 120, 126

handling headaches, 67–72

headaches

colonic irrigation as treatment for, 116–19, 152–53

learning how to deal with, 67–73, 75–77, 109, 119–20

minor stroke, 532

need for ileostomy bag, 562

need for prostatectomy, 234

pneumonia, 84, 563, 571, 573, 579

aspiration pneumonia, 563, 564

possible heart attack, 573

problems relating to aging catching up in 2001, 524–27

sleeplessness, 32, 120–26, 153

methods for handling, 122–26

streptococcus infection, 63–67

tonsillitis with complications, 63–78

use of hearing aids, 525

wobbly legs, 524, 532

See also hospitalizations

healthy consequences, 135, 176

healthy negative feelings, 31, 139, 239, 242, 244, 532

hearing aids, 525

heart attack, 573

Heath Avenue, East Bronx, 34, 165–66, 191

Hebrew, Albert Ellis learning, 257

hedonism, 188

Heidegger, Martin, 243

Heinie, Albert Ellis's uncle, 206

Henry Street Playhouse, 311

Herbert, Victor, 208, 254, 501, 518

heterosexuality, 85–86

high frustration tolerance (HFT)

Albert Ellis having, 19, 141, 143, 157, 159, 194, 251–52, 281, 327

examples of in his songwriting, 209, 213, 217

impact on sex life, 277

using HFT to handle LFT, 195, 249, 252

biological basis of, 251

interest in drawing cartoons, 500
presentations on humor, 536
sale of cassette and songbook of
    rational humorous songs, 217
"Humor and Psychotherapy" (pre-
    sentation by Ellis and Pelusi in
    2001), 536
"Humor in Psychotherapy" (presen-
    tation by Ellis and Harper at
    APA in 1976), 499–500

IBs. *See* irrational beliefs
I Don't Like Asparagus (Bard), 481
"If I Loved Thee as I Love Me"
    (lyrics by Ellis), 211–12
impatience of Albert Ellis, 204, 205,
    526–27
impotence, treating, 55
impulsivity of Albert Ellis, 204, 323,
    391
independence of Albert Ellis, 60
Independent (magazine), 453
"Indian Love Call, The" (song from
    Rose Marie), 501
Infidelity (Boylan), 494
insomnia, Albert Ellis's, 32, 120–26,
    153
    methods for handling, 122–26
Institute for Rational Living, 459
Institute for Sex Research at Indiana
    University, 309
insulin, 14, 17, 171, 525, 562, 565
    Ellis's difficulties getting insulin at
        Jamaica Hospital, 495–98
    See also diabetes
intelligence of Albert Ellis, 193, 249,
    281, 368, 377, 389–90
International Journal of Sexology, 313
In the Hall of the Mountain King
    (Grieg), 212
"Intimacy in Psychotherapy: Gallant
    Goal or Hollow Hoax?"
    (Harper Symposium), 449, 450

Intimate Enemy, The (Bach), 478
in vivo desensitization, 183–85,
    186–87, 189, 358
    and fear of meeting women,
        283–84, 287–89, 303
    and public speaking, 262–64
"I Push My Ass," 217
IQ tests, 249, 368
irrational beliefs, 154
    all patients having, 362
    creating anxiety and depression,
        200
    disputing of, 124, 175–78,
        179–80, 181
        dealing with depression, 155
        dealing with separation anxiety,
            135–39, 155
        using realistic and anti-
            absolutistic methods,
            180–81, 246
    as a way to rethink, 186
irritation as a healthy negative
    feeling, 139
Isabel (lover), 317
itching. *See* eczema and severe
    itching
"I Wish I Were Not Crazy" (lyrics
    by Ellis), 79–80, 216

Jack (Gertrude's husband), 400–401,
    402, 403, 405, 406, 408, 410,
    414, 417, 418, 421–22, 423,
    425–26
Jacobson, Edmund, 97, 98
Jamaica Hospital, 495–98
Janet (apartment mate and long-term
    lover), 38–39, 232, 240, 305,
    331, 510–11, 575–76
    leaving the relationship, 527–30, 532
    moving out, 331, 511, 512
    serving as manager at the Albert
        Ellis Institute, 331, 510–11,
        527

having a rebellious streak, 199,
203, 247
having scarlet fever, 210
impact of father's remarriage on, 256
letters from Albert Ellis to, 440–41
Pavlov, Ivan, 187
"Peace Be with Love" (lyrics by
Ellis), 213
Peale, Norman Vincent, 57
Pelusi, Nando, 536
Penthouse, 476
"Perfect Rationality" (lyrics by
Ellis), 214
Perkins, Maxwell, 386
Perls, Fritz, 90, 504, 555
Phadke, Kishor M., 479, 485–86
Philadelphia Society of Clinical Psychologists, 462, 463
Phil Donahue Show, 502
Philip (son of Karyl and Albert
Ellis), 391
philosophy and Albert Ellis
early development of, 27, 29,
60–61
attitude toward life's hassles,
163
in order to avoid pain and deprivation, 203
not getting early exposure to
philosophers, 26–27
and stoicism, 67, 108, 119, 125,
132, 152, 352–53, 565
reinventing the Stoic philosophy,
56–57
phobias, overcoming, 263
fear of approaching strange
women, 277, 278, 283–89,
303, 326, 328
fear of public speaking, 262–64,
277, 278–82, 326
Watson experiments on overcoming children's fears of animals, 262, 287

physical activities, Albert Ellis not
involved in, 78, 83, 168, 207,
248, 495
physical therapy, 567, 568
Pickford, Mary, 165, 168, 443
Pittsburgh, Albert Ellis's early years
in, 23–30, 164, 435
Plato, 444
PMA. *See* "I Push My Ass"
pneumonia, 84, 563, 571, 573, 579
aspiration pneumonia, 563, 564
poetry
Albert Ellis's compulsive interest in
rhyming, 79–83
comic verses published in *New
York Post*, 336, 337
poems for his wife Debbie, 514–18
See also songwriting and Albert
Ellis
Pogo (cartoon character), 19
political thoughts of Albert Ellis
Albert Ellis's dislike of capitalism,
264, 265, 266
deciding a lesser evil than collectivism, 270
learning to prefer capitalistic liberalism, 273
anti-communist beliefs, 221, 234
becoming a revolutionist, 253–75
on bigotry and racism, 204–205
favoring unpopular causes,
492–94
influence of Harold Lasswell on,
268–69
libertarian leanings of, 270, 271
moving toward becoming a sexual
revolutionist, 270–71, 273–75,
325–26, 335
on nationalism, 205
revolutionist ideas of, 221, 268,
325–26, 335–36
application to join Socialist
Party, 339

TA. *See* transactional analysis
Tales from the Vienna Woods
    (Strauss), 211
Tchaikovsky, Pyotr Ilyich, 209, 210
"Tea for Two" (Youmans), 215
Teenie, Albert Ellis's aunt, 206
television and radio, Albert Ellis
    appearances, 501–502
Temple University, 485
Tenzin Gyatso. *See* Dalai Lama
"terriblizing" situations, 124, 134,
    238, 356, 549, 553, 554–55
    See also "awfulizing" situations;
    "catastrophizing" situations
Thackeray, William Makepeace, 166
therapy sessions
    as art or science, 146–47
    dealing with a potential suicide,
    180
    importance of self-therapy, 328
    therapist choosing how to inter-
    pret client, 145
    See also sex therapy
thinking, need to change, 186
Thomas, Norman, 268, 270
Thoreau, Henry David, 26
Three Musketeers, The (musical),
    501
Thurber, James, 205
Thurston the Magician, 166
Tillich, Paul, 362, 368, 385, 530
tolerance. *See* high frustration toler-
    ance; low frustration tolerance
Tono-Bungay (Wells), 17
tonsillitis with complications, 63–78
Tony (Karyl's husband after Ellis
    annulment), 389, 391, 392, 393
"too damned bad" factor, 557
"Totem Tom Tom" (Friml), 520
transactional analysis, 130
Treaker, Larry, 456
Treatment Manual (Beck), 464–65,
    466

Trimpey, Jack, 483
"Triolet on Love" (verse by Ellis), 81
"Triolet on Wealth" (verse by Ellis),
    81
Trotsky, Leon, 268, 269, 335
Trotter, Tom, 219
Trumbo, Dalton, 454
Twayne Publishers, 474
*Twisted Thinking: A Guide to the
    Emotional Disorders* (Beck),
    460, 461, 462

ULA. *See* Unconditional Life-
    Acceptance
Ulysses (Joyce), 494
Unconditional Life-Acceptance, 546,
    550, 553
Unconditional Other-Acceptance, 41,
    382, 472, 546, 550, 553, 555
    taking it too far, 547–48
Unconditional Self-Acceptance, 19,
    200, 395, 472, 481, 546, 550,
    553
    Albert Ellis not having in relation-
    ship with Karyl, 348, 368
    belief in alleviating anxiety,
    201–202
    concept coming from existential-
    ists, 368, 530–31
unfairness of the world, 36
"Unfuck it" as a pejorative term, 238
Unger, Andrew, 562, 566
unhappiness
    choosing not to be unhappy,
    56–57, 61–62
    unhappiness with relationship with
    Karyl, 349, 353, 354, 361,
    370
Unhappiness and Depression
    (Simon), 490
unhealthy consequences, 135
unhealthy negative feelings, 31, 136,
    139, 242, 244, 532

writing and Albert Ellis, 13, 43
desire to become a writer, 285,
336, 406
desire to write an opera based on
Romeo and Juliet, 566
enjoyment of writing, 327–28
feeling too much pain to be able to
write, 568
interest in writing song lyrics and
rhymes. *See also* songwriting
and Albert Ellis
comic verses published in *New
York Post*, 336, 337
publishing a cassette and songbook of Ellis's songs, 217
samples of, 79–83, 209, 210–17
productiveness of, 147, 159, 551
in professional life, 109–10, 251
quantities of letters written, 251.
See also letters from Albert
Ellis
viewed as one of most influential
writers on sex revolution of
1960s, 275
writing college papers quickly to
overcome procrastination,
250–51
wrong. *See* right and wrong, defining
of determines feelings of guilt

"Yankee Doodle Dandy" (Cohan),
214–15

"Yankee Doodle Dandy" (folksong),
498
Yates, Aubrey, 146
YCL. *See* Young Communist League
of America
Yipsels. *See* Young People's Socialist
League
yoga exercises, 97, 154, 357
"You for Me and Me for Me" (lyrics
by Ellis), 215
Youmans, Vincent, 215
Young, Loretta, 286
Young America, 261–64, 265,
278–80
controlled by New America,
266–67
interest in writing song lyrics and
rhymes, 335
Socialist Party attempts to take
over, 268
Young Communist League of
America, 261, 278
Young People's Socialist League,
269–70
Your Erroneous Zones (Dyer),
486–90

Zeig, Jeffrey K., 484, 490
Zen Buddhism, 277
Zeno of Citium, 56, 187
Zilbergeld, Bernie, 478
Zimmerman, Horst, 486

About the Authors

Albert Ellis was born in Pittsburgh and raised in New York City. He held MA and PhD degrees in clinical psychology from Columbia University. He has held many important psychological positions, including chief psychologist of the state of New Jersey and adjunct professorships at Rutgers and other universities. He was founder and president of the Albert Ellis Institute in New York City; has practiced psychotherapy, marriage and family counseling, and sex therapy for sixty years; and practiced at the Psychological Center of the Institute in New York. He is the founder of Rational Emotive Behavior Therapy (REBT), the first of the now-popular cognitive behavioral therapies (CBT).

Dr. Ellis served as president of the Division of Consulting Psychology of the American Psychological Association and of the Society for the Scientific Study of Sexuality. He has also served as officer of several professional societies, including the American Association of Marital and Family Therapy, the American Academy of Psychotherapists, and the American Academy of Sex Educators, Counselors, and Therapists. He is a diplomat in clinical psychology on the American Board of Professional Psychology and of several other professional organizations.

Professional societies that have given Dr. Ellis their highest professional and clinical awards include the American Psychological Association, the Association for the Advancement of Behavior Therapy, the American Counseling Association, and the American Psychological Association. He was ranked as one of the "most influential psychologists" by both the American and Canadian psychologists and counselors. He has served as consulting or associate editor of many scientific journals and has published over eight hundred scientific papers and more than two hundred audio materials and videocassettes. He has written or edited eighty books or monographs, including a number of best-selling popular and professional volumes. Some of his best-known works include *How to Live with a Neurotic*; *The Art and Science of Love*; *A Guide to Rational Living*; *Reason and Emotion in Psychotherapy*; *How to Stubbornly Refuse to Make Yourself Miserable about Anything—Yes, Anything*; *Overcoming Procrastination*; *Overcoming Resistance*; *The Practice of Rational Emotive Behavior Therapy*; *How to Make Yourself Happy and Remarkably Less Disturbable*; *Feeling Better, Getting Better, and Staying Better*; *Overcoming Destructive Beliefs, Feelings, and Behaviors*; *Anger: How to Live with and without It*; *Rational Emotive Behavior Therapy: It Works for Me—It Can Work for You*; *The Road to Tolerance*; and *The Myth of Self-Esteem*.

DEBBIE JOFFE ELLIS

Debbie Joffe Ellis was born and raised in Melbourne, Australia. She is affiliated with several major psychological associations and societies, including being a member of the Australian Psychological Society and an international affiliate member of the American Psychological Association. For several years, she worked with her husband, Dr. Albert Ellis, giving public presentations and professional trainings in Rational Emotive Behavior Therapy (REBT), as well as collaborating on writing and research projects, until his death in 2007. She now continues to present, practice, and write about his groundbreaking psychotherapeutic approach of REBT. She currently has a private practice in New York City and also delivers lectures, workshops, and seminars throughout the United States and across the globe.